Inside APPN and HPR

The Essential Guide to New SNA

Fourth Edition

The ITSO Networking Series

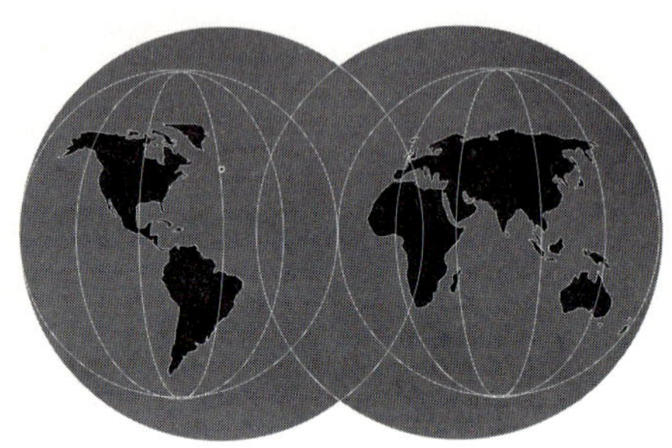

TCP/IP Tutorial and Technical Overview
by Murphy, Hayes, and Ender

Asynchronous Transfer Mode (ATM)
by Dutton and Lenhard

High-Speed Networking Technology
by Dutton and Lenhard

www.security: How to Build a Secure World Wide Web Connection
by Macgregor, Aresi, and Siegert

Internetworking over ATM: An Introduction
by Dorling, Freedman, Metz, and Burger

The Internet and the World Wide Web
by Kressin

Inside APPN and HPR: The Essential Guide to New SNA, fourth edition
by Dorling, Lenhard, Lennon, and Uskokovic

Inside APPN and HPR

The Essential Guide to New SNA
Fourth Edition

BRIAN DORLING ■ PETER LENHARD ■
PETER LENNON ■ VELIBOR USKOKOVIC

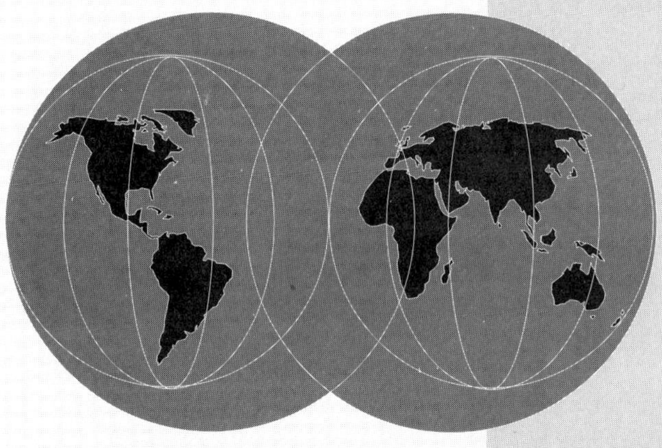

IBM

PRENTICE HALL PTR, UPPER SADDLE RIVER, NEW JERSEY 07458

Take Note!
Before using this information and the product it supports, be sure to read the general information in Appendix E, "Special Notices" on page 431.

Fourth Edition (June 1997)

This edition applies to IBM Advanced Peer-to-Peer Networking Architecture and Product Family.

Comments may be addressed to:
IBM Corporation, International Technical Support Organization
Dept. HZ8 Building 678
P.O. Box 12195
Research Triangle Park, NC 27709-2195

Published by Prentice Hall PTR
Prentice-Hall, Inc.
A Simon & Schuster Company
Upper Saddle River, New Jersey 07458

Prentice Hall books are widely used by corporations and government agencies
for training, marketing, and resale.
The publisher offers discounts on this book when ordered in bulk quantities.
For more information, contact: Corporate Sales Department, Phone: 800-382-3419;
FAX: 201-236-7141; E-mail: corpsales@prenhall.com
Or write: Corp. Sales Dept., Prentice Hall PTR,
1 Lake Street, Upper Saddle River, NJ 07458

Printed in the United States of America
10 9 8 7 6 5 4 3 2 1

ISBN 0-1-13-761511-6

Prentice-Hall International (UK) Limited, *London*
Prentice-Hall of Australia Pty. Limited, *Sydney*
Prentice-Hall Canada Inc., *Toronto*
Prentice-Hall Hispanoamericana, S.A., *Mexico*
Prentice-Hall of India Private Limited, *New Delhi*
Prentice-Hall of Japan, Inc., *Tokyo*
Simon & Schuster Asia Pte. Ltd., *Singapore*
Editora Prentice-Hall do Brasil, Ltda., *Rio de Janeiro*

Contents

Preface

Foreword

While the growth and glamor of the Internet and its associated TCP/IP protocol suite eclipse SNA in the trade press daily, SNA unobtrusively continues its vital role as the workhorse of enterprise networking. SNA applications and networks exist in enormous numbers today, running critical business and governmental applications worldwide. New SNA applications and networks are being deployed, and SNA will continue to grow for a long time.

It is estimated that over twenty trillion dollars have been invested in SNA applications in over 40,000 enterprises worldwide. According to surveys, SNA accounts for 61% of wide area network enterprise traffic and 68% of enterprise WAN budgets. Contrary to the image portrayed by some of the trade press, SNA is alive and well. Fifteen years of annual surveys find no decrease in SNA penetration or any significant plans to convert SNA applications. SNA remains a vital solution for customers in their mission-critical applications. In fact, it continues to grow, with a reported 4.7 million units of SNA client software shipped in 1995 and an estimated 5.38 million in 1996. Existing single-enterprise SNA networks may have as many as one million terminals and logical units and an average of 435,000 active sessions.

Customers have come to depend on the stability, predictability, reliability, dependability, interoperability, and high resource utilization that SNA networks provide, and they increasingly want the high availability and performance provided by APPN/HPR.

IBM's first release of SNA in 1974 did for networking what System/360 had done for IBM computing a decade earlier. It brought order by providing commonality and structure through a single architecture for data communications, and ended the anarchy of the multitude of disparate methods and link protocols then in use for connecting devices to host systems. Originally designed for the "glass house," subarea SNA's hierarchical structure connected many simple devices to one powerful mainframe. IBM added multiple-host networking in 1977 and transmission priority in 1980. Priority allowed more important (for example, interactive) traffic to proceed before less time-critical (for example, batch) traffic, improving link utilization. In 1982 IBM introduced Advanced Program-to-Program Communication (APPC) so applications could embrace the new distributed transaction programming paradigm.

SNA provides a base that promotes reliability, efficiency, ease of use, and low cost of ownership; enhances network dependability; improves end-user productivity; allows for resource sharing; provides for network security and resource management; protects network investments; simplifies problem determination; accommodates new facilities and technologies; and lets independent networks communicate. SNA can be very frugal with expensive networking resources such as links. With careful tuning, link utilizations as high as 98% have been reported. Subarea SNA also allows for extremely large networks; enterprises with tens to hundreds of thousands of attached terminals and applications are not uncommon. All these features made it a favorite for mission-critical corporate and governmental applications.

While APPC let programmers write distributed programs, the original hierarchical SNA network structure inhibited any-to-any connectivity, since all data had to flow through one or more host-controlled subareas. To address this, IBM introduced SNA's second generation, Advanced Peer-to-Peer Networking (APPN) in 1986. Today APPN runs on virtually all of IBM's current computing and networking platforms, and is available on products from a wide variety of vendors, including implementations for PC-based 3270 emulators, various non-IBM computing platforms, and networking hardware (routers, etc.) This broad-based investment by the industry underscores the continuing importance of SNA applications and networks.

APPN is an open data networking architecture that is easy to use, has decentralized control with centralized network management, allows arbitrary topologies, has connection flexibility and continuous operation, and requires no specialized communications hardware. It replaces the coordinated system- definition required in subarea SNA with automatic configuration definition, and fully embraces the peer-to-peer and client-server paradigms. It provides sophisticated route selection and dynamic topology updates, and upholds SNA's virtues, readily accommodating existing subarea networks. In 1994 IBM added the Dependent Logical Unit Requester (DLUR), allowing APPN networks to carry all types of subarea SNA traffic. Recognizing that customers were best served by an open architecture, in 1993 IBM sponsored the first APPN Implementers' Workshop (AIW), a consortium of networking vendors sharing an interest in APPN. As the standards body for SNA technologies, the AIW continues to meet three times a year. The latest updates on APPN can be found on the World Wide Web at:

`http://www.networking.ibm.com/app/aiwhome.htm`

To improve APPN availability and performance, IBM developed High-Performance Routing (HPR). This third-generation SNA is a fully compatible upgrade to APPN. Building upon APPN's topology and directory services, HPR adds nondisruptive rerouting and improves routing performance, while reducing memory and processor use in intermediate nodes. SNA applications can take full advantage of the features of HPR, without modification. HPR merges the best attributes of connection-oriented SNA and APPN, and connectionless IP, and then adds advanced rate-based congestion control to provide state-of-the-art networking.

In 1992 and 1994, IBM developed Peripheral and Extended Border Nodes for partitioning very large networks into smaller subnets. Border nodes allow directory searches and sessions to span interconnected subnets, while limiting topology flows. They replace SNA network interconnect (SNI), providing a secure way to divide or interconnect networks according to any policies or criteria.

In 1996, the AIW approved *HPR Extensions for ATM Networks*. This standard lets customers exploit Asynchronous Transfer Mode Quality of Service from existing SNA applications, giving them a way to meet response time goals for business-critical applications over ATM while minimizing link costs. This is done by matching each application's needs with an ATM virtual circuit with specific characteristics, such as reserved bandwidth or best effort. SNA applications are in a unique position to take advantage of QoS, because SNA is the only protocol with class of service in its application programming interface.

In 1997 IBM added native multilink transmission groups to HPR products. This popular feature from subarea SNA tunes network capacity by aggregating low-speed links, dials extra bandwidth on demand, and maintains the integrity of a transmission group despite individual link failures.

To meet the need to grow an individual APPN network to encompass many thousands of branch sites, IBM introduced Branch Extender in 1997. Branch network nodes maximize the efficiency of APPN protocols on expensive peripheral links and allow direct branch-to-branch data flow, greatly reducing telecommunications costs, without sacrificing the ability to centrally manage all branch devices.

Now that APPN matches or exceeds every major feature of subarea SNA, customers increasingly recognize that it is a worthy heir to SNA. Furthermore, APPN is the vehicle for meeting 100 percent host availability requirements and exploiting the powerful capabilities of the System 390 Parallel Enterprise Server. The coming years will see further APPN developments as IBM harnesses today's network resources to make the largest assemblage of data content, on IBM servers, available for fruitful collaboration on the World Wide Web. Universal access from any client or browser will replace today's glamorous but diluted Web content. New linkages to the corporation's most valuable information resources, the corporate MIS databases, will enable electronic commerce to thrive. Even as companies jump on the Internet bandwagon, APPN preserves the continuing immense value of their mission-critical SNA applications.

January 2, 1997

Marcia Peters
Chuck Brotman, AIW chair
IBM Corporation
Research Triangle Park, North Carolina

The Team That Wrote This Book

The fourth edition of this book was produced by a team of specialists from around the world working at the Systems Management and Networking ITSO Center, Raleigh.

Brian Dorling is an Advisory ITSO Specialist for Communications Architectures at the Systems Management and Networking ITSO Center, Raleigh. Brian is responsible for a broad range of IBM communication architectures including Advanced Peer-to-Peer

Networking (APPN), Multiprotocol Transport Networking (MPTN), Networking Broadband Services (NBBS), and Switched Virtual Networking (SVN). Since joining IBM in 1978, Brian has worked as a Customer Engineer and Systems Engineer in the networking field in the UK and Germany.

Peter Lenhard is an Advisory Systems Engineer in NS Marketing, IBM Germany. After joining IBM in 1973, he gained broad experience in SNA and telecommunications supporting IBM customers in the automotive industry. From 1991 through 1995, he was IBM's technical liaison and support for communications architectures at the ITSO Raleigh Center. He holds a masters degree in mathematics from the University of Hamburg, Germany.

Peter Lennon is a Network Consultant in IBM South Africa. In his first 17 years as an SNA specialist in the UK, Europe and USA he served as systems engineer, network performance expert, writer, instructor, software author and product manager. Later he became Team Leader in IBM Software Services with responsibility for APPN projects. Before joining IBM, Peter was a schoolmaster, then an Antarctic scientist. He holds BSc and ARCS degrees in Physics from Imperial College, London.

Velibor Uskokovic is an Advisory I.T. Specialist, responsible for pre- and post-sales technical support in IBM South Africa. After working seven years in Montenegro (Yugoslavia) as a Data Communications Systems Engineer, for the last three years he has enjoyed life in South Africa as part of the IBM Networking Division team there. He holds an Honors BSc in Electronics from the University of Podgorica, Montenegro.

The authors of the previous editions of this book were:

Paul Berdowski	IBM The Netherlands
Bernd Kampmann	IBM Germany
Vokke Kreuk	IBM The Netherlands
Peter Lenhard	IBM Germany
Martin Numan	IBM The Netherlands
Rachel Pickering	IBM United Kingdom
John Purrington	IBM Germany

Thanks to the following people for the invaluable advice and review comments provided in the production of this book:

Michael Allen	Formerly IBM Research Triangle Park
Marilyn Beumeler	Formerly IBM Research Triangle Park
Ray Bird	IBM Research Triangle Park
Ray Boyles	Formerly IBM Research Triangle Park
Roy Brabson	IBM Research Triangle Park

Rachel Brue	IBM Rochester
David Bryant	Formerly IBM Research Triangle Park
Ralph Case	IBM Research Triangle Park
Mark Cossack	Formerly IBM Rochester
Joe Czap	IBM Research Triangle Park
Gary Dudley	IBM Research Triangle Park
Candace Elder	IBM Research Triangle Park
Jim Fletcher	IBM Research Triangle Park
Johnathan Harter	IBM Research Triangle Park
Lap Huynh	IBM Research Triangle Park
Doyle Horne	Formerly IBM Research Triangle Park
John Klonowski	IBM Research Triangle Park
Arthur Majtenyi	IBM Research Triangle Park
Keith Meyer	IBM Research Triangle Park
Thomas Moore	IBM Research Triangle Park
Robert E. Moore	IBM Research Triangle Park
James Perkins	IBM Kingston
Marcia Peters	IBM Research Triangle Park
Larry Plank	IBM Rochester
Gary Schultz	IBM Research Triangle Park
Suvas M. Shah	IBM Research Triangle Park
Wolfgang Singer	IBM Austria
Bill Stoddard	IBM Research Triangle Park
Ed Tremblay	IBM Research Triangle Park
Shawn Walsh	ITSO Raleigh Center
The Editing & Graphics Team	ITSO Raleigh Center

Chapter 1. APPN Overview

This chapter gives a short introduction to Advanced Peer-to-Peer Networking, describes the position of APPN in relation to LEN and SNA, and introduces the basic terminology used with APPN.

1.1 LEN and APPN

A network can be very simple, for example, two PS/2s connected by a telephone line, as shown in the figure below.

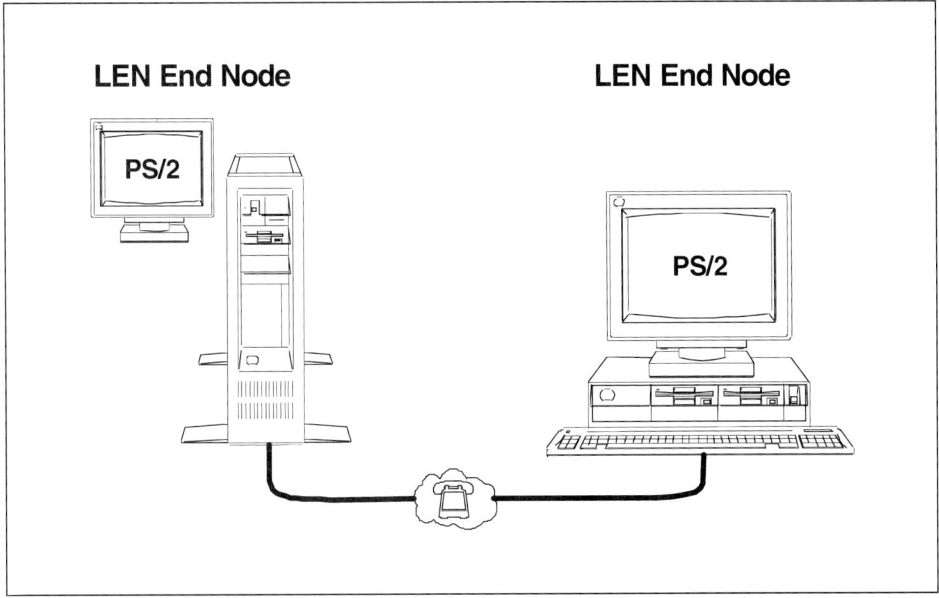

Figure 1. Two PS/2s Forming a LEN Connection

The purpose of connecting these two systems is to exchange data between two end users. An end user could be a person working with this system, a program running on the system, or a printer controlled by the system.

The end user gains access to the network through the logical unit (LU). Before the two LUs are able to exchange data, they must start an LU-LU session. For program-to-program communication, this session would typically be an LU 6.2 session.

In the case above, when the two systems (PS/2s) establish a *low-entry networking* (LEN) connection, the two connecting systems are known as *LEN end nodes*. Using the architectural terms, the configuration above could be drawn as shown in Figure 2 on page 2.

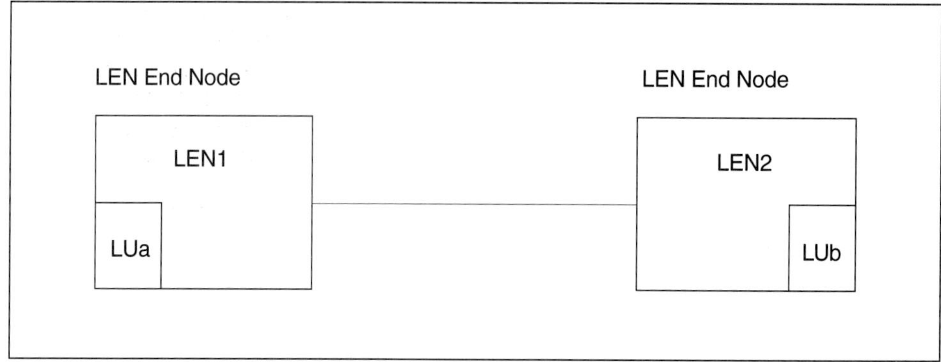

Figure 2. The Basic LEN Connection

Several systems can be configured as LEN end nodes, such as VTAM and NCP, AS/400 and PS/2. LEN end nodes provide the minimum functions required to:

- Provide a connection between LEN1 and LEN2
- Establish a session between the LUs named LUa and LUb
- Transport data

The relation between LEN end nodes is truly peer-to-peer. Either side may activate a connection or start a session to the partner.

A significant feature of the LEN architecture is that there are only *two* adjacent nodes involved in a LEN connection. No matter how many nodes there may be in the network, a LEN connection recognizes only two of them.

Obviously, there must be functions in addition to LEN if a network with more than two nodes is to be built. One of these functions is the capability to act as an intermediate node (that is, a node that can receive data that is not for itself and can pass it on to the destination node). This principle is shown in Figure 3.

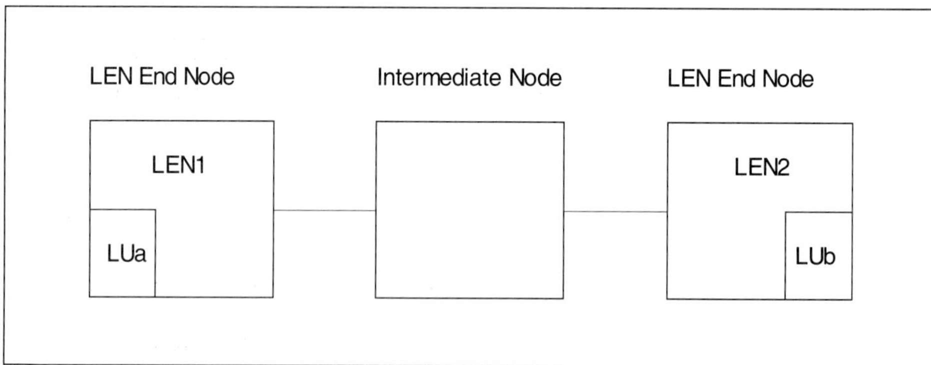

Figure 3. LEN End Nodes Connected to an Intermediate Node

According to the LEN architecture, the relation between LEN end nodes is always a "*two*-node peer relationship." LUs residing on nonadjacent LEN nodes can establish sessions and exchange data because the intermediate node presents itself as a LEN node owning all LUs residing on nonadjacent nodes. As seen from LEN1, the intermediate node is just a normal LEN end node, and LEN2 is not visible at all from LEN1. For LEN1, the LU named LUb seems to be in the intermediate node.

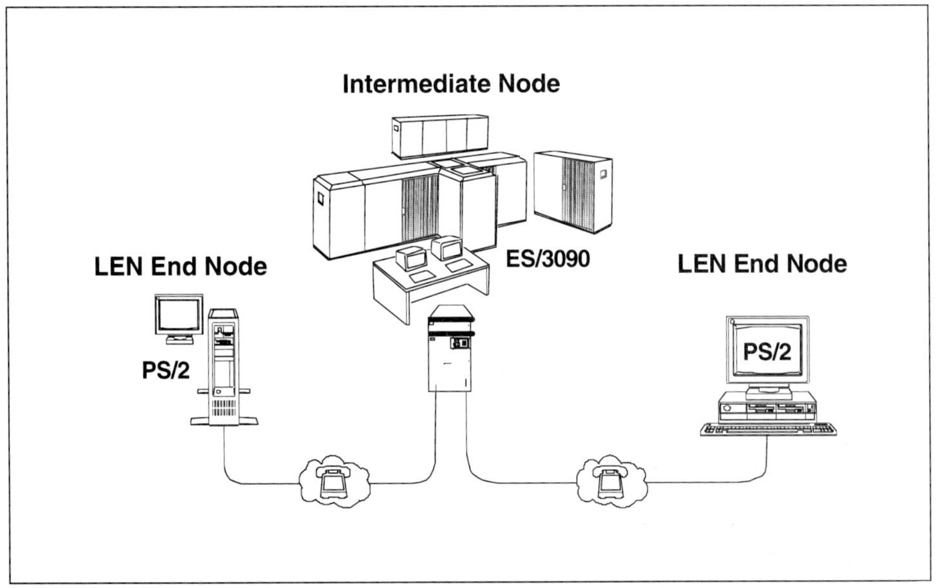

Figure 4. VTAM/NCP Providing the Intermediate Routing Function for LEN End Nodes

VTAM and NCP support the LEN end node function and also provide intermediate routing between LEN end nodes. Figure 4 gives an example of this configuration with VTAM on an ES/3090 as intermediate node.

The functions of LEN nodes are limited; for example, they are not able to exchange topology and configuration data. Additional functions are needed to reduce the number of definitions and the maintenance effort when building larger networks. For this purpose the Advanced Peer-to-Peer Networking (APPN) architecture was developed and published as an extension to SNA (Systems Network Architecture).

APPN architecture defines two basic node types:

APPN End Node

The APPN end node is similar to a LEN end node, except that the control point (CP) of the end node exchanges information with the CP in the adjacent *network node*. The communication over the CP-CP sessions reduces the requirement for network definitions, and thus makes installation and maintenance of the network easier.

APPN Network Node

The APPN network node has intermediate routing functions and provides network services to either APPN or LEN end nodes that are attached to it. It establishes CP-CP sessions with its adjacent APPN network nodes to exchange network topology and resource information. CP-CP sessions between an APPN network node and an adjacent APPN end node are required only if the APPN end node is to receive network services (such as partner location) from the APPN network node.

APPN architecture also describes the connection of LEN end nodes to APPN network nodes or APPN end nodes.

Figure 5 shows the basic form of an APPN network and gives an example of the services provided by the APPN network node. When LUa requests a session with LUc, the network node will locate the partner LU and assist in establishing the session.

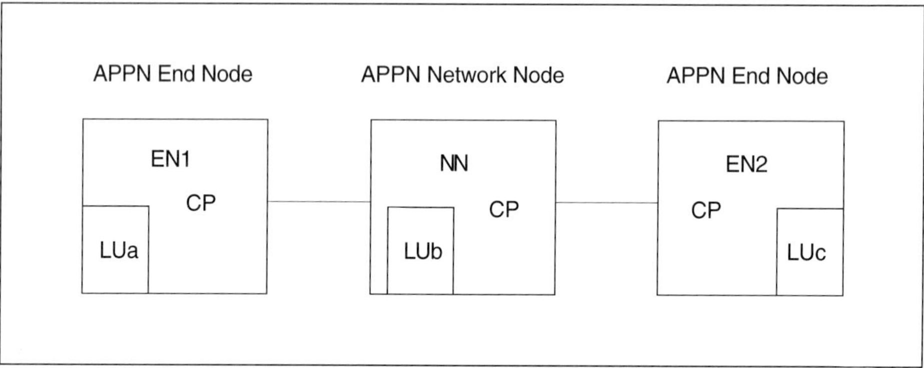

Figure 5. Advanced Peer-to-Peer Networking with Three Nodes

Figure 5 shows the basic form of an APPN network. However, APPN networks can be much more complex. The architecture does not limit the number of nodes in an APPN network nor does it explicitly limit the number of intermediate APPN network nodes through which LU-LU sessions are routed. One restriction exists, however: the length of the Route Selection control vector (RSCV) describing a physical session path is limited to 255 bytes. See 5.7.1.3, " The Route Selection Control Vector" on page 104 for a detailed discussion.

Figure 6 on page 5 shows a backbone structure of APPN network nodes to which end nodes connect. The APPN nodes communicate using CP-CP sessions between adjacent nodes. User sessions can be established from any LU to any LU.

Note: NAU names must be unique within an APPN network. To ensure this uniqueness you need a consistent naming convention.

1.4.1.2 Network Identifiers

You can divide your "network" into partitions in order to simplify your resource name administration. Each partition will have a network identifier (network ID), 1 to 8 bytes long. Net IDs are used throughout SNA, in both subarea and APPN parts of networks. Because names of LUs and CPs have to be unique only within the scope of a network ID, you can assign and administer them independently for each partition.

Registering can help your network administrators ensure the uniqueness of a network ID. IBM provides a worldwide registry for network IDs. Information on the registration process can be obtained from your IBM representative.

IBM-registered network IDs should have an 8-character name of the form `cceeeenn`, where:

cc is the country code (according to ISO Standard 3166).

eeee is the enterprise code (unique within a country).

nn is the network suffix code (unique within one enterprise).

1.4.1.3 Network Names

A *network name* is an identifier of a network resource. Each CP, LU, link, and link station in an SNA network has a network name. The network names are assigned through system definition. In an APPN node, the system definition is done using the node operator facility (NOF).

1.4.1.4 Network-Qualified Names

A resource's *network-qualified name* identifies both the resource and the network in which the resource is located. It is a concatenation of the network ID and the network name of the resource. For example, NETA.LUA, NETA.LUB, NETB.LUA, and NETB.LUB are all valid network-qualified names, and they refer to four different entities.

1.5 Addresses

Addresses are used in all SNA networks for routing data correctly between session partners. There are big differences, however, in the ways addresses are used in traditional subarea SNA on the one hand and APPN on the other, and differences again between basic APPN and HPR.

1.5.1.1 Addresses in Subarea Networks

In traditional subarea SNA, each resource is assigned its own distinct network address. The subarea number part of this is used by VTAM and NCP nodes in the network to route data to the correct destination subarea. There, local addressing takes over. The boundary function of the VTAM or NCP node concerned converts the network addresses to local addresses. These are seen in the transmission headers of packets on boundary links.

1.5.1.2 Addresses in APPN Networks

In an APPN network, routing information is session oriented throughout. The *address* used in an APPN transmission header is an identifier unique on the given TG for a particular session, rather than the address of the NAU. The identifiers are locally defined for each pair of adjacent routing nodes and are only *temporarily* assigned. They are assigned at session initiation, and released when the session ends. The session initiation request (BIND) carries routing information about the full session path that determines the sequence of links used from origin to destination. The local session identifier stored in each intermediate node in a session path is contained in a *session connector* and kept only for the life of the session.

The session identifier is associated with:

- A particular session
- A transmission group between two nodes

Figure 9 shows a session between two LUs, LUa and LUb, residing on two nonadjacent APPN end nodes. The session data is routed through two intermediate network nodes. The session can be thought of as a sequence of three session stages or *hops* with a distinct session identifier assigned to each session stage.

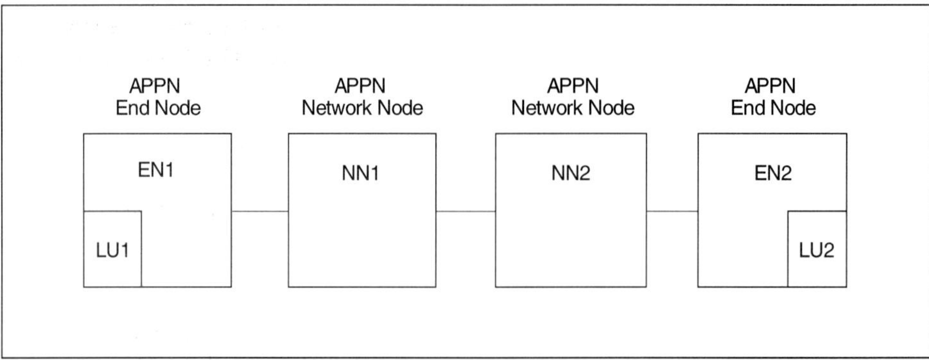

Figure 9. Session with Several Session Stages

Session identifiers vary at different session stages, which is why they are called *local-form session identifiers* (LFSIDs). The LFSID is set up during session establishment by the address space manager component of the CP and assigned for the lifetime of an LU-LU (or CP-CP) session. Details may be found in Chapter 3, "Address Space Manager" on page 47.

Each session is uniquely identified by a network-unique identifier, the fully qualified procedure correlation ID (FQPCID), which is described in 7.2, "Fully Qualified Procedure Correlation Identifier (FQPCID)" on page 140.

1.5.1.3 Addresses in HPR Networks

In an HPR network, a new form of routing is used, which is called *automatic network routing* (ANR). ANR is a source-routing protocol, which means the sender of a packet provides the information about the physical path the packet will use through the network in the network header. As HPR provides the ability to do nondisruptive path switching, the HPR architecture handles the case where the route changes in mid-session.

ANR uses a new form of addressing to identify the route through an HPR network. However, unlike the APPN session-oriented addresses (LFSIDs), the addresses in ANR are based purely on the TGs that make up the route. The network header contains a list of ANR labels that identify the route through the network. Each ANR label describes a TG that is to be taken to exit a node. This is described in more detail in 8.3, "Automatic Network Routing" on page 166.

In addition to the ANR labels, there are still addresses that are associated with sessions in HPR. Each session will have a pair of unique session addresses, one for each direction. Unlike the LFSID that identifies each stage of the APPN session, the HPR session addresses are used only on an (HPR) end-to-end basis. They are known as *enhanced session addresses.*

The process of supporting the end-to-end sessions across the HPR network is called rapid transport protocol or RTP. This is described in more detail in 8.4, "Rapid-Transport Protocol" on page 173.

In a network that is supporting both existing APPN nodes and HPR nodes, both the APPN and the HPR methods of addressing are used. This is described in more detail in 8.9.2, "Routing in APPN/HPR Networks" on page 213.

1.6 Domains

A domain is an *area of control.* A domain in an APPN network consists of the control point in a node and the resources controlled by the control point. Consequently, all APPN networks are multidomain networks.

Though all APPN nodes are peers with respect to session initiations and do not rely on other nodes to control their resources, APPN end nodes and LEN end nodes do use the services of network nodes. The domain of an APPN end node or LEN end node contains the node's own (local) resources. The domain of an APPN network node contains its local resources *and* the resources of those nodes that use the network node's services. Thus, the domains of the APPN end nodes and LEN end nodes are included in the domains of their respective network node servers.

Note: In traditional subarea networking, a domain is the part of the network owned by a VTAM System Services Control Point (SSCP). Within this document, when using the term domain, we refer to an APPN domain unless explicitly stated otherwise.

1.7 Node Types

Before and after its announcement in 1986, the LEN end node was known by many names. Some of the names for the LEN end node that are found in various publications are:

LEN end node
LEN node
Peer node
PU type 2.1
PU 2.1
SNA PU 2.1
SNA Type 2.1 node
Type 2.1
T2.1

All the names mentioned above are synonyms for *LEN end node*. They all refer to the same function set. With the APPN extensions to SNA, two other types of nodes, *APPN end node* and *APPN network node*, have been introduced. Because VTAM as an APPN node identifies itself as a T5 node to the APPN network, it is no longer valid to use the term *T2.1 node* when referring to an APPN node. Throughout this document we will use the term *APPN or LEN node* to refer to any of these three types of nodes, and use the term *APPN node* when referring to either an APPN network node or an APPN end node.

1.7.1 APPN Network Node

An APPN network node provides distributed directory and routing services for all LUs that it controls. These LUs may be located on the APPN network node itself or on one of the adjacent LEN or APPN end nodes for which the APPN network node provides network node services. Jointly, with the other active APPN network nodes, an APPN network node is able to locate all destination LUs known in the network.

A facility known as *central resource registration* allows an APPN network node to register its resources at a central directory server. Once a resource is registered, APPN network nodes can locate the resource by querying the central directory server instead of using a broadcast search, thus improving network search performance during session establishment.

After the LU is located, the APPN network node is able to calculate the route between origin and destination LU according to the required class of service. All network nodes exchange information about the topology of the network. When two adjacent network nodes establish a connection, they exchange information about the network topology as they know it. In turn, each network node broadcasts this network topology information to other network nodes with which it has CP-CP sessions.

Alternatively, if the connection between network nodes is deactivated, then each network node broadcasts this change to all other active adjacent network nodes. An APPN network node that is taken out of service will be declared inactive and, after some time, removed from the topology information in all network nodes together with its routing capabilities to other nodes.

The APPN network node is also capable of routing LU-LU sessions through itself from one adjacent node to another adjacent node. This function is called intermediate session routing.

1.7.2 APPN End Node

An APPN end node provides limited directory and routing services for its local LUs. It can select an adjacent APPN network node and request this network node to be its *network node server.* If accepted by the network node, the APPN end node may register its local resources at the network node server. This allows the network node server to intercept Locate search requests for the APPN end node's resources and pass these requests to the APPN end node for verification.

Without a network node server an APPN end node can function as a LEN end node and establish LU-LU sessions with a partner LU in an adjacent APPN or LEN node.

When it needs to find an LU it does not already know, an APPN end node sends a Locate search request to its network node server. The network node server uses its distributed directory and routing facilities to locate the LU (via directed, central directory, or broadcast searches) and calculates the optimal route to the destination LU from the APPN end node.

The APPN end node may have active connections to multiple adjacent network nodes. At any given moment, however, only one of the network nodes can be acting as its network node server. The APPN end node establishes CP-CP sessions with a network node to select that network node as its network node server.

On APPN network nodes, APPN end nodes are categorized as either *authorized* or *unauthorized.* An authorized APPN end node may send registration requests to register local network accessible resources at a network node server, a facility known as *end node resource registration*, and may, in addition, request that these resources be registered with the central directory server. If during session establishment a network node server does not know where an LU is located, it will query authorized APPN end nodes within its domain that have indicated they are willing to be queried for unknown resources. Network accessible resources on unauthorized nodes require explicit definition at the network node server, either statically as part of its system definition, or dynamically by the network node server's operator. To avoid unnecessary explicit definitions of resources of authorized APPN end nodes at their network node servers, you should have them register their resources, or be set up to allow the network node servers to query them for unknown resources.

An APPN end node can attach to any LEN or APPN node regardless of its network ID.

1.7.3 LEN End Node

A LEN end node provides peer-to-peer connectivity to other LEN end nodes, APPN end nodes, or APPN network nodes. A LEN end node requires that all network accessible resources, either controlled by the LEN end node itself or on other nodes, be defined at the LEN end node. LUs on adjacent nodes need to be defined with the control point name of the adjacent node. LUs on nonadjacent nodes need to be defined with the control point name of an adjacent network node, as LEN end nodes assume that LUs are either local or reside on adjacent nodes.

Unlike APPN end nodes, the LEN end node cannot establish CP-CP sessions with an APPN network node. A LEN end node therefore cannot register resources at a network node server. Nor can it request a network node server to search for a resource, or to calculate the route between itself and the node containing a destination resource. It does, however, use the distributed directory and routing services of an adjacent network node indirectly. It does this by predefining remote LUs, owned by nonadjacent nodes, with the CP name of an adjacent APPN network node. The session activation (BIND) request for that remote LU is sent by the LEN end node to the adjacent network node. The network node, in turn, automatically acts as the LEN end node's network node server, locates the actual destination LU, calculates the route to it, and uses this route to send the BIND.

A LEN end node can attach to any LEN or APPN node regardless of its network ID.

1.7.4 Other Node Types

In SNA, a node represents an endpoint of a link or a junction common to two or more links. The LEN end node, APPN end node, and APPN network node are endpoints of a link. Each node has a distinct role in an APPN network.

Besides these node types you will find references in the APPN literature to other node types that are either synonyms for nodes as seen from a subarea network, represent a specific junction in the network, or represent an APPN node with additional functions. The following is not a complete list, but it does contain all types found when creating this document:

- Boundary and peripheral node
- Composite node
- Interchange node
- Virtual Routing node
- Peripheral border node
- Extended border node
- HPR node
- Branch network node

1.7.4.1 Boundary and Peripheral Node

In traditional subarea SNA networks, resources are controlled through hierarchical structures. Nodes in these networks are categorized as *subarea* and *peripheral* nodes.

An example of such an SNA network is an IBM System/390 mainframe running VTAM with a 3745 communication controller running NCP, and 3270 terminals attached via IBM 3274 controllers. The VTAM and NCP nodes are both referred to as subarea nodes. The VTAM subarea node contains the System Services Control Point (SSCP). Like the APPN control point, the SSCP controls all the resources in its domain.

Attached to these subarea, or *boundary*, nodes are the peripheral nodes. The peripheral node is either a PU T2.0 or an APPN or LEN node. The PU T2.0 node, for instance one of the IBM 3274 clusters in our example network, is a traditional hierarchical node that requires the support of an SSCP to establish sessions, and of the boundary function for its addressing.

Traditional subarea SNA allowed LEN connections only; CP-CP sessions could not be established between VTAM and the APPN nodes.

With the introduction of APPN VTAM, a VTAM or a composite network node (subarea network consisting of one VTAM and one or more NCPs) is able to present an APPN image to other APPN nodes. APPN VTAM allows CP-CP sessions with APPN nodes attached to the VTAM or NCP boundary function to gain full APPN connectivity. The term *peripheral* node has lost its value in a network that is truly peer-to-peer.

1.7.4.2 Composite Node

The term *composite node* is used in some publications to represent a group of nodes that appear as one APPN or LEN node to other nodes in an APPN network. For example, a subarea network consisting of a VTAM host and some NCPs is a multiple-node network, but when connected to an APPN node, appears as *one* logical APPN or LEN node.

A subarea composite node may appear as either a LEN end node or as an APPN network node. In the former case, the term composite LEN node is used; in the latter case the term composite network node (CNN) is used.

1.7.4.3 Interchange Node

A VTAM host acting as an interchange node (ICN) can be a stand-alone APPN VTAM node or a composite network node. The ICN routes sessions from APPN nodes into and through the subarea network using subarea routing, without exposing the subarea implementation to the APPN part of the network. This is accomplished by making the APPN VTAM node, plus all its owned resources, appear to other nodes as a single APPN network node with multiple connections. At the same time the ICN, and the NCPs it owns, will maintain their subarea appearance to other subarea nodes.

The ICN supports SSCP-SSCP sessions with other VTAM nodes as well as CP-CP sessions with adjacent APPN network nodes and end nodes. This support allows the ICN to use both APPN and subarea data flows to locate LUs and to provide the best route between nodes. APPN session setup protocols, which flow on CP-CP sessions, are converted to the corresponding subarea protocols that flow on SSCP-SSCP sessions, and vice versa.

To an ICN, see for example VTAM1/NCP in Figure 10, multiple VTAMs and NCPs may connect using subarea protocols. Session establishment is possible between any LU in the subarea network and any LU in the APPN network. The VTAM host to which APPN nodes attach, or the VTAM host owning the NCPs to which APPN nodes attach, must have implemented APPN VTAM, as it is responsible (as an *interchange node*) for the conversion of subarea to APPN protocols and vice versa. Other VTAMs within the subarea network may be backlevel VTAMs. From the viewpoint of the APPN nodes, LUs owned by VTAMs (for example, VTAM2 or VTAM3) other than the VTAM providing the interchange function are considered to reside on APPN end nodes.

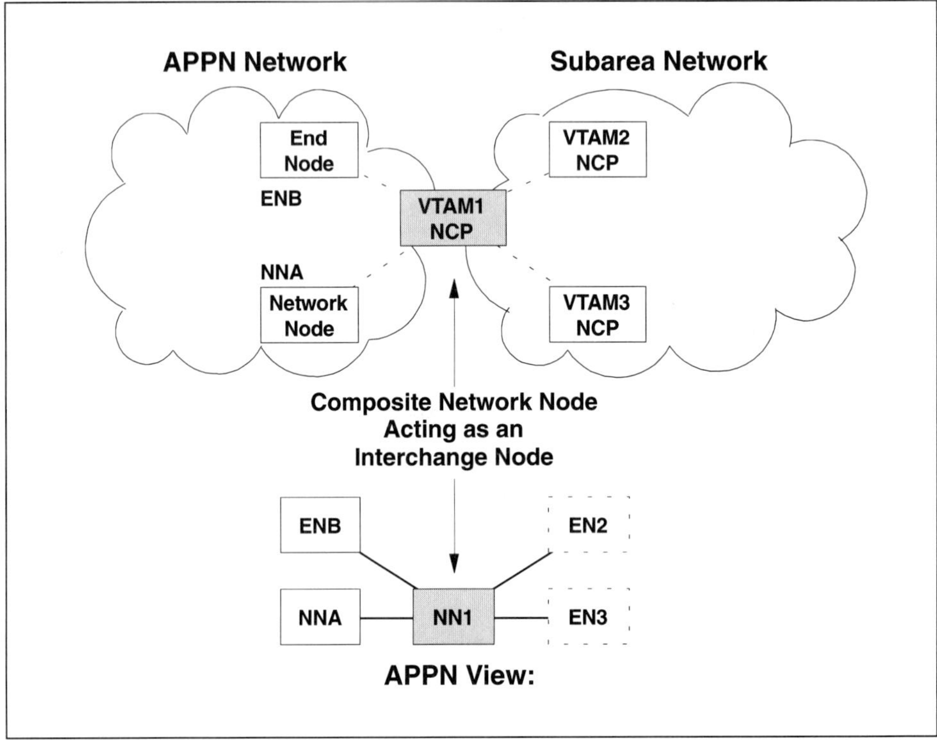

Figure 10. Composite Network Node Acting As an Interchange Node

Note: Figure 10 shows the basic form of connecting APPN and subarea networks using a composite network node acting as an interchange node. For more details see Appendix C, "APPN VTAM" on page 409.

1.7.4.4 Virtual Routing Node

APPN allows APPN nodes to reduce the addressing information stored at each node connected to a shared-access transmission facility (SATF), such as a token-ring, by allowing each node to define a virtual routing node (VRN) to represent its connection to the shared facility and all other nodes similarly configured. The SATF and the set of nodes having defined a connection to a common virtual routing node are said to comprise a *connection network*.

A virtual routing node (VRN) is not a node, but it is a way to define an APPN node's attachment to a shared-access transport facility. It reduces end node definition requirements by relying on the network node server to discover the common connection and supply necessary link-level signaling information as part of the regular Locate search process. LU-LU session data can then be routed directly, without intermediate node routing, between APPN nodes attached to the SATF. For more information see 4.6, “Connection Networks and Virtual Routing Nodes” on page 66.

1.7.4.5 Border Node

Base APPN architecture does not allow two adjacent APPN network nodes to connect and establish CP-CP sessions when they do not have the same net ID. The border node is an optional feature of an APPN network node that overcomes this restriction.

A border node can connect to an APPN network node with a different net ID, establish CP-CP sessions with it, and allow session establishment between LUs in different net ID *subnetworks*. Topology information is not passed between the subnetworks. Similarly a border node can also connect to another border node. Two types of border node are defined in the APPN architecture: peripheral border node and extended border node. For more information see Chapter 10, “Border Node” on page 231.

1.7.4.6 Peripheral Border Node

The peripheral border node enables the connection of network nodes with different net IDs and allows session establishment between LUs in different, adjacent, subnetworks.

A peripheral border node provides directory, session setup and route selection services across the boundary between paired subnetworks with different net IDs while isolating each subnetwork from the other network's topology information. This reduces the flow of topology updates and the storage requirements for the network topology database on network nodes in each of the network partitions. For more information see 10.2, “Peripheral Border Node” on page 233.

1.7.4.7 Extended Border Node

The extended border node allows the connection of network nodes with different net IDs, and session establishment between LUs in different net ID subnetworks that need not be adjacent.

An extended border node provides directory, session setup and route selection services across the boundary between paired or cascaded nonnative net ID subnetworks. An extended border node can also partition a single net ID subnetwork into two or more clusters or topology subnetworks with the same net ID, thus isolating one from the topology of the other. For more information see 10.3, "Extended Border Node" on page 244.

1.7.4.8 HPR Node

An HPR node is an APPN node that has implemented the optional HPR functions. An HPR node can be an APPN end node or an APPN network node.

In a mixed APPN and HPR topology network, a group of interconnected HPR nodes is sometimes referred to as an *HPR subnetwork* or an HPR subnet. When an HPR link is activated between a pair of adjacent HPR nodes, an HPR subnet is formed.

In addition, the terms base APPN subnetwork and base APPN subnet may also be used when referring to a part of the network that is not an HPR subnet. HPR subnets are not separated from the other parts of the topology database.

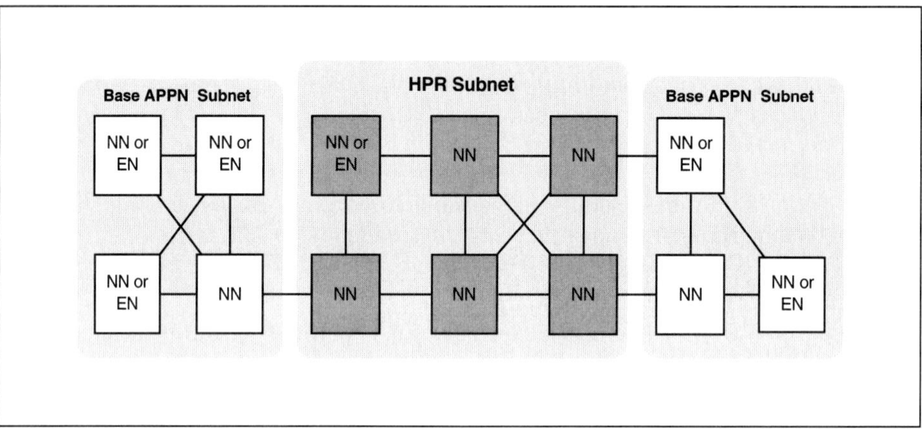

Figure 11. HPR Nodes and HPR Subnets

Figure 11 shows a backbone HPR subnet with two adjacent base APPN subnets. The six nodes in the HPR subnet are interconnected with HPR links.

If any of the nodes are to provide intermediate session routing, then they must be network nodes. But if a node acts only as a session endpoint, it can be a network node or an end node. The HPR nodes are exactly the same as APPN nodes in this respect.

If a product supports HPR, it can choose to implement only the base HPR function, or the HPR base function and optional functions. The base HPR function provides ANR routing, so as a minimum an HPR node can always act as an intermediate node in an

HPR network. An HPR node that is providing only ANR routing will always be a network node. For more information, see 8.2, "HPR Base and Options" on page 162.

1.7.4.9 Branch Extender

Branch network node is a new function that enhances network node functionality. A branch network node is a network node that acts as a network node to the APPN nodes downstream of it, but presents an end node image to the APPN nodes upstream of it. By appearing as an end node to the backbone network, the number of network nodes in the backbone is reduced. This function reduces the number of network nodes in the backbone network. This greatly reduces the topology updates that flow through the backbone, which in turn decreases the traffic on WAN links. For more information, see 10.5, "Branch Network Node" on page 252.

Chapter 2. APPN and LEN Node Structure

This chapter describes the structure and components of APPN and LEN nodes. The structure of a LEN end node, APPN end node, or APPN network node is shown in Figure 12 on page 22. The components in the figure are described below:

Node Operator
: This component defines all information required by the node (for example, on links to adjacent nodes, and on LUs within its domain) and causes activation and deactivation of the node and its resources (for example, links). It may also query the status of a node's resources. See 2.1, "Node Operator Facility (NOF)" on page 23 for more details.

Node Operator Facility (NOF)
: The function of this component is to allow communication between the node operator and the control point (CP), intermediate session routing (ISR), and LUs. NOF initializes the CP and ISR components when the node is started. It also performs functions such as the following when requested to do so by the node operator:

- Defining (creating) and deleting (destroying) LUs
- Activating and deactivating links
- Querying the CP and ISR for database and status information

Application Transaction Program (TP)
: These programs communicate with other local or remote application transaction programs (TPs) to perform user-defined functions. Communication is accomplished by establishing conversations between TPs. Data is then exchanged between the TPs using an LU verb interface.

Control Point (CP)
: The function of the CP is to manage the resources of the node. It creates the path control (PC), rapid-transport protocol (RTP), network connection layer (NCL), and data link control (DLC) components. The CP also manages session resources and provides facilities such as directory and topology information. The CP is created by NOF when the node is started.

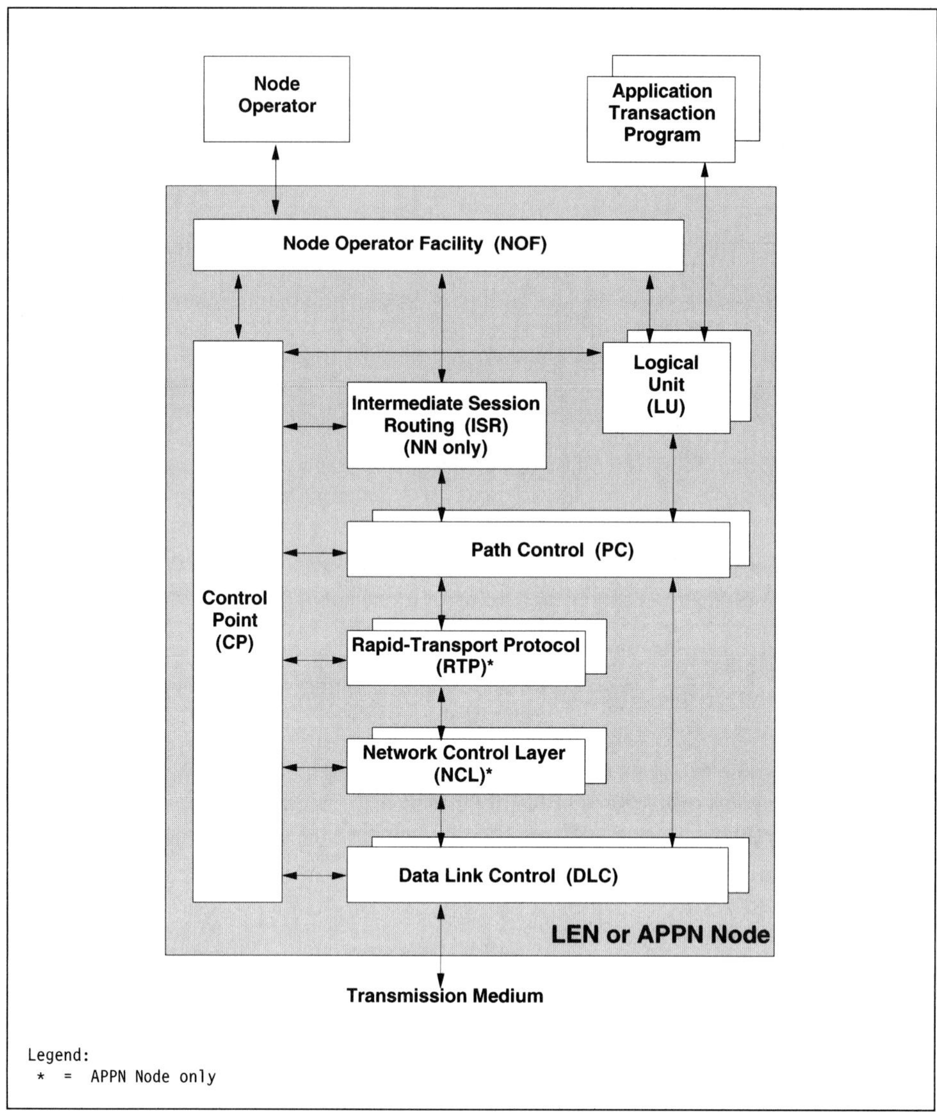

Figure 12. Structure of an APPN or LEN Node

Intermediate Session Routing (ISR)

The intermediate session routing (ISR) component is present only in an APPN network node. The primary function of ISR is to route session traffic received from one node and destined to another node. ISR is created by NOF when the node is started.

Logical Unit (LU)

The LU serves as a port into the network for one or more application transaction programs. It establishes sessions with other LUs. Conversations are allocated on these sessions that allow communication between TPs.

Path Control (PC)

This component routes message units from LUs, ISR, and CP within the node to RTP for transmission over an RTP connection or, when not using HPR, to DLC for transmission to adjacent nodes. Messages received by path control from DLC or RTP are routed to the appropriate component (CP, LU, or ISR). PC also routes message units between LUs within the local node.

Rapid-Transport Protocol (RTP)

RTP provides the protocols necessary to ensure reliable delivery of messages between RTP connection endpoints. Its functions include end-to-end error recovery, nondisruptive path switch, and end-to-end flow and congestion control. RTP routes messages received from PC to NCL and those received from NCL to PC. RTP is present only in an APPN node that supports the RTP functions for HPR.

Network Connection Layer (NCL)

NCL uses automatic network routing (ANR), which is a source-routing protocol. A message received from RTP or DLC is forwarded to DLC or RTP according to the routing information in the message's NCL header. NCL is present only in an APPN node that supports the HPR base functions.

Data Link Control (DLC)

DLC provides the protocols necessary for reliable or unreliable (for NCL packets when not using link-level error recovery) delivery of messages between link stations in adjacent nodes attached to a common transmission medium. DLC also controls the node attachment to various types of transmission media.

For a detailed description of RTP and NCL see Chapter 8, "High-Performance Routing" on page 155.

2.1 Node Operator Facility (NOF)

The node operator facility provides an interface to the APPN or LEN node so that node operators can control the operation of the node. For example, the node operator may activate and deactivate link stations, define and delete LUs, query the control point about links and another node's resources, and receive diagnostic information.

The node operator can be:

A human operator using an interactive display to issue commands.

A system-specific dialog manager converts the information entered by the human operator into node operator commands and forwards the commands to the node operator facility. The dialog manager receives the command results from the node operator facility and shows those results on the display in a human-readable form.

A file containing a list of commands.

An implementation-specific file interpreter reads the command file, converts the file records into node operator commands, and forwards the commands to the node operator facility. The file interpreter logs or discards the command results after receiving them from the node operator facility. Command files are very useful when a series of commands must be repeated periodically (for example, a command file may be used to load the initial configuration when a node is started). The file interpreter may discard the results because the node operator facility will log commands and their results upon request.

A transaction program handling remote requests from a partner transaction program in another node.

Remote operations of the node are allowed by permitting node operator commands to be issued by transaction programs. The local transaction program receives a command from a partner transaction program, converts it from the transaction-specific format into a node operator command, and issues it. The local transaction program receives the command result from the node operator facility and forwards this result to the remote transaction program.

All three types of node operators make use of a program within the system to interact with the node operator facility. Figure 13 on page 26 illustrates the different cases.

2.1.1 Node Initialization

At node initialization time the node operator facility creates and initializes the control point components in a controlled manner using installation-defined parameters. The node initialization is started with one or more of the following parameters:

- The node type (network node, LEN or APPN end node)
- The network-qualified name of the control point
- Whether negotiable link stations are supported
- Whether segment reassembly is supported
- Whether BIND reassembly is supported
- Whether the node's resources should be registered with its network node server (APPN end node only)
- Whether segmenting is supported
- Whether mapping of mode name to class of service and transmission priority is supported
- Type of management services node (entry point or focal point)

- The name of management services major vector file for generic alerts
- The name of the management services log file
- The type of resource registration supported (network node only)
- Whether the node is a central directory server (network node only)
- Whether incremental update to route-selection tree cache is allowed (network node only)
- The name of the topology database file
- The name of the class-of-service (COS) definition file
- Maximum number of route-selection trees cached (network node only)
- Maximum number of out-of-sequence TDUs accepted from adjacent node (network node only)
- List of resource types this node can be searched for by its network node server (LU is the only resource type currently supported)
- Maximum number of LU-LU sessions ISR can support (network node only)

In the chapters describing the various control point components, reference will be made to the node's initialization parameters.

The components that NOF creates and the order of their creation are:

1. Address space manager
2. Session services
3. Directory services
4. Configuration services
5. Management services
6. Topology and routing services
7. Session connector manager of ISR (network node only)
8. Session manager of the control point (except LEN nodes)
9. Session manager of each LU

2.1.2 Node Operator Facility Commands

The node operator facility interfaces with the control point components to define, change, or delete the node's resources, start and stop transmission groups, or obtain the status of resources. Where appropriate, references are made in this document to specific commands and their function.

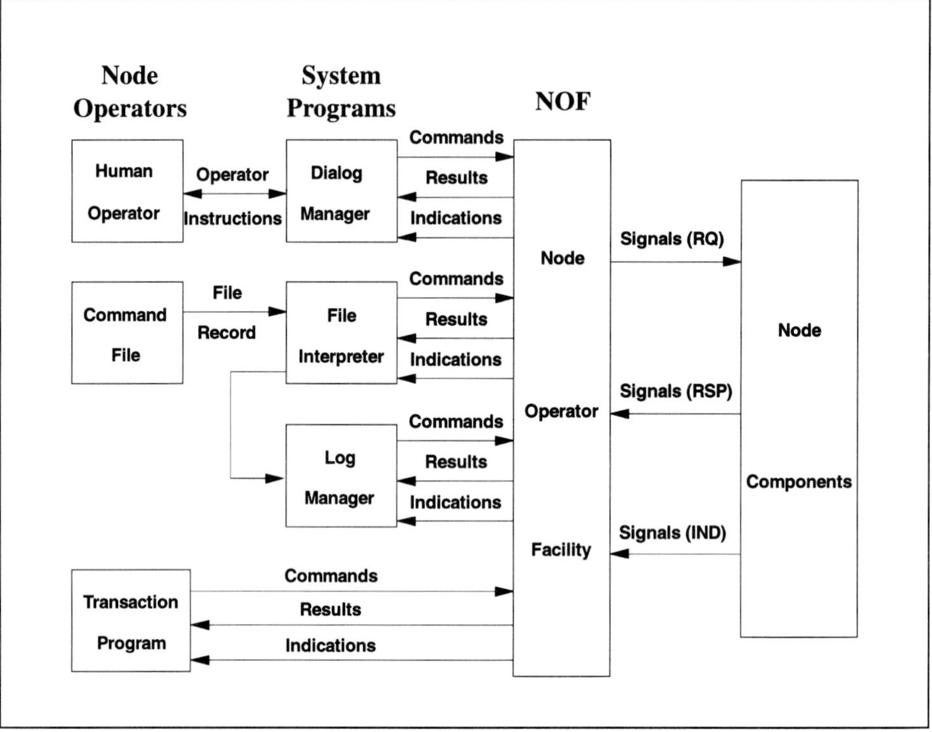

Figure 13. Node Operators. Interaction between node operators, the node operator facility, and the node components.

The available node operator facility commands (base set 090) are:

- Define/Delete adjacent node
- Define/Delete class of service (COS)
- Define/Delete connection network (CN)
- Define/Delete directory entry
- Define/Delete data link control instance
- Define/Delete link station
- Define/Delete local LU
- Define/Delete mode
- Define/Delete partner LU
- Define/Delete port
- Define/Delete TP
- Initialize/Change/Reset session limit
- Query class of service (COS)
- Query connection network (CN)
- Query data link control instance
- Query link station
- Query port

- Query statistics
- Start node
- Start TP
- Start/Stop data link control instance
- Start/Stop link station
- Start/Stop port

The following node operator facility commands (base set 091) apply only to network nodes:

- Define/Delete intermediate session routing tuning parameters
- Define/Delete node characteristics

For more information on node operator facility commands see Chapter 3, "Node Operator Facility" in *SNA APPN Architecture Reference*, SC30-3422.

2.2 Control Point (CP)

The control point (CP) is responsible for managing the node and its resources. It activates links to adjacent nodes, exchanges CP capabilities when establishing CP-CP sessions with adjacent nodes, and interacts with the node operator through the node operator facility. For its local LUs, the control point finds the partner LU's location and provides routing information. The services of the control point are described in detail later in this document. They can be categorized as follows:

Configuration Services (CP.CS)
Configuration services manages the links to adjacent nodes.

Topology and Routing Services (CP.TS)
In LEN end nodes and APPN end nodes, topology and routing services collects information on links and adjacent nodes. In APPN network nodes, topology and routing services additionally collects and exchanges information on other network nodes and the links between them. For LU-LU sessions, it provides the best route between the two LUs.

Directory Services (CP.DS)
The directory services component is responsible for locating network resources throughout the APPN network. On LEN end nodes, directory services searches only the node's local database for defined resources. On APPN end nodes, directory services searches its local database first. Then, if unsuccessful, it uses the distributed search facilities provided by the APPN network node with which it has established CP-CP sessions. Although an end node can have active links to more network nodes, it maintains CP-CP sessions only with its current network node server.

In order to locate network resources, directory services at each node collects resource information from the node operator and maintains this information in the local directory database. On request of an authorized APPN end node for which it provides network node services, directory services at the APPN network node registers the APPN end node's resources in its local directory database.

Session Services (CP.SS)
The session services component is responsible for activating and deactivating the CP-CP sessions that are used by CP components to exchange network information. It is also responsible for maintaining and assigning unique session identifiers to sessions and assisting logical units in activating and deactivating LU-LU sessions.

Address Space Manager (CP.ASM)
The address space manager administers addresses used by path control to identify sessions on links. It interacts with LUs and ISR at BIND/RSP(BIND) and UNBIND/RSP(UNBIND) time. Optional features of address space manager are BIND reassembly and adaptive BIND pacing.

Management Services (CP.MS)
Management services monitors and controls the node's resources. Upon malfunction it will receive or generate alerts and forward these alerts to the network operator in its own node or a focal point node.

Note: APPN optional function set 1012 (LU Name = CP Name) allows the node control point to serve as an LU for end-user sessions. This is strictly a product implementation option and in this book the CP and LU are treated as distinct roles. However, merging the CP and LU roles has the following implications:

- The CP and LU roles are distinguished only by mode names. CPSVCMG denotes the CP-CP session and all other mode names denote the LU-LU role.
- The NOF operator interface and protocol boundaries with other nodes may be extended to accommodate the merged case by allowing all LU functionality to apply to the merged CP/LU. LU logic does not distinguish between the CP and LU roles, so all verbs may apply to either context.
- The merged CP/LU can support local application transaction programs and be treated as both CP and LU by partner nodes, using the mode to distinguish contexts.
- The merged CP/LU may be entered into a directory as a CP and as an LU. The same name would be listed under both resource types, with the CP entry being the parent of the LU entry.
- In the case of a network node, the location of the CP/LU can be learned from the topology database, avoiding a broadcast search when the DLU is not known.

2.2.1 CP-CP Sessions

To perform directory services, session services, and topology and routing services, adjacent nodes throughout the APPN network use pairs of parallel CP-CP sessions to exchange network information. All these CP-CP sessions use LU 6.2 protocols. In all cases, each session partner is the *contention winner* on one of the pair of sessions, and the *contention loser* on the other. Both sessions must be active in order for the partner CPs to begin or continue their interactions.

Once the CP-CP sessions are established, the *capabilities* of the control points are exchanged.

Network nodes use CP-CP sessions to keep track of the network topology and also for directory and session services, and management. A network node establishes CP-CP sessions with (selected) adjacent network nodes and with each client APPN end node. It is recommended that an NN not establish CP-CP sessions with *every* adjacent NN (for example, when a large number of NNs is connected to a shared-access transport facility like a LAN). An APPN end node establishes sessions with a single adjacent network node acting as its current server. CP-CP sessions cannot be established between APPN end nodes. A LEN end node does not support CP-CP sessions.

The term *send session* refers to a CP-CP session that is used, for example, to send a Locate search or a registration flow to a partner CP (for details, see Chapter 6, "Directory Services" on page 107). The send session corresponds to the contention-winner CP-CP session. A *receive session* is a CP-CP session that is used, for example, to receive a Locate search reply or a registration reply. The receive session corresponds to the contention-loser session. On the adjacent node, the CP-CP sessions are matched in the obvious complementary fashion with respect to sending and receiving. Each CP sends the session activation (BIND) request for its own contention-winner session.

All CP-CP sessions are used to conduct directory searches. In addition, end node to network node CP-CP sessions may be used to register resources and to pass alerts between management services components. CP-CP sessions between adjacent network nodes are also used to exchange topology information.

During link activation (see 4.4, "Link Activation" on page 61) APPN network nodes indicate whether they support CP-CP sessions to particular APPN nodes on the link. During link activation APPN end nodes indicate whether or not they support CP-CP sessions, or whether they support *and* request CP-CP sessions, over the link. APPN end nodes may defer the establishment of CP-CP sessions, for example if they want to select a network node server at a later time.

CP-CP sessions between APPN network nodes can be established if both nodes have the same net ID, or if at least one of them supports a border node function. This is described in Chapter 10, "Border Node" on page 231. An APPN end node can have CP-CP sessions with a network node server that has a different net ID.

2.3 Logical Unit (LU)

The logical unit (LU) serves as a port into the network and acts as an intermediary between the end user and the network. The LU is engaged in session establishment with one or more partner LUs and manages the exchange of data with partner LUs.

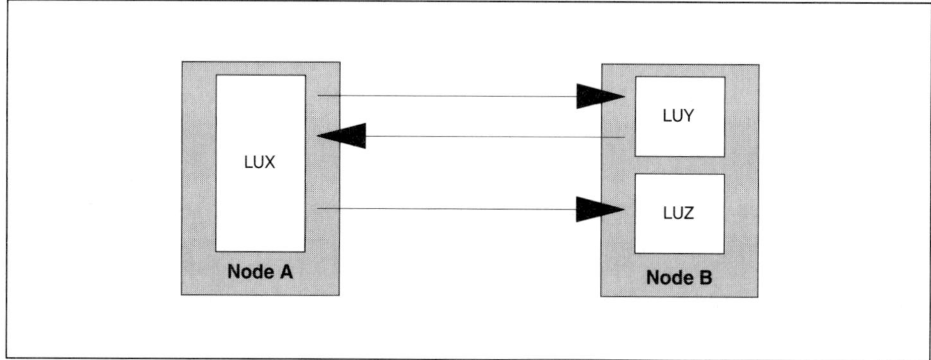

Figure 14. Multiple and Parallel Sessions

LUs on APPN and LEN nodes can accept session initiation requests from other LUs or initiate those sessions themselves. The BIND sender is referred to as the primary LU (PLU); the BIND receiver is referred to as the secondary LU (SLU). A session starts when the PLU sends a BIND and the SLU responds with a RSP(BIND), and stops when UNBIND and RSP(UNBIND) are exchanged. The UNBIND may be sent by either LU.

For a discussion of dependent and independent LUs, see 2.3.1, "Dependent and Independent LUs."

Figure 14 shows the distinction between *multiple* and *parallel* sessions. LUX has multiple sessions: two parallel sessions with LUY and one, single session, with LUZ. The direction of the session arrow shows the PLU-SLU relationship. In this example, LUX is the PLU for its session with LUZ and one of its two parallel sessions with LUY. At the same time LUX is the SLU for its other session with LUY.

2.3.1 Dependent and Independent LUs

Logical unit types define the sets of functions in an LU that support end-user communication. The most flexible LU type is type 6.2, also known as LU 6.2, or *APPC*. LU 6.2, because of its peer-oriented communication support, is particularly suited to today's environment in which processing power is widely distributed throughout a network. That is the reason that LU 6.2 was the only LU type originally supported in APPN networks.

Earlier LU types evolved within a hierarchical (subarea) network and depend on a system services control point (SSCP) for establishing LU-LU sessions. These are called *dependent LUs*. An *independent LU* is able to activate an LU-LU session without assistance from an SSCP. LU 6.2 is the only LU type that can also be an independent LU.

Dependent LUs feature an asymmetry in the roles of the partner LUs, with the host-based LU having the primary role with respect to session activation and recovery.

The LU 6.2 avoids this limitation by allowing either partner to assume the primary role and activate communication over a session.

One or more independent LUs may reside in a node. If there are two or more, a node must support intranode sessions between them. This function (option set 1011) is useful during the development of networked applications.

In order to migrate existing subarea networks to APPN there is, however, the need to support the vast number of dependent LUs (for example, 3270-type LUs) currently installed in subarea networks. See C.6, "Dependent LU Support" on page 427 for a discussion of the evolving support of dependent LUs in APPN networks.

2.4 Intermediate Session Routing (ISR)

At a session endpoint it is the role of the LU, in conjunction with control point services, to establish sessions with a session partner and route session data back and forth to the partner LU. If the partners reside on nonadjacent nodes, the data will pass through intermediate (network) nodes. As these intermediate nodes do not control either of the LU endpoints, LU services cannot be invoked on these nodes. Their responsibility, as intermediate nodes, is to forward the data along the session path. This is done either by the network connection layer, if the session data flow on an RTP connection, or by the intermediate session routing (ISR) function.

The structure of intermediate session routing is shown in Figure 15 on page 32. The components of ISR are the session connectors (one for each session passing through the node) and a session connector manager.

Updates on dynamic node characteristics, which define the ability to perform intermediate session routing, are exchanged among APPN network nodes. Network nodes in an APPN network use node and TG characteristics in choosing routes. Two node characteristics are reported:

- Route-addition resistance
- Congestion status

Route-addition resistance defines the desirability for a network node to perform additional intermediate session routing. The higher the value defined for this attribute, the less desirable the node becomes for additional intermediate session routing purposes.

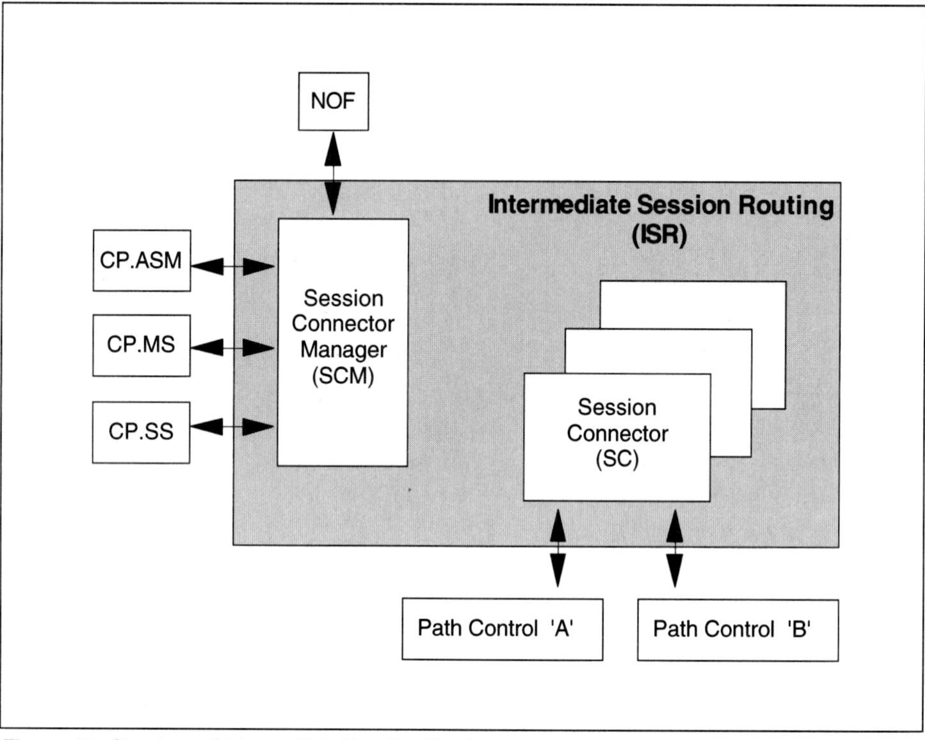

Figure 15. Structure of Intermediate Session Routing

Congestion is determined so that new sessions can be directed away from a node when, for example, 90% of the defined maximum number of sessions using the node as an intermediate node has been reached. A node is considered no longer congested when the number of routed sessions drops below, for example, 80% of the maximum number. When a node actually signals being congested or no longer congested is determined by implementation and installation definition. Node congestion may or may not allow additional sessions to be routed through a network node but it does indicate to all the other network nodes that alternative routes are preferred.

2.4.1 Session Connector Manager (SCM)

SCM manages session connectors for sessions passing through the node. Its main functions are:

- To interface with the address space manager to obtain an LFSID for the TG in the direction of the destination LU.
- To perform intermediate BIND processing. RU sizes within the BIND will be updated if they exceed the maximum RU size allowed for the intermediate node. Session-level pacing will always be set to adaptive pacing, and window sizes will

only be changed if an installation has defined specific values for the intermediate node.

- To create a session connector. The session connector will contain, among other parameters, the fully qualified procedure correlation ID (FQPCID) of the session and the LFSIDs used by the session on the incoming and outgoing TGs.
- To connect the session connector to the two path control instances when the session is activated.

For example, see Figure 16 on page 35, and assume an LU at ENA wants to establish a session with an LU at ENC. After having selected an LFSID(i), SCM forwards the BIND request unit, with LFSID(i) in its TH, to NNB. Routing information, to be more specific, the Route Selection control vector (RSCV), is contained within the BIND. The address space manager at NNB receives the BIND and passes it to the ISR component, as the destination LU is not located on NNB.

After NNB has changed the BIND according to its installation-defined parameters and a new LFSID(j) has been obtained, the LFSID(j) is entered in the TH (replacing LFSID(i)) and the BIND is forwarded to the next node.

2.4.2 Session Connector

The session connector (SC) connects two stages of a session. The main functions of the SC are:

- The routing of session traffic, in the form of path information units (PIUs), by performing address swapping on the address fields in the transmission header based on the LFSIDs stored during session activation along the route.
- Session-level pacing, either adaptive or fixed, of session data flowing on both stages of the session.

  With **fixed** session-level pacing, the maximum number of messages sent in one window is predefined at BIND time; with **adaptive** session-level pacing, the receiver dynamically adapts the number of messages sent in one window.

  If a network node has implemented APPN option 1301 (Nonpaced Intermediate Session Traffic) the session connector manager can accept nonnegotiable BINDS and RSP(BIND)s requesting the node to receive nonpaced session traffic. Otherwise, such sessions would be deactivated. For information on congestion control see *SNA Technical Overview*, GC30-3073.
- Intermediate reassembly of the inbound (received) basic information unit (BIU) segments (optional in end nodes).

  Note: The reverse process, segmenting a basic information unit (BIU) into BIU segments (each in its own PIU) of the appropriate size for the outgoing TG, is a function of path control (optional in end nodes).

2.4.3 Local-Form Session Identifier (LFSID) Swapping

Session traffic, in the form of path information units (PIUs), is routed through an intermediate node by performing address swapping on the address fields in the transmission header (TH), based on the LFSIDs stored during session activation along the route. This is illustrated in Figure 16 on page 35 and explained in the notes.

For each TG on which a node can send and receive message units, a separate path control instance and corresponding address space of *local-form session identifiers* (LFSID) is maintained. Each path control instance handles addresses only from its corresponding address space.

APPN or LEN nodes associate each session using a given TG with a 17-bit LFSID taken from the address space corresponding to that TG. On a specific TG, adjacent nodes use the same LFSID to identify the message flow for a given session. They map the LFSID into transmission headers (THs) in a defined way. On each session stage (or *hop*) between the endpoints, each pair of adjacent nodes uses a distinct LFSID to identify the session. An LFSID is assigned, when the BIND flows to activate the session, by each node that forwards the BIND on a specific TG. The assignment endures for the life of the session, with *address swapping* in the TH occurring on each hop as subsequent session traffic flows over the route.

Chapter 3, "Address Space Manager" on page 47 discusses the LFSID assignment algorithm.

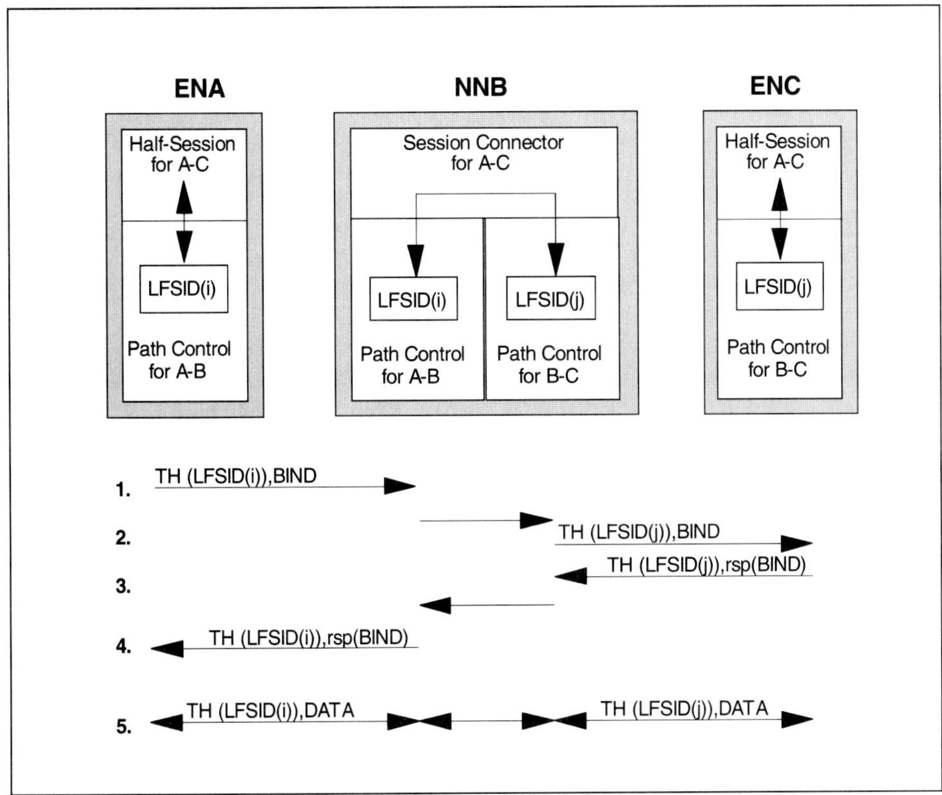

Figure 16. BIND Sets Up Address Swapping

Figure 16 shows the assignment of LFSIDs as the BIND flows along the session path. Each step corresponds to the numbers shown in the figure:

1. The half-session in ENA is to be connected with the half-session in ENC to activate an LU-LU session. A BIND goes from ENA to NNB, carrying a TH that contains an LFSID created in ENA. In NNB, the BIND invokes upper-layer management components (address space manager and session connector manager) and creates entries in the newly activated session connector and in both path control components (one for the incoming TG and one for the outgoing TG). NNB creates a new LFSID(j) for the session stage to ENC.

2. The BIND continues to ENC, but with new address fields, representing LFSID(j), in the TH.

3. ENC accepts the BIND and returns a positive response. The LFSID values used in the TH are reversed for the return path at each session stage.

4. The response continues to ENA with swapped address values in the TH.

5. Now the rest of the PIUs on the session can flow through NNB without rising above the session connector layer. The session PIUs pass through the session connector layer for the pacing function and to switch path control components. The addresses in the THs are swapped as noted in accordance with the information stored at BIND time.

2.5 Path Control (PC)

The path control component delivers message units (MUs) between session-layer components in the same or different nodes. Session components consist of half-sessions in LUs and CPs (collectively referred to as *network accessible units*, or *NAUs*), as well as session connectors residing in intermediate network nodes. (See Figure 17 and Figure 18 on page 37.) The path control component allows these components to exchange MUs without concern for the underlying configuration of nodes and links. Note that path control in an intermediate node is not involved in the routing of network layer packets for data flowing on RTP connections through that node.

Path control routes two types of message unit traffic:

- Session traffic. Requests and responses transmitted between paired session components.
- Nonsession traffic. Requests and responses between paired session components, including session activation and deactivation message units, for example, BIND, UNBIND, BIND-pacing Isolated Pacing Message.

The PC components support a transmission priority function for outgoing message units. Higher-priority messages are passed to data link control (DLC) before lower-priority messages.

One PC instance, a *process* initiated by CP configuration services, exists per transmission group (TG). A separate PC instance serves as a connection between logical units (LUs) in the same node. This latter PC instance is called the *intranode* PC; all others are *internode* PCs.

At the DLC layer, a single DLC process may serve multiple adjacent link stations. Each adjacent link station (ALS) is represented by its own ALS identifier and control block within its managing DLC process. A PC instance interacts with DLC using a DLC process ID and ALS designation for its adjacent link station.

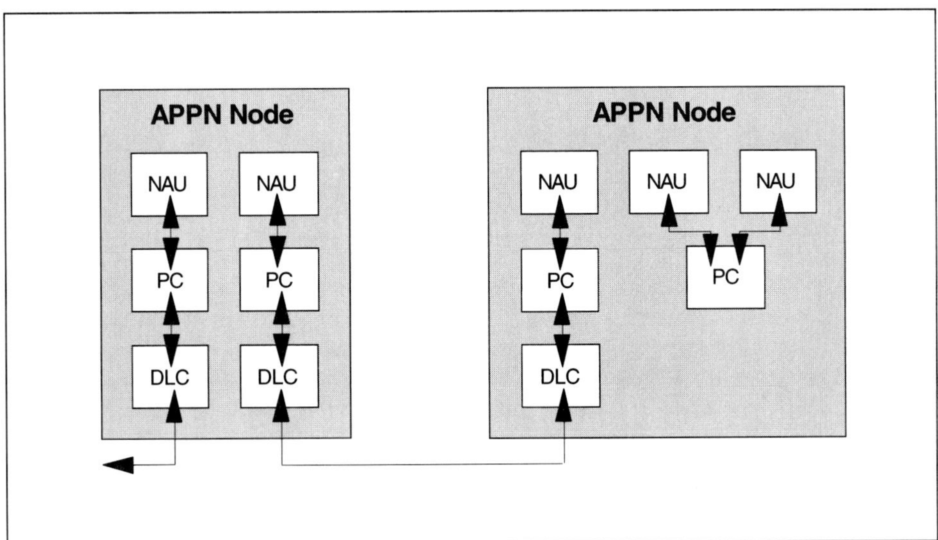

Figure 17. Internode and Intranode Path Control Connections

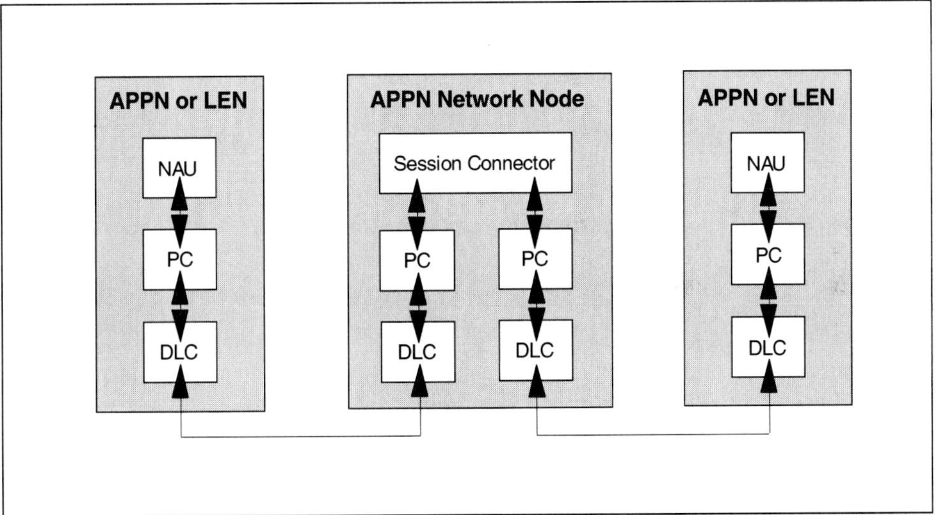

Figure 18. Intermediate Session Routing. The session connector interfaces with two PC instances.

Figure 19 on page 38 shows the structure of a PC instance and its interactions with other components.

The address space manager (ASM) sends session-connection and session-disconnection information to a path control manager, causing it to change the set of half-sessions connected to the path control instance. Each PC instance has its own address space from which the address space manager assigns local-form session identifiers (LFSIDs) to half-sessions connected to that PC instance.

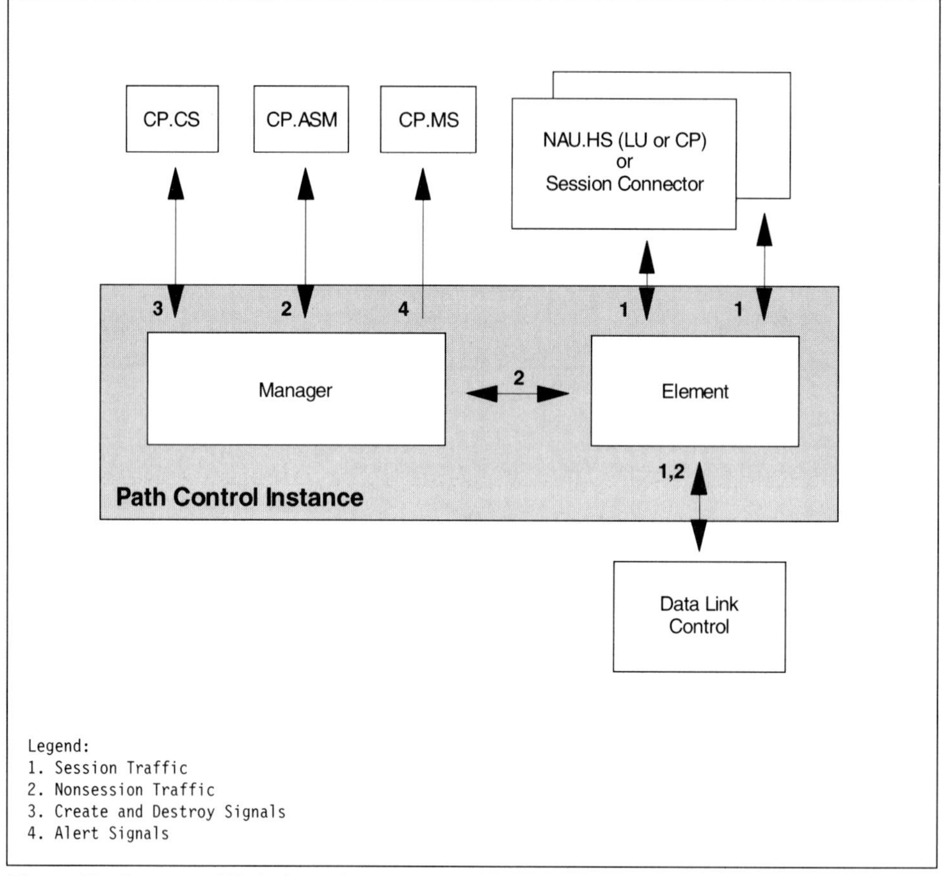

Figure 19. Structure of Path Control

The functions of the path control manager are:

Session connection and disconnection.
When notified, it establishes or breaks a connection to the specified half-session or session connector.

Data flushing.
Upon request, it stops outbound traffic after sending out all pending messages (those residing in path control queues) to data link control. This function is used when a link is being deactivated gracefully.

The path control element is responsible for:

Message routing.
It routes session traffic between session connectors, LU and CP half-sessions and DLC components.

In order to perform its routing functions, path control maintains awareness of its connected session components. PC tables show the relationship between session components in the node connected to a PC instance and their assigned LFSIDs; PC uses this information to build or interpret TH addresses.

Message transformation.
It converts message units received from DLC to a form that can be processed by the CP and LU, and, conversely, it converts message units received from the CP and LU to a form that can be processed by DLC.

Segment generation.
It generates basic information unit (BIU) segments for outbound session traffic when required (done only if segment generation is supported by the local node and reassembly by the adjacent node). The reassembly of BIU segments into BIUs for inbound message units is performed after the message units have been passed to the session component or to ASM, as appropriate (done only if segment reassembly is supported by the node). The ASM is invoked when PC has received nonsession data, for example BINDs.

Error checking.
It performs error checking (to find TH errors) on message units received from the data link.

Transmission Priority.
It enqueues outgoing messages to DLC according to session priority. Transmission priority support is optional in end nodes.

2.5.1 Session RU Segmenting and Reassembly

Session traffic and nonsession traffic are segmented if segmenting is supported by the node. Segmenting of BIUs into smaller BIU segments is performed by path control in order to transmit message units longer than the maximum size BTU allowed on a particular TG. These segments are reassembled into complete BIUs at the partner node. The LU learns from session services of the segment generation and reassembly capabilities of its node and all adjacent nodes, as well as the maximum BTU size of the TG. With this information, it prevents any message units from being passed to PC that would exceed the maximum BTU size when segment generation is not possible.

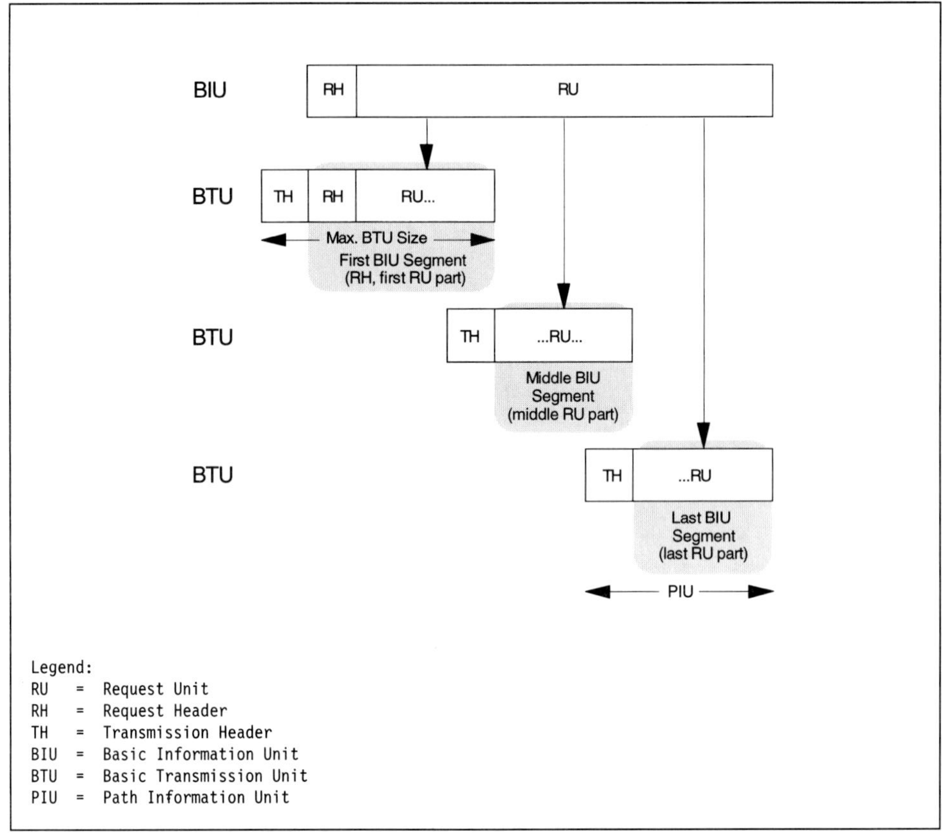

Figure 20. Segmenting of Basic Information Units

Note: Normally a BTU is a single PIU. The exception is on the S/390 channel, where *blocking* permits multiple PIUs in a single BTU.

Segment Generation:

A sender segments a BIU if the link receive buffer in the adjacent node is not large enough to allow the node to receive the whole BIU.

Segments are generated as illustrated in Figure 20. The mapping field in the TH of each BTU is set to indicate whether it contains the first, middle or last segment of the BIU. If the BIU has not been segmented, the Mapping field indicates that the BTU contains the whole BIU. Nodes that do not support segmenting make a mandatory check for a Mapping field value that does not indicate a whole BIU; if such a value is found, the node sends a negative response if possible.

All the segments of a BIND or RSP(BIND) are sent contiguously, not interleaved with other traffic.

In HPR, PIUs are divided into PIU segments. Figure 21 on page 41 shows a PIU segmented into several segments that are transported in NLPs.

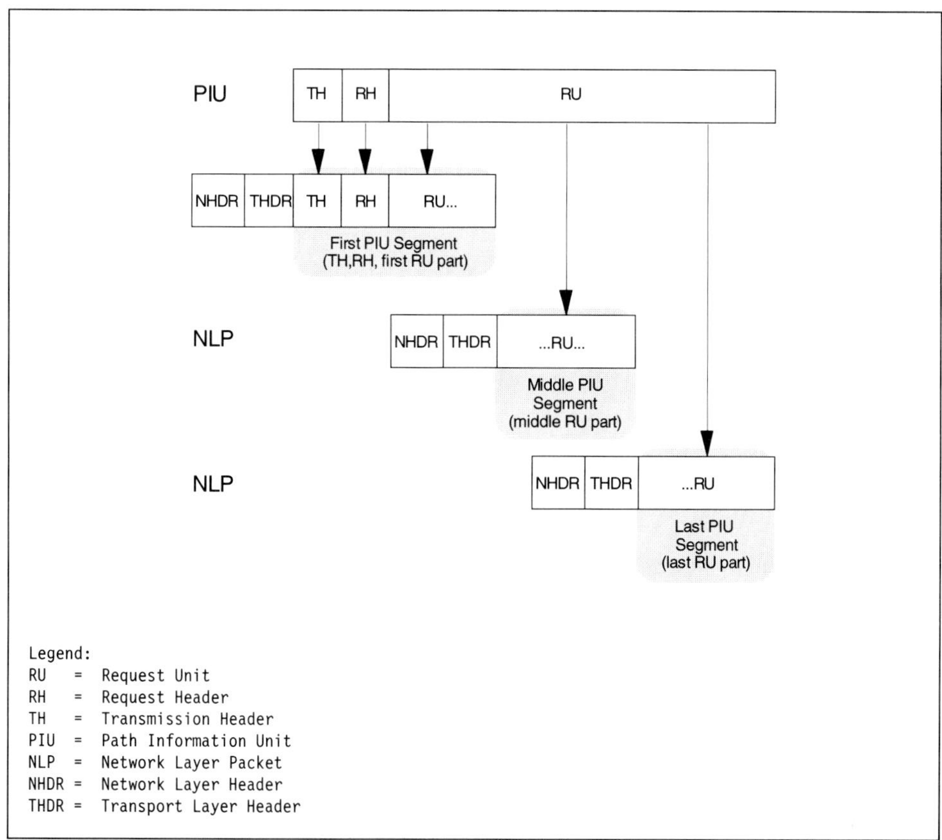

Figure 21. Segmenting of Path Information Units in HPR

Segment Reassembly:
Segment reassembly is done according to the Mapping field in the TH of each BTU. Nodes do reassembly on a session basis in order to properly reassemble segments interleaved from different sessions.

2.5.2 Transmission Priority

Transmission priority provides a mechanism for specifying on a session basis the priority (network, high, medium, low) at which all outgoing messages on a session are to be transmitted (except isolated pacing messages, or IPMs, which are always transmitted at network, or highest, priority). The transmission priority is indicated in the message unit passed to PC. The message's priority dictates the order in which PC hands over the messages to DLC.

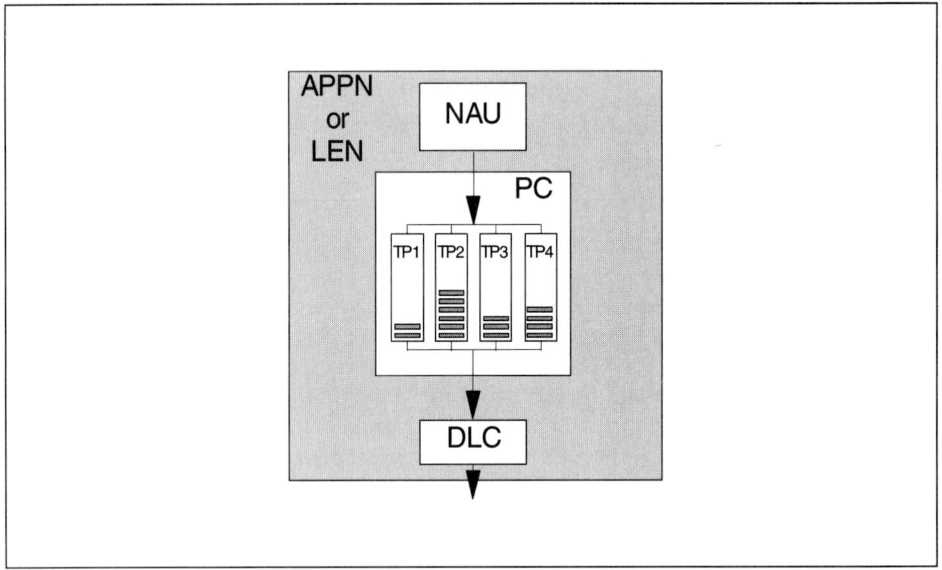

Figure 22. Transmission Priority Queues

The PC components provide four queues (one for each transmission priority) for outgoing message units. Implementations may vary in their selection algorithms; for example, higher-priority queues may be served more frequently, or an aging mechanism may be chosen that guarantees a minimum bandwidth for lower-priority traffic.

2.5.3 Routing Actions

To route messages through an SNA network, path control adds a transmission header (TH) to each BIU. SNA path control uses format identifier type 4 (FID4) headers to route messages over subarea TGs, format identifier type 2 (FID2) headers to route messages over peripheral, APPN, and LEN TGs, and format identifier type 5 (FID5) headers to route messages over RTP connections.

For incoming messages, the addressing information in the TH is used to relate the message to a specific half-session or (for APPN FID2 TH only) to a session connector. For outgoing messages, path control uses the LFSID to generate the appropriate addressing information for the FID2 TH.

Table 1. Mapping of LFSID Fields into TH		
1) Mapping of LFSID Fields for Message Unit (MU) Flows		
	TH Fields	
Direction of MU Flow	DAF'	OAF'
BIND sender to BIND receiver	SIDL	SIDH
BIND receiver to BIND sender	SIDH	SIDL
Note: The ODAI in both the LFSID and TH has its value set by CP.ASM in the BIND sender's node.		
2) LFSID to TH Mapping for BIND-pacing IPMs		
	TH Fields	
Direction of Isolated Pacing Message (IPM) flow	DAF'	OAF'
From primary link station	SIDL	SIDH
To primary link station	SIDH	SIDL
Note: The ODAI in both the LFSID and TH has the value 0.		
Legend: SIDL = Session identifier low SIDH = Session identifier high DAF' = Destination Address Field prime OAF' = Origin Address Field prime ODAI = OAF'-DAF' Assignor Indicator		

APPN and LEN nodes use FID2 transmission headers for the internode routing of data traffic (except when forwarding data over a VR-TG through the subarea network or over an RTP connection). A FID2 TH contains three address fields:

- A one-bit OAF'-DAF' Assignor Indicator (ODAI)
- An eight-bit Destination Address Field prime (DAF')
- An eight-bit Origin Address Field prime (OAF')

The 17-bit LFSID and the three TH addressing fields are mapped as follows. Path control uses a one-to-one mapping between the leftmost bit of the LFSID and the ODAI field. Mapping between the remaining 16 bits of the LFSID, composed of two eight-bit fields, SIDH and SIDL, as well as the DAF' and OAF' fields, is shown in Table 1 (see also 3.3, "Local-Form Session Identifier (LFSID)" on page 49).

2.6 Data Link Control (DLC)

The DLC layer is responsible for the node-to-node protocols necessary to ensure reliable delivery of information between paired stations in nodes attached to a common communication medium. These protocols are provided for sequencing, acknowledgment, error recovery, and the establishment and maintenance of synchronization between the paired stations. HPR-capable links offer the option not to use error recovery, acknowledgment, and sequencing of network layer packets.

There is one DLC manager and element for each DLC layer instance (a *process* started by the CP); see Figure 23 on page 44. DLC provides, protocols for SDLC, X.25, frame-relay, LAN (token-ring, Ethernet, and FDDI), ISDN, S/390 channel connections, and ATM.

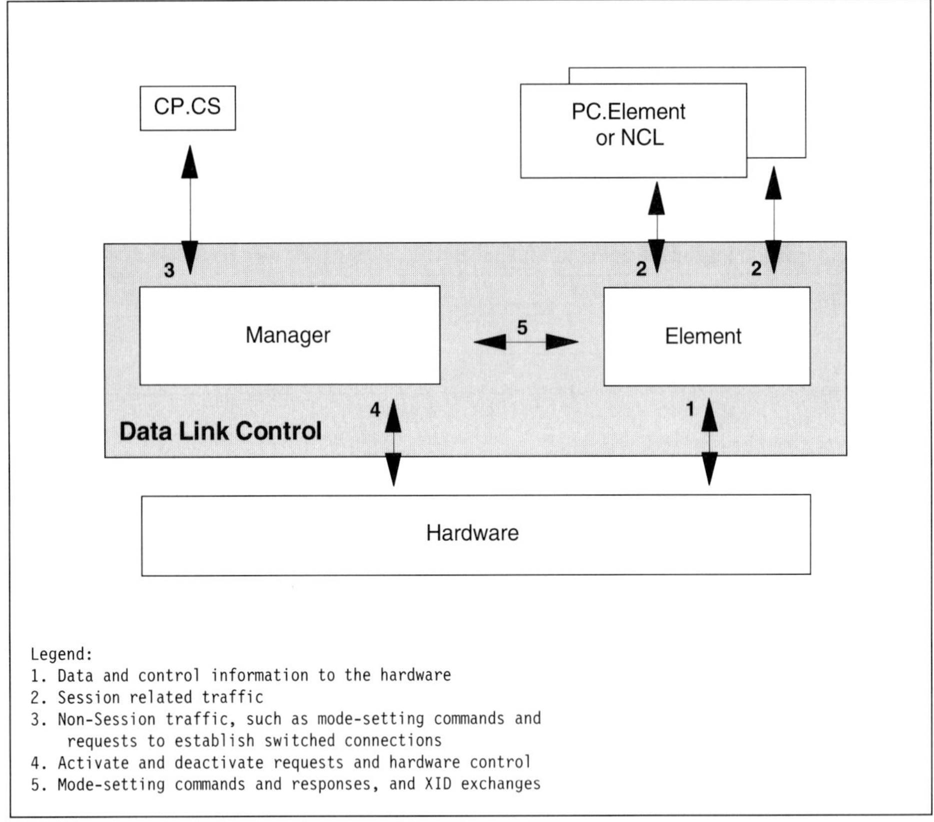

Figure 23. Data Link Control

The functions of the DLC manager are:

- Activate and deactivate the DLC element
- Activate and deactivate links
- Manage the DLC portion of the CP-DLC protocol boundary
- Coordinate the actions performed by the DLC element in response to the service request from the CP
- Notify the CP whenever a station or port becomes operative or inoperative
- Coordinate activation and deactivation of switched circuits

The functions of the DLC element are:

- Exchange data traffic with adjacent DLC elements, subject to any fixed-window agreements and retransmitting when necessary
- Manage the DLC portion of the PC-DLC or PC-NCL protocol boundaries
- Transfer data to the physical medium
- For data networks, exchange data traffic with the data network access data switching exchanges (DSEs)

Chapter 3. Address Space Manager

The address space manager (ASM) is one of the components in the control point (CP) of an APPN network node or APPN end node. ASM's functions include:

- Managing the session address (called *local-form session identifier, or LFSID*) used by local path control for the routing of session traffic.
- Routing the session-activation messages (BIND, RSP(BIND)) and session-deactivation messages (UNBIND, RSP(UNBIND)) between the session managers or session connector managers (SCMs) and path control components within the node.
- Reassembling segmented session-activation messages (BIND, RSP(BIND)) received by the node into whole messages.
- Performing flow control of the session-activation messages (BIND).
- Notifying the appropriate session managers in the node when a link connection or link station fails.

3.1 Function Overview

The address space manager is created by the node operator facility at node initialization time. The node operator facility passes the following parameters to the address space manager:

- The name of the control point
- The network ID
- Whether or not BIND reassembly is supported

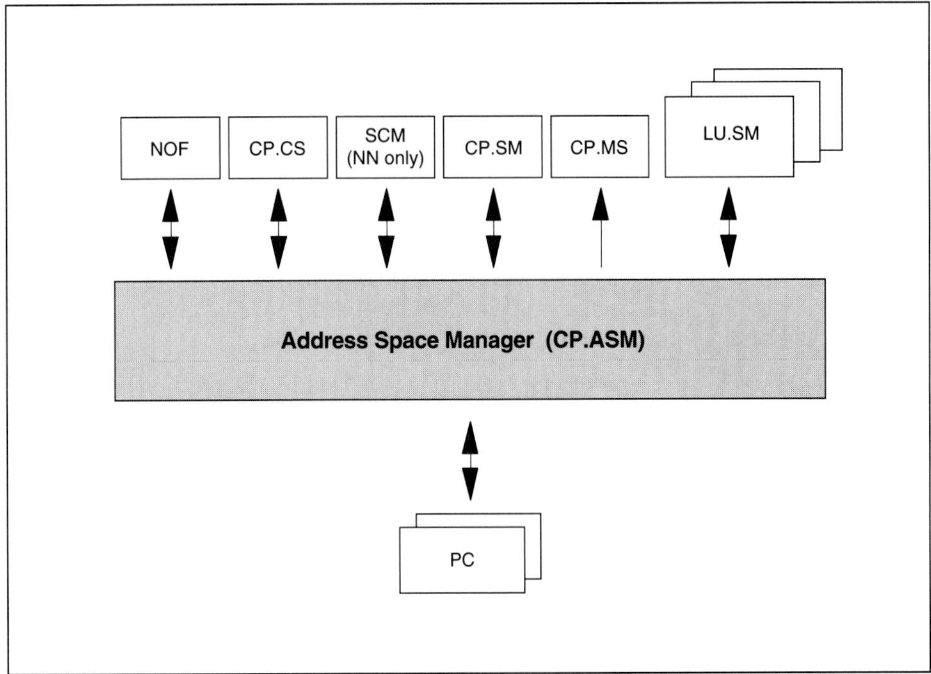

Figure 24. Overview of ASM Interaction with Other Components in the Node

3.2 Address Space

For each TG attached to the node, ASM defines an address space consisting of 2^{17} (131 072) LFSIDs that may be assigned (with some restrictions, see Figure 25 on page 51) to sessions routed over the TG. Each TG is associated with a unique path control instance (*process*), and the identifier for the TG's path control instance is also used as the identifier for the TG's address space.

When configuration services (CS) activates or deactivates a TG, it informs ASM. ASM then creates or removes, respectively, the control table it uses to manage the TG's address space. In this control table, for each LFSID in the address space, ASM saves an indication of whether or not the LFSID is assigned to a session.

The two nodes connected by a TG share that TG's address space. When a session is initiated over the TG, ASM in the node that forwards the BIND selects the LFSID. To keep ASM in the two nodes from selecting the same LFSID for two sessions being initiated at the same time by BINDs flowing in opposite directions, the address space is divided into two partitions; ASM in one node selects LFSIDs from one partition, and ASM in the other node selects LFSIDs from the other partition. The partition is determined by the setting of one bit (the ODAI) of the LFSID. See the discussion of ODAI in the next section for more information about partitioning.

3.3 Local-Form Session Identifier (LFSID)

A transmission group between adjacent nodes can be used by multiple sessions. In order to relate the messages to a particular session, adjacent path control instances use unique session identifiers (LFSIDs) in the messages. On each session stage (or *hop*) between two session endpoints, each pair of adjacent nodes uses distinct session identifiers to identify a session; therefore, the term *local-form session identifier (LFSID)* is used.

The LFSID is a 17-bit identifier used by path control to route session traffic; see Figure 25. The LFSID is composed of a 1-bit *ODAI* (OAF'-DAF' Assignor Indicator) field and two 8-bit fields: *SIDH* (Session Identifier High) and *SIDL* (Session Identifier Low). The ODAI divides the LFSID address space into two distinct partitions. The ASMs in the two nodes connected by a TG select LFSIDs from that TG's address space with different ODAI values, so that they never select the same LFSID. The ODAI value determination is a by-product of link station role negotiation during XID exchange. ASM in the node with the primary link station selects LFSIDs with an ODAI value of 0, and ASM in the node with the secondary link station selects LFSIDs with an ODAI value of 1.

The SIDH and SIDL allow ASMs a possible 2^{16} (65 536) session identifiers for each TG, with some restrictions. For details see the next section.

3.3.1 Address Space Management

For CP-CP or independent LU-LU sessions, the session manager (SM) components in the CP or LU request an LFSID from ASM. For sessions routed through an intermediate node, the session connector manager (SCM) invokes ASM to obtain an LFSID. ASM selects an LFSID that is not currently in use by another session, assigns it to the particular session and informs the SM or SCM of the assigned LFSID.

Dependent LU-LU sessions are treated as independent LU-LU sessions on all session stages other than the stage connecting the boundary function and the node containing the secondary LU. That is, the SM of the primary LU and SCMs at intermediate routing stages are dynamically paired with LFSIDs. At the BF-SLU stage, however, a static relationship exists between LFSIDs and SMs of secondary LUs. This relationship is established through a coordinated system definition for both the node containing the secondary LU and the node providing boundary function support.

ASM assigns LFSIDs according to the partitioning of the address space described below; Figure 25 on page 51 illustrates this partitioning.

1. If boundary function support for dependent LUs is provided or received over the TG, the LFSID with SIDH = X'00' and SIDL = X'00' is used for the SSCP-PU session or in the FID2 TH preceding an HPR route setup RU; otherwise, this LFSID is not used.

2. If boundary function support for dependent LUs is provided or received over the TG, LFSIDs with SIDH = X'00' and SIDL values in the range from X'01' to X'FF' (inclusive) are used for SSCP-LU sessions; otherwise, these LFSIDs are not used.
3. The LFSID with SIDH = X'01', SIDL = X'00', and ODAI=0 is used for BIND flow control (that is, adaptive BIND pacing).
4. If boundary function support for dependent LUs is provided or received over the TG, LFSIDs with SIDH = X'01' and SIDL values in the range from X'01' to X'FF' (inclusive) are used for dependent LU-LU sessions for secondary LUs that receive boundary function support over this link; otherwise, these LFSIDs are not used.

   Note: Some older implementations use this LFSID range for CP-CP sessions and independent LU-LU sessions if boundary function support is not provided or received over the TG. This policy of LFSID assignment has been retired from the architecture.
5. LFSIDs with SIDH values in the range from X'02' to X'FE' (inclusive) are used for CP-CP and independent LU-LU sessions.
6. LFSIDs with SIDH = X'FF' are reserved.

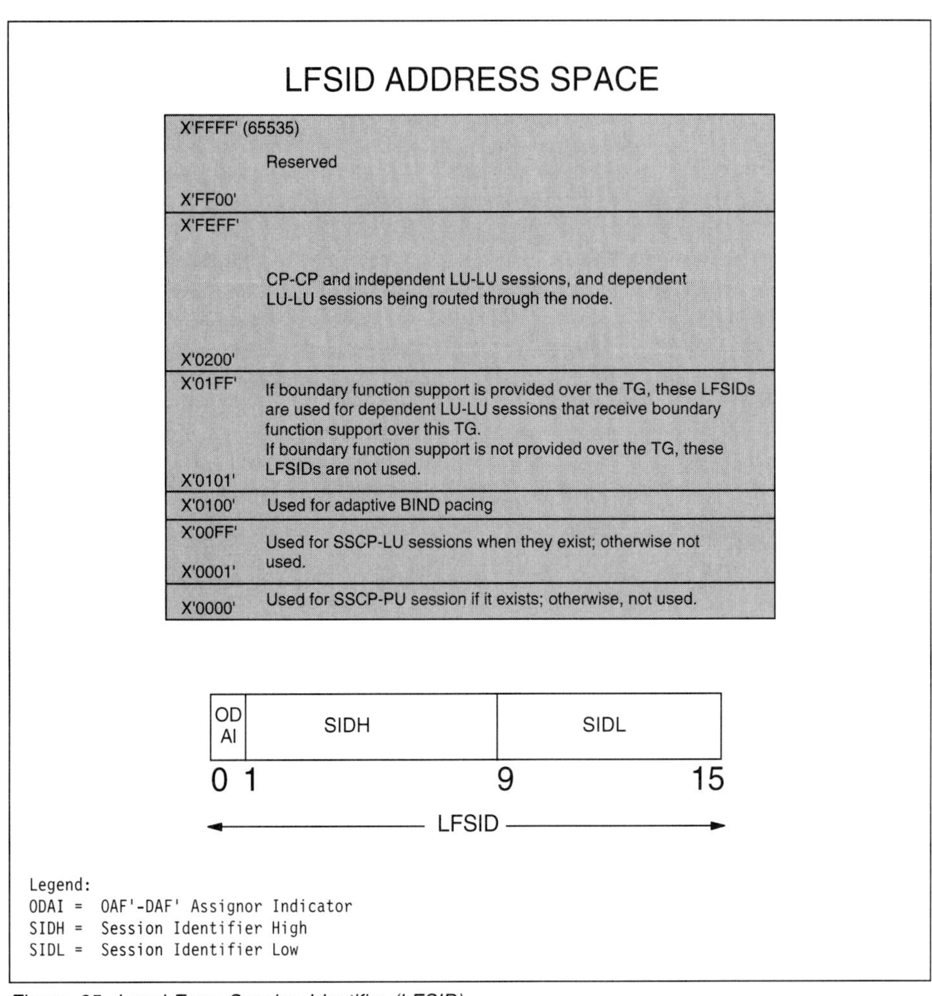

Figure 25. Local-Form Session Identifier (LFSID)

This partitioning of the LFSID address space enables a node that contains dependent LUs to accept ACTPU, ACTLU, and BIND requests from a VTAM or NCP boundary function.

Each node forwarding a BIND request (that is, the node owning the PLU and each intermediate node), assigns an available LFSID from the appropriate LFSID address space. The LFSIDs assigned to a session, one per TG, are valid only for the lifetime of the session. Available LFSIDs include those released by sessions terminations. This happens when Path Control informs ASM that an UNBIND or RSP(UNBIND) has been sent, or when session managers inform ASM that session activation has failed.

The two nodes connected by a TG share that TG's address space. When a session is initiated over the TG, ASM in the node that forwards the BIND selects the LFSID. Path control on either side of the TG inserts this session identifier in the transmission headers of all the basic information units (BIUs) for that session.

Note: The usage of LFSIDs is similar to that of *logical channels* in X.25. Session identifiers allow path control instances on two adjacent nodes to multiplex data on TGs connecting the nodes, and relate the data received to specific half-sessions or session connectors (for intermediate session routing). The session identifiers have *local* significance only. If an LU-LU session is routed through intermediate nodes, a different LFSID will be assigned for each TG along the path between the nodes owning the LUs.

3.4 BIND Segmenting and Reassembly

APPN and LEN nodes optionally support segmenting and reassembly of BIND requests and responses. Path control performs the segmenting, while the address space manager (ASM) performs the reassembly. Like segmenting and reassembly for other basic information units (BIUs), BIND segmenting and reassembly uses the Mapping field in the FID2 transmission header. For details, see *Systems Network Architecture Formats*, GA27-3136.

When configuration services (CS) activates a transmission group to an adjacent node, it negotiates with configuration services at the other node the maximum message (BTU) size that can be sent across the transmission group. If the BIND message is larger than the BTU size selected for the transmission group, path control performs BIND segmentation. However, path control cannot perform BIND segmentation unless ASM at the adjacent node is capable of BIND reassembly. Knowledge of whether or not the receiver is capable of BIND reassembly is exchanged between nodes at TG activation time as part of the XID exchange.

If the address space manager does not support BIND reassembly, it will discard any segmented BIND request or response and instruct configuration services to deactivate the TG.

3.5 Bind Flow Control

When a node activates a large number of sessions across a TG in a short period it may fill up all buffers at the adjacent node. As a consequence, the adjacent node may run into a deadlock situation, as it can no longer obtain free buffers to respond to the activation requests or receive new BIND requests.

To circumvent these types of problems, the address space manager can perform flow control for all BINDs sent and received across a transmission group. The flow control mechanism is called *adaptive BIND pacing* and is similar to adaptive session-level pacing. For details, see *SNA LU 6.2 Reference: Peer Protocols*, SC31-6808 and *Systems Network Architecture Formats*, GA27-3136.

Adaptive BIND pacing uses two algorithms, a sender and a receiver algorithm. Both are window based, which means that the sender can send only a limited number, or *window*, of messages per grant of permission-to-send from the receiver. As long as this permission has not been given, the sender must defer sending messages. After receiving permission the sender may send the next window of messages. Because the pacing algorithm allows the window to expand and contract, the term *adaptive* is used.

Chapter 4. Configuration Services

The configuration services (CS) component of the CP in an APPN or LEN node manages the node's local resources, such as the links to adjacent nodes. Most of the functions are the same for LEN end nodes, APPN end nodes, and APPN network nodes. Where there are differences, they will be pointed out in this chapter.

Configuration services creates path control instances, which it associates with specific transmission groups as it activates them, and destroys the path control instances after having deactivated the associated transmission groups. It also creates the intranode path control process, which is used for routing messages between LUs that reside in the local node. Configuration services provides information, acquired as a result of its functions, to other components of the node.

4.1 Function Overview

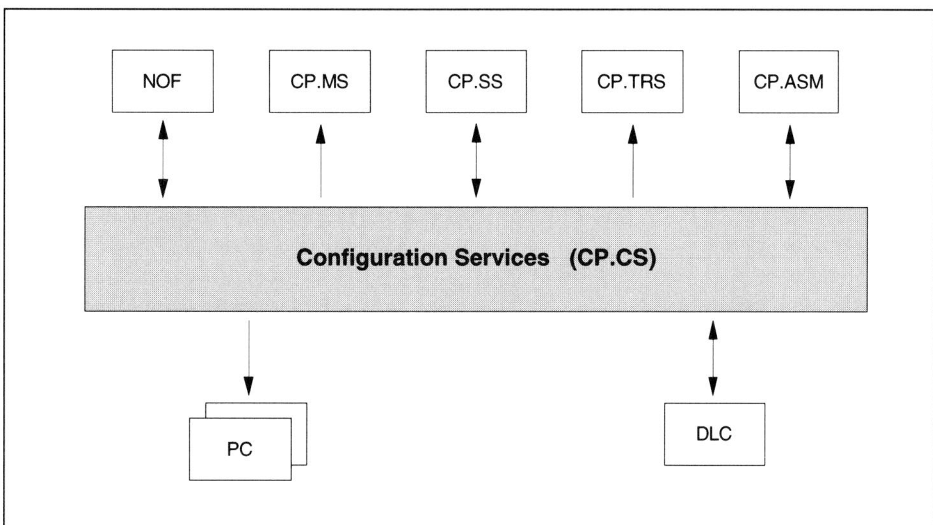

Figure 26. Overview of CS Interaction with Other Components in the Node

The basic functions performed by configuration services are:

- Definition of the node's configuration:
  - Types of data link control (DLC)
  - Ports
  - Adjacent link stations
  - Attached connection networks
  - Adjacent nodes

- Link activation (including XID exchange)
- Nonactivation XID exchange
- Link deactivation
- Link queries
- Connection networks (not supported in LEN end nodes)

The node operator facility (NOF) initializes configuration services. NOF also defines, starts, stops, and queries the components of configuration services. The following information is passed to configuration services when it is initialized:

- The node's CP name.
- The node's network ID.
- The node's product set ID, containing information such as machine type, machine serial number, software product number, date of link-edit.
- Whether or not negotiable link stations are supported. (Defining a link station as negotiable allows the link station to be either primary or secondary. The actual role is determined during link activation.)
- Whether or not parallel TGs are supported.

4.2 Data Link Control

The DLC layer is responsible for the node-to-node protocols necessary to ensure reliable delivery of information between paired stations in nodes attached to a common communication medium. These protocols are provided for sequencing, acknowledgment, error recovery, and the establishment and maintenance of synchronization between the paired stations. See 8.5.5, "HPR Link Activation" on page 201 for a description of DLC functions in an HPR node.

There is one DLC manager and element for each DLC layer instance (a *process* started by the CP). Each DLC layer instance, or process, may manage one or more ports. For details, see 2.6, "Data Link Control (DLC)" on page 43.

4.2.1 Ports

A port represents a physical connection to the link hardware. The specific component it represents is sometimes referred to as an *adapter*. Each port is associated with a DLC process.

Ports are defined by the node operator facility using the following types of information:

- Associated DLC process.
- Information specific to the port, like link station activation limits and time-out values.
- Information that is common to all link stations associated with the port, for example TG characteristics (modem class, security) and receive buffer size.

Some of the information is not needed for link activation, but is used for route calculation by route selection services. For details, see 5.7, "Route Computation: Overview" on page 95.

- Information about any connection network (discussed in 4.6, "Connection Networks and Virtual Routing Nodes" on page 66) if one or more is defined on the port.

4.2.2 Links

A link represents a connection between a local link station and a link station in an adjacent node. It includes the data link control (DLC), the port, and the link station components. The associated link station in the adjacent node is locally referred to as the *adjacent link station* (ALS).

Note: The term link, or physical link, is often used to refer to the physical components that enable two adjacent nodes to communicate. Within APPN a link should be considered as a logical association between two entities in distinct nodes.

A link between two nodes may require that one link station takes the role of *primary* link station and one link station takes the role of *secondary* link station. This role setting does not imply that the link stations maintain a *master-slave* relationship; see 4.4, "Link Activation" on page 61.

Link roles are coordinated at link activation time. The link station roles must either be predefined or negotiated during link activation. Predefinition of link station roles requires that the definitions at both ends match. If both nodes define the local link station as primary or both define the local link station as secondary, link activation will fail. Defining a link station as *negotiable* means that the link station role can be either primary or secondary and that the actual role will be determined during link activation. If both ends are defined as negotiable, the final roles are decided on the basis of node identification fields exchanged between the two link stations, during link activation.

4.2.2.1 Point-to-Point and Multipoint

Links can be either *point-to-point* or *multipoint*. Implementations may provide the ability to add secondary link stations to existing point-to-point connections through dynamic reconfiguration. This type of connection is called a multipoint capable connection.

Point-to-point links are links between two and only two link stations. The link station role, primary or secondary, can be negotiated during link activation. There is no need to define the secondary link station address. If the value is needed, it will be acquired during XID negotiation.

Multipoint, or multipoint-capable, links are links between one link station at one end, which is always the primary link station, and one or more adjacent link stations, which are always the secondary link stations. Multipoint links require predefinition of the link station role. Negotiable stations are not usable on multipoint or multipoint-capable link connections because they use the broadcast address to avoid defining the secondary address when they do not know which end will be the secondary station. Any station receiving the broadcast address will respond to it. Multipoint, or multipoint-capable, links require explicit definition of the secondary station addresses.

Note: The data link layer protocol on a point-to-point connection can be either a *balanced* or an *unbalanced* protocol. Unbalanced protocols presume a *master slave* relation; balanced protocols presume a peer relation. The DLC layer on a multipoint connection always uses unbalanced link protocols. Examples of balanced DLC protocols are LAPB and LAPD, while an example of an unbalanced DLC protocol is SDLC.

4.2.2.2 Switched and Nonswitched

Links can be either *switched* or *nonswitched.* Switched links require some kind of *dial* procedure before link activation can take place. Nonswitched links can be activated immediately after a port has become active. Switched link connections are always point-to-point links, but nonswitched links can be either point-to-point or multipoint. Multiple simultaneous switched connections may be supported through a single port.

A switched link may support *auto-activation*, to automatically activate a link when sessions are established using that link station.

A switched link may also be defined as a *limited resource*, to automatically deactivate a link when no sessions use the link. For example if an X.25 network provider charges its users for the period a switched connection is kept active, network administrators may decide that X.25 links should be deactivated if the link is not used.

Examples of switched link connections are the links between nodes attached to an X.25 public switched data network (PSDN) using switched virtual circuits.

Examples of nonswitched link connections are links between adjacent nodes connected by a leased line, or nodes attached to an X.25 public switched data network (PSDN) using permanent virtual circuits.

4.2.3 Transmission Groups

A transmission group (TG) corresponds to a connection with a single adjacent link station. Base APPN architecture supports only hp1.single-link TGs. See 1.3, “Transmission Groups” on page 8 for explanations of the transmission group terminology, and 8.5.4, “Multilink Transmission Groups” on page 198 for a description of the multilink transmission group support in APPN HPR. This section will describe the TG support in base APPN.

Each TG has a TG number assigned to it during link activation. The TG number must be unique between a pair of CPs. This allows a TG to be uniquely identified by a pair of (network-qualified) CP names and a TG number.

Table 2. TG Number Space		
Parallel TGs supported	**Range**	**Function**
No	0 to 20	Predefined
Yes	1 to 20	Predefined
Yes or No	21 to 239	Negotiated
Yes or No	240 to 255	Reserved

Table 2 shows the general rules for determining the TG number. When parallel TGs are not supported between two nodes, any integer between 0 and 255 is permissible as a TG number. When parallel TGs are supported between two nodes, any integer from 1 to 255 is allowed as a TG number. The number 0 is excluded as a valid TG number when parallel TGs are supported, since it has special meaning for the TG negotiation itself.

Any TG less than or equal to 20 is set aside to represent a TG that has been predefined between two nodes. Predefined TGs are used when it is important to match the characteristics of the link stations on both ends of the TGs. TG numbers greater than 239 have a special meaning and must not be used. For example, a subarea network may connect to an APPN network using a VTAM interchange node (ICN). To provide transparency to the other nodes in the APPN network, all LUs in or accessible through the subarea network are presented as if they reside on an end node that connects to the ICN using TG number 254. See Appendix C, "APPN VTAM" on page 409.

TG numbers from 21 to 239 are selected during TG number negotiation, which is performed during link activation (see 4.4, "Link Activation" on page 61). The list below summarizes the rules for determining the TG number:

- For connections that are being reactivated, the TG number that was used for the previous activation is reused, if possible.
- If one node sends a TG number of 0, then it is willing to accept the TG number of the other side.
- If both nodes send TG numbers of 0 and parallel TGs between them are not supported, then the TG number is set to 0.
- If both nodes send TG numbers of 0 and parallel TGs between them are supported, then the node with the higher network-qualified CP name picks a valid TG number.
- If neither node sends a TG number of 0, then the number that was sent by the node with the higher network-qualified CP name is used.

4.3 System Definitions

A node is responsible for its own local definition of supported links and their characteristics, node capabilities, and the control point names of the node that can be directly attached. This and other information is maintained by CS in its database.

A link station is a combination of hardware and software that allows a node to control a link. Some characteristics must be defined explicitly through the node operator facility, while others can be either defined explicitly or negotiated with the adjacent link station during link activation.

A node requires the following system definition for a local link station:

- Link station name
- Link station role: primary, secondary, negotiable
- Local link station address for any secondary or negotiable station
- Modem equalization delay value
- Inactivity timer
- Retry limit for mode-setting command (SNRM, SABM)

Certain nodes can act only as primary link stations and require the attaching node to assume the secondary role. This requirement is defined by the network administrator at system definition time for the attached node.

The components of a link (DLC, port, link station) are defined individually. DLC must be defined before its associated ports are defined, and ports must be defined before associated adjacent link stations are defined. More than one adjacent link station may be defined on a port.

An adjacent link station is either defined explicitly, by the node operator facility, or dynamically, using a set of default parameters assigned to them. *Dynamic link stations* may be defined because session services (SS) has required the activation of a link, or as a result of an adjacent node activating a link.

A dynamic link station is treated as a *limited resource*, meaning that when no sessions are using the link between the local and the dynamic link station, the link can be deactivated. No CP-CP sessions are supported on connections using dynamic link stations since CP-CP sessions normally need to be kept up continuously.

Information about the adjacent link station is used when the link station is activated, deactivated or its status queried. To activate a link, the DLC, port, and link station must be activated. Dynamically defined link stations cannot be activated by the operator.

4.3.1 DLC, Port and Link Station Interrelationship

Figure 27 on page 61 shows how CS maintains information about DLC processes, ports, and link stations. There can be one or more DLC processes per node, one or more ports used by DLC, and one or more link stations per port.

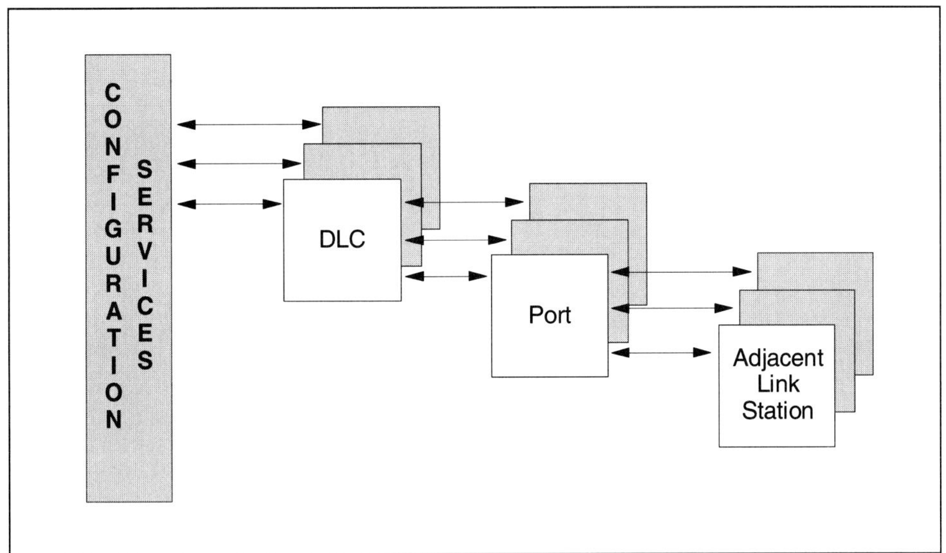

Figure 27. DLC, Port, and Link Station Interrelationship

4.4 Link Activation

Link activation is initiated locally by an operator command or by following a session setup request, or by the adjacent node. DLCs and ports must be defined before they can be activated. Adjacent link stations must be defined before they are activated, except in the case of dynamic link stations. A DLC is always activated before its associated ports, and ports are always activated before their associated adjacent link stations.

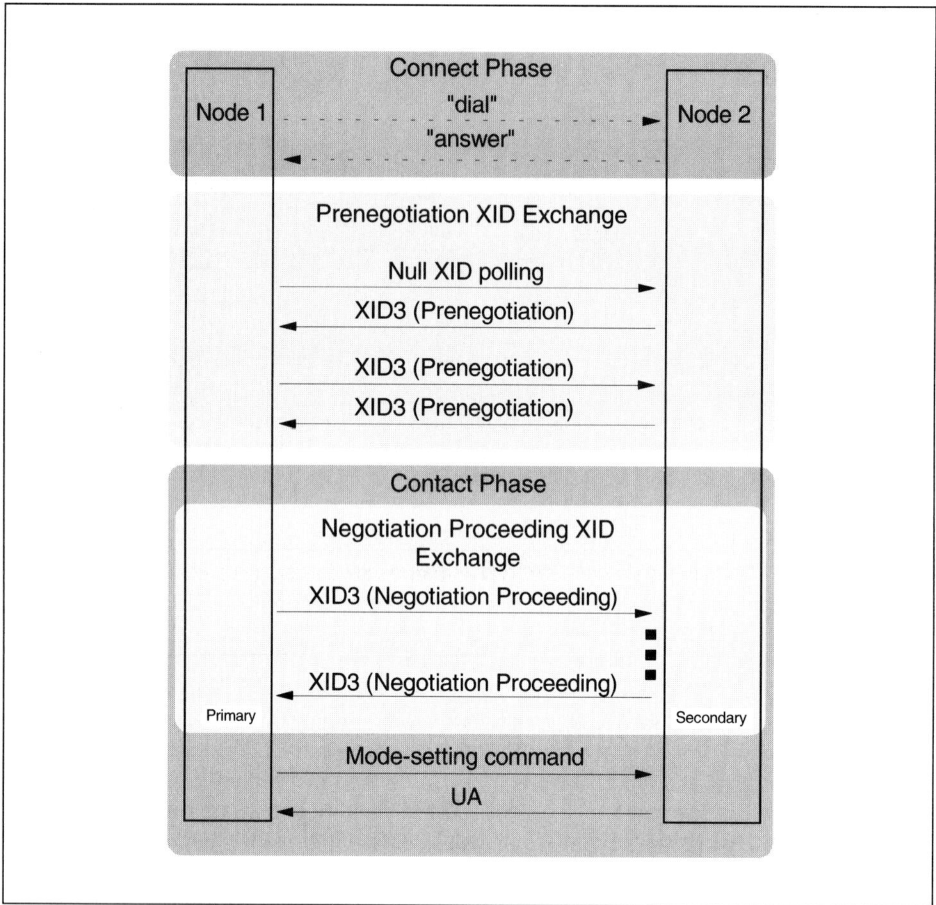

Figure 28. Link Activation

Link activation encompasses the activation of the physical link connection and the adjacent link station. It consists of (at most) three phases (see Figure 28):

- Connect Phase
- Prenegotiation XID Exchange
- Contact Phase

The connect phase allows initial establishment of communication between nodes. The connect phase is optional and DLC dependent. For switched connections, one may think of *dial* and *answer* procedures; for example, the establishment of a virtual circuit if nodes are attached to an X.25 packet switching network. Once the connect phase has completed, the two nodes are able to exchange and establish node characteristics via XID exchanges.

The exchange of *prenegotiation* XIDs is optional as well. It allows a node to determine if the adjacent station is active and to verify the identity of the adjacent node. Node identification fields and, optionally, the CP name will be exchanged. As an example, for switched connections, VTAM will select switched major node definitions based on information obtained during this phase.

APPN nodes use two types of XIDs. The null XID determines whether the adjacent station is active. The XID3 performs the *prenegotiation* and *negotiation-proceeding* processes, which are part of the contact phase. For format details, see *Systems Network Architecture Formats*, GA27-3136.

As part of the contact phase, the partner nodes will start an XID3 negotiation process to establish primary and secondary roles of the link stations, the TG number, and other characteristics of the link. The result of the primary-secondary role negotiation determines which node will send the mode-setting command (SNRM, SABM) and is also used in setting the ODAI field in the LFSID (see 3.3, "Local-Form Session Identifier (LFSID)" on page 49).

The *negotiation-proceeding* XID3 exchange completes once the link station role negotiation and the TG number negotiation have completed, and when each node has sent and received at least one *negotiation-proceeding* XID3.

After the link-activation XID exchange has completed successfully, CS creates a new path control instance and instructs the address space manager (ASM) to activate a new address space. When the address space has been created, CS instructs DLC to perform the DLC mode-setting exchange and notifies topology and routing services (TRS) that a TG has become active. Finally, if during link activation the adjacent node has indicated that CP sessions are either supported and/or requested, CS notifies session services (SS). SS may then activate CP-CP sessions if necessary.

The link is active from the perspective of both nodes when a mode-setting command has been sent and a response returned.

The link can be deactivated from either end, via the node operator facility, or after failures have been detected on the link station or port. A link defined as a *limited resource* will be deactivated after the number of sessions using the link falls to zero.

4.4.1 XID3 Negotiation

The contact phase consists of the negotiation-proceeding XID3 exchange and the mode-setting sequence.

The XID exchange reduces the requirement for system definition of the adjacent node. During the negotiation-proceeding XID exchange, link station roles and the TG number used to represent the link are resolved cooperatively by the two link stations.

The following information, where applicable, is communicated to the adjacent node:

- Adjacent link station (ALS) name
- CP capabilities:
  - Network node providing services over this link
  - Network node not providing services over this link
  - End node supporting CP-CP sessions over this link
  - End node not supporting CP-CP sessions over this link
  - End node supporting and requesting CP-CP sessions over this link
- CP name
- Link characteristics
- TG number
- Subarea PU name
- Product set ID
- Node capabilities:
  - Parallel TG support
  - DLC support

4.4.1.1 Basic Transmission Unit (BTU) Size

Each link station determines its own maximum send basic transmission unit (BTU) size. It is based on local node definitions and XID information received from the DLC and the adjacent link station. The smallest of the following values will become the actual maximum send BTU size:

- Locally defined send BTU size
- Maximum BTU size as set by DLC
- Maximum receive BTU size of the adjacent link station

When the partner does not support BIND reassembly, the maximum BTU size must be at least 265 if the partner node is an APPN end node or LEN end node, or at least 521 if an APPN network node.

When path control supports segmenting, it segment outgoing messages that are longer than the maximum BTU size. Figure 20 on page 40 shows how the maximum BTU impacts this segmenting process.

Note: Normally a BTU is a single PIU. The exception is on the S/390 channel, where *blocking* permits multiple PIUs in a single BTU.

4.5 Nonactivation XID Exchange

Information associated with an already active link may change. To communicate these changes, adjacent link stations use a *nonactivation* XID3 exchange. Possible reasons to start a nonactivation XID3 exchange are as follows:

- Network node server change
- SSCP takeover
- TG quiescing

All nodes support the receipt of nonactivation XID3s when they contain the secondary link station on a connection, but not all implementations support the receipt of nonactivation XID3s when assuming the primary link station role. The capability of a primary link station to receive an XID from the secondary station when no XID command has been issued is declared in the XID3 during link station activation. Unless both nodes indicate support for this function, secondary-initiated nonactivation XID3 exchanges cannot occur.

When a nonactivation XID3 exchange occurs, the parameters relating to the physical characteristics of the connection and the connecting nodes have already been established. Table 3 shows the XID parameters that, during a nonactivation XID3 exchange, will never change, may change without a CP name change, or may change but only together *with* a CP name change.

Table 3. XID3 Parameters. Requested link station changes.

Field	Never Changed	Without CP Change	With CP Change
ACTPU Suppression	X		
Link Station Role	X		
CP-CP Session Requested		X	X
CP-CP Session Supported		X	X
TG Number			X
CP Name			X
CP Name Change Requested		X	X
TG Quiescing		X	X

No IBM implementation uses the nonactivation XID3 exchange to change network node server. Instead, this can be achieved using SS-initiated protocols (see 7.3, "CP-CP Session Activation" on page 141).

SSCP takeover

A function of subarea networks that allows one SSCP to gain ownership of NCP boundary function connections that were previously owned by the same or another SSCP, without breaking the connections or disrupting existing LU-LU sessions on the connections. Once the new SSCP has taken over a connection, it processes all session requests that come from or are destined for LUs on that connection. A CP name change, and possibly a TG number change, takes place during a VTAM SSCP takeover.

The fundamental role that nonactivation XID3 exchanges play during SSCP takeover requires that the NCP must have the capability of initiating a nonactivation exchange whether it assumes the primary or secondary link station role on a connection. All APPN nodes support the receipt of nonactivation XID3s when they contain the secondary link station, but do not generally support secondary-initiated exchanges when they contain the primary link station on a connection, the NCP providing the boundary function must assume the primary link station role during link activation. NCP only allows role negotiation on SDLC switched connections, and the NCP logic works in a way as to almost always become the primary end of SDLC switched connections. For nonswitched connections, the link station role must be predefined in NCP, so the user can force the NCP to be the primary end. In case of NCP-NCP connections, one of the NCPs must assume the role of the secondary link station. This will not be a problem since the NCP will support secondary-initiated nonactivation XID3 exchanges.

TG quiescing
Will be done by an NCP when the VR, which is used by its SSCP-PU session with a VTAM interchange node, is deactivated. Since other APPN nodes have no knowledge of VRs, they will still assume a path to this composite network node is available and continue to send BINDs. To avoid this, NCP will send a nonactivation XID3 with TG quiescing set to ON to inform adjacent APPN nodes. It is up to the adjacent (network) nodes to include the *quiescing* status in the network topology database and send topology database updates (TDUs) accordingly, informing other APPN network nodes in the network. The processing of the TDU for TG quiescing is part of the base APPN network node support.

4.6 Connection Networks and Virtual Routing Nodes

A *shared-access transport facility* (SATF), such as a token-ring, allows direct connectivity between any pair of link stations attaching to the facility. Direct connectivity avoids session traffic being routed through intermediate network nodes but requires link definitions at a node for any node to which connectivity is required. See, as an example, (A) in Figure 29 on page 67. ENA and ENB have a direct link and, although they need the assistance of a network node server to establish a session, the session data is exchanged directly between the two nodes. No link has been defined between ENA and ENC and session data will always be routed through at least one intermediate network node.

If any-to-any direct connectivity is required to avoid routing through intermediate network node(s) and sending the same message more than once across the SATF, then the number of definitions required is proportional to the square of the number of nodes on the SATF, which, as the number of nodes grows, will become very high. See, as an example, (B) in Figure 29 on page 67. Each node requires definitions to all other nodes.

Another drawback of increasing the number of direct links between APPN network nodes is that the number of topology database updates (TDUs) flowing in the network grows rapidly and may degrade the performance of the network. An APPN network node broadcasts TDUs to all adjacent network nodes and after having received a TDU forwards the TDU to all adjacent APPN network nodes; for details, see 5.4.1, "Topology Database Updates" on page 81. As an example, see (C) in Figure 29. NN1 will send TDUs to all network nodes that will then forward the TDU to all other network nodes. So, instead of receiving one copy, NN2, NN3 and NN4 receive the TDU three times. Flow reduction mechanisms prevent the network nodes from continuing to forward the TDUs.

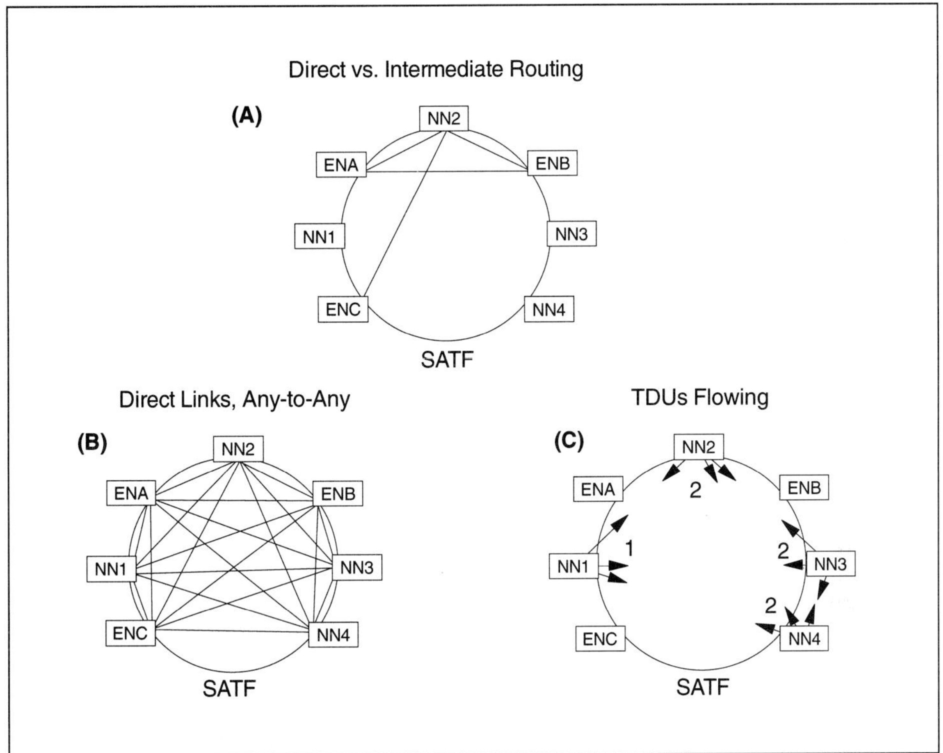

Figure 29. Shared-Access Transport Facility (SATF) without VRN

Thus, defining any-to-any links on an SATF provides optimal session routing but requires a high number of definitions and results in high volumes of TDUs.

To alleviate these problems, APPN allows nodes to define a *virtual routing node* (VRN) to represent their attachment to an SATF. Session traffic between two nodes that have defined the VRN can be routed *through* the VRN without passing through any real network node. TDUs will never be exchanged with a VRN.

The SATF and the set of all nodes defined as having a connection to a common virtual routing node representing the SATF are said to comprise a *connection network*. NOF defines a connection network (CN) and specifies a network-qualified name for it. This CN name is used as the CP name of the virtual routing node.

It is important to realize that session setup data and TDUs are routed through an APPN network using CP-CP sessions. Nodes can establish CP-CP sessions neither *with* nor *through* a VRN, as it is not a real node. Two nodes can establish CP-CP sessions only if a direct link has been defined between them.

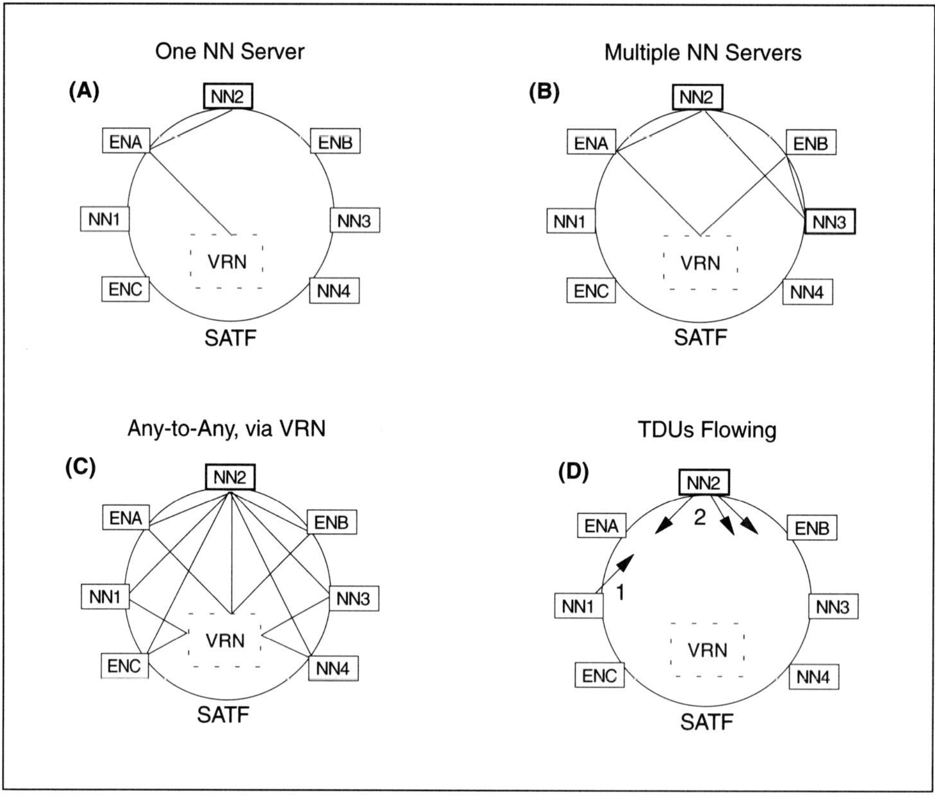

Figure 30. Shared-Access Transport Facility (SATF) with VRN

Session establishment between LUs owned by APPN end nodes requires assistance from a network node server if no direct link has been defined between the APPN end nodes. As the APPN end nodes cannot have CP-CP sessions with a network node server through a VRN, it is necessary for them to have defined links to their respective network node servers, as well as defined connections to the VRN. (A) in Figure 30 shows the minimal definition requirements for an APPN end node. ENA has defined two connections: one to the VRN and one to its network node server NN2.

Network nodes cannot establish CP-CP sessions through a VRN. Therefore, if two APPN end nodes (ENA and ENB) do not share the same network node server, session establishment between LUs on ENA and ENB is possible only if their network node servers have CP-CP connectivity. See (B) in Figure 30. The latter is also required to allow session establishment between LUs on two network nodes. CP-CP connectivity between two network nodes requires that the two network nodes have defined a link between each other and CP-CP sessions have been established between the two nodes, or that the two network node servers can exchange data via one or more intermediate network nodes with active CP-CP sessions between each pair of adjacent network nodes.

The benefits of defining a VRN can be seen in (C) in Figure 30 on page 68. To have any-to-any connectivity without session data being routed through real network nodes requires only two link definitions in each node: one to the VRN and one to a common network node as depicted in the figure as NN2. NN2 is the only node that requires link definitions to all nodes. NN2 assists only in session setup; no session data will be routed through it. For performance and backup reasons, more than one *common* network node can be defined.

TDUs flow only between network nodes that have CP-CP sessions to each other. Link definitions in a network node can be limited to the link to the VRN and to one other network node. (D) in Figure 30 on page 68 depicts a situation where network nodes NN1, NN3, and NN4 have CP-CP sessions with only one NN2 network node. A TDU from NN1 will be sent to NN2 and, after receipt, forwarded to NN3 and NN4. So instead of receiving multiple copies, each network node receives only one copy of the TDU. When the CP-CP connectivity between network nodes is extended, the number of TDUs flowing through the network will increase.

4.6.1 The Virtual Routing Node

A *virtual routing node* (VRN) is not a node, but is simply a way to define an APPN node's attachment to a shared-access transport facility. It allows LU-LU session data to be routed without intermediate node routing through APPN network nodes. It reduces definition requirements and the number of TDUs flowing through the network.

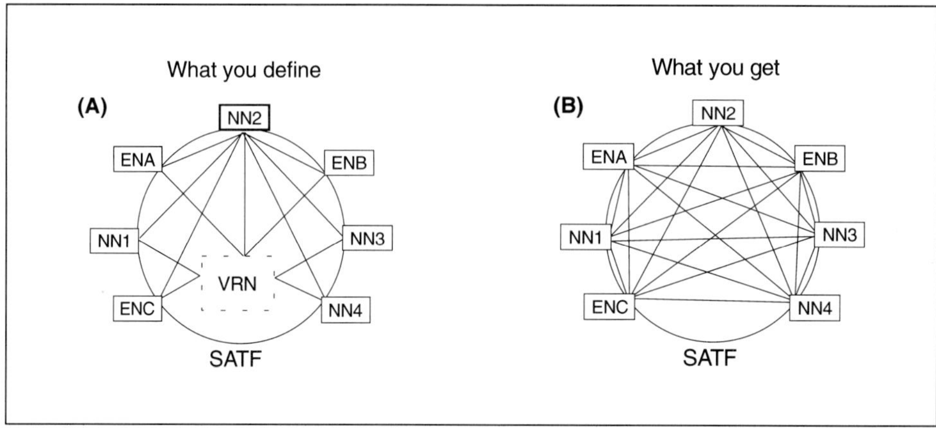

Figure 31. Virtual Routing Node

During LU-LU session establishment, the end nodes report their VRN connections, along with local DLC-signaling information such as token-ring MAC and SAP addresses to their network node server. The information is carried in the TG vectors, which are explained in Chapter 5, "Topology and Routing Services" on page 71. The TG vectors describing the *link* to the VRN allow the network node server responsible for route computation to determine that two nodes can communicate directly. The node owning the primary LU receives the DLC-signaling information of the adjacent node, which it can use to activate a dynamic link to the adjacent node, if none is already active. After the link is activated, a session BIND and BIND(RSP) will flow on this link.

Nodes attaching to a shared-access transport facility (SATF) may define direct connection to other nodes attached to the same SATF, define a *connection network* (CN), or do both. An APPN end node must define at least a connection to its network node server.

Multiple CNs may be defined per port and a single CN may be defined on multiple ports. All adjacent link stations on a CN are *dynamic* link stations. All dynamic link stations associated with a particular port on the CN share the same characteristics.

The activation of actual connections through a connection network is triggered either by session services (as part of session establishment) or by a remote node. The node operator facility cannot activate connections through a connection network.

Chapter 5. Topology and Routing Services

The topology and routing services function (TRS) resides in every APPN network node and, in a reduced form, in every APPN end node and LEN end node.

In an APPN network node, TRS is responsible for creating and maintaining the class-of-service (COS) database and for creating and maintaining a copy of the *network topology database*. The network topology database contains information on network node connections to VRNs and other network nodes. In an end node, TRS is responsible for creating and maintaining the class-of-service database (only if the end node supports the class-of-service/transmission-priority-field (COS/TPF) option set), and for maintaining the *local topology database* (which TRS in a network node also maintains). The local topology database contains information on connections involving the end nodes EN-to-EN, EN-to-VRN, and EN-to-NN.

During LU-LU session establishment, TRS is invoked to compute an optimal route through the APPN network between the two nodes on which the LUs reside. TRS in an end node will use the local database to select possible TGs (single hop) from the end node to adjacent nodes. TRS in a network node will use the information provided by the two end nodes, together with the information in the network node's COS and network topology databases to select an end-to-end route.

The scope of functions differs among node types. For LEN end nodes, they are very simple, while APPN network nodes can use large databases and sophisticated program logic.

Note: Directory Services is invoked to *locate* a session partner, and Topology and Routing Services is invoked to *compute* an optimal route to the session partner once it has been located.

5.1 Function Overview

As you can see in Figure 32 on page 72, TRS consists of three components:

Topology Database Manager (TDM)
: The TDM is responsible for maintaining the topology databases that include a local topology database on both end nodes and network nodes, and a network topology database on network nodes.

Class-of-Service Manager (COSM)
: The COSM provides support for the COS/TPF function. It is responsible for creating and maintaining the COS databases and provides the capability to translate a *mode name* to a COS name and an associated transmission priority. The COSM is a required component of TRS on network nodes. On end nodes, the COSM exists only if the COS/TPF option set (036) is supported. COSM shares the COS database with route selection services (RSS).

Route Selection Services (RSS)
RSS is responsible for route computation.

Note: A *route* is an ordered sequence of nodes and TGs that represents a path from an origin node to a destination node.

Figure 32 depicts the node functions that interface with TRS. The class-of-service manager (COSM) function is optional in end nodes, and the interface between directory services (CP.DS) and TRS exists only in APPN network nodes.

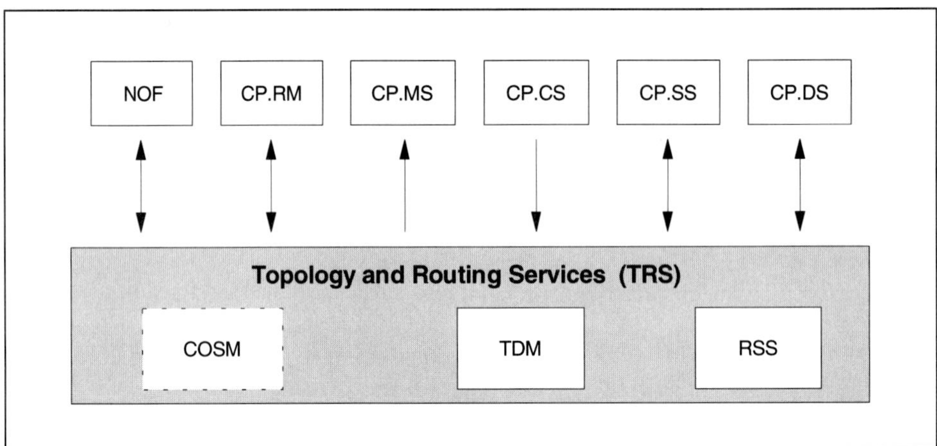

Figure 32. Overview of TRS Components and Protocol Boundaries

Topology and routing services (TRS) is initialized by the node operator facility (NOF). NOF passes the following parameters during initialization:

- Type of node
- CP name of this node
- Network ID of this node
- Indication of whether the COS/TPF function is supported
- The COS database file name
- The topology database file name

The main function of TRS, or actually RSS, is to compute the optimal route between two nodes in an APPN network. RSS interacts with the two other TRS components, COSM and TDM, to obtain the necessary information before being able to perform a route computation.

To allow the computation of an optimal route, several databases are maintained. Figure 33 on page 73 depicts the various types of databases involved in route calculation and how these are used by the components of topology and routing services.

Route computation is a coordinated activity between TRS components on several APPN nodes. In the following sections, we give more details about the information maintained by TRS and explain which components of TRS are invoked, and on which nodes, to make it possible to calculate an optimal route.

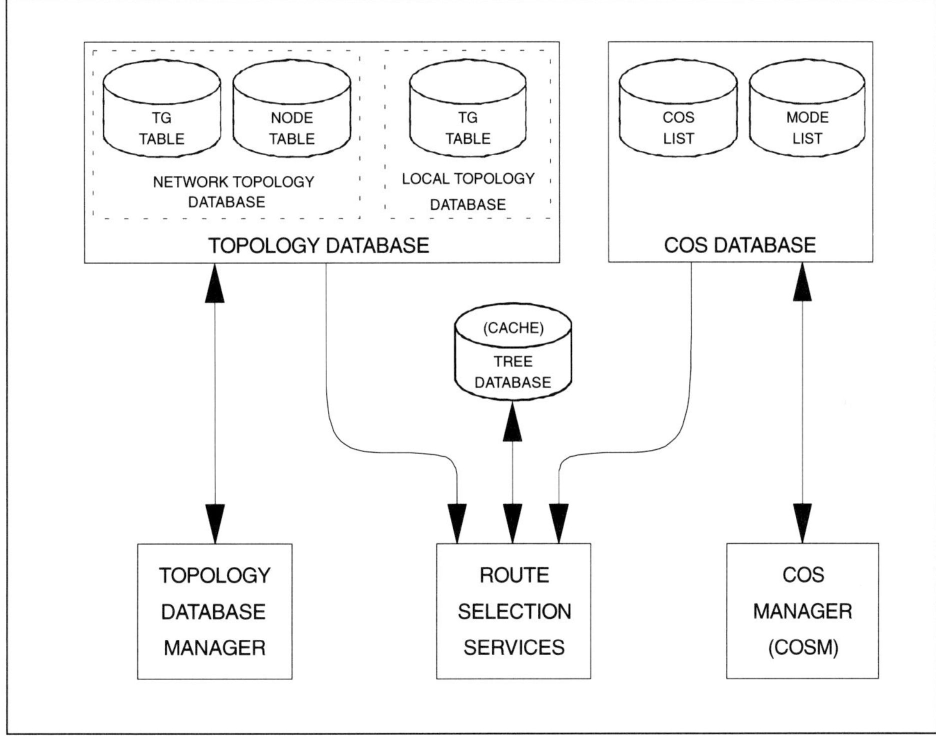

Figure 33. Databases and Subcomponents of Topology and Routing Services

5.2 Resource Characteristics

In order to calculate the optimal route, which means the physical path that best fits the user's requirement for an LU-LU session path, the *actual* node and transmission group (TG) characteristics have to be compared with the *required* route characteristics.

For both TGs and nodes, APPN has defined a set of properties that specify their characteristics. APPN also defines the values that can be assigned to each of these properties. To define the resource characteristics, two different data structures are used:

- Binary-valued properties such as operational/nonoperational status are encoded as property flags (bits).
- Multi-valued properties such as bandwidth are encoded as property indices (bytes). Some indices (such as cost per byte) can have any value within an allowed range, while others (such as security class) take one of a predefined set of values.

Note: Some resource properties, for example the TG bandwidth, are static, while others, congestion for example, are dynamic and are periodically updated.

5.2.1 TG Characteristics

Table 4 depicts the TG characteristics. The values are either static (S) or dynamic (D) and can assume binary (B) or multiple (M) values.

Table 4. TG Characteristics

Property	**Dynamic (D) or Static (S)**	**Binary (B) or Multiple (M)**
Cost per Byte	S	M
Cost per Connect Time	S	M
Security Level	S	M
Modem Class	S	M
Effective Capacity	S	M
User Defined-1	S	M
User Defined-2	S	M
User Defined-3	S	M
Propagation Delay	S or D	M
Quiescing	D	B
Operational	D	B

The TG characteristics are stored in the topology database and exchanged in topology database updates (TDUs) using control vector (CV) X'47'. For format details, see *Systems Network Architecture Formats*, GA27-3136. Some fields are described below:

Cost per Byte
: This is a single-byte value in the range 0 to 255 that expresses the relative cost of transmitting a byte over the associated TG. The units for cost per byte are user-defined.

Cost per Connect Time
: This is a single-byte value in the range 0 to 255 that expresses the relative cost of using a TG. The units for cost per connect time are installation-defined and are typically based on the applicable tariffs of the transmission facility used by the TG.

Security Level
: This is an indication of the level of security protection provided by the TG. The security values are architecturally defined to provide consistency across all networks. The default is X'01', indicating no security.

Currently, the following security levels are defined:

- X'C0' guarded conduit containing the transmission medium; protected against physical and radiation tapping
- X'A0' link-level encryption is provided
- X'80' guarded conduit protected against physical tapping
- X'60' secure conduit; not guarded
- X'40' underground cable; located in a secure country
- X'20' public switched network; no predetermined route that traffic will take
- X'01' all others; for example, satellite connection or located in an insecure country

Effective Capacity
: Is the highest bit-transmission rate that the TG will be allowed to attain before being considered overloaded. The effective capacity, defined as a one-byte floating point value, is expressed in units of 300 bps.

User Defined 1,2,3
: These are up to three user-defined values in the range 0 to 255.

Propagation Delay
: Is the time it takes for a signal to travel from one end of the TG to the other. Propagation delay, defined as a one-byte floating point value, is expressed in units of 1 microsecond.

5.2.2 Node Characteristics

Table 5 depicts the node characteristics. The values are either static (S) or dynamic (D) and can assume binary (B) or multiple (M) values.

Table 5. Node Characteristics		
Property	**Dynamic (D) or Static (S)**	**Binary (B) or Multiple (M)**
Central Directory Support	S	B
Node Congested	D	B
Intermediate Routing Resources Depleted	D	B
Quiescing	D	B
Node Type	S	M
Route-Addition Resistance	D	M

The node characteristics are stored in the topology database and exchanged in topology database updates (TDUs) using control vectors (CVs) X'44' and X'45'. For format details, see *Systems Network Architecture Formats*, GA27-3136.

Central Directory Support
This characteristic indicates that the node acts as a central directory server (optional function 1106). See 6.2.2.2, "Central Resource Registration (CRR)" on page 112 for more information.

Node Congested
This characteristic is set and reset by a node based upon one or both of the following congestion measures:

- Cycle utilization of the hardware
- Total buffer utilization (control blocks, message buffers, etc.)

When either of these measures crosses a specified threshold the congestion bit is set. It is not reset until the node is out of the congested state for all of the measures that the node maintains.

The *reset* threshold should be significantly below the *set* threshold. This is necessary to prevent the node from flooding the network with TDUs when congestion measures are oscillating around their threshold levels.

Intermediate Routing Resources Depleted
This characteristic indicates whether the node's pool of resources is depleted to the extent that it cannot support additional routes that traverse it but do not terminate at it. The node monitors the set of session connector control blocks, which are required for intermediate routing.

Quiescing
The quiescing bit indicates whether the network operator wants the node to be drained of existing sessions traversing the node to shutdown. When this bit is set, the node is excluded from subsequent route computations.

Node Type
This characteristic indicates the node type.

Route-Addition Resistance

This characteristic is a binary number between 0 and 255 used as a *node weight* during route calculation. The value is user defined and can be dynamically changed, but implementations may choose to keep it fixed for a node. The lower the value, the more likely it is that this node is used as an intermediate routing node.

This node characteristic could be used, for example, to assign low values to the set of nodes over which the network administrator wants the majority of traffic to flow. This then has the effect of defining a *backbone* network.

5.3 Topology Databases

APPN networks consist of a *backbone* structure of network nodes interconnected by TGs, known as *intermediate-routing* TGs, and TGs connecting end nodes to adjacent network nodes, virtual routing nodes, or end nodes, known as *endpoint* TGs. For an example, see Figure 34 on page 78. All TGs attached to either EN1 or EN2 are endpoint TGs, and all TGs between two adjacent network nodes are intermediate-routing TGs.

Information about the backbone structure of the APPN network is kept within the *network topology database*, which resides on every APPN network node. Information about endpoint TGs is contained within *local network topology databases*, which reside on every APPN node or LEN end node.

The primary use of local and network topology databases is to enable route calculation when an LU residing in one APPN node wishes to establish a session with an LU residing in another APPN node. The topology databases enable TRS to determine all possible routes between the nodes. The local topology database contributes the end node's TGs, while the network topology database supplies the information on network nodes and the TGs between them.

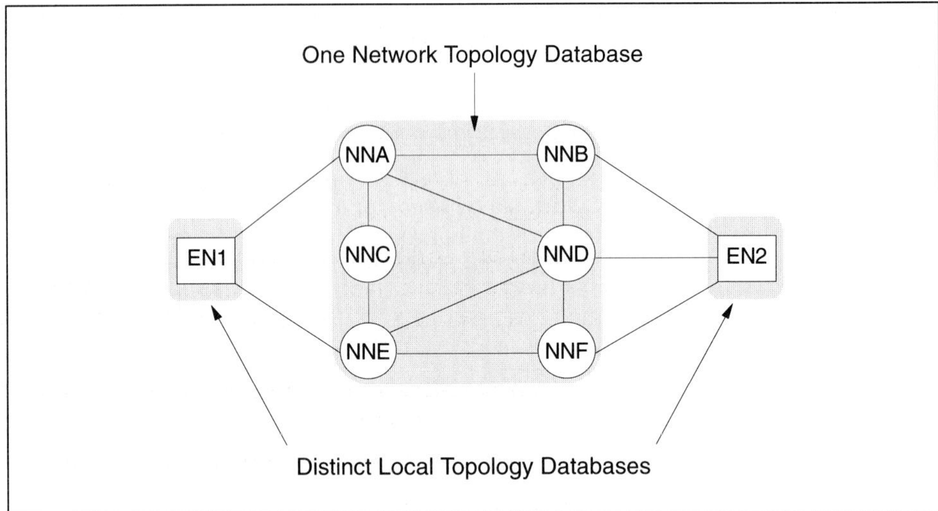

Figure 34. Network and Local Topology Databases

Figure 34 shows an example of an APPN network and how network topology information is maintained in local and network topology databases.

5.3.1 Local Topology Databases

Each end node maintains information about every endpoint TG attached to the end node itself. The information is kept in a database called the *local topology database*. The local topology database is created and maintained by TDM. It is not saved across IPLs and is rebuilt when the node initializes.

An APPN end node uses its local topology database:

1. When there is no CP-CP session to a network node server, for example, when a CP-CP session is being established.
2. To send information on endpoint TGs to its network node server to complement the network node's knowledge during the route selection processes.
3. When establishing sessions to predefined LUs without the help of a network node server.

The local topology database contains information on *endpoint TGs*. An endpoint TG is not included in the network topology database.

5.3.1.1 End Node Topology Database Manager

The topology database manager (TDM) creates and maintains the topology database. Entries in the topology database are created automatically, when configuration services informs TDM about newly activated or changed TGs. The operator updates the topology database through configuration services. The topology database is searched by TDM when it receives a query from route selection services or from session services.

5.3.2 Network Topology Database

Each network node maintains information about all network nodes and all intermediate-routing TGs in the APPN network in a database called the *network topology database*. The network topology database does not include information on LEN end nodes, APPN end nodes, or the TGs attached to them. It includes information only on network nodes and their connections to virtual routing nodes and other network nodes.

The network topology database is fully replicated on all APPN network nodes. APPN protocols for the distribution of network topology information ensure that every network node is provided with a complete view of the network backbone topology.

In addition, the local copy of the network topology database contains information on the other local TGs of the APPN network node itself. This information is kept locally only and not sent to adjacent network nodes.

The network topology database is created and maintained by TDM and saved across IPLs by the *safe-store of network TDB* function.

5.3.2.1 Node Table

The network topology database contains the following information about the network nodes in the network:

- The network-qualified CP name of the node.
- Node characteristics, summarized in 5.2.2, "Node Characteristics" on page 75
- A pointer to the list of records describing node-attached TGs.
- A resource sequence number (RSN). See also RSN on page 85.

5.3.2.2 TG Table

Both network and local topology databases contain information about TGs. TG database entries, consisting of a TG vector and a TG record, are direction dependent, and two entries exist for each TG. One entry describes the TG in one direction, and another entry describes the TG in the opposite direction. (See the note under 5.4, "Network Node Topology Database Manager" on page 80.)

The TG record contains the following information:

- A pointer to the TG vector
- A pointer into the weight index structure (see below)

The TG vector contains the following information:

- The TG number
- The partner-node CP name

- A status indicator (active or inactive)
- Whether CP-CP sessions are supported and active
- CP-CP session status (if the node supports function set 086)
- The partner-node type: real or virtual routing node (VRN)
- TG characteristics, as described in 5.2.1, "TG Characteristics" on page 74
- The resource sequence number (RSN). See also RSN on page 85.
- DLC-signaling information

  For TGs to virtual routing nodes (VRNs), DLC-signaling information is also maintained. For example, for token-ring attached nodes, the MAC address of the node is stored.

  The DLC-signaling information is used to allow a station to dynamically establish a connection through a VRN to a remote station when using a shared access transport facility (SATF). For details, see 4.6, "Connection Networks and Virtual Routing Nodes" on page 66.

5.3.2.3 The Weight Index Structure

TG weights have to be calculated to compute the optimal route between an origin and destination endpoint. This can be a time-consuming process that has to be repeated for each session setup. For performance reasons, APPN provides an option to cache the TG weights. This option is called the TG weight index structure.

Refer to *SNA APPN Architecture Reference*, SC30-3422 for details about the weight index structure.

5.4 Network Node Topology Database Manager

A network node topology database manager (NNTDM) component resides in every network node and is responsible for maintaining the local copy of the network topology database.

Note: Each node is considered the *resource owner* of itself and of its locally attached TGs. In order to ensure that every resource in the network has only one owner, in turn to prevent topology database update loops, every TG is regarded as two unidirectional pipes with one owning node at each end. The node owning a TG in a given direction is the *sender* of data flowing in that direction.

Each NNTDM creates and broadcasts topology database updates (TDUs) about its resources to adjacent network nodes using its CP-CP sessions. NNTDM stores the information from incoming TDUs in its copy of the network topology database, and forwards the TDUs to adjacent network nodes. This allows every NNTDM in the network to maintain a consistent copy of the network topology database.

5.4.1 Topology Database Updates

The NNTDMs in two adjacent nodes can start to exchange TDUs after the CP-CP sessions between the nodes have been established. The TDUs contain:

- Resource identifiers
- Resource characteristics
- Resource sequence numbers (RSNs)

When a network node connects to the network for the first time, it has no knowledge of remote resources and has only information about its local resources. It will receive a copy of the current network topology database from the adjacent network node and send TDUs with information about itself, its locally-attached intermediate-routing TGs, and connection networks (VRNs). The adjacent network node receiving this information will broadcast these TDUs into the network.

When two network nodes reconnect after having been temporarily disconnected, only the changed information within the local copies of the network topology database will be exchanged. See the discussion about Flow-Reduction Sequence Numbers (FRSNs) on page 86.

Whenever a network node detects a change in its own state, or in the state of a locally-attached intermediate-routing TG, it updates the resource entry in its own copy of the network topology database, increments the RSN for that resource to the next even value, and informs its adjacent network nodes by broadcasting TDUs. The reason for using an *even* value here is that an *odd* value would have a special meaning; it would signal that the sender of a TDU has become aware of an inconsistency in the information held collectively about the resource, and would prompt the network node owning the resource to resolve this inconsistency. (See 5.4.1.4, “Processing Topology Database Updates (TDUs)” on page 82.)

When no information is received about a resource for 15 days, it becomes eligible for *garbage collection*. See page 87 for more information.

5.4.1.1 Processing Topology Database Queries

Directory services, session services, and route selection services interface to the NNTDM in order to obtain information from the topology database. Whenever NNTDM updates or deletes a resource, it notifies the route selection services (RSS) component of topology and routing services, to enable RSS to update routing information that has been cached.

5.4.1.2 Virtual Routing Node (VRN)

Because VRNs are merely representations of connection networks and do not really exist, they cannot broadcast resource updates. Where a network node has TGs that connect into VRNs, the network node broadcasts the TG and VRN information on their behalf. The node characteristics for a virtual routing node have architecturally defined default values.

5.4.1.3 Preventing TDU Wars

A *TDU war* occurs when two or more network nodes contend over the contents of the same resource records in their topology databases, resulting in a degradation of network performance. Unless the TDU war is stopped, two contending nodes continuously broadcast TDUs correcting a resource's information received in a TDU from the other node.

To prevent TDU wars in a network, network nodes use the following rules regarding the broadcasting of TDUs:

1. An NN can modify and broadcast topology information about a resource owned by another NN *only* if it believes that inconsistent information exists in the network about that resource and the NN owning the resource is no longer present in the network.
2. If after performing step 1 above, the NN receives a TDU correcting the same resource record it originally modified, it does not issue a new TDU but accepts the information in the received TDU as being correct.
3. If an NN receives a resource update for a resource it owns and the information in that update is not identical with the stored information in its topology database, it has to create and broadcast a new TDU containing the stored information.

These three rules prevent TDU wars from occurring except when two (or more) NNs exist in the network that have the same CP name (which is a configuration error, because CP names have to be unique in a network) or if an NN erroneously modifies the content of a TG or node record before transmitting the resource information in a TDU.

To prevent such TDU wars, function set 1203 (Detection and Elimination of TDU Wars) was created. NNs implementing this function increment a *resource contention counter* for every resource owned by the local node whenever they receive a TDU from another NN trying to modify information about that resource. If a counter then exceeds 10 for a resource, the NN owning this resource stops correcting TDUs received for that resource and issues an alert indicating that condition.

First after 15 minutes, then 30 minutes, and finally every 60 minutes a new TDU with information about the resource is broadcast and a new alert generated if the contention condition still exists to remind the network operator that the problem still persists in the network. Once a day, during garbage collection, any currently existing resource contention counters are erased.

5.4.1.4 Processing Topology Database Updates (TDUs)

When a network node receives a TDU, the TDU may contain information for resources local to that network node or remote from it. In either case the network node decides what to do with the information by comparing resource sequence numbers (RSNs) in the TDU with those in its existing network topology database, as follows:

Local resource information in TDU:
As the owner of the resource, the receiving network node is responsible for providing the network with valid information on that resource, especially if it detects an inconsistency between the information received in a TDU and the information stored in its topology database, or if some other node indicates an inconsistency for a resource by broadcasting a TDU with an odd RSN.

- If the RSN in the TDU is less than the RSN in the database, then
  - The network node discards the received resource information and builds a new TDU with the RSN from the database and using the information from its database.
- If the RSN in the TDU is equal to the RSN in the database and the resource information received is identical to the information in the database, then:
  - The network node discards the associated resource information from the TDU.
- If the RSN in the TDU is equal to the RSN in the database but the resource information received is not identical to the information in the database, then:
  - The network node treats this as an attempt by another NN to modify a locally owned resource as described below.
- If the RSN in the TDU is greater than the RSN in the database and the resource is an inoperative or inconsistent TG (in the database) and marked for garbage collection in the TDU, then:
  - The received information is discarded if the TG is already marked for garbage collection in the topology database.
  - The received information is stored in the topology database and a new TDU is built if the TG is not already marked for garbage collection in the topology database.
- If the RSN in the TDU is greater than the RSN in the database and the resource is not an inoperative or inconsistent TG (in the database) or not marked for garbage collection in the TDU, then:
  - the network node treats this as an attempt by another NN to modify a locally owned resource as described below.
- If another node attempts to modify information describing a resource owned by the local node, then:

  The network node increments the resource contention counter by one (or creates one with the initial value of one if none exists).

If the resource contention counter is ≤ 10, the network node builds a new TDU with an even RSN that is greater than the RSN received, using the information from its database, which, being the owner of that resource, it knows is valid.

If the resource contention counter has exceeded 10 (indicating that a TDU war is occurring), an alert is generated and the information received is discarded.

Whenever a new TDU is built, it is then broadcast to all adjacent network nodes to ensure that all copies of the network topology database are again synchronized.

Remote resource information in TDU:

In this case, the receiving network node assumes that the TDU carries valid information about the resource from the resource's owner. It nevertheless checks the received information and RSNs against the information and RSNs in its database.

- If the resource is not currently contained in the network node's database, then:
  - The network node stores the information from the TDU (including the RSN) in its database and rebroadcasts the resource information in a TDU to all adjacent network nodes.
- If the RSN in the TDU is greater than the RSN in the database, then:
  - The network node stores the information from the TDU (including the RSN) in its database and rebroadcasts the resource information in a TDU to all adjacent network nodes.
- If the RSN in the TDU is equal to the RSN in the database and the resource information received is identical to the information in the database, then:
  - The network node discards the associated resource information from the TDU.
- If the RSN in the TDU is even and equal to the RSN in the database but the resource information received is not identical to the information in its database, then:
  - The network node builds a new TDU using the information from its database. In the new TDU, the RSN from the received TDU is incremented by one, thus forcing the RSN to an odd value. This is used to signal other network nodes that the information about the resource is inconsistent, and that the resource should not be included in route calculations. The owner of the resource will then resolve the inconsistency by resending the valid information from its database, as described above on page 83.

- If the RSN in the TDU is odd and equal to the RSN in its database, then:
  - The network node discards the associated resource information from the TDU.
- If the RSN in the TDU is less than the RSN in the database, then:
  - The network node discards the associated resource information from the TDU. A new TDU is then built with information from the database (including the RSN) and broadcast to all adjacent network nodes or, optionally, just to the node from which it received the smaller RSN.

5.4.2 Flow Reduction Considerations

The numbers of topology database updates (TDUs) flowing between network nodes in a large network may be of concern. Several mechanisms have been put in place to reduce the numbers of TDUs. The mechanisms are described below:

TDUs for VRNs, Network Nodes, and Intermediate-Routing TGs Only
TDUs will never contain node information for end nodes or TG information for endpoint TGs. The information that network nodes maintain in the network topology database about local endpoint TGs is never broadcast.

TDUs for Connection Networks
A network node does not broadcast a TDU for activation or normal deactivation of a TG to another network node going by way of a virtual routing node. Only if such a TG fails (abnormal deactivation) are TDUs generated, in order to exclude this TG from route computation.

Resource Sequence Numbers (RSNs)
An RSN is associated with the current information about each node and TG in the network topology database. This RSN is assigned by the network node that owns the resource. A network node owns node definitions for itself, and TG characteristics in the direction of adjacent nodes. See the note under 5.4, "Network Node Topology Database Manager" on page 80 for an explanation of TG ownership.

Whenever a network node detects a change in the state of one of its resources, it increments the RSN to the next even value. It then creates a TDU including the new resource information and its associated RSN and broadcasts it to all its adjacent network nodes.

The use of RSNs in TDUs and the network topology database allows a network node to determine whether resource information has been received before. Resource information in a TDU is discarded and not rebroadcast if the resource's RSN in the TDU is equal to the RSN in the existing topology database and the information in the TDU is the same as in the database. This prevents endless retransmission of resource information. See also 5.4.1.4, "Processing Topology Database Updates (TDUs)" on page 82.

The RSN is an unsigned even integer in a circular number space. The range is 2 to 2^{32} - 1. Odd values, also known as "inconsistent sequence numbers," are used to signal that the information about a remote resource is inconsistent. This will trigger recovery. See 5.4.1.4, "Processing Topology Database Updates (TDUs)" on page 82.

Flow-Reduction Sequence Number (FRSN)

Each network node tracks that TDUs it broadcasts to each of its adjacent network nodes and that TDUs it receives from each of its adjacent network nodes using flow-reduction sequence numbers (FRSNs). FRSNs are associated with TDUs and known only by a network node and its adjacent network nodes, as opposed to RSNs which are associated with resources and distributed to all network nodes in a topology subnet. The FRSN is an unsigned integer in the range of 1 to 2^{32} - 1.

FRSNs tend to eliminate unnecessary TDU flows when network nodes re-establish their CP-CP sessions following failures using the method described in the following paragraphs.

Whenever a node broadcasts a TDU to its adjacent network nodes, it increases its local FRSN by one and includes this FRSN in the TDU. For each modified or newly created resource included in a TDU. This TDU's FRSN is then added to the resource's topology database entry for later reference. New FRSN values are not assigned to entries that have not been modified, and are included in a TDU, for example, during initial topology exchange.

For each adjacent network node, a network node remembers which TDUs it has sent and received by saving in its topology database the last FRSN sent and received. If a network node becomes disconnected from an adjacent network node and the two subsequently re-establish their CP-CP sessions, they will exchange their respective last-received FRSNs. Both nodes will then compare the adjacent node's last-received FRSN with the local current FRSN, scan their topology database for entries that have FRSNs that are higher than the adjacent node's last-received FRSN, and send the new information in TDUs to one another. This will effect a complete re-synchronization of the topology databases.

The use of FRSNs allows a pair of network nodes to exchange only those topology updates that cannot be sent while the two nodes are disconnected, instead of exchanging the contents of their entire topology databases. A node may, however, indicate that it wants a complete copy of its adjacent node's topology database by indicating that the last-received FRSN is zero. This might be necessary when a node is restarted that does not support safe-store of its topology database.

Garbage Collection

Garbage collection is the process of purging obsolete network topology database entries, thus reclaiming the storage allocated to them and preventing any further TDU flows based on them.

In the original APPN architecture, garbage collection is passive. When an APPN backbone resource first enters the network, its owning network node creates a network topology database entry for it with a *time-left* field, which is initially set to 15 days. The entry is propagated to all the other network nodes' copies of the network topology database by means of TDUs, as usual. The network nodes will all automatically decrement the time-left field once a day, and will delete the resource if its time-left goes to zero. The owning network node sends out a *heartbeat* TDU for the resource every five days to prevent this, as long as the resource entry remains valid. The effect of the heartbeat TDU, or any other TDU concerning the resource, is to put the time-left back to 15 days once more. An obsolete resource will therefore be discarded finally from all copies of the network topology database between 10 and 15 days after becoming obsolete, provided it is not mentioned in *any* TDU in the intervening period.

This original garbage collection method, in practice, can fail to purge obsolete network topology database entries. Additional network node functions known as *enhanced garbage collection* have now been added to the architecture. Network nodes having the enhanced functionality will work alongside others having the basic functionality to reduce the impact of *persistent garbage*. The problem will be eliminated altogether when all network nodes implement the new functions.

5.4.2.1 Enhanced Garbage Collection

The remainder of this section illustrates how the *persistent garbage* problem occurs.

On Monday morning (Diagram A in Figure 35 on page 88), two network nodes, NNA and NNB, have records of node NNX in their copies of the network topology database. The last time they heard of node NNX was 13 days ago. It could be, for instance, that node NNX was renamed at about that time, or de-installed, or that it was only ever intended to be a temporary node for some specific test. Whatever the reason, NNX has 2 days left according to nodes NNA and NNB.

On Monday afternoon (Diagram B in Figure 35 on page 88), network node NNC joins the network and establishes CP-CP sessions with its neighbor NNA. NNA sends TDUs to NNC to create NNC's copy of the network topology database. One of these TDUs concerns NNX. The effect is that NNX is recorded in NNC's database as having *15* days left.

On Wednesday (Diagram C in Figure 35 on page 88), NNX drops to zero days left in NNA and NNB, and is duly deleted. It persists, however, in NNC's database where it now has 13 days left.

On Thursday (Diagram D in Figure 35 on page 88), node NND joins the network and connects to nodes NNC and NNB. TDUs flow as illustrated. As well as putting NNX into NND's copy of the database, they also re-insert NNX into NNA's and NNB's copies of the database, with a full 15 days to live again.

The process is capable of repeating itself indefinitely if, for instance, network nodes continue to be added to the configuration every week, or if there are restarts involving network nodes that do not support safe-store of the topology database and therefore require full updates every time. This can make it practically impossible to effect a final deletion of a *garbage resource* such as NNX.

The example has a network node in the role of a garbage resource, but this works the same way with an intermediate-routing TG.

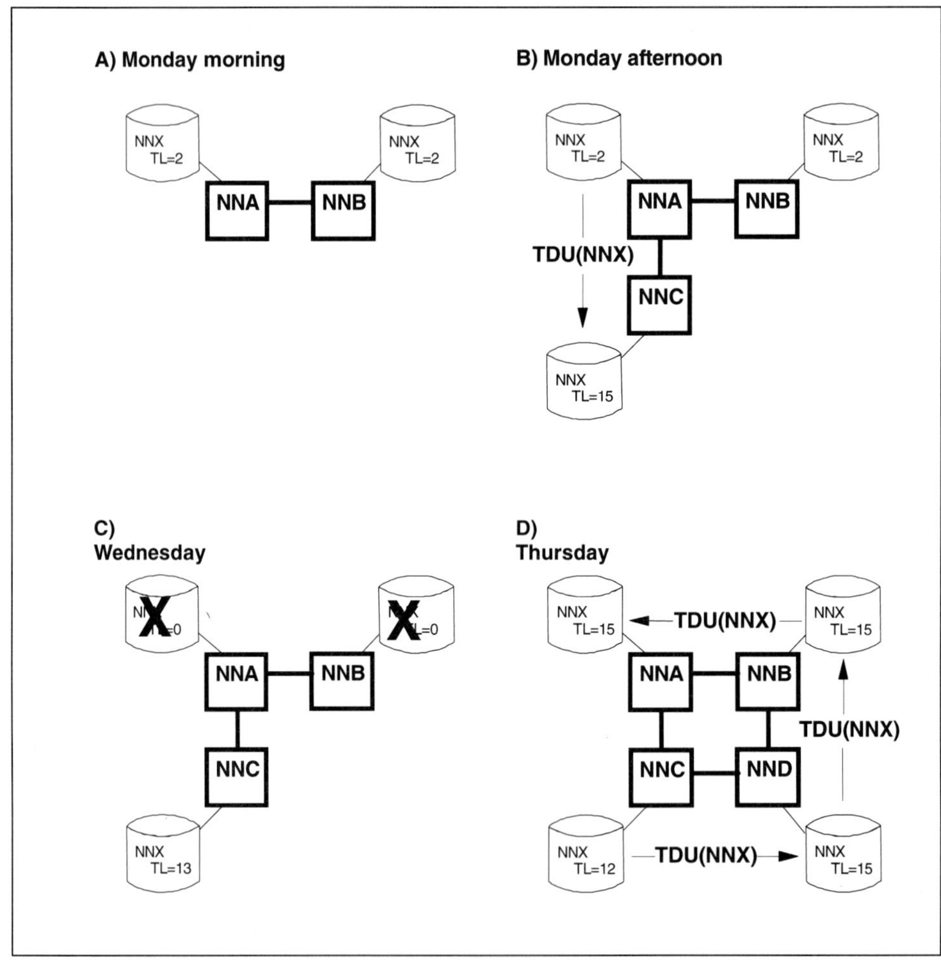

Figure 35. An Example of Persistent Garbage

The solution to the problem is to include two new pieces of information in TDUs: a *garbage collection indicator* in the characteristics control vectors (CVs 45 and 46, concerning respectively network nodes and intermediate-routing TGs), and a new *topology resource descriptor* vector (CV48), which indicates the time-left value. The garbage collection indicator will allow obsolete resources to be marked as such immediately and thereby excluded from route computations across the network. Inclusion of the time-left value in TDUs will mean that a newly-made copy of the network topology database can accurately reflect existing knowledge rather than simply giving all updated resources 15 days to live. Nodes implementing enhanced garbage collection may additionally use odd RSNs in TDUs concerning an obsolete resource. This would make such a resource unusable for routing purposes by the receiving node even if the receiving node itself had not implemented enhanced garbage collection. (See page 81 for more information.)

One additional detail is that the topology resource descriptor vector (CV48) will come as an *unknown control vector* to a network node not implementing the function. A network node having enhanced garbage collection must take care not to broadcast TDUs containing CV48 unless all its adjacent network nodes support receipt of unknown control vectors. It must first find out. A new bit in the CP capabilities vectors exchanged during CP-CP session setup has been allocated for this purpose.

5.5 Class-of-Service Database

The COS database and the class-of-service manager (COSM) exist in all APPN network nodes, and in those APPN end nodes that support the *COS/TPF function*. A node having the COS/TPF function is capable of translating a mode name to a COS name and an associated transmission priority.

Using the information in the COS database, TRS is able to select optimal routes between session endpoints. An optimal route is the physical path that most closely matches the COS requirements for a specific LU-LU session.

The COS database includes:

A list of mode names
Each entry contains a mode name and a pointer to the corresponding COS name.

A list of COS names
Each entry contains a COS definition. This represents one or more sets of acceptable characteristics to which actual TG and node characteristics will be compared. The entry also contains the transmission priority and the weight index value assigned to the COS.

Weight index structure
This structure allows actual TG weights to be computed once and then stored, rather than having to be computed each time a route is requested.

The COS database is maintained independently at each node and can be updated using the node operator facility (NOF).

5.5.1 Mode Name

When an LU starts a session, it uses a mode name to indicate the session characteristics and the class of service (COS) it wants for the session. COSM will use the mode name to obtain a COS name from the COS database, allowing route selection services (RSS) to select an appropriate route.

In the COS database, COS and mode entries exist. Each mode entry, referenced by a mode name, contains a pointer to a corresponding COS entry.

The ability to specify a mode name at session establishment time provides a considerable amount of flexibility. IBM provides several predefined mode names and corresponding COS names and COS definitions. See 5.8, "SNA Defined Modes and Classes of Service" on page 106.

5.5.2 Class of Service (COS)

For each COS, the COS database contains:

- COS name
- Transmission priority:
  - High
  - Medium
  - Low

  APPN distinguishes four transmission priorities. The highest transmission priority, *network priority*, cannot be specified for user-data LU-LU sessions and is reserved for network control messages or CP-CP sessions.
- Several rows of COS definitions for TGs, consisting of:
  - Ranges (pairs of high and low values) for the following TG characteristics:
    - Cost per byte
    - Cost per connect time
    - Effective capacity
    - Propagation delay
    - Security level
    - User defined-1
    - User defined-2
    - User defined-3
  - A weight field
- Several rows of COS definitions for nodes, consisting of:
  - Ranges (pairs of high and low values) for the following node characteristics:
    - Route-addition resistance
    - Congestion

– A weight field

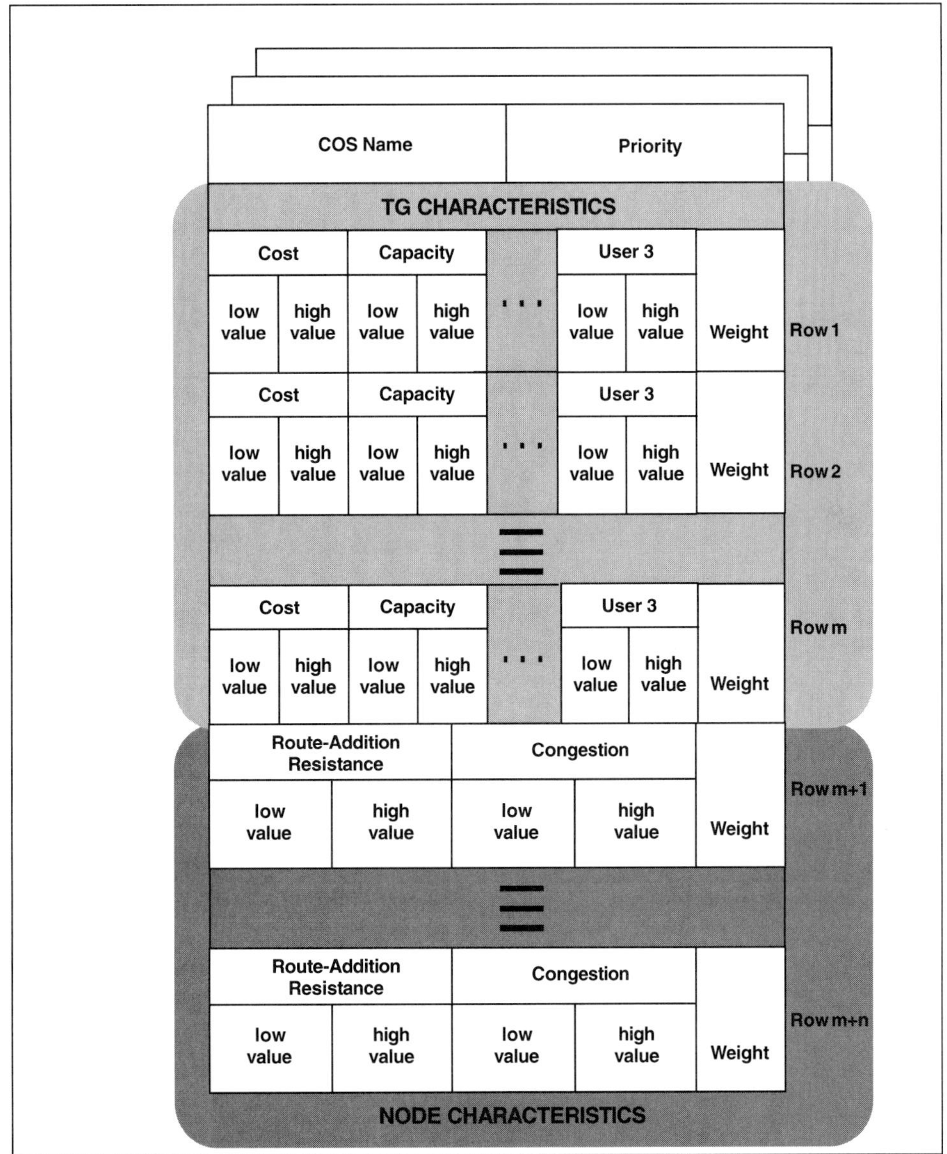

Figure 36. COS Entry with m Rows of TG Characteristics and n Rows of Node Characteristics

Note: The figure shows, for a given COS, the transmission priority and three rows of required TG characteristics. For each of the rows, a weight is also included.

As shown in Figure 36, each COS entry in the COS database consists of a transmission priority and one or more rows of TG characteristics. Each row indicates a *range* of acceptable values for each of the TG characteristics. Each row has an associated weight.

During route calculation, RSS uses the TG characteristics to decide which TGs are acceptable and which are not, for this class of service. A TG is considered *acceptable* if all the *actual* TG characteristic values obtained from the topology database fall within the range of *required* TG characteristics obtained from the COS database. A TG is considered *unacceptable* if at least one of the actual TG characteristics falls outside the range of the required TG values.

A COS may define multiple rows of *required* TG characteristics with a weight assigned to each of the rows. The TG weight is a quantitative measure of how well the actual TG characteristics satisfy the session requirements specified by the COS definition. If a TG satisfies the criteria specified by a row of TG characteristics within a COS definition, then the weight of this specific row is used as a TG weight for route computation. If a TG is considered acceptable for more than one row, the lowest weight is assigned to the TG. If a TG does not satisfy the criteria specified by any row of TG characteristics, the TG is assigned an infinite weight.

More information about TG weight assignment and route calculation is described in 5.7, "Route Computation: Overview" on page 95.

Note: Instead of defining fixed TG weight values per row, implementations may allow the invocation of a function that calculates the TG weight value, giving the user more control over the TG weight assignment process.

5.6 Tree Database

Building and maintaining a tree database is an optional function. It allows an APPN network node to cache *optimal* routes from the APPN network node to all other network nodes (*tree caching*). (The term *tree* or *sink tree* is obtained from graph theory. Graph theory is a mathematical discipline that, among other things, allows optimal route calculation in a network.)

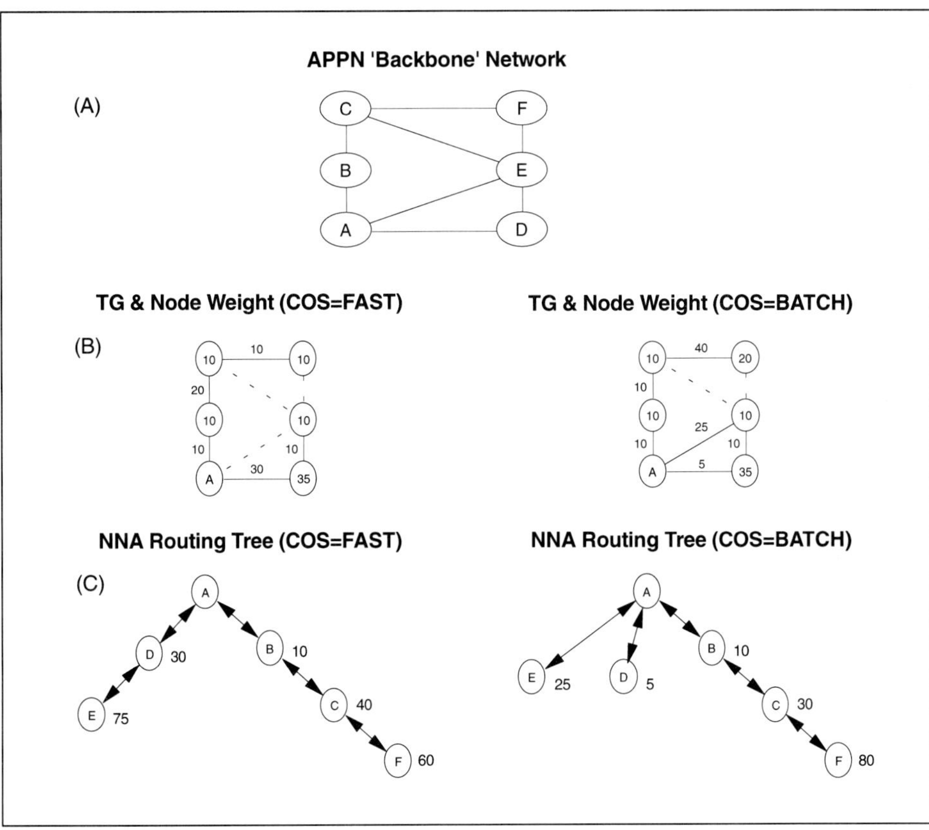

Figure 37. Tree Database at Network Node A for Different Classes of Service

For a given node, the optimal routes to all other nodes in a network can be represented in a tree-like structure. See, for example, (C) in Figure 37. In an APPN network, routing trees are COS-dependent, and the tree database contains one tree per root network node per class of service.

(C) in Figure 37 shows two tree structures for network node A derived from the APPN network depicted in (A). The network node A, for which the routing tree is valid, is shown at the top.

A tree is computed from the perspective of the node; see network node A in Figure 37, drawn at the top. It is unidirectional (the optimum routes are from top to bottom) and includes network nodes and their connecting TGs. For each of the network nodes, a route weight is stored for the route, from the *top* node to the network node itself.

For example, the shortest path from network node A to network node F for COS=FAST has a weight of 60 and uses network node C and network node B as intermediate network nodes using the TGs drawn. Note that, although not shown in the figure, the actual TG numbers between adjacent nodes are included in the tree database.

The route weight is the sum of the weights assigned to each of the components, TGs and nodes, that make up the route. Route weights are COS-dependent because TG weights are COS-dependent. Route weights are also direction-dependent. As for each TG, two sets of TG characteristics have been defined; one in either direction. Each node has a node weight, equal to the *route-addition resistance* value assigned to the node (see 5.2.2, "Node Characteristics" on page 75).

Note that the tree database contains optimal routes between network nodes. When an optimal route has to be computed between two APPN end nodes, route selection services first checks its tree database to see if routes already have been computed between network nodes adjacent to both end nodes. If so, route selection services uses this routing information, together with routing information obtained from the end nodes, to compute the optimum end-to-end route. If no information can be obtained from the tree database, route selection services computes new trees and stores them.

The tree database is derived from the network topology database and the COS database. Whereas the network topology database is replicated throughout all network nodes, the tree database is unique for each node. For each COS, a routing tree can be calculated *from* the node at the top to each network node within the tree.

The tree database is introduced for performance reasons. It saves the overhead of recomputing the optimal tree for each route request. The tree database can be kept in cache. When no tree database is maintained, trees have to be computed from scratch for each route request.

Trees may be removed when the database is full, after topology changes, after an implementation-defined number of uses, or for load distribution among equally weighted routes. The latter may be done with the expectation that equally weighted routes are randomly selected each time the tree is recalculated (*randomized route calculation*).

5.6.1 Routing Trees

Routing trees represent the *least-weight*, or *shortest path*, from the node at the top to each network node within the tree.

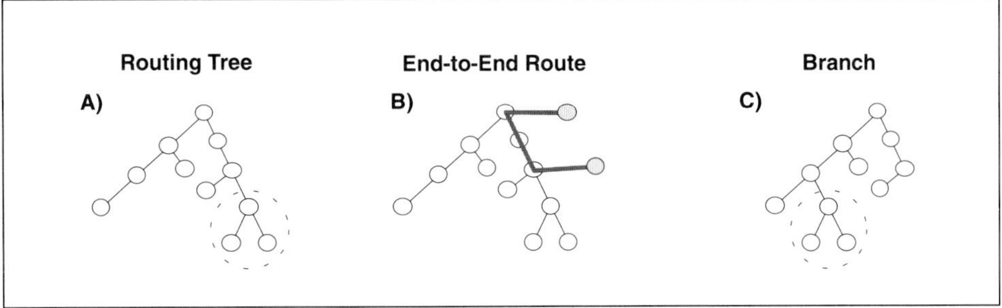

Figure 38. Routing Trees

A few interesting features should be pointed out:

- A routing tree can be computed partially. As soon as the requested destination has become part of the tree, the computation can be stopped.
- The endpoint TG vectors of end nodes can be added to an existing routing tree allowing fast computation of end-to-end routes. See (B) in Figure 38.
- A routing tree is expandable (*incremental updates to tree*). Adding a network node to a (partial) tree can be done, in many cases, without having to compute a new tree.
- If intermediate TGs become (in)active. In most cases, whole *branches* accessible through another TG can be moved to another part of the routing tree, allowing fast re-computation of the tree. See (C) in Figure 38.
- The time to compute a routing tree is proportional to the number of TGs, while the number of network nodes is less important (of course, more network nodes means more TGs).

5.7 Route Computation: Overview

APPN networks consist of a backbone structure of network nodes interconnected by TGs, known as *intermediate-routing* TGs. End nodes are connected to this backbone structure. The TGs connecting the end nodes to adjacent network nodes or end nodes are known as *endpoint* TGs.

A *route* in an APPN network is an ordered sequence of nodes and TGs that represent a path from an origin node to a destination node. To compute the *optimal* route between two nodes, an APPN network node needs to do a number of things:

1. Obtain the *required* route characteristics.
2. Obtain characteristics of all resources, TGs and network nodes, that make up possible routes.
3. Exclude from route computation every resource, TG or network node, where use of the resource is not acceptable.

4. Calculate all possible routes and select the optimal, or most preferred, route.

These steps are explained in detail in the following sections:

Obtain Required Route Characteristics

It is essential in APPN route calculation that an optimal route be calculated on a session basis. A route between two APPN nodes that is the optimal route for one session can be far from optimal for a second session.

At session establishment time, an LU indicates, by using a mode name, which type of route is required for the session requested. For example, by using the mode name FAST, an LU could indicate that a route is required for an interactive application requiring a speedy and predictable response. The mode name BATCH could be used for bulk traffic for which response time is less important than throughput.

To enable TRS to select routes on the basis of a given mode name, COSM will use this mode name to obtain a class of service (COS) and a transmission priority from its COS database. Each COS contains one or more sets of *required* TG characteristics, expressed in terms of costs, propagation delay, capacity, and so on. For details, see 5.5.2, "Class of Service (COS)" on page 90.

To allow route computations, a weight factor has been assigned to each set of required TG characteristics.

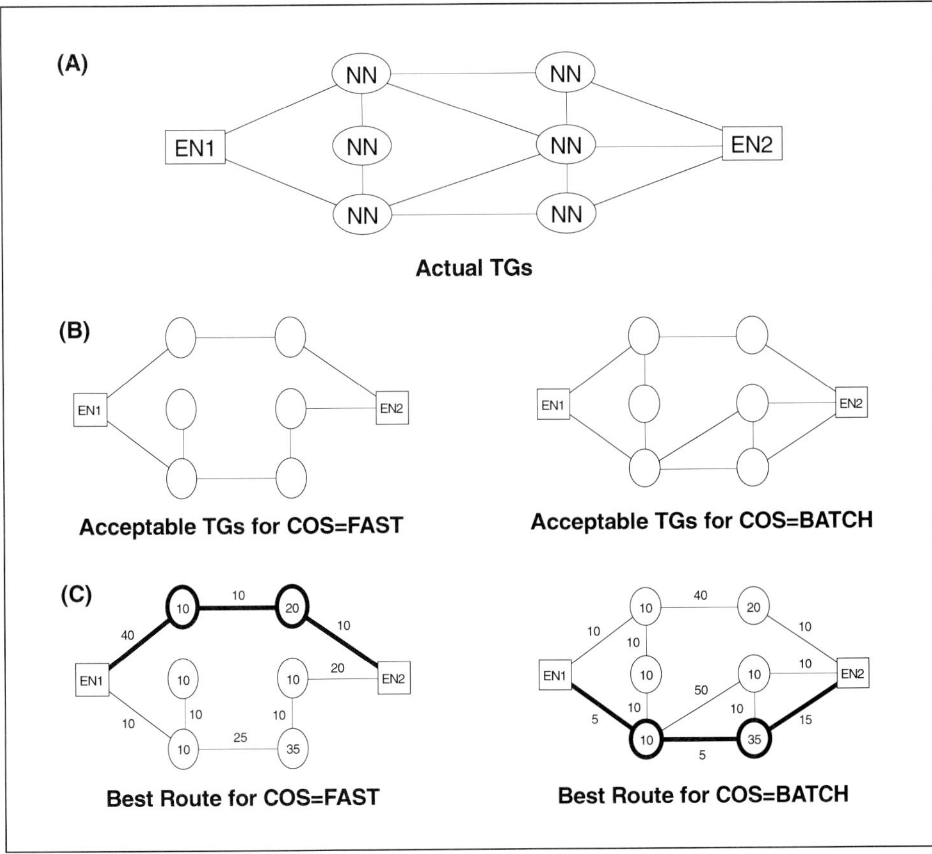

Figure 39. COS-Dependent Route Selection

Obtain Characteristics of All TGs and Network Nodes that Make Up Possible Routes

To enable TRS to calculate all possible routes between two endpoints, information is required from the network topology database and from the local databases at each of the endpoints. To be specific:

1. Information about network nodes and intermediate-routing TGs

   This information is obtained from the network topology database at the origin network node server.

2. Information about the endpoint TGs of the origin APPN end node to adjacent network nodes and virtual routing nodes

   This information is obtained from the local topology database at the origin end node. (In the case of a LEN or unauthorized APPN end node, the endpoint TG information is obtained from the origin network node server's local topology database.)

3. Information about the endpoint TGs of the destination APPN end node to adjacent network and virtual routing nodes and to the origin end node

   This information is obtained from the local topology database at the destination end node. (In the case of a LEN or unauthorized APPN end node, the endpoint TG information is obtained from the destination network node server's local topology database.)

Note: Information about endpoint TGs of the destination node to the origin end node allows TRS to compute direct routes if two end nodes are adjacent.

As an example, see (A) in Figure 39 on page 97. In order to calculate a route from EN1 to EN2, endpoint TGs are obtained from the local topology databases on both EN1 and EN2. Information about intermediate-routing TGs and network nodes is obtained from the network topology database, a copy of which is maintained at every NN.

Exclude All Unacceptable TGs and Network Nodes

Before starting to compute all possible routes, TRS will exclude the network nodes and TGs that are considered unacceptable for the desired route.

Excluding a node from route calculation depends on the characteristics of the node as maintained in the network topology database. Nodes may, for example, be excluded from route calculations if their intermediate-routing resources are depleted.

A TG is excluded from route computation if, for a given COS, TRS has assigned an infinite weight to the TG. The TG weight assignment process is COS-dependent. TRS will assign an infinite weight to the TG if the actual TG characteristics do not match the TG characteristics defined in the COS. For details, see 5.5.2, "Class of Service (COS)" on page 90.

After the exclusion of unacceptable TGs and network nodes, all possible routes can be calculated.

(B) in Figure 39 on page 97, shows a graph of the network after all unacceptable resources have been removed. Note how this graph depends on the COS used during the route calculation.

Compute All Routes and Select the Optimal Route

To compute the optimal route requires a method of quantifying the resources, TGs and nodes, that make up the potential routes. APPN architecture allows TRS to assign a weight to each node and TG. By adding up all weights, a route weight can be calculated and the optimal route, the route with the *least weight*, selected. This route is also known as the *shortest path*. If the minimum weight (for a given COS) is not the exclusive property of any one route, but is possessed by two or more routes, then one of these routes is selected at random. This random selection will evenly distribute sessions requesting the same class of service over multiple paths with the same weight to provide session distribution.

Note: While it is not architecturally required, products usually cache routing trees and reuse them several times to reduce the CPU overhead of route selection processing. Thus when equivalent routes exist, they are not necessarily chosen randomly.

A routing tree is generally updated only when needed for route selelection after one or more TDUs affecting that tree have arrived since last use, or when a configured reuse count or timer expires (the latter occurs only if choices existed when the tree was built). Some products, for example VTAM, further optimize by updating routing trees incrementally. A product may place an upper limit on the number of trees stored (for example, AS/400's limit is 30 and CS/2 limit is 20) but it is doubtful that these limits will be exceeded in most networks. VTAM *REUSAGE* defaults to 100 with a legal range of 0–2 × 10^9 and *NUMTREES* defaults to 100, with a range of 2 – 10,000. 6611, 2210, 2216, and 3746-950 default to 2 reuses; AS/400 defaults to 5. CS/2 maintains its 20-tree cache on a least-recently-used basis.

The weight of a network node is obtained from the network topology database. This weight is fixed and is not session- or COS-related.

The weight factor assigned to an individual TG is COS-related. TRS assigns COS-dependent TG weights using the TG characteristics from topology databases and COS definitions from the COS database.

After TRS has computed a weight for each of the components that make up possible routes, the optimal (*least-weight*) route can be selected. (C) in Figure 39 on page 97, shows the assigned resource weight and the dependency between *optimal* route and COS.

To compute an optimal route between two end nodes in an APPN network requires the coordinated invocation of TRS, or more precisely, the components of TRS (COSM, RSS, and TDM) on several APPN nodes. To understand in what order TRS components are invoked, and on which nodes, requires some insight into how LU-LU sessions are established in an APPN network.

5.7.1 Session Establishment and TRS

This section gives a brief and simplified description of how LU-LU sessions are established in an APPN network in order to point out which components of TRS are invoked at the various stages.

In base APPN, LU-LU session establishment is triggered by the LU known as the *originating LU (OLU)*. The requested session partner is referred to as the *destination LU (DLU)*. Both LUs are controlled by control points (CPs), called the CP of the OLU, CP(OLU), and the CP of the DLU, CP(DLU).

The essential difference between a LEN end node and an APPN end node is the fact that the APPN end node maintains CP-CP sessions with its network node server and is able to request assistance in session establishment from its network node server. Network node servers are referred to as either NNS(OLU) or NNS(DLU). Benefits of the CP-CP session between an APPN end node and its network node server are that locations of DLUs can be learned dynamically and routes computed that are truly end-to-end. Note that an APPN end node that does not maintain CP-CP sessions with a network node server should be considered a LEN end node for the topics discussed in this chapter.

We limit ourselves to a description of the two cases where both LUs reside on either LEN end nodes or on APPN end nodes.

5.7.1.1 LUs Residing on LEN End Nodes

Session establishment and invocation of TRS components between two LUs residing on LEN end nodes are explained using Figure 40 on page 101.

The figure shows a case where the CP(OLU), which does not support Locate search requests, relies on NNS(OLU) to build a Locate request and to find the DLU. In this example, the route taken by the Locate request is:

NNS(OLU) .. -> .. NNS(DLU)

If NNS(OLU) and NNS(DLU) are not adjacent, the Locate request will be routed through intermediate network nodes.

The route taken by the BIND request is:

CP(OLU) -> NNS(OLU) .. -> .. NNS(DLU) -> CP(DLU).

If NNS(OLU) and NNS(DLU) are not adjacent, the BIND request will be routed through intermediate network nodes. Because of optimal route calculation for this session, the session data (including the BIND) may follow a different route from NNS(OLU) to NNS(DLU) than the Locate search request. Session data is routed along the optimal route, and the Locate search flows along the shortest (minimum hops) path.

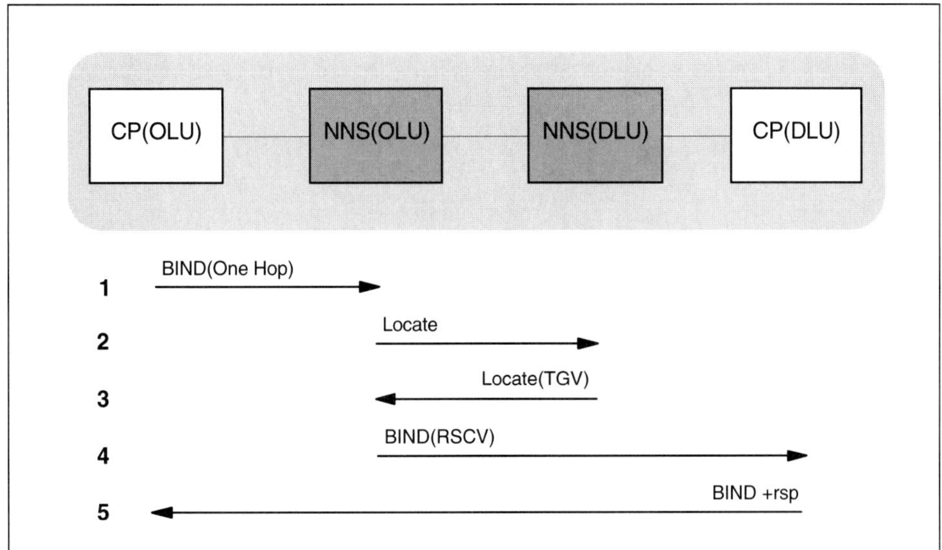

Figure 40. Session Establishment between LUs on LEN End Nodes (Simplified)

On CP(OLU), the DLU must be explicitly defined and is assumed to reside on NNS(OLU). Two components of TRS will be invoked on CP(OLU), namely:

1. COSM, optionally, to perform the mode name to COS name mapping
2. TDM to select the endpoint TG to NNS(OLU)

   Note: LEN end nodes do not support parallel TGs.

A BIND, optionally containing the COS name, will be sent to NNS(OLU) on the TG selected.

NNS(OLU) will send a Locate search request to NNS(DLU). The Locate search request will be a directed search or a broadcast search, according to whether or not NNS(OLU) knows that NNS(DLU) is the network node server of CP(DLU). For details, see 6.4.2, "Network Searches" on page 118.

On NNS(DLU) the DLU must be explicitly defined, because NNS(DLU) maintains no CP-CP sessions with CP(DLU) and, therefore, the location of DLU cannot be learned dynamically. NNS(DLU) does not forward the Locate request to CP(DLU); instead, TDM will be invoked to obtain the endpoint TG between NNS(DLU) and CP(DLU). NNS(DLU) returns a positive Locate/Found reply and, within the reply, the TG vector describing the connection to CP(DLU).

On NNS(OLU), COSM is invoked to perform the mode-to-COS name translation (if not already done), and to obtain the contents of the COS entry from the COS database. TDM will be invoked to obtain TG and node characteristics from the network topology database. Using this information, the TG on which the BIND has been received from

CP(OLU), and the endpoint TG information returned by NNS(DLU), RSS computes an "optimal" route between CP(OLU) and CP(DLU). The computed route will be added, in the form of a Route Selection control vector (RSCV), to the BIND which, is then forwarded along the computed route to CP(DLU).

CP(DLU) receives the BIND request and returns a positive response.

Note: The route on which the session data flows is not necessarily an end-to-end optimal route, as NNS(OLU) and NNS(DLU) will always be part of the route selected.

5.7.1.2 LUs Residing on APPN End Nodes

Session establishment and invocation of TRS components between two LUs residing on APPN end nodes are explained using

This figure shows the case where the CP(OLU), since it supports Locate search requests, sends a Locate search request to its network node server, NNS(DLU), when a session is required. In this example, the route taken by the Locate request is:

CP(OLU) -> NNS(OLU) .. -> .. NNS(DLU) -> CP(DLU)

If NNS(OLU) and NNS(DLU) are not adjacent, the Locate request will be routed through intermediate network nodes.

The route taken by the BIND request is:

CP(OLU) -> NN .. -> .. NN -> CP(DLU)

The BIND is routed along an end-to-end optimal route that may be different from the route taken by the Locate request. The network nodes in the session path are optional if links exist between the end nodes, or if both end nodes are attached to the same connection network (VRN), session data (including BIND) may be routed directly between the two nodes.

Note: As part of the session establishment, CP(OLU) and CP(DLU) forward all endpoint TGs to adjacent network nodes, and CP(DLU) forwards all possible endpoint TGs to CP(OLU). The endpoint TGs, if available, allow NNS(OLU) to compute a direct route between the end nodes.Figure 41 on page 103 .

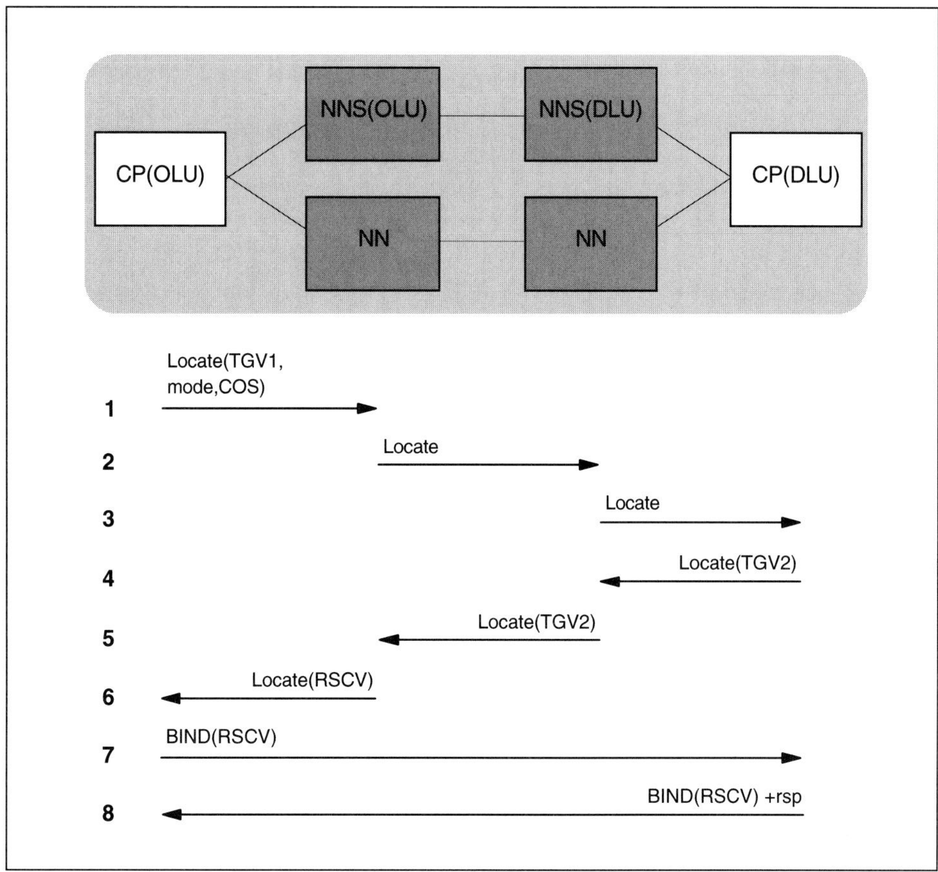

Figure 41. Session Establishment between LUs on APPN End Nodes (Simplified)

Before sending a Locate request to NNS(OLU), two components of TRS will be invoked on CP(OLU), namely:

1. TDM, to obtain endpoint TGs from CP(OLU) to adjacent network nodes and end nodes

   Note: CP(OLU) includes all TGs leading to adjacent network nodes or connection networks that can be used for sessions. It does not include the TGs leading to adjacent APPN end nodes.

2. COSM, optionally, to perform the mode name to COS name mapping

CP(OLU) will send a Locate request for the DLU, using its contention winner CP-CP session, to NNS(OLU). This Locate request contains an (optional) COS name and a TG control vector (TGV1), which describes the endpoint TGs from CP(OLU).

NNS(OLU) will forward the *Locate* request to NNS(DLU). The Locate request will be sent directly to NNS(DLU) if NNS(OLU) knows the network node server of the DLU. If not, the Locate request will arrive on NNS(DLU) as a result of a network broadcast search started by NNS(OLU). For details, see 6.4.2, "Network Searches" on page 118.

On CP(DLU), TDM will be invoked to obtain the endpoint TGs connecting CP(DLU) to adjacent network nodes and end nodes. This information is added as a TG control vector (TGV2) to the Locate reply returned, via intermediate network nodes, to NNS(OLU).

Note: CP(DLU) includes all TGs leading to adjacent network nodes or connection networks and also includes all TGs to CP(OLU).

On NNS(OLU), COSM is invoked to perform the mode-to-COS name translation (if not already done), and obtain the contents of the COS entry from the COS database. TDM will be invoked to obtain intermediate-routing TG and node characteristics from the network topology database. Using both TGVs (TGV1 and TGV2) and intermediate resource information obtained from its network topology database, RSS on NNS(OLU) will compute an optimal route between CP(OLU) and CP(DLU). It will return this information in a Route Selection control vector (RSCV), added to the Locate reply, to the CP(OLU).

After receiving the Locate reply, CP(OLU) will construct a BIND to start the session. Among other information, the BIND will contain the RSCV obtained from the NNS(OLU). The BIND will be routed to the CP(DLU) using the routing information within the RSCV. The BIND response will be returned on the reverse path.

5.7.1.3 The Route Selection Control Vector

A Route Selection control vector (RSCV) is carried in the BIND and Locate requests and replies, and other RUs to describe a route through the APPN network. A distinction has to be made between the RSCV used for BIND routing, also called *session RSCV*, and the *Locate RSCV*, which is used to route Locate search requests through the network. For details about Locate search requests, see 6.4.2, "Network Searches" on page 118.

A Locate RSCV contains a list of CP names from an origin to a destination node, as opposed to a session RSCV, which contains a list of CP names and TGs between each adjacent pair of nodes along a route from an origin to a destination node. The Locate RSCV contains the *shortest* route (minimum hops) over which CP-CP sessions are active, whereas the session RSCV yields an *optimal* route. TG information is not required in a Locate RSCV, as the Locate request is forwarded using CP-CP sessions between adjacent network nodes.

The BIND is forwarded to the destination node using a method called *source routing*. Source routing relies on routing information contained in the message itself. Intermediate nodes do not require knowledge about the final destination, they learn from the message itself what the next node is along the route and how to get there. Source routing provides a very fast method of routing messages through a network, as the processing required in intermediate nodes is minimal. Networks offering *connectionless* services often rely on source routing.

The opposite of source routing is the use of *virtual circuits*. Virtual circuits imply a *connection-oriented* network service. A virtual circuit assumes an end-to-end connection that has to be established before messages can be sent. The use of virtual circuits typically depends on routing tables maintained in intermediate nodes to route messages from an origin to a destination node. Each message contains a logical channel identifier, which is used by intermediate nodes to index their routing tables and find what the next node is along the route and how to get there. The logical channels do not have end-to-end meaning and may vary (be *swapped*) between pairs of adjacent node.

As mentioned, an example of source routing is the method used to forward a BIND in an APPN network. The session RSCV is used by each intermediate node to obtain the next node and a TG to the node, along the route. Session data, however, is routed over a virtual circuit. During BIND flow, intermediate nodes will initialize their routing tables and assign logical channels, or local-form session identifiers (LFSIDs), for each TG along the route. Session data routed between two LUs contains an LFSID, which is then used for intermediate routing. LFSIDs have only local significance and vary between each pair of nodes along the route. Intermediate network nodes will swap LFSIDs within the header of the message, on each TG, as the session data is routed towards the destination node. For details, see 3.3, "Local-Form Session Identifier (LFSID)" on page 49.

The maximum number of APPN nodes and TGs a session may traverse is limited by the size of the RSCV. The RSCV has a maximum length of 255 bytes. Bytes 1 and 2 contain the vector header and bytes 2 and 3 the maximum and current hop counts, leaving 251 bytes for TG Descriptor control vectors. The length of each of these control vectors depends on the length of the net ID and CP names, and also on whether or not the route passes through a border node. Assuming that all CP names and net IDs are 8 characters long and that both the OLU and DLU have the same net ID, the first TG Descriptor control vector would have a length of 23 bytes (having a network-qualified CP name of 17 bytes). If subsequent CPs have the same net ID only the CP name would be required in the TG Identifier subfield giving a length of 14 bytes for all other TG Descriptor subvectors. This would give a maximum possible hop count of 16. If, however, CP names are shorter than 8 characters, this number increases slightly. If the net ID changes along the route, the maximum possible number of hops decreases.

5.7.1.4 Route Selection Using Virtual Routing Nodes

APPN end nodes that have defined a connection network will include the endpoint TG to the virtual routing node in the TG control vectors (TGVs) added to the Locate request or reply. The TGVs also contain DLC-signaling information such as the end node's MAC address on a token-ring.

RSS on NNS(OLU) will detect if both APPN end nodes have defined a TG to the same VRN and, optionally, if no lower weight routes exist, select the route *through* the VRN as the optimal route.

Being connected to the same connection network indicates that both APPN end nodes attach to the same *shared-access transport facility* (SATF), and session data can be sent directly, without intermediate node routing, between the APPN end nodes.

5.8 SNA Defined Modes and Classes of Service

Generally speaking, each installation is free to choose its mode names, COS names, and COS definitions; however, because definitions on one node may imply definitions on a second node, synchronization of definitions is sometimes required. For example, when an end node performs mode name to COS name mapping, it assumes the COS definitions are present in its network node server.

To simplify table maintenance, SNA has defined default mode names, related COS names and COS definitions for the various classes of service.

Below is a list of the SNA-defined names. The contents of the COS tables are described in *SNA APPN Architecture Reference*, SC30-3422. The contents of the modes are described in *SNA LU 6.2 Reference: Peer Protocols*, SC31-6808.

Mode Name	Corresponding COS Name
Default	#CONNECT
#BATCH	#BATCH
#INTER	#INTER
#BATCHSC	#BATCHSC
#INTERSC	#INTERSC
CPSVCMG	CPSVCMG
SNASVCMG	SNASVCMG
CPSVRMGR	SNASVCMG

Notes:

1. If no mode name is specified during a session establishment request, implementations use COS name #CONNECT.
2. The "#" character represents the hexadecimal value X'7B'.

In most cases, the default values in the IBM-supplied table will be adequate. In particular, small networks will not realize much benefit from modifying the standard tables. In larger networks, modifications may be required in order to achieve the desired amount of load distribution, if the nodes do not support randomization during route selection.

Chapter 6. Directory Services

The directory services component of the control point is responsible for the management of the directory database and the search for network resources throughout an APPN network.

6.1 Function Overview

The major components of directory services (DS) are:

Directory Database Function (DDB)
: The directory database function is responsible for the database lookup and database maintenance logic of DS. Part of the database maintenance logic is the resource registration (RR) function. RR is responsible for sending and receiving requests for resource registration.

  The DDB component is not available on LEN end nodes.

Maintain CP Status Function (MCPS)
: The maintain CP status function is responsible for keeping DS aware of other control points that it wishes to communicate with. In the case of an APPN end node, the MCPS function maintains awareness of the sessions with the node's network node server. In the case of an APPN network node, the MCPS maintains awareness of APPN end nodes and LEN end nodes within the APPN network node's domain, and additionally, other APPN network nodes to which it has CP-CP sessions.

Network Search Function (NS)
: The network search function is responsible for sending and receiving resource search requests to and from other APPN nodes in the network.

  This DS component is not available on LEN end nodes.

Figure 42 depicts the node functions that interface with DS.

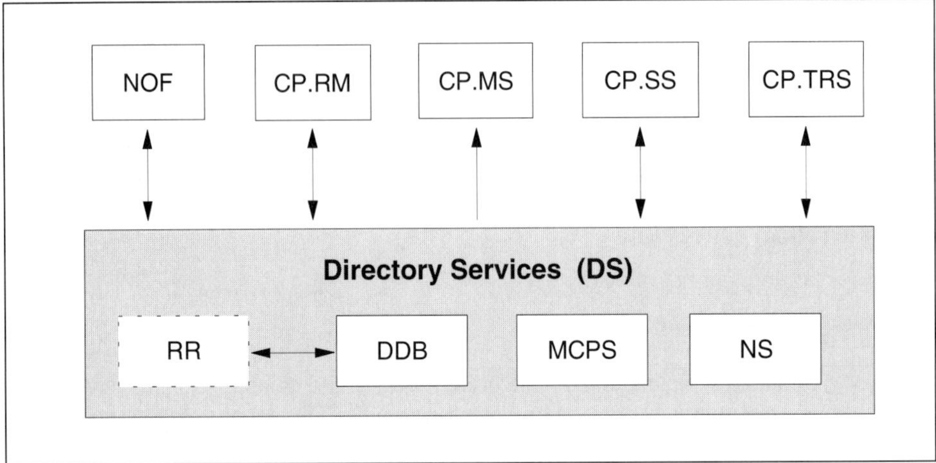

Figure 42. Overview of DS Components and Protocol Boundaries

Directory services (DS) is created and initialized by the node operator facility (NOF) at node initialization time. NOF passes the following parameters to DS at initialization time:

- Node type (LEN end node, APPN end node, or APPN network node)
- The network ID of the node
- The control point name of the node
- Whether or not resources should be registered

  APPN end nodes may register resources at their network node server, and APPN network nodes may register resources at a central directory server.

6.2 Directory Database Function

Each node uses a *local directory database* to maintain awareness of network resources and their location in the APPN network. The directory database function on each node is responsible for maintaining the local directory database and locating resources in either the local directory database or directory databases residing on other nodes. Resources can be *local*, *same-domain* or *other-domain* to a specific node.

When trying to locate a resource, DS does not restrict itself to resource information maintained locally, but also tries to use information contained in remote directory databases. The term *network directory database* or *distributed directory database*, is used to refer to a *virtual* database containing all resource information contained within the network. The phrase "DS is responsible for locating a resource in the network database" refers to a coordinated effort of DS on one or more nodes to obtain the resource information from any local directory database on each of the nodes.

An APPN or LEN end node is responsible for maintaining database entries for:

- Local resources
- Local resources on adjacent nodes with which it wishes to have peer-to-peer sessions, that is, establish sessions without the support of an APPN network node

An APPN end node may choose to inform its network node server of some or all the resources located on itself, a process known as *end node resource registration*. APPN architecture does not allow an APPN end node to register resources on its network node server that are owned by other end nodes. Directory database entries on an end node are entered via the node operator facility (NOF).

An APPN network node is responsible for maintaining database entries for:

- Local resources (that means, LUs)
- End node resources within the APPN network node's domain
- End node or network node resources outside the APPN network node's domain

An APPN network node may choose to inform other network node servers of some or all the resources located on itself or within its domain, a process known as *central resource registration*. Directory database entries on an APPN network node are entered via the node operator facility (NOF), by resource registration, or by caching information obtained via network searches.

Each DS is responsible for maintaining directory information about network resources. This information includes:

- Network-qualified resource name

  For a resource of type LU, the LU name is given. For a resource of type control point, the CP name is given.

- The resource type, either:
  - LU
  - APPN or LEN end node CP
  - APPN network node CP
- Indicator specifying whether resource registration is required and the registration status, which is either:
  - Not registered
  - Registration in progress
  - Registered

Resources are either unique or nonunique within a network. SNA requires that any network accessible unit (NAU) can be distinguished from other resources in the network. NAUs are resources of the type LU, APPN network node CP, APPN end node CP, and LEN end node CP. It is strongly recommended to use a consistent naming convention for NAUs, to prevent duplicated names. Duplicate names will lead to errors and degrade the performance of the network.

In the directory database, a resource "hierarchy" is maintained. For example for a resource of type LU, the database contains pointers to the CP name of the node owning the LU and the CP name of the network node server.

Directory database entries are entered by system definition, by resource registration, or by caching information obtained from network searches.

6.2.1 System-Defined Resources

Although APPN directory services (DS) is very dynamic and resource knowledge can be obtained dynamically, each resource must at least be defined at the node where it resides.

LEN end nodes lack the support for CP-CP sessions and resources on other nodes cannot be learned dynamically; therefore, LEN end nodes require that all network resources that will be accessed by local resources be defined in the local directory database of the LEN end node. Alternatively, if a LEN end node is connected to an APPN network node, then all LEN end node resources that need to be accessed from or through the APPN network node must be defined at the network node. To simplify this registration, directory services provides a facility using *generic names* and *wildcards*:

Wildcards
: Wildcards are represented with an asterisk (*). An asterisk results in a match for each network resource that is searched for by directory services.

Generic names
: Partially specified names are represented by one or more start characters of the resource name followed by an asterisk. For example, if all network resources on a LEN end node start with the characters *ITSC*, then the partially specified name could look like *ITSC**.

For details on how the use of wildcards impacts DS search logic, see 6.4.3.1, "Wildcards" on page 125.

Network accessible unit resources owned by an APPN end node must always be defined at its network node server if the APPN end node is defined as an *unauthorized* end node. A network node server will never query unauthorized APPN end nodes to locate resources, and does not allow session establishment initiated by LUs on the end node if the LU is not explicitly defined.

In addition, APPN network nodes may define same-domain APPN end node's resources and other-domain resources to improve network search performance.

6.2.1.1 LU Name Equal CP Name

If a node supports APPN option 1012 (LU Name = CP Name), installations may choose to select the same name for an LU as the CP name of that node. This reduces the system definition at the local node. Another advantage of using LU names equal to the CP name is when a directory search is required.

Function set 1104 (Topology-Based Directory Nonverify) requires that the network node server of the node owning the OLU check with topology and routing services to see whether the DLU name is equal to one of the control point names known in the network topology database before it searches its local directory database for the destination LU. If the LU name is equal to a CP name of an active network node, then directory services does not need to perform a directory database or network search (unless a Locate/CD-Initiate carrying a session key used for session cryptography needs to be returned by the DLU). The topology database is only queried by the network node starting the resource search procedure. Since the network topology database contains only network nodes, defining an LU name equal to a CP name will limit resource search time only if the target LU is contained in a network node.

6.2.2 Resource Registration

Two types of resource registration are defined in APPN:

1. End Node Resource Registration

   APPN end nodes register local resources at their network nodes.

2. Central Resource Registration

   APPN network nodes register local and same-domain resources at a network node known as the *central directory server.*

The reason for resource registration is to improve network search performance. Details about end node and central resource registration will be given in the following sections.

6.2.2.1 End Node Resource Registration

End node resource registration is an optional facility on APPN end nodes, which allows an APPN end node (registration requester) to register network accessible resources at its network node server (registration server). Supporting the receipt of the registration request is a base function for APPN network nodes. APPN network nodes allow registration requests only from APPN end nodes that have been defined as *authorized* end nodes.

Note that resources on end nodes that do not perform resource registration must be system defined at the network node server.

Following CP-CP session establishment, when CP capabilities are exchanged between the APPN end node and its serving network node, an authorized APPN end node may then register resources that it wishes to make available to the network.

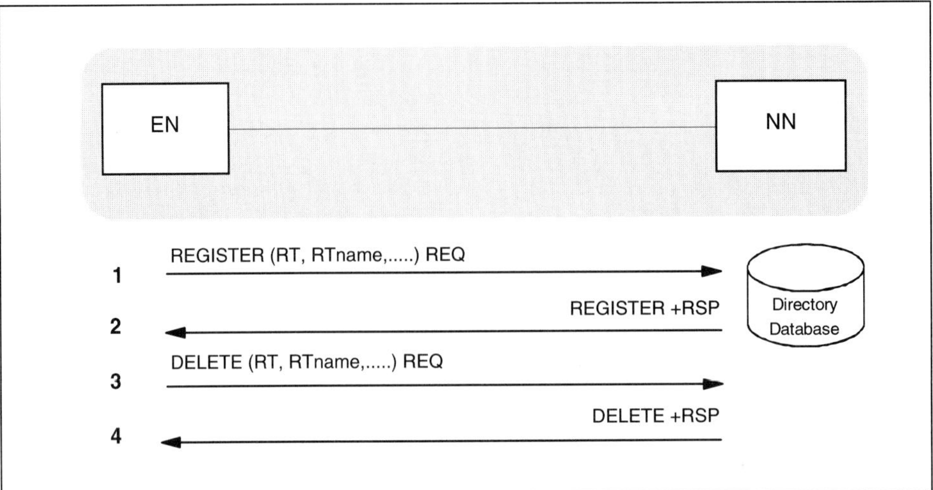

Figure 43. Resource Type (RT) and Name Registration

The register request may contain control vectors describing multiple resources; however, the total length of the Locate/Register must not exceed 1024 bytes. The end node will not initiate an additional registration request until it has received a reply from the previous registration request. The network node server may use this function to control the rate at which it receives registration requests. The network node will send a reply to show the success (or failure) of the resource registration operation (see Figure 43).

When DS sends a resource registration request, DS changes the status of the resource to *registration pending*. The status becomes *registered* or *not registered* when the APPN end node receives respectively a positive, or a negative reply to the registration request.

An APPN end node may delete resources from its network node server's directory database using an explicit deletion request (see Figure 43). Directory services will also remove resources registered by an APPN end node when the CP-CP sessions between the APPN end node and the network node server are terminated.

To change a resource entry, the APPN end node must first delete the old entry and then completely register the resource again.

6.2.2.2 Central Resource Registration (CRR)

The APPN *central resource registration* architecture allows one or more network nodes in a network to act as central *directory servers*. Instead of trying to locate a resource themselves, network nodes query their closest central directory server. The central directory server then takes responsibility for locating the resource, either by querying its own cache, querying other central directory servers, or by initiating a network search. The central directory server concept maximizes the sharing of cached directory entries and, therefore, minimizes the number of network searches.

Central resource registration (CRR) depends on two functions, which are:

1. Registration server
2. Registration requester

CRR allows a network node (registration requester) to register resources at a central directory server (registration server). Both the registration requester and server function are optional functions in an APPN network.

For performance and reliability reasons, more than one central directory server may be present. Central directory servers defined as having equal capabilities are referred to as *alternate* directory servers.

The APPN topology database (TDB) is used to allow identification of central directory servers and their capabilities to every network node. Directory servers identify themselves with an indicator in the topology database update (TDU) messages when connecting to the network, thereby informing all network nodes in the same topology subnetwork of their presence. Only APPN network nodes that support the resource registration requester function recognize the server capabilities data included in the TDU. APPN network nodes that do not support the resource registration requester function do not recognize the server capabilities data within the TDU and just store and forward the TDU as they receive it.

Central resource registration allows a network node to register its resources at a directory server, eliminating the need for broadcast searches to locate registered resources. Once the resource is registered, all network nodes may find the resource by sending a directed Locate search request to the central directory server. Resource registration reduces the number of network broadcasts considerably.

Note: The difference between a broadcast search and a directed search will be explained in 6.4.2, "Network Searches" on page 118.

When registering its resources with its network node server, an APPN end node indicates which of those should be centrally registered, as specified in its local definitions. Since it is optional for end nodes to register resources with their network node servers, any unregistered resources may still require a broadcast search to locate the resource, preventing total elimination of broadcast searches.

Since no direct sessions exist from the directory services of a network node to the directory services of a central directory server, the existing CP-CP sessions and network search service transaction programs provide the means for transporting registration data. By adding register variables to a directed Locate search request sent to the central directory server, a network node is able to register its resources at the directory server. Intermediate network nodes will only look at the routing information within the Locate request and ignore the appended register variables.

The register request may contain control vectors describing multiple resources; however, the total length of the register must not exceed 1024 bytes.

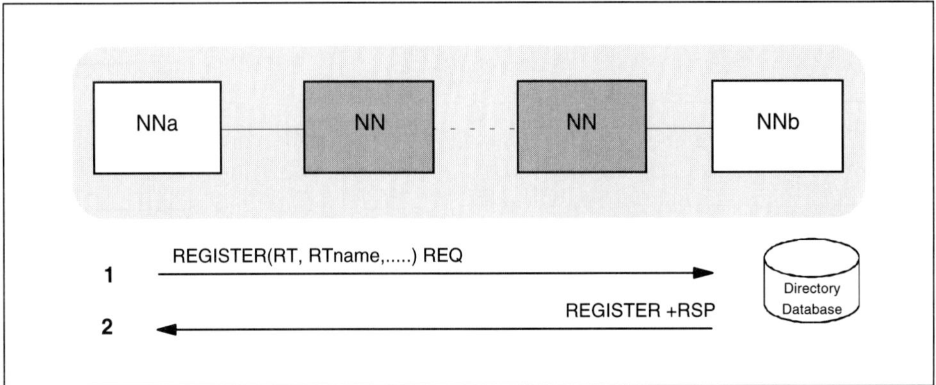

Figure 44. Central Resource Registration. Registration requester (NNa), registering resource type (RT), and RT name at a registration server (NNb).

Registration of resources by the CRR function will result in those resources being cached at the central directory server, and will be handled appropriately. For example,the resources are replaced by least-recently-used (LRU) algorithms or overlaid by new information, without requiring explicit registration information. The central directory server will send a reply to show the success (or failure) of the resource registration operation (see Figure 44). A negative response, indicating registration failure, will contain error information.

The origin network node will not register any additional information until it has received a reply from the previous registration request. The central directory server may use this function to control the rate at which it receives registration requests from a particular node.

CRR is handled differently from end node registration. It does not require an explicit delete with a subsequent register operation to change resource information registered at the central directory server. Information can be updated simply by submitting a register request that will overlay the existing information. Deletion of information will happen as a consequence of NN search requests.

Optionally, implementations save registered directory entries across IPLs.

6.2.3 Cached Directory Entry

APPN network nodes dynamically increase the information in the directory database by caching the results of directory searches. Figure 45 on page 115 depicts the concept of resource caching.

Session services in CP(OLU) invokes DS to locate the DLU. Assuming CP(OLU) has no system-defined entry for the DLU, DS sends a one-hop Locate request for the DLU to DS on its network node server, NNS(OLU). The Locate search request also contains information about the OLU, enabling NNS(OLU) to cache a directory entry for the OLU

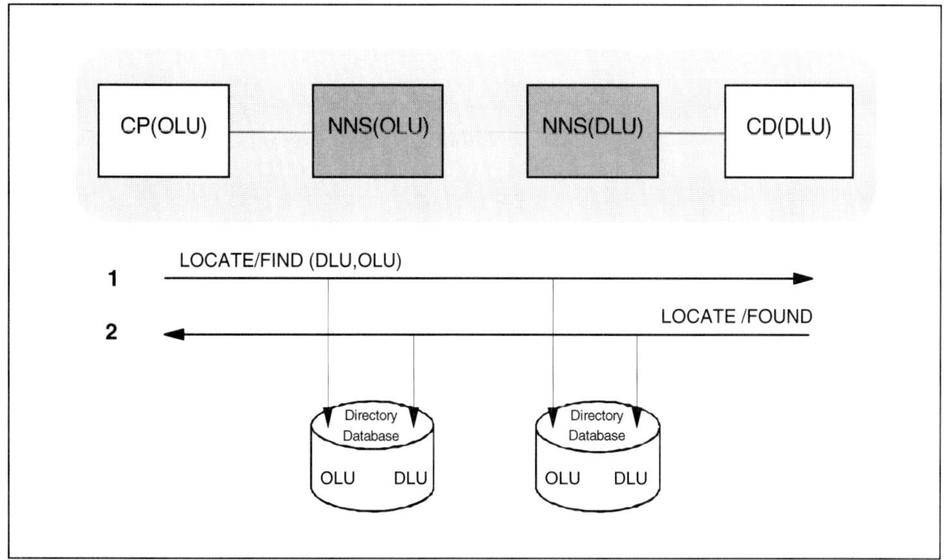

Figure 45. Resource Caching

before starting a network search for the DLU. The search request may either be a directed (DLU location known in NNS(OLU) directory) or a broadcast search (DLU location unknown). When the network node server of CP(DLU), which is the NNS(DLU), receives the Locate request and NNS(DLU) is able to locate the DLU, NNS(DLU) will cache a directory entry for both OLU and DLU, and return a positive response to NNS(OLU). NNS(OLU) will cache a directory entry for the DLU and return a positive response to CP(OLU).

The information retrieved through caching may ultimately result in huge local directory databases and even include resource entries that are no longer in use or up-to-date. It is up to the implementation of the APPN network node function to decide how the cache entries are maintained, when they are deleted or replaced, and whether entries are saved across IPLs (*safe-store of DS cache*).

For example, the Network Services/2 product (APPN for OS/2) saves its cache directory to disk every 20 updates. In addition, it allows for a total of 255 cached directory entries. If all 255 cache entries are in use, new entries to be cached will replace the oldest cache entries first.

An APPN network node that caches resource entries that are owned by end nodes for which it provides network node services, deletes these entries when the CP-CP sessions with the end node are deactivated.

6.2.4 End Node Caching

In order to avoid connection charges for session setup flows between an EN and its NN server in a switched environment (for example, X.25 networks), ENs that implement the EN caching optional function will be able to cache LU location information and RSCVs obtained through normal session establishment flows, but may only cache information that was provided in a response from its NN server. Since a session establishment flow includes the Locate/Found and CD-Initiate with an RSCV, the EN is able to cache the DLU name, the associated resource hierarchy, the RSCV, and, if the EN supports the RTP functions for HPR, the received NCE.

EN cached entries are maintained in the same manner as NN cached entries. They are stored in a least-recently used fashion and updated when new information is obtained. Since RSCVs, however, are specific to a destination node, it is only necessary to store RSCVs per destination EN or NN and by COS. Because the network topology can change dynamically, cached RSCVs that include multiple hops may not remain optimal over an extended period of time. For this reason, ENs will only cache RSCVs that specify an entry to an adjacent node (this includes routes through a connection network). The reasoning behind this being that the EN can then establish the session across a switched network with a single connection directly to the target node, so reducing connection charges.

When SS in an EN receives a session initiation request from a local LU, it asks DS to obtain the target LU location. DS may now return the location obtained from the local directory database indicating that verification was not performed. SS then uses this information to determine the first hop, have it activated, and return the appropriate Cinit response to the requesting LU (see 7.5.2, "Directory Search and Route Computation" on page 147).

Since it is possible that the BIND for this type of session initiation fails because of out-dated cached information, the LU must be prepared to redrive the session request, this time requiring verification. This means that the nonverify function described in 6.5, "Nonverify Function" on page 131 is a prerequisite of end node caching.

6.3 Maintain CP Status Function (MCSF)

All APPN nodes that exchange information on CP-CP sessions are interested in the enabled status of partner CPs. Among other things, CP-CP sessions are required for resource registration and to locate resources. The maintain CP status function (MCSF) in DS is present in APPN end nodes and network nodes; it maintains a list of CPs on adjacent APPN nodes and, on network nodes only, a list of active central directory servers.

MCSF learns about the central directory server from the network topology database; for details, see 6.2.2.2, "Central Resource Registration (CRR)" on page 112. Status changes of a directory server CP in the network topology database are reflected in the information MCSF maintains about this directory server.

Entries for APPN (network node or end node) CPs are maintained dynamically as CP-CP sessions are established and terminated. Session services informs DS whenever a CP-CP session is established or deactivated.

End nodes are either *authorized* or *unauthorized* end nodes. APPN network nodes accept Register requests only from authorized end nodes.

In order to locate a resource, an APPN network node will query only authorized end nodes. APPN end nodes do not always support the receipt of Locate requests for resources that have not been registered or cached at the network node server. An APPN network node will not query adjacent APPN end nodes that have indicated they are not willing to accept, and handle, Locate requests for such resources. Note that all APPN end nodes support the receipt of Locate search requests for registered or cached resources, for example, to verify that a resource is active and to return the end node TG vectors.

Entries of adjacent LEN end nodes cannot be learned on the basis of CP-CP sessions, but can be optionally cached when BINDs are received from the adjacent LEN end node with an undefined LU as PLU. They have to be defined by system definitions if they shall act as SLUs before they themselves request a session through the network node server. Because of the lack of CP-CP sessions, LEN end nodes cannot support resource registration and Locate search requests; therefore, DS on an adjacent APPN network node is not interested in the authorization status or Locate support of LEN end nodes.

6.4 Network Search Function (NS)

The primary function of the network search (NS) function in DS is to locate network resources and to control the flow of search requests and replies through the network.

When handling a directory search request, the NS function invokes the directory database function to determine the knowledge that the CP has about the resource in question. Depending on that knowledge, the NS function may choose to reply to the request or to forward the request to another node. When the NS function chooses to send a request to another node, its exercises its transport logic. This logic controls the sending of directory messages carrying search requests and replies. These messages are called *Locate searches.*

Additionally, the Locate searches are capable of carrying non-DS data and can be used by other CP components for the transport of their control data. Such other components are termed DS users or DS applications. For example, session services (SS) acts as a DS user when requesting a directory search; for example, to locate an LU and delivery of SS variables. Examples of SS variables that may be included when session services requests DS to locate an LU are as follows:

- The fully qualified procedure correlation identifier (FQPCID)
- The destination LU

- The origin LU
- Mode name
- COS name
- Endpoint TG vectors

Endpoint TG vectors are included in a Locate search by SS(OLU), but not forwarded beyond session services of OLU's network node server; SS(DLU) then sends endpoint TG vectors in the Locate reply back to NNS(OLU).

6.4.1 Search Terminology

The DS user, or DS application, refers to the process or CP component that asks DS to find a target resource.

Locate search refers to the signals that DS components in one node send to DS components in other nodes when looking for resources.

Historically, the originator of a search request is referred to as the originating CP(OLU). We refer to the destination node as CP(DLU), to the network node server of CP(OLU) as NNS(OLU) and to the network node server of CP(DLU) as NNS(DLU). Note that the *network node server* of a network node is the network node itself and CP(OLU) and CP(DLU) may have the same network node server.

6.4.2 Network Searches

Directory services (DS) will be invoked to obtain the location of a resource. If the local directory database function indicates that the CP has no knowledge of the resource, the request may be forwarded to another node. The messages used by DS on different nodes are *Locate searches.* Locate search requests are always sent on the *conwinner* CP-CP session to an adjacent CP.

There are three types of Locate search requests:

1. One-hop search
2. Directed search
3. Broadcast search

After describing each type of Locate search request in the following sections, we will continue with a description of how the various types of Locate searches are used on LEN end nodes, APPN end nodes and APPN network nodes.

6.4.2.1 One-Hop Search

A one-hop search is a Locate search request that is exchanged between an APPN end node and its network node server. The one-hop search is sent on the CP-CP session between the control points (see (A) in Figure 46 on page 120). The one-hop is conceptually simpler than the two other types of searches (broadcast and directed) because no routing information is needed.

6.4.2.2 Directed Search

A directed Locate search request is a request that is sent along a predefined path from one network node to another network node. The origin network node calculates a path of CP-CP session hops to the target network node and appends the routing information to the search. Each network node along the path relies on that routing information for choosing the next hop and ensuring that the search travels directly to the destination network node.

The routing information for the directed Locate search request is contained within a *Locate RSCV*. A Locate RSCV (Route Selection control vector) defines the nodes on the search path including a series of network node names. A locate RSCV describes the shortest path, that is, the path with the least number of hops, to a destination node.

A directed search is used by:

1. NNS(OLU), when NNS(OLU) has a directory entry indicating that the destination resource is an other-domain resource.
2. NNS(OLU), when invoking a central directory server.
3. A central directory server, when the central directory server has a directory entry indicating the destination location is an other-domain resource.
4. A central directory server, to query alternate directory servers.

The reason for sending a directed Locate search in 2 and 4 is to obtain resource information from DS on the remote node. The reason for sending a directed Locate search in 1 and 3 is to verify the accuracy of directory information and to obtain the endpoint TGs of the end node that owns the destination resource. This procedure is known as *resource verification*. Because of the optional *nonverify function*, a network node server (point 1) may decide not to perform resource verification, whereas a central directory server (point 3) always performs resource verification. For details about the nonverify function, see 6.5, “Nonverify Function” on page 131.

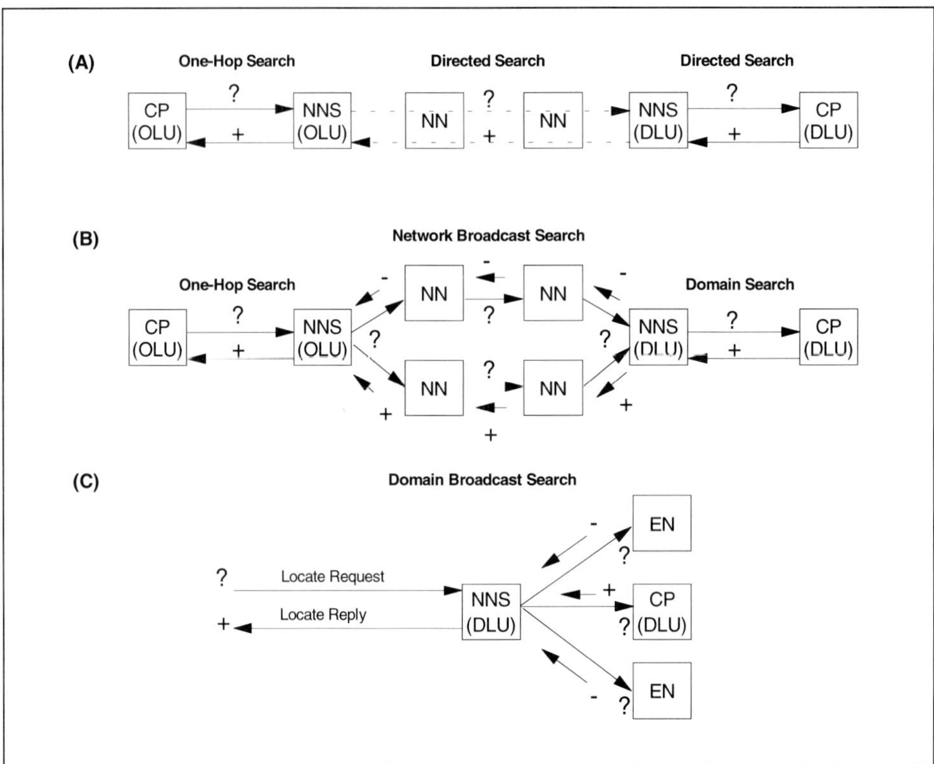

Figure 46. Locate Search Requests

Example (A) in Figure 46 depicts a directed Locate search request. NNS(OLU) determines from its directory database the network node server of the DLU, calculates a route to NNS(DLU), adds the routing information to the request and forwards the Locate search to the next network node on the calculated route. Intermediate network nodes forward the Locate search along the route, using routing information within the Locate RSCV, to NNS(DLU).

6.4.2.3 Broadcast Search

When the DLU is unknown and no central directory server is present, broadcast searches are used by network nodes to send Locate search requests to multiple CPs. A central directory server uses a broadcast search to locate a resource when it has no cached information about this resource. If a central directory server is present in a topology subnet and all network nodes in this topology subnet query a central directory server for unknown resources, then the central directory servers are the only nodes that will use broadcast searches to locate resources. There are two types of broadcast searches:

- Domain broadcast: to query APPN end nodes in the network node's domain

- Network broadcast: to query all network nodes in the network

Broadcast searches are always done in parallel, which allows DS to locate a resource quickly.

Domain Broadcast Search

A network node that starts a domain broadcast search will send a Locate search for the destination resource to adjacent APPN end nodes. See (C) in Figure 46 on page 120.

APPN end nodes will be included in an APPN network node's domain search only if the APPN end nodes have been defined as authorized end nodes, and during the exchange of CP capabilities the end nodes have indicated they are willing to be included in a domain search of their network node server.

A domain broadcast cannot be distinguished at an end node from a directed search. An end node receiving the search has no awareness of which other nodes are being searched; it simply searches its database and returns a reply. The coordination of the domain broadcast is the responsibility of the network node. If more than one positive reply is returned, DS uses the *first* positive reply. Note that receiving more than one positive response on a domain search indicates a definition error.

Network Broadcast Search

By performing a network broadcast search, a network node is able to query all APPN network nodes in the network. As Locate search requests always flow on CP-CP sessions, which can only be established between adjacent nodes, a network node starts a network broadcast search by sending a Locate request to all adjacent network nodes to which it has CP-CP sessions active. The adjacent network nodes forward the request to their adjacent network nodes and so on until every network node has received a copy of the Locate request.

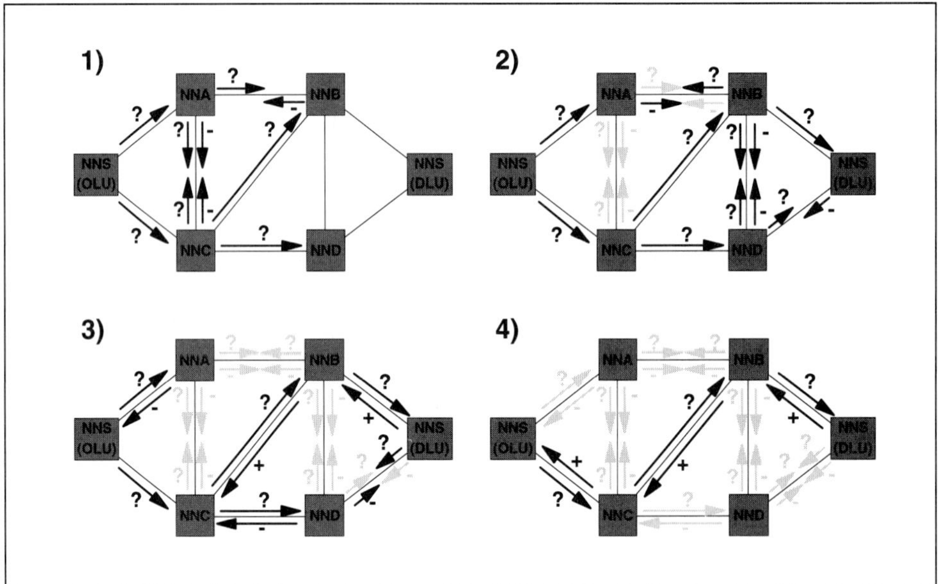

Figure 47. Network Broadcast

For an example network broadcast search see Figure 47:

1. NNS(OLU) starts a broadcast search by sending the Locate request to NNA and NNC. NNA propagates the Locate request to its neighbors NNB and NNC, and NNC propagates the Locate request to NNA, NNB, and NND. Because NNA and NNC have received the request already from NNS(OLU), they both send a negative reply to each other. The request from NNC arrives first in node NNB, so that NNB answers with a negative reply to the request received from NNA.

2. NNB and NND forward the request to all their neighbors. NNB and NND send a negative reply to each other because they have received the request before from NNC. NNB also sends the request to NNA and gets a negative reply. The request from NNB arrives first in node NNS(DLU), so that NNS(DLU) answers with a negative reply to the request received from NND.

3. NNA and NND have received a negative reply from all their respective neighbors, so they can now send a final negative reply to NNS(OLU) and NNC, respectively. Before checking its directory database, NNS(DLU) forwards the request to NND and, of course, receives a negative reply. Because NNS(DLU) knows about the DLU, it sends a positive reply to NNB, which in turn forwards this positive reply to NNC. NNB's positive reply could indicate that it is an incomplete reply if NNB has not yet received the replies from NNA and NND.

4. NNC forwards the positive reply from NNB to NNS(OLU). This reply might be incomplete, however, in which case it is followed by a final reply after NNC has received the (final) replies from NNA, NNB, and NND.

A network broadcast search is used:

- When the NNS(OLU) has no directory entry for a destination resource, and the resource location cannot be found differently; for example, via a domain search or by querying a central directory server.
- When a central directory server has no directory entry for a destination resource and the resource location cannot be found differently, for example via a domain search or by searching alternate directory servers.

A network broadcast search, sending a Locate search to each adjacent network node, is the search of last resort because the broadcast search floods the network with requests for the location of the target resource and therefore has negative performance implications for the network. A network node will perform a network broadcast only if it is not able to locate a resource differently. Network nodes capable of querying a central directory server, which optionally performs a network broadcast search itself, will never perform a network broadcast search.

As each network node forwards the request to all its neighbor network nodes, except to the node from which the request has been received, network nodes can receive multiple copies of the same request. A simple mechanism prevents unnecessary forwarding of the broadcast request. All Locate requests are uniquely identified by an FQPCID (fully qualified procedure correlation ID). By temporarily storing FQPCIDs, comparing stored values with the FQPCID within broadcast requests received, and returning a negative reply to duplicate requests, each network node makes sure that only one copy of the Locate request is forwarded.

As depicted in Figure 47 on page 122, NNS(OLU) starts the network broadcast search by sending a Locate search request to its adjacent network nodes. Each receiving network node should propagate the Locate search to its neighbor network nodes before checking local resources to allow the network search to progress rapidly, but an implementation may decide to check local resources first.

Each network node maintains a status of all broadcast search requests sent to adjacent network nodes. Normally, the replies from the adjacent nodes are consolidated and as soon as all replies are received, a reply is sent to the originator of the broadcast search. However, the broadcast algorithm requires that positive replies be returned immediately (in APPN good news travels fast). Therefore, if the target resource is a local resource, the resource has been found within the node's domain, or the node receives a positive reply from a neighbor node, then the node returns a positive reply immediately, regardless of whether all nodes have replied.

A Locate search reply can be *complete* or *incomplete*. A complete reply indicates that this is the last reply to be returned, whereas an incomplete reply is sent by a node that has information to be sent immediately but has not received a reply to all requests forwarded. Each node will send a final reply, preceded optionally by one or more (positive) incomplete replies.

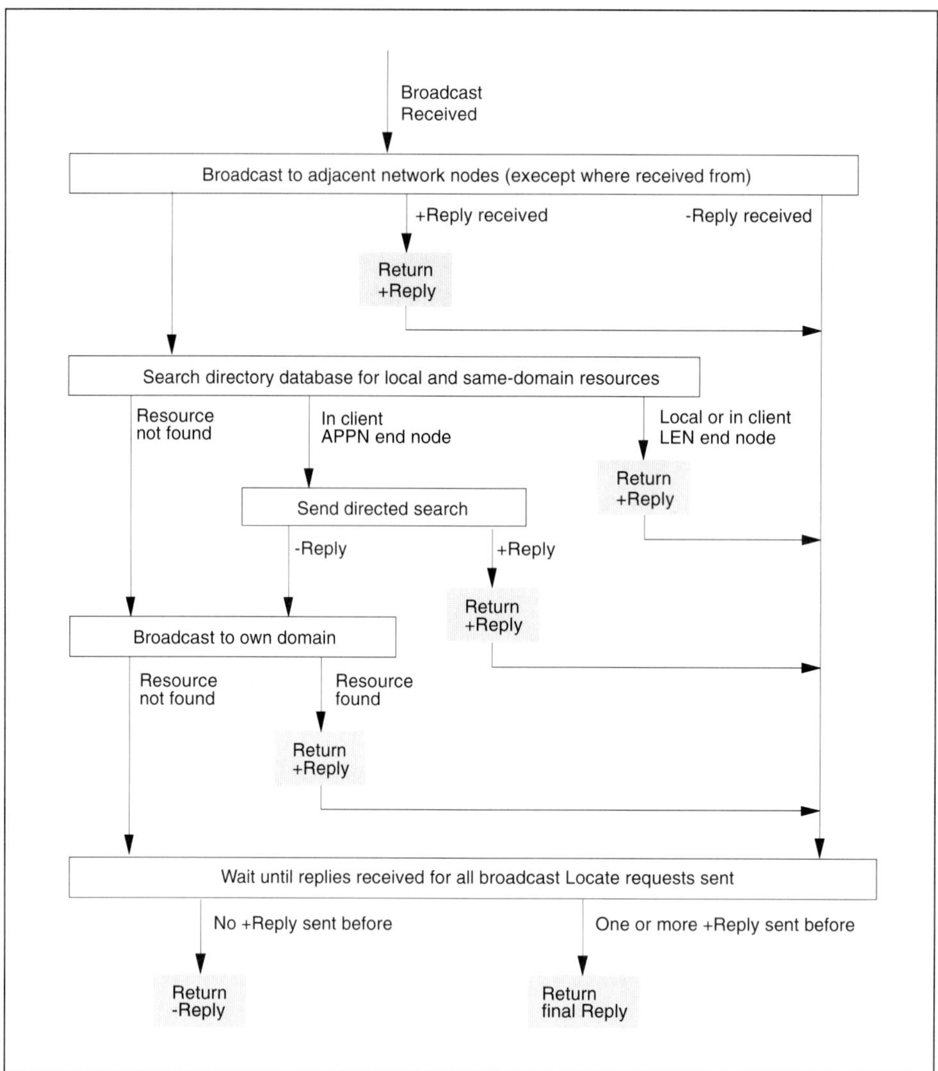

Figure 48. DS Search Logic during Broadcast Search

Each network node will consider a broadcast search to be completed when all adjacent network nodes have returned a complete reply. The broadcast originating node may receive more than one positive reply after a broadcast search because of the target resource being defined on multiple nodes. Duplicate definitions are not necessarily erroneous; for example, a LEN end node's resources may be defined, either explicitly or using wildcard definitions, on all network nodes to which the LEN end node is connected. The broadcast originating node will use the *first* positive reply that results from an explicit definition, or if none is received, the first reply indicating a wildcard definition. See also 6.4.3.1, "Wildcards" on page 125.

Figure 48 on page 124 depicts the DS search logic on a network node during a network broadcast search.

6.4.3 LEN End Nodes

Locate search requests originating on a LEN end node are restricted to a search of the local directory database only. If the LEN end node cannot locate the resource in its local directory database, directory services at the LEN end node returns a Locate failure to the initiator of the request. Entries within the directory database of a LEN end node for resources not located on the LEN end node itself can only be the result of system definition.

Any resource not located on the LEN end node itself has to be defined as being located on an adjacent node although the actual location may be anywhere in the network. A BIND is then sent to the adjacent node that will locate the destination node using its normal search and session setup logic.

6.4.3.1 Wildcards

All the LEN end node's resources to be accessed as DLUs must be defined on the LEN end node's serving network node. In the case of a LEN end node that supports a large number of resources; for example, a subarea network attached as a LEN end node to an APPN network, a large number of definitions will be required.

To alleviate this definition problem on such a network node, directory services provides generic and wildcard routing. For example, in the network node directory, there could be entries for RAL* and *. For details on how to define resources using generic (partially specified) names and wildcards, see page 110.

When a network node receives a Locate search request for a resource, the network node checks the directory entries that have fully specified resource names. If the resource cannot be found, the resource name is compared with the partial entries. Any LU name beginning with "RAL" would, for example match "RAL*." Finally, if no match can be found, the directory is checked to see if a wildcard entry "*," which matches all resources, has been defined. Once a match has been found, a positive Locate search reply is returned.

Problems may arise when a network broadcast search is sent and more than one network node, using either explicit, partially specified, or wildcard resource definitions, returns positive Locate search replies. A solution to this problem is that the network node returning the positive reply will indicate if the resource was found using a wildcard definition. The network node from which the broadcast search originated, differentiates between the replies. DS will return to the DS user, for example session services, the first positive reply based on an explicit definition (which could be a partial definition) or, if none was received, the first positive reply as a result of a wildcard definition.

Care should be taken and, most important, a consistent naming convention is required when using wildcards. Although it reduces the number of definitions it can easily lead to errors. Only one network node in a network should ever define a wildcard entry.

6.4.4 APPN End Nodes

Directory services at an APPN end node, in conjunction with directory services at its network node server, offers distributed search facilities throughout the APPN network. If a search request fails at the APPN end node, the APPN end node automatically sends a one-hop search request to its network node server. Directory services at the APPN network node is responsible for a Locate search through the network.

Locate search requests will be received by APPN end nodes in the following two cases:

1. Its network node server is handling a search request and has information, either system-defined, registered, or cached, that the end node owns the destination resource.
2. Its network node server is handling a search request, has no information, either system-defined, registered, or cached and has, therefore, started a domain search.

   When CP-CP sessions are established between an end node and its network node server, authorized APPN end nodes may request to participate in domain search requests that originate from the network node server.

When receiving a Locate search request, the APPN end node will check its directory for the target resource. A positive reply will include the TG vectors of the end node.

6.4.5 APPN Network Nodes

For an overview of the DS search logic on APPN network nodes, see Figure 49 on page 127 and Figure 50 on page 128. The first figure depicts the search logic on the network node server of the node from which the resource search originates. The second figure depicts the search logic on the network node server of the node owning the destination resource. An APPN network node may receive Locate search requests, from:

1. DS users within the node itself or from served APPN end nodes, using a one-hop search request

   The network node will check its directory database and return a positive reply if the destination resource is a local resource or resides on an adjacent LEN end node. A same-domain resource on an adjacent APPN end node will be verified by sending a Locate search request. When supporting the (optional) nonverify function, a network node server will not perform the resource verification if the request indicates this. For details, see 6.5, "Nonverify Function" on page 131.

   The network node will send a directed Locate search request to the network node server of the destination resource if the directory database search indicates the resource was other-domain.

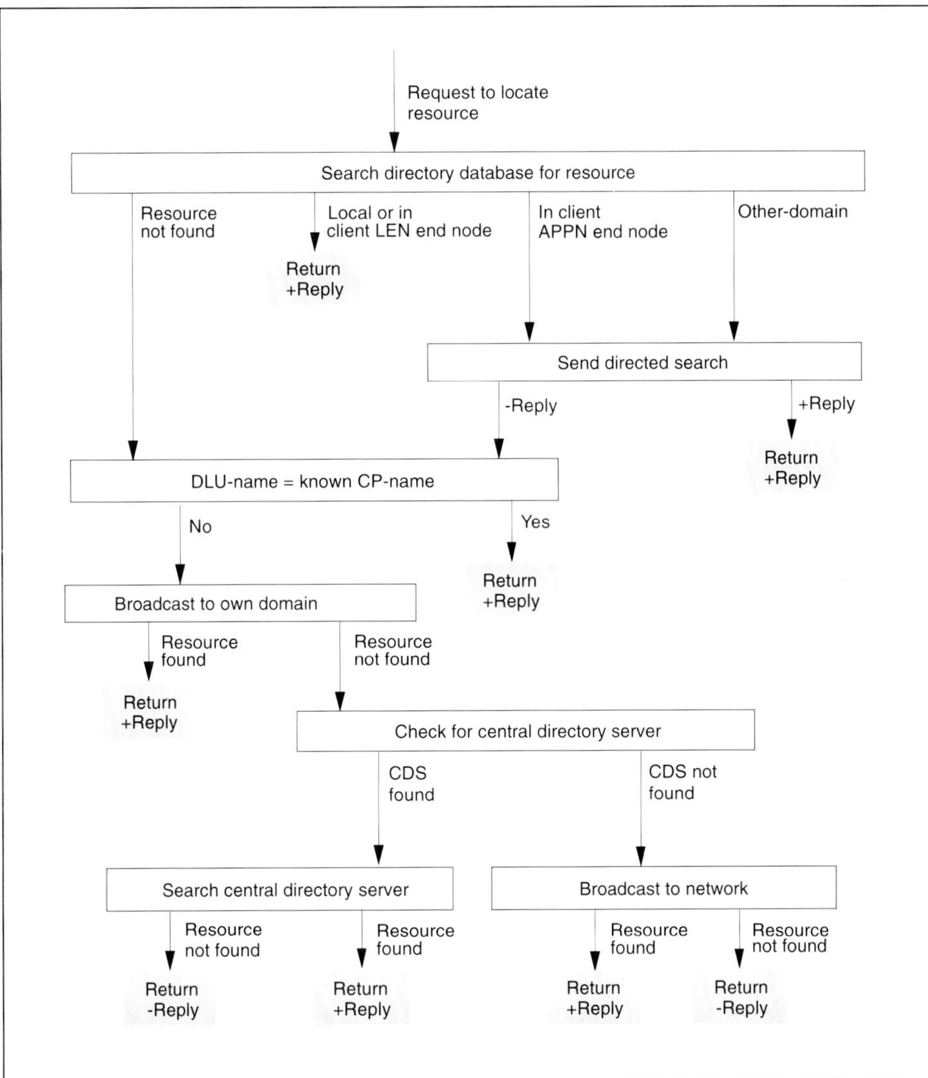

Figure 49. NNS(OLU) Search Logic

If the resource cannot be found in the directory database, resource verification is not successful, or the other-domain directed Locate search fails, the network node starts a domain broadcast search.

If the domain broadcast is not successful, the network node will either start a network broadcast search or send a directed request to the closest (minimal-weight route) directory server. The latter will be done only if central directory servers exist in the network and the network node supports querying a directory server. A

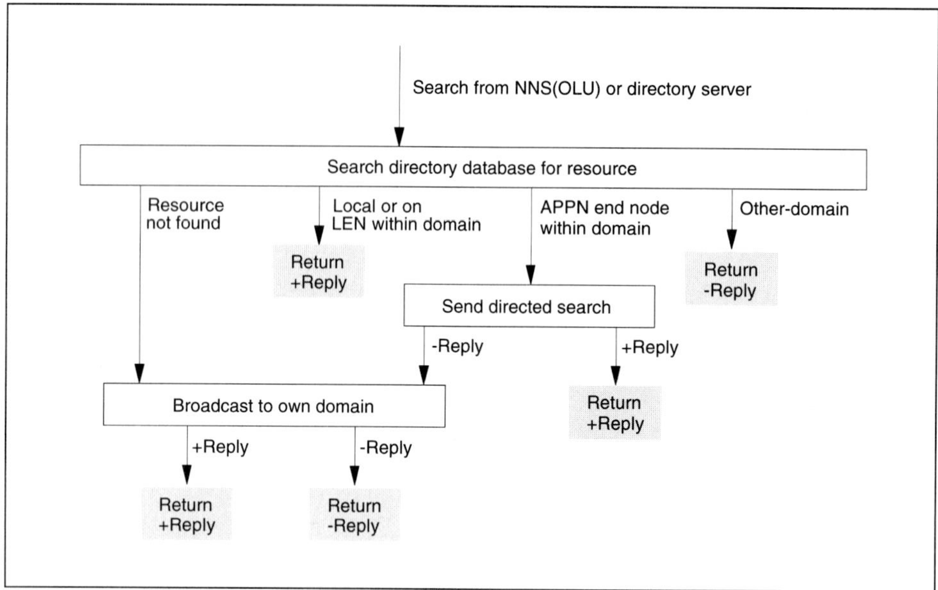

Figure 50. NNS(DLU) Search Logic

network node will never start a network broadcast after querying a central directory server.

2. Network nodes performing a network broadcast search

   The network broadcast algorithm has been described in 6.4.2, "Network Searches" on page 118. As part of the broadcast search, the network node will perform the local activities mentioned in 1 on page 126, that is, checking the directory database for local or same-domain resources, (optionally) verifying the resource, and, if necessary, starting a domain search.

3. Network nodes performing a directed search

   An APPN network node will receive a directed search if the sending network node assumes the resource is within the domain of the receiving network node or if the sending network node has no directory entry for the resource and the receiving network node performs the function of central directory server. A network node performing the function of central directory server is described in 6.2.2.2, "Central Resource Registration (CRR)" on page 112.

   When the network node receives a directed Locate search request it will perform the local activities mentioned in 1 on page 126, that is, checking the directory database for local or same-domain resources, (optionally) verifying the resource, and, if necessary, starting a domain search. Implementations may decide to start the domain search before checking the directory database.

Figure 49 on page 127 depicts the DS search activities on the network node serving the node that owns the OLU. Figure 50 depicts the DS search activities on the network node serving the node that owns the DLU.

6.4.6 Search at a Central Directory Server

The search procedure acting as a central directory server at a network node is described in this section. See Figure 51 on page 130 for an overview. is as follows.

The central directory server's directory is searched for an entry that matches the query. If the search is successful, the resource will be verified by sending a directed Locate search request to the NNS(DLU) to obtain the endpoint TG vectors and verify the accuracy of the directory entry. A central directory server will always perform resource verification, even if the nonverify function is supported. For details, see 6.5, "Nonverify Function" on page 131.

If the resource has not been found or resource verification indicates an erroneous directory entry, the central directory server checks the network topology database for alternate central directory servers. The central directory server will send a directed Locate search to all alternate central directory servers in parallel.

The central directory servers will use the *first* positive reply to verify the resource and obtain the endpoint TG vectors. Verification is done by sending a directed Locate to the network node server of the destination resource.

During verification it is possible that other replies will be returned as a result of the multiple alternate central directory servers being queried. These replies will be discarded if they indicate the same resource location as the one currently being verified. The replies are stored if they indicate a different resource location. Verification will be retried until the stored replies are exhausted or a successful verify occurs.

If after the previously described actions the resource has not been located and/or resource verification was not successful, then the central directory server will start a network broadcast search.

6.4.7 Alternate Central Directory Server

Central directory servers with equivalent capabilities will be queried by the central directory server, which is referred to as the *origin* central directory server.

When an alternate central directory server is queried, it searches the local directory and, optionally, a domain search is started. The domain search is optional since it is the intention of this search to treat the directories of alternate central directory servers as an *extended cache*.

If the alternate central directory server locates the resource in its local directory as being in its domain, it may optionally verify that resource. In this case, the origin central directory server is informed that verification was successful. An alternate central

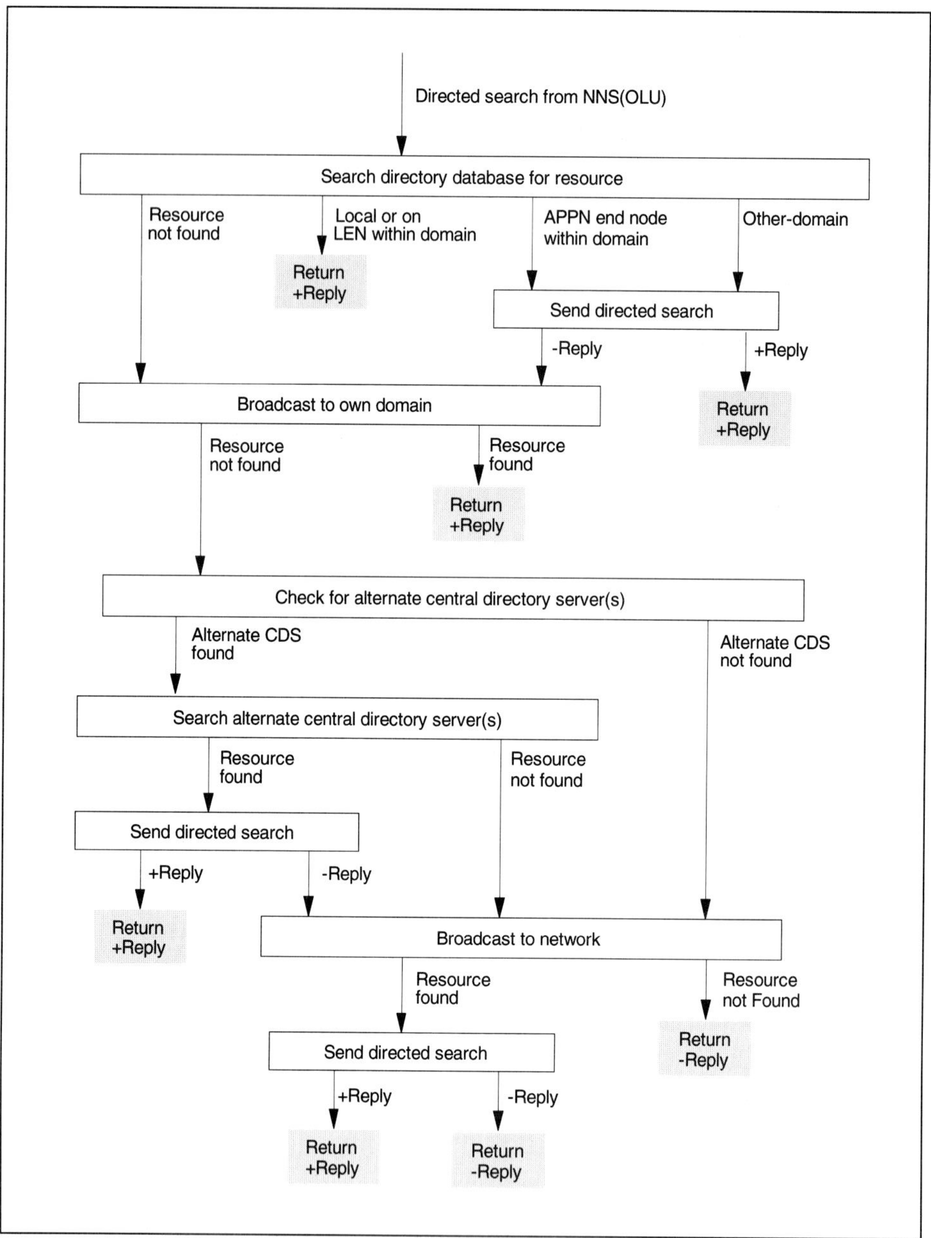

Figure 51. Central Directory Server Search Logic: Overview

directory server will not perform a network broadcast search for a resource it cannot find locally; the network broadcast search will be done by the central directory server that was queried first by the NNS(OLU).

6.5 Nonverify Function

In the base APPN architecture, a network node that receives a session initiation request will send a Locate search request to the node containing the destination LU even if the session request does not need to be delivered to the destination LU (for example, the session request is for a PLU-initiated session without resource reservation). This is done for two reasons:

- To ensure the accuracy of directory cache entries

  If the cached information is incorrect, the directed Locate search will fail and the network node will send a directed search to a central directory server or will start a broadcast search.

- To obtain the endpoint TG vectors of the node containing the destination LU

In base APPN, there is only one exception from this verification requirement. If the destination LU is an NN control point (that also acts as an application LU), then the topology database contains sufficient information to send a BIND directly to the target LU without a preceding directed Locate. This is the topology-based nonverify function described in 6.2.1.1, "LU Name Equal CP Name" on page 110.

Note: If cryptography, for example, is requested on the session, the topology-based nonverify function is bypassed in order to allow the Locate/CD-Initiate carrying the session key to be returned by the DLU.

In order to reduce both the network traffic and the time required to establish the session, the nonverify function (option set 1108) introduces an optional indication on a session request that verification of a destination resource, via directed Locate (either at the NNS(OLU) or the NNS(DLU)), is not necessary. The session manager (SM) component of the LU has to indicate that verify is not required when passing a session request to session services of the CP(OLU). A nonverify session initiation attempt may only be requested for PLU-initiated sessions that do not require resource reservation.

Verification is always required if any of the following is true:

- The DLU's real NN server has to be obtained.
- The session requires a secure class of service.
- Cryptography is requested.
- Application-supplied dial parameters are provided.
- A Locate is sent during an HPR nondisruptive path switch.

When nonverify is requested by an LU, SS in the originating CP must determine whether all the necessary information is available to perform a nonverify session initiation attempt. If not, verification is performed. In an EN, the nonverify attempt may use cached information about the DLU if the EN supports end node caching (see 6.2.4, "End Node Caching" on page 116).

If the session initiation attempt should fail where verification was not performed, the LU's SM will redrive the session initiation indicating that verification now is required (unless the sense data returned indicates that the initiation request will also fail).

6.5.1 Registration of Resource Characteristics

The nonverify function introduces new indicators for an LU's *status* and *stability*. An LU's status may be either *available* (accepting session requests, which is the default) or *unavailable* (not accepting session requests). An LU's stability is the length of time that it is expected to remain in its current state. The stability indicator can be zero, a finite value, or infinite. These values are set by the LU or by an operator. They are used by the nonverify function in other nodes to reduce the number of directory searches.

If both the end node and its NN server support the nonverify function, the EN includes a Directory Entry Characteristics control vector when registering an LU with its NN server. This control vector indicates whether an LU is available or unavailable, and how many seconds it will remain in that state. Additional Register requests are sent whenever an LU's availability status changes. An LU is available when it is enabled (that is, accepts new session requests). Products may indicate that an LU is unavailable when it has reached its session limit. An LU should only be re-registered to indicate a new state (available or unavailable). If an LU must be verified for every session, its characteristics are set as “available for zero time.”

If an end node supports the RTP functions for HPR (see Chapter 8, “High-Performance Routing” on page 155), an LU's NCE is included on that LU's Register request. Whenever the NCE for a registered LU changes, the LU is re-registered to indicate the new NCE.

When an LU is registered with the NN server, the NN server may register it with a central directory server (CDS). The Directory Entry Characteristics control vectors may optionally be included with the central registration flows, but are not returned by the CDS on Locate replies. They may optionally be used like cached DLU entries by the CDS in its role as NNS(OLU).

Only registered directory entries (at the NNS(DLU)) prevent searches for an unavailable LU. If an LU is cached as unavailable, the search still takes place.

6.5.2 EN TG Vector Registration

During CP-CP session activation, an NN indicates in the CP Capabilities GDS variable that it supports the nonverify function. When both the EN and its NN server support the nonverify function, the EN registers its endpoint TG vectors with its NN server. After successful CP-CP session establishment with the NN server the EN will send endpoint TG vectors in topology database updates (TDUs) to its NNS. Note that ENs register *all* endpoint TG vectors with their NNS, including TG vectors (TGVs) for parallel TGs, TGVs to connection networks, TGVs to other NNs and TGVs to other ENs.

Since the EN TG Vector registration process is one way only (ENs cannot receive TDUs) and NNs do not propagate domain TGVs into the subnet, a subset of TRS Flow Reduction techniques are needed. ENs that register their TGVs may set the LAST_FRSN_SENT field to zero in the first TDU sent to its network node server. This serves as an indicator to the NNS to purge all the previously registered TGVs for that EN and accept the new list associated with this CP-CP session. If the EN has reestablished a CP-CP session with the same NNS, and the NNS has indicated a FRSN not equal to zero, the EN may send TDUs that contain TGVs with FRSNs higher than the last FRSN that the EN sent to the NNS. ENs may include Resource Sequence Numbers (RSNs) within their resource updates. However, the NNS just accepts the resource updates and applies them to the EN's Topology database. There is no need for the NNS to execute the Resource Sequence Number (RSN) logic. The EN does not implement receive logic and the EN topology database is logically separate from the network topology database and not propagated between network nodes.

6.5.3 Endpoint TG Vectors on Locate Flows

When all endpoint TG vectors are registered with the NN server, an EN does not normally include any endpoint TG vectors in Locate flows. If any are included, they are used for route selection in preference to registered endpoint TG vectors. But endpoint TG vectors provided in Locate flows are not cached, do not replace registered entries, and are not used for any subsequent sessions. This gives an EN, in its role as CP(OLU) as well as CP(DLU), flexibility to influence the route selection process in special cases.

6.5.4 Network Node Information Caching

Base APPN architecture (as described in 6.2.3, “Cached Directory Entry” on page 114) dictates that a network node creates or updates cache entries in its directory database when its role in a directed or broadcast search is the network node serving either the search origin or the search target. Those cache entries are made for the search origin as well as the search target.

A node supporting the nonverify function includes stability information (carried in a Directory Entry Characteristics control vector) in all Locate/Find and Locate Found/requests, indicating whether a resource is available or unavailable, and how many seconds it will remain in that state. This stability information will be cached by other NNs (also by NNs that do not support the nonverify function), and forwarded to other nodes whenever the corresponding cached directory entry is used to respond to a Locate request.

Each cache entry has a timer to control the local node's use of the cache entry information. This timer is initialized to the smaller of the node's internal default timer value and the value received for the resource's stability. If no information about a resource's stability is present, the resulting cache entry indicates that the resource is available and its timer value is initialized to the implementation-defined default. In this case, the cached stability information is only used for the node's internal processing and not forwarded to other nodes.

Stability information, as introduced by the nonverify function, indicates only whether a *known* resource is available or unavailable. But repeated searches for *unknown* resources can severely affect a network's availabilty. For example, repeated attempts of thousands of users trying to logon to their IMS system that died together with its supporting VTAM would (if not controlled) create huge volumes of broadcast traffic. In order to limit the repetition of broadcasts for unknown resources, ACF/VTAM V4R2 introduced a *search reduction* function. But due to the complexity of determining whether a resource really is nonexistent or simply not found due to parameters contained in the search itself (such as COS, PCID, PCID modifier, etc.), search reduction is currently considered a *product feature* of VTAM and not approved APPN architecture.

A network node caches the resource location information contained in a Locate/Find request or in a Locate/Found reply unless it has already registered information about that resource. If it supports the nonverify option, it also caches (in the directory database) the endpoint TG vectors of an EN containing the resource, if present. The intention is to have cached the most recent information so that it can be used to satisfy other (nonverify) Locate requests.

6.5.5 Network Node Cache Maintenance

As in base APPN, a network node deletes the least-recently used cache entries first, when the cache is full and new entries have to be added. To further improve cache maintenance, network nodes supporting the nonverify function have implementation-specific values for a reference count (optional) and a reference timer (required). Whenever a cache entry is created, a timer value and (optionally) a reference count are associated with that entry.

Whenever a node references a cache entry, it decrements the entry's reference count. When an entry is referenced and its reference count reaches zero or the timer value has been exceeded, the entry has expired. When an expired entry is referenced, the node uses the entry's location information to refresh the entry. This is done by sending a directed search and, if that search fails, performing normal network search logic. The result will either be an available or unavailable entry with current location information and endpoint TG vectors. The associated timer and optional reference count are initialized again as described before.

A cache entry can also change its indication of whether a resource is available or unavailable through the normal caching process. If the network node receives a Locate request or reply and a cached entry for a referenced resource exists, the values received in the Locate will replace the cached values.

6.5.6 NNS(OLU) Search Request Processing

When a network node acting as the NNS(OLU) receives a session initiation request, its actions are based upon the content of its cache entry for the DLU and whether verification is required:

- If verification is required, base APPN search processing is performed.
- If there is no cache entry for the target resource, normal network search logic is performed using the setting of the *verify not required* indicator from the received search request.
- If a cached entry exists for the target resource, but the entry is expired or indicates that the resource is unavailable, the cached location information is used to send a directed search to the NSS(DLU) to obtain the most recent availability information. If the NNS(DLU) responds with:
  - Resource available, this information is cached and session establishment proceeds.
  - Resource unavailable, this information is cached and session establishment does not proceed.
  - Resource not found, the NNS(OLU) deletes its cached entry for that resource and continues with normal search logic.
- If verification is not required and a valid (not expired) cached entry exists for the target resource indicating that the resource is available, the node attempts to calculate an RSCV for the session using the DLU's cached endpoint TG vectors (as described below).

Whenever an NNS(OLU) returns a search reply to the OLU node, the *verify not performed* indicator is set as it was on the search reply received from another node. When the reply is generated by the NNS(OLU) (that is, the search did not contact the owner of the target resource), the *verify not performed* indicator is set.

6.5.7 NNS(DLU) Search Request Processing

In its function as server for a destination LU, a network node may receive a Locate request indicating that verification is not required if the originating network node lacked the information needed to satisfy that search request. If the originating network node did not know the DLU's location, its Locate request is in the form of a broadcast search; if it knew the location, but was unable to compute an RSCV or had to refresh the cache entry for that resource, its Locate request is in the form of a directed search. A search (directed or broadcast) will always arrive at the NNS(DLU) if the NNS(OLU) does not support the nonverify function, unless the DLU is a NN CP (this is the topology-based nonverify function, see 6.2.1.1, "LU Name Equal CP Name" on page 110).

When a network node receives a Locate request specifying that verification is not required, its processing depends on a number of factors:

- When the DLU is located on the receiving network node itself or on a LEN end node (regardless of whether verification is required), a positive Locate reply is returned indicating that verification was performed.

- If the NN does not know the location of the target resource, it will perform the normal NNS(DLU) search function. The search reply will indicate that verification was performed.
- If the NN has a valid (cached or registered) directory entry indicating that the DLU is available on a domain EN and has registered endpoint TG vectors for that EN, the search reply is generated without forwarding the search to that EN. This search reply indicates that verification was not performed and includes only those endpoint TG vectors that would else have been returned by the EN (that is, TGs to NNs, VRN(s), and direct TGs to the EN(OLU)).
- If the NN knows that the DLU is on a domain EN but does not have *registered* endpoint TG vectors, or the (registered or cached) directory entry is expired, the NN will forward the search to the appropriate EN. The search reply then will indicate that verification was performed.
- If the NN receives a Locate for a resource that is *registered* as unavailable, it sends a negative Locate reply without forwarding the request to the EN.
- If the NN receives a Locate for a resource that is *cached* as unavailable, it forwards the Locate request to the EN. The reply from the EN is used to update the cache.

When a Locate request is forwarded to an EN and the Locate reply from the EN contains endpoint TG vectors, those are returned to the origin in preference to any registered endpoint TG vectors. This allows the EN to select specific TGs based on the origin LU or the class of service in the request.

A search reply generated by a network node supporting the nonverify function will always include stability and availability information from the node's directory database.

6.5.8 NNS(OLU) Search Reply Processing

If a network node supporting the nonverify function has performed a broadcast search, it will no longer automatically accept the first explicit positive reply (as is done in base APPN). Instead, it will use the first *verified* explicit positive reply (that meets any other criteria) or, if none is received, the first nonverified acceptable reply.

Although in some cases this may impose a slight delay, it will ensure that existing connections are used whenever possible. If the NNS(OLU) has a choice between a verified and a nonverified reply, selecting the verified one will decrease the probability that a new switched connection has to be activated to the DLU node.

6.5.9 Path Calculation

The network node server of the origin LU calculates the session path using the network topology database and the endpoint TG vectors of the OLU and DLU nodes. It can obtain the OLU node's endpoint TG vectors either from its local topology database (if they have been registered) or from the session request. If they are present in the session request, they should always be used to calculate the session path for that session.

The endpoint TG vectors of the DLU node for a nonverify session request can come from a variety of sources:

- If the NNS(OLU) directly answers the session request (because it has all the information), they come from its directory cache (or from its local topology database if it is also the network node server of the DLU).

  In order to detect any direct connectivity between the origin and destination node, the NNS(OLU) must check its local topology database for any such connection when using cached information (because it might not have been present in a previous search).

- If the NNS(OLU) forwards a nonverify request into the network, they come from the local topology database of the NNS(DLU) (if they were previously registered) or directly from the CP(DLU).

If no route can be calculated for the requested COS, the network node server of the OLU redrives the search, this time requiring verification. When the search completes, the verified reply with the then-calculated RSCV is returned to the OLU.

Chapter 7. Session Services

The session services component of the control point generates unique session identifiers, activates and deactivates CP-CP sessions, and assists LUs in initiating and activating LU-LU sessions.

7.1 Function Overview

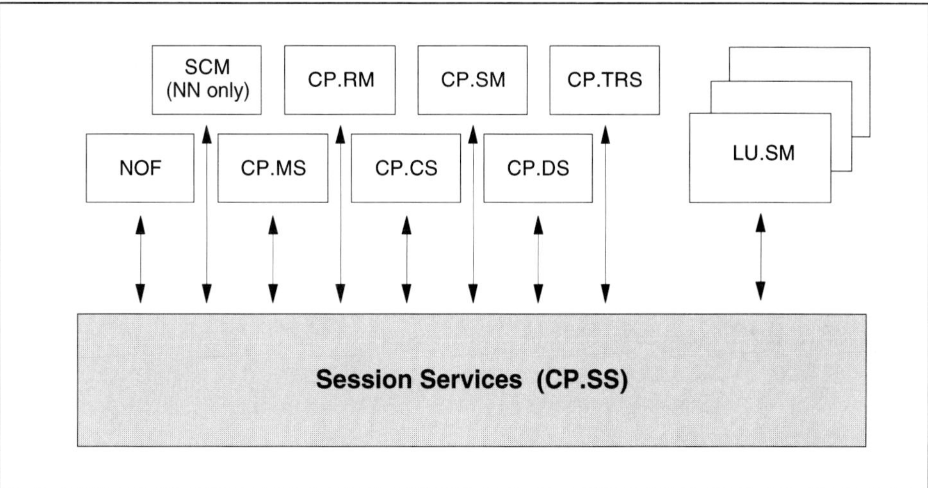

Figure 52. Overview of SS Interaction with Other Components in the Node

The following information is passed when session services is initialized by the node operator facility (NOF):

- Type of node
- CP name of this node
- Network ID of this node
- Indication if the COS/TPF function is supported

  The COS/TPF function allows a node to translate a mode name to class-of-service (COS) name and an associated transmission priority (TP). For more information, see 5.5.2, "Class of Service (COS)" on page 90.

- Indication if the node is to be included in a network node domain search

  If a network node server is not able to locate a resource it may decide to query all authorized APPN end nodes within its domain. Only the APPN end nodes that have explicitly indicated they want to be searched, will be included in the domain search. For more information, see 6.4.2, "Network Searches" on page 118.

Session services (SS) generates unique session identifiers, activates and deactivates CP-CP sessions, and provides LU-LU session initiation assistance and information to the session managers (SM) representing the LUs at the endpoints of a session. SS invokes directory services (DS) to locate a partner LU, invokes topology and routing services (TRS) to calculate an optimum route between an origin and destination node, informs management services (MS) about newly activated or deactivated CP-CP sessions, and may invoke configuration services (CS) to activate TGs. Each of these functions will be described in the following sections.

7.2 Fully Qualified Procedure Correlation Identifier (FQPCID)

Session services assigns network-unique session identifiers, also called the *fully qualified procedure correlation identifier* (FQPCID), for the following reasons:

- To correlate requests and replies sent between APPN nodes.

  Examples are resource registration requests, topology database updates (TDUs), and Locate requests exchanged during session initiation. Note, that the term *session identifier* is somewhat confusing, as the FQPCID is also used to identify non-session type data.

- To identify a session during cleanup or recovery procedures.
- To identify a session for problem determination.
- To identify a session for accounting, auditing, and performance-monitoring purposes.

The FQPCID is assigned at the node from which a session establishment or non-session request originates. A session related FQPCID identifies a particular session as long as this session remains active and all requests and replies that relate to this particular session (Locate, BIND, UNBIND) include its FQPCID.

To ensure uniqueness throughout the network, the FQPCID consists of a fixed-length (8-byte) PCID field concatenated with the length and the qualified network name of the control point that generated the FQPCID. The PCID contains a 4-byte value derived (using a hashing function) from the qualified network name of the CP and a 4-byte sequence number. The sequence number is incremented by 1 each time session services assigns an FQPCID. The initial value of the sequence number is either derived (also using a hashing function) from the time-of-day (TOD) clock, or for implementations that do not have a suitable clock, a monotonically increasing number (until wrapping occurs) with the last value safely stored across IPLs. A detailed description of the FQPCID generation process can be found in *SNA APPN Architecture Reference*, SC30-3422.

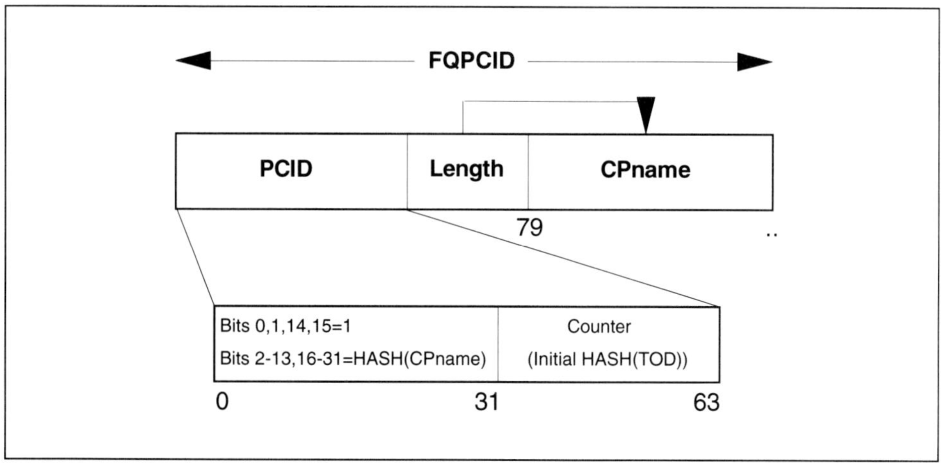

Figure 53. Fully Qualified Procedure Correlation Identifier (FQPCID)

Although the FQPCID is intended to be unique, collisions may occur because of the nature of hashing. When a collision is detected, a negative response is returned to the originating node. The node generating the colliding FQPCID is responsible for resolving the collision. When a collision occurs, a new PCID is generated by adding a random number in the range 1-255 (8 bits) to bits 0-31 of the PCID and forcing the format bits (0, 1, 14, and 15) to 1. This new value is then retained as a seed value in future PCID generation.

Note: Collisions of FQPCIDs may occur only when duplicate CP names have been assigned.

7.3 CP-CP Session Activation

CP components, specifically topology and routing services (TRS), directory services (DS), session services (SS), and management services (MS) use CP-CP sessions between adjacent APPN nodes to exchange information with their counterparts in other APPN nodes. Examples of CP-CP session usage are the exchange of network topology updates (TDUs), distribution of Locate search requests, and the exchange of CP capabilities. Note that CP-CP sessions are established between adjacent nodes only. If a CP component communicates with a peer component on a nonadjacent node, the information to be exchanged travels via multiple CP-CP sessions.

CP-CP sessions are always logical unit type 6.2 (LU 6.2) sessions. Using this session type, a contention situation could arise if both session partners attempted to allocate a conversation at the same time. This situation is resolved by defining one of the sessions the *contention-winner*, also often called *conwinner* session and the other the *contention-loser*, or *conloser* session. The primary session partner refers to its session as the contention-winner session, and the secondary session partner refers to that same session as the contention-loser session. For more information on LU 6.2 protocols see *SNA LU 6.2 Reference: Peer Protocols*, SC31-6808.

CP-CP sessions are always established in parallel, such that each partner maintains a conwinner and a conloser session. Each node will use its conwinner session to transmit requests and to send replies.

Basic APPN architecture designates exchanges of XID3s as the means of requesting CP-CP sessions with adjacent nodes. When a link between two adjacent APPN nodes is activated, each node indicates, as part of an XID exchange, if CP-CP sessions are required and supported. Configuration services, at each node, then signals session services that CP-CP sessions are required, causing SS to initiate the conwinner CP-CP session between the two nodes. This occurs asynchronously at both ends, resulting in the activation of the parallel CP-CP sessions between the two nodes.

End nodes and network nodes that support function set 1015 (CP-CP Session Activation Enhancements) will now determine, independently from the information given in the XID3 exchange that CP-CP sessions are requested, whether to send a BIND to the adjacent node for CP-CP sessions. As before, an end node is responsible for determining which network node it will select to be its network node server. It indicates its choice of server by sending a BIND for its conwinner CP-CP session to an adjacent network node, which then accepts its role as a network node server by sending a BIND for its conwinner session (see Figure 54 on page 144). This design allows for a simple recovery from failed CP-CP sessions between an end node and its network node server. The end node selects the next network node capable of being its network node server and simply sends a BIND for the conwinner CP-CP session.

Earlier versions of the APPN architecture only indicated whether CP-CP sessions were supported between two APPN nodes. Based on the assumption that two network node server would always have CP-CP sessions if a link between them supported CP-CP sessions, TRS used this information to *infer* the CP-CP session status when computing RSCVs. Network nodes that support function set 086 (Topology Awareness of CP-CP Sessions) now have a direct method of determining which TGs support CP-CP sessions, and which TGs have CP-CP sessions active over them. In addition, network nodes supporting function set 086, upon receiving notification that their Contention Loser session has been activated, will activate their Contention Winner session, if their Contention Winner session is not already active. This allows for a simple recovery of failed CP-CP sessions between adjacent network nodes.

When SS initiates a CP-CP session, it notifies DS that the session is pending-active so that DS may queue any network operations involving the CP-CP session partner, for example, directory searches, until the contention-winner session becomes active. SS notifies the resource manager to activate the CP-CP contention-winner session with the adjacent node. The session manager of the CP invokes SS to do its normal session initiation (for example, assign FQPCID) with a mode name *CPSVCMG*, which indicates a CP-CP session.

In order for one node to consider an adjacent node enabled, for example to send it Locate search requests, both CP-CP sessions with it must be enabled. The contention-winner CP-CP session is considered to be enabled when SS receives its partner node's CP capabilities on that session. The contention-loser CP-CP session is considered to be enabled when SS has sent its CP capabilities on that session.

When many NNs in a network have a high number (more than 4) of adjacent NNs, with which they establish CP-CP sessions, many redundant broadcast messages (TDUs and broadcast searches) can temporarily flood the network and degrade network performance. Because it is doubtful that establishing CP-CP sessions with more than two adjacent NNs provides much benefit for the majority of networks, it is recommended that network administrators limit the number of CP-CP sessions when configuring their network. (Note that the number of CP-CP sessions between ENs and their NN servers has no effect on the amount of TDU traffic in the network.)

7.3.1 Control Point Capabilities

Immediately following the activation of the CP-CP sessions between the CPs in the two nodes, a CP capabilities exchange occurs on the CP-CP sessions. This exchange determines the extent of network services that each node supports, and provides the basis for future CP-CP communication between the nodes.

Each node requests the CP capabilities of its partner node over the CP-CP session it has initiated (contention-winner session), and it includes its own CP capabilities in the request. Each node also sends its own CP capabilities when it receives a request for them over its contention-loser CP-CP session. The exchange of control point capabilities is done using service transaction programs.

Figure 54 on page 144 shows how session services in each node activates its contention-winner session with the other node. Session services activates a session by sending a BIND command to the partner node of the session partner; the session partner accepts the session by returning a BIND response. On receipt of the BIND response, the nodes will exchange control point capabilities with each other.

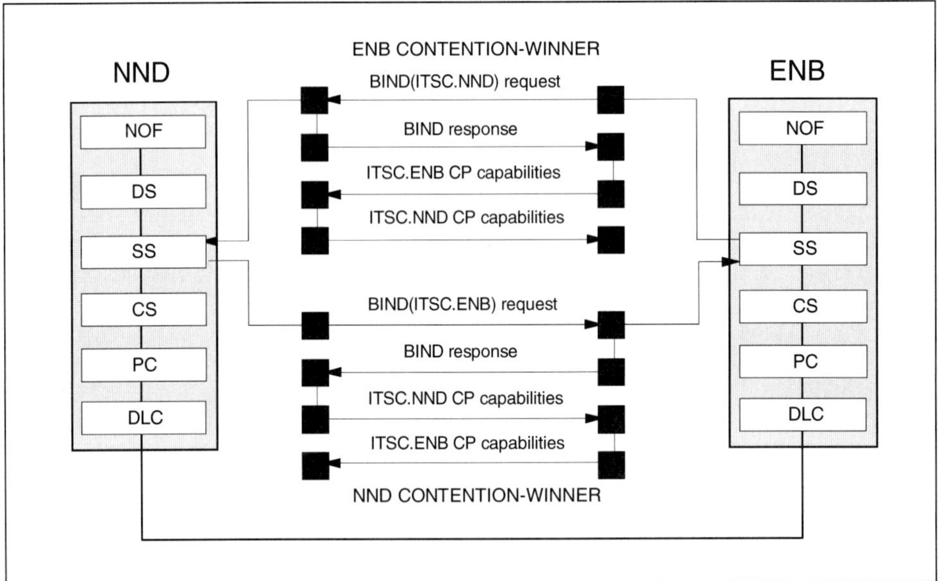

Figure 54. Session Services Activates CP-CP Session

After the CP-CP sessions have been established, the nodes exchange their control point capabilities. Among other things, the following information is exchanged:

Topology database update (TDU) receipt supported
: The sending CP supports receipt of TDUs. This indication is set by network nodes.

Flow reduction sequence number (FRSN)
: The flow reduction sequence number identifies the latest CP capabilities or topology database update GDS variable received by the sender of this CP capabilities GDS variable. It is included only when TDU receipt is supported. For details, see 5.4.2, "Flow Reduction Considerations" on page 85.

Request/reply management data support
: The sending CP supports receipt of request for management services data and sending replies to the requests.

CP-CP session activation enhancements support

Resource search capability
: This parameter is set by APPN end nodes that support a domain search from their network node server. It specifies the resource types for which the end node may be searched for by its network node server. Currently only resource type *LU* is supported. For more information, see 6.4.2, "Network Searches" on page 118.

Topology awareness of CP-CP sessions support
This parameter is set by network nodes that support topology awareness of CP-CP sessions.

Recognizes unknown control vectors in a topology database update (TDU) variable
The sender indicates that it supports the receipt of unknown control vectors in TDU variables.

Bypass of directed locate not allowed indicator supported
This parameter allows an end node to indicate that the Locate search must occur.

When a network node server receives an end node's capabilities, they are retained only if the end node is authorized to provide its own CP capabilities. Otherwise, the CP capabilities defined locally (by NOF) at the network node for the end node are retained. End node authorization at a network node is specified at system-definition time when NOF defines the end node to the network node.

7.4 CP-CP Session Deactivation

A session services component with active CP-CP sessions may receive requests to deactivate CP-CP sessions with an adjacent node. The main reasons to deactivate CP-CP sessions may be:

- Normal CP-CP session deactivation

  Normal deactivation may be the case if the node itself or the partner node no longer requires the CP-CP sessions. For example, an APPN end node may decide to switch to another network node server or one of the session partners may be taken out-of-service.

- Abnormal CP-CP session deactivation

  Abnormal CP-CP session deactivation is needed when a link failure or serious protocol violations occur on the CP-CP sessions.

In both cases, the CP-CP session will be deactivated. However a link failure will be regarded as a recoverable error and session services will immediately activate the CP-CP session again. If the link failure persists, session services will retry the CP-CP session activation until the retry limit is exceeded. The setting of the retry limit is implementation-dependent.

7.5 LU-LU Session Initiation

As described in 2.3, "Logical Unit (LU)" on page 29, APPN and LEN nodes support LUs that can both initiate sessions and respond to session activation requests. The BIND sender is referred to as the primary LU (PLU); the BIND receiver is referred to as the secondary LU (SLU). A session starts when the PLU sends a BIND and the SLU responds with RSP(BIND) and stops when UNBIND and RSP(UNBIND) are exchanged.

The UNBIND may be sent by either LU. The PLU specifies in the BIND request information like:

- The network-qualified name of the PLU
- The network-qualified name of the SLU
- Session characteristics such as maximum RU size and pacing windows
- The route through the network towards the SLU
- The unique session identifier (FQPCID)

Besides using the terms *primary* LU (PLU) and *secondary* LU (SLU), the terms *origin* LU (OLU) and *destination* LU (DLU) are often used as well to indicate which LU (actually the node owning the LU) is responsible for locating the partner LU. The request to locate a session partner flows from OLU to DLU, and the reply in the opposite direction.

In base APPN, the OLU is always the PLU and the DLU is always the SLU. By using the terms OLU and DLU, session setup procedures can be adequately described. However, with the introduction of APPN VTAM, sessions are no longer limited to PLU-initiated sessions. APPN VTAM allows session initiation from the PLU, the SLU, or from a third-party LU. The term, *initiating LU* (ILU), is used to indicate the LU that initiates an LU-LU session. Although a BIND request always flows from PLU to SLU, the Locate search request to find a session partner may originate from either side, depending on which LU has initiated the session.

As only APPN VTAM has implemented *session services extensions*, which among other things allows SLU and third-party session initiation in an APPN network, we have chosen to describe base APPN session services separately from the functions contained within session services extensions. For a description of session services extensions, see 11.1, “Session Services Extensions” on page 263.

Note: Base APPN does cover the situation when a VTAM system connects to an APPN network as a LEN end node.

7.5.1 CD-Initiate Processing

Session services (SS) provides LU-LU session initiation assistance and information to the session managers (SM) representing the LUs at the endpoints of a session. Among other things, SS will invoke directory services (DS) to locate a destination LU. DS uses Locate search requests to find a resource. DS allows DS users, such as session services, to exchange data using the Locate search requests.

The primary means of communicating session initiation information between session endpoints in separate nodes is the Cross-Domain Initiate (CD-Initiate) GDS variable. SS will add the CD-Initiate GDS variable to the Locate search request. A Locate search request containing the CD-Initiate GDS variable is sometimes also called a *Locate/CD-Initiate*.

Listed below are the CD-Initiate fields that are modified or referenced by SS at the session endpoints. For a detailed description, see *Systems Network Architecture Formats*, GA27-3136.

Session polarity
Indicates which LU is expected to be the BIND sender (PLU), either OLU or DLU. In base APPN, the PLU is always identical with the OLU.

Mode name
The mode name, allowing a COS to be selected for the LU-LU session requested.

Additional control vectors

- COS/TPF control vector The COS/TPF control vector is included in the CD-Initiate. Session establishment requests from an end node contain this information only if the end node supports the COS/TPF function. For details, see 5.7.1, "Session Establishment and TRS" on page 99.
- Route Selection control vector, RSCV

  The route to the DLU is calculated, and a Route Selection control vector (RSCV) is built by the network node server of the node containing the originating LU. The RSCV will be used to route the BIND request from the PLU to the SLU.
- TG Descriptor control vector

  An APPN end node includes endpoint TG information in the Locate search request (that is, from the CP(OLU)) and reply (that is, from the CP(DLU)). The CP(OLU) includes TG information about endpoint TGs between the end node and adjacent network nodes and connection networks. The CP(DLU) includes TG information about endpoint TGs from the end node to adjacent network nodes and connection networks but also TG information for TGs to the CP(OLU). For details, see 5.7.1, "Session Establishment and TRS" on page 99.

7.5.2 Directory Search and Route Computation

SS of the origin node initiates the route computation by invoking DS to search its directory for the DLU. DS will search its local directory, which contains entries for LUs residing in the end node or in an adjacent end node. If the local search is successful, and if the LU resides in an adjacent end node, TRS is invoked by SS to generate an RSCV containing the single TG (hop) to the peer node. This RSCV is returned to the OLU in a Cinit.

If the local search is not successful, DS of an APPN end node passes the Locate/CD-Initiate to its network node server, which initiates a distributed search of the network for the DLU. If the distributed search is successful, TRS of the network node server computes the route and provides an RSCV in the Locate/CD-Initiate reply to the APPN end node; see 7.5.4, "Examples" on page 148.

Note: On LEN end nodes, all destination LUs have to be defined as residing on adjacent nodes. LUs that do not actually reside on adjacent nodes need to be defined as if they reside on an adjacent network node. A LEN end node starts a session by passing a BIND to the adjacent node on which it assumes the destination LU resides. If a network node receives a BIND, the network node then takes the necessary steps to locate the DLU and forward the BIND.

7.5.3 Route Activation

After the route has been computed and the RSCV provided to SS of the origin node, the TG on which the BIND has to be sent may not be active. SS, of the origin end node, inspects the RSCV for the first TG (hop) and, optionally, invokes CS to activate that TG. After the TG is successfully activated, SS sends the session information to the session managers (SM) representing the LUs, so that the BIND can be sent to the SLU.

7.5.4 Examples

To establish a session between two LUs requires the invocation of directory services (DS), topology and routing services (TRS), and session services (SS) components on several APPN nodes, namely:

- Node owning the OLU: CP(OLU)
- Network node server of the OLU: NNS(OLU)
- Network node server of the DLU: NNS(DLU)
- Node owning the DLU: CP(DLU)

In the following two sections we describe the session establishment between two LUs residing on a LEN end node, and between two LUs residing on APPN end nodes.

7.5.4.1 LUs Residing on LEN End Nodes

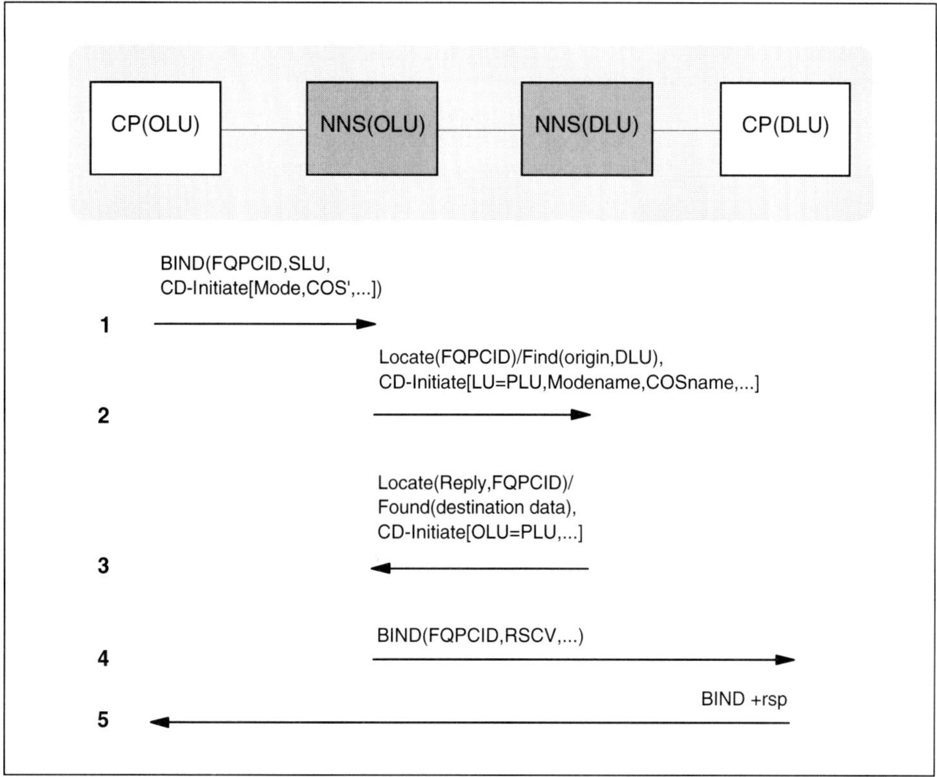

Figure 55. Session Establishment between LUs on LEN End Nodes

Figure 55 depicts the internode sequences involved in session establishment between two LUs residing on LEN end nodes.

Note: The "NNS(OLU)" of an origin LEN end node is the network node that receives the BIND by which a session from a LEN end node is started. The "NNS(DLU)" of a destination LEN end node is the network node to which the LEN end node connects and on which the DLU has been defined.

The figure shows a case where the CP(OLU), which cannot support Locate search requests, relies on NNS(OLU) to build a Locate request, to add the CD-Initiate variable, and to find the DLU. In this example, the route taken by the Locate request is:

NNS(OLU) .. -> .. NNS(DLU)

If NNS(OLU) and NNS(DLU) are not adjacent, the Locate request will be routed through intermediate network nodes.

The route taken by the BIND request is:

CP(OLU) -> NNS(OLU) .. -> .. NNS(DLU) -> CP(DLU).

If NNS(OLU) and NNS(DLU) are not adjacent, the BIND request will be routed through intermediate network nodes. Because of optimum route calculation for this session, the session data (including the BIND) may follow a different route from NNS(OLU) to NNS(DLU) from the Locate request.

Figure 55 on page 149 illustrates the session establishment process, the following list explains this process. The list items correspond to the numbered items in the figure. These are:

1. To CP(OLU,) all destination LUs appear to be adjacent, so the LEN end node sends the BIND to its network node server. The BIND contains the session parameters requested by the OLU, as well as the DLU name, the FQPCID, the mode name and, optionally, the COS name. The COS name will be included only if CP(OLU) supports the COS/TPF function.

2. NNS(OLU) examines the BIND and extracts the DLU name. Since the DLU is not in this node, NNS(OLU) searches its directory database. NNS(OLU) will send a directed Locate request to verify the DLU when the DLU location can be obtained. NNS(OLU) will perform a central directory server search or, if no central directory server is present, a broadcast search to locate the DLU if no information can be found. See also Chapter 6, “Directory Services” on page 107.

   Note: A *cached* directory entry is an entry stored by the network node as a result of a previous search operation revealing the DLU's location; its presence in the directory allows NNS(OLU) to perform a *directed Locate*.

   Before sending a directed Locate request, NNS(OLU) computes a route to NNS(DLU) and provides an appropriate *Locate RSCV*. A Locate RSCV contains a list of CP names from an origin to a destination network node server, as opposed to a *BIND*, or *session RSCV*, which contains a list of CP names and TGs between each adjacent pair of nodes along a route from an origin to a destination endpoint node. The Locate RSCV contains the *shortest* route (minimal hops) between NNS(OLU) and NNS(DLU), whereas the session RSCV contains an *optimum* route for the requested class of service between PLU and SLU. TG information is not required in a Locate RSCV as the Locate request is forwarded using CP-CP sessions between adjacent nodes.

   NNS(OLU) builds all variables that have to be added to the Locate search request. It includes the FQPCID obtained from the BIND, the OLU and DLU name from the BIND, the CP name of CP(OLU) and NNS(OLU), and the mode and COS names. The COS name is obtained from the BIND or, if not present, obtained from the COS database on NNS(OLU), based on the mode name.

3. NNS(DLU) searches its directory database and finds an entry that indicates that DLU is located on a LEN end node within its domain. NNS(DLU) returns a positive reply to the Locate request including endpoint TG information of the TG between NNS(DLU) and CP(DLU).

4. NNS(OLU) receives the Locate reply and uses its network topology database, the TG on which the BIND has been received from CP(OLU), and the endpoint TG vectors received from NNS(DLU) to compute the optimum session route using either the COS obtained from the BIND, or, using the mode name, the COS obtained from its local COS database. Among other things, the Route Selection control vector (RSCV) indicating the session route is appended to the BIND and sent along the route to CP(DLU).

5. CP(SLU), which in base APPN is always CP(DLU), returns a positive response to the BIND that is sent along the session path to CP(PLU).

7.5.4.2 LUs Residing on APPN End Nodes

Figure 56 on page 152 depicts the internode sequences involved in session establishment between two LUs residing on APPN end nodes.

This figure shows the case where the CP(OLU), since it supports Locate search requests, sends a Locate search request to its network node server, NNS(DLU), when a session is required. In this example, the route taken by the Locate request is:

CP(OLU) -> NNS(OLU) .. -> .. NNS(DLU) -> CP(DLU)

If NNS(OLU) and NNS(DLU) are not adjacent, the Locate request will be routed through intermediate network nodes.

The route taken by the BIND request is:

CP(OLU) -> NN .. -> .. NN -> CP(DLU)

The BIND is routed along an end-to-end optimum route, which may be different from the route taken by the Locate request. The network nodes in the session path are optional; if links exist between the end nodes, session data (including BIND) may be routed directly between the two nodes. Note that, as part of the session establishment, CP(OLU) forwards all endpoint TG vectors for connection networks and adjacent network nodes, and CP(DLU) forwards all endpoint TG vectors for connection networks and adjacent network nodes and possible endpoint TG vectors for CP(OLU). The latter, if available, allows NNS(OLU) to compute a direct route between the end nodes.

Figure 56 on page 152 illustrates the session establishment process, the following list explains this process. The list items correspond to the numbered items in the figure. These are:

1. In this configuration, CP(OLU) sends a Locate request to its network node server. The Locate/CD-Initiate contains all of the end node's endpoint TG vectors, as well as the DLU name, the FQPCID, the mode name and, optionally, the COS name. The COS name is included only if CP(OLU) supports the COS/TPF function.

2. NNS(OLU) searches its directory database as described in the previous example and sends a Locate/CD-Initiate request, and either a directed or (if no central directory server is present) a broadcast search request, to NNS(DLU). For details, see annotation 2 on page 150.

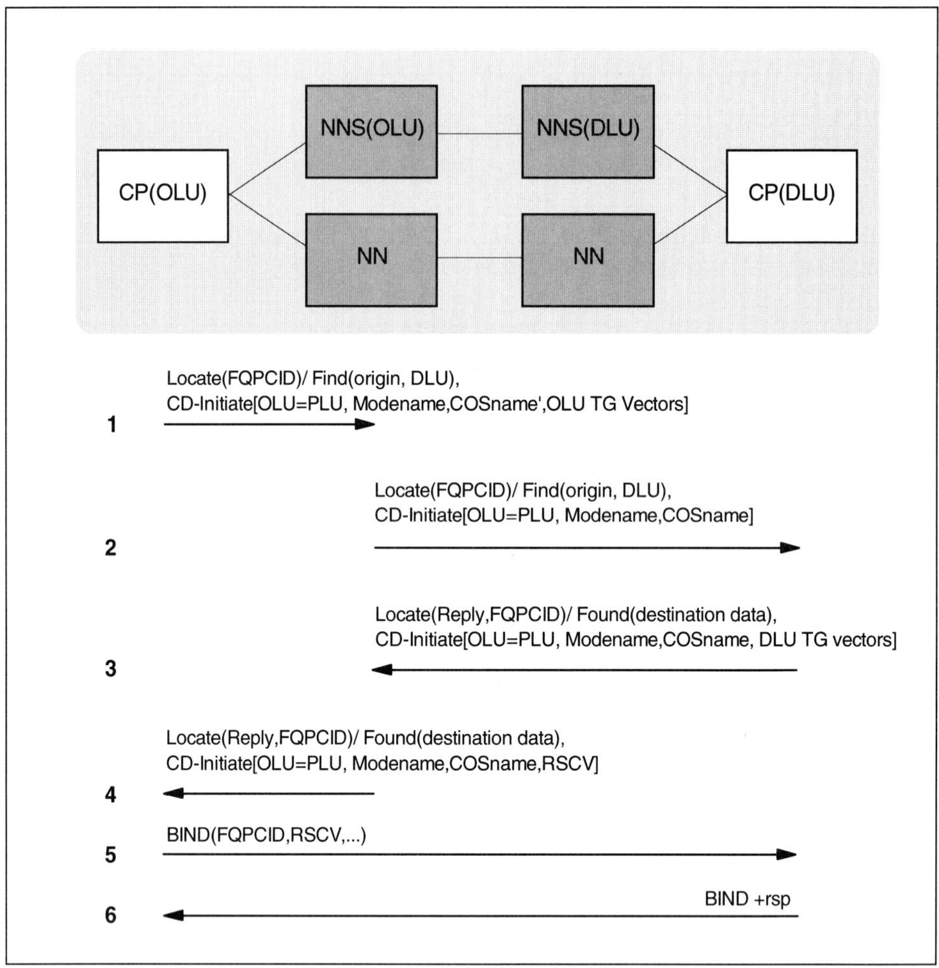

Figure 56. Session Establishment between LUs on APPN End Nodes

NNS(DLU) forwards the Locate/CD-Initiate to CP(DLU).

3. CP(DLU) returns a Locate/CD-Initiate reply including endpoint TG vectors, confirming the location of the DLU.

4. NNS(OLU) receives the reply with the destination node's endpoint TG vectors. It uses the TG vectors in conjunction with its topology database to compute the optimum route using the COS, which is either obtained from the BIND, or, using the mode name, obtained from its local COS database. The resulting RSCV is appended to the Locate/CD-Initiate reply, which is returned to CP(OLU).

5. CP(PLU), which in base APPN is always CP(OLU), constructs a BIND and copies the RSCV from the Locate/CD-Initiate reply into the BIND. CP(PLU), and, subsequently, each intermediate network node along the session route, examines

the RSCV to determine how to route the BIND request and initialize the session path.

6. CP(SLU), which in base APPN is always CP(DLU), returns a positive reply to the BIND that is sent along the session path to CP(PLU).

Chapter 8. High-Performance Routing

High-performance routing or HPR is an addition to the APPN architecture. It enhances APPN data routing performance and reliability, especially when using high-speed links.

To support emerging high-speed communications facilities, certain changes to the APPN architecture are required to allow switching in intermediate nodes to be done at a lower layer and much faster than can be achieved in base APPN. HPR changes the existing intermediate session routing (ISR), which is done in APPN by using a routing algorithm that minimizes the storage and processing requirements in intermediate nodes. The level of error recovery that is done in APPN for the slower-speed lines used today is unnecessary for high-speed, more-reliable lines. HPR addresses this by reducing the amount of error recovery done on individual lines and instead providing an end-to-end level of error recovery. HPR also enhances APPN by implementing a nondisruptive path switch function, which can switch sessions around failed links or nodes.

One of the general design principles of HPR is that it should have functional equivalence with the base APPN architecture. It was also a requirement that a node that supports HPR should be able to interoperate with existing APPN nodes. These two features will result in a seamless migration to HPR from an installed APPN network.

8.1 HPR Overview

The two main components of HPR are the rapid-transport protocol and automatic network routing.

8.1.1.1 Rapid-Transport Protocol (RTP)

RTP is a connection-oriented, full-duplex protocol designed to support data in high-speed networks. *RTP connections* are established within an HPR subnet and are used to carry session traffic. These connections can be thought of as *transport pipes* over which sessions are carried. RTP connections can carry data at very high speeds by using low-level intermediate routing and minimizing the number of flows over the links for error recovery and flow control.

The RTP functions include:

Nondisruptive path switch

An RTP connection's physical path can be switched automatically to reroute sessions around a failure in the network. The RTP connection is reestablished over a new physical path that bypasses the failing link or node, and the sessions' traffic flow is resumed on the RTP connection nondisruptively. Any data that was in the network at the time of the failure will be recovered automatically using RTP's end-to-end error recovery.

End-to-end error recovery

In base APPN, error recovery is done on every link in a network. To address the emerging high-speed lines with lower bit error rates, HPR removes the requirement to do link-level error recovery and instead does error recovery on an end-to-end basis. This will improve performance by reducing the number of flows required to do the link-level error recovery on every link. RTP also supports selective retransmission, where only missing or corrupted packets are re-sent, and not all packets since the failure occurred.

RTP also handles the in-order delivery of data. If there is a multilink transmission group (MLTG) in the path, the packets may arrive at the endpoint out of sequence. The RTP endpoints will re-sequence the data in this case.

End-to-end flow control and congestion control

Flow control in APPN networks is also done on each stage of the session by using adaptive session-level pacing. This method provided the best performance for networks comprised of a mixture of link types, with differing speeds and quality. However, for high-speed networks, adaptive session-level pacing is not adequate because of the amount of processing required in each node.

HPR uses a protocol suitable for high-speed routing called adaptive rate-based (ARB) flow/congestion control. It regulates the flow of traffic over an RTP connection by adaptively changing the sender's rate based on feedback from the receiver. This protocol allows for high link utilization and prevents congestion before it occurs, rather than recovering from congestion once it occurs.

Figure 57 on page 157 shows an RTP connection that is carrying multiple sessions. Traffic from many sessions requesting the same class of service can be routed over the same RTP connection. If an HPR node is an intermediate node on a session path, then it must be a network node, just as in base APPN.

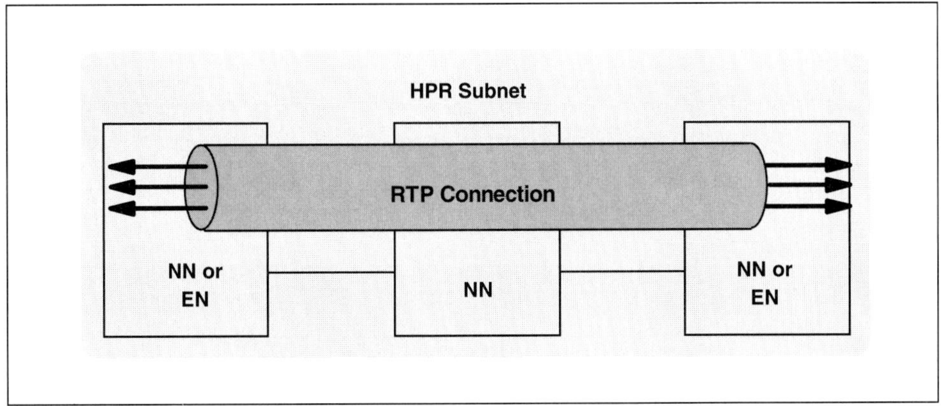

Figure 57. RTP Connection Supporting APPN Sessions. Multiple sessions using the same class of service can share the connection.

8.1.1.2 Automatic Network Routing (ANR)

ANR is a new routing mechanism to minimize storage and processing requirements for routing packets through intermediate nodes.

The ANR functions include:

Fast packet switching
: ANR takes place at a lower layer than APPN intermediate session routing and will significantly improve performance in the intermediate nodes. Functions such as link-level error recovery, segmentation, flow control, and congestion control are no longer performed in the intermediate nodes. Instead, these functions are performed at the RTP connection endpoints.

No session awareness
: Intermediate nodes are not aware of the SNA sessions or the RTP connections that are established across the nodes. This means that there is no requirement to keep the routing tables for session connectors that are kept in base APPN (APPN sessions require between 200 and 300 bytes per session per node). This saving on intermediate storage will be essential in the future, when HPR nodes supporting high-speed links will be carrying many more intermediate sessions than APPN nodes do today.

Source routing
: ANR is a source-routing protocol and carries the routing information for each packet in a network header with the packet. Each node strips off the information it has used in the packet header before forwarding onto the link, so the next node can easily find its routing information at a fixed place in the header. This means that switching packets through a node can be done more quickly than in the routing table lookup method used in base APPN. There is no restriction on the number of hops in ANR.

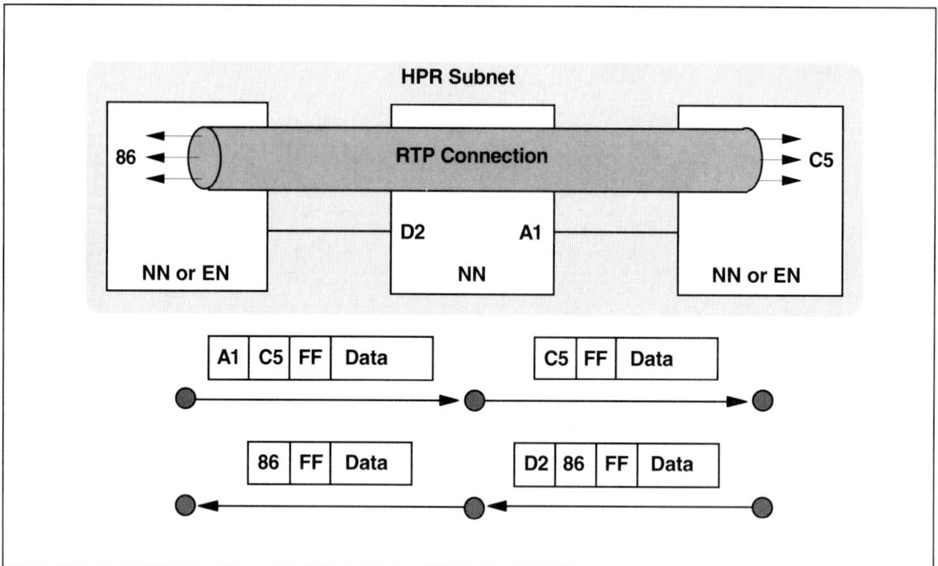

Figure 58. ANR Routing. Intermediate nodes strip routing information from the header at every stage through the network.

Figure 58 shows the principle of ANR. The intermediate network node strips the first routing label (A1) from the network header before forwarding the packet on link A1. The address of C5 represents the endpoint in the last HPR node. The intermediate network node can route packets very quickly, with no need to reserve storage or buffers, or to do link-level error recovery.

8.1.2 General APPN/HPR Operation

By way of a general overview, an example of the setting up and operation of an APPN session that passes through an HPR subnet is given here. The details of the HPR parts of the route and session setup are explained in the later parts of this chapter.

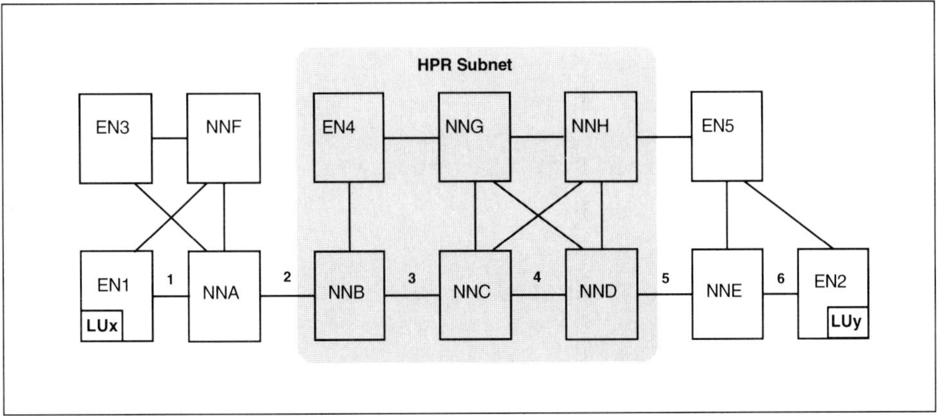

Figure 59. Overview of the Operation of an APPN/HPR Network. NNA is the network node server for EN1 and NNE is the network node server for EN2. The assumption is that LUx on EN1 wants to establish a session with LUy on EN2.

8.1.2.1 APPN Topology

CP-CP sessions are established between adjacent nodes as in base APPN. The CP-CP sessions between the network nodes are used to broadcast the topology database updates. In the example, it is assumed that the CP-CP sessions between network nodes are fully meshed and so there will be CP-CP sessions between the following pairs of network nodes:

> NNA-NNB, NNB-NNC, NNC-NND, NND-NNE, NNG-NNH, NNA-NNF, NNC-NNG, NNC-NNH, NND-NNG and NND-NNH.

The APPN topology database is fully replicated on all the network nodes, and the structure of it is the same on the APPN nodes and the HPR nodes. Nodes in the base-APPN subnets see the HPR nodes and links as base-APPN nodes and links. However, nodes in the HPR subnet can distinguish between the base-APPN and the HPR nodes and links.

8.1.2.2 Directory Search

EN1 will send the Locate search request for LUy to its network node server NNA. If NNA has no previous knowledge of the location of LUy, and there is no central directory server in the network, then NNA will perform a broadcast search. The broadcast search will be sent to all the APPN and HPR network nodes in the network, using the CP-CP sessions in the usual way. NNE will send a reply indicating the location of LUy on EN2.

8.1.2.3 Route Computation

NNA, acting as the network node server for EN1, will calculate the route to be used through the whole network. The route calculation will be done in exactly the same way as in base APPN, using class of service and the topology database to select the least-weight route through the network. NNA has no knowledge that the HPR subnet is any different from the rest of the network. For the example, it is assumed that the route selected by NNA uses the following path:

EN1 - 1 - NNA - 2 - NNB - 3 - NNC - 4 - NND - 5 - NNE - 6 - EN2

The BIND from EN1 will be sent through the network with the RSCV, which was calculated by NNA. The RSCV is composed of a list of CP and TG vectors, as in base APPN.

8.1.2.4 BIND Routing through the HPR Subnet

Routing the BIND in the base-APPN subnets is always done using the RSCV. The BIND is sent to NNB using the RSCV calculated by NNA.

When the BIND reaches the APPN/HPR boundary function in NNB, an RTP connection will be set up, which crosses the HPR subnet and finishes in NND. If an RTP connection already exists between nodes NNB and NND for the requested class of service, this existing RTP connection will be used and a new RTP connection is not set up.

The routing of the BIND over the RTP connection through the HPR subnet is done using ANR rather than using the RSCV. After the BIND has left the APPN/HPR boundary function in NND, the RSCV routing continues for the last part of the route through the network.

The BIND response is sent on the reverse path. It uses the APPN connectors set up during the BIND request in the base-APPN subnets, and it uses the RTP connection set up across the HPR subnet.

HPR does not change the APPN route selection process. The RTP connection will follow the same route through the HPR subnet as was indicated in the RSCV calculated by NNA, and so will take the following path:

NNB - 3 - NNC - 4 - NND

However, if a failure occurs in NNC or either of the intermediate links 3 or 4 get disconnected, then a nondisruptive path switch will cause a different route for the RTP connection to be set up between NNB and NND. In this case, NNB or NND will calculate the new route for the RTP connection.

8.1.2.5 LU-LU Session Routing

The session traffic can then begin, and this will follow the path as described above. In the base-APPN subnets, the routing is done with intermediate session routing, using the session connectors set up during the BIND process. In the HPR subnet, the routing is done using ANR across the RTP connection.

As the APPN class of service is used to calculate the route through the HPR subnet, the transmission priority requested in the class of service is used in HPR when traffic is flowing through the network. HPR nodes establish queues for the four transmission priorities per out-going transmission group to prioritize traffic at the link level. In addition to this, the new ARB congestion control that is used in the HPR subnet will regulate the HPR traffic and so the performance in the HPR subnet will be improved.

NNC, as an intermediate node on the path of the RTP connection, has no knowledge of the RTP connection, nor of the sessions that pass across it. It can route the packets of the LU-LU session traffic based on the ANR routing information that is contained in every packet.

8.1.3 Changes to the APPN Architecture

The two main components of HPR are the rapid-transport protocol and automatic network routing.

Apart from these two new components, HPR requires only minor changes to previously defined APPN functions. The main changes introduced by HPR are discussed in this chapter.

8.2 HPR Base and Options

The HPR function is an extension to the APPN architecture and can be added to an existing APPN end node or APPN network node.

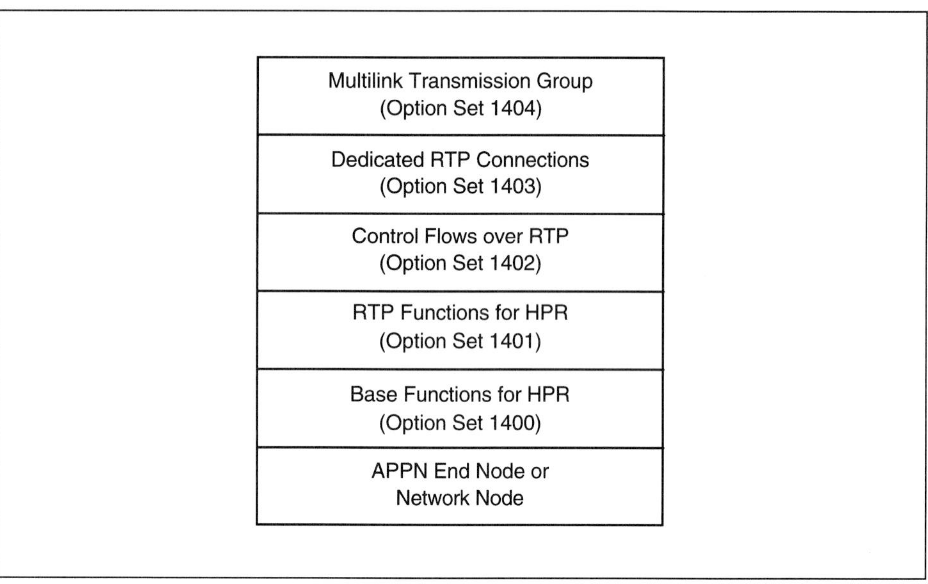

Figure 60. HPR Base and Options

8.2.1 Base Functions for HPR

The primary role of the HPR base functions (APPN option set 1400) is to support ANR. Products that implement only the HPR base functions will act as intermediate ANR routing nodes for RTP connections. Such nodes cannot act as endpoints for RTP connections. As APPN intermediate routing is done only by APPN network nodes, it follows that a node that is only supporting ANR must be an APPN network node. An APPN end node that implemented only the HPR base could not make use of the HPR ANR routing functions.

The following lists the HPR base functions:

Intermediate routing of network layer packets using ANR

HPR network layer packets (NLPs) flowing on RTP connections and using ANR may be efficiently routed through the node.

Using FID2 routing for CP-CP sessions and route setup requests

All CP-CP session traffic between a base HPR node and its neighbors flows (as in base APPN) using FID2 PIUs.

Prior to establishing an RTP connection, a route setup protocol is executed in order to obtain the necessary ANR information associated with each link along the path. Every node along the path, including base HPR nodes, participates by adding the appropriate ANR information. When the route setup messages are exchanged between an HPR base node and its neighbors, they flow in FID2 PIUs.

FID2 PIUs and NLPs share a link
Both FID2 PIUs and NLPs may flow over a single link. They are distinguished by the first 3 bits in the packet (B'001' for a FID2 PIU and B'110' for an NLP).

Using FID2 routing for LU-LU sessions that use intermediate session routing (as opposed to ANR)
APPN LU-LU traffic not flowing over RTP connections continues to use FID2 PIUs.

HPR capability exchange via XID3
During XID3 exchange, an HPR node indicates its level of HPR support.

A maximum packet size of at least 768 bytes on an HPR link.
Any link that supports HPR must be capable of transporting packets at least as big as 768 bytes.

TDUs indicate level of HPR support
TDUs for TGs and nodes are sent indicating the appropriate level of HPR support.

Calculation of HPR-only routes
HPR network nodes are able to calculate routes that contain only nodes and TGs that support HPR.

Link-level error recovery support
Link-level error recovery is always required for the following link types (not using link-level error recovery on these link types is not allowed or possible):

- IBM-compatible parallel and ESCON channels
- X.25
- SDLC

The ability to send packets over a link without using link-level error recovery is required support for all other link types (not listed above) supported by HPR. Using link-level error recovery on these links is optional.

8.2.2 RTP Functions for HPR

Rapid-transport protocol (RTP) is the transport protocol used in HPR for transporting data across HPR subnets.

A node that supports the RTP functions for HPR (APPN option set 1401), in addition to the HPR base functions, can act as an endpoint of an RTP connection. RTP connections can only be established between nodes that support the RTP functions. To be able to make use of HPR in a network, there must be an HPR subnet with at least two nodes that support the RTP functions. If all the nodes in a network support only the

HPR base functions, then no RTP connections can be established and the network will run base APPN protocols.

The endpoint of an RTP connection can be in an APPN end node or an APPN network node, and so the RTP functions for HPR could be implemented in either node type.

The following lists the RTP functions for HPR option set:

Rapid-transport protocol (RTP)
: This is the transport protocol used in HPR for transporting data across HPR subnets.

Nondisruptive path switch
: If the current path used by an RTP connection fails, the connection may be automatically switched to a new path. Sessions that are transported over the RTP connection are not disrupted.

APPN/HPR boundary function
: APPN (FID2 PIU traffic) is mapped to HPR (NLP) traffic and vice versa.

Directory reply with LU's network connection endpoint (NCE) identifier
: An NCE identifier is an ANR label that allows an NLP to be routed to a specific component within a node. The component is uniquely identified by the label. A search reply for an LU contains the NCE identifier associated with that LU.

Of course, all the base functions for HPR are also supported by a node that implements the RTP functions for HPR.

8.2.3 Control Flows over RTP

A node that implements the HPR control flows over RTP option (APPN option set 1402), in addition to the RTP functions for HPR option set, will support the use of:

- RTP connections for CP-CP sessions
- RTP connections for route setup requests and responses

In each case, these RTP connections terminate in the adjacent nodes. Only when both HPR nodes, connected by one or more HPR links, support the control flows over RTP option, will RTP connections and network layer packets be used to transport the CP-CP session flows and route setup requests and responses; otherwise, FID2 routing will be used.

Note that because FID2 routing is not supported over HPR multilink transmission groups, both nodes connected by a multilink transmission group have to support the control flows over RTP option.

8.2.4 A Sample HPR Network

Figure 61 shows a sample network that includes different possibilities of HPR base and options.

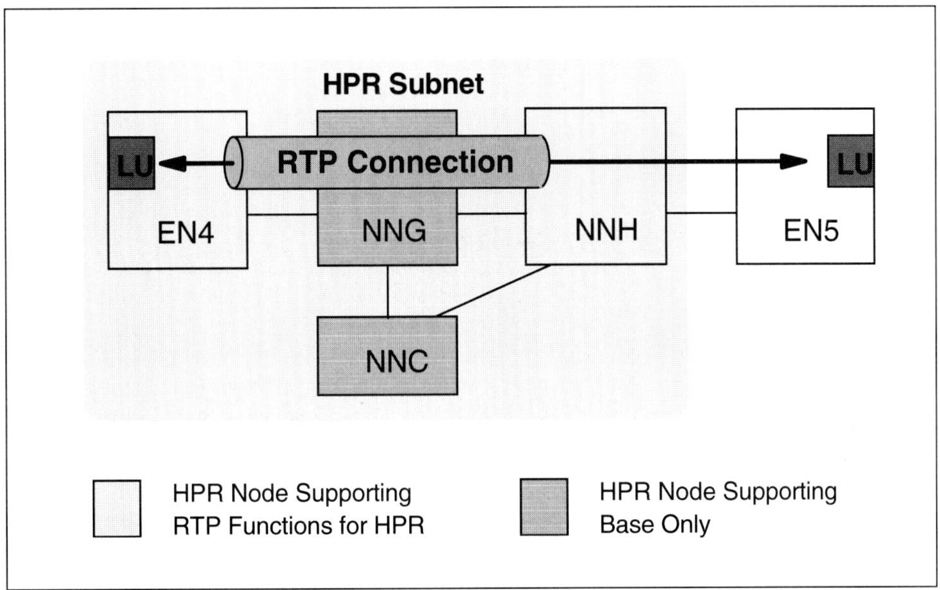

Figure 61. HPR Base and Options Example

In this example, it is assumed that the end nodes are attached to their network node servers via unreliable lines that require link-level error recovery. The network nodes are assumed to be connected via a backbone of high-speed, reliable lines that do not require link-level error recovery.

The link between EN4 and NNG is an HPR link, and to support the unreliable link, link-level error recovery is used on the link. The link between NNH and EN5 is an APPN link and so link-level error recovery is provided as part of base APPN.

EN4 and NNH provide endpoints for the RTP connection and so require the RTP functions for HPR. NNG supports ANR for the RTP connection and NNC may provide ANR after a nondisruptive path switch. Thus, NNG and NNC need the HPR base function, but because they are not RTP connection endpoints, they do not require the RTP functions for HPR.

Thus the HPR options are implemented in the nodes in the HPR subnet in Figure 61 on page 165 as follows:

EN4 HPR base and RTP functions for HPR
NNG HPR base
NNH HPR base and RTP functions for HPR
NNC HPR base

8.3 Automatic Network Routing

HPR uses the automatic network routing (ANR) mode to route session traffic through an HPR network or subnet, between nodes that support the RTP functions for HPR. ANR provides point-to-point transport between these nodes.

HPR uses a route setup protocol when establishing an RTP connection through the network. Each network layer packet is routed independently by carrying the complete routing information to navigate the packet through the network in a network layer header (NHDR). This allows processing of packets to be handled at a lower functional layer in intermediate nodes compared to base APPN's ISR, with a minimum of processing and storage requirements.

8.3.1 Network Layer Packets

ANR supports variable-length network layer packets that have a network layer header as shown in Figure 62 on page 167.

The first 3 bits of the network layer header are always B'110' and so an HPR node can distinguish between a network layer packet and a FID2 PIU that always starts with B'0010'. The network layer header itself is also of variable length and depends on the length of the ANR routing field.

The sender sets the *transmission priority field* to the priority associated with the RTP connection (that is, to the transmission priority of the sessions being carried over that RTP connection). Because the (possible) transmission priority values are the same for FID2 and network layer packets, priority queueing can be done when transmitting both FID2 and network layer packets over the same TG.

The *time-sensitive packet indicator* is set when an NLP cannot tolerate excessive delays along the path. For example, any product-specific blocking functions should flush all data currently blocked so that a time-sensitive packet may be processed and forwarded immediately. The time-sensitive packet indicator is set for all packets that contain a status requested indicator or a Status segment in the transport header (THDR).

The *Slowdown1* and *Slowdown2 indicators* may optionally be set to *on* by any node along the path when a congestion condition exists along the path (for example, in a frame-relay subnet). This information is then used by the RTP endpoints to regulate the adaptive rate-based flow/congestion control algorithm (see 9.4, "Optional Intermediate Node Interaction with ARB" on page 228).

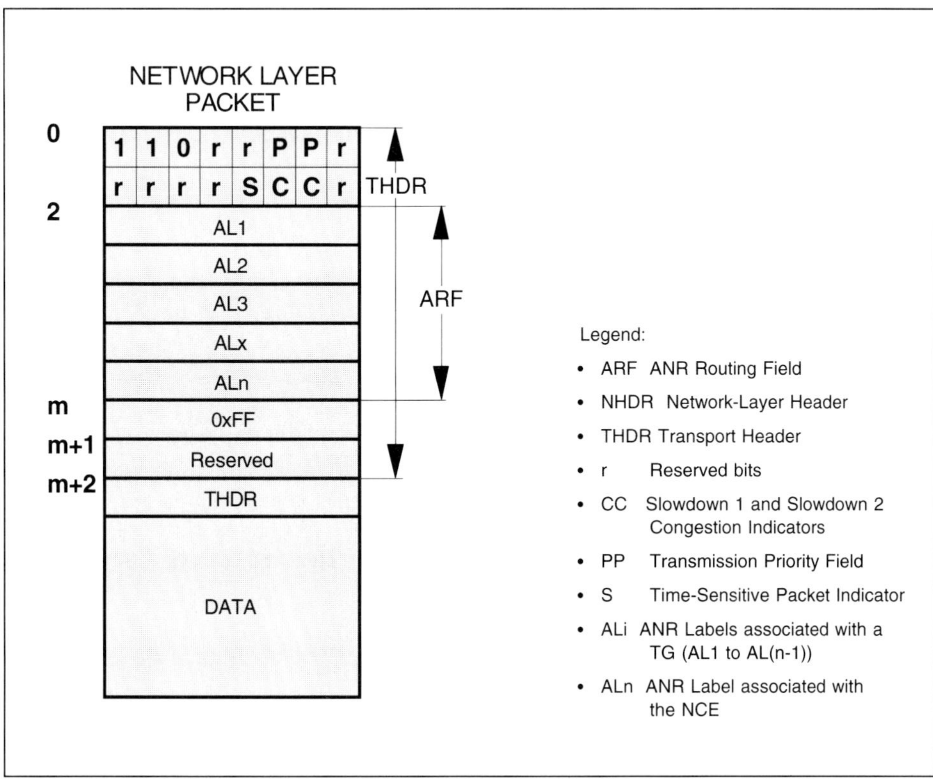

Figure 62. Network Layer Packet Formats

8.3.2 ANR Routing Field

ANR is a source-routing protocol, and the ANR routing information is determined through a route setup protocol (see 8.4.2, "HPR Route Setup" on page 182 for details).

The ANR routing field in the NHDR is comprised of a string of ANR labels. These labels describe the path of a packet through an HPR network or subnet. An HPR node looks at the first ANR label in the ANR routing field and uses that label to select the link (TG) over which to send the packet. The HPR node will remove this first label from the ANR routing field before forwarding the packet out onto the link. This means that the length of the ANR routing field will decrease as a packet passes through an HPR network.

The end of the ANR routing field is indicated by an X'FF' delimiter. The last ANR label in the ANR routing field before the X'FF' indicates the network connection endpoint (NCE) that is the destination component in the HPR endpoint. There are no delimiters between the ANR labels in the ANR routing field. The ANR routing field does not have a maximum length, as there is no restriction as to the number of HPR links over which an RTP connection can pass.

ANR labels are assigned internally within a node and are not the same as TG numbers; they do not appear in the topology database. Each HPR link is assigned two ANR labels, one at each end of the link. The ANR label only has significance in a node, so ANR numbers do not have to be unique across a network. However, the ANR labels within an HPR node must be unique. The first (high-order) bit of an ANR label is reserved and always set to "1."

The size of the ANR label can vary from 1 to 8 bytes, but will typically be 1 or 2 bytes, and the length can be different among nodes in an HPR network. The ANR label length can even vary within an HPR node, as long as the labels are unambiguous. X'FF' is never allowed within an ANR label, because it would be interpreted as the ANR routing field delimiter.

8.3.3 Network Connection Endpoints (NCEs)

ANR requires a new form of address within an HPR node, called the NCE label. The network connection endpoint (NCE) identifies the component within the node that is to process the received network layer packet. The NCE label is included as the last ANR label in the ANR routing field. In Figure 62 on page 167, ALn is the last ANR label before the X'FF' delimiter and represents the NCE. An NCE can be one of the following:

- Control point (CP)
- Route setup function
- APPN/HPR boundary function
- LU

The NCE label will allow the destination HPR node on an RTP connection to route the packets to the correct function. The NCE labels of the components within an HPR node are set internally at node and link-activation time.

CP NCEs
: Each node that implements the control flows over RTP option to support the transport of CP-CP sessions over an RTP connection assigns an NCE label for its CP. Adjacent nodes exchange the NCE labels of their respective CPs during link activation (on XID3). All CP-CP session traffic is then sent with an ANR routing field containing the CP's NCE label of the destination node. Any packet received with the CP NCE label in the ANR routing field is internally routed to the CP. See 8.8.1, "CP-CP Sessions" on page 207 for more information.

LU NCEs
: When the destination LU is located in a node that supports the RTP functions for HPR, LU-LU session traffic is sent with an ANR routing field whose last label addresses the LU (the LU's NCE label). Any packet received by the destination node containing an LU's NCE label is internally routed to the appropriate LU. The LU's NCE label identifies the component within the node that processes all packets received for that LU.

There can be at most one NCE label assigned to an LU; that is, a single LU cannot have two NCE labels assigned to it at the same time. An implementation may internally allocate an NCE label for each LU, for a group of LUs, or for all LUs residing in that node.

An LU's NCE label is learned during a directory services search when a target LU resides on an HPR node, and in this case, the LU's NCE address is sent on the Locate search reply; but an LU NCE may also be learned during the route setup process. See 8.8.2, "LU-LU Sessions" on page 209 for more information.

APPN/HPR Boundary Function NCE

An APPN/HPR boundary function NCE label is used to identify the component that performs the transforms from base APPN flows to HPR flows (and vice versa) in an HPR node at the border between the HPR subnet and the base-APPN subnet. The HPR/APPN boundary function is required to support TGs to APPN nodes or to HPR nodes that do not support the RTP functions for HPR. An HPR/APPN boundary function NCE label may be assigned for each such TG, for a group of such TGs, or for all such TGs in a node. An APPN/HPR boundary function NCE label is learned during the route setup process. See 8.9, "Combined APPN/HPR Networks" on page 211 for a description of the APPN/HPR boundary function.

Route Setup NCEs

HPR employs a route setup protocol in order to obtain ANR and RTP connection information. If adjacent nodes both support the control flows over RTP option the route setup messages flow over a link's route setup RTP connection; otherwise, they flow within the FID2 messages between the adjacent nodes on the network control (NC) flow. The component within a node that processes route setup messages over an RTP connection is identified by the route setup NCE label. Route setup NCE labels are exchanged when links are activated. For a description of the route setup function, see 8.4.2, "HPR Route Setup" on page 182.

8.3.4 Intermediate Node Routing

When an incoming network layer packet is received, the HPR DLC will pass control to the ANR component. ANR inspects the ANR routing field and determines whether to send the packet to a local NCE or outboard on another link. If the packet is to be switched onto a link, ANR will remove the first ANR label in the ANR routing field. The DLC for the outboard link will compute the CRC and add a link header and trailer.

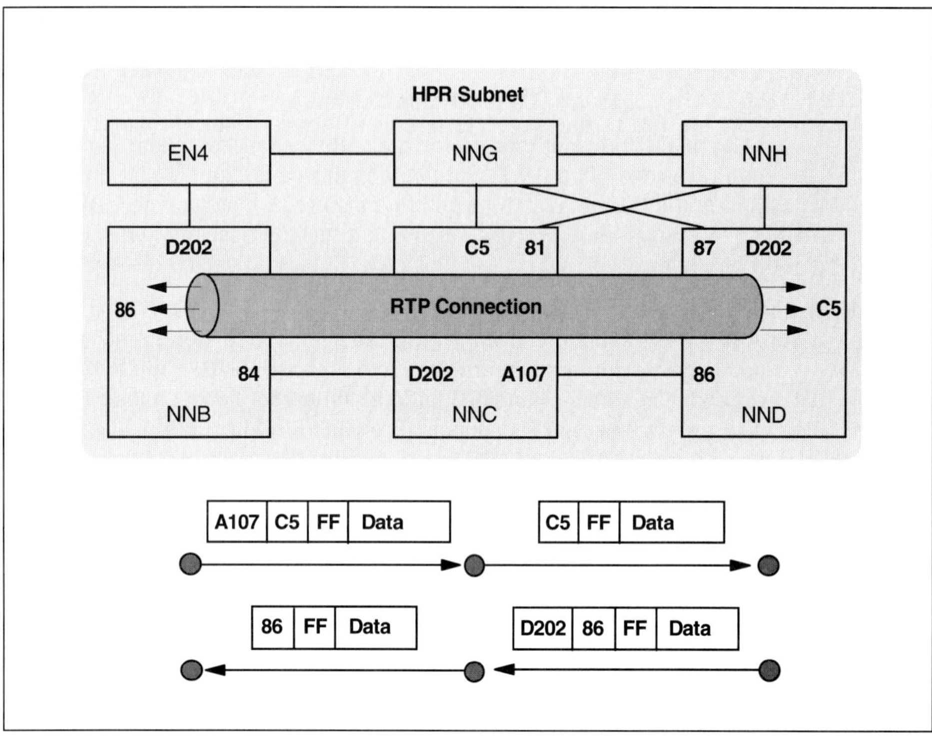

Figure 63. ANR Routing through an HPR Subnet

Figure 63 shows the ANR routing field when a packet is routed from an RTP connection endpoint (NCE) label 86 in NNB to an NCE address C5 in NND. These NCEs can be either LUs or APPN/HPR boundary functions (if the session continues into a base-APPN subnet). The NCEs of the other endpoints and components of HPR nodes are not shown. It is assumed that the RTP connection and the LU-LU sessions have already been established.

Each packet that is sent between the two nodes will contain the ANR routing fields as shown in each stage of the RTP connection. For the packets flowing between NNB and NND, the ANR labels consist of:

84 ANR label of link leaving NNB
A107 ANR label of link leaving NNC
C5 ANR label of destination NCE in NND

The packet is forwarded to the link with ANR label 84 (NNB to NNC). Before sending the packet out on this link, NNB removes the ANR label 84 that was used to route internally within node NNB. When the packet arrives at NNC, the first ANR label is A107, and NNC routes the packet to its link with ANR label A107 (NNC to NND). Before sending the packet, NNC removes the ANR label A107 from the ANR routing field.

When the packet arrives at NND, the last ANR label C5 represents the NCE of the endpoint of the RTP connection (an LU or an APPN/HPR boundary function).

Similarly, each packet sent from NND back to NNB along the RTP connection will have an ANR routing field that represents the reverse route. The ANR labels of the reverse route consist of:

86 ANR label of link leaving NND
D202 ANR label of link leaving NNC
86 ANR label of destination NCE in NNB

The first ANR label 86 in the reverse route, which represents the link out of NND, is removed by NND before sending out the packet on the link to NNC. NNC strips its first ANR label from the incoming packet, which is D202, before forwarding the packet out on link D202. Finally, the ANR label 86 represents the NCE of the destination endpoint in NNB. There is no conflict between the two ANR labels with value 86 in the reverse route, because they are each interpreted by different nodes.

Note that NNC has a link with an ANR label C5 (NNC to NNG). The first packet was routed through NNC with an ANR routing field that also contains an ANR label C5 for the destination NCE. There is no confusion between the ANR label representing a link in NNC, and the same ANR label representing the NCE in NND. When NNC is performing ANR, it looks only at the first ANR label in the incoming ANR routing field (A107) and so does not see the subsequent ANR label C5 in the routing field.

Note also that each of NNB, NNC and NND have a link with an ANR label D202. Again, this will not cause confusion because the ANR labels along an ANR route have significance only in the node, and not in the entire network.

Finally, the length of the ANR labels is shown in the example as being 1 or 2 bytes (2 or 4 hexadecimal digits) and in some nodes both lengths are used. As long as the labels are unambiguous within a node, there is no problem with having different ANR label lengths. For example, in NNC the ANR label of 81 is allowed, but an ANR label of A1 would not be allowed, because then NNC would not be able to distinguish between it and the link with ANR label of A107.

8.3.5 Transmission Priority

The network layer header contains a transmission priority field that is used by intermediate HPR nodes. Note that in base APPN, intermediate nodes establish session connector control blocks for sessions passing through the node to store, among other information, the transmission priorities to be used for the particular sessions. There is then no need to carry the transmission priority in the (FID2) header of every packet. HPR intermediate nodes (as intermediate nodes in subarea INN routing) have no session awareness, and hence the transmission priority has to be marked in every packet.

The transmission priority field specifies one of the four values: network, high, medium, or low. The network priority is reserved for control traffic such as topology database updates and directory searches. The setting of the priority field in the network layer header for LU-LU sessions comes from the COS selected by the origin LU. HPR does not change the APPN COS selection, which is described in 5.5.2, "Class of Service (COS)" on page 90.

APPN nodes keep queues for each priority on every link, and higher-priority network layer packets can overtake lower-priority ones. The priority queues will support both ANR and FID2 traffic. To ensure that lower-priority packets are not permanently held in queues while higher-priority traffic is serviced, an aging mechanism can be used on the queues. The aging mechanisms in APPN are implementation-dependent.

8.3.6 ANR and FID2 Routing

HPR nodes can support the routing of network layer packets and FID2 PIUs on the same HPR link (except on links that are part of an HPR multilink transmission group). The first 4 bits of the headers in each case are different and so the DLC supporting the link will be able to tell whether to use ANR or intermediate session routing.

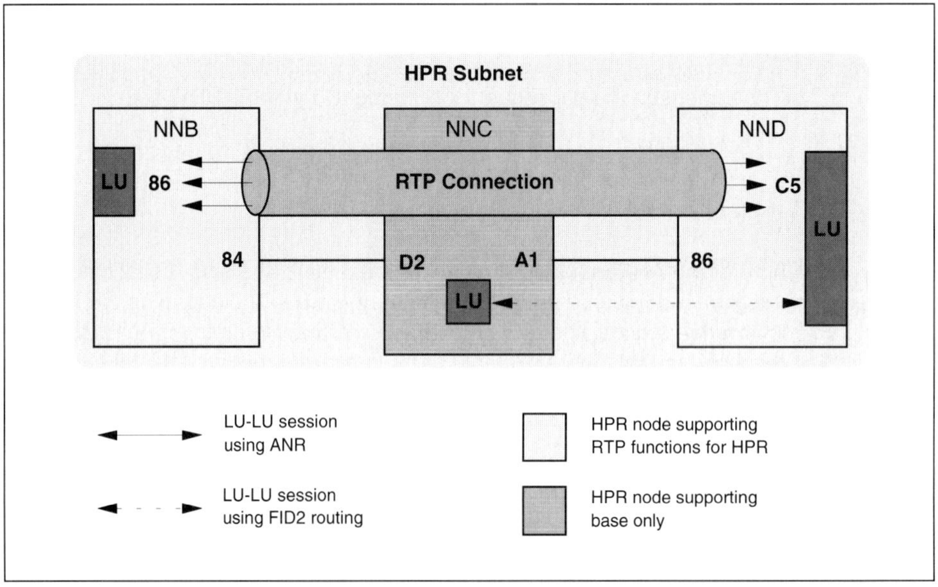

Figure 64. HPR Links Support ANR and FID2 Routing. It is assumed that NNC supports only the HPR base and not the RTP functions for HPR.

If the header indicates a network layer packet, then the DLC will pass control to the ANR component, which inspects the ANR routing field and determines whether to send the packet to a local NCE or outboard on another link. If the header indicates a FID2 PIU, then the DLC will hand over to path control, which then uses the LFSID from the FID2 to select the half-session or session connector (if using APPN intermediate session routing).

Figure 64 on page 172 shows an LU-LU session using FID2 routing that is sharing the HPR link NNC-NND with the RTP connection. The ANR labels 86 in NNB and C5 in NND describe the endpoints of the RTP connection (the LUs' NCE addresses). Note that an LU can support multiple sessions whose routing is done with both HPR and intermediate session routing. The LU does not see any difference between the two types of sessions.

NNC can do ANR for any intermediate LU-LU sessions that pass through the node. However, as NNC does not support the RTP functions for HPR (and the control flows over RTP option) it cannot be the endpoint of RTP connections. So, NNC must use FID2 routing and not network layer packets for the following traffic:

- LU-LU sessions that have an endpoint in NNC
- CP-CP sessions
- Route setup requests

8.4 Rapid-Transport Protocol

Rapid-transport protocol (RTP) is a connection-oriented, full-duplex protocol designed to transport data in high-speed networks. HPR uses RTP connections to transport LU-LU and (optional) CP-CP session traffic. RTP provides reliability, in-order delivery, segmentation and reassembly, and adaptive rate-based flow/congestion control. Because RTP provides these functions on an end-to-end basis, it eliminates the need for these functions on the link level along the path of a connection.

8.4.1 RTP Connections

RTP connections are established in an HPR subnet and are used to transport session traffic. They provide a full-duplex logical connection between two nodes over a specific path through the HPR subnet.

Each RTP connection supports session data for a specific class of service as specified in a BIND. An RTP connection is not used for more than one COS to simplify the nondisruptive path switch process, and also to enforce that all traffic on an RTP connection uses a single transmission priority. A node may activate multiple RTP connections for one COS to the same partner either because there may be an implementation dependent limit on the number of sessions being carried over one RTP connection or because the route selection algorithm tends to evenly distribute sessions over multiple paths that have the same weight (to achieve some load balancing).

All the traffic from one particular session must flow over a single RTP connection in an HPR subnet, and multiple sessions of the same COS will be multiplexed onto one RTP connection. This means that the route setup process is done only once for multiple sessions. RTP connections can be used for traffic in either direction. If an existing RTP connection for the required class of service and the required route already exists, then sessions can be started from either end, regardless of which endpoint activated the RTP connection.

Note that the RTP connection actually is established between two NCEs. Only sessions flowing between these two NCEs may be multiplexed onto their RTP connection.

8.4.1.1 RTP Transport Header

Figure 62 on page 167 shows the format of the network layer packet that flows over an RTP connection. The RTP packet consists of the RTP transport header (THDR) and the data.

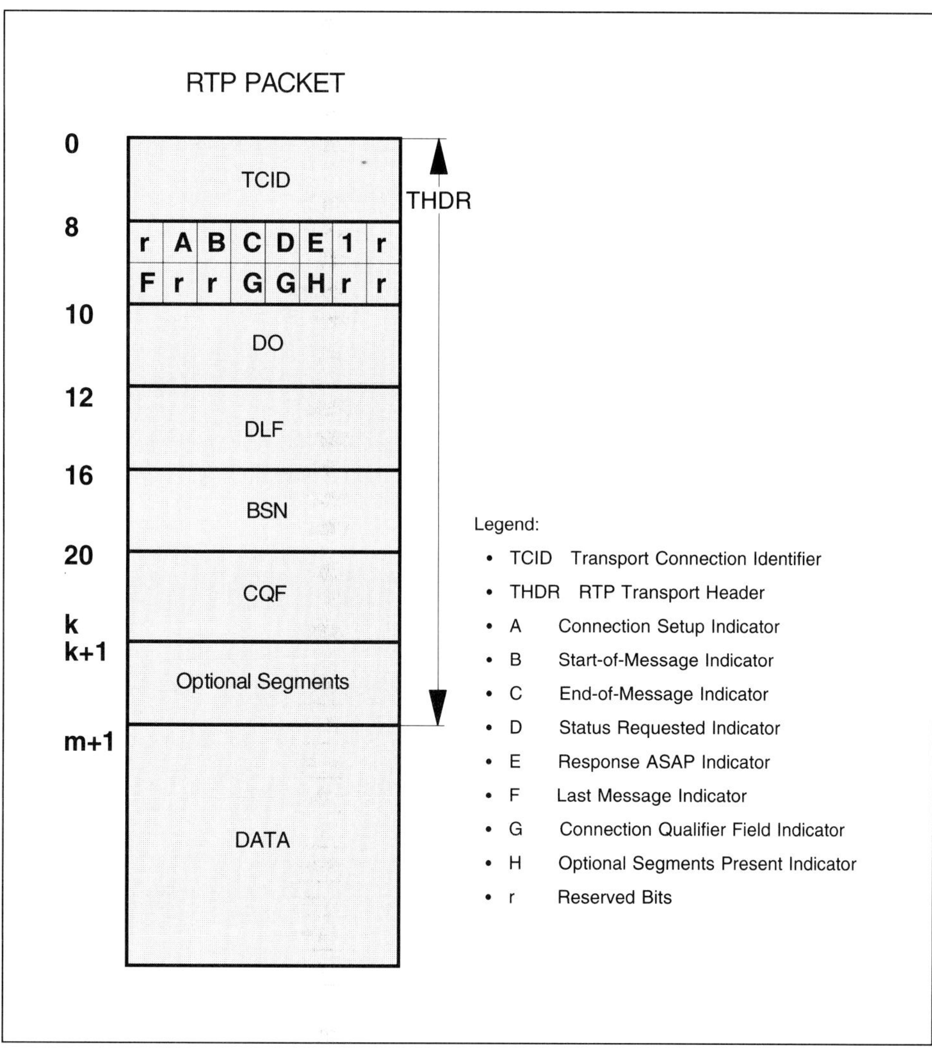

Figure 65. RTP Transport Header Format

The RTP transport header (as shown in Figure 65) contains information necessary for creating and maintaining an RTP connection. The header consists of a main header and optional segments, and all parts are of variable length. The *main RTP transport header* includes the following:

Transport Connection Identifier (TCID)
The TCID identifies an RTP connection in an HPR node, sometimes qualified by a CQF (see below).

Connection Setup Indicator
Used to indicate that a Connection Setup segment is present in the THDR.

Start-of-Message Indicator
Used by RTP for segmenting and reassembly.

End-of-Message Indicator
Used by RTP for segmenting and reassembly.

Status Requested Indicator
Used to request a Status segment (acknowledgment) from the endpoint of the RTP connection.

Respond ASAP Indicator
Used to request that a Status segment be sent immediately.

Retry Indicator
Used to indicate whether the sender will support retransmission. In HPR, the Retry indicator is always set to B'1' indicating that retransmission is supported for all messages.

Last Message Indicator
Used to mark the last message on an RTP connection.

Data Offset (DO) Field
The position of the Data field relative to the beginning of the THDR. This position is always constraint to be a multiple of 4 bytes. The DO field carries the data offset value divided by 4.

Data Length Field (DLF)
The exact number of bytes carried in the Data field.

Byte Sequence Number (BSN)
Each data byte is (conceptually) assigned a sequence number relative to the beginning of the data stream sent over the RTP connection. The BSN field carries the sequence number of the first byte of the Data field. When the Data field is empty (not present), this is the sequence number of the first byte of the next non-empty Data field.

Connection Qualifier (CQF) Field
Used to further identify the node and is used during a nondisruptive path switch. The *optional segments* in the RTP transport header are used to carry control information for the RTP connection and may include:

Connection Setup Segment
The Connection Setup (CS) segment is used to activate an RTP connection.

Status Segment
The Status segment is used to acknowledge data when a response is requested, and it will be piggybacked with user data, if there is any to send. It is also sent as an unsolicited request for retransmission of parts of the data stream after a gap is detected in the data stream.

Connection Identifier Exchange (CIE) Segment
The CIE is used during the RTP connection activation process to exchange a TCID between RTP connection endpoints.

Switching Information (SI) Segment
The Switching Information segment is used to send the route's forward and reverse path information (ANR labels) to the other endpoint during RTP connection activation.

Adaptive Rate-Based (ARB) Segment
The ARB segment is used to exchange ARB control information between the RTP connection endpoints.

Client Out of Band (COB) Segment
The COB segment is used during the deactivation of an RTP connection.

Connection Fault Segment
The Connection Fault segment is used to send sense information to the partner endpoint of an RTP connection when one endpoint detects a protocol violation. Normally, this RTP connection will then be deactivated.

8.4.1.2 RTP Connection Activation

An RTP connection is set up when an HPR node is establishing a session and a suitable RTP connection does not already exist. The requirements for a suitable existing RTP connection are as follows:

- The class of service must be the same.
- The RSCV (or the HPR subnet portion of the RSCV) must be the same.

If no suitable RTP connection exists or no routing information is remembered, the HPR node will go through the route setup process to determine the characteristics of the path to be used (see 8.4.2, "HPR Route Setup" on page 182). The HPR node will then assign its *Transport Connection Identifier* (TCID) for this RTP connection. The HPR nodes at each end of the RTP connection independently assign their TCID for the RTP connection. A TCID has local significance only; when sending data over an RTP connection, the sending node has to include the TCID assigned by the receiving node in the RTP transport header.

An RTP connection is not a session; it does not require a BIND in its own right. The process of sending the Connection Setup segment and exchanging TCIDs, with the appropriate acknowledgments, activates an RTP connection.

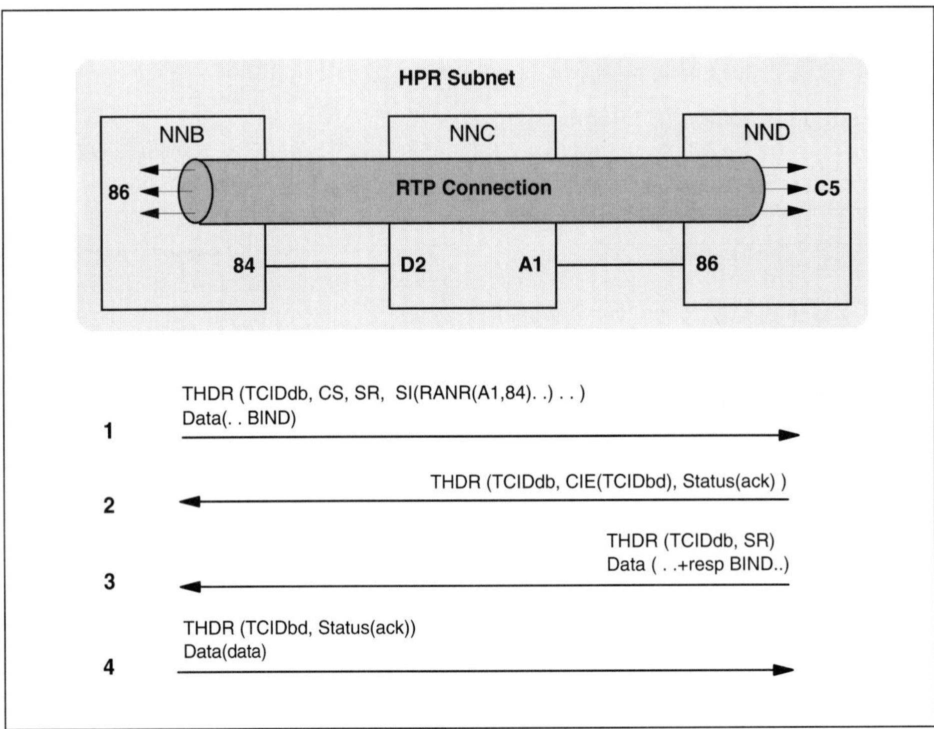

Figure 66. RTP Connection Setup and Session Establishment. Optional segments in the RTP transport header are used to reduce the number of exchanges in RTP.

Figure 66 illustrates the steps involved in RTP connection setup and session establishment, the following list explains these steps. The list items correspond to the numbered items in the figure. These are:

1. The first exchange sets up the RTP connection and may also carry the BIND for the first LU-LU (or CP-CP) session.
   - The RTP transport header contains TCIDdb that NND will subsequently use when it returns traffic to NNB.
   - The presence of the Connection Setup (CS) segment indicates that a new RTP connection is being activated. The Connection Setup segment contains a field for the class-of-service name for the LU-LU session. In the case of RTP connections for CP-CP sessions or route setup requests, this field contains a globally defined name.
   - The Status Requested (SR) message is always requested during connection setup to create an acknowledgment.
   - The SI segment, which includes the reverse ANR (RANR) for the route to be used on all traffic from NND to NNB, is sent to NND in this first exchange.
2. The second exchange is an acknowledgment.

- The TCIDdb value in the RTP transport header is the value that was sent in the first exchange.
- The CIE segment indicates the TCIDbd value, assigned by NND, that NNB should use from now on when sending data to NND on this RTP connection.
- The Status segment acts as acknowledgment for the full RTP packets, including both the RTP connection setup message and the BIND message.

3. The third exchange is sent when the BIND response is available.
   - The Status Requested message is present to request acknowledgment.
4. The fourth exchange is an acknowledgment.
   - This acknowledges the BIND response, and implicitly the receipt of TCIDbd received in exchange 2.
   - The Data field in the packet can contain the first user data of the session if there is anything to send.

If the BIND response is available immediately, it could happen that steps 2 and 3 are combined in one exchange. Thus the RTP connection has been activated, the first session established, and data has begun to flow in only three or four message exchanges.

When the BIND is sent over the RTP connection, the RSCV is transported at the end of the BIND in the usual way. The BIND and the RSCV are transported as data inside the network layer packet. The RTP connection endpoint that sends the BIND (NNB in Figure 66 on page 178) will increase the hop count indicator in the RSCV of the BIND to the end of the HPR subnet. So, the intermediate nodes along the RTP connection do no processing of the BIND, and in fact have no session awareness at all.

The actual endpoints of the RTP connections are the network connection endpoints (NCEs) and not the HPR node or CP. So, multiple RTP connections could exist between the same two nodes to reach different LUs, or different APPN/HPR boundary function instances. The combination of the NCE and the TCID will uniquely identify the endpoint of an RTP connection in an HPR node.

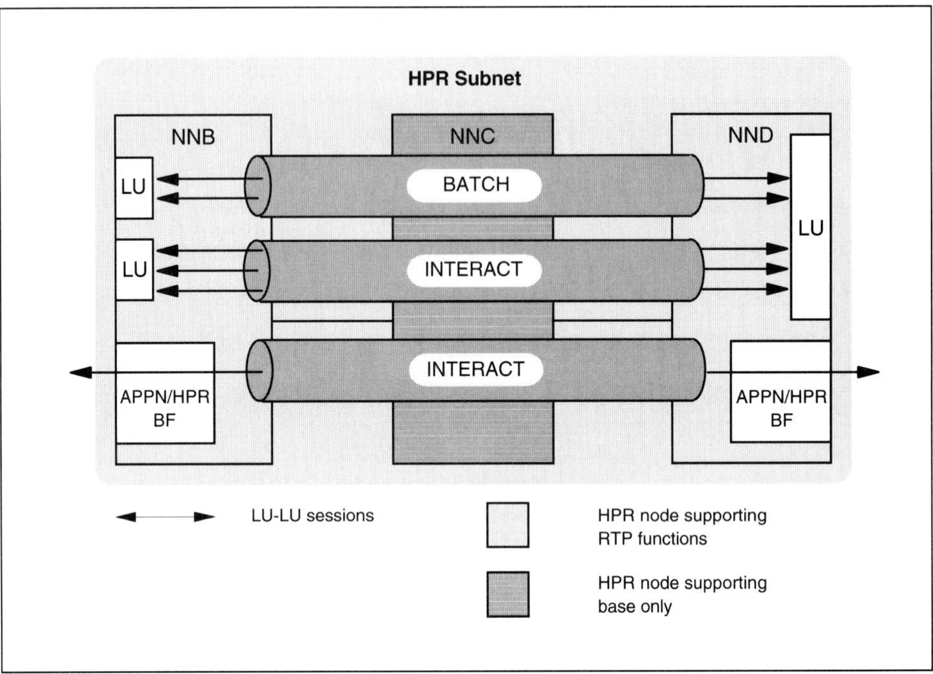

Figure 67. Multiple RTP Connections between Two HPR Nodes. Different classes of service require separate RTP connections.

Figure 67 shows three RTP connections between nodes NNB and NND in the sample network. The first two groups of sessions require separate RTP connections because some are using the class of service INTERACT and some are using class of service BATCH. The third session is also using the class of service INTERACT. However, it is a session that is routed across the HPR subnet between two base-APPN nodes. So, each endpoint of the third RTP connection does not represent an LU but the APPN/HPR boundary function, and as typically this has a separate NCE address (unless a product implementation decides to use the same NCE for both functions), it cannot share the RTP connection used for the other INTERACT traffic.

8.4.1.3 Route Setup RTP Connections

Every HPR (single-link or multilink) TG between HPR nodes that support the control flows over RTP option will have an RTP connection to be used for the route setup protocol. This RTP connection is used for the route setup requests and route setup replies flowing between the two adjacent nodes and stays active as long as the TG is active. It is activated only when needed for a first route setup request to be forwarded over a TG and will never carry a session because the flows between the route setup functions are *connectionless* and do not use CP-CP sessions.

As the links over which the route setup requests flow may not be using link-level error recovery, the route setup RTP connections always request reliable transport. This is done by requesting acknowledgments for the route setup requests and replies. See 8.4.3.2, "Reliable Transport" on page 186 for more details.

8.4.1.4 RTP Connection Deactivation

An RTP connection is deactivated when the number of active, pending-active or pending-deactivate sessions goes to zero. The RTP endpoint that originally activated an RTP connection is initially responsible for deactivating it. The optional Client Out of Band (COB) segment in the RTP transport header is used to deactivate the RTP connection. No data will be carried on these flows, because the UNBINDs for the sessions must have already completed before starting to deactivate the RTP connection.

If the other RTP endpoint is not ready to deactivate the RTP connection, it sends back a COB signal that is then used to pass control for the RTP connection deactivation from one endpoint to the other. This situation might occur if the second endpoint had sent a BIND onto the RTP connection, just as the first endpoint started to deactivate the RTP connection.

8.4.1.5 Enhanced Session Addressing

An enhanced session addressing algorithm has been developed for sessions passing through HPR networks or subnets. This applies to CP-CP sessions and LU-LU sessions. Each CP, LU or APPN/HPR boundary function at the endpoint of an RTP connection will assign a session address that is used to identify traffic received from the session partner. So, each session will have two session addresses, one for each direction.

These addresses are used in the new *FID5 transmission header*. As is shown in Figure 68 on page 182, the FID5 header is very similar to the FID2 header with the new session addresses replacing the existing OAF, DAF and ODAI addresses that make up the LFSID. The PLU (or the boundary function at the primary side) will assign its session address first and this will be sent to the SLU (or the boundary function at the secondary side) in the FID5 header on the BIND request for the session. This session address is then used (in the FID5 TH) by the secondary side when sending session traffic (BIND response, session traffic, etc.). The SLU (or boundary function at the secondary side), after receiving the BIND, will assign its session address (to be used by the primary side when sending session traffic) and will send this to the primary side in a new Session Address control vector on the BIND response.

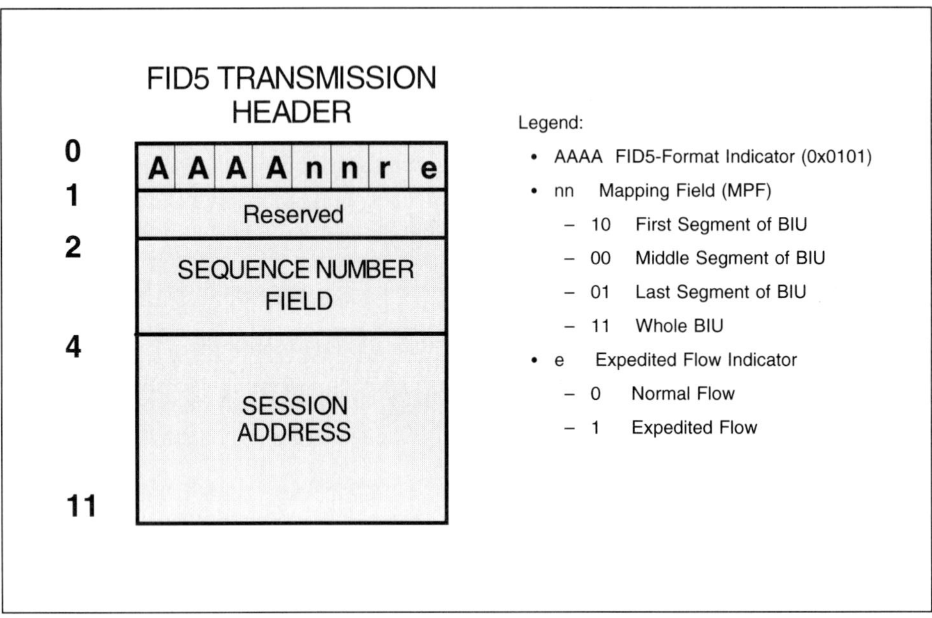

Figure 68. FID5 Transmission Header Format

The session addresses apply to this session only and can be reused after the session has been deactivated. As multiple sessions of the same class of service can use the same RTP connection, the session addresses must be unique for each RTP connection in an HPR node.

When a message is passed to the endpoint of an RTP connection, RTP uses the enhanced session address from the FID5 header to decide which half-session or session connector to pass it to.

8.4.2 HPR Route Setup

The route setup protocol is initiated to obtain information about a route between HPR nodes, prior to establishing an RTP connection. The protocol consists of a route setup request and a route setup reply, and the messages flow over the exact path that is to be used for the session.

HPR does not change the APPN route calculation process. An HPR node that supports the RTP functions for HPR will inspect the RSCV that is included in the BIND at session activation time. This will be done either by the HPR node that contains the PLU, or the first HPR node (the APPN/HPR boundary function) along the session activation path. To activate an RTP connection between two HPR nodes, both nodes must support the RTP functions for HPR. So the HPR node that is inspecting the BIND will csan the RSCV looking for the first non-HPR capable link, and sends the route setup to the last RTP-capable node found before finding the non-HPR link.

The HPR node then performs the route setup protocol to find out the routing information for the HPR subnet. A route setup request is sent to the last node along the path that supports the RTP functions for HPR, which is part of the contiguous HPR subnet. The route setup requests do not flow on sessions. Every HPR node has a route setup function, and the route setup requests and route setup replies flow as GDS variables, hop by hop through the network between the route setup functions. The route setup function in an HPR node knows the address to be used for the adjacent route setup function from the XID3.

The RSCV that was calculated for the LU-LU session is also used to navigate the route setup request through the HPR subnet. The part of the RSCV that describes the path through the HPR subnet (including the TG control vector that describes the hop leaving the HPR subnet) is carried in the route setup request to indicate to each route setup function along the HPR subnet that TGs and nodes are to be used. Thus, the route setup request flows along the same path that the LU-LU session will use over its RTP connection.

Figure 69 on page 184 shows the sample network with the route setup RTP connections that are used for the route setup protocol. If NNB receives an incoming BIND from an adjacent APPN node that is destined for NNC, then NNB inspects the RSCV attached to the BIND and finds that the next link is an HPR link. It then looks at the next node and finds that NNC is an HPR node. However, NNC is also the last node in the RSCV and, as it does not support the HPR RTP functions for HPR, it cannot be the endpoint of an RTP connection. So an RTP connection cannot be used for this session and thus NNB will provide normal intermediate session routing for the session.

If NNB receives an incoming BIND from an adjacent APPN node that is destined for NND, then NNB inspects the RSCV attached to the BIND and finds that the next link is an HPR link. It then looks at the next node and finds that NNC is an HPR node. The next link is another HPR link and the final node NND is an HPR node. NND does support the RTP functions for HPR, and can be the endpoint of an RTP connection. So an RTP connection will be used for this session and NND will go through the route setup protocol.

If two adjacent HPR nodes support the HPR control flows over RTP option (in addition to the RTP functions for HPR), then the route setup requests will flow over an RTP connection (the route setup RTP connection), and will use network layer packets. If the nodes do not both support the control flows over RTP option, then the route setup requests will use FID2 PIUs. If the HPR subnet contains a mixture of HPR nodes with and without the HPR control flows over RTP option, the route setup request will use both network layer packets and FID2 PIUs on the different hops through the subnetwork.

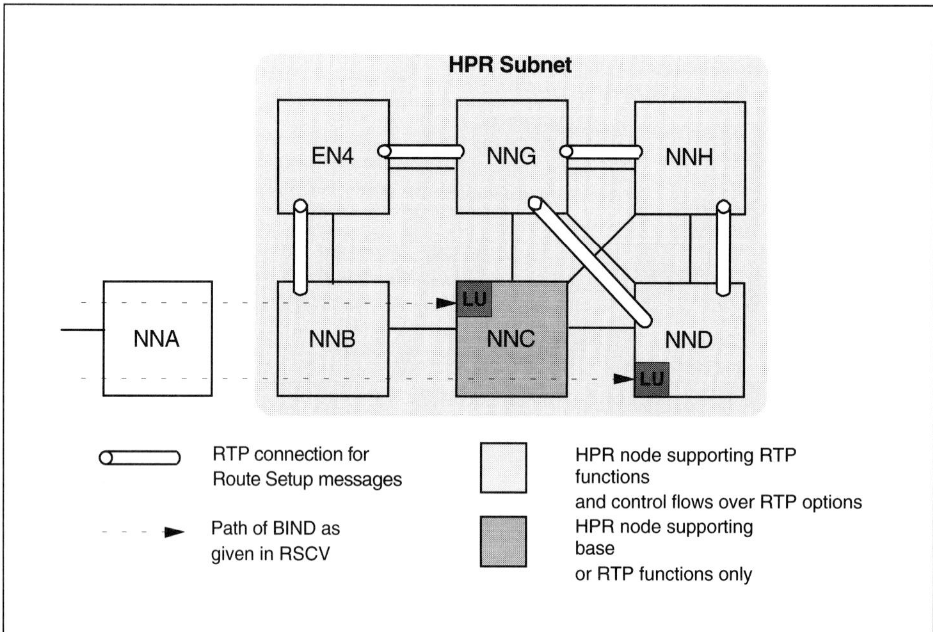

Figure 69. Route Setup Protocol in an HPR Subnet

In the two examples in Figure 69, the route setup messages will flow as FID2 PIUs because NNC is a base HPR node and does not support the control flows over RTP option. In both cases, the route setup messages flow over the same route that the LU-LU session will take.

The route setup protocol will find out various pieces of information about the path to be used for an RTP connection:

- The ANR labels of the links to be used in both directions along the path.
- The maximum packet size of each link along the route, so that a minimum maximum value for end-to-end segmentation can be calculated.
- Whether an MLTG exists along the path.
- If the endpoint of the RTP connection is an APPN/HPR boundary function, rather than an LU, then the NCE address is learned at this time.

When the information in the route setup reply is received, the new RTP connection can be activated.

Figure 70 on page 185 shows how the route setup protocol passes along the path of the RTP connection to be set up between NNB and NND. The forward ANR labels are added to the route setup request and the reverse ANR labels are added to the route setup reply. Other information, such as maximum packet size, is also collected as the messages flow through the network.

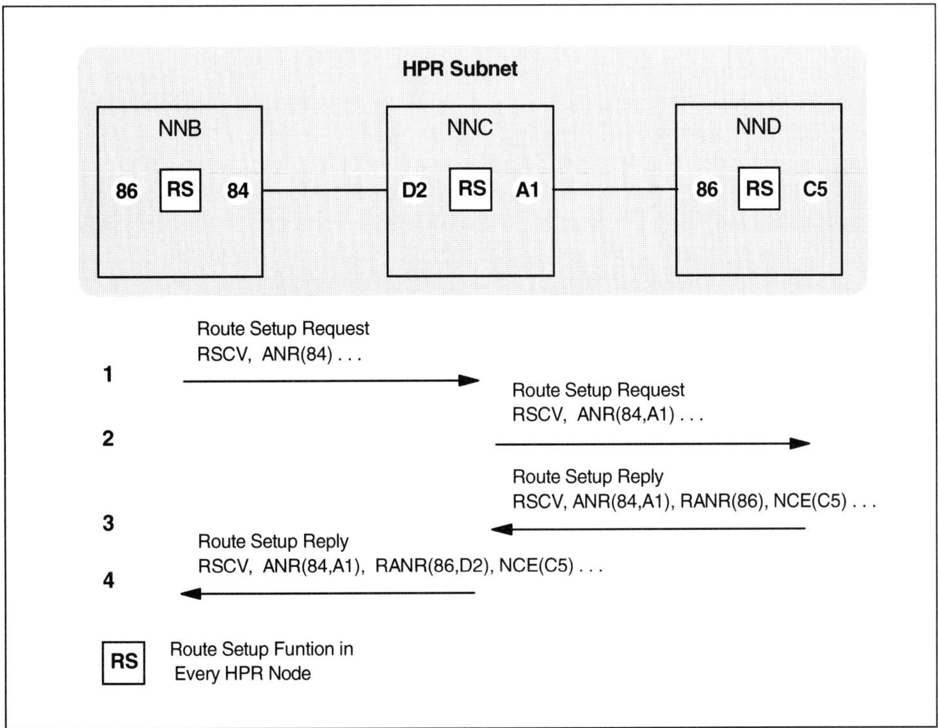

Figure 70. HPR Route Setup

When the route setup reply is received by NNB, the destination NCE addresses are added to the ANR and reverse ANR label strings to complete the ANR routing fields. In the reply, NNB will find the maximum packet size to be used for the RTP connection and the segment size is chosen. The RTP connection can then be activated (see 8.4.1.2, “RTP Connection Activation” on page 177).

8.4.3 RTP End-to-End Protocols

RTP enhances the performance across an HPR subnet by performing many functions on an end-to-end basis over an RTP connection, instead of on a hop-by-hop basis as in base APPN.

8.4.3.1 RTP End-to-End Error Recovery

In base APPN, error recovery is done on every link. When using higher-speed links with lower error rates, this is no longer necessary; therefore, base HPR supports links where no link-level error recovery is done. But even when no link-level error recovery is used, the cyclic redundancy check (CRC) in the link trailer is checked and a packet will be discarded if an error is detected. To allow for the possibility of no link-level error recovery, HPR nodes at the endpoints of RTP connections always do end-to-end error recovery.

RTP uses a byte sequence numbering protocol for the life of an RTP connection. That means that a packet is identified by the byte sequence number of the first user data byte in that packet counted from the beginning of the data stream on this RTP connection. The byte sequence number and the length of user data of a packet are included in the THDR and used by the receiver to calculate the byte sequence number of the next packet to be expected. If the byte sequence number of the next received packet is higher than expected, then the receiver knows that there is a gap in the data stream received, but does not know how many packets are missing (there are no packet sequence numbers in RTP). When an RTP connection endpoint detects a gap in an incoming byte stream, it uses the optional Status segment to inform the sender of the byte sequence number of the first packet missing (that is, the first byte of the gap). This then allows the sender to begin retransmitting from the start of the gap.

RTP supports *selective retransmission.* So, rather than requesting retransmission of *all* packets following the start of the gap (as would be necessary with the window mechanism in base APPN), the receiver indicates in the Status segment the length of the gap and also supports indicating multiple gaps (support of at least two gaps is required in HPR). The sender then will retransmit only those packets that are missing in the data stream.

8.4.3.2 Reliable Transport

All APPN traffic is carried reliably over RTP connections. The Retry indicator and the Status Requested indicator in the RTP transport header and the associated acknowledgments are used to provide this reliability.

Retry Indicator

The Retry indicator is set in the RTP transport header to indicate that the sender can retransmit data if it is not successfully received. The sender keeps a copy of unacknowledged data in its send buffers for the RTP connection, so that it can be resent if necessary.

Status Requested Indicator

The Status Requested indicator is set in the RTP transport header when the sender wishes to get an acknowledgment of data previously transmitted. If a positive acknowledgment is received, the sender can then flush out the copies of data in its send buffers. An RTP connection endpoint can decide to request acknowledgments for various reasons:

- There is no more data to send (that is, the send queue is empty). This ensures that the loss of the last packet(s) sent can immediately be detected.
- The send buffers allocated to this RTP connection are depleted or are becoming depleted. This is done to allow the sender to free the buffers

of those packets that have been successfully received. The status should be requested early enough to allow continuous transmission on the connection.

- An ARB rate request is included in the THDR of the packet. See Chapter 9, "Adaptive Rate-Based Flow/Congestion Control" on page 217 for more information.

When a packet is received that includes a status request, the receiver responds immediately by sending a Status segment. The Status segment is included in the THDR of the next user data packet (piggybacked) if any such data is queued. If no user data is queued, a packet with the Status segment is sent without any user data.

8.4.3.3 RTP Segmentation and Reassembly

RTP connections may traverse a series of HPR links and nodes, and each link in the path may have a different maximum BTU size. APPN intermediate session routing provides segmentation over each APPN link to handle this. However, in HPR, the RTP connection endpoints will perform segmentation and reassembly for the whole RTP connection on an end-to-end basis.

The RTP connection endpoints learn the maximum BTU size of each link on the selected path during the route setup process. The smallest value of all the maximum BTU sizes is taken and referred to as the *minimum maximum link size*. RTP will segment all messages that are to use an RTP connection into segments of the minimum maximum link size of the connection. Each segment includes a network layer header, an RTP transport header and portions of the data. The receiving RTP connection endpoint is responsible for reassembly of the segments. The RTP transport header indicates the first, middle or last segment of a message.

If the RTP connection path is altered due to a nondisruptive path switch, RTP will be informed of the new minimum maximum link size and will change the segment size for the RTP connection accordingly.

8.4.3.4 RTP Resequencing

RTP was designed to operate in connection-oriented networks, and so it expects the network to deliver data in sequence. A packet out of sequence is therefore considered to be an error. However, when using multilink transmission groups (MLTGs), it is very likely that packets will arrive out of sequence, because packet sizes will vary and also because the line speeds in an MLTG can be different. HPR nodes perform ANR routing only and, in contrast with subarea SNA, will not perform resequencing at the end of the MLTG. Packets will get out of sequence at the end of the MLTG and will be transported out of sequence to the RTP connection endpoint. The RTP receiver would normally interpret this as a gap in the data stream and request retransmission from the sender.

To avoid unnecessary retransmissions, RTP handles the MLTG case by delaying the error recovery process. The presence of an MLTG on the path of an RTP connection is detected during the route setup process. If a packet then arrives out of sequence, RTP will wait a period of time that is governed by the Re-FIFO timer (see 8.4.5.3, "Re-FIFO Timer" on page 194) before the normal error recovery is started, allowing time to fill any gaps caused by the MLTG(s).

8.4.3.5 Flow/Congestion Control

HPR uses no hop-by-hop flow control mechanism to regulate the traffic of RTP connections. For HPR, a new adaptive rate-based (ARB) flow and congestion control algorithm was developed (see Chapter 9, "Adaptive Rate-Based Flow/Congestion Control" on page 217).

8.4.3.6 Adaptive Session-Level Pacing in HPR

In HPR, multiple sessions requesting the same class of service are multiplexed over one RTP connection. The ARB mechanism will provide fairness between multiple RTP connections crossing a single link or node. However, the ARB algorithm cannot provide fairness at the session level.

HPR uses the existing adaptive session-level pacing mechanism to provide fairness among the multiple sessions that use a single RTP connection. This will stop one session from using resources such as buffers unfairly compared to the other sessions on the RTP connection. Adaptive session-level pacing for a session that crosses an HPR subnet is done between the half-sessions that represent the LUs, and the RTP connection appears as a one-hop *virtual link*. If an RTP connection endpoint is an APPN/HPR boundary function, then it does adaptive session-level pacing with an adjacent APPN node in the same way as base APPN (see 8.9.1, "APPN/HPR Boundary Function" on page 211).

8.4.4 Nondisruptive Path Switch

The HPR nondisruptive path switch function is used to automatically route RTP connections around failed links or nodes. This function operates only in an HPR subnet, and not within or across a base-APPN subnet. When a failure occurs and an HPR-only alternate path exists that satisfies the requested class of service (COS), the traffic of the RTP connection using the failed path is rerouted over the new alternate path in a manner that is transparent to the sessions being carried over the RTP connection.

If the original HPR path recovers before a path switch occurs, then the path will not be switched.

Figure 71 on page 189 shows a failure in a sample network on the link between NNC and NND.

Which RTP partner initiates the path switch depends on the partner types. *Mobile* partners prefer to initiate a path switch, whereas *stationary* partners yield to the partner's wishes. There are then three possible combinations:

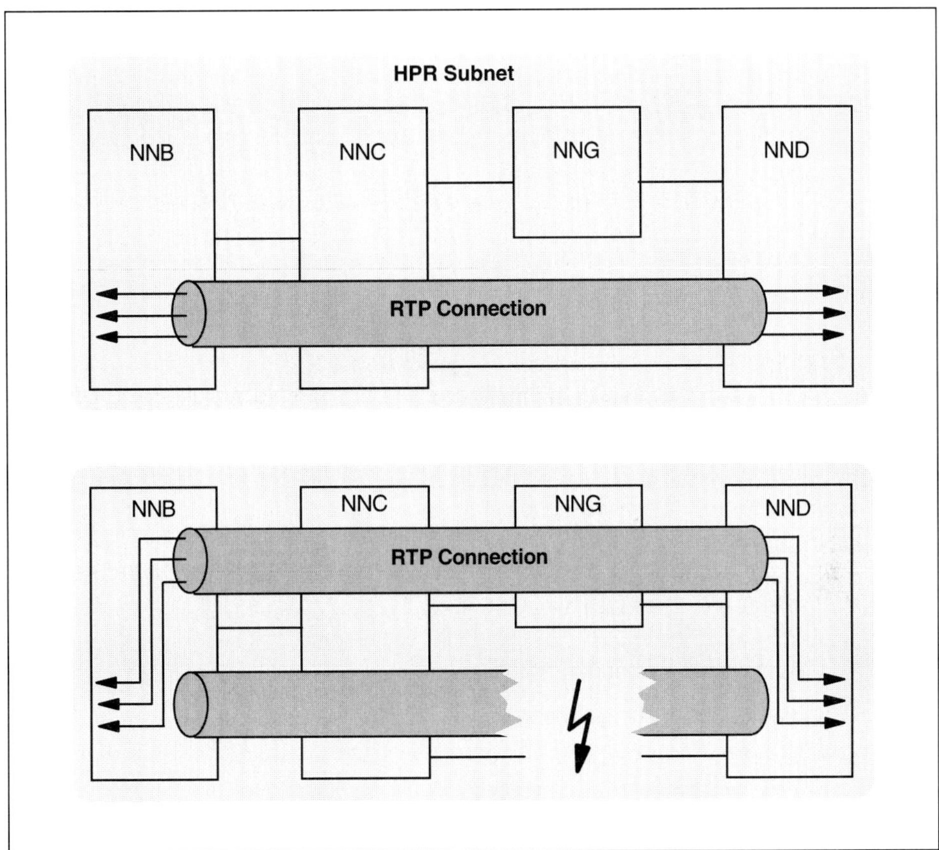

Figure 71. Nondisruptive Path Switch in an HPR Subnet

- If both partners are stationary or both are mobile, either partner may initiate a path switch.
- If one partner is stationary and the other is mobile, then:
  - Only the mobile partner initiates the path switch when a connection failure is detected.
  - Either partner may initiate the path switch in the other cases described in the next section.

The RTP origin (the node that initiates the RTP connection) communicates its type (mobile or stationary) during RTP connection setup in the Switching Information (SI) segment. The RTP destination communicates its type in the route setup reply.

8.4.4.1 Path Switch Triggers

Various circumstances can trigger a nondisruptive path switch:

RTP connection failure detection

If a message is sent requesting an acknowledgment and the Short-Request timer expires before a reply is received, the sender attempts to determine whether the partner is still reachable. (See 8.4.5.2, "Short-Request Timer" on page 193 for a description of the Short-Request timer.) A state exchange message is sent including the status of the sender and asking for the status of the receiver. If the Short-Request timer expires again for this message it is retried until the retry limit is reached. Finally the sender concludes that the connection has failed and triggers a path switch.

Support for this trigger is required in all nodes implementing the RTP functions for HPR.

Local link failure

If a local link being used by an RTP connection fails, it may trigger a path switch. This allows RTP connections to be switched faster than waiting for each RTP connection on a link to time out individually.

Support of this trigger is optional.

Remote link failure

If a TDU is received indicating that a remote link used by an RTP connection has failed, this may trigger a path switch. This can happen only when the local node is an NN (ENs don't receive TDUs) and for RTP connections that end in NNs (ENs don't send TDUs).

Support of this trigger is optional.

Operator request

The node operator or a network management operator requests that the path be switched. This request may be done for a specific path. This function is especially useful for switching an RTP connection back to its original path after a nondisruptive path switch has occurred and once the original path is operational again.

Support of this trigger is optional.

Automatic time interval switch

After a certain (network administrator definable) time period, an attempt is made to obtain a path that has a lesser weight as calculated by the TRS route selection algorithm. If a better path is available, the RTP connection is switched to it. Investigation of this path switch trigger is still in progress.

Support of this trigger is optional.

8.4.4.2 Path Switch Timer

Once it is determined that a path switch needs to be done, a path switch timer is started. This timer indicates the time allowed to accomplish the switch. If this timer expires and the path has not been successfully switched, the RTP connection is deemed to have failed.

The path switch timer time-out value is usually associated with the transmission priority. Suggested timer default values for each priority are:

- 1 minute for network priority
- 2 minutes for high priority
- 4 minutes for medium priority
- 8 minutes for low priority

Note that the use of a path switch timer handles the case where a path switch is attempted before the TDU, indicating the link failure that caused the path loss has arrived in all nodes. In this case, the same (bad) route might be calculated again and the RTP retries will fail again. This procedure could be repeated several times before the TDU arrives and a good path can be calculated. For this reason, products may find it desirable to wait between path switch attempts.

Nondisruptive path switch can be disabled by setting the path switch timer to a value of zero. In this case, RTP will not attempt a path switch when the RTP connection fails.

8.4.4.3 Obtaining a New Path

When an attempt is made to obtain a new path for an RTP connection during a path switch, the new path has to be an *HPR-only* path (that is, a path between the two RTP endpoints that contains only HPR-capable links supporting ANR routing). New paths are represented by RSCVs (just as in base APPN). Obtaining a new path may involve some or all of the following functions:

Directory search
: The target resource used for directory searches is always the CP name of the remote RTP partner. A new indicator on the directory search request specifies that an HPR-only path is requested.

RSCV calculation
: All HPR NN servers (NNs that support the HPR base function) can calculate HPR-only paths. Route selection services will select the *lowest-weight HPR-only route*. If there are two possible routes for the required class of service, one that passes into a base-APPN subnet and one that only uses the HPR subnet, then the HPR subnet route will be selected, even if the weight is higher.

  Note that if an HPR EN is connected to both an HPR NN and to a base-APPN NN, but the base-APPN NN happens to be its NN server, the request to obtain an HPR-only path might fail because the base-APPN NN does not understand the request to calculate an HPR-only path. The EN then has to check whether the path is indeed HPR-only, if it is not the RTP connection is failed. HPR-only paths can be recognized by examining the returned RSCV to see if all the links in the RSCV are HPR capable.

Route setup protocol
: The route setup must always be performed to obtain information for the new path.

8.4.5 Timers

RTP maintains a number of timers that are used by the different functions necessary to ensure proper operation of an RTP connection. This section describes the use and purpose of the different timers.

8.4.5.1 Alive Timer

The Alive timer is used to check that both endpoints of an RTP connection and the path between the two endpoints are still operational after a period of inactivity. When this timer expires and no packet has arrived from the partner since it was last started, a packet with a Status Request indicator will be sent and the Short-Request timer will be started. If a Status segment is received (that is, the RTP connection is still operational) the Short-Request timer is stopped. When the Short-Request timer expires, the status request is retransmitted. If after a (user-defined) number of retransmissions no answer is received, a nondisruptive path switch will be initiated to find a new path for this RTP connection. If the partner is not operational or there is no suitable path to the partner, the sender will eventually terminate the RTP connection.

The main purpose of the Alive timer is to detect hung conditions, that is, to recover from link failures on the path of an RTP connection, or to clean up an RTP connection when the partner is no longer operational. A second purpose is to keep limited-resource links active. Limited-resource links are automatically deactivated in HPR, when no traffic flows over them for a specified period of time (link deactivation timer period). In order to keep these links active while RTP connections are using them, traffic must flow to keep the link deactivation timer from expiring. If there is no user data traffic, RTP uses a liveness message, which is sent at intervals set by the Alive timer. After the last RTP connection using a limited-resource link is deactivated, no RTP liveness messages flow and the link will be disconnected upon expiration of the link deactivation timer.

The following describes how the Alive timer is used for different types of RTP connections:

RTP connection for CP-CP or LU-LU sessions with no limited-resource links along the path

The Alive timer is used to detect a hung condition and, upon detection, trigger a path switch. The Alive timer value may be dependent on COS and transmission priority, or there may be one value used for all RTP connections ending in a node. The default value for the Alive timer is 3 minutes but may be overridden by the network administrator.

RTP connection for CP-CP or LU-LU sessions with one or more limited-resource links along the path

The Alive timer is used both to detect a hung condition and to keep limited-resource links active. The recommended default value for this case is 45 seconds but may be overridden by the network administrator. It is advisable that the limited-resource timer for a link not be made too small because of the possibility that the timer may expire and the link be deactivated before the RTP connection is set up.

When the route setup protocol is performed, the smallest limited-resource timer is obtained for the entire path and is used by the RTP endpoints to govern the sending of RTP liveness messages. The RTP endpoints set the value of the Alive timer to one half of the smallest limited-resource timer returned in the route setup reply.

RTP connection for route setup

Liveness messages are never sent on these connections. These RTP connections are one-hop between adjacent nodes only. They are activated over each link and are deactivated when the link is taken down. There is no path switch done for those connections and thus the Alive timer is not needed to detect a hung condition. In addition, a route setup connection should not keep limited-resource links active.

8.4.5.2 Short-Request Timer

The Short-Request timer is used to perform error recovery. When a sender of a packet requesting status (acknowledgment) receives no response within a Short-Request timer interval, the sender will initiate a state exchange. If after a number of retries (default is 6), there is still no response, the sender will initiate a nondisruptive path switch.

The Short-Request timer is initialized to 1 second ($SRTT_0 = 1$) when the connection setup message is sent or received. After the connection has been established the Short-Request timer is estimated dynamically based on an algorithm widely used in TCP/IP networks to estimate the round-trip delay. This algorithm is adapted for RTP and works as follows:

- Sample the round-trip delay each time a status request is sent. This is done by marking the time S_i when a status request is sent. When the associated status response is received at time R_i, the round-trip delay obtained as $RTT_i = R_i - S_i$.

  Note that as a result of the ARB algorithm, status requests are sent at least periodically every time an ARB rate request is sent (see Chapter 9, "Adaptive Rate-Based Flow/Congestion Control" on page 217).

- Use exponential filtering to smooth the round-trip time. Let $SRRT_{i+1}$ be the smoothed round-trip time at time $i+1$, then $SRTT_{i+1} = \alpha \times SRTT_i + (1 - \alpha) \times RTT_{i+1}$, where ($SRTT_0 = 1$). The parameter α ($\alpha \leq 1$) is used here to determine how quickly we want to adapt to changes in *RTTs* with respect to past estimates of *SRTT*.

- Set the Short-Request timer to be $\beta \times SRTT_i$ with $\beta \geq 1$. SRTT is essentially the median of the round-trip time and β takes into account the variance.

- Use an exponential back-off mechanism when a time-out occurs, that is, double the Short-Request timer for every retry until an RTP state exchange completes successfully. The Short-Request timer will then be set to the timer period it has when the state exchange finally succeeds. It will be dynamically adjusted again based on the conditions of the path.

  When the number of retries is high, this exponential back-off could result in a high value for the Short-Request timer, leading to an unacceptably long time until a nondisruptive path switch is initiated. For this reason, the Short-Request timer should not exceeded four times the Short-Request timer period used before the first time-out occurs. That means that if the number of retries is six, the third through sixth retries will use the same Short-Request timer period as the one computed for the second retry.

The factors α and β are set to 0.875 and 2, respectively. Studies have shown that these values are quite effective in estimating the round-trip delay in networks without requiring a lot of overhead (the calculations can be done with shift and add operations). In HPR, the mechanism used for flow control and congestion avoidance is ARB, rather than the time-outs (based on round-trip delay) used by other protocols like TCP/IP. Additional overhead is not necessary to get a more accurate estimate of the round-trip delay.

8.4.5.3 Re-FIFO Timer

The Re-FIFO timer defines the time period that the RTP receiver waits, delaying error recovery procedures, when a gap is detected in the data stream and there are one or more multilink transmission groups on the path of the RTP connection. The value for the Re-FIFO timer should be configurable by the network administrator, because it is dependent on the link speeds of the multilink transmission groups. The optimum values vary with the speed of the slowest links within any multilink transmission group (the slower the links, the larger the optimum Re-FIFO timer period).

The default value for the Re-FIFO timer is ten times the value of the Short-Request timer. (Note that this value varies throughout the life of an RTP connection because the Short-Request timer changes dynamically.) This relatively large value will handle almost all types of MLTGs, including those where the disparity of link speeds is high.

8.4.5.4 Path Switch Timer

The Path Switch timer is used to monitor the length of time that RTP should attempt a nondisruptive path switch for an RTP connection upon detecting its failure. 8.4.4, "Nondisruptive Path Switch" on page 188 describes the path switch mechanism and the Path Switch timer in detail.

8.4.5.5 Dally Timer

The Dally timer is used by an RTP endpoint to make sure that its partner receives the last acknowledgment that it sent. Once the timer expires, the connection context can be safely released or reused for a new connection. The Dally timer is based on the Short-Request timer that is associated with the RTP connection and with the number of retries *K*. Its value is set to *Dally timer* $= K \times (4 \times$ *Short-Request timer)*.

8.5 Configuration Services

Configuration Services in HPR nodes basically works the same as in base APPN. There are only a few additions necessary to support HPR specifics.

8.5.1 HPR Data Link Control

HPR is an enhancement to APPN and can operate over links supported by base APPN. Therefore, hardware adapters and DLCs currently being used for APPN can be used for HPR. The actual DLCs supported for HPR is a product implementation decision.

8.5.1.1 Maximum Packet Size

The maximum packet size supported for any HPR link frame must be at least 768 bytes. The NHDR and THDR cannot be segmented; therefore the supported maximum packet size on any link must accommodate the largest possible (within reason) NHDR/THDR combination. The size of the NHDR depends on the number of hops (TGs) and the size of the ANR labels used. The largest possible THDR is the one used when activating an RTP connection. A maximum packet size of 512 bytes would satisfy the above in almost all cases, but would not leave much space for future expansion. The maximum packet size of at least 768 bytes bytes was therefore chosen to ensure that route setup requests and replies are never segmented.

Because any given network layer packet has to be able to be sent over any link in an HPR multilink transmission group, the maximum packet size must be the same for all links within an MLTG.

8.5.1.2 HPR Link Formats

Some changes are required in the link header to support traffic with no link-level error recovery. This is discussed in more detail in 8.5.6, "Link Data Traffic" on page 203. The link trailer is unchanged and contains the frame check sequence field that is the result of cyclic redundancy checking (CRC). The CRC applies to both the link header and the packet. On HPR links that are not using link-level error recovery, the CRC is the only integrity check and is therefore always required in HPR.

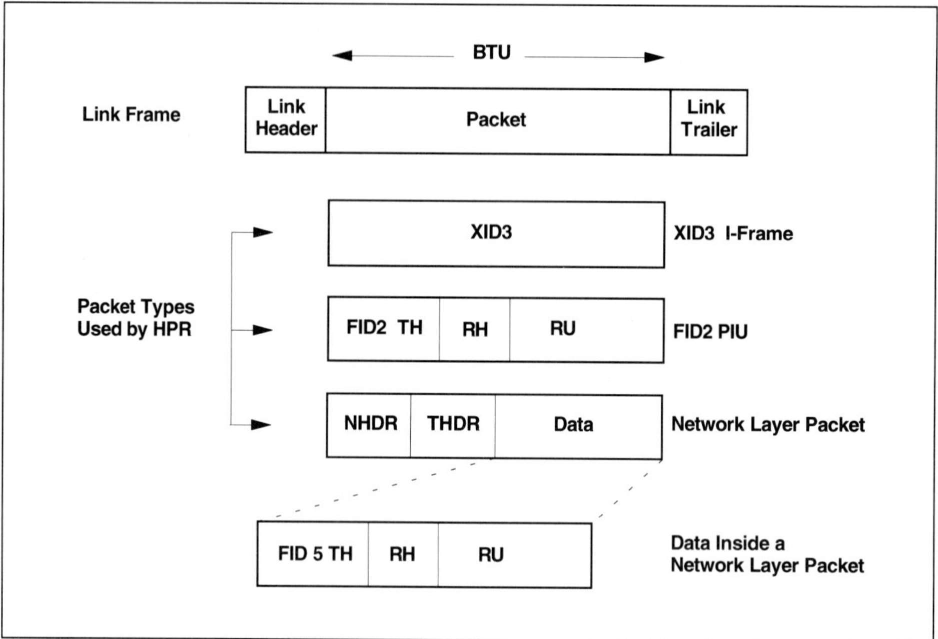

Figure 72. HPR Packet Formats

Figure 72 shows the different packet types that are used by HPR. Each of these is discussed below:

XID3 I-Frame
The XID3 format is similar to the existing format, with the addition of a new HPR Capabilities control vector.

FID2 PIU
FID2 PIUs are still supported in HPR and the structure of them is exactly the same as in base APPN. HPR uses FID2 PIUs in the following circumstances:

- LU-LU sessions transported using intermediate session routing (not HPR)
- CP-CP sessions between nodes that do not both support the HPR control flows over RTP option
- Route setup requests between nodes that do not both support the HPR control flows over RTP option

Network Layer Packet
The new network layer packet is used by HPR when doing ANR for an RTP connection. Two new headers are used in HPR for ANR and to control the RTP connection:

NHDR
This is the network layer header that contains the ANR routing information.

THDR
This is the RTP transport header that contains the RTP transport information.

The data inside a network layer packet can itself be of two types:

- LU-LU or CP-CP session traffic. This session traffic will use a new FID5 transmission header in place of the base APPN FID2 header.
- Route Setup messages in the form of GDS variables.

An HPR node can support ANR and FID2 routing on the same HPR link. This support is part of the base HPR function.

8.5.2 Limited Resource

HPR nodes support limited-resource links (see 4.2.2.2, "Switched and Nonswitched" on page 58 for a description of the existing APPN support). HPR nodes that contain the RTP connection endpoints have session awareness and can deactivate limited-resource links based on session usage.

HPR network nodes can also act as intermediate nodes doing ANR routing. HPR intermediate nodes have no session awareness and so cannot use the existing support to deactivate limited-resource links. So, HPR nodes will deactivate a limited-resource link when *both* the following are true:

- No known sessions are using the link (as FID2 sessions may still be supported over an HPR link).
- No traffic has used the link for a certain period of time.

8.5.3 HPR Connection Network Support

An RTP connection that supports LU-LU sessions can pass over a connection network. In base APPN, the TG that describes the link across the connection network to the real partner node is set up at session activation time. If an HPR route setup request needs to pass over a connection network, the TG to the real partner node is required. This means that the TG needs to be activated earlier in the session establishment process for HPR.

The TG across the connection network is activated at route setup time. After the TG is activated, and if both nodes connected by the TG support the HPR control flows over RTP option, a long-lived RTP connection is established between the real nodes. If at least one node does not support the HPR control flows over RTP option, then FID2 packets are used to forward the route setup request. In either case, the route setup request is sent to the real partner node, and the ANR labels of the link are added at this time. For more details, see 8.4.2, "HPR Route Setup" on page 182.

Note that the dial information to establish the direct link to the real partner node is used only when activating the TG, just as in base APPN. This dial information is obtained from the RSCV as in base APPN, only now it is carried in the route setup request. Once the link is activated the route setup RTP connection could be established across the link (if both adjacent nodes support the control flows over RTP option) and the route setup request is forwarded over the link.

8.5.4 Multilink Transmission Groups

A multilink transmission group (MLTG) consists of multiple DLC-level connections between two nodes made to appear to higher layers as a single connection. An MLTG is available for service as long as one or more of its constituent links are available. See 1.3, “Transmission Groups” on page 8 for explanations of the transmission group terminology.

Multilink transmission groups are supported in traditional subarea SNA networks and in APPN HPR networks, but not in base APPN.

Although superficially similar to multilink transmission groups in subarea networks, MLTGs in APPN HPR networks are significantly different in operation. This section describes HPR MLTGs.

8.5.4.1 HPR MLTG Requirements

Multilink transmission groups (MLTGs) have advantages over single-link TGs and parallel TGs in a number of cases:

Where the traffic demand can exceed existing TG capacity

Traffic demand can exceed existing TG capacity when a single session reaches the point at which it needs more bandwidth than the TG can provide. Aggregate available bandwidth can be raised simply by the addition of more links dynamically. If the demand subsequently falls, the extra bandwidth can be taken back by deletion of the extra links, saving network charges. Parallel TGs cannot help in this circumstance.

The need may also arise because of varying loads placed on a TG by a collection of sessions, rather than any single session. In this instance, adding parallel TGs *might* be an alternative solution, or not, depending on class-of-service and route selection implementations. But a single session could not use more capacity than the link offers that carries this session.

Where multiple lower-speed links are less expensive than a single higher-speed link

There are cases where multilink transmission groups prove less expensive than single-link TGs. In certain countries circuit capacities of 64 Kbps and 2 Mbps are available, but nothing in between. If you live in one of these countries and have to provide 100 Kbps of bandwidth, for example, you may find it costs less to put two 64 Kbps links into a multilink transmission group than to have a single 2 Mbps link.

Where individual links are unreliable

Although HPR provides a fast nondisruptive path switch capability, not even this will be necessary if your TGs never fail. If you are considering MLTGs to avoid TG failures however, you must plan for the potential effects of temporarily reduced TG capacity. When one of several active links in an MLTG fails, effective capacity will be reduced even though the TG does not itself fail.

Where you have a subarea network including multilink transmission groups

If you have grown used to having the multilink transmission group facility in subarea networks you may feel more comfortable about migration to APPN HPR, knowing a similar facility is there.

Additional design objectives of the MLTG architecture include:

- The need to support mixed link types within MLTGs

  All supported SNA link types are also supported in HPR MLTGs.

- The need to support mixed link speeds within MLTGs
- The need to minimize system definition

8.5.4.2 HPR MLTG Overview

The critical parameter determining whether two links belong to one MLTG or to two parallel TGs is TG number (given of course that the links connect the same pair of nodes). If the links share the same TG number, then they belong to an MLTG; if they have different TG numbers, then they belong to parallel TGs. In this regard, subarea SNA and HPR do not differ.

One of the architectural problems with subarea multilink transmission groups was the need for resequencing of packets. Higher layers required DLC to guarantee delivery of packets, hop-by-hop, and to guarantee FIFO order. This dictated, among other things, that SNA subarea nodes had to act as *store-and-forward* switches, being unable to make forward routing decisions until entire packets had been safely received. It could easily happen that two packets, transmitted on different links within a multilink transmission group, would reach this point in reverse order of their initial order. The receiving node would have to buffer the second packet, pending the arrival of the first. This TG resequencing function could impose large processing overheads, especially where there were widely varying line speeds, propagation delays, or packet lengths, or where there were significant line error rates. In today's high-speed networks, resequencing delays en-route would be unacceptable.

HPR eliminates the need for TG resequencing and for hop-by-hop error recovery by shifting these functions to RTP endpoints. When a VR-based transmission group (VR-TG) crossing the subarea network includes a subarea multilink transmission group, resequencing is not done for HPR network layer packets transported over that subarea MLTG.

In the HPR MLTG architecture, error recovery on individual links is optional, and TG resequencing en route is absent. Because FID2 packets have to be transmitted reliably and in sequence, HPR MLTGs do not support any FID2 traffic. HPR MLTGs must carry ANR network layer packets exclusively. This means, in turn, that RTP connections must be used for CP-CP sessions and route setup flows. Both nodes connected by an HPR MLTG must hence support the control flows over RTP option.

As regards routing and ANR labels, MLTGs are treated the same as single-link TGs. See 8.3, “Automatic Network Routing” on page 166. An MLTG is assigned one ANR label for each direction.

MLTGs and single-link TGs are also considered alike by TRS when it comes to the generalities of topology databases, TDUs, and route calculations. Differences show up when an MLTG's characteristics change *in flight*; for instance, when a new link is added. Such circumstances cannot arise in single-link TGs. When MLTG characteristics do change, topology database records are modified and TDUs generated. See 8.6.2, “MLTG Characteristics and TDU Reporting” on page 206.

Some functions are not supported in HPR MLTG:

- Limited resource
- Connection networks
- Nonactivation XID

Much of the HPR MLTG architecture revolves around the handling of TG number and other characteristics governed by XID3 exchanges during link activation. In particular, it deals with the exceptions that can occur when differently defined links are put together.

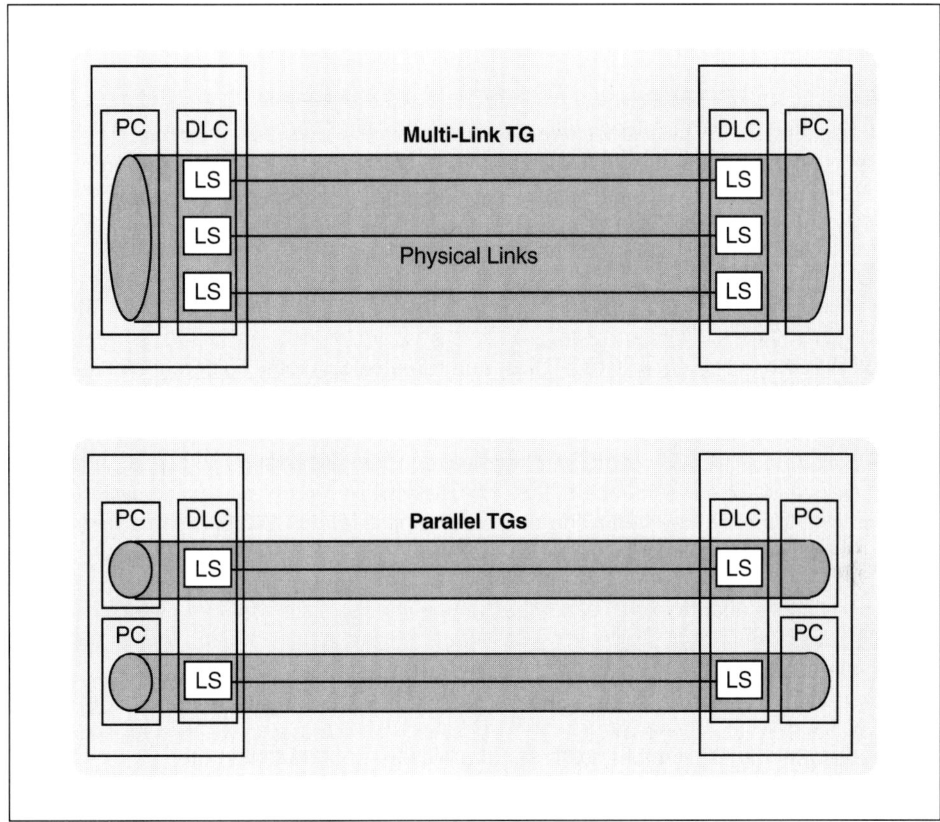

Figure 73. Multilink and Parallel TGs

8.5.5 HPR Link Activation

At link activation time, DLCs are started by HPR in the same way as in base APPN. XID3s are exchanged and the appropriate set mode signals are sent when the exchange is complete. See 4.4, "Link Activation" on page 61 for a description of the existing APPN support.

The HPR DLC adds a new *HPR Capabilities control vector* to the XID3 used during the negotiation-proceeding phase. This control vector indicates the following:

- Whether link-level error recovery is required on this link.
- Whether the RTP functions for HPR is supported by the node.
- Whether the HPR control flows over RTP option is supported by the node.
- Whether MLTG is supported and it is desired that this link become part of the specified MLTG (as indicated by the XID TG number).

The presence of the new control vector indicates base HPR support. If both nodes send the control vector in their XID3, the link is known as an *HPR link*.

If one node is an HPR node and the other is a base APPN node, then this link is an APPN link and the HPR protocols are not used. It is also possible (although not generally recommended) for an HPR node to activate a link in the APPN way, without including the new HPR control vector in the negotiation-proceeding XID3. This might be desirable in some environments to run very slow-speed links the APPN way because of constraints on link buffer sizes and bandwidth.

CP-CP session activation is triggered by link activation in the same manner as in base APPN.

8.5.5.1 MLTG Negotiation

An MLTG may be one of up to 20 *explicit* MLTGs connecting a pair of nodes, or it may be the only *default* MLTG. The difference between them lies simply in the TG number used: explicit MLTGs use numbers 1-20 inclusive, while the default MLTG uses TG number 240, formerly reserved. The point of having a *default* MLTG is explained in 8.5.5.2, "Advantages of the Default MLTG" on page 203.

The nodes agree about which TG number to use in essentially the same way as base APPN nodes agree about single-link TGs, that is by exchanging XIDs. This is described under 4.4, "Link Activation" on page 61. One modification is needed: an MLTG-supported indicator is now carried in the HPR Capabilities control vector in XID3.

The nodes use the TG number fields and the MLTG-supported bit in the negotiation-proceeding XID3 exchanges to determine whether a link being activated belongs to an MLTG, and, if so, to which one. The following tabulates the various possibilities:

Table 6. MLTG Negotiation

Side X	Side Y	Result
M, 0	M, 0	Add link to default MLTG (240)
M, 0	M, 1-20	Add link to explicit MLTG identified by Side Y
M, 1-20	M, 1-20	Add link to MLTG identified by both sides if the numbers match; otherwise reject activation
M, 0	¬M, any	Activate link as a single-link TG, negotiating TG number as usual
M, 1-20	¬M, any	Activate link as a single-link TG if the numbers match; otherwise reject activation

Key:

M = MLTG support indicator ON

¬M = MLTG support indicator OFF

8.5.5.2 Advantages of the Default MLTG

The idea of the default MLTG is to enhance operational flexibility. It can also reduce system definition effort. If you have the nodes at both ends of an MLTG default, you will eliminate TG number definitions altogether. If, on the other hand, you have a need for parallel MLTGs where you must, of course, use more than one TG number, you can have one side default and define the TG numbers on the other.

The default MLTG will be particularly useful in client/server environments where you might otherwise spend a lot of time administering TG numbers for your many client/server connections.

8.5.6 Link Data Traffic

The DLC formats used for network layer packets (NLPs) depend on the type of data link control and whether link-level error recovery is used on a link or not. (Note that FID2 PIUs are always sent using link-level error recovery, just as in base APPN.) Whether link-level error recovery procedures for NLPs for a link shall be used is determined during the XID3 exchange. HPR will change the existing DLC format used by base APPN only if no link-level error recovery is being done on the link.

At present, the HPR architecture describes the following DLCs:

Frame relay

If no link-level error recovery is used on a frame relay link, then base support is to carry NLPs in frames with the level 2 protocol identifier indicating that no IEEE 802.2 header is present. The HPR NLP then immediately follows the level 3 protocol identifier for HPR.

Multiple HPR links can optionally be multiplexed in a single frame relay virtual circuit by using different SAP fields in the 802.2 header. This support may be chosen to simplify the interface to a frame relay network and to reduce WAN connection costs (when using a frame relay carrier). In this case, NLPs are carried in frames with the level 2 protocol identifier indicating the presence of an 802.2 header. The 802.2 header then contains the SAP associated with the individual link and the UI command code (if not using link-level error recovery).

LANs

For performance reasons a separate SAP, different from the SAP currently being used for APPN traffic, is normally used to transmit NLPs with no link-level error recovery. (The default is X'C8'.) The SAPs to be used for NLPs with no link-level error recovery are exchanged between the two nodes activating a LAN link during the XID negotiation proceeding phase. NLPs requiring link-level error recovery use the same SAP as existing APPN traffic. If the HPR SAP is configured to have the same value as the APPN SAP, then NLPs with no link-level error recovery are sent as UI frames. Even though there might be two different SAPs to separate HPR and base-APPN traffic, there is logically only one link station. All traffic travels along the same physical path. Because there is only a single link station, all LLC commands and responses (XID, SABME, DISC, etc.) flow using the APPN SAP.

SDLC

There are no changes required to run HPR over SDLC. It might be possible to transmit NLPs over SDLC links without using link-level error recovery by sending them as UI frames, but the benefit (especially on multipoint connections) appears to be minimal. Since SDLC is not considered one of the high-speed link protocols of the future, no HPR enhancements are being made to it.

X.25

All the individual links through an X.25 network as well as the access links provide link-level error recovery. There is no way to de-activate this link-level error recovery since it is part of the X.25 recommendations and under control of the X.25 network. X.25 DTEs have a choice of using either QLLC or ELLC. ELLC provides an additional layer of error recovery end-to-end between the DTEs that operates on top of the link-level error recovery. QLLC relies on the underlying X.25 link-level error recovery and does not provide additional error recovery.

PPP

RFC 1700 defines four code points to be used for SNA traffic over PPP. Code point X'004B' (SNA over 802.2) is used for APPN FID2 and HPR NLP packets that require link-level error recovery. Code point X'004D' (SNA) is used for HPR NLP packets that do not require link-level error recovery.

ATM

For a complete description of the native ATM DLC for HPR refer to Chapter 12, “APPN Support in ATM Networks” on page 277.

8.5.7 After Link Activation

If both nodes support the HPR control flows over RTP option, then an RTP connection is set up between the adjacent HPR nodes over every link that is activated. This RTP connection is used during route setup, to carry the route setup requests and it remains active for as long as the link remains active (hence the term *long-lived RTP connection*). The route setup requests and the route setup RTP connection are explained in 8.4.2, “HPR Route Setup” on page 182. A link's long-lived RTP connection is established when the first route setup request arrives that has to be forwarded over this link.

CP-CP sessions are also activated after link activation. If both the adjacent nodes support the HPR control flows over RTP option, then an RTP connection is set up to carry the CP-CP sessions. If the nodes do not both support the HPR control flows over RTP option, then the CP-CP sessions will use FID2 protocols as in base APPN (see 8.8.1, “CP-CP Sessions” on page 207).

8.5.8 Link Failure Detection

When link-level error recovery is implemented, failure of a link is immediately detected. If a packet sent is not acknowledged, it is retransmitted for a defined number of times. If then no acknowledgement is received the link is inactivated and its changed status reported to topology and routing services. But when not using link-level error recovery for any packets sent over a link, this mechanism will not work simply because packets do not request an acknowledgment.

Since it is still necessary to detect link outages, a *link inactivity timer* is used. When no packets have been received for a certain time, an inactivity message is sent over the link requesting an acknowledgment. If this inactivity message then is not acknowledged within a given time (and after a number of retries), the link is inactivated and its changed status is reported to topology and routing services. The overall time to detect a link outage must be shorter than the end-to-end RTP connection timeouts in order for nondisruptive path switch to work properly. When a new path for an RTP connection affected by the link outage is calculated, the information about the link's status change must have been distributed in TDUs to all network nodes in the network.

There are actually three parameters that govern how long it will take to detect a link failure:

- When no packets have been received for the interval set by the *inactivity timer*, an inactivity message is sent to check if the link is still alive.
- The *send timer* defines how long the sender will wait for an acknowledgment of the inactivity message sent.
- The *number of retries* parameter defines how often the inactivity message is resent when it is not acknowledged within the send timer interval.

8.6 Topology and Routing Services

HPR nodes use topology and routing services in the same way as base APPN nodes. Only some minor additions are necessary to support HPR.

8.6.1 Topology Database Manager

The topology database is used in the same way as in base APPN as described in 5.3, "Topology Databases" on page 77. The only change made by HPR is the addition of the HPR capabilities to the TG vectors that describe HPR links in the topology database:

- This TG goes to an HPR node that supports the RTP functions for HPR.
- This TG goes to an HPR node that supports the control flows over RTP option.

APPN nodes that do not support HPR will see these new types as reserved combinations. Therefore, APPN nodes will not see any difference between HPR nodes and links and APPN nodes and links.

8.6.2 MLTG Characteristics and TDU Reporting

Like a single-link TG, an MLTG is reported in TDUs when it becomes active or inactive. Additionally, however, it must be reported when its characteristics change. It will become more attractive for session routing when capacity is increased, or less attractive when capacity is reduced.

Note: You must take care when deleting links from an MLTG. This may compromise the ARB calculations done during route setup over the MLTG (described under Chapter 9, "Adaptive Rate-Based Flow/Congestion Control" on page 217). It may even result in a violation of the COS rules for sessions set up while the route was at its maximum capacity, and which still exist. In either case, there may be serious performance implications.

What happens is that the characteristics of a route are calculated and fixed at route setup time, and sessions are then mapped to it if it meets COS criteria. If a link within an MLTG is lost through any cause, the endpoints of RTP pipes traversing the TG can continue to pump data into those pipes at the same rates as before. Congestion may follow. If it does, ARB will come into play and reduce the allowed sending rate.

Note: A TG's security level may not be altered.

When characteristics do change, the new ones are computed as shown in the following table:

Table 7. MLTG Characteristics

Characteristic	How Computed
Security	Unchanged
Capacity (bps)	Sum
Cost per connect time	Weighted average
Cost per byte	Weighted average
Propagation delay	Weighted average
User-defined (1, 2, 3)	Unchanged

Note: An example of *weighted average* is if Link 1 has capacity 100 and cost 2, while Link 2 has capacity 50 and cost 5, the weighted average cost will be ((2*100) + (5*50)) / (100+50); which is 450/150 or 3.

8.6.3 Route Selection Services

The logic used by route selection services to calculate the initial route (as opposed to a backup route) through an HPR network or an APPN/HPR combined network is unchanged. The network node, which is the NNS(OLU) or the CP(OLU) (if the OLU resides in the network node), is still responsible for the initial route calculation.

The only change to RSS was necessary to support nondisruptive path switch. An HPR network node that is the NNS(OLU), the CP(OLU), or the APPN/HPR boundary function between a base-APPN subnet and an HPR subnet will need to calculate a new route through the HPR subnet. The changes in route selection services to support this are discussed in 8.4.4, "Nondisruptive Path Switch" on page 188.

HPR does not artificially make HPR links appear more attractive by lowering their weight in any way, which could have an adverse effect on the whole network. A small change in the characteristics of one link could change the distribution of traffic throughout the whole network. Instead, it is assumed that when an HPR node activates an HPR link, the node characteristics as broadcast in the topology database update will have a weight that reflects the desirability of the link compared with all the other links. The weight of HPR links should be defined to reflect this, and if applicable, the customer could give HPR links lower weights than base APPN links when defining their TG characteristics.

8.7 Directory Services

The directory database is used in the same way by an HPR node as described in 6.2, "Directory Database Function" on page 108. There is a change in Locate search replies if an HPR node contains the LU that is the target of a directory search.

- All HPR nodes that contain the target LU will include the LU's network connection endpoint (NCE) address on the Locate search reply. This address is used to distinguish between the different components in an HPR node, and is explained in 8.3.3, "Network Connection Endpoints (NCEs)" on page 168.
- HPR end nodes that contain the target LU will include the HPR capabilities of TGs in the end node TG vectors. The use of the end node TG vector is described in 5.7.1.2, "LUs Residing on APPN End Nodes" on page 102. This information will be used by route selection services during a path switch, but only if the NNS(OLU) or CP(OLU) is an HPR node. This is because the end node TG vectors are sent only to the NNS(OLU) or CP(OLU) and not kept by any intermediate nodes.

The changes in route selection services to handle nondisruptive path switch are discussed in 8.4.4, "Nondisruptive Path Switch" on page 188.

8.8 Session Services

Session services needed only a few extensions to support session setup for CP-CP and LU-LU sessions over RTP connections.

8.8.1 CP-CP Sessions

The CP-CP sessions in HPR are triggered in the same way as in APPN, after link activation, and if requested in the XID. If both HPR nodes indicate that they support the HPR control flows over RTP option, then an RTP connection is activated to support the CP-CP sessions. Contention-winner and contention-loser LU 6.2 sessions are activated between the nodes. If both nodes support the HPR control flows over RTP option, then either one or two RTP connections will be activated for the CP-CP sessions, depending on the timing of the session activations. If a node activates an RTP connection for its contention-winner CP-CP session, and the partner node recognizes this before activating its RTP connection, then a single RTP connection will be used.

The RTP connection for the CP-CP sessions can be set up without going through the route setup process. This is because CP-CP sessions are between adjacent nodes, and the information required for the RTP connection activation is known from the XID3 exchange done at link activation time (see 8.4.1.2, “RTP Connection Activation” on page 177 for details).

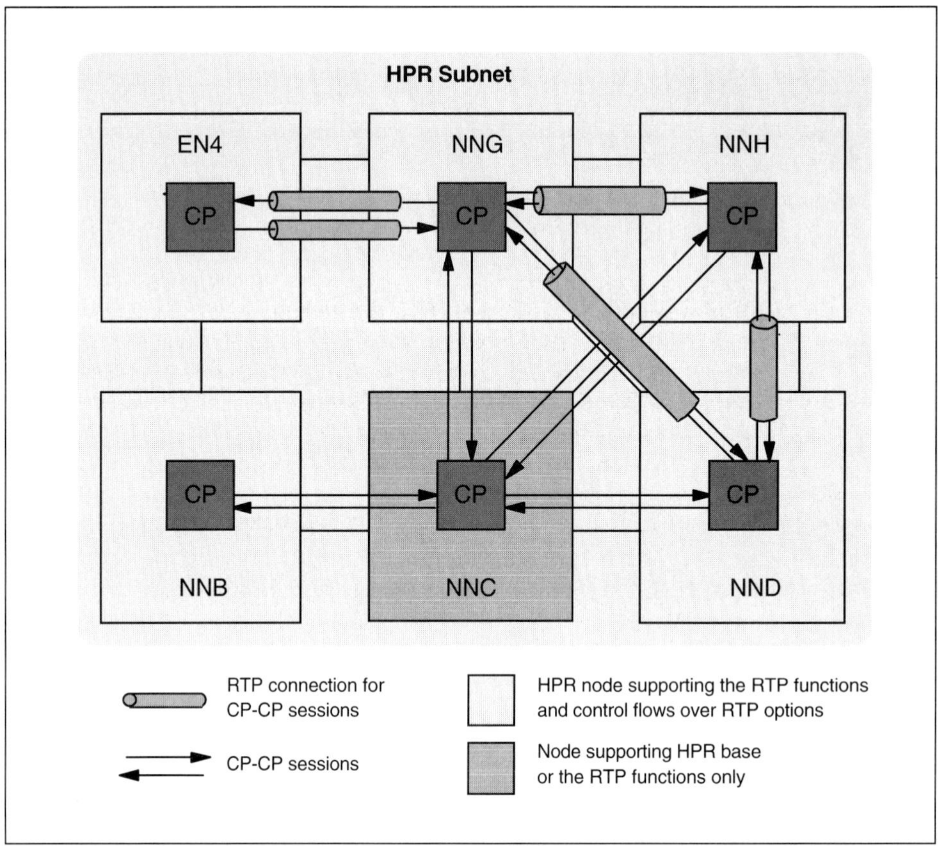

Figure 74. CP-CP Sessions in an HPR Network. The CP-CP sessions between a pair of nodes can run over one or two RTP connections depending on the timing of the activation.

Figure 74 shows the CP-CP sessions which are set up in the sample network after the HPR links are activated. It is assumed that NNC supports only the HPR base or RTP functions for HPR and not the HPR control flows over RTP option. So, NNC cannot set up RTP connections and its CP-CP session must use FID2 routing. The following CP-CP sessions will, therefore, be set up using FID2 routing:

NNC-NNB, NNC-NND, NNC-NNG and NNC-NNH

All the other nodes in the HPR subnet are assumed to support the RTP functions for HPR. So HPR nodes NNB, NND, EN4, NNG and NNH will activate RTP connections for their CP-CP sessions. It is assumed that the CP-CP sessions between the network nodes are to be fully meshed. The following CP-CP sessions will be carried over RTP connections:

NND-NNG, NND-NNH, EN4-NNG and NNG-NNH

Note that EN4 only activates CP-CP sessions to NNG, which is assumed to be the network node server for EN4.

The CP-CP sessions in an HPR subnet support all the functions of CP-CP sessions in APPN, such as CP capabilities, topology database updates and Locate search requests. To support HPR, new control vectors and subfields are added to the existing GDS variables used on the CP-CP sessions.

If a function such as a topology database update or a Locate search request flows through an HPR subnet with a mixture of nodes that have implemented the HPR base function only, the RTP functions for HPR, or the control flows over RTP option, then the formats of the packets will change from FID2 PIUs to network layer packets as they pass between CPs. There is no additional function required in the HPR nodes to do this changing of packet formats. It is handled by path control that strips the headers off all packets before passing messages to the CP. For example, in Figure 74 on page 208, a directed Locate search that flows from NNC to EN4 would use a FID2 PIU on the hop from NNC to NNG and a network layer packet on the hop from NNG to EN4 (assuming the NNC uses the direct link to reach NNG). In NNG, the FID2 path control strips the FID2 header off the incoming packet before passing the Locate to the CP, and then FID5 path control adds the FID5 header before passing the packet to the RTP connection.

Nondisruptive path switch is always supported for CP-CP sessions.

8.8.2 LU-LU Sessions

Activating an LU-LU session that originates in an HPR node requires the following steps:

- Find the location of the target LU (using Locate searches if necessary).
- Calculate the RSCV to be used to reach the target LU.
- Perform the route setup process (if necessary).
- Activate an RTP connection (if necessary), or send the BIND on an existing RTP connection.

The logic used during the first two steps is the same as in base APPN, with the addition of the new control vectors and subfields used by HPR. After the RSCV has been calculated, the HPR node will inspect the RSCV to determine if the first TG on the path is an HPR link. If the first TG is an HPR link, then this HPR node will continue to inspect the RSCV until it finds the end of the HPR subnet (which may or may not be the end of the RSCV). The HPR node will then require an RTP connection and if one exists already for the required class of service, the BIND is sent on the RTP connection. If an

RTP connection does not exist, then a new RTP connection is activated and the BIND sent at the same time (see 8.4.1.2, "RTP Connection Activation" on page 177).

If the first TG in the RSCV is not an HPR link, then it must be an APPN TG, and the normal APPN route setup logic is used to establish the session, and the BIND is sent out over the APPN link.

At some later point during the session setup, the BIND may pass through an intermediate HPR node that supports the RTP functions for HPR. An HPR node that receives a FID2 BIND will inspect the RSCV before it builds the APPN session connectors. If the intermediate HPR node detects that there is an HPR link in the RSCV as it leaves this node, then it will continue to inspect the BIND until it has found the end of the HPR subnet (which may or may not be the end of the RSCV). The intermediate HPR node will then require APPN/HPR boundary function between the base APPN subnet and HPR subnet (see 8.9.1, "APPN/HPR Boundary Function" on page 211). Finally, the RTP connection is activated, or an existing RTP connection is used.

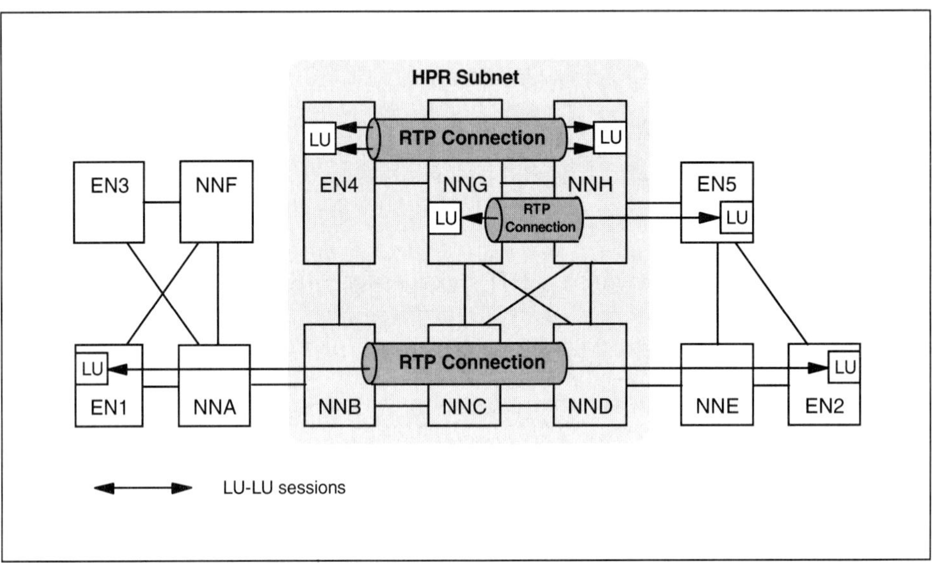

Figure 75. LU-LU Sessions in an APPN/HPR Network. Multiple sessions can be multiplexed over a single RTP connection if they all use the same class of service.

An intermediate HPR node that supports only the HPR base will not inspect the RSCV in a FID2 BIND for HPR subnets. This is because it cannot provide the APPN/HPR boundary function or be the endpoint of an RTP connection. So, if a base HPR node receives a FID2 BIND, it will act as a normal APPN intermediate network node and use APPN intermediate session routing.

Each RTP connection in an HPR subnet can transport session data for one specific class of service as specified in a BIND. Multiple sessions of the same class of service can use an RTP connection. The APPN transmission priority is stored as part of the class of service and so all the traffic using a single RTP connection will have the same priority. Different classes of service require different RTP connections.

Sessions can originate in APPN nodes or HPR nodes and can be destined for APPN nodes or HPR nodes. There is no restriction on the number of APPN and HPR subnets that an APPN session can cross. The endpoint of an RTP connection can be an HPR end node or an HPR network node. If an HPR node is an intermediate node on a session path, then it must be a network node, just as in base APPN. Figure 75 on page 210 gives examples of three different kinds of sessions using RTP connections:

- Both session endpoints are in HPR nodes.
- One session endpoint is in an HPR node and one is in a base APPN node.
- Both session endpoints are in base APPN nodes.

There is no change required in the applications or subsystems at the session endpoints, when LU-LU sessions pass over HPR subnets. The LU-LU sessions will see the benefits of the improved performance in the network, without having to make any changes to support HPR.

Nondisruptive path switch is always supported for LU-LU sessions.

8.9 Combined APPN/HPR Networks

To provide a seamless migration from (base) APPN to HPR and also to provide interoperability between HPR nodes and (base) APPN nodes that do not support HPR, every HPR node that implements the RTP functions for HPR supports the APPN/HPR boundary function.

8.9.1 APPN/HPR Boundary Function

If a session passes from a base-APPN subnet to an HPR subnet, the HPR node will provide APPN/HPR boundary function. This function is provided by an HPR node with the RTP functions for HPR. All the protocols between the HPR node and APPN nodes are the base APPN protocols. All the protocols between the HPR node and other HPR nodes in the HPR subnet are HPR protocols.

The APPN/HPR boundary function provides a session connector to support intermediate session routing across a base-APPN subnet (see 2.4.2, "Session Connector" on page 33). The APPN/HPR boundary function between each base-APPN subnet and HPR subnet will change the routing from intermediate session routing to ANR. The APPN/HPR boundary function uses the normal APPN session connector, and so the adjacent APPN nodes will see the HPR node with APPN/HPR boundary function as a normal intermediate network node.

Figure 76 on page 212 shows the APPN/HPR boundary function that is set up in NNH to support an LU-LU session between NNG in the HPR subnet and EN5 in the base-APPN subnet. The half-sessions in an end node represent the LU (see Figure 16 on page 35 for a description of how APPN sets up half-sessions). The session connector in the APPN/HPR boundary function connects the APPN path control to the HPR path control instances. The EN5 sees NNH as a normal APPN intermediate node in the session path.

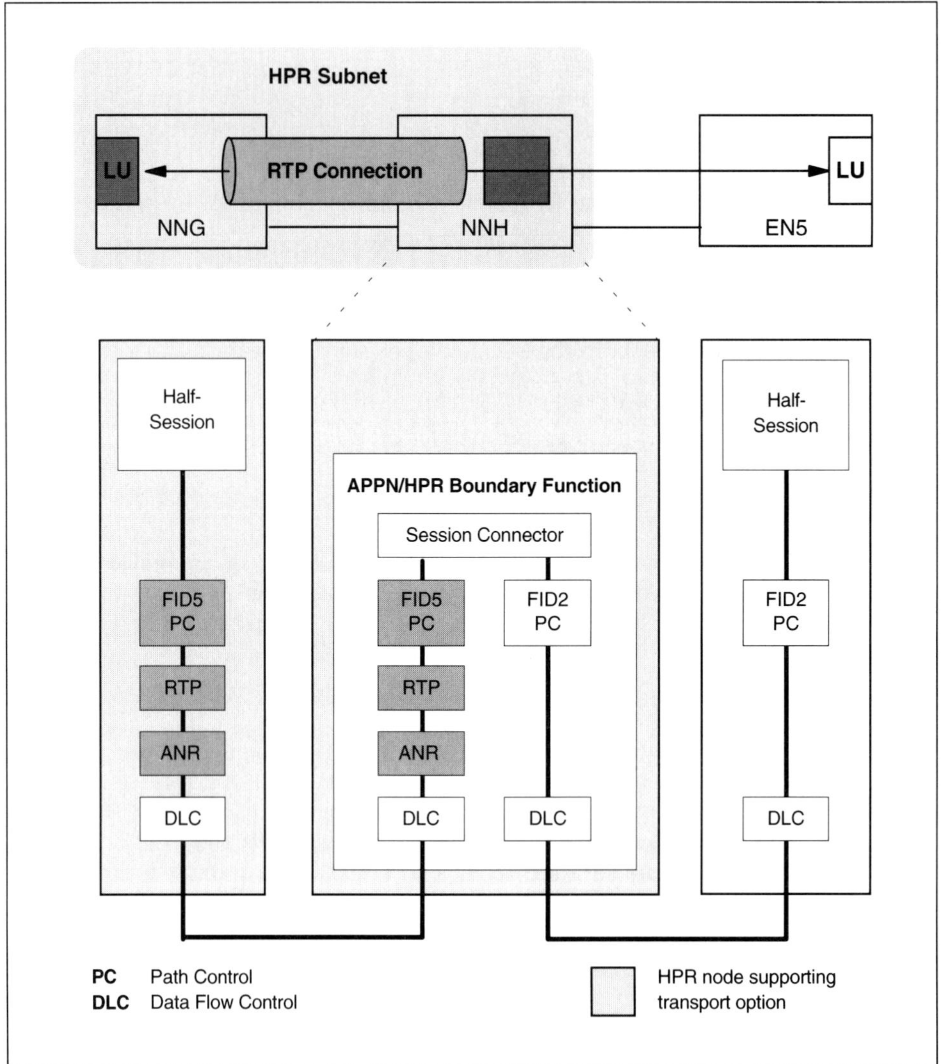

Figure 76. APPN/HPR Boundary Function

8.9.2 Routing in APPN/HPR Networks

When a session passes across multiple base-APPN subnets and HPR subnets, an HPR node with the RTP functions for HPR will provide APPN/HPR boundary function at each boundary between the different subnets. ANR is done in the HPR subnets and intermediate session routing is done in the base-APPN subnets.

At session establishment time, the RSCV that is calculated in the normal way is transported end-to-end along the session path with the BIND. The RSCV is used to establish the route through the base-APPN subnets in the normal way. The HPR route setup process uses the RSCV to calculate the path through the HPR subnets, and the RTP connections are activated along this path (see 8.4.2, "HPR Route Setup" on page 182).

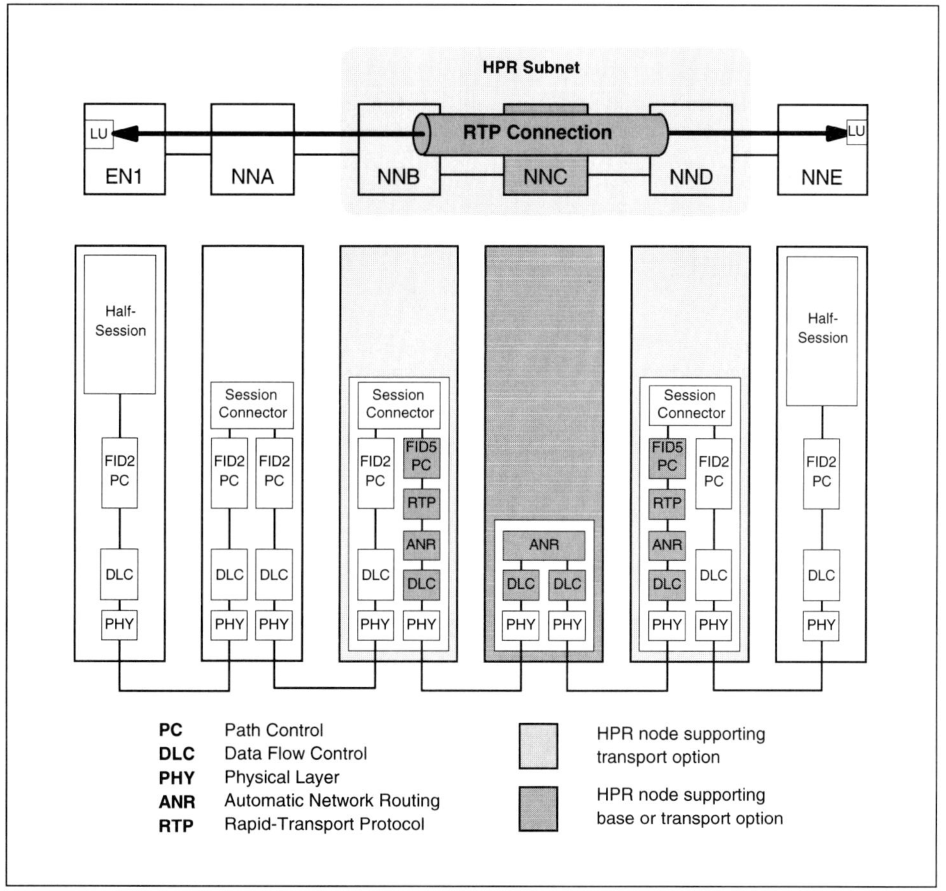

Figure 77. Intermediate Session Routing and ANR Routing

Figure 77 shows the components used in the APPN and HPR nodes, to support an LU-LU session between EN1 and NNE. The LU-LU session traffic is routed using intermediate session routing in the base-APPN subnets and using ANR in the HPR subnet. The APPN/HPR boundary functions provide session connectors that are used to support the APPN intermediate session routing. The ANR in the HPR subnet is done at a lower layer than the intermediate session routing.

8.9.3 HPR Migration

There are no configuration restrictions about how an APPN network is migrated to support HPR. As soon as an HPR subnet is formed, the benefits of HPR can be achieved. A customer may add new HPR nodes, or upgrade existing APPN nodes to APPN in any manner.

To take full advantage of the HPR function, though, the customer should plan to upgrade APPN nodes to HPR nodes so that HPR subnets are formed. High-speed links with the heavy traffic, such as backbone links, would benefit from the reduced flows and the omission of link-level error recovery.

As soon as two adjacent APPN nodes migrate to HPR, the following benefits can be achieved:

- Nondisruptive path switch
- Adaptive rate-based congestion control
- Reduction in traffic flows to support error recovery
- Selective retransmission after errors
- Multilink transmission group support

When additional nodes migrate to HPR so that an HPR node with at least two HPR links can perform ANR instead of intermediate session routing, then the other benefits of HPR can be obtained:

- Fast intermediate node routing with priority
- Reduction in intermediate node storage

As HPR is an extension to APPN, HPR uses the existing APPN control point protocols, using CP-CP sessions and the APPN route selection algorithm. This reduces the amount of code that will be required to migrate to HPR, particularly at the APPN/HPR boundary. The fact that HPR nodes and links appear as APPN nodes and links in the topology databases of APPN nodes means that the migration to HPR can be orderly and will not affect the other APPN nodes in the network.

The desirability of HPR links should be reflected in terms of their TG characteristics, for example, using one of the three user-defined characteristics. If HPR links are higher speed than the existing links, then their weights should reflect that. HPR will not automatically select HPR links in preference to APPN links if their weights are the same. If the selection of HPR links in preference to APPN links is a requirement, it can be done by the appropriate definition of the TG characteristics.

HPR insulates the upper layers and the user from any awareness of the RTP connections and ANR routing in the network. The LU-LU sessions will see the benefits of the improved performance in the network, without having to make any changes to support HPR. Any existing applications supported by independent LUs will be supported by HPR networks. For example, if an HPR node also supported the dependent LU requester, then dependent LU sessions could be carried over an RTP connection to an HPR node that supported the PLU.

Chapter 9. Adaptive Rate-Based Flow/Congestion Control

The adaptive rate-based (ARB) congestion and flow control algorithm is designed to let RTP connections make efficient use of network resources by providing a congestion avoidance and control mechanism.

The basic approach used in this algorithm, as the name implies, is to regulate the input traffic (offered load) of an RTP connection based on conditions in the network and at the partner RTP endpoint. When the algorithm detects that the network or the partner endpoint is approaching congestion and the path becomes saturated, resulting in increased delays and decreased throughput, it reduces the rate at which traffic on an RTP connection is allowed to enter the network until these indications go away. When the network or partner endpoint is sensed to have enough capacity to handle the offered load, the algorithm allows more traffic to enter the network without exceeding the rate that the slowest link on the path of an RTP connection or that the receiver can handle.

9.1 ARB Operating Region

Figure 78 on page 218 shows the network throughput as a function of the offered load for a given path.

The *knee* (point K) is the point beyond which the path starts to get saturated because transmission queues are developing, resulting in higher network delays. An increase in offered load (such as the sending rate) then does not correspond to an increase in throughput which is reflected in the receiving rate. ARB detects this saturation condition and adjusts (reduces) the sending rate accordingly, thus preventing operation beyond the *cliff* (point C). Because HPR does not use a hop-by-hop flow/congestion control algorithm (as base APPN does with adaptive session-level pacing), intermediate nodes will drop packets when their buffers are depleted. The cliff reflects the point beyond which there is a significant loss of packets because of excessive queueing along the path. An increase in offered load beyond this point results in a drastic decrease of throughput because of packet retransmissions.

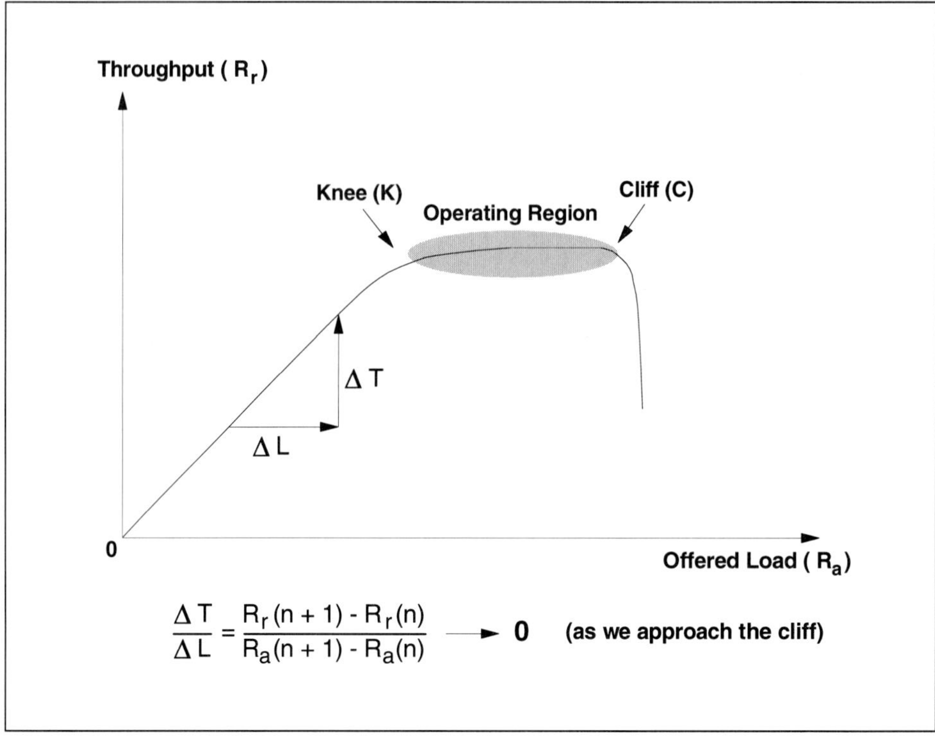

Figure 78. ARB Operating Region

9.2 ARB Principles

The ARB algorithm has the following properties:

- It is adaptive to network conditions in such a way as to maximize throughput and minimize congestion.
- It smooths the input traffic into the network by avoiding large bursts when the physical capacity of the access link is larger than the allowed sending rate. This prevents long queues from developing in the network and helps minimize oscillation in the network traffic patterns.
- It provides effective end-to-end flow control between RTP endpoints.
- It is simple to implement and requires minimum overhead, both in processor cycles and network bandwidth.
- It is generally fair in providing equal access to network resources between all RTP connections.

The ARB algorithm employs a closed-loop, distributed control mechanism based on information exchanged between the two endpoints of a connection. Figure 79 on page 219 shows the relationship between an ARB sender and an ARB receiver over an RTP connection between two RTP endpoints.

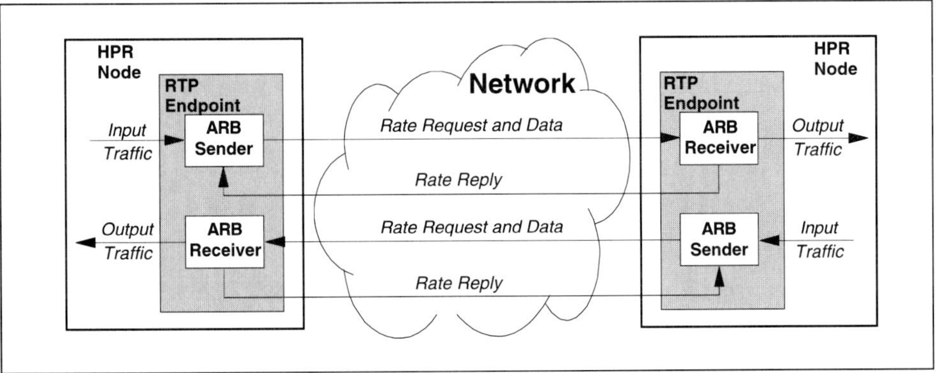

Figure 79. ARB Closed Loop

The ARB algorithm is implemented in the endpoints of an RTP connection. At each endpoint there are two components, an ARB sender and an ARB receiver. The ARB procedures performed by the sender and receiver at one end are the same as those performed by the sender and receiver at the other end respectively. (Note that intermediate nodes have no awareness of the ARB protocol and do not participate in it.)

The ARB algorithm always regulates the rate at which data is flowing from the ARB sender to the ARB receiver. The sender continually queries the receiver, by sending a *rate request* (along with user data) in order to obtain information about the state of the network and the state of the node containing the receiver. The receiver responds by sending back a *rate reply*. The sender then adjusts its send rate based on the information in the rate reply. The sender may reduce its send rate to relieve congestion or increase it to take advantage of the available network capacity.

Fixed characteristics of the path (that is, the speed of the slowest link along the path and the total transmission delay over the entire path) are factored into the ARB algorithm at both the sender and the receiver. These path characteristics are communicated in the ARB setup message during RTP connection establishment (including nondisruptive path switch). The ARB messages (rate request, rate reply, and setup) are transmitted in the ARB optional segment of the THDR and piggybacked (whenever possible) onto normal data packets.

9.3 ARB Algorithm

As is illustrated in Figure 80 on page 220, at regular intervals approximating the round-trip delay on the RTP connection, the ARB sender sends a rate request in an ARB segment, which is always added to a packet containing user data. (When no user data is flowing on an RTP connection, there is no need to measure the RTP connection's performance.) This rate request includes the *sender's measurement interval*, which is the time that has elapsed since the last request was sent. Upon receipt of the request, the receiver determines whether any delay has occurred in the network. It does so by calculating the difference between the sender's measurement interval and the *receiver's measurement interval*, which is the time that has elapsed since the last rate request was received.

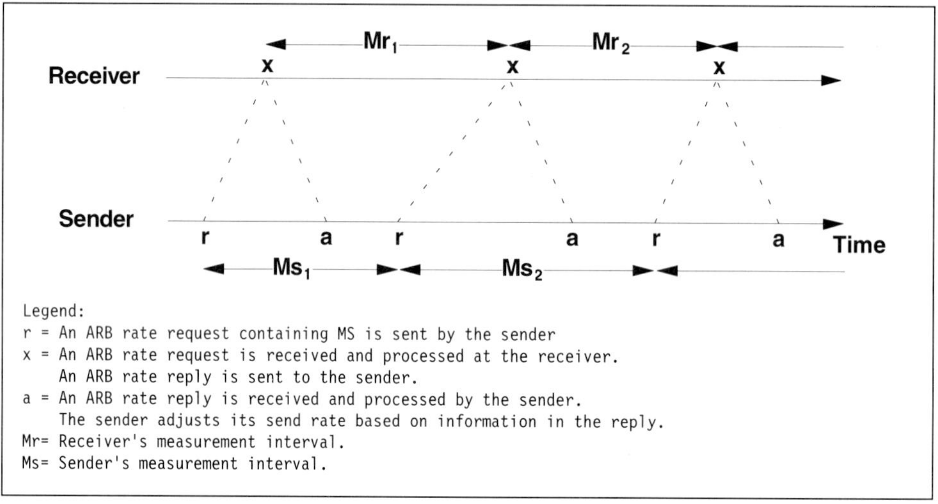

Figure 80. Overview of ARB Algorithm

The receiver also takes into account previous delays remembered from earlier rate request messages. Based on the measured changes in network delay, the receiver will then recommend appropriate actions to be taken by the sender. These recommended actions are communicated in a rate reply message that enables the sender to adjust its send rate appropriately. The ARB segment containing the rate reply may be either carried in the THDR of a packet with user data or, if none is available, sent alone as a packet without user data. The receiver, in addition to deriving its recommendations based on network delays, can also tell the sender to adjust its send rate based on conditions within the receiving node (for example, buffer depletion).

9.3.1 ARB Initialization

When an RTP connection is being established, or during a nondisruptive path switch, a number of parameters have to be set on both sides of the RTP connection for both the sender and the receiver logic. Because the setting of those parameters is mainly derived from the characteristics of the links on the path of the RTP connection, the node that receives the route setup reply (normally the node that requests the RTP connection) will decide on the values of the basic parameters and communicate them to its partner in an ARB (setup) segment that is carried in the THDR of the very first packet sent either on a new RTP connection or after a nondisruptive path switch. From these basic parameters, others can then be derived using a common logic on both sides.

The following gives an overview of the parameters that have to be initialized before the ARB algorithm can start working to regulate the user data flow. (Not mentioned are a number of parameters used to keep track of the internal state of the algorithm.) Note that these parameters are set independently for both directions.

Range begin time
: This is the amount of delay on the RTP connection indicating that the beginning of the ARB operating region (point K, the knee, in Figure 78 on page 218) is reached. The value of this parameter is set to the time that it takes to transmit 8000 bits (1000 bytes) over the slowest link on the path of the RTP connection.

Range end time
: This represents the end (point C, the cliff, in Figure 78 on page 218) of the ARB operating region. The value of this parameter is set to the time that it takes to transmit 80000, 120000, or 160000 bits over the slowest link. The higher values will be chosen to accommodate longer paths (that is, many hops) or paths with more than one slow link. This is done to allow high throughput for longer paths and also to allow connections with longer paths to compete fairly with those connections that traverse shorter paths.

Maximum send rate
: This is the maximum rate at which the sender is (initially) allowed to send data. It is set to the capacity (link speed) of the slowest link on the path of the connection. This is not the maximum rate at which the sender *ever* is allowed to send because the system definitions for the link speeds might not reflect the actual link speed, or the accumulated bandwidth of an MLTG can change as its links are activated and deactivated.

Send rate
: This is the rate at which the sender is currently allowed to send data. The send rate is initialized to 10% of the maximum allowed send rate for a new RTP connection and to 5% after a nondisruptive path switch. The smaller value after a path switch was chosen to avoid congestion on the new path since there may also be many other RTP connections switching to the same path.

: The initial allowed sending rates are deliberately kept small because it is assumed that during stable network operation the links along the path are being heavily (80-90%) utilized. Therefore, new connections being put on these links should start slowly in order to minimize bursting and thus avoid congestion for existing connections.

Minimum and maximum rate increment
: These are the minimum and maximum values used to increment the send rate. The values are typically set to 0.2% and 0.8%, respectively, of the maximum send rate.

The minimum rate increment is to allow for small oscillations (within a few percent of the path's capacity) in the operating region of ARB. The maximum rate increment is to allow the send rate to reach the operating region relatively quickly.

Rate increment
This is the value used to increment the sender's send rate. This value determines how quickly the send rate is increased. It is initially set to the maximum rate increment so that the send rate is increased at the maximum rate.

Burst size
This is the maximum number of bits of user data permitted to be sent by an ARB sender in the allotted burst time. It has a value of 65536 (8 KB). Only for very high send rates will it be adjusted to a larger value.

Burst time
This is an interval of time during which the ARB sender may send the number of bits defined in the burst size. The burst time is calculated by dividing the burst size by the current send rate. At high send rates the resulting value can become smaller than the minimum timer tick interval. When that happens, the burst size will be adjusted to allow the burst time to remain at the system minimum timer tick interval.

9.3.2 ARB Send Operation

Within each burst time interval, the ARB sender may send a maximum of 65536 bits (8 KB) of user data. The burst time interval is recalculated every time the burst time expires by dividing the burst size (normally 65536 bits) by the current send rate. This recalculation is necessary because the send rate may have been adjusted according to the recommendations received in a rate reply message since the last start of a burst interval.

At regular intervals of burst time duration the ARB sender is given permission to send burst size number of bits. If the burst timer expires several times in succession without any data being sent, the ARB sender is still limited to sending burst size number of bits (that is, the number of bits allowed does not accumulate). This is an important feature of the ARB algorithm. It tightly controls the rate at which data is allowed to enter the network by introducing gaps between blocks when a number of successive blocks are ready for transmission. This *smoothing effect* minimizes queueing that occurs within the network and thus increases throughput and maintains stable response times.

Figure 81 on page 223 shows an example illustrating the mechanism to ensure that the ARB sender maintains its currently allowed send rate within one sender's measurement interval. There are four blocks of user data to be sent: block A has a size of 10 KB; block B of 4 KB; blocks C and D of 8 KB each. There are five equal burst time intervals (B_1 through B_5). At the beginning of each burst time interval the sender is granted the right to send up to 8 KB of user data. Network and transport layer headers are not counted, but SNA transmission and request headers are (they are considered user data on the RTP connection). Note that the data is always sent at the physical (peak) rate of the outbound link, which is always greater than or equal to the allowed send rate.

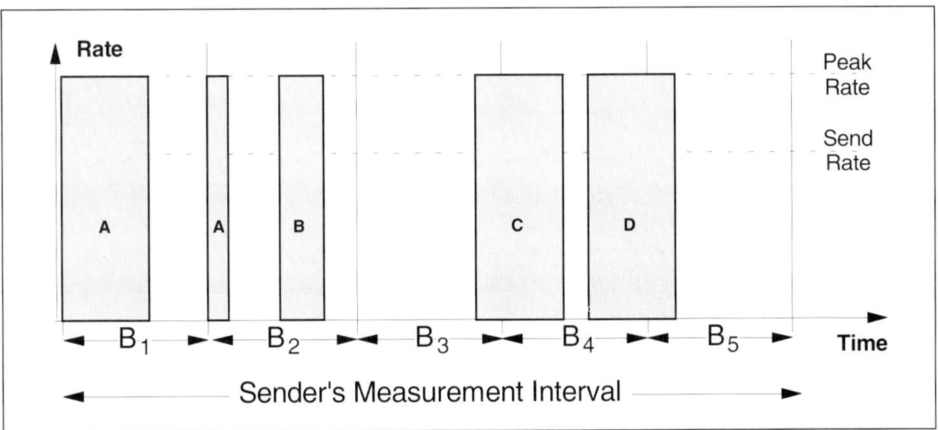

Figure 81. ARB Send Operation

When data block A arrives, the first 8 KB are sent in burst time interval B_1. Note that the largest message ever sent by RTP is either 8 KB (plus the network and transport layer header) or the largest packet size (including headers) allowed over the connection path, whichever is smaller. Thus, the 10 KB block of data in this example is segmented into 8 KB and 2 KB pieces. The remaining 2 KB of block A are sent starting at the beginning of burst time interval B_2

Note that in reality, data is passed to data link control (DLC) and the DLC will send it as soon as it is able to. Because there may be other RTP connections using the same outbound link, sending by the ARB sender actually means queueing a packet for transmission according to the RTP connection's transmission priority. The ARB sender's logic operates asynchronously to the DLC process so that it is possible that other events may occur and be processed by the ARB sender while the DLC is in the process of sending the data.

During burst time interval B_2, data block B arrives and is sent immediately because the 8 KB maximum is not exceeded. Near the end of interval B_3, data block C arrives and is sent. Block C is still being sent (by DLC) after interval B_4 has begun. Immediately after block C is sent, block D arrives and is sent. Note that during interval B_4, more than 8 KB of data may be sent by DLC (at the physical link speed). However, on the average, there is never more than 8 KB of data sent per burst time interval on one RTP connection.

9.3.3 Send Rate Adjustment

Whenever a data packet is ready to be sent, the ARB sender checks the amount of time that has elapsed since the last rate request message was sent. If this time interval is larger than the Short-Request timer period (which is the smoothed round-trip delay), the sender sends (along with the current packet which is being sent) a request for rate information to the receiver. The request is carried in the ARB optional segment of the RTP header and includes the sender's measurement interval (Ms), that is, the time that actually has elapsed since the last rate request was sent. Note that because rate requests are only sent when a user data packet is ready to be sent, the sender's measurement interval is no fixed value but will vary with the characteristics of the user data stream.

Upon receipt of the rate request, the receiver calculates the delay change (*dc* in Figure 82), which is the difference between the sender's measurement interval (Ms) and the receiver's measurement interval (Mr). This delay change represents the difference in network delay between the current (just received) rate request and the previously received rate request. A positive delay change indicates that the current rate request took longer to traverse the network than the previous one. If the change in delay is large enough, it will cause the sender's send rate to be lowered.

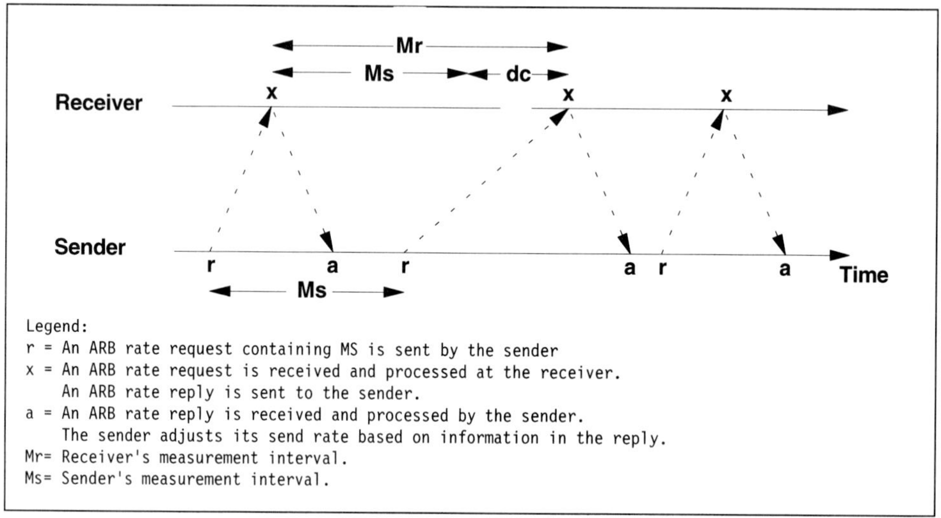

Figure 82. ARB Send Operation

Network delay can build up in two ways:

Sudden build-up

The current rate request took much longer to reach the receiver than the previous one (that is, the delay change is large). This can occur when traffic from other RTP connections suddenly causes build-up of queues in one or more intermediate nodes and the rate request gets stuck in those queues.

Gradual build-up

Small increases in delay occur over a series of rate requests. Each successive rate request experiences a little more delay than the previous one until finally there is significant delay and action needs to be taken.

The ARB algorithm accounts for both sudden and gradual delay build-up by keeping a running total of the delay changes. (Of course, this running total has to be cleared once action has been taken.)

Depending on the accumulated delay changes, the receiver will recommend appropriate actions to be taken by the sender. These actions will enable the sender to adapt the sending rate to network conditions. The actions taken and the recommendations given by the receiver depend on the value of the sum of the delay changes.

Sum of delay changes ≤ 0

This happens when there previously was queueing delay in the network and the queues have either disappeared or decreased in size when the current rate request was sent. It is desirable to increase the send rate to take advantage of the available network capacity. The receiver returns a *Normal* indication to the sender and resets the sum of delay changes to zero.

0 < sum of delay changes ≤ range begin time

The sum of delay changes is positive, indicating that some delay has occurred, but is less than the range begin time (see 9.3.1, "ARB Initialization" on page 220 for a description), which indicates the beginning of the ARB operating region. In order to reach the operating region, the receiver returns a *Normal* indication to the sender.

Range begin time < sum of delay changes ≤ range end time

This is the desired operating region, so the send rate should not be changed. The receiver returns the *Restraint* indication to the sender.

Range end time < sum of delay changes ≤ 4 × range end time

The end of the operating region has been exceeded. If the receiver detects that it has remained two consecutive times in this area and there is still positive delay change, then an indication of *Slowdown1* is returned (because delay is persistently building up in the network). Otherwise, an indication of *Restraint* is returned. When *Slowdown1* is returned, the sum of delay changes is reset to zero to ensure that this RTP connection does not reduce its send rate another time before other RTP connections have reduced their send rates first.

4 × range end time < range end time

As the probability of reaching this region because of a sudden build-up of network delay is relatively low, the reason for reaching this region will, at most, be internal delays in the RTP endpoints on either side. The sender will return an indication of *Restraint* because there is no reason to slow down the send rate when there is (most probably) no real network delay. If the network actually is the problem, then not slowing down the send rate will eventually lead to packet losses and the send rate will be reduced drastically.

In addition to returning an indication to the sender based on the accumulated delay changes, the receiver will also decide which indication to return based on conditions at the ARB receiver node. The algorithm for determining the indication is implementation dependent. For example, the indication could be set based on usage of the buffer pool as follows:

- *Normal* if the buffer usage is between 0% and 75%
- *Restraint* if the buffer usage is between 75% and 80%
- *Slowdown1* if the buffer usage is between 80% and 85%
- *Slowdown2* if the buffer usage is between 85% and 90%
- *Critical* if the buffer usage is above 90%

The rate reply will be piggybacked with a user data packet whenever possible. But because the rate reply has to be sent immediately to ensure that the round-trip delay (Short-Request timer) is correctly calculated, the rate reply will be sent as a stand-alone packet only with a transport header including the ARB segment carrying the rate reply message, if no data packet is currently queued for transmission.

Three *operating modes* determine how the send rate is adjusted by the sender based upon the feedback information. The operating mode is set to:

- GREEN when
  - The rate reply indication is *Normal* or *Restraint* and the current state is YELLOW
  - The RTP connection is idle (no data has been sent during the Alive timer interval)
- YELLOW when
  - The rate reply indication is *Normal* or *Restraint* and the current state is RED
  - The rate reply indication is *Slowdown1* or *Slowdown2* and the current state is GREEN or RED
- RED when
  - The rate reply indication is *Critical* and the current state is GREEN or YELLOW
  - No acknowledgment to sent data has been received as expected within the Short Request timer period and the current state is GREEN or YELLOW
  - The ARB sender has received a Status segment from the ARB receiver indicating that data has been lost and the current state is GREEN or YELLOW

In all other cases, the operation status remains unchanged.

The adaptation of the sending rate is based on the sender's current operating mode and the receiver's feedback.

- If the receiver's feedback is *Normal* and the current operating mode is GREEN, the send rate can be increased additively by an amount of rate increment. But it is increased only if the measured actual send rate is more than half the allowed send rate. (Why increase the allowed rate if it is not used anyhow?)
- If the receiver's feedback is *Normal* and the current operating mode is not GREEN, the send rate is not increased. This is done to avoid oscillation. Only the operating mode is changed from RED to YELLOW or YELLOW to RED respectively.
- If the receiver's feedback is *Restraint*, the send rate is not increased. Only the operating mode is changed from RED to YELLOW or YELLOW to RED respectively.
- If the receiver's feedback is *Slowdown1*, the send rate is reduced by 12.5%, if the maximum send rate is greater than 128 Kbps, or else by 25%. The operating mode is set to YELLOW.

  When the maximum send rate (the capacity of the slowest link along the path) is ≤ 128 Kbps, the minimum rate increment is initialized to a relatively large value of 1 Kbps, which is significantly larger than 0.2% of 128 Kbps. This makes the rate increases quite aggressive. Since the ARB algorithm operates in units of bits/ms, anything less than 1 increases its complexity. This problem is solved by countering an aggressive increase with an aggressive decrease.
- If the receiver's feedback is *Slowdown2*, the send rate is reduced by 25%. The operating mode is set to YELLOW.
- If the receiver's feedback is *Critical*, or no acknowledgment to sent data has been received as expected within the Short Request timer period, the send rate is reduced by 50% (but not to a lower value than 1 Kbps). The operating mode is set to RED.
- If the ARB sender has received a Status segment from the ARB receiver indicating that data has been lost and the current operating mode is YELLOW or GREEN, the send rate is reduced by 50% (but not to a lower value than 1 Kbps). The operating mode is set to RED.
- If the connection is idle (no data has been sent during the Alive timer interval) the send rate is reduced by 12.5% but not to a lower rate than the initial send rate. The operating mode is set to GREEN.

When the sender increases the send rate 16 times without any intervening decreases, the rate increment is increased additively by the minimum rate increment value (until it reaches the maximum rate increment). Increasing the send rate 16 times is an indication that bandwidth is available and the sender should increase its send rate as quickly as possible in order to reach the ARB operating region.

When the sender has either lowered (as a result of a non-critical condition) or not changed the send rate for a total of 16 times, the rate increment is decreased to half its current value. This condition occurs normally when operating within the ARB operating region. It is then desirable to use a small rate increase to minimize oscillation of the send rate and thus increase overall network throughput.

9.4 Optional Intermediate Node Interaction with ARB

It is desirable for an intermediate node to indicate when congestion is occurring in the case where the normal end-to-end ARB protocol is not otherwise able to detect it. This can occur, for example, when the committed information rate (CIR) is exceeded over a frame-relay link.

In Figure 83 on page 229, an RTP connection exists between nodes A and D, and is carried over a virtual circuit through a frame-relay network between nodes B and C. The ARB sender in node A has increased its (allowed) send rate to a value that is greater than the CIR defined for the frame-relay virtual circuit. When then the actual send rate exceeds the CIR, the frame-relay network sets the forward error congestion notification (FECN) bit, but as long as the frame-relay network has enough bandwidth available data will arrive in node C with no additional delays. Because the ARB receiver in node D does not measure an increase in delays, it will notify the ARB sender in node A to further increase the send rate. The ARB sender in node A will continue increasing its send rate until it exceeds the excessive information rate (EIR), which is the maximum rate allowed over the frame-relay virtual circuit. The frame-relay network discards packets that are in excess of EIR, which in turn (because packets are lost) causes the ARB sender in node A to cut its send rate drastically (by one half). Because there are still no measured delay increases, the ARB sender will again increase its send rate beyond EIR and will have to cut back after a number of measurement intervals. This wide oscillation in the send rate is undesirable because it reduces overall throughput.

The preferred method of operation in this scenario is to notify the ARB sender when congestion starts to occur (that is, when CIR is exceeded). This then causes the ARB sender to moderate its send rate such that it never exceeds EIR (thus avoiding packet losses). This minimizes oscillation and increases overall throughput. To achieve this, the frame-relay DTE in node C, when receiving the FECN indication, maps the FECN bit into the network layer header (NHDR) Slowdown indicator. This eventually causes the ARB sender to reduce its send rate.

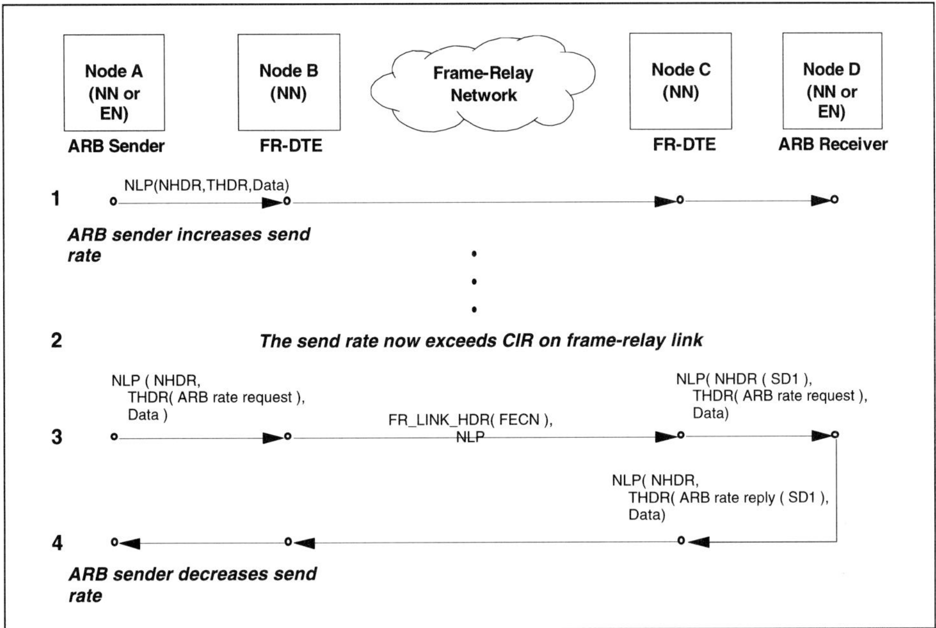

Figure 83. Intermediate Subnet Causing ARB Send Rate Reduction

Figure 83 explains how the optional intermediate node interaction works in detail:

1. The ARB sender in node A is sending network layer packets (NLPs) and keeps increasing its send rate because there are no delays in the network.
2. At this point, the send rate exceeds the CIR over the frame-relay virtual circuit.
3. The frame-relay network sets the FECN indicator on the frame-relay link header (FR_LINK_HDR) in every packet that exceeds the CIR. When node C receives a packet with the FECN indicator, it sets the *Slowdown1* (SD1) indicator in the NHDR (that is, it maps the FECN indicator into the Slowdown1 indicator). The ARB receiver in node D observes SD1 when it is set in an NLP that contains an ARB rate request (the SD1 indicator is ignored in NLPs that do not contain an ARB rate request).
4. The ARB receiver reflects the SD1 condition by setting the *Slowdown1* indication in the ARB rate reply. This causes the ARB sender in node A to reduce its send rate and prevent packet loss by not allowing EIR to be exceeded on the frame-relay virtual circuit.

9.5 RTP Connection Fairness

As the ARB algorithm detects congestion starting to occur, it reduces the sending rate until the network has the capacity to handle the offered load again. The objective of the

ARB algorithm is to smooth the traffic flow through the network, rather than allowing traffic throughput in the network to oscillate.

When multiple RTP connections use the same network resources, there are different mechanisms which affect the network performance. If two RTP connections share the same link, and the transmission priorities are different, then the higher-priority traffic will always be scheduled for transmission before lower-priority traffic. As links reach their maximum capacity, the queues for lower-priority traffic (starting with transmission priority 0) will start building up and their delays will start to increase first. Consequently, RTP connections for lower transmission priorities will decrease the allowed send rate while RTP connections for higher transmission priorities are not affected or might even increase their send rate.

If two RTP connections share the same link, and the transmission priorities are the same, then as traffic builds up, the throughput of both RTP connections will start to decrease. The ARB functions in both RTP connections will then reduce the flow of traffic in parallel by the same percentage. This means that the RTP connection with the higher send rate will decrement its send rate faster than the RTP connection with the slower send rate. This eventually leads to both RTP connections stabilizing at the same send rate. This process works regardless of whether the whole paths taken by each RTP connection are the same or not. Even if two RTP connections share only one common link, the individual ARB processes will handle congestion over both paths.

Chapter 10. Border Node

This chapter describes the optional APPN functions for network nodes, known as the *peripheral border node*, *extended border node*, and *branch network node* functions and also introduces the concept of *subnetworks* and *clusters*.

In the base APPN architecture, network nodes within an APPN network must share the same net ID (as opposed to end nodes, which may have a net ID different from their adjacent node's net ID).

The border node functions allow the connection of APPN networks having different net IDs, thus allowing session setup across subnetwork boundaries. Border nodes also allow the partitioning of single-net-ID networks into (topology) subnetworks. This reduces the size of topology databases and the flow of topology update traffic, allowing network nodes with limited resources to participate in APPN networking.

The peripheral border node is supported on AS/400 in OS/400 Version 2 Release 1 and above and the extended border node is supported in VTAM Version 4 Release 2 and above.

10.1 Subnetworks and Clusters

The following list is a description of some of the terms used in this chapter. Figure 84 on page 233 is an illustration of the first four terms described below:

Subnetwork or subnet
: Within the APPN context, a subnetwork or subnet is a collection of interconnected nodes and links with some logical association and which are part of a larger composite network.

Composite Network
: A composite network is a network consisting of two or more subnetworks.

Net ID subnetwork
: A net ID subnetwork is an APPN (or subarea) network in which all the nodes have the same network identifier or net ID.

APPN topology subnetwork
: An APPN topology subnetwork is an APPN subnetwork in which all the network nodes share the same topology database.

APPN cluster
: An APPN cluster is an APPN topology subnetwork which is a proper subset of some APPN net ID subnetwork. This term is generally used when referring to the topology subnets of a partitioned APPN subnet.

Native subnetwork (or native subnet)
Native subnetwork (or native subnet) and nonnative subnetwork are relative terms. The subnetwork in which a resource resides is that resource's native subnet and other subnets in its composite network are nonnative subnets to that node.

Intermediate subnet
An intermediate subnet, as its name suggests, is a subnet that supports intermediate network routing for sessions with endpoints in two other subnets.

Peripheral subnet
A peripheral subnet is a subnet that may contain an endpoint of an intersubnet session, but never acts as an intermediate subnetwork to connect two different subnetworks.

Figure 84 on page 233 illustrates the following:

- Networks 2, 3, 4, 5 and 6 are all subnetworks.
- Networks 1 and 2 are composite networks.
- Networks 3, 4, 5 and 6 are all topology subnetworks.
- Networks 3 and 4 are clusters of NETA.

The peripheral border node function does not allow adjacent subnets to have the same network identifier (net ID). In Figure 84 on page 233, peripheral border nodes could connect subnet 5 with 6 and both 5 and 6 with subnets 3 and 4. However, a peripheral border node could not connect subnets 3 and 4 while keeping them as separate topology subnets. A peripheral border node in either subnet 3 or 4 connecting with a network node or peripheral border node in the other would in fact merge them into one larger topology subnet (here, it is subnet 2).

The extended border node function allows partitioning of an APPN network into two or more subnetworks each having the same net ID. Extended border nodes could connect all subnets shown in Figure 84 on page 233, including subnets 3 and 4, while still keeping them as separate topology subnets or clusters.

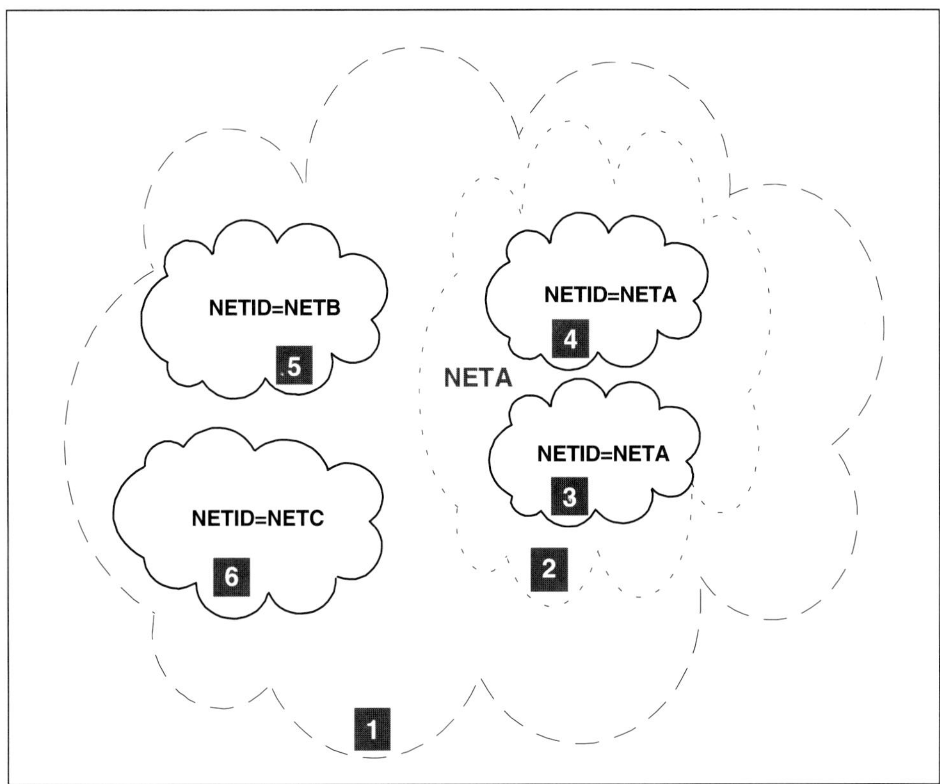

Figure 84. Subnetworks and Clusters

The following sections describe the two types of border node as defined in the APPN architecture.

10.2 Peripheral Border Node

A peripheral border node is an APPN network node that includes the APPN optional function set 1014 (Peripheral Border Node). The current border node support for AS/400 is based on the peripheral border node function. A network node in the nonnative network that connects to a peripheral border node requires function set 1013 (Interoperability with Peripheral Border Node). This function set, or at least a part of it, also is required in every network node in the two networks that calculates an RSCV for a session crossing a subnet border.

Note: This requirement also applies for sessions going through extended border nodes.

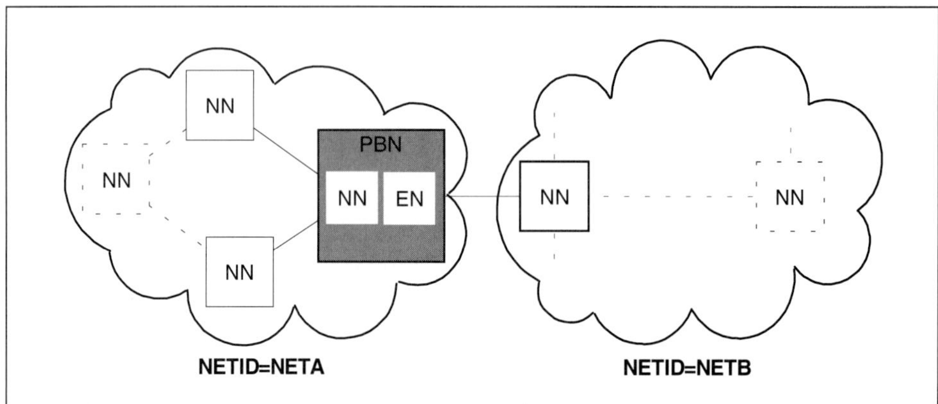

Figure 85. Peripheral Border Node Connection

Figure 85 shows the basic form of two subnets being interconnected by a peripheral border node. The peripheral border node (PBN) has one CP with an NN image to its native network and an EN image to the nonnative network.

A peripheral border node does not pass topology information between its native network and nonnative networks. A peripheral border node portrays itself as a network node to native partner network nodes and as an end node to nonnative network nodes; thus, topology database update messages can only be sent to, and received from, network nodes within the native subnet.

A peripheral border node can connect either to a network node or a border node in the nonnative subnetwork. In this section, border nodes will be considered to be peripheral border nodes. Extended border node and peripheral border node connectivity is discussed in 10.3, "Extended Border Node" on page 244.

When two peripheral border nodes are connected (see Figure 86), one of them will present a network node image to the other in order to keep the asymmetrical connection required by the peripheral border node function. Which peripheral border node will assume which role is decided during XID exchange. The peripheral border node with the *lower* net ID will present the end node image and the node with the *higher* net ID will portray a network node (see Figure 86 on page 235).

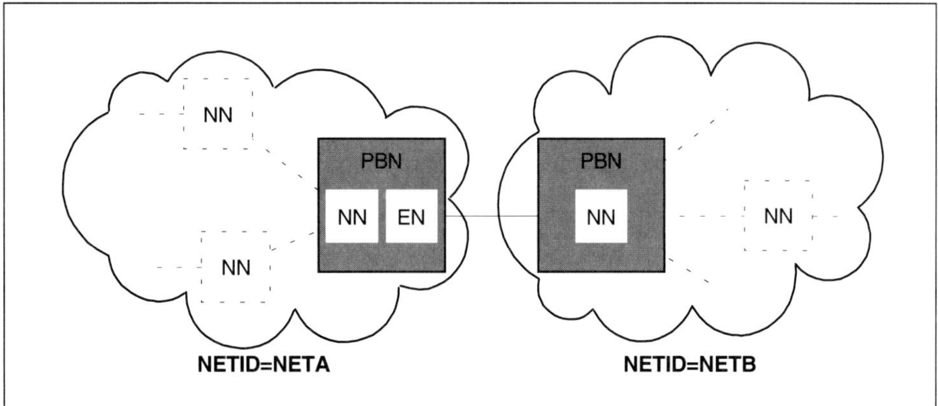

Figure 86. Peripheral Border Node to Peripheral Border Node Connection

Figure 87 on page 236 shows two subnets with multiple peripheral border nodes connected in parallel providing enhanced internetwork availability and bandwidth. The figure illustrates parallel connections where A) multiple peripheral border nodes reside in the same subnet, and B) where both subnets each have one peripheral border node.

A peripheral border node can be connected to both network nodes and end nodes in nonnative subnets. However, only connections to network nodes (or other peripheral border nodes) will provide a connection between the two networks through which sessions can be established between LUs residing on any nodes in either subnet. Figure 88 on page 237 illustrates two examples of how a peripheral border node can connect several subnets.

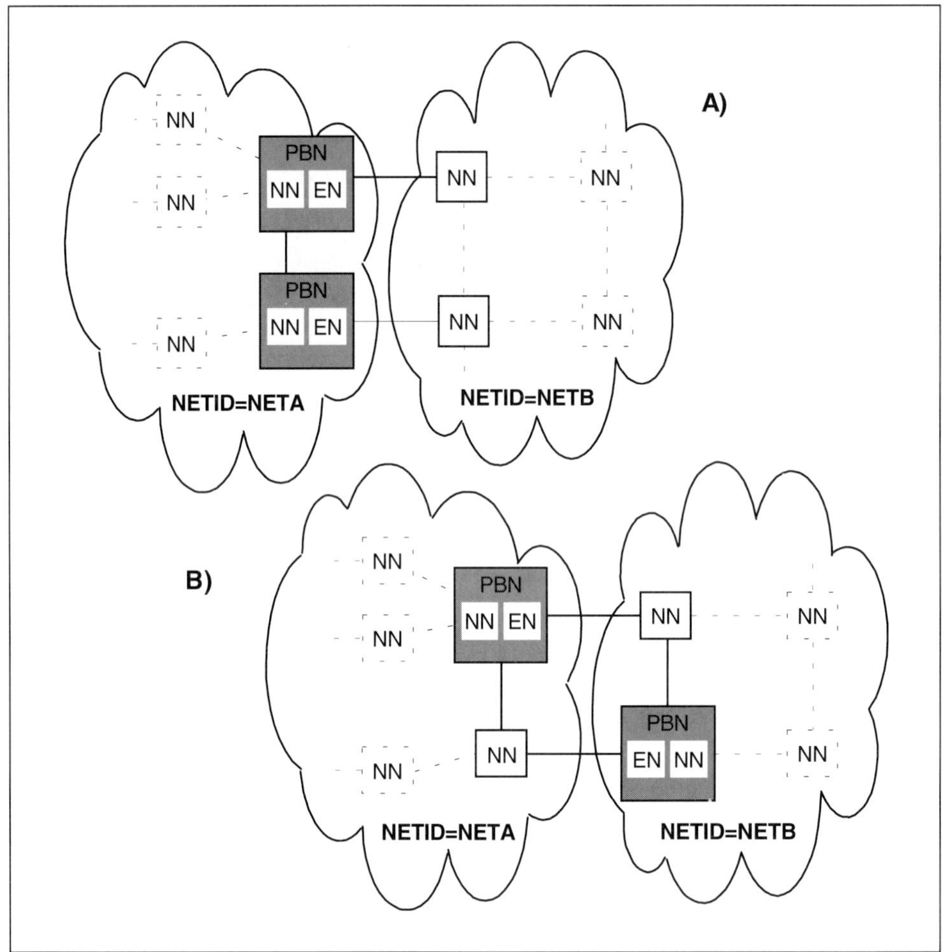

Figure 87. Parallel Peripheral Border Node Connections

The peripheral border node in NETA connects to network nodes in NETE and NETC. The network nodes in both subnets will serve as the network node server of the peripheral border node, NNS(PBN), for their respective subnets. The peripheral border node in NETD shows the case when the PBN portrays itself as an APPN end node to a network node in one subnet (NETE), and as an APPN network node to a peripheral border node (acting as an end node) in another subnet (NETC).

Because of a peripheral border node limitation, described below, no sessions can be established between LUs residing in NETA and NETD, nor between LUs residing in NETC and NETE.

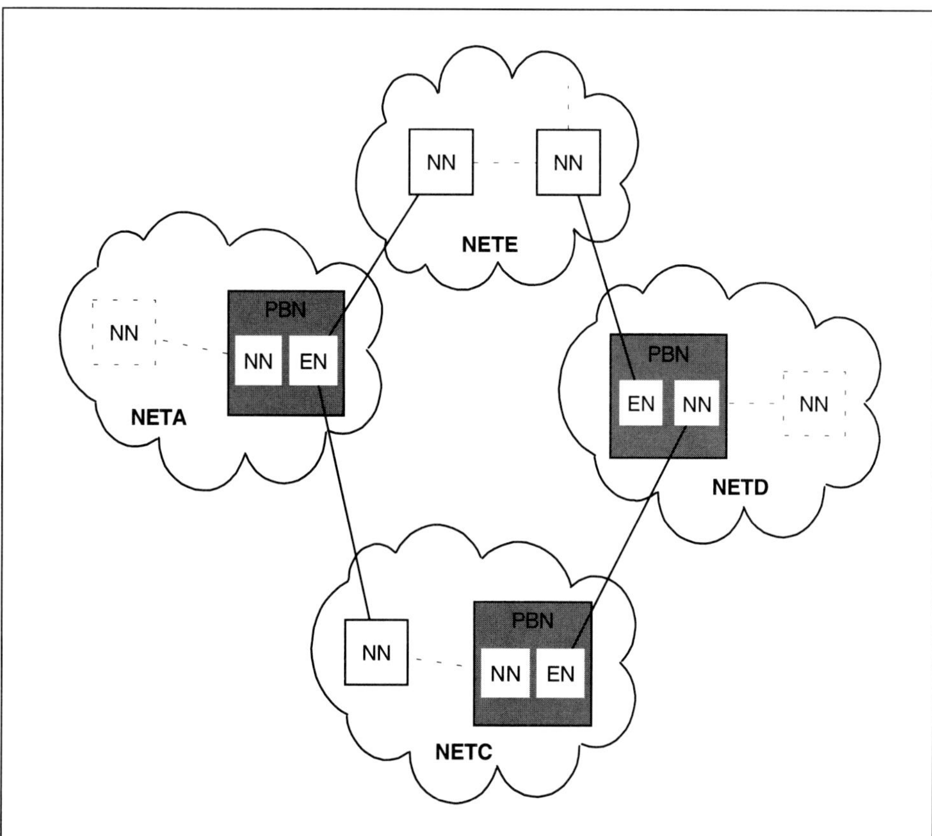

Figure 88. Peripheral Border Node Connections to Multiple Subnets

10.2.1 Multisubnet Searches

The border node concept allows session setup between LUs residing in different subnetworks. With the peripheral border node function, cross-network sessions are only possible between session partners that reside in adjacent subnetworks.

In APPN, the destination LU (DLU) must be located with a Locate search request, before a session BIND can flow between the session partners. A peripheral border node that provides the end node image on its connection to an adjacent network node or peripheral border node will forward Locate search requests over an intersubnetwork link only if the net ID of the origin LU matches the peripheral border node's native net ID and if the net ID of the destination LU matches that of the node receiving the Locate request over that link.

Note: This limitation will not apply if the peripheral border node is connected to an extended border node. Peripheral border node and extended border node connectivity is discussed in 10.3, "Extended Border Node" on page 244.

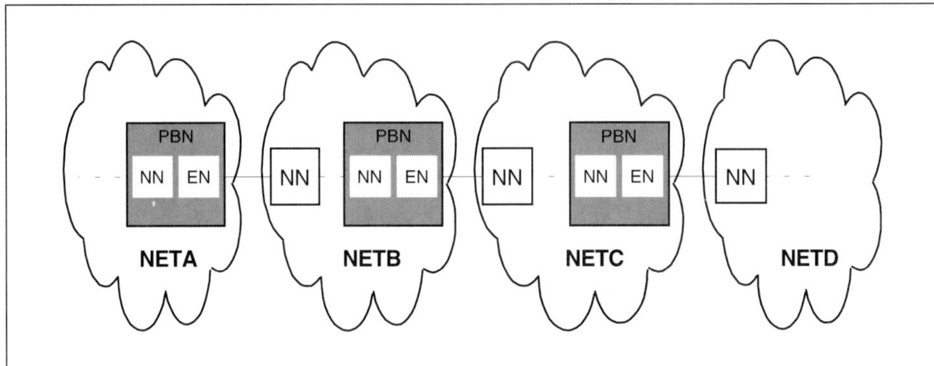

Figure 89. Cascaded Networks with Peripheral Border Nodes. LUs in NETC and NETD are not able to establish sessions with LUs in NETA, nor are LUs in NETA or NETB able to establish sessions with LUs in NETD.

To allow a border node to control searches across subnet boundaries, border node architecture defines two functions during the Locate search flows in addition to base APPN architecture:

- The initiator of a search procedure can indicate in the Locate request that the search should be restricted to the native network. A border node will not accept a Locate request received over an intersubnetwork link, nor will it forward a Locate request across an intersubnetwork link, if this has been specified.
- Since peripheral border nodes do not support intermediate network routing, the scope of searches needs to be limited to the origin network and its adjacent networks. A peripheral border node, its EN side to be specific, will add the information to a Locate request, before forwarding it across an intersubnetwork link, that this request has already crossed a subnetwork border. If a peripheral border node (again, its "EN side") finds this information in a Locate request received across an intersubnetwork link, it sends back a negative reply and does not propagate this search request into its native subnetwork. This has the effect that sessions across subnetwork boundaries are (with the peripheral border node function) limited to sessions between LUs residing in adjacent subnetworks.

10.2.2 Parallel PBN Connections and Duplicate Search Collisions

Because border nodes route search requests into adjacent subnets, it is possible that multiple Locate search requests enter the destination subnet; for example, when a broadcast search occurs in the origin subnet and multiple peripheral border nodes provide connections between the origin and destination subnet.

The impact is deemed to be minimal because, once a resource has been located, the network node server of the originating LU will cache information associated with a specific peripheral border node, and subsequent searches will not collide.

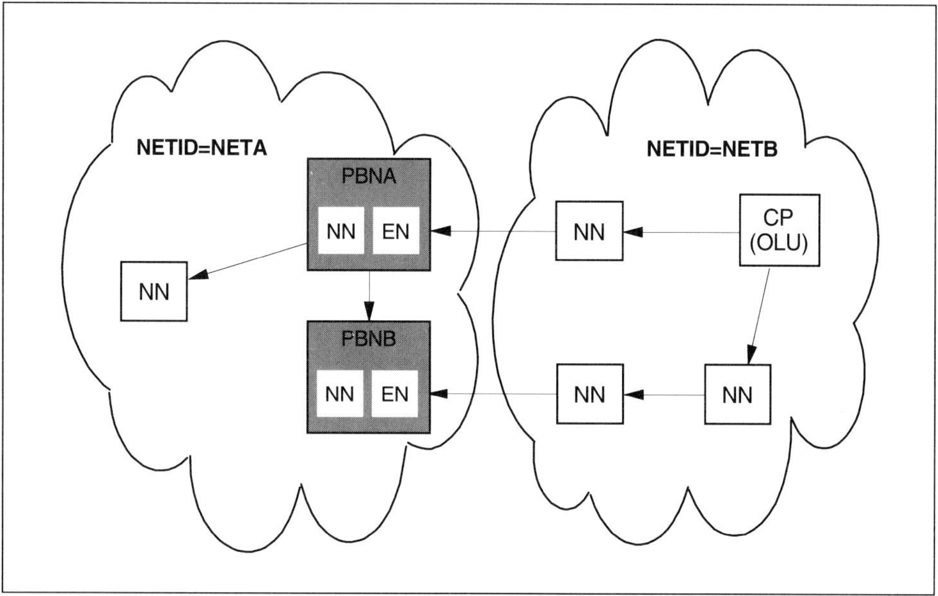

Figure 90. FQPCID Caching with Parallel Peripheral Border Nodes

To minimize the impact of this collision problem, the concept of FQPCID caching has been developed. A peripheral border node that implements FQPCID caching does two things:

FQPCID Caching
A peripheral border node caches the FQPCIDs of all those searches received from adjacent network nodes in its native subnetwork that have already crossed a subnetwork boundary (according to the information in the Locate request).

FQPCID Checking
A peripheral border node receiving a Locate request across an intersubnetwork connection rejects this request if the FQPCID is contained within its FQPCID cache, indicating that this request has been forwarded into its native subnetwork already through an alternate peripheral border node.

The benefit of FQPCID caching is shown in Figure 90 on page 239. A broadcast search is started in subnet NETB from CP(OLU). The search request will eventually reach both peripheral border nodes in subnet NETA. As the search request, in our example, has to pass one more node before reaching PBNB, there is a good chance that PBNA receives the search request earlier than PBNB. PBNA then will start a broadcast search in subnet NETA using the FQPCID from the search in NETB. If this broadcast search in NETA arrives in PBNB before the search request from subnet NETB, PBNB will not initiate a broadcast search in subnet NETA because it already knows about the search when checking its FQPCID cache.

10.2.3 Route Selection

Internetwork routing through peripheral border nodes is accomplished by calculating two piece-wise optimal routes, as illustrated in Figure 91 on page 241.

In both case A and case B in Figure 91 on page 241 the first calculation will take place at the network node server of CP(OLU), NNS(OLU), and result in an optimal route from CP(OLU) to the peripheral border node (PBN). The second route computation will take place at the PBN (NNS(PBN)) in case A and at the PBN in case B and results in an optimal route from the peripheral border node to CP(DLU). These two routes together form a continuous end-to-end route, which is piece-wise optimal in each subnet but not necessarily end-to-end optimal.

Note: The above section refers to the *network node server of the peripheral border node*, this is the non-native network node adjacent to the peripheral border node

Furthermore, each of the optimal routes is calculated by a node according to its (local) COS definitions for the COS name carried in the session request and according to the node and TG characteristics within the given subnet. To provide COS definition independence in each subnet, border nodes use the COS name specified in the Locate/CD-Initiate and map them to COS names specific to their native subnet. Unrecognized COS names will be mapped to some (definable) default COS name. Base APPN nodes that are connected to nonnative border nodes are not able to provide this mapping function for their native subnet and hence must support the COS name specified in the session initiation flow received from the border node.

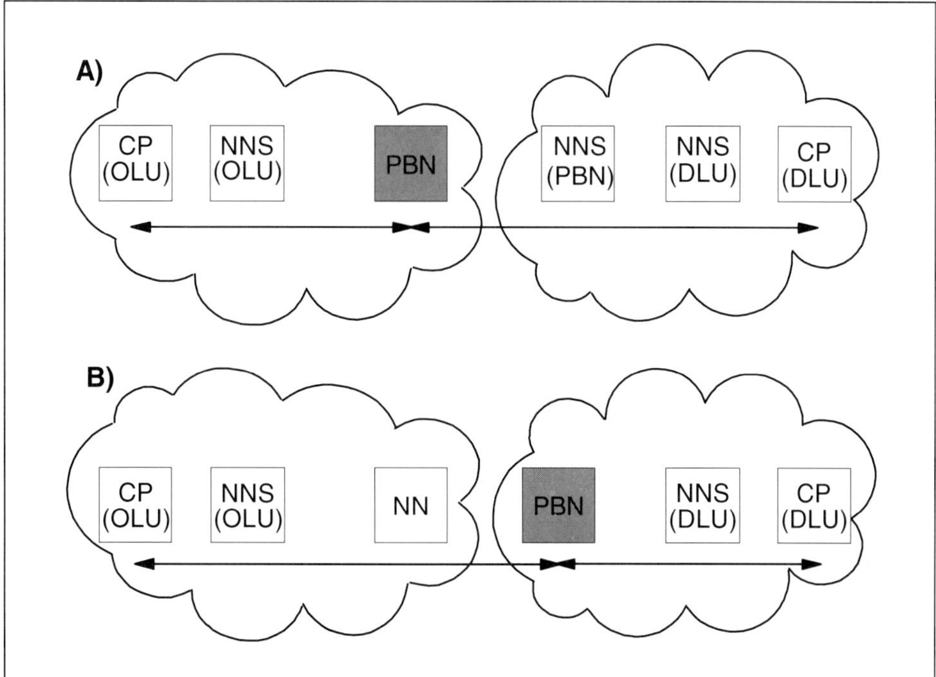

Figure 91. Piece-Wise Optimal Route Calculation

For this reason, we strongly recommend that border nodes be configured to support all IBM-architected default COS names without mapping.

10.2.4 Session Initiation

Because the only implementation of the peripheral border node function is currently on AS/400, and AS/400 does not support the session setup flows for SLU-initiated (dependent LU) sessions, we restrict the discussion in this section to PLU-initiated sessions (that is, OLU=PLU). A PLU is said to be native if it resides in the same subnet as the peripheral border node, and nonnative if not. Because the session initiation flows are slightly different for the two cases, they are described separately in the two following sections.

10.2.4.1 Native PLUs

When a peripheral border node receives a search request from within its subnet (this is case A in Figure 91), it performs the base-APPN search logic. If it is necessary to forward the search into the adjacent subnet, it caches the FQPCID and other information associated with the OLU. When forwarding the Locate/Find to its nonnative NNS, it indicates that the NNS(OLU) is the *real* network node server and replaces any existing endpoint TG vectors with endpoint TG vectors representing all TGs from itself to NNs (including PBNs emulating ENs) in the destination subnet.

The NN receiving this Locate/Find then acts as the normal network node server for a connected EN and presents itself as the NNS(OLU) associated with the real CP(OLU) in the origin network. If the COS name specified in the Locate is defined at this NN, the request is propagated into this NN's subnet (or else it is rejected).

Once the DLU has been located, the NNS(DLU) caches information indicating that the OLU is located on the real CP(OLU) served by the NNS of the peripheral border node. It then returns a Locate/Found with the endpoint TG vectors of the CP(DLU).

When receiving this Locate/Found reply, the NNS of the peripheral border node caches information about the DLU, which can be used in future search requests. It then calculates a route from the PBN to the CP(DLU) and passes the Locate/Found with this RSCV back to the PBN. Note that this route can use any of the TGs connecting the peripheral border node with this NN's native subnet.

The peripheral border node caches this RSCV, the COS information, and the associated FQPCID for use on the subsequent BIND. It then modifies the resource hierarchy to indicate that the DLU has been found on the real CP(DLU) with itself as the network node server and the NNS(DLU) as the real network node server. In addition, it appends an endpoint TG vector representing the first TG of the received RSCV. This TG will appear as a TG from itself to an EN with the CP name of the CP(DLU). The Locate reply is then returned to the NNS(OLU)

The NNS(OLU) calculates a route to the real CP(DLU) in accordance with base-APPN architecture, based upon the endpoint TG vector returned from the peripheral border node. Since this is the only endpoint TG vector in the reply from the peripheral border node, the route calculated is guaranteed to traverse this peripheral border node. The Locate/Found is then passed back to the CP(PLU), which uses it to send the BIND for the requested session.

When this BIND is received from the native PLU, the PBN uses the FQPCID to check its cache for an RSCV to the CP(DLU). If it is found, the peripheral border node replaces the RSCV in the BIND with the cached RSCV for the destination subnet, builds a session connector, and forwards the BIND using the new RSCV towards the CP(DLU). If no RSCV can be found for the FQPCID (for example, because the cached entry has been purged from the cache), then the peripheral border node removes the RSCV from the BIND and forwards it to its nonnative NNS. This NNS then treats this BIND like a *surprise* BIND coming from a LEN node and initiates the proper session establishment protocols.

On returning the BIND response, the peripheral border node includes all the information that is expected by the session origin (for example, swapping back the original RSCV).

10.2.4.2 Nonnative PLUs

When a peripheral border node receives a search request from a nonnative partner NN (this is case B in Figure 91 on page 241), it arrives on the EN interface of the peripheral border node. If the net ID of the DLU matches its own net ID, this search request has to be forwarded into its subnet (or else the search is rejected). It then modifies the associated resource entries in the Locate/Find to indicate that it is the NNS(PLU) of the real (nonnative) CP(PLU) and the NNS(PLU) as the real NNS(PLU). The peripheral border node also uses the COS information that may be present and maps the COS name to some natively significant COS. If the COS name in the Locate is not recognized, the peripheral border node maps this to some native default COS definition. The peripheral border node must cache the nonnative COS information received with the associated FQPCID, so that it can be returned on the Locate reply.

Once the DLU has been located, the NNS(DLU) caches the OLU information indicating that the OLU resides on the real nonnative CP(PLU), which is an EN served by the peripheral border node. It then sends a Locate/Found response (with the appropriate endpoint TG vectors included) back along the search path to the peripheral border node.

When the Locate/Found reply is received at the peripheral border node, it caches the DLU's resource information and, acting as the NNS(PLU), calculates an RSCV to the CP(DLU). This RSCV is then cached together with the COS information and the associated FQPCID. If the DLU resides on an NN in the native subnet, the peripheral border node modifies the resource information such that the CP(DLU) appears to be an EN with the NNS(DLU) as the real network node server. The peripheral border node then replaces the endpoint TG vectors in the Locate/Found reply with endpoint TG vectors that represent all the TGs from itself to NNs in the origin subnet.

The nonnative network node server of the peripheral border node indicates itself as the NNS(DLU) when forwarding the Locate/Found to the NNS(PLU).

The NNS(PLU) caches the DLU as residing in CP(DLU), which appears to be an EN served by the network node server of the peripheral border node. But because the endpoint TG vectors are TGs to the peripheral border node, the NNS(PLU) then calculates a route to this peripheral border node and returns the calculated RSCV in the Locate/Found to the CP(PLU). The CP(PLU) constructs a BIND and sends it on the session path towards the peripheral border node.

When this BIND is received at the peripheral border node, it uses the FQPCID to check its cache for an RSCV to the CP(DLU). If it is found, the peripheral border node replaces the RSCV in the BIND with the cached RSCV, builds a session connector, and forwards the BIND using the new RSCV towards the CP(DLU). If no RSCV can be found for the FQPCID (for example, because the cached entry has been purged from the cache), the peripheral border node treats this BIND like a *surprise* BIND coming from a LEN node and initiates the proper session establishment protocols.

On returning the BIND response, the peripheral border node includes all the information that is expected by the session origin (for example, swapping back the original RSCV).

10.3 Extended Border Node

Extended border node is the second stage of the APPN border node function. An extended border node is an APPN network node that includes the APPN optional function set 1016 (Extended Border Node). Options sets 1014 (Peripheral Border Node) and 1063 (Session Services Extensions Network Node Server Support) are prerequisites of this function. Extended border nodes support intermediate network routing while being able to limit the number of subnetworks being traversed. The border node support for APPN VTAM is based on extended border node. Figure 92 shows the basic form of two subnets being interconnected by an extended border node.

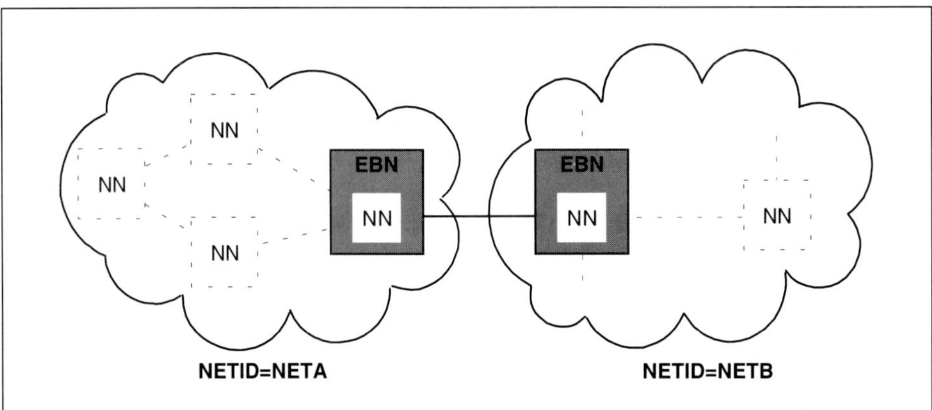

Figure 92. Extended Border Node Connection

Major enhancements in comparison with the peripheral border node are:

- Extended border node allows session establishment between LUs residing in nonadjacent subnets.
- Extended border node allows partitioning of net ID subnets into two or more topology subnets or clusters with the same net ID.

Other differences compared to peripheral border nodes are:

- An extended border node presents a network node image to other extended border nodes; it appears as an end node to peripheral border nodes and network nodes in other (peripheral) net ID networks.
- FQPCID caching, see page 239, becomes a mandatory function.
- An extended border node identifies itself as such by its CP capabilities boundary node identifier to adjacent nonnative extended border nodes and all other network nodes in its native network.

10.3.1 Intersubnet TGs and Topology Isolation

An extended border node presents an NN image to all extended border nodes and to all network nodes in its native network. Similar to a peripheral border node, an extended border node presents an EN image to adjacent nonnative network nodes. When activating a link to a nonnative peripheral border node, it will not negotiate its image, but will always present itself as an end node

An extended border node determines its partner nodes subnet affiliation during XID prenegotiation in two ways:

1. If the net ID portion of the partner's CP name is not the same as its own net ID, then this is a subnet boundary and the partner node is in a different subnet.
2. If the prenegotiation XID3 contains a TG Descriptor control vector this will be checked to see if the TG is defined as an *intersubnet TG*. (Extended border nodes will always include a TG Descriptor control vector in the prenegotiation XID3.) If the TG is defined as an intersubnet TG, then this will be a subnet boundary regardless of the net ID. The definition of an intersubnet TG by one of the nodes will suffice to define a subnet boundary.

Figure 93 shows an example of a net ID subnetwork partitioned into two topology subnetworks or clusters. This reduces the size of topology databases and results in fewer topology updates broadcast through the network. Clustering can be helpful in large networks where topology databases have become too large and/or the flow of topology updates is too great. Thus, it allows network nodes with limited resources to participate in APPN networking.

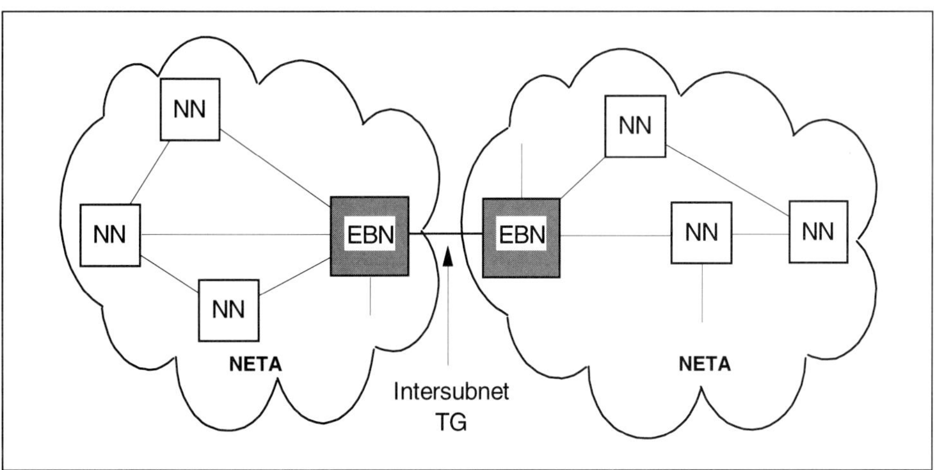

Figure 93. Net ID Subnet Partitioned into Two Clusters (Topology Subnets). The transmission group linking the two extended border nodes will need to be defined as an intersubnet TG in at least one of the extended border nodes.

Since an extended border node presents an NN image to native network nodes, it will exchange topology update information with network nodes in its native subnet. However, as one of the functions of an extended border node is to provide topology isolation between distinct subnets, it will not forward topology updates from its native subnet to an adjacent subnet. An extended border node will, however, send a TDU containing a Node Characteristics CV across an intersubnet TG to its partner extended border node. TDUs received over an intersubnet TG will never be propagated into the native network.

10.3.2 Intermediate and Peripheral Subnets

The terms *intermediate* and *peripheral subnet* were introduced with the extended border node function. An intermediate subnet supports intermediate network routing for sessions with endpoints in two other subnets. See NETB and NETC in Figure 94. A peripheral subnet is a subnet that may contain an endpoint of an intersubnet session, for example NETA and NETD in Figure 94, but never acts as an intermediate subnetwork to connect two different subnetworks.

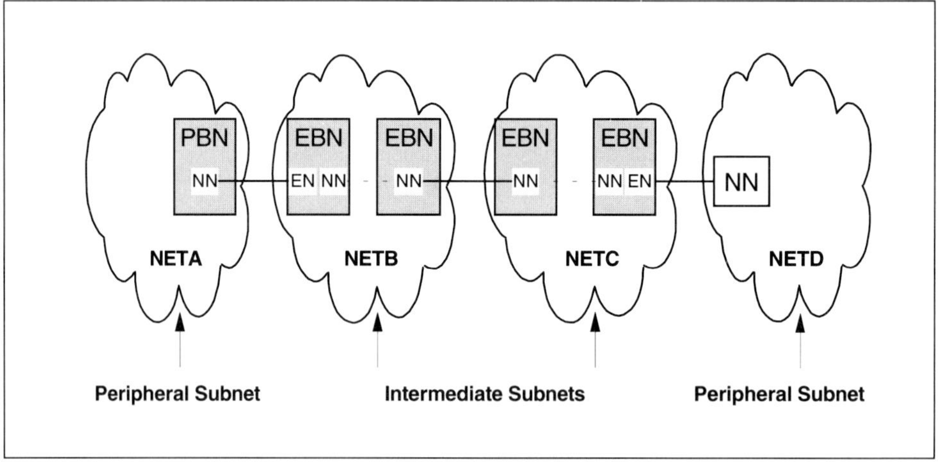

Figure 94. Cascaded Network Support (Extended Border Node)

Only extended border nodes can be at the boundary of intermediate subnets. Either an *ordinary* network node or a peripheral border node can be at the boundary of a peripheral subnet (see Figure 94).

10.3.3 Multisubnet Searches

The border node concept allows session setup between LUs residing in different subnetworks. The extended border node, unlike a peripheral border node, allows cross-network sessions between session partners that reside in cascaded subnetworks.

When an extended border node receives a Locate search, it must decide whether to do a border node search or not. A border node search is a search of additional subnets beyond the local directory and domain. A search of additional subnets is possible if a subnet list is defined and contains a list of at least one border node (or net ID) outside of the native subnet to which a search for a resource (with a given net ID) can be forwarded. In the absence of a subnet list, implementation options include:

- No searches outside local subnet (unless location is cached)
- Limiting of searches to adjacent subnets only
- Sending unrestricted searches to all adjacent subnets, which may then, depending on the subnet lists in other extended border nodes, be forwarded throughout the network

A border node search may include a broadcast search of the native subnet. Each extended border node in a search path acts independently of searches initiated at other extended border nodes occurring earlier in the path.

When an extended border node receives a search across an intersubnet TG, it will check its subnet list for the destination's net ID. If the subnet list includes an entry for the extended border node receiving the search itself, a broadcast search of this extended border node's native subnet will be done. If this broadcast search fails or if the subnet list does not include the extended border node itself, the search will be forwarded across intersubnet links directly attached to the extended border node and to other extended border nodes in the native subnetwork according to the entries in the subnet list.

When an extended border node receives a search from its native subnetwork, it will only forward the search across directly attached intersubnet TGs (again, according to the entries in its subnet list) because other extended border nodes in its native subnetwork will also receive the search and forward the search to their attached nonnative subnetworks.

If the resource is not found in the local search and if the border node search is not run, the extended border node replies with a *not found*.

10.3.4 Route Selection

Intersubnet routing across subnets and through border nodes (BNs) is accomplished by calculating piece-wise optimal routes. Routes are calculated across subnets from an entry BN to the BN exiting that subnet. Exit BNs must route to an adjacent BN, which will be the entry BN to the adjacent subnet. For PLU-initiated sessions, intrasubnet route computation is performed by the NNS(PLU), by the entry extended border nodes along the tentative session path, and/or by the peripheral border node or network node connected to the last exit extended border node. Intra-subnet route computation also defines a COS-acceptable route from the CP(OLU) to the CP(DLU) (see Figure 95 on page 248), as described in 10.2.3, "Route Selection" on page 240.

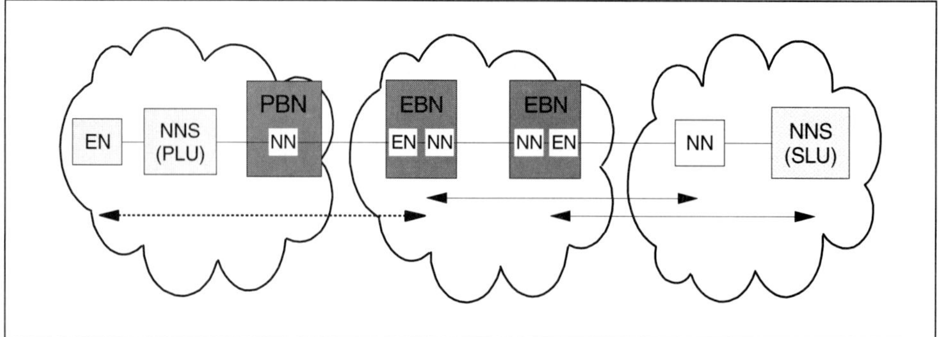

Figure 95. Route Selection with Extended Border Nodes

10.3.5 Session Initiation

In order to provide consistency with session setup flows within a subnetwork (as defined by base-APPN architecture), a border node must modify information carried on Locate and BIND flows. For example, COS/TPF information may be altered to ensure a correct selection of a multi-subnet session path. This section describes the functions performed on the intersubnet connection between extended border nodes for a PLU initiated session. The functions performed on connections from extended border nodes to peripheral border nodes or to NNs (in peripheral subnets only) where the extended border node assumes an EN role are described in 10.2, "Peripheral Border Node" on page 233.

Whenever an extended border node receives a search request (Locate/Find) (independent of its location on the search path), it will first decide whether to do a BN search or not. If it must forward the search, it must forward the search to the designated node only if it can find a COS-acceptable route (or intersubnetwork TG) to that node.

The origin BN (that is, the BN in the origin subnet) modifies the associated resource entries in the Locate/Find to indicate that it (the BN itself) is the NNS(OLU) with the CP(OLU) appearing as an EN connected to the BN, and the NNS(OLU) as the real NNS(OLU).

Extended border nodes at every entry point into a subnetwork must ensure that the COS/TPF information in the Locate/Find is replaced with information that has meaning for the local subnet. If the COS-name is not recognized it is mapped to some defined default COS definition. The COS/TPF information received is stored with the associated FQPCID for reference when the Locate reply arrives.

Extended border nodes at every exit point from a subnetwork indicate themselves as the NNS(OLU) before forwarding the Locate/Find across the intersubnetwork TG.

The destination border node (that is, the extended border node in the destination subnet) indicates itself as the NNS(OLU) and adds an endpoint TG vector for the intersubnetwork TG, over which the Locate/Find was received.

Once the DLU has been located, the NNS(DLU) will cache the OLU's information, append the appropriate endpoint TG vector(s) of the CP(DLU) and return a Locate/Found back to the destination border node.

The destination border node modifies the resource information of the DLU to indicate that it (the BN itself) is the NNS(DLU) with the CP(DLU) appearing as an EN connected to the BN, and the NNS(OLU) as the real NNS(DLU). A COS-acceptable route is calculated to the CP(DLU) and the resulting RSCV cached associated with the FQPCID in order to properly route the forthcoming BIND.

Every border node, before forwarding the Locate/Found to its partner border node, indicates itself as the NNS(DLU).

The origin border node (that is, the extended border node in the OLU's subnet) indicates itself as the NNS(DLU) and adds an endpoint TG vector for the intersubnetwork TG, over which the Locate/Find was received.

The NNS(OLU) will cache the information about the DLU indicating that the DLU resides on the nonnative CP(DLU). It will then calculate a route to the (as it thinks) CP(DLU) through the origin border node using the endpoint TG vector describing the intersubnetwork TG (provided by the origin border node). The resulting RSCV is then included in the BIND sent towards the origin border node.

All border nodes receiving the BIND translate the destination information (for example, information about the NNS and CP of the DLU) that may have previously been cached during the Locate flows. If the destination information is not available (cached), the border node must perform the normal Locate functions to obtain the destination data, build an RSCV (if not cached), append the RSCV to the BIND, and forward the BIND.

All exit border nodes should strip all RSCV information concerning the local subnet from the BIND before forwarding the BIND across a subnet boundary.

All entry border nodes receiving the BIND across a subnet boundary do a COS/TPF mapping or use the default and place the appropriate local COS/TPF information in the BIND. The RSCV to the next border node on the path should be recovered from the cache if available. Otherwise, an RSCV is calculated to the next border node on the path (if cached), and appended to the BIND.

The destination border node (in the DLU's subnet) must use its cache to determine the location of the destination, generate an RSCV, and append it to the BIND. The BIND is then sent to the destination.

10.4 HPR Support for Border Nodes

With the current design of (peripheral and extended) border node functions, separate RSCVs are calculated for every subnet and not propagated across intersubnetwork TGs (ISTGs). This was done to hide each subnet's topology from other subnets as a security measure. When migrating to HPR, this then has the effect that RTP connections cannot cross subnet boundaries even when both border nodes connected by an intersubnetwork TG have implemented HPR functions and could support the routing of NLPs. In a pure HPR environment across all connected subnets, separate RTP connections would be set up within every subnet and high-speed ANR routing would be done inside the subnets, but to cross a subnet boundary, NLPs had to be converted into FID2 PIUs in the exit border node, transmitted over the ISTG, and converted into NLPs again. This process (at every subnet boundary) would impact the performance of intersubnet sessions and is not adequate for a high-speed networking environment.

The HPR support for border nodes modifies the functions of extended border nodes in a way that:

- RSCVs for the entire route can be passed across subnet boundaries.
- ANR labels for the entire route can be passed across subnet boundaries.
- RTP connections can be established across subnet boundaries.

The goal for the design of the HPR support for border nodes is to provide cross-subnet connectivity with full HPR functions and performance. HPR border nodes support at least the HPR base functions to support routing of NLPs using ANR.

10.4.1 LU-LU Session Establishment

Before an LU can establish a session with a partner LU, that LU must be located using base APPN search request procedures with the existing border node extensions to them. The Locate reply then returns an RSCV to the origin RTP node that contains an endpoint TG vector with a new Composite Route Selection subfield (CRSS) describing the complete cross-subnet route. Once the destination is located, the composite RSCV obtained from the Locate and placed in the BIND is used to navigate the route setup messages along the RTP connection path (if a new RTP connection must be established for the session).

If the BIND contains an RSCV with an CRSS, the node that establishes the RTP connection uses the CRSS together with the RSCV to create an intersubnet RSCV, which traverses more than one subnet. The part of this RSCV that goes to the partner RTP node is used to route the route setup messages. HPR border nodes always indicate that the origin and destination RTP endpoints reside in ENs, so that in the case of a path switch, a Locate will be sent to find the partner instead of searching the topology database first.

For PLU initiated sessions, the CRSS is accumulated by HPR border nodes at each ISTG along the path when processing the Locate reply. As the Locate/Found reaches each entry (extended) border node (the first border node in a subnet in the PLU-to-SLU direction), the border node calculates (or obtains from cache) an RSCV describing the path from itself to the exit border node, including an endpoint TG vector representing the ISTG exiting the local subnet (or if terminating in the local subnet to the destination CP). If a CRSS from a previous subnet crossing is included in the destination endpoint TG vector, that CRSS is removed from the endpoint TG vector and the RSCV carried in that CRSS is concatenated to the end of the newly created RSCV. The resulting (intersubnet) RSCV is reduced in size as much as possible and incorporated into a new CRSS.

The new CRSS is then included in the endpoint TG vector describing the intersubnetwork TG (or in all endpoint TG vectors, if more than one connection exists into the adjacent subnet), which is returned in the Locate/Found.

If the CP(OLU) is an HPR node supporting the RTP functions for HPR, it will remove the CRSS from the endpoint TG vector received in the Locate reply and append the RSCV information from that CRSS to the RSCV calculated (by the NNS(OLU)) for the local subnet. The CRSS route is appended directly after the TG (intersubnetwork TG) that contained the CRSS. The resulting RSCV then is an intersubnet RSCV, which spans the entire route from origin CP to destination CP, and is used by the CP(OLU) in the BIND and for the route setup (if necessary).

If the CP(OLU) does not support the RTP functions for HPR, it includes the RSCV calculated (by the NNS(OLU)) for the local subnet in the BIND. This RSCV contains an endpoint TG vector with the CRSS as the last hop. The BIND will be forwarded on the session path until it reaches the first node on the path that supports the RTP functions for HPR. This HPR node then processes the RSCV in the same way as in the previous case and replaces the local RSCV with the intersubnet RSCV and activates an RTP connection if necessary.

Extended border nodes acting as ENs can only be adjacent to peripheral subnets and process the Locate replies as described above for the (pure) extended border node case, with only one exception. An exit border node acting as an EN (the last border node in the direction of the DLU) is seen by its partner NN in the adjacent subnet as a client EN and provided with an RSCV for the adjacent (peripheral) subnet. This RSCV includes the ISTG as the first hop. The border node will create an endpoint TG vector representing the ISTG with a CRSS that is built from the received RSCV without the first-hop ISTG.

When there is an extended border node along a session path that has no HPR support for border nodes (a base-APPN BN) the complete intersubnet RSCV will not be carried in a BIND across the intersubnetwork TG. This is because APPN BNs delete the RSCV from one subnet before forwarding the BIND across the ISTG. No RTP connection will cross an ISTG to or from an APPN BN. RTP connections may be established on either side of the ISTG controlled by an APPN BN in the normal manner. RSCVs cached by APPN BNs include the CRSS attached to endpoint TG vectors will be inserted once the

BIND arrives across the ISTG and converted by the next node supporting the RTP functions for HPR on the session path into an intersubnet RSCV.

10.5 Branch Network Node

10.2, “Peripheral Border Node” on page 233 and 10.3, “Extended Border Node” on page 244 gives details of how to structure large APPN networks using peripheral border node and extended border node. Those solutions are not optimal for all configurations since large APPN networks with thousands of network nodes are not uncommon.

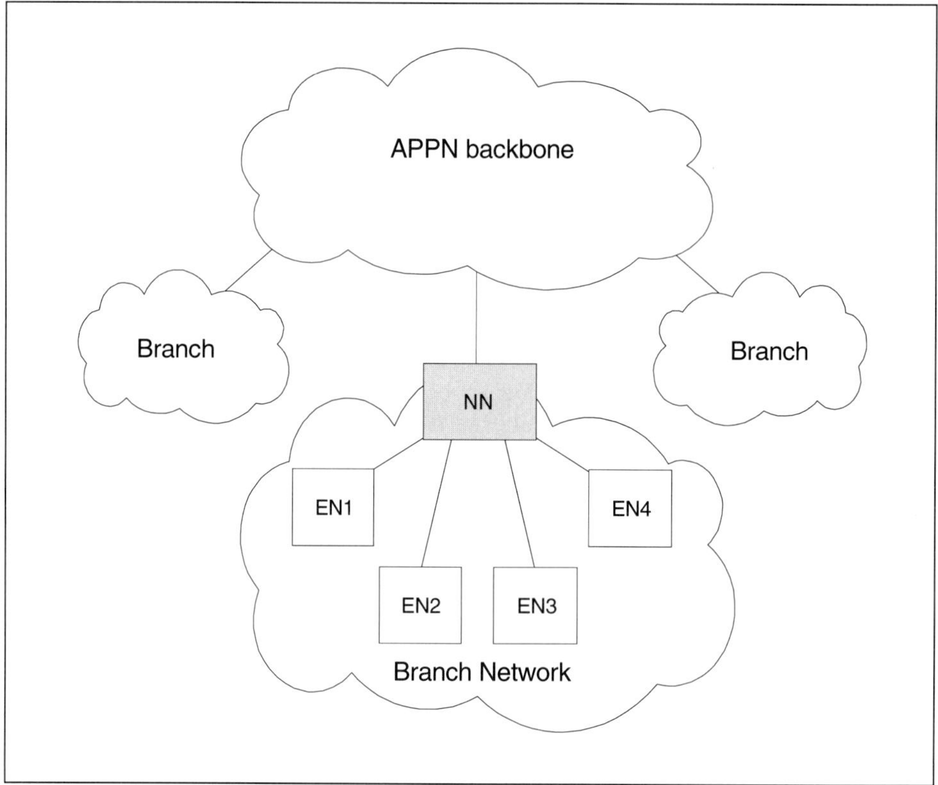

Figure 96. Branch Access Configuration

Figure 96 shows a typical branch access configuration.

A single network node or multiple network nodes connect downstream dependent and independent traffic from ENs and LEN ENs to WAN links. A network node must be used to allow intermediate session routing, but this network node then exchanges TDUs with all other network nodes in the APPN network. Most of these branch access devices have limited topology database storage. There is no reason for topology updates to flow from the WAN backbone into the branch office, or for directory searches into the branch office for resources that are located somewhere else. Such traffic consumes bandwidth on the (usually low-speed) WAN links to the branch office.

Isolating branch locations from the APPN backbone with a border node function, divides the APPN network into different networks and would stop TDU flows between them. At the same time it would increase directory search traffic, since a CDS can not be seen across subnet boundaries. If there are multiple links to a branch, searches may come into the branch on one link and leave on another, without finding the target in the branch. Extended border node is complex and, therefore, difficult to implement on branch platforms. As mentioned before, today there is only one implementation of the peripheral border node architecture (AS/400), and one of the extended border node architecture (VTAM 4.2). A smaller, less complicated design is the solution.

IBM's solution is a network node that has implemented the APPN option set 1121 (Branch network node). This is also known as the Branch Extender feature. It works well at the edge of a network; for example, in bank branch environments. We refer to network nodes that have implemented the branch network node function set as branch network nodes (BrNN).

A BrNN is designed to connect a BrNN branch office to an APPN backbone network. All its TGs are logically defined as *branch uplink, branch downlink* or *other* (for connection network TGs). Logical branch uplink TGs (referred to as uplinks) are connected to the APPN backbone network, while logical downlink TGs (referred to as downlinks) are connected to the BrNN's local domain. It is this act of defining a link as a branch uplink, branch downlink, or other that activates the BrNN function. When the node is defined as a branch network node, TGs default to downlinks, unless otherwise defined.

10.5.1 Branch Network Node Characteristics

A branch network node is a network node with two node type representations (see Figure 97 on page 254). To its APPN backbone (uplink), it always presents an end node image. To its local domain (downlink), it presents a network node image. Although it is a network node, a BrNN presents an end node image to its uplink NNS by setting the EN parameters to *On* in XID exchanges on its uplinks. Like any normal APPN EN, BrNN can have only one TG with CP-CP sessions on the uplink side (it can have other uplink TGs without CP-CP sessions).

10.5.1.1 Branch Uplinks:

On its uplinks (see Figure 97 on page 254), the BrNN is connected to the APPN backbone. A BrNN can have more than one uplink; its partners may be of any node type. Like a standard APPN EN, it can only have CP-CP sessions to a single NNS. A BrNN uses standard EN server-selection logic to find a new NNS should the current NNS become unavailable. The uplink to the NNS is used for all requests that cannot be resolved locally.

Since the BrNN presents an EN image on its uplink, it is isolated from topology updates in the APPN backbone. The NNS will not send its TDUs to the BrNN. Therefore, a

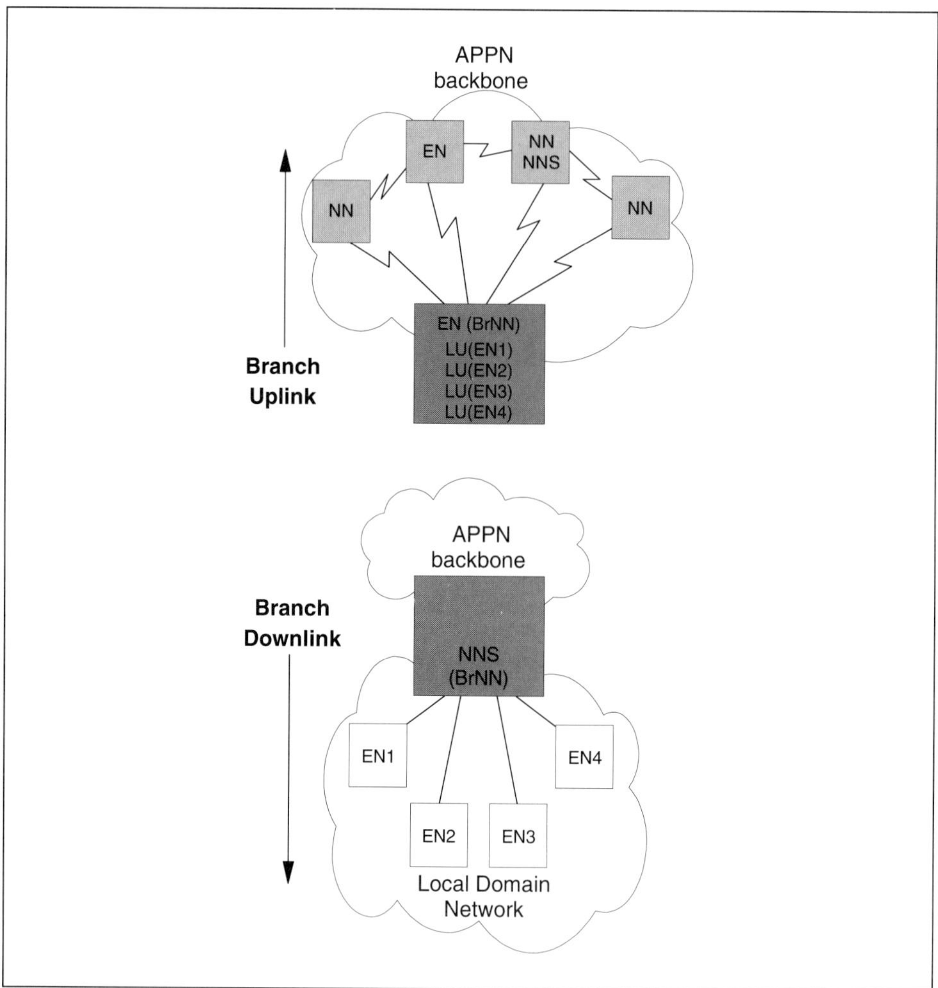

Figure 97. Logical Views of Downlinks and Uplinks

BrNN has no knowledge of a central directory server (CDS), or other network nodes and their TGs. This prevents network node broadcasts from being sent over the WAN links to BrNN and its local domain.

A BrNN presents itself to the uplink side as the owner of all resources in its local domain. To appear as the owner of these resources, a BrNN uses a procedure called *resource hierarchy modifications*, whereby it downgrades resource types of local nodes from EN to LU; for example, domain ENs become BrNNs LUs. After modifications, devices in the APPN backbone network cannot see the downlink hop between a BrNN and its local domain ENs. This also means that a BrNN must change endpoint TG vectors, to add the missing hop between the BrNN and its local domain nodes.

10.5.1.2 Branch Downlinks

On the downlink side (see Figure 97 on page 254), a BrNN presents a network node image and supplies network node services to its domain ENs. Domain ENs do not need to know that their NNS is actually a BrNN. From their point of view, they are connected to the uplink network via a regular NN, which is their NNS with which they have normal CP-CP sessions.

10.5.2 Branch Network Node Connectivity

While the BrNN logical links are divided between uplink and downlink, the number and type of physical links over which it provides APPN services to the local domain or APPN backbone are unchanged from base APPN.

Although a typical BrNN local domain is a single LAN, that domain may consist of any combination of one or more of any DLCs supported by APPN.

The same physical medium may support BrNN uplinks and downlinks simultaneously, as long as the medium supports simultaneous multiple logical connections. Examples of logical addressing are SDLC multipoint station addresses, IEEE 802.2 Logical Link Control type 2 (LLC2) connections identified by unique SSAP/DSAP pairs, and Frame Relay Data Link Control Identifiers (DLCIs).

In the branch network node's local domain, the only active network nodes allowed are other BrNNs (acting as ENs). All other nodes in the local domain must be ENs, LEN nodes, or T2.0 nodes, all of which must use a BrNN as their NNS or DLUR.

Nodes that provide APPN or subarea network interconnection (peripheral border node, extended border node, or interchange node) are not allowed in the local domain. This restriction is to prevent search looping.

Multiple BrNNs in a branch are allowed. Multiple BrNNs in one branch may be desirable for capacity and load distribution, and for non-disruptive rerouting around link failures.

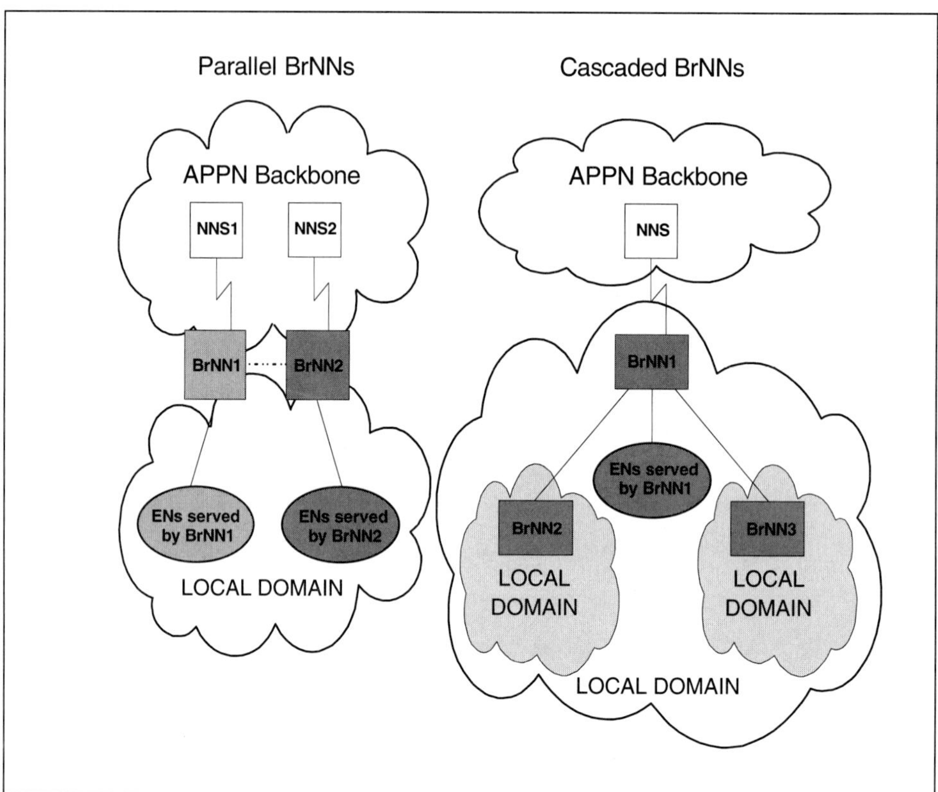

Figure 98. Multiple BrNNs Configuration Examples

Two multiple branch network node configurations are supported (see Figure 98).

Parallel BrNNs

Where the link between the BrNNs is configured as an uplink, and they appear as ENs to each other. Domain ENs can establish CP-CP sessions and register their resources with either BrNN to which they have connectivity. The BrNN with which an EN currently has CP-CP sessions is its NNS. Only this BrNN replies positively to Locate requests for that EN's resources.

Cascaded BrNNs

Where the upper BrNN (BrNN1 at the border to APPN backbone) defines the links to the BrNNs (BrNN2, BrNN3) in its local domain as downlinks, and assumes a network node role for those branch network nodes. The lower BrNNs define these links as uplinks and assume an EN role. Each BrNN may be the NNS for other resources on its own downlinks.

All DLUR support in a local domain is provided by the BrNN. No DLUR support may be provided by any node downstream of a BrNN. If BrNNs are cascaded, this still applies, but only the BrNN connected to the APPN backbone can be a DLUR. Dependent LUs and PUs in the local domain use a *gateway* function to access the DLUR functions in the BrNN.

They provide added advantages by presenting an EN image to the APPN backbone, and thereby reducing the number of network nodes in the network, BrNN complements the connection network model by enabling direct branch-to-branch connectivity over a WAN connection network.

10.5.3 Branch Network Node Route Selection

The BrNN is responsible for all APPN sessions entering or leaving the branch and session setup inside the local domain. LU-LU sessions between two ENs in the same local domain are managed and connected without the intervention of an NNS in the APPN backbone. A BrNN is the only network node and the only NNS in that local domain. Route calculation and connection establishment are handled locally.

While a BrNN knows the topology of its local domain, it knows nothing of uplink topology. To connect LU-LU sessions between LUs in different local domains, or between LUs in the local domain and the backbone, the BrNN relies on its APPN backbone NNS to calculate the best route. When it is necessary, BrNN supports a pass-through for Locates, Registers, Deletes, BINDs and UNBINDs, MS Capabilities, MDS Transport and HPR Route Setups.

Since a BrNN appears as an EN and the owner of local domain LUs, NNS, has no knowledge of the hop between the BrNN and its local domain ENs. The BrNN handles uplink Locates, BINDs and Route Setups so that local domain ENs look like LUs in the BrNN. Traffic flows from a BrNN must appear to be correct so as not to confuse the uplink network. The BrNN modifies Locate request CVs so that the uplink network sees BrNN as the CP(DLU or OLU) and domain ENs as LUs in the BrNN. It must also substitute the endpoint TG vector (received from the uplink) by adding the missing hop between the BrNN and local domain ENs. The following two examples show how BrNN does that.

10.5.3.1 Locate Request and Bind from Local Domain

Figure 99 on page 258 shows a configuration where the OLU is in the local domain and issues a Locate/Find for a DLU outside of the local domain.

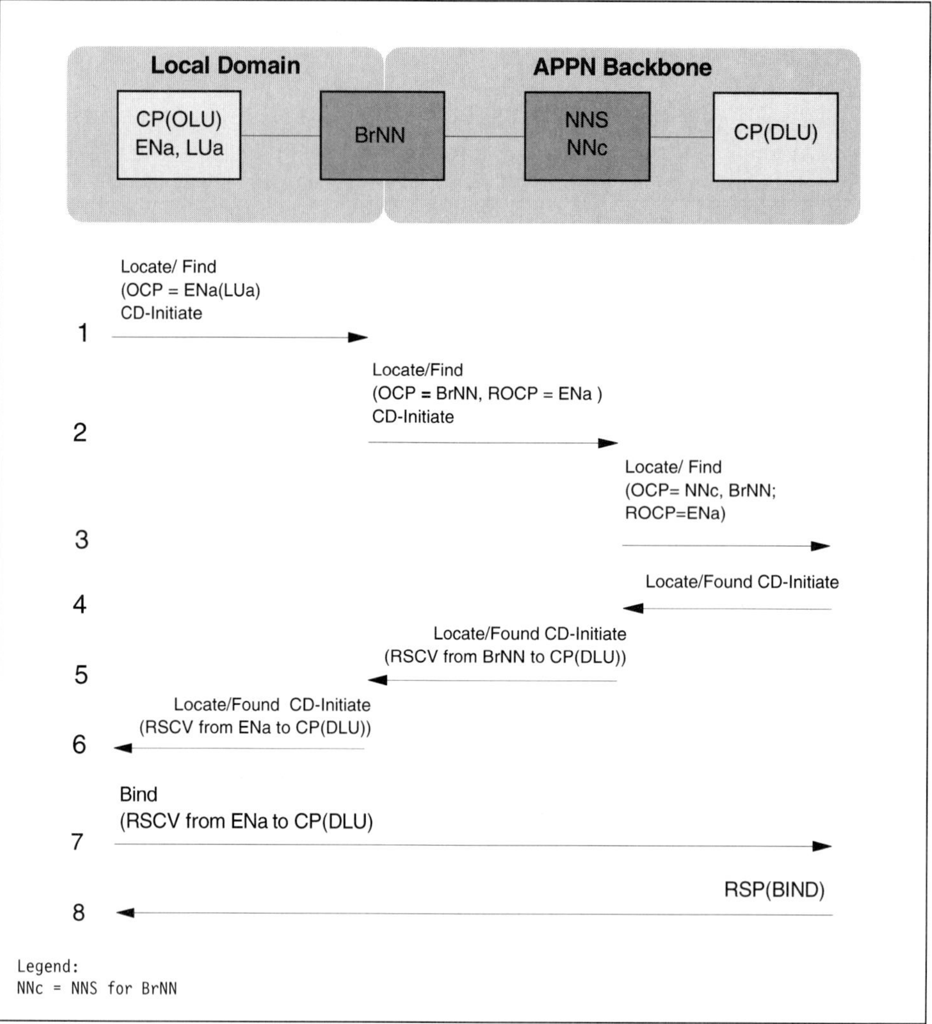

Figure 99. Request from the Downlink Network

The following list describes in detail the flows marked 1-8 in Figure 99.

1. A local domain EN sends a normal Locate request. The OLU resource hierarchy is ENa, LUa.
2. The first modification takes place on the BrNN when the Locate request arrives. BrNN substitutes BrNN's CP name for the ENa name in the hierarchy and puts the ENa name into a new CV ROCP (real origin CP). Now the BrNN has become the OLU(owner of ENa(LUa)) for NNc.
3. NNc forwards the Locate to the network.

4. When the Locate reply comes back from the network, NNc computes an RSCV from the BrNN(OLU) to CP(DLU).
5. This RSCV is sent back to the BrNN. It points to the BrNN as the OLU of LUa.
6. The second modifications take place when the Locate reply arrives at the BrNN from NNc with an RSCV pointing to the LUa as being in the BrNN. This RSCV must now be corrected before the ENa uses it for BIND or Route setup. BrNN modifies the RSCV by inserting the missing hop between ENa and BrNN and delivers the correct RSCV to ENa.

   For an base-APPN EN, BrNN is the only node capable of fixing the RSCV. If a local domain EN is HPR capable, it could also correct the RSCV. As BrNN doesn't know if the EN will use HPR on this path, it always fixes the RSCV. The RSCV is complete and correct when the CP(OLU) gets it, so it can be used directly for BINDs or ROUTE Setups.
7. Now the local domain ENa can send a BIND with the correct RSCV from itself all the way to the CP(DLU). When BrNN receives this BIND, it performs standard network node logic. It simply creates a session connector, updates the current pointer in the RSCV and forwards the BIND to the next hop uplink, not necessarily on the default routing link.

10.5.3.2 Locate Request and Bind from the Uplink Network

Figure 100 shows a configuration where the DLU is in the local domain and an OLU outside of the local domain issues a Locate/Find CD-Initiate for that LU.

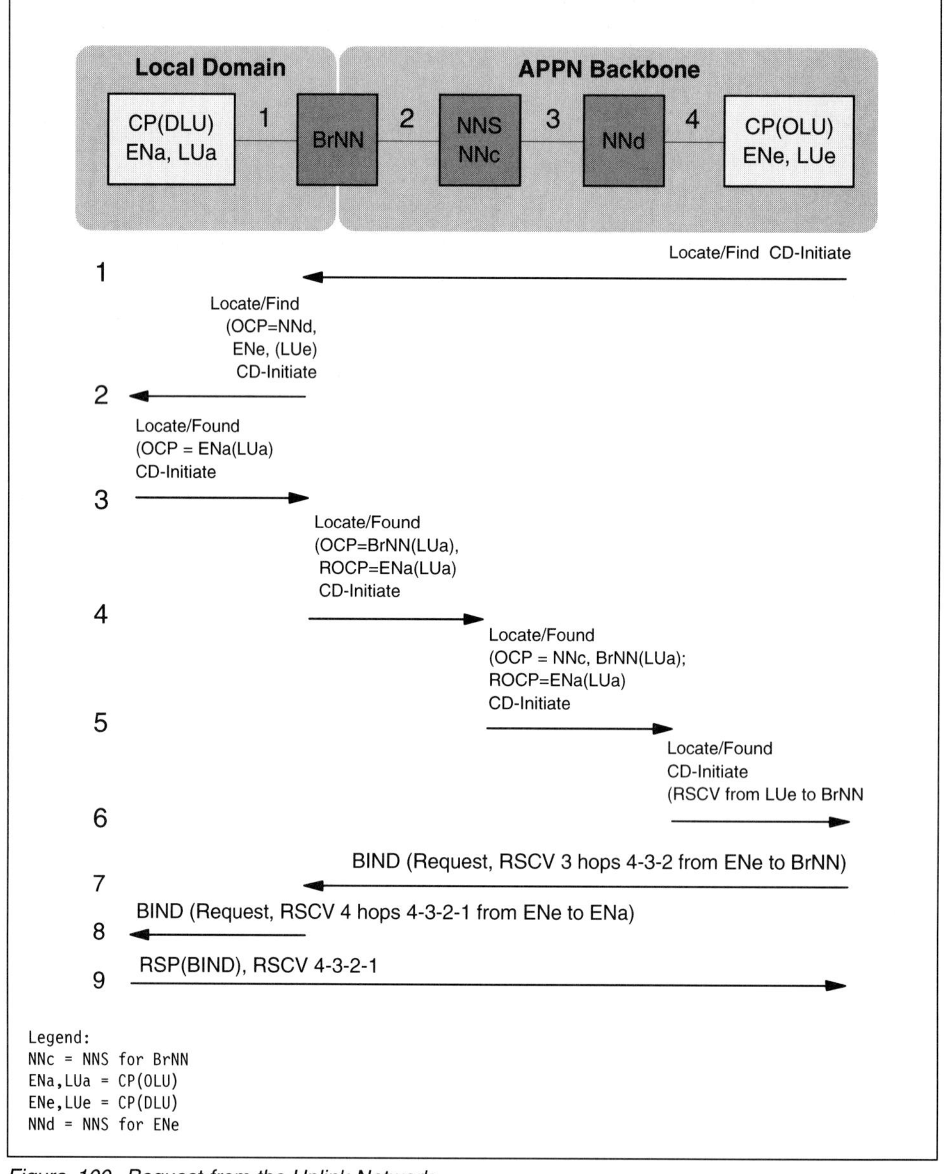

Figure 100. Request from the Uplink Network

The following list describes in detail the flows marked 1-9 in Figure 100.

1. ENe sends a normal Locate request to find LUa. It gets to NNc and is sent to BrNN (maybe because BrNN had previously registered LUa in the NNc directory).
2. BrNN forwards the Locate to ENa without modifying the LUe resource hierarchy.
3. ENa sends back the Locate reply. This reply also includes the TG vectors to the BrNN. BrNN uses these vectors to compute a route between BrNN and ENa. This route is encoded in a CRSS (as in the HPR border node function), and included in the TGVs that BrNN returns to NNc.
4. Now BrNN modifies the hierarchy, substituting the BrNN's CP name for ENa, and becoming the CP(DLU) for the uplink network.
5. NNc completes the hierarchy and forwards the reply.
6. NNd computes a route from ENe to the apparent CP(DLU), which is now the BrNN.
7. If ENe is HPR capable it will use the CRSS to expand the RSCV to include the hop between BrNN and ENa. Otherwise, ENe will use the incorrect RSCV (it ends at BrNN) to send a BIND.
8. If the BrNN receives a BIND containing a CRSS for the last hop to ENa, it performs RSCV expansion and inserts the missing hop from the BrNN to ENa. After creating a normal session connector, BrNN then forwards the BIND to ENa.
9. ENa receives an RSCV containing the complete route. If ENa returns an RSCV in RSP(BIND), it is complete and no special BrNN processing of RSP(BIND) is necessary.

Chapter 11. Dependent LU Support

Previous chapters have focused on the base APPN support of independent LUs (SSCP-independent LUs). This chapter describes extensions to APPN to support SSCP-dependent LUs.

The APPN base architecture only supports type 6.2 logical units that do not require the services of a system services control point (SSCP) (SSCP-independent LUs or more commonly independent LUs). Independent LUs are able to start a session by sending a BIND and by so doing become the primary logical unit (PLU) of that session. APPN base architecture does not support other LU types, nor provides functions such as SLU-initiated sessions, session queuing, or third-party initiation, which are widely used in subarea SNA.

SSCP-dependent LU types (dependent LUs) evolved within a hierarchical (subarea) network and require a system services control point (SSCP) for establishing (and managing) LU-LU sessions.

Dependent LUs have an asymmetric relationship where the primary LU, which is always host-resident, is responsible for session activation and recovery. The secondary LU can, with the help of the SSCP, request that the primary LU activate a session and a third-party can request that an LU-LU session be started.

Session services extensions are optional APPN functions that may be implemented to support dependent logical units and provide additional services for independent logical units.

The dependent LU server and dependent LU requester are optional APPN functions that provide more flexibility in connecting dependent logical units to their owning system service control points.

11.1 Session Services Extensions

The APPN option sets for session services extensions are:

- 1060 Prerequisites for Session Services Extensions CP Support
- 1061 Prerequisites for Session Services Extensions NNS Support
- 1062 Session Services Extensions CP Support
- 1063 Session Services Extensions NNS Support
- 1064 Session Services Extensions PLU Node Support
- 1065 Session Services Extensions CP(SLU) (SSCP) Support

Enabling session services extensions for LU-LU sessions requires the implementation of the appropriate function at each of the nodes on which session endpoints reside. Also, base function set 060 (Locate Chains - Locate(keep)) is required in all intermediate routing nodes along the path of directed searches and base function set 105 (Intermediate Session Routing for Dependent LU Sessions) on all nodes along the session path.

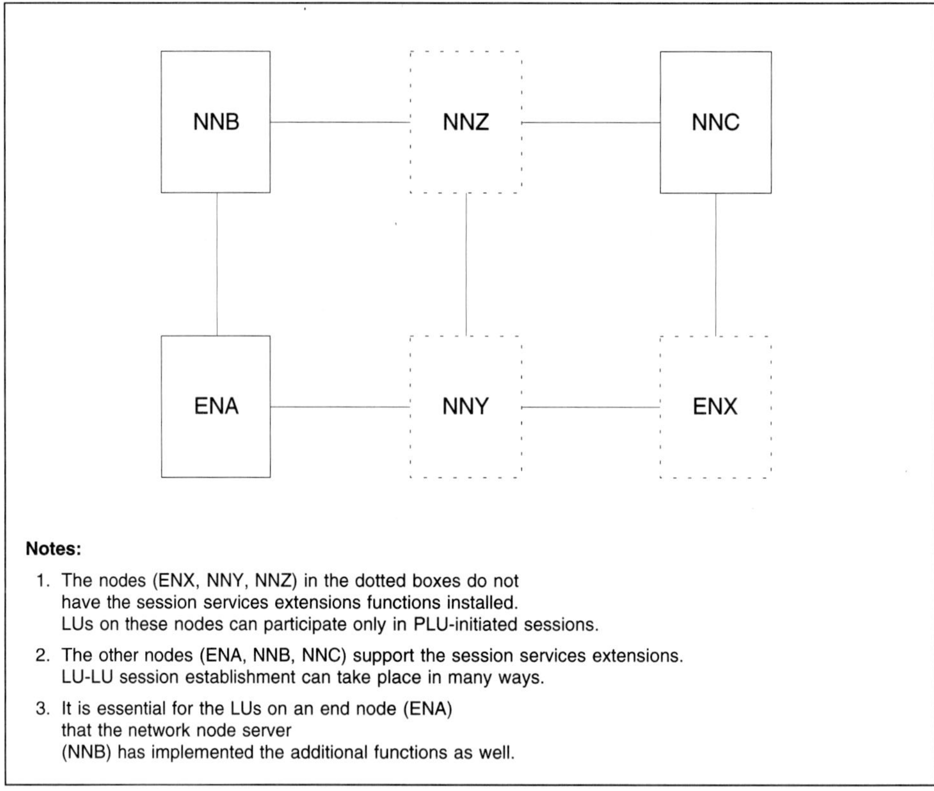

Notes:

1. The nodes (ENX, NNY, NNZ) in the dotted boxes do not have the session services extensions functions installed. LUs on these nodes can participate only in PLU-initiated sessions.
2. The other nodes (ENA, NNB, NNC) support the session services extensions. LU-LU session establishment can take place in many ways.
3. It is essential for the LUs on an end node (ENA) that the network node server (NNB) has implemented the additional functions as well.

Figure 101. Session Services Extensions

Note: Only VTAM currently supports session services extensions; therefore, in Figure 101, ENA, NNB, and NNC can only be VTAM or composite (VTAM/NCP) nodes. For details about the APPN implementation in VTAM, see Appendix C, "APPN VTAM" on page 409.

Details about session services extensions are given in 11.1.1, "Additional Functions" on page 265.

Implementing the session services extensions:

- Enhances the support provided for LU 6.2 sessions
- Is required to fully support the attachment of dependent LUs to APPN networks

- Is necessary on the interchange node (see the discussion of interchange node in Appendix C, "APPN VTAM" on page 409) connecting APPN and subarea networks in order to provide transparency to the LUs in subarea networks

11.1.1 Additional Functions

Session services extensions defines additional information in the cross-domain initiate (CD-Initiate) GDS variable in order to support functions currently available and widely used in subarea networks: These functions are:

Additional Types of Session Initiation

SLU Initiate

An SLU must be able to initiate sessions, and a node that attaches dependent LUs must be able to provide mode names, COS names, BIND images, and device characteristics when required.

Queuing

Session queuing is the process of suspending the establishment of an LU-LU session until a needed resource (either an LU or a session with that LU) is available. There are two basic reasons for the queuing of a session initiation request, and it may be queued for either or both reasons. The reasons are:

Queue for Enabled:

A session initiation request may be queued because the PLU or SLU is not enabled for a session (for example, a printer is powered off or an application program is not initialized). Queuing for enabled is performed once the destination LU has been found.

Queue for Session Limit:

When an LU has the capability to have only a limited number of sessions and this number is reached, subsequent session initiation requests may be queued. Once a current session is terminated, the node containing that LU will dequeue the first session initiation request that was queued for session limit.

Session initiation requests that are queued require that the Locate chain be maintained between the nodes of the session partners as long as the request is queued. Once the required resource becomes available, the node managing that LU dequeues pending session initiation requests for that LU and resumes the network flows needed to establish the sessions.

Session requests indicate the queuing position for the request, should it become queued. Normally, requests are queued FIFO (first in, first out). This allows session requests to be dequeued in the order they are received. However, to support VTAM's version of third-party initiate (CLSDST PASS), LIFO (last in, first out) is used to ensure that the SLU is directly passed from the current PLU to the next PLU indicated in the request.

Third-Party Initiation

A function, limited to PLUs, that allows the LU to establish a session between an LU it is currently having a session with, and a third LU. The LU being passed must be the SLU in the new session. The LU initiating the session setup request may be a menu server, a help function, or some other application program that might have reasons to end its session with the SLU and, in its place, initiate a session between the SLU and some other application program.

Automatic Logon

Sessions provided via automatic logon are useful for a device such as an automatic teller machine which should be kept in session with a controlling application, or for assuring that terminals are connected to a menu or security application program when powered on. Automatic logon provides a method for automatically establishing a session between an SLU and a designated controlling PLU whenever the SLU is enabled and below its session limit.

If the SLU is single-session capable, a determination of whether to reestablish the SLU's automatic logon session must be made whenever the SLU's current session terminates. The automatic logon session will be reestablished unless the SLU has a request queued for session limit, which will then be dequeued.

If the SLU is multisession capable, automatic logon establishes a session between the SLU and the controlling PLU whenever such a session does not already exist.

Session Release Request

A PLU may initiate a session with an SLU and indicate in the request that, if the SLU is at its session limit, the current PLU should be notified that another PLU would like a session with the SLU. The PLU that sends the new session initiation request must indicate that the request may be queued. If the SLU is enabled and not at its session limit, the session will be initiated. If the SLU is at its session limit, the session request will be queued and the current PLU will be notified. The current PLU may terminate its session with the SLU or ignore the request.

This function is normally used to improve the availability of printers shared by different application programs. The PLU receiving the release request will terminate its session, for example, if no output is queued for the (printer) SLU, or once the current listing is finished.

Request LU Status

This function allows an OLU (which has to be the PLU) node to request LU status information, in a session initiation request of type *search only*, by setting the *LU status requested* indicator in the CD-Initiate GDS variable that it sends. The DLU node, if it supports this function, will include an *LU status control list (X'01')* in the

CD-Initiate GDS variable that it sends in reply to provide status information of the DLU.

11.1.2 Initiating LUs and Initiate Types

With the extensions described, the number and kinds of session initiation procedures have grown significantly. The initiating LU (ILU) can be either the PLU, the SLU, or a third-party LU currently in session with the SLU. Furthermore, inquiries may be sent by an LU to retrieve information regardless of intended session role.

In order to support the different session initiation requests described in the previous section, additional initiate types have to be specified in Locate/CD-Initiate requests that are not necessary in base APPN architecture where only the PLU can request a session, and this session request fails when the SLU is not available. The initiate types that may be requested are:

Search Only (S)

The request origin is attempting to locate an LU but there is no implication that a session will be established. The origin is not requesting a session, but rather requesting information (for example, DLU available or not available, at its session limit or not at its session limit) that may allow it to establish a session.

Initiate Only (I)

The request origin is attempting to establish a session. If the DLU does session-limit management, resource reservation (that means, reservation of an available session) is requested. If the resources are currently not available, then the session request should fail.

This is the normal session initiation type in base APPN.

Initiate or Notify (I/N)

The request origin is attempting to establish a session. If the DLU does session-limit management, resource reservation is requested. If the requested LU is not enabled (that means, currently not willing to accept or send a BIND), then the request origin requests notification when it is enabled. Once the DLU becomes enabled, CP(DLU) remembers that CP(OLU) requested notification and sends a Locate notify (Resource Enabled) to CP(OLU), which then restarts the session initiation procedure.

This type is used when an automatic logon is attempted.

Initiate or Queue (I/Q)

The request origin is attempting to establish a session. If the DLU does session-limit management, resource reservation is requested. If the resources are currently not available, then the request origin is willing to have the session initiation queued. Queueing conditions are queue for enabled, queue for session limit, or both.

This type is used, for example, when a VTAM application program requests a session with an SLU that is a printer or display currently being powered off. The IBM 3174 control unit notifies the SSCP that the device is enabled for sessions when that device is powered on. Thus the SSCP can resume the session setup procedure at this time and dequeue the session request. Using this type of session initiation procedure the PLU has to request the session only once instead of periodically having to request a session.

Queue Only (Q)
The request origin is attempting to establish a session, but the session initiation request is to be queued, since the request origin is not yet ready. The queueing conditions available to the request origin are queue for enabled, queue for session limit, or both.

The permitted combinations are shown in Table 8.

Table 8. Session Services Requests

	S	I	I/N	I/Q	Q
PLU Initiated	X	X (1)		X	X
SLU Initiated		X	X (2)	X	X
Third-Party Initiated				X	X

Note:

1. The only type of session initiation request supported in base APPN is a PLU originated Locate/CD-Initiate with *Initiate Only.*
2. Used for automatic logon support.

11.1.3 Session Characteristics

In order to support SLU-initiated sessions, some of the information that is maintained by the SLU must be transferred in a Locate request or reply to the PLU node, so the PLU can properly establish a session with the SLU without having to predefine this information at the PLU. The information that needs to be transferred includes the BIND image, which contains session parameters, and device characteristics. This data will be copied into the BIND flowing from the PLU to the SLU.

11.1.3.1 BIND Image

In adding support to APPN for LU types other than 6.2, BIND images need to be passed from the SLU node to the PLU node. For a non-LU 6.2 session, the node owning the SLU will always provide a BIND image on either a Locate request (SLU-initiated session) or on a Locate reply (PLU-initiated session).

For an SLU-initiated session, the BIND image will always be provided by the SLU node regardless of the LU type. For a PLU-initiated session, the BIND image is always provided by the SLU node for session types other than LU 6.2.

In the subarea architecture, the SSCP of the SLU always sends the BIND image (via the SSCP of the PLU) to the PLU regardless of the session type, even for an LU 6.2 session.

The BIND image is carried in the BIND Image (X'31') control vector that is included in the Locate/CD-Initiate request or reply flowing from the CP(SLU) to the CP(PLU).

11.1.3.2 Device Characteristics

Device characteristics for non-SNA devices (such as BSC 3270 terminals) are required for application programs to interact properly with the device. Some fields in the device characteristics such as the terminal model number are used to derive a default display screen size, buffer size for the terminal, and so on, even though the preferable way is to use the information that can be supplied in the session parameters.

Other fields in the device characteristics, such as terminal type and the device addresses needed for the 3270 copy function, do not have appropriate counterparts in the BIND image.

The device characteristics will be included in the Locate request or reply from the SLU node to the PLU *when and only when* the BIND image is included.

11.1.4 Search Procedure Identification

The Fully Qualified Procedure Correlation ID (FQPCID) is used as a universal identifier for session-related procedures. That is, an FQPCID is assigned at initiation and used on all flows (for example, Locate, BINDs, and UNBINDs) to identify the referenced session. It is also used for network management as the unique identifier for a session.

Depending on the type of session initiation, a number of subprocedures need to be done, details of which are beyond the scope of this document. To distinguish between the various subprocedures, the PCID Modifier control vector is used in the Locate request/reply. It contains the Procedure Resubmit Number (PRN) and the PCID Modifier List. This information is used by the FQPCID caching logic in APPN VTAM or subarea VTAM nodes (see page 239) to avoid duplicate searches for resources in, or accessible through, the subarea network.

11.2 Dependent LU Requester/Server

While the session services extensions function (described previously) allows dependent LUs to use APPN networks for LU-LU sessions, the following restrictions still apply:

- SSCP-PU and SSCP-LU sessions cannot use APPN connectivity.
- The PU T2.0, APPN or LEN node containing the LU must be adjacent to a subarea boundary node.
- The node containing the LU must have subarea connectivity to its owning SSCP.

See Figure 102.

The dependent LU server and dependent LU requester functions together remove the current restriction that a PU T2.0, APPN or LEN node supporting dependent LUs be adjacent to a subarea boundary node.

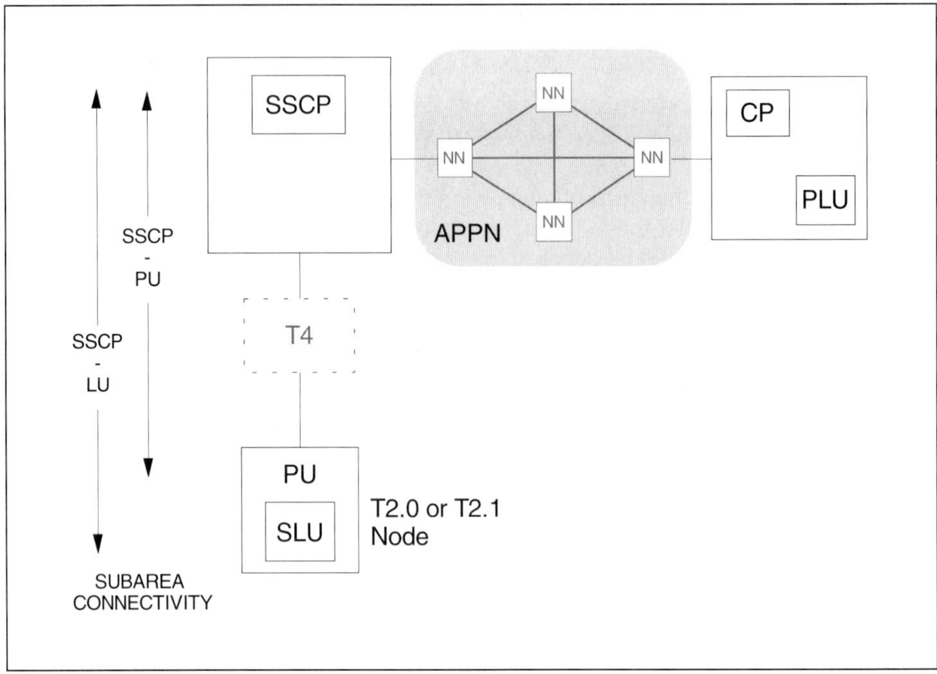

Figure 102. Dependent LU SSCP Connectivity without Dependent LU Requester/Server. The SLU-PLU session can use APPN between the composite network node and the node containing the PLU but must use subarea connectivity for SSCP-PU and SSCP-LU sessions.

11.2.1 Dependent LU Server

The dependent LU server function (option set 1066) is a product feature of an interchange node or a T5 network node supporting session services extensions. This function provides server support for dependent LU requester clients in which SSCP-PU and SSCP-LU flows to a PU T2.0, APPN or LEN node externally attached to the requester, or a PU T2.0, APPN or LEN node image within the requester, are encapsulated within LU 6.2 sessions.

11.2.2 Dependent LU Requester

The dependent LU requester function (option set 1067) is an enhancement for an APPN end node or network node. This function is the client side of the dependent LU server function in which SSCP-PU and SSCP-LU flows to a PU T2.0, APPN or LEN node attached to the requester are encapsulated within LU 6.2 sessions.

The requester function provides a remote boundary function for dependent LUs. This option set relieves the restriction that PU T2.0 nodes be directly attached (or bridged, or data link switched, or frame relayed) to the VTAM or NCP boundary function. The dependent LU requester function may reside in the same node as the secondary LU or be provided by a node adjacent to and upstream from the secondary LU (see Figure 103).

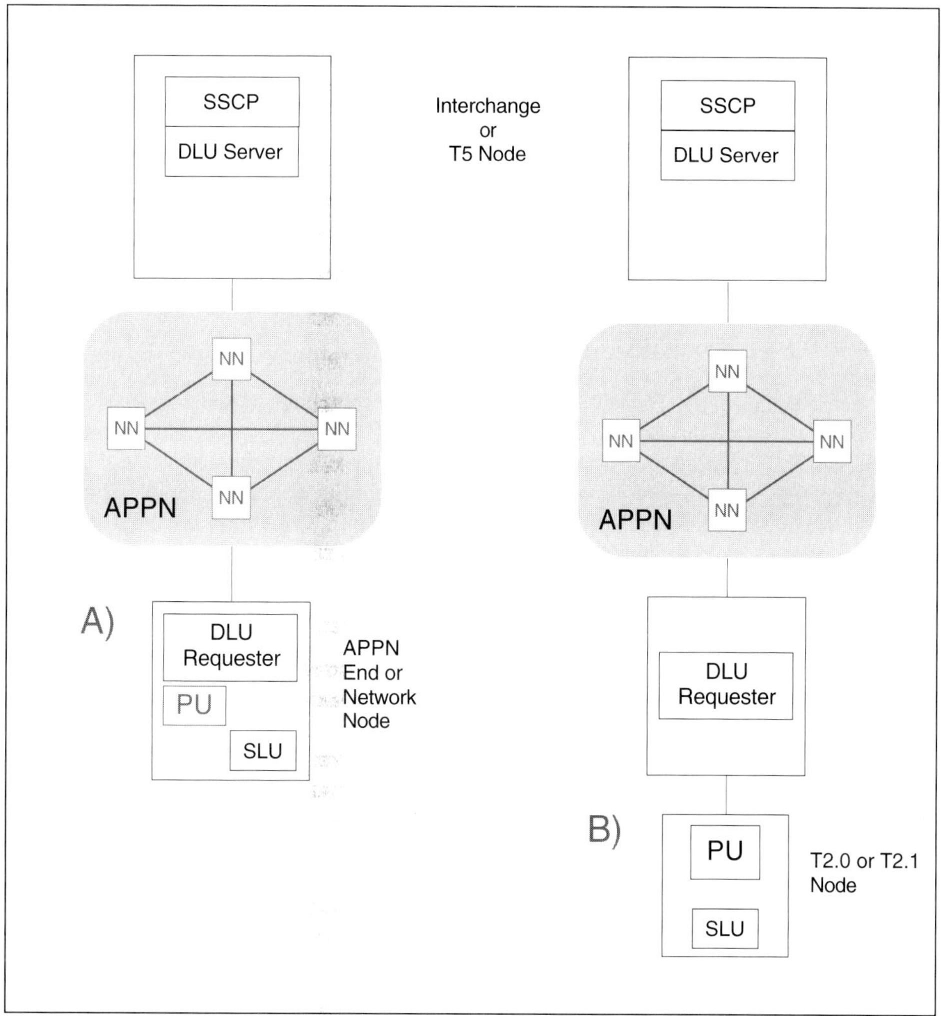

Figure 103. Dependent LU Requester/Server

Note:

A) The dependent LU requester is in the same node as the dependent LU(s).
B) The dependent LU requester is in an APPN end node or network node directly connected to the PU T2.0, APPN or LEN node containing the dependent LU(s).

11.3 CP-SVR Pipe

The CP-SVR pipe is the term used to describe the LU 6.2 sessions encapsulating the SSCP-PU and SSCP-LU session flows between the dependent LU server and the dependent LU requester. These sessions are similar to CP-CP sessions in that each node has a contention-winner and contention-loser session to the other. The CP-SVR pipe is established using a new mode called CPSVRMGR which uses the SNASVCMG COS. The dependent LU requester will need to know its dependent LU server, and the dependent LU server will need to know which dependent LU requester to contact for a particular PU activation.

SSCP-PU and SSCP-LU flows required to set up and manage a dependent LU-LU session are carried encapsulated inside the CP-SVR pipe between the requester and server. The CP-SVR pipe can carry encapsulated SSCP-PU and SSCP-LU sessions for multiple PUs (see Figure 104).

Either the dependent LU server or the dependent LU requester may initiate the CP-SVR pipe. CP-SVR sessions are only initiated when some form of PU activation is required (and no CP-SVR pipe already exists). The CP-SVR pipe is deactivated when it is no longer required. The CP-SVR pipe cannot cross through a subarea subnet. The node initiating the Locate must set the Suppress Subarea Search bit in the Locate and the Prevent Subarea Search bit in the Find.

Note: The resulting LU-LU sessions between dependent LUs can be routed over a different path (option set 105, Intermediate Session Routing for Dependent LU Sessions) from the encapsulated SSCP flows.

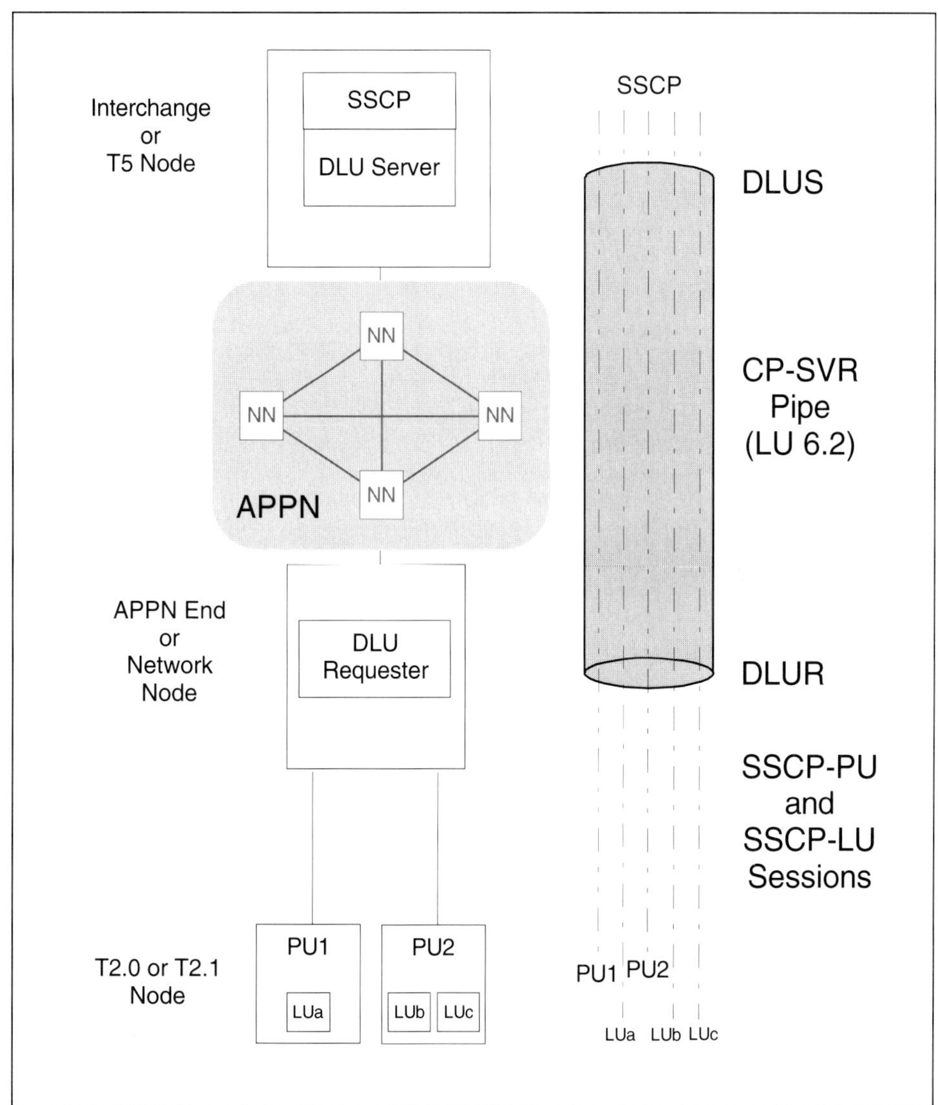

Figure 104. CP-SVR Pipe and Encapsulated SSCP-PU and SSCP-LU Sessions

11.4 Sample Configurations

Figure 105 shows a configuration where the dependent LU resides in a PU T2.0, APPN or LEN node downstream from the dependent LU requester providing the remote boundary function.

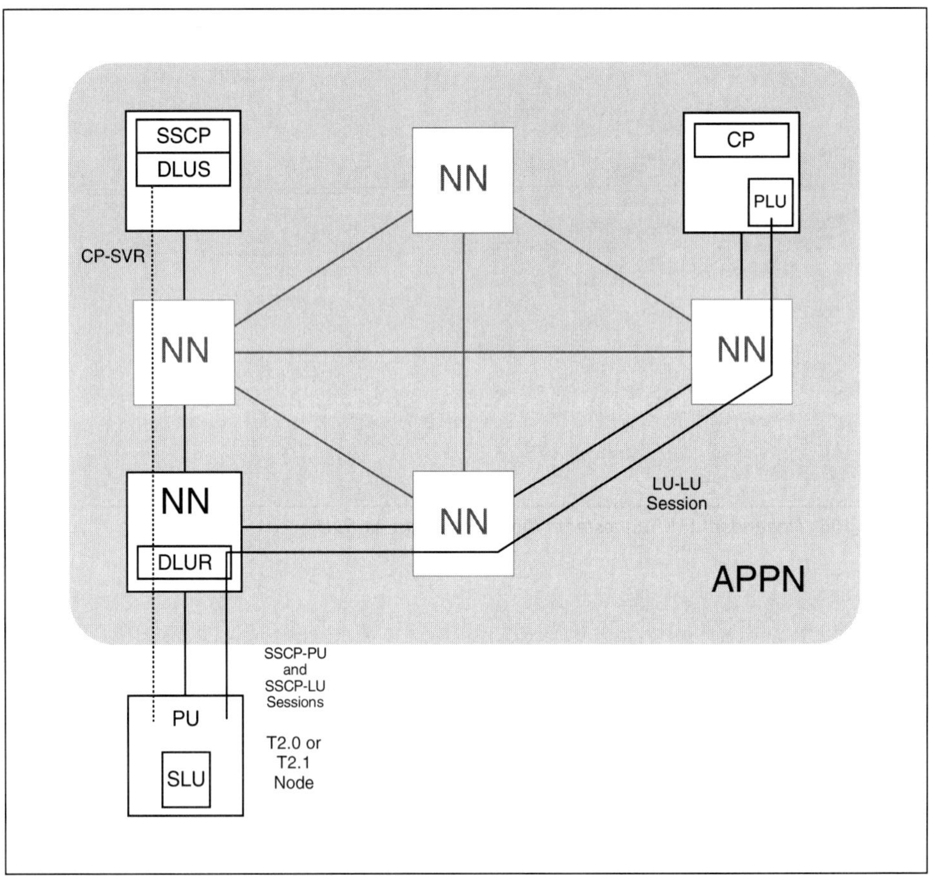

Figure 105. SLU in a Node Adjacent to the Dependent LU Requester

The PU T2.0, APPN or LEN node must be adjacent to the dependent LU requester node. The BIND and data flows on the LU-LU session between the SLU and PLU need not use the same route as the SSCP-PU and SSCP-LU sessions.

Figure 106 shows a configuration where the dependent LU requester resides in the same APPN end node or APPN network node as the dependent secondary logical unit.

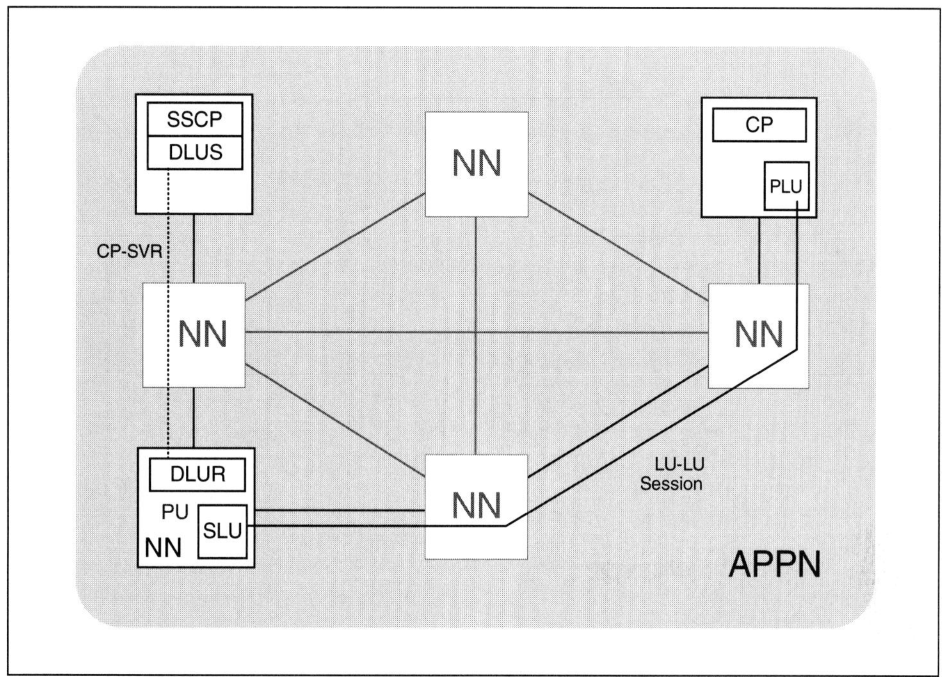

Figure 106. Dependent LU Requester in the Same Node As SLU

The BIND and data flows on the LU-LU session between the SLU and PLU need not use the same route as the SSCP-PU and SSCP-LU sessions.

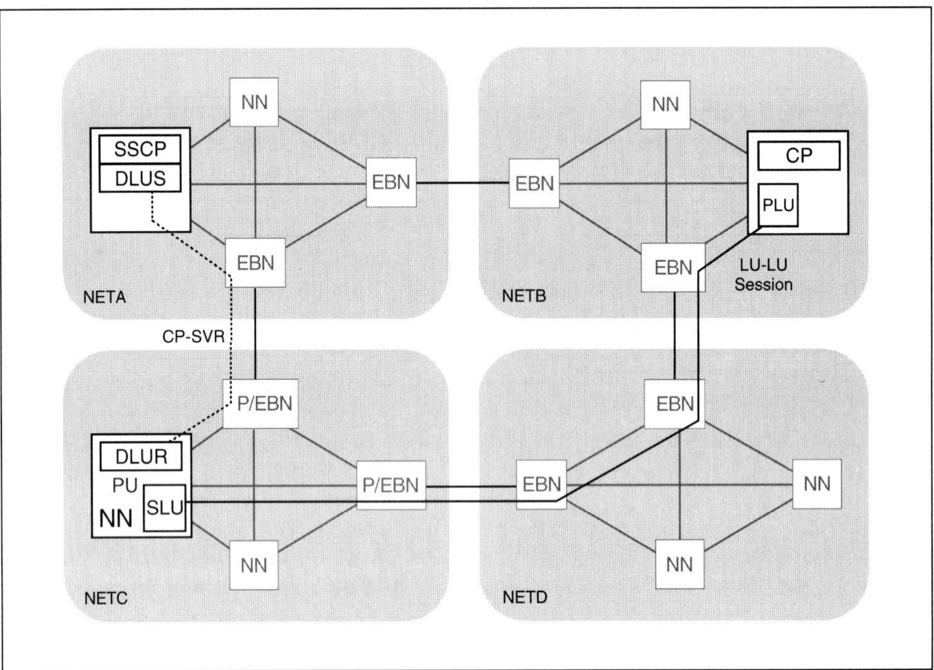

Figure 107. Dependent LU Requester, Dependent LU Server and PLU in Different Subnets

Figure 107 shows a configuration where the dependent LU requester, the dependent LU server and the PLU all reside in different subnets. All the BNs in subnets NETA, NETB, and NETD must be extended border nodes, whereas all nodes in NETC connecting NETC to NETA and NETD can be extended border nodes, peripheral border nodes, or even simple NNs. The CP-SVR pipe between the dependent LU requester and dependent LU server may traverse APPN subnets but not subarea subnets.

Chapter 12. APPN Support in ATM Networks

In November 1996 IBM, in conjunction with the APPN Implementers' Workshop (AIW) and ATM Forum, completed work on enhancements to the APPN architecture that describe a native DLC for APPN nodes to access asynchronous transfer mode (ATM) networks. These enhancements will allow existing APPN applications to gain access to ATM quality-of-service (QoS) and traffic contracts without changes to the applications themselves. In addition, a method for transporting other protocols on the same ATM virtual circuit (VC) as APPN data is being defined. This method does not involve encapsulation of one protocol inside another, but allows true multiplexing on a single ATM VC. Native access to ATM networks will afford existing APPN nodes the full benefits of ATM without use of an enabling protocol such as multiprotocol over ATM (MPOA).

The scope of these enhancements is limited to APPN/HPR products. IBM's current strategy for subarea products is to access ATM through migration to APPN/HPR, through LAN emulation or through frame relay interworking.

The ATM Forum's Signalling Working Group reviewed the sections of the AIW document "HPR Extensions for ATM Networks" dealing with ATM Signalling. The ATM Forum considers those sections to be a valid implementation of ATM Forum Signalling specifications.

The information in this chapter gives an overview of the native ATM DLC for HPR.

12.1 Native ATM DLC

A native ATM DLC is the most straightforward approach to APPN over ATM. The LAN emulation approach by comparison is indirect and restrictive. For example, ATM addresses would be associated with links and included in the topology databases and endpoint TG vectors. Native ATM DLCs do, however, require changes to the higher-layer protocol software (for example, to accept ATM addresses at the MAC driver interface).

The following prerequisites have been defined for APPN communication over native ATM DLCs:

- The base functions for APPN architecture Version 2 (see Appendix A, “APPN Base and Option Sets” on page 335)
- High-Performance-Routing (HPR) enhancements including the Rapid Transport Protocol (RTP) and Control Flows over RTP option sets

The decision to use HPR was made because the *go-back-n* error recovery mechanism used by IEEE 802.2 type 2 LLC (LLC2) is not good enough for high-speed ATM links. Instead *selective retransmission* is needed. Selective retransmission can be provided by

RTP or an LLC such as the service specific connection-oriented protocol (SSCOP). Having HPR as a prerequisite eliminates the need for a high-function LLC. A new logical data link control (LDLC) has been designed to provide functions such as reliable delivery of XIDs.

Unlike LAN emulation, a native ATM DLC allows APPN to fully exploit ATM's guaranteed bandwidth services. Frame relay interworking can provide similar services, but only on a subscription basis until frame relay SVC interworking is defined. In addition, a native ATM DLC would allow APPN to exploit ATM services for real-time transport and multicast, functions not provided by a frame relay service. The current AIW proposal for a native APPN DLC does not support real-time traffic or multicast.

For time-critical transactions, reserved-bandwidth variable bit rate connections with controlled delay and error rates could be allocated, whereas batch file transfers could use the cheaper less predictable unspecified bit rate (UBR) connections. SNA allows HPR to match an ATM connection's quality of service (QoS) to the COS needs of an application.

12.2 Native ATM DLC Implementation

When APPN/HPR runs over an ATM DLC, it is better able to exploit the features of ATM such as its quality of service (QoS). There are, however, many considerations (for example, which AAL type to use for the user plane). Exploitation also requires enhancements to APPN. The following sections describe these considerations and enhancements.

12.2.1 Node Structure

Figure 108 on page 279 shows the node structure for a node supporting nonshared SVCs that supports only APPN/HPR traffic using the base LDLC function. There will be variations in different platforms based on platform characteristics such as:

- Whether multiple higher-layer protocols have access to ATM services, or whether APPN is the only higher-layer protocol in the node
- The function split between ATM adapters and main processors
- Whether a higher-layer protocol requires reliable link-level delivery

The node structure for support of other protocols (for example, IP) has also been defined. The native ATM DLC includes the ATM signalling and LDLC components. The ATM signalling component converts configuration services (CS) signals into the signals defined on the interface to the Port Connection Manager (PCM) (typically located on the ATM adapter) and vice versa. The low-level ATM interface (LL ATMI) defines such an interface. Logical Data Link Control (LDLC) is a subset of IEEE 802.2 LLC type 2 (LLC2). LDLC encapsulates HPR traffic within an LLC2 frame; this provides for SAP multiplexing. SAP multiplexing allows multiple links to share an ATM VCC. There is an instance of LDLC for each link, and incoming packets are passed to the correct instance of LDLC based on the SAPs in the LLC2 header. In addition, SAP multiplexing enables multiple logical nodes, each with its own SAP, to share an ATM port.

LDLC also provides other functions; reliable delivery is provided by LDLC for a small set of APPN flows (XID, XID_DONE and DEACT). Error recovery for HPR RTP packets is provided by the protocols at the RTP endpoints. LDLC, using the HPR network header, multiplexes traffic from CS with HPR RTP traffic.

The HPR network control layer (NCL) uses the automatic network routing (ANR) information in the HPR network header to pass incoming packets to either RTP or to an outgoing link. RFC 1483 defines multiprotocol encapsulation over ATM; it provides for encapsulation of HPR NLP packets within LLC frames; thus each HPR packet is encapsulated within two LLC frames.

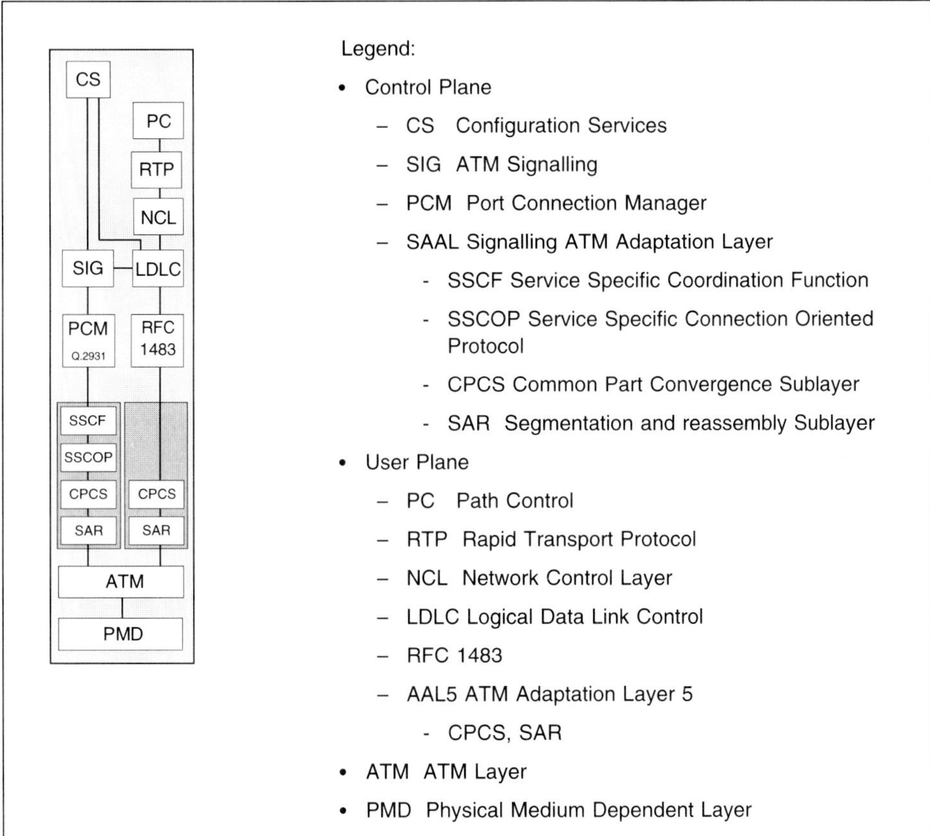

Figure 108. Node Structure

12.2.1.1 Low- Level ATM Interface (LL ATMI)

The native ATM DLC approach requires an interface to ATM that gives higher-layer protocols the ability to request the full range of ATM services. APPN products are free to implement any such interface.

IBM has proposed the *low-level ATM interface* to the ATM Desktop Alliance. The LL ATMI provides a common semantics platform for access to the native services of ATM as defined by the ATM Forum's *User-to-Network Interface Specification, Version 3.1.* The specification (file name ATMIXPS.ZIP) is available via anonymous FTP at:

`ftp://ftp.efficient.com/pub/desktopapi`

The LL ATMI is an interface between the network adapter driver and the higher-layer protocols (perhaps using a common connection manager). The interface provides a formal description of the interface semantics and operating system-independent message encodings. This interface is for both the signalling and user planes. The LL ATMI's positioning is platform-specific for both the user and control planes. For signalling, it is typically positioned between the higher-layer protocols or their common connection manager and the Q.2931 port connection manager. For the node structure in Figure 108 on page 279, it is typically positioned immediately above the AAL 5 for the user plane.

The LL ATMI should not be confused with a UNI, which defines the interface between an ATM end station and the public or private ATM network equipment over which signalling information and data are exchanged. The LL ATMI is an interface within an ATM end station over which the higher layers gain access to ATM services.

12.2.1.2 Control Plane

In order for an APPN node to dynamically establish, maintain and terminate SVC connections through an ATM network, the node uses ATM signalling procedures to exchange information with the network, for example, the ATM adaptation layer type to be used for the SVC. Depending on whether the network is private or public, the interface is referred to as either a private UNI or public UNI. UNI signalling is standardized by the ATM Forum in ATM UNI 3.1 and by the ITU. Q.2931 is the layer 3 protocol used to control the UNI. The component providing Q.2931 signalling is called the port connection manager (PCM). Q.2931 runs on top of the signalling ATM adaptation layer (SAAL), which defines how to transfer the signalling information reliably using cells of the ATM layer on signalling virtual channels. This is described in ITU-T recommendation Q.2100, B-ISDN Signalling ATM Adaptation Layer Overview Description. Currently a dedicated point-to-point signalling virtual channel with VCI=5 and VPI=0 is used for UNI signalling.

SAAL consists of a service-specific part and a common part (see Figure 108 on page 279). The service-specific part further consists of a UNI service-specific coordination function (SSCF) and a service-specific connection-oriented protocol (SSCOP). The UNI SSCF maps the particular requirements of Q.2931 to the requirements of the ATM layer. This is defined in ITU-T recommendation Q.2130,

B-ISDN ATM Adaptation Service Specific Coordination Function for Signalling at the User-to-Network Interface. SSCOP provides mechanisms for the establishment, release and monitoring of signalling information exchange connections between peer signalling entities. This is described in ITU-T recommendation Q.2110, B-ISDN ATM Adaptation Layer Service Specific Connection-Oriented Protocol. SAAL uses the common part convergence sublayer (CPCS) and the segmentation and reassembly sublayer of AAL type 5.

12.2.1.3 User Plane

The ATM adaptation layer (AAL) supports higher-layer functions of both the user and control planes. The SAAL, described earlier, is used for the control plane.

There are several AAL types defined for the user plane. AAL type 3/4 and AAL type 5 are used for variable bit rate (VBR) data. The AAL type used for a given SVC is defined with the signalling protocols in the AAL information element (IE). The structure for the user plane is shown in Figure 108 on page 279.

The CPCS performs functions common to all AAL users. The service-specific requirements of different classes of users are implemented in the service-specific convergence sublayer (SSCS). For user classes that do not require any service-specific function, the SSCS may be null. The SSCS for a given connection is specified with the signalling protocols in the AAL IE.

The native ATM DLC for APPN uses AAL type 5 with a null SSCS.

12.2.1.4 Logical Data Link Control (LDLC)

LDLC is a base function for the native ATM DLC, but can also be used for other DLCs (for example, Ethernet, token ring, frame relay, and X.25).

LDLC is a new LLC type defined to be used in conjunction with HPR (with Control Flows over RTP option set 1402) over reliable links that do not require link-level error recovery. Using LDLC eliminates the need for LLC2 and its associated cost (adapter storage, longer path length, etc.) by using an LLC2 subset that uses only TEST, XID, DISC, DM, and UI frames.

LDLC performs the following functions:

Reliable delivery of XIDs
: As done by LLC on today's APPN links, LDLC delivers XID3s reliably.

Indication of when the XID exchange is complete
: This is analogous to the set mode function (for example, SABME and UA) and is required because configuration services (CS) needs to synchronize the completion of the XID exchange with the partner.

Deactivation of the link
: This function enables the APPN/HPR link to be deactivated without deactivating other non-SNA links over a shared circuit (SVC or PVC).

NLP Routing
: NLPs of type ANR (that carry all HPR session and control traffic) are sent and received over the link in UI frames. LDLC routes received NLPs of this type to the appropriate upper-layer component (NCL). LDLC does not guarantee successful delivery of these packets as this function is provided by RTP.

Link INOP processing
: On many link types (for example, ATM and frame relay) failure notification is provided by the service provider subnet when the link connection fails. On these link types, LDLC receives an INOP message when the link connection fails. For example, when an ATM SVC or PVC fails, the ATM signalling component sends an INOP message to LDLC. LDLC cleans up the link when an INOP is received.

Liveness Protocol
: LDLC may optionally check that the partner is alive by periodically sending *test* commands and receiving, if the partner is alive, a test response. The format of these commands is defined in the IEEE 802.2 standard. However, this *liveness* protocol is unique to LDLC.

These functions are the only ones required since all other traffic (CP-CP session, LU-LU session, and route setup) is delivered reliably by RTP.

LDLC Instances and SAP Multiplexing: There is an instance of LDLC associated with each link. A link is uniquely identified by the standard identifiers (such as port address) and the SAP pair. The SAP pair is carried in the 802.2 header which resides in every LDLC packet. The SAP pair can be used to multiplex many links over a single physical connection, which is referred to as *SAP multiplexing*.

12.2.1.5 Error Recovery Positioning

Error recovery can be provided either by the ATM network, using an SSCS, or at a higher layer such as LLC. For APPN transmissions over a native DLC, error recovery will not be provided by the ATM network. This choice was made for the following reasons:

- When a VCC is established, its SSCS is specified by signalling or definition and used for all data flowing over the VCC. Thus, if the reliability mechanism is associated with that SSCS, it is the only one available for all data streams. Alternatively, with a null SSCS and reliable delivery provided at the DLC layer, each traffic stream can have its own reliable delivery mechanism (or none at all); thus, traffic streams with different reliable delivery mechanisms can be multiplexed over a single VCC.
- Multiprotocol encapsulation, as defined by RFC 1483 (and extensions), expects to run over AAL type 5 with a null SSCS (see Figure 108 on page 279). Placement of SSCOP as an SSCS would prevent interoperability with other vendor's products, which are expected to use RFC 1483 for multiprotocol data.

Rapid transport protocol (RTP) for APPN/HPR also provides error recovery and selective retransmission. Thus, RTP data does not require error recovery by LLC. To eliminate the need for a high-function LLC, HPR and RTP were made prerequisites for the native ATM DLC function. In addition, the HPR control flows over RTP option set was also made a prerequisite; HPR CP-CP sessions and route setup traffic will therefore flow only over RTP connections. Therefore, no error recovery function needs to be provided by the LLC.

APPN/HPR requires guaranteed delivery across its links for XID3 traffic. For this reason, current DLCs used for XID3 traffic include an LLC that can provide this function. In order to provide reliable delivery for XIDs, LLC typically sends XIDs as unnumbered commands (with the poll bit set to 1) and responses. A similar technique must be provided across the user plane for ATM links. This function will be provided by the native DLC in a new logical data link control (LDLC) component.

To support frame relay service interworking, products may optionally support IEEE 802.2 LLC type 2 (LLC2). XID is used to determine whether LLC2 or LDLC will be used.

Optional link-level error recovery is allowed when using LLC2 instead of LDLC over ATM's low error-rate links.

12.2.1.6 Internal Routing of Frames

When LDLC is used, APPN/HPR passes outgoing RTP traffic through its LDLC component. XID, XID_DONE, and DEACT are processed by the LDLC reliable delivery function (see Figure 109 on page 285).

The mechanism for routing frames received over an ATM network to the proper component within a node is as follows:

- All frames are encapsulated within an RFC 1483 header (see Figure 110 on page 286).
- The 1483 header indicates the higher-layer protocol to which the frame should be passed.
- When the 1483 header indicates the higher-layer protocol is HPR, the RFC 1483 header is removed, and the packet is passed to the correct instance of LDLC (SAP demultiplexing); that is, RFC 1483 decides which instance of LDLC is correct by looking at the SAPs in the second LLC header, and not the SAPs in the RFC 1483 header. LDLC examines the LLC header and the HPR network header.
  - When the LLC header indicates XID, TEST DISC or DM, or the LLC header indicates unnumbered information (UI) and the network header indicates function routing, the packet is processed by the LDLC reliable delivery function. LDLC forwards XID, XID_DONE and DEACT frames to APPN configuration services (CS).

- When the LLC header indicates UI and the network header indicates ANR routing, the packet is passed to NCL. NCL examines the ANR information and passes the packet either to RTP or to an outgoing link.

12.2.1.7 ATM User Plane Frame Formats

The native ATM DLC will operate over AAL type 5 with a null SSCS. The network control layer of HPR will pass data network layer packets (NLP) to LDLC. How control NLPs are passed to LDLC, and internal data formats, are both implementation-dependent. Figure 109 on page 285 shows a basic representation of how packets are passed down through the various layers.

The data unit passed from the RFC 1483 encapsulation function to AAL type 5 is called the CPCS service data unit (CPCS-SDU). CPCS pads the CPCS-SDU and adds an 8-byte CPCS trailer. The resulting data unit is a multiple of 48 bytes in length and is called the CPCS protocol data unit (CPCS-PDU). SAR segments the CPCS-PDU into 48-byte SAR-PDUs, which it passes to the ATM layer. The ATM layer adds its 5-byte header to each SAR-PDU to create a 53-byte ATM cell.

Figure 110 on page 286 depicts the various frame formats. All transmissions on an ATM TG will be in an IEEE 802.2 LLC frame that begins with an 8-byte header. The contents of this header are defined by RFC 1483 and ATM Forum Implementation Agreement 94-0615, which is called an RFC 1483 header. When DSAP, SSAP and Control Field are coded X'FEFE03', the fourth byte is a network layer packet identifier (NLPID). An NLPID of X'09' indicates that the NLPID is followed by a 2-byte layer 2 protocol identifier (L2) and a 2-byte layer 3 protocol identifier (L3), the format of which complies with broadband low-layer information specified in ITU-T Recommendation Q.2931. The values of L2 and L3 are defined in ATM Forum Implementation Agreement 94-0615. An L2 value of X'4C80' indicates the use of IEEE 802.2 as the L2 protocol, and an L3 value of X'7085' indicates that HPR is the layer 3 protocol.

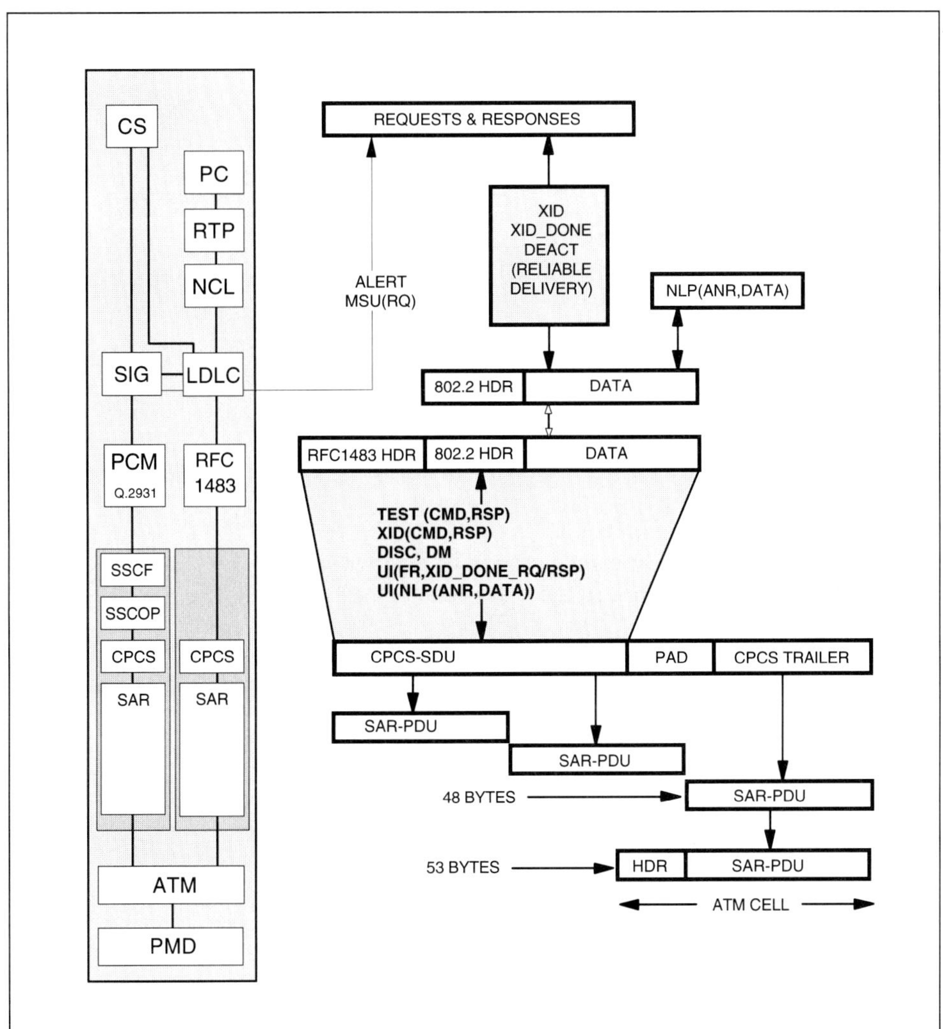

Figure 109. Internal Routing of Frames

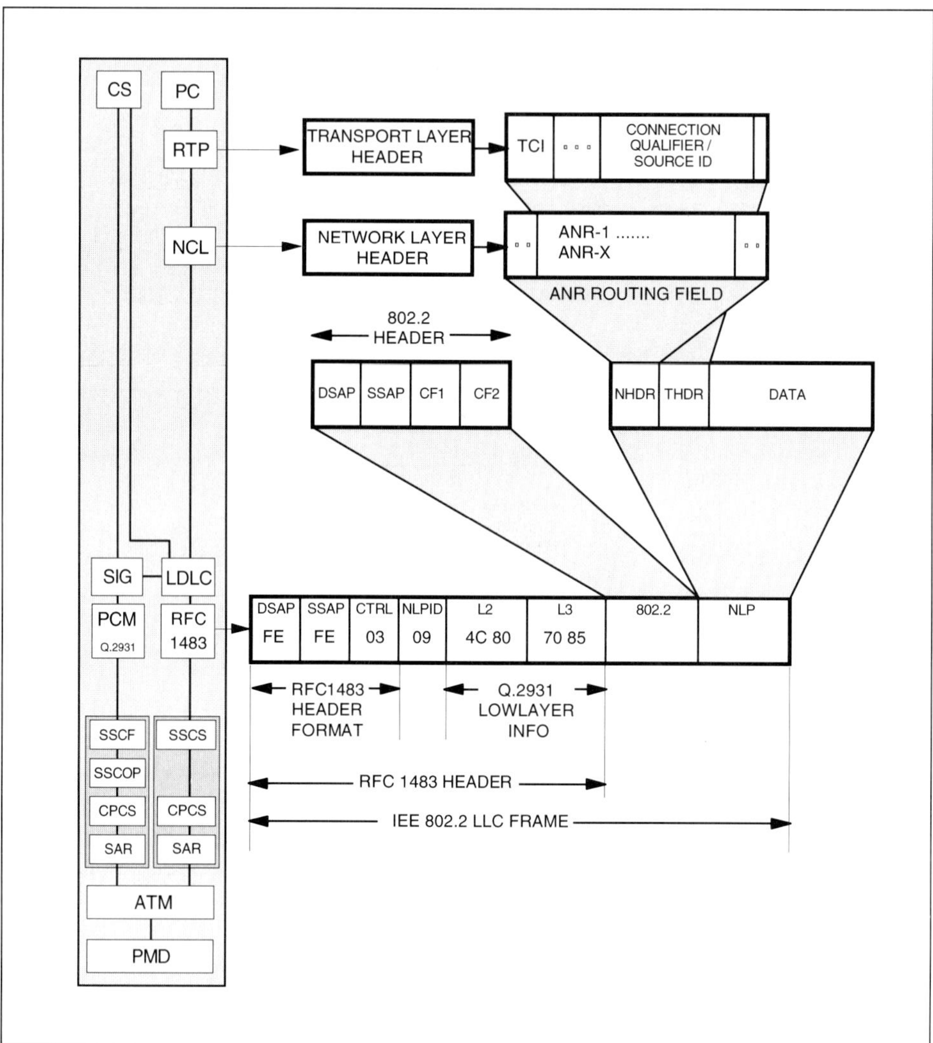

Figure 110. Frame Formats

Typical formats for data and control NLPs on a single protocol SVC are shown in Figure 111 on page 287. A value of X'101' in the switching mode field of the network layer header (NHDR) indicates the mode is function routing. For function routing, a value of X'1' in the function type field of the NHDR indicates that the function type is LDLC. When the function type is LDLC, there is no transport header (THDR) and a 1-byte function routing header follows the NHDR.

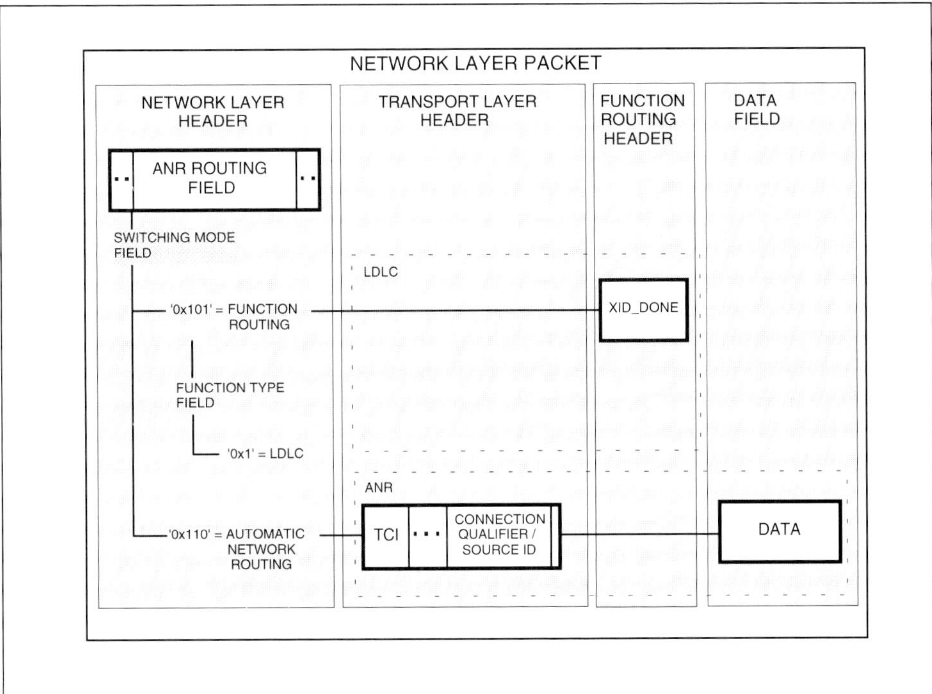

Figure 111. NLP Formats

12.3 ATM Connection Networks

In the connection network model, a virtual routing node (VRN) is defined to represent the shared access transport facility (SATF). Each node attached to the SATF defines a single TG to the VRN rather than TGs to all other attached nodes.

The following extensions to the connection network model for LANs are required for ATM connection networks:

- For LANs, the DLC signalling information, which consists of the MAC address and the LLC SAP address, is sufficient to establish a connection; however, this is not the case for ATM switched facilities. The DLC signalling information for ATM includes the ATM address, but other information, which may be either included in the DLC signalling information or defined locally, is required to establish a call. For example, the QoS class for the forward direction is locally defined at the node placing the call.
- The connection network model for LANs allows only one TG between a port and a VRN. For ATM, multiple TGs between a port and a VRN are allowed in order to support separation of traffic for different classes of service.

- The LAN connection network model assumes the same characteristics for each connection crossing the LAN. For ATM when multiple TGs are defined to a VRN, each may have different associated call request parameters. In addition, ATM connections across the same TG to different destination nodes may have different call request parameters based on parameter definition for the paired connection network TG.
- Normally, one connection network is defined on a LAN (that is, one VRN is defined.) For ATM, separate connection networks are required for best-effort service and reserved bandwidth connections. In addition, a separate connection network may be defined between the nodes connected to a private campus ATM network.

Two types of SVCs, *dedicated* and *nondedicated*, can be established for ATM connection networks. Support for dedicated SVCs is a product option. If a route selected for a session needing dedicated SVC services crosses a connection network between two nodes that support dedicated SVCs, an SVC dedicated to that session is established using the specified throughput and QoS characteristics.

12.4 ATM Traffic Contracts and Quality of Service (QoS) Classes

ATM networks are expected to support a variety of data types with different characteristics. Design and operation of network control functions such as call admission, bandwidth reservation, and congestion control require accurate source characterization to achieve high resource utilization. However, some sources are unable to provide a detailed description of their traffic behavior. Hence, there is a trade-off between how much information should and can be defined to characterize a source.

The ATM UNI provides the protocol for establishing a virtual channel connection (VCC) on demand. A bidirectional traffic contract (one for each direction) specifies the negotiated throughput characteristics of an ATM connection at the UNI. The APPN node requesting the setup of the VCC selects a QoS class for each direction from the set of QoS classes supported by the ATM network. Upon agreement, the network commits to meet the requested QoS for a direction as long as the user complies with the traffic contract for that direction.

An SVC for APPN traffic needing guaranteed throughput would usually request specified QoS class 3, which is defined to support service class C, connection-oriented data transfer.

There is also an unspecified QoS class 0 used with best-effort service for which no explicit characteristics are negotiated with the network. For best-effort service, there are no traffic throughput guarantees; the only parameter specified is the peak cell rate, which is used by the other endpoint.

Note: Unlike ATM UNI 3.0 and ATM UNI 3.1, Q.2931 signalling specified by ITU-T only supports the unspecified QoS class.

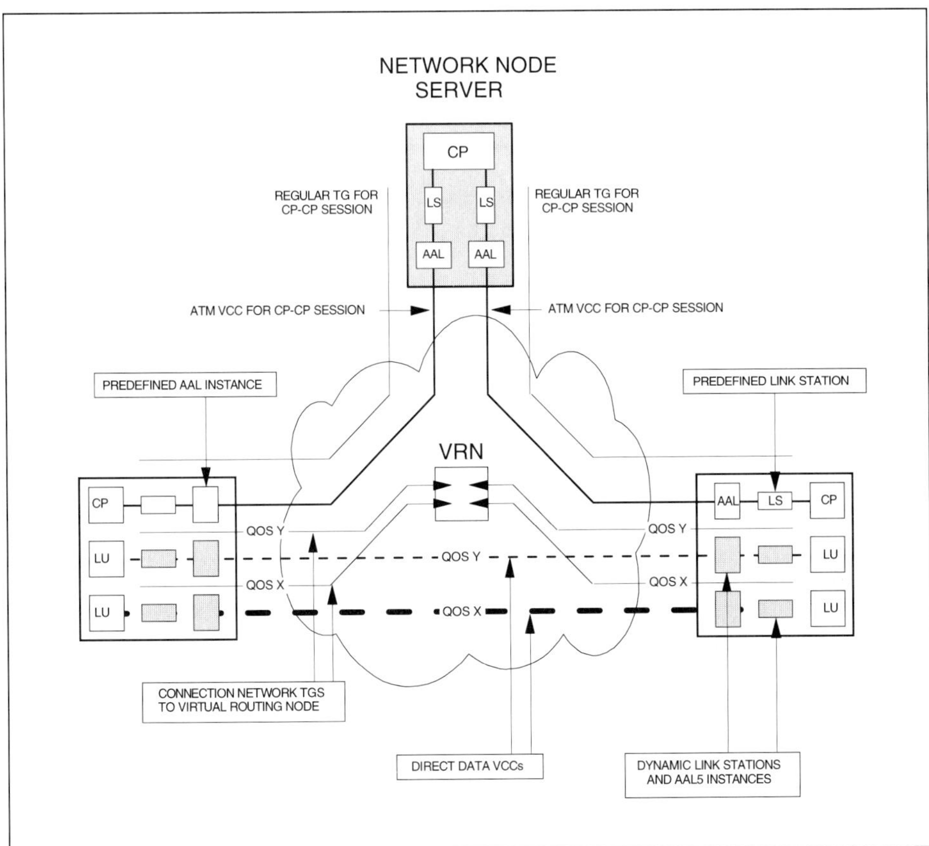

Figure 112. Connection Network Example

12.5 Adaptive Rate-Based Congestion Control Parameters

Adaptive rate-based congestion control (ARB) is an HPR Rapid Transport Protocol (RTP) function that controls the data transmission rate over RTP connections. ARB also provides fairness between the RTP traffic streams sharing a VCC. For ARB to perform these functions in the ATM environment, it is necessary to coordinate the ARB parameters with the ATM setup parameters.

When the HPR route setup protocol is used to establish an RTP connection across an ATM SVC or PVC, the value for the minimum link capacity received in Route Setup (request or reply) is lowered to the effective capacity of the ATM link with a 10% deduction for ATM cell overhead as defined for the TG characteristics (unless the received value was already lower) before the Route Setup is forwarded across the ATM link. For a reserved bandwidth VCC, the capacity parameter is based on the sustainable cell rate in the direction the Route Setup is flowing. For a best effort connection, it is based on the peak cell rate which should be the same for both directions.

ATM switches may use the settings 010 and 011 of the Payload Type (PT) field in the ATM cell header (for both best effort and reserved virtual connections) of data packets as an explicit forward congestion indication (EFCI). The ATM Forum has not standardized the use of EFCI; therefore, some ATM switches will not set these values, and those that do may use the settings under somewhat different conditions. HPR products treat EFCI like forward explicit congestion notification (FECN) for frame relay; as a result, ARB at the source RTP connection endpoint may be requested to slow down. For ATM, the mechanism for each direction of flow on an RTP connection works as follows when congestion is detected:

1. A cell flowing through the ATM subnet encounters congestion causing EFCI to be set in the cell's PT field.
2. The HPR node at the edge of the ATM subnet detects EFCI in one or more cells of a reassembled packet and turns on the slowdown 1 congestion indicator in the packet's HPR network header.
3. The packet arrives at the RTP receiver endpoint node.
   - If the packet contains an ARB request segment in the RTP transport header, then a slowdown 1 rate adjustment action is returned in the ARB reply segment.
   - If the packet does not contain an ARB request segment, the indicator in the network header is ignored.
4. When the ARB reply segment is received at the RTP sender endpoint node, ARB reduces the send rate.

There is some concern because the congestion notice takes on the order of round trip time to reach the RTP sender. The ATM Forum is currently discussing the mechanisms by which an ATM network will indicate congestion for available bit rate (ABR) service. The mechanisms under discussion will provide this notification to the ATM endstations at both ends of the connection; that is, both forward and backward congestion indicators will be provided. The backward congestion indication could be used to decrease the time required for ARB to respond to congestion. It should be possible to use the same mechanism to notify the RTP sender of forward congestion as used for EFCI. However, a more complex algorithm would be required to take advantage of a backward congestion indication; such an algorithm would not guarantee significantly improved performance. Note that HPR intermediate (that is, ANR) nodes do not have RTP connection awareness and cannot generate a flow back to the RTP sender. Also, note that when a network header with a congestion indicator is received, the RTP endpoint assumes that it applies to traffic the endpoint is receiving, not the traffic it is sending.

ATM adapters will have greater capability than frame relay to queue data before sending it into the subnet. This queueing will result in delay that is detectable by ARB; this delay detection reduces the need to provide congestion notification to the RTP sender.

12.5.1 Enhanced Session-Level Pacing

For the native ATM DLC, enhanced session-level pacing is a required function for LU 6.2 in HPR nodes; it is an optional function for ISR session connectors. Session-level pacing, as currently defined, can be a bottleneck preventing sessions from fully using the bandwidth available for an ATM VCC. The enhanced session-level pacing algorithm increases the pacing window, more rapidly allowing sessions to take advantage of the available bandwidth. ARB prevents the sessions from causing congestion in the ATM network.

12.6 Multiprotocol Encapsulation

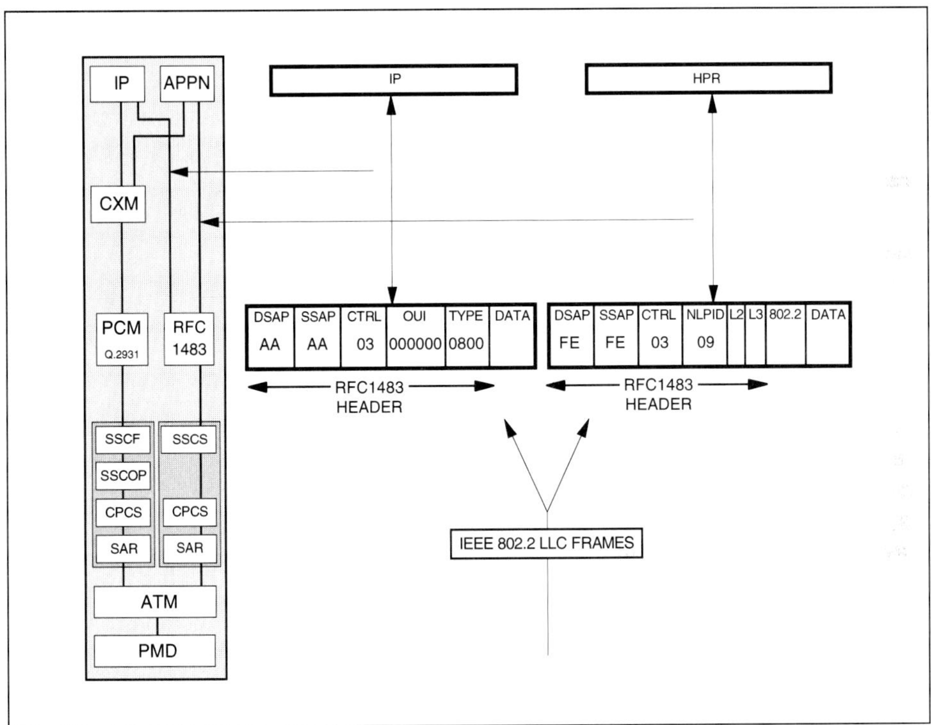

Figure 113. Multiprotocol Encapsulation on SVCs

Multiprotocol encapsulation provides a flexible method for carrying multiple protocols on a given ATM connection. The method is useful when customers desire *parallel* transport of data from multiple higher-layer protocols (that is, data from one protocol is not encapsulated within the headers of a second protocol). Otherwise, separate VCCs must be established for each protocol. Figure 113 shows the basic node structure for supporting multiprotocol encapsulation (in this case, IP and APPN). A common connection manager (CxM) supports signalling for the multiple higher-layer protocols.

RFC 1483, *Multiprotocol Encapsulation over ATM Adaptation Layer 5*, describes multiprotocol encapsulation for connectionless network interconnect traffic and for routed and bridged protocol data units (PDUs). IBM has submitted ATM Forum contribution 94-0615, *Multiprotocol over ATM Adaptation Layer Type 5 Implementation Agreement*, that extends RFC 1483 to cover connection-oriented protocols. The implementation agreement adds code points for the following protocols:

- Subarea SNA (FID4)
- Peripheral SNA (FID2)
- APPN (FID2)
- APPN/HPR
- NetBIOS

These extensions are currently under consideration by the ATM Forum. The extensions were also presented at the APPN Implementers Workshop (AIW).

RFC 1483 encapsulates packets of the various protocols within 802.2 LLC type 1 frames (see Figure 110 on page 286).

Chapter 13. Network Management

Network management is the process of planning, organizing, monitoring, and controlling an APPN network. The architecture provided to assist in network management of SNA systems is called *management services* and is implemented as a set of functions and services designed to capture and use the information needed for effective management. For details about SNA management services see *Systems Network Architecture Management Services Reference*, SC30-3346.

13.1 Network Management Categories

Network management can be divided into the following categories:

- Configuration management
- Problem management
- Change management
- Performance and accounting management
- Operations management

13.1.1.1 Configuration Management

Configuration management is the control of information necessary to identify network resources. This identification includes information such as machine type and serial number (hardware), program number, release and maintenance level (software or microcode), vendor and service organization, etc.

The configuration information may assist other network management categories, for example:

- Problem management may use the configuration data to determine the physical identity and location of a network resource, and the organization responsible for service.
- Change management may use the configuration data to schedule changes and analyze the effects of these changes.

13.1.1.2 Problem Management

Problem management is the process of managing a problem or potential problem from its detection through its final resolution. The term problem denotes an error condition resulting in an actual or potential loss of availability of a system resource that is visible to the end user. Problems may originate in hardware, software, or as a result of external causes such as user procedures.

The elements of problem management are:

Problem determination
: This is the element of problem management that detects the problem or impending problem and isolates the problem to the failing component.

Problem diagnosis
: Is the element of problem management that determines the exact cause of the problem and identifies the action required to resolve the problem.

Problem bypass and recovery
: Is the element of problem management that implements a partial or complete circumvention of the problem, while the original problem is being diagnosed and a permanent solution is being worked on. For example, when a leased telephone line fails, the bypass could be to use a switched connection until the leased line has been repaired.

Problem resolution
: Is the element of problem management that schedules and tests the repair action and reports the problem as closed and the resource back in service.

Problem tracking and control
: Is the element of problem management that tracks the problem from problem determination until final resolution.

13.1.1.3 Change Management

Change management is the process of planning and controlling changes in a network. A change is defined as an addition, modification, or deletion of a network component. The component being either hardware (including microcode) or software. The software could be either system or application (vendor supplied or user written).

The elements of change management are:

Change planning
: Is the element of change management that encompasses all the activities required to take place before changes can be distributed and installed.

Change control
: Is the element of change management that distributes change files to entry points and installs them there. These changes may be either installed on a trial basis or in production.

Node activation
: Is the element of change management that reactivates altered entry points according to the change management plan.

13.1.1.4 Performance and Accounting Management

Performance and accounting management is the process of quantifying, measuring, reporting, and controlling the responsiveness, availability, utilization, and costs of network components.

13.1.1.5 Operations Management

Operations management provides the capability to control distributed network resources. Activating and deactivating resources, as well as setting resource clocks are all functions that are included in this category. In addition, a cancelation function has been defined that enables previously sent commands (including those executing at the target) to be terminated.

As an implementation option, operations management commands may be initiated as a result of system notification forwarding.

13.2 Management Services Roles

In terms of management services, SNA nodes fall into two basic categories, which help explain the nodes' role in the network. An *entry point* is an SNA node that provides distributed network management support. It may be a T2.0, T2.1, T4, or T5 node. It sends SNA-formatted network management data about itself and the resources it controls to the second major type of node, known as *focal point*, for centralized processing. The entry point also receives and executes focal-point-initiated requests to manage and control its resources. The network management data, or management services (MS) data, can be *solicited* (requested by the focal point) or *unsolicited* MS information on events occurring within the entry point. An example of unsolicited information would be an *alert* sent by an entry point as notification of a link failure.

The concept of a focal point permits centralized management of a distributed network. A focal point is an entry point that provides centralized management and control for other entry points for one or more network management categories.

Focal points and entry points have relationships with each other for one or more categories of network management. Relationships between a focal point and entry points for problem management may or may not be the same as those established for change management, for example. A single communications system or network may have multiple focal points.

The manner in which the focal points and entry points interact to accomplish the goal of network management is introduced in the following sections.

13.2.1 Focal Point Concepts

When a focal point to entry point relationship needs to be established to enable the sending of unsolicited data from the entry point, *MS capabilities* major vectors are exchanged between the focal and entry point. These exchanges establish the relationship between the focal and entry point for a particular category of management services. The set of nodes having this relationship with a focal point is known as the *sphere of control* (SOC), of the focal point, and each of the individual nodes directly in the sphere of control is known as an *SOC node*.

Note: For the change management category, the relationship between an entry and a focal point is not established by the exchange of MS capabilities.

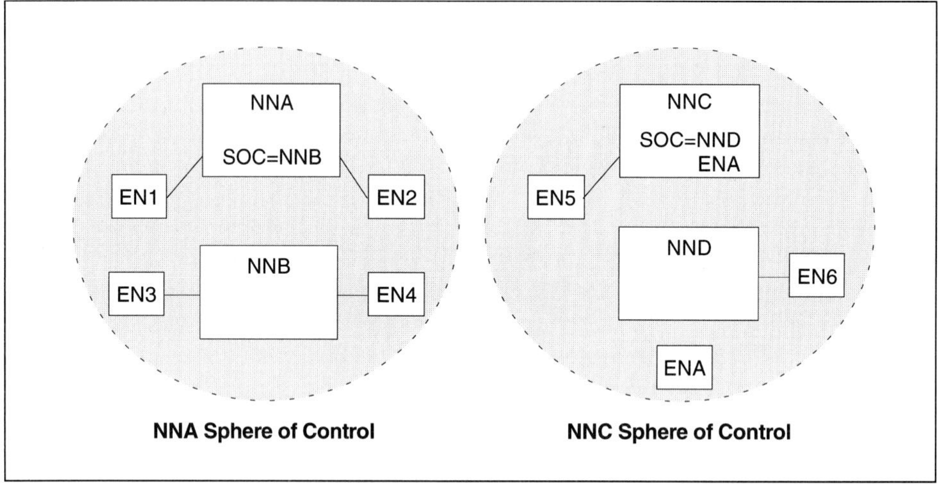

Figure 114. Sphere of Control (SOC)

APPN network nodes are SOC nodes both for themselves and for their served end nodes. The network node provides focal point notification messages to its served end nodes. This simplifies network administration and reduces network startup overhead, since focal points need to be aware of only the network nodes in their SOC. However, end nodes may optionally provide the same level of support as network nodes and be SOC nodes themselves.

It is possible for a focal point to have no SOC nodes, in which case it is said to have a *null sphere of control*.

A network may have multiple focal points. These focal points may have responsibility for the same or different categories of management service data. However, the spheres of control for multiple focal points may not overlap.

Nodes can be assigned to a focal point's sphere of control, or can be acquired independently of network operator definition (for example, from the topology of the network). In the first case, the focal point is an *assigned* focal point; in the second case, the focal point is referred to as a *default* focal point.

Assigned Focal Point

An *explicitly* defined sphere of control is one that is defined at the focal point. The focal point is responsible for initiating and establishing this focal point (FP) to entry point (EP) relationship. The FP type for an explicit FP-EP relationship is called *explicit primary*.

An *implicitly* defined sphere of control is one that is defined at the various entry points. It is not explicitly defined at the focal point. The entry points are responsible for initiating and establishing this focal point to entry point relationship. The FP type for an implicit FP-EP relationship is called *implicit primary*.

Default Focal Point

A *default* focal point does not have a sphere of control explicitly assigned. Instead, it learns of the identity of APPN network nodes by examining the network topology. Network nodes will only accept the services from a default focal point, if no other focal point has been assigned. The default FP-EP relationship applies only to EP nodes that are network nodes. The FP type for a default FP-EP relationship is called *default primary*.

Backup Focal Point

A *primary* focal point is the preferred destination for unsolicited data for a particular management services category. A *backup* focal point is one that provides management services for a node in the event that the services of the primary focal point are unavailable. The FP type for an implicit (backup) FP-EP relationship is called *backup*.

Host Focal Point

A *host* FP-EP relationship may be established if the EP node can establish an SSCP-PU session to a host node. No MS capabilities are exchanged.

Nested Focal Point

The relationship of focal-entry points may be nested; that means a focal point can be an SOC node in another focal point's sphere of control. The relationship between a *nesting* focal point (see, for example, NNE in Figure 115 on page 298) and a *nested* focal point (NNA or NNC) is established the same way as the relationship between any focal point and the nodes in its sphere of control. Notice that since a focal point is the focal point for itself, it would never accept a request from a default focal point. Nesting focal points must always be assigned.

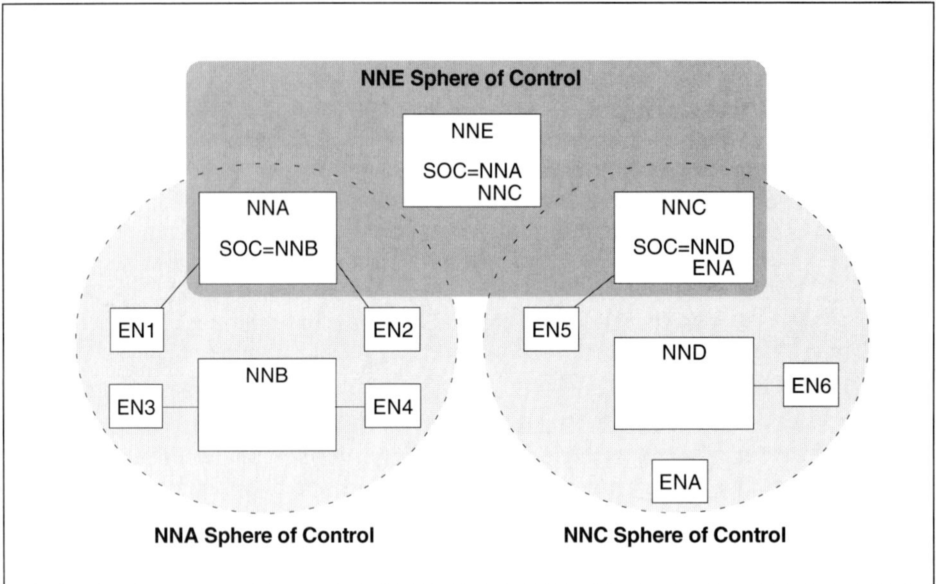

Figure 115. Nested Focal Points

The sphere of control relationship between focal points allows the lower-level focal point to forward network management information that it does not filter to its higher-level focal point. Nesting focal points cannot have overlapping spheres of control. This means that nodes in the sphere of control of the nested focal point are not in the sphere of control of the nesting level focal point.

13.3 Management Services Components

Management services distinguishes three components. These are:

- Local management services, hereafter referred to as LMS
- Control point management services, hereafter referred to as CPMS
- Physical unit management services, hereafter referred to as PUMS

  Note: The functions of PUMS as described in this chapter cover the management services of an SNA Type 2.0 node. Similar functions, although performed by a CP, are performed in a T2.1 node attached to a VTAM or NCP boundary function.

13.3.1 Local Management Services

LMS is the network management portion that is implemented in components and layers of a T2.1 node; see Figure 116 on page 299 below and Figure 117 on page 301. The LMS function is implemented in control point components such as topology and routing services, directory services, and session services, but also in the SNA layers such as data link control and path control. The LMS in each component or layer gathers information and forwards this information to its CPMS. The interface used between the CPMS and LMS is implementation-dependent. The LMS also receives and executes network management requests from the CPMS. The results of the network management requests are returned to the CPMS for further processing.

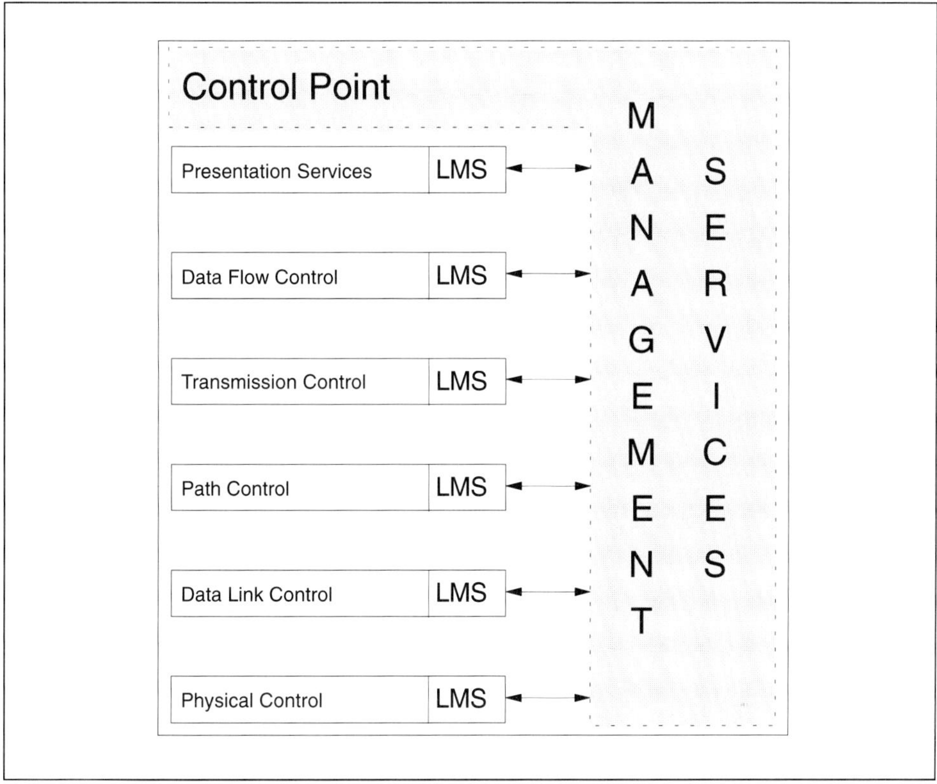

Figure 116. Local Management Services (LMS)

13.3.2 Introduction to Control Point Management Services (CPMS)

Control point management services (CPMS) is implemented in every T2.1 node. CPMS is a CP component of a T2.1 node that assists a network operator in the management and control of the node. The CPMS receives commands from the network operator or other CPMS instances, converts these commands in installation unique formats, and routes these to the appropriate LMS function for further processing. Information received from LMS, either solicited or unsolicited, is converted to standardized management services formats and routed to either the network operator or other CPMS instances.

In an APPN network, every APPN node contains CPMS. In an APPN end node, CPMS acts only as an entry point; in an APPN network node, CPMS can act as an entry point or a focal point.

13.3.2.1 CPMS: Overview

Figure 117 on page 301 illustrates the components with which CPMS in an APPN network node exchanges data. The following list items correspond to the numbered items in the figure. These are:

1. Session Services (SS)
   - Upon request, SS provides information about the currently active sessions.
   - Upon request, SS assigns FQPCIDs to CPMS. The FQPCID is required on the interface to directory services.
   - SS in a network node provides unsolicited notification to CPMS when CP-CP sessions to served end nodes change status.
   - SS in an end node provides unsolicited notification to CPMS when CP-CP sessions to the network node server become active or inactive.
   - SS provides unsolicited notification of problems detected by the component.
2. Configuration Services (CS)
   - Upon request, CS provides configuration information about its domain.
   - CS provides unsolicited notification of problems detected by the component.
3. CP Session Manager
   - Upon request, the CP session manager provides information about the currently active LU 6.2 sessions for which the CP is a session endpoint.
4. CP Resource Manager
   - Upon request, the CP resource manager provides information about conversations on sessions for which the CP is a session endpoint.
5. Address Space Manager (ASM)
   - Upon request, ASM provides the names of all active LUs at this CP.
   - ASM provides unsolicited notification of problems detected by the component.
6. Topology and Routing Services (TRS)
   - TRS provides unsolicited notification of all nodes for which connectivity has just been required.
   - TRS provides unsolicited notification of problems detected by the component.
7. Directory Services (DS)
   - Upon request, DS provides the names of active LUs.
   - Upon request, DS locates network resources for CPMS.
   - DS provides unsolicited notification of problems detected by the component.

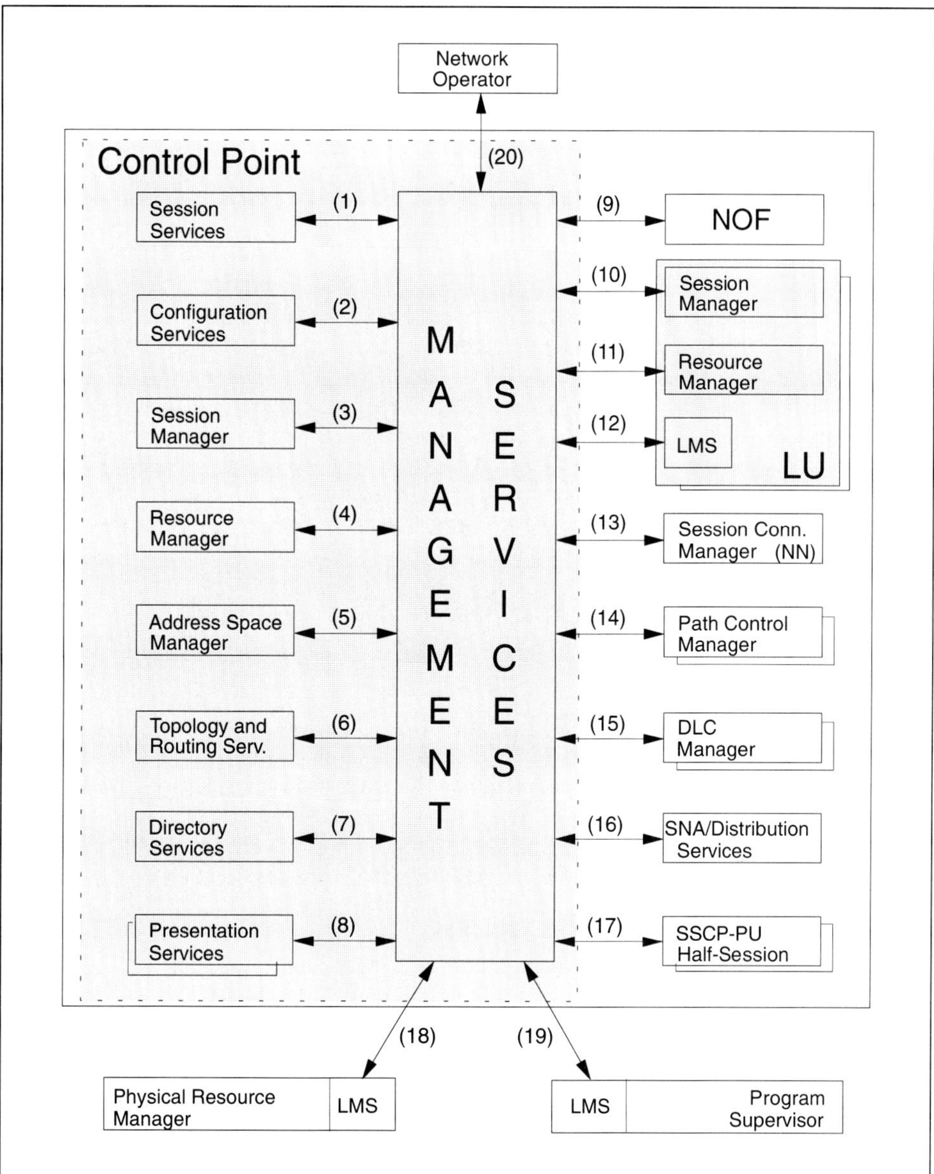

Figure 117. CP Management Services Boundaries with Other Components

8. CP Presentation Services

   - CP presentation services provides the LU 6.2 protocol boundary used by MS service transaction programs that communicate over CP-CP sessions.

9. Node Operator Facility (NOF)

   - The NOF is the component that provides operator control of the local node, such as initialization of other CP components (including management services).

10. LU Session Manager

    - Upon request the LU session manager (LU 6.2 only) provides information about the currently active sessions for which the LU is a session endpoint.

11. LU Resource Manager

    - Upon request the LU resource manager (LU 6.2 only) provides information about conversations on sessions for which the LU is a session endpoint.

12. Logical Unit Local Management Services

    - The LU LMS provides unsolicited notification of problems detected by the LU.

13. Session Connector Manager (SCM)

    - Upon request SCM provides LU session data for sessions passing through the node.
    - SCM provides unsolicited notification of problems detected by the component.

14. Path Control Manager Local Management Services

    - The path control manager provides unsolicited notification of problems detected by the component.

15. Data Link Control Local Management Services

    - Upon request data link control (DLC) tests resources, for example, links and modems, sets or retrieves management services parameters, and provides traces.
    - DLC provides unsolicited notification of errors and traffic statistics when problems associated with links and link stations are encountered, or when a counter threshold is exceeded.

16. SNA/Distribution Services

    - SNA/DS provides the capability to send and receive CP-MSUs, SNA/File Services (SNA/FS) agent objects, and SNA/FS files (bulk data) over an LU-LU session using LU 6.2 protocols.

      The change management category uses SNA/FS and SNA/DS for distribution of potentially large files, and issues the commands to manipulate them. For more details, see 13.4.4, "SNA Distribution Services" on page 310.

17. SSCP-PU Half-Session

    - The SSCP-PU half-session provides communication with PUs within the CP's domain (only if the T2.1 node has implemented SSCP functions).

18. Physical Resource Manager Local Management Services

    - The physical resource manager LMS provides unsolicited notification of problems with the node physical resources, for example, tapes, disks, storage and microcode.

19. Program Supervisor Local Management Services (LMS)

    - On request, the program supervisor LMS alters software and microcode components.

20. Network Operator

    - The network operator requests management services from CPMS.
    - The network operator receives management services from PUMS in a Type 4 or Type 2.0 node, either unsolicited or upon request. This data may have been received directly from PUMS on an SSCP-PU session, or received indirectly from PUMS via a controlling CPMS on a CP-CP session.
    - The network operator receives management services data from CPMS in an APPN network node either unsolicited or upon request. This data may have been received from CPMS in an SSCP-PU or CP-CP session, or received indirectly via a controlling CPMS or a serving CPMS on a CP-CP session.

    Note: The term network operator actually refers to the programming which supports an operator, either human or programmed.

13.3.3 Introduction to Physical Unit Management Services (PUMS)

Physical unit management services (PUMS) is the component of an SNA *physical unit* (PU) responsible for providing general management services to the node and its associated resources. The functions of PUMS as described in this section cover the management services of an SNA Type 2.0 node. Similar functions, although performed by the CP, are present in T2.1 nodes that attach to a VTAM or NCP boundary function. In a T2.1 node, the CP acts as a PU for the purpose of management services.

PUMS requires an SSCP-PU session with its controlling *System Services Control Point* (SSCP) to forward network management data from the SSCP or receive network management requests from the SSCP. The management services commands received from the SSCP are converted to installation unique formats and forwarded to the LMS for further processing. Information received from the LMS, solicited or unsolicited, is converted to a network management vector transport (NMVT) and sent across the SSCP-PU session to the SSCP.

13.3.3.1 PUMS: Overview

Figure 118 on page 305 gives an overview of the PU management services boundaries with other components within an SNA node. The following list items correspond to the numbered items in the figure. These are:

1. PU Session Manager
   - Upon request, the PU session manager provides information about the currently active sessions managed by the PU.
2. PU Configuration Services
   - Upon request, PU configuration services provides information that uniquely identifies the hardware and the software of the node and provides a list of active LUs.
   - PU configuration services provides unsolicited information when the SSCP-PU session becomes active.
3. SSCP-PU Half-Session
   - The SSCP-PU half-session provides communication (over SSCP-PU sessions) with a resource's controlling CPMS.
4. LU Local Management Services
   - Upon request, the LU LMS sets response-time measurement parameters and provides response-time data.
   - The LU LMS provides unsolicited notification of problems within the LU and unsolicited response-time data.
5. SNA/Distribution Services
   - SNA/DS provides the capability to send and receive CP-MSUs, SNA/File Services (SNA/FS) agent objects, and SNA/FS files (bulk data) over an LU-LU session using the LU 6.2 protocol.

     The change management category uses SNA/FS and SNA/DS for distribution of potentially large files and issues the commands to manipulate them. For more details, see 13.4.4, "SNA Distribution Services" on page 310.
6. Data Link Control Local Management Services
   - The DLC manager LMS provides unsolicited notification of problems with links.
7. Physical Resource Manager Local Management Services
   - The physical resource manager LMS provides unsolicited notification of problems with the node physical resources, for example, tapes, disks, storage and microcode.
8. Program Supervisor Local Management Services
   - Upon request, the program supervisor LMS alters software and microcode components.

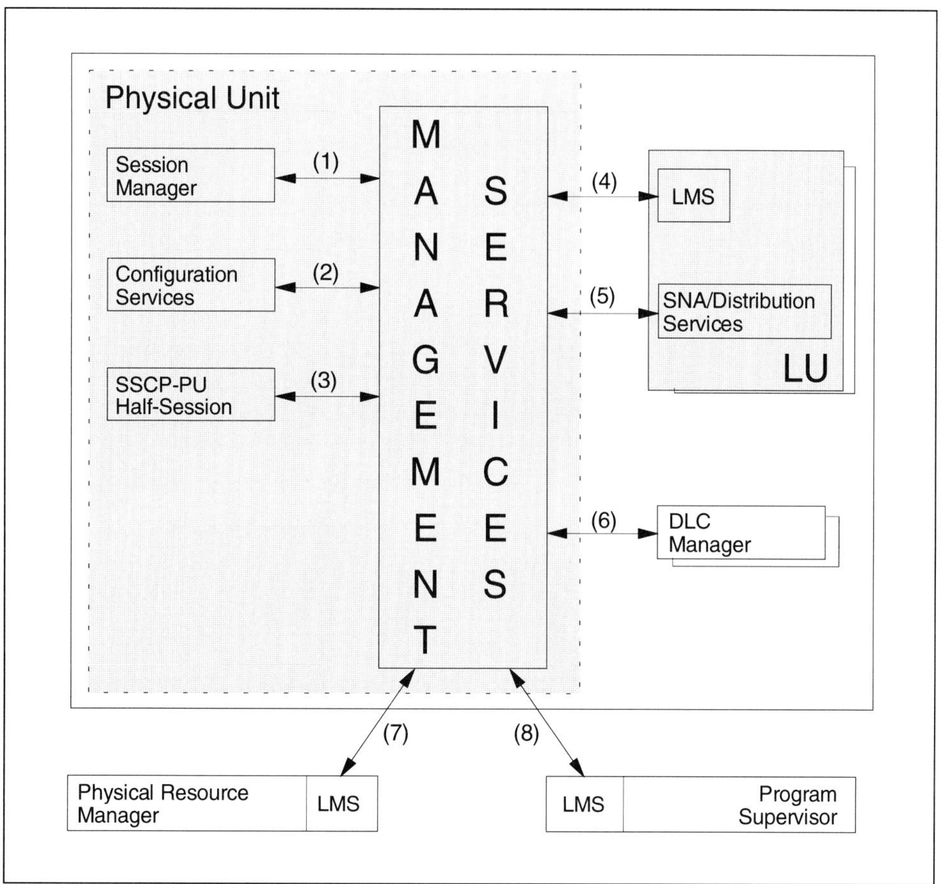

Figure 118. PU Management Services Boundaries with Other Components

13.4 Transport of Management Services Data

The SNA network management services function is provided by the combined functions of the control point management services, physical unit management services, and local management services components. The following sections describe the options available to management services application programs for transporting management services data. A distinction can be made between:

Transport of Management Services Data on the SSCP-PU Session

A T2.1 node may optionally have established an SSCP-PU session. The SSCP-PU session is used for transferring management services data between a control point and a physical unit. Note that CPMS in a T2.1 node that uses the SSCP-PU session for its management services communication with the SSCP performs the same function as PUMS in a Type 2.0 node.

SNA Distribution Services
The change management category uses SNA/File Services and SNA/Distribution Services for distribution of potentially large files, requests to manipulate them, and reports to track the distribution and installation. These employ LU-LU sessions.

Multiple Domain Support
The third type of management services transport, defined for the transfer of MS data between control points, is called MULTIPLE_DOMAIN_SUPPORT (MDS). This transport provides the transaction routing between management services application programs via CP-CP or LU-LU sessions.

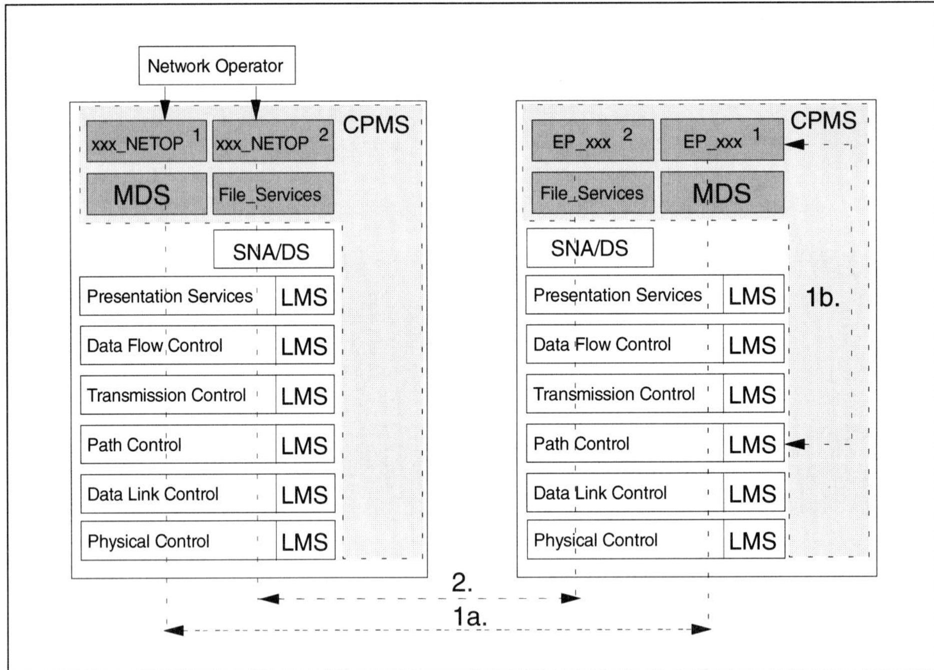

Figure 119. Communication between CPMS Instances

Figure 119 gives an example of how two CPMS instances may communicate. Focal point MS functions xxx_NETOP[1] and xxx_NETOP[2] communicate with entry point MS functions EP_xxx[1] and EP_xxx[2], respectively. Communication is possible via MDS (see 1a. in Figure 119) or SNA/DS (see 2.). Within the entry point an LMS instance (for example, path control, see 1b.) communicates with EP_xxx[1]. Communication of focal point function xxx_NETOP with an entry point LMS instance is always via EP_xxx.

13.4.1 Management Services Formats

Two ways exist to encode management services formats. A management services unit (MSU) is a management services encoding that is formatted according to a major vector, subvector, subfield scheme (see Figure 120). The other way of encoding a management services format uses a non-MSU scheme, and therefore does not use the major vector scheme.

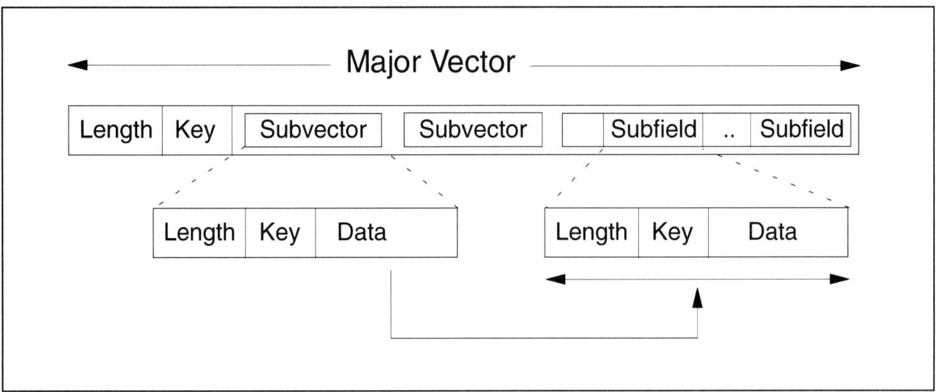

Figure 120. Overview of a Management Services Major Vector

The MSU that flows on an SSCP-PU session is called a *network management vector transport (NMVT)*. In addition, some management services request units that do not exhibit the MSU encoding scheme may flow on an SSCP-PU session. They are termed non-MSU management services request units. For details see *Systems Network Architecture Management Services Reference*, SC30-3346.

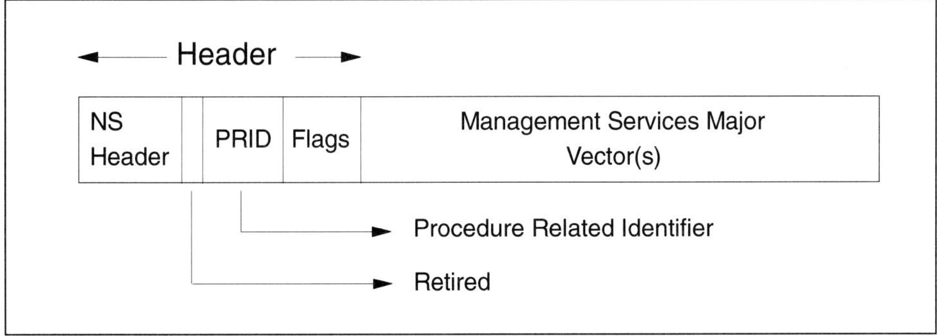

Figure 121. The NMVT Message Unit Format

The MSUs transported on CP-CP and LU-LU sessions between CP instances are general data stream (GDS) variables, which adhere to the encoding rules for GDS variables (for details see *Systems Network Architecture Formats*, GA27-3136). Figure 122 on page 308 shows the CP-MSU GDS variable format.

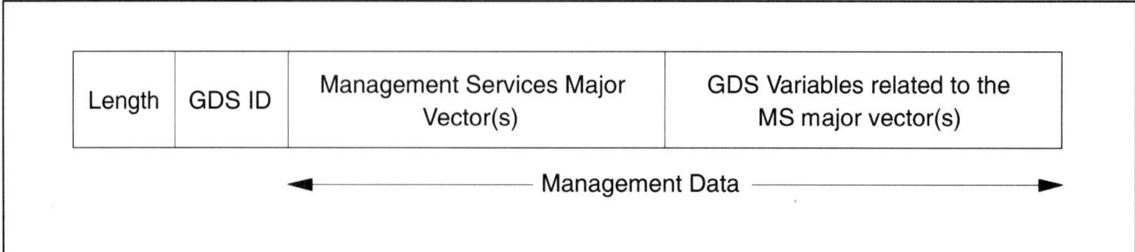

Figure 122. The CP-MSU GDS Variable Format

The *multiple-domain support message unit* (MDS-MU) GDS variable is used for the transport of non-bulk MS data in APPN networks. The MDS-MU has two components: the MDS header and the MS application program data; see Figure 123. The MDS header consists of MDS routing information (origin and destination names) and a correlation variable. The latter allows MDS and MS application programs to correctly correlate MDS-MUs.

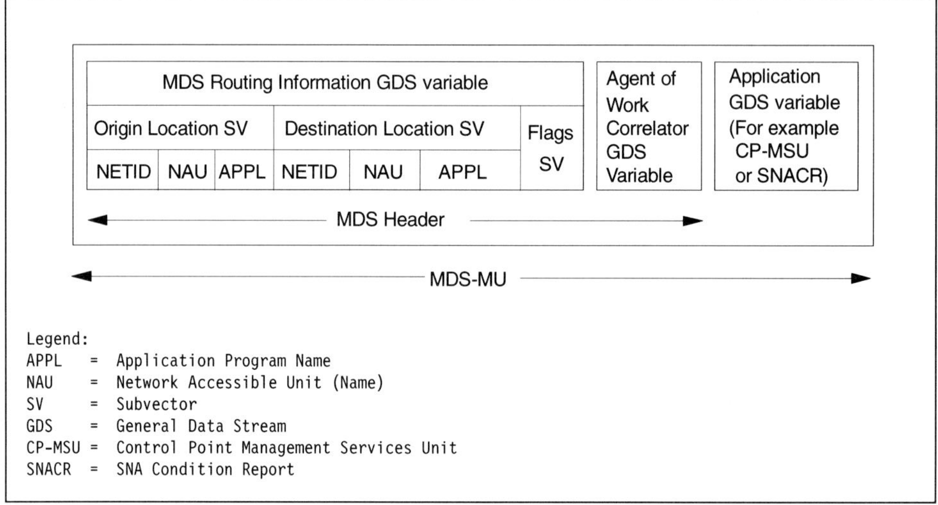

Figure 123. The MDS Message Unit Format

The *control point management services unit* (CP-MSU) is a GDS variable that can be used for transmitting either non-bulk data in the MDS-MU variable or transmitting bulk data using SNA/DS.

The following list shows when management services information is exchanged:

- A network operator communicating with an instance of CPMS
- Communication between instances of CPMS in different nodes via MDS on CP-CP or LU-LU sessions using LU 6.2 protocols
- CPMS communicating with PUMS on a control point to physical unit (SSCP-PU) session

- Both CPMS and PUMS communicating directly with an instance of LMS
- Bulk data being transported between CPMS and PUMS, or between instances of CPMS, using SNA/DS protocols on LU-LU sessions

13.4.2 Transport of Management Services Data on the SSCP-PU Session

The primary path for transport of SNA management services (SNA/MS) data between CPMS and PUMS is the SSCP-PU session. SNA/MS plays no role in the establishment of this session. Since the session is established when a PU is activated, it is already present when PUMS comes up. From the point of view of PUMS, the SSCP-PU session is simply a pipe through which management services requests and data can be exchanged with the PU's controlling SSCP.

13.4.3 Multiple-Domain Support

The service provided by CPMS that provides the routing of data between MS application programs over CP-CP and LU-LU sessions is called multiple-domain support (MDS). MDS consists of a router and multiple service transaction programs. The *MDS router* routes message units between MS application programs residing in the same node and uses the MDS service transaction programs (STPs) to route message units between MS application programs residing in different nodes. Example A in Figure 124 depicts the sessions used by MDS for default routing in an APPN network. MDS default routing uses LU-LU sessions (mode SNASVCMG) between network nodes (including focal points) and CP-CP sessions (mode CPSVCMG) between network node servers and their client end nodes. An LU-LU session directly from a focal point to an end node may also be used as shown in example B below.

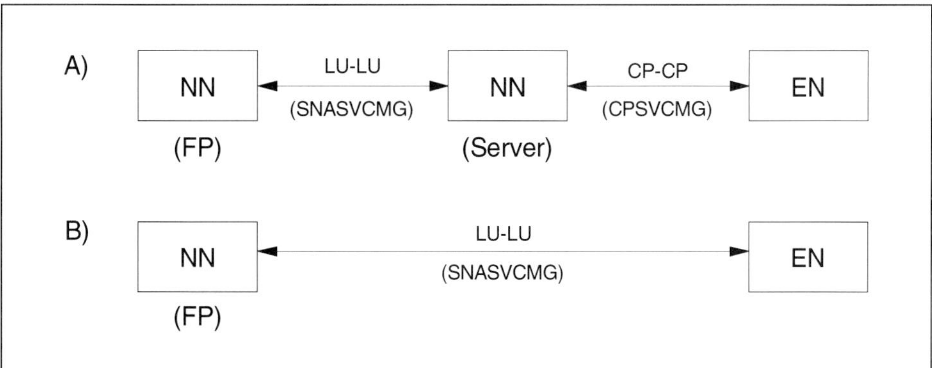

Figure 124. Sessions Used by MDS in an APPN Network

Notice that to exchange messages between management service transaction programs in the focal point and the end node, the data may flow through the network node server as shown in example A.

13.4.4 SNA Distribution Services

SNA management services uses SNA/DS for the transport of requests, reports, and bulk data. An LU-LU session directly from a focal point to an entry point is used to exchange data as shown in Figure 125.

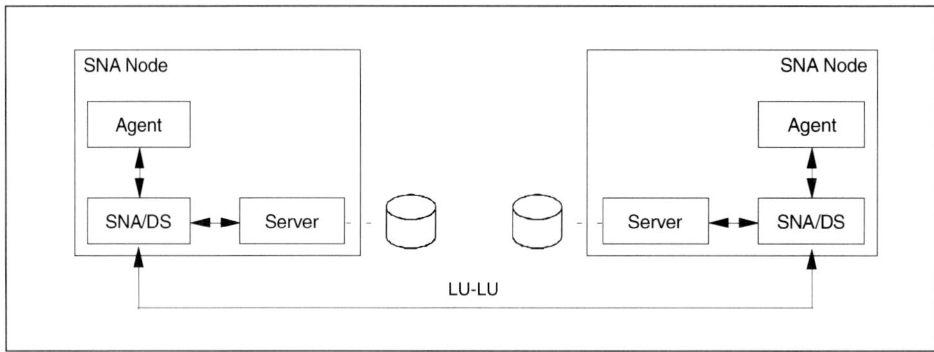

Figure 125. SNA Distribution Services

This figure shows an application transaction program, or *agent* in SNA/DS terminology, which uses SNA/DS as a transport mechanism. For a detailed description of SNA/Distribution Services, refer to *SNA Distribution Services Reference*, SC30-3098. The *server*, also provided by SNA/DS, is invoked to handle staging and destaging of (typically large) files to the system storage facilities.

The building and parsing of the object handled by the server (the server object) for network management is not different from that for other SNA/DS agents. For this reason, architecture has been developed for the server, called *SNA/File Services* (SNA/FS). For a detailed description of SNA/File Services, refer to *SNA File Services Reference*, SC31-6807.

13.5 Network Management Functions

Network management architecture addresses the management services for different SNA nodes. The differences in SNA nodes are not only the SNA node types, for example, T2.1, T4 (NCP), T5 (VTAM), but also the difference in functions and capabilities implemented for each SNA node type. For example, a T2.1 SNA node may be either a LEN end node, an end node, or a network node. Therefore, the network management architecture has split the management services into *function sets*. A management services function set is a collection of services that together perform an overall management services function. Each MS function has a mandatory or *base subset* that all implementations of that function set must support. The rest of the function set is composed of *optional subsets*. Implementations of that function set can choose to support some or all of the optional subset, depending on their *role* requirements. Defined MS roles are:

- CPMS in an APPN end node
- CPMS in an APPN network node
- PUMS in a Type 2.0 node
- CPMS in a node implementing an SSCP (for example, AS/400)
- PUMS in a Type 4 node
- PUMS in a Type 5 node (for example, VTAM)

This document discusses only the first three MS roles.

Note: In order to clearly distinguish names of MS function sets when they appear in this publication, they are generally given descriptive multiple-word names, capitalized, and connected with underscore characters. For example, the function set that describes how PUMS sends data over the SSCP-PU session is denoted by the name SEND_DATA_SSCP_PU.

13.5.1 Electives

Certain functions can be implemented in more than one way. If the effect can be observed at the MS protocol boundary, then that choice is called an *elective*. Electives are not optional functions, but are choices that regulate how or when a function is provided. If another component can observe the effect of an elective choice, then that component must also be able to support all of the possible effects of the elective choices. Product implementations make elective choices for performance or development-cost reasons.

13.5.2 Function Sets for CPMS and PUMS

Figure 126 and Figure 127 on page 312 depict the base and the optional MS function sets for PUMS in a Type 2.0 node and CPMS in an APPN node, respectively. The figures also show how the various function sets relate, such that each function set requires the function sets in its lower layers.

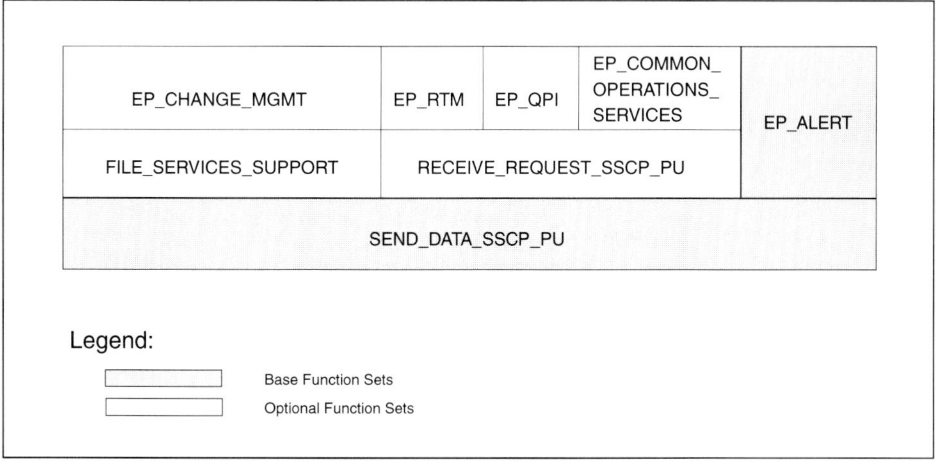

Figure 126. PUMS Function Sets in a Type 2.0 Node

Note: CPMS in a T2.1 node attached to NCP's or VTAM's boundary function performs the same function as PUMS in a Type 2.0 node.

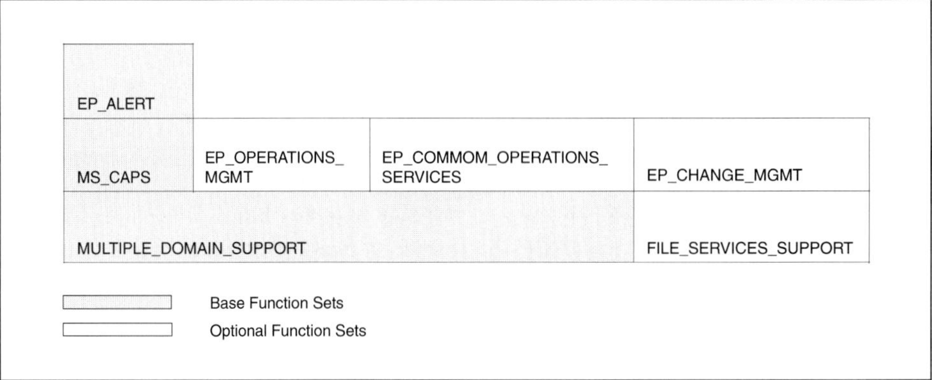

Figure 127. CPMS Function Sets in APPN Network and End Nodes

13.5.3 Function Sets: Description

Table 9 gives an overview of the MS function sets relevant for CPMS on APPN nodes or PUMS on a Type 2.0 node. It mentions the general management function sets and the specialized function sets for entry points.

Table 9. General and Specialized Function Sets

General Function Set	**Specialized Function Set for Entry Points**
MULTIPLE_DOMAIN_SUPPORT	EP_ALERT
MS_CAPS	EP_RTM
FILE_SERVICES_SUPPORT	EP_QPI
SEND_DATA_SSCP_PU	EP_CHANGE_MANAGEMENT
RECEIVE_REQUEST_SSCP_PU	EP_COMMON_OPERATIONS_SERVICES
	EP_OPERATIONS_MGMT

The remainder of this section gives a short description of each of the generalized function sets and specialized function sets for entry points mentioned in Table 9.

MULTIPLE_DOMAIN_SUPPORT

It provides the capability to send management services requests and data between management functions in the same or different nodes. It consists of a set of functions that are common to implementations in network nodes and end nodes, two subsets that are mandatory depending on a node's role, and two optional subsets:

End Node Support (Optional Subset 1)

The end node support is applicable to end nodes only. It consists of the MDS router functions for the entry point.

Network Node Support (Optional Subset 2)
The network node support is applicable to network nodes only. It consists of the MDS router functions for network nodes.

High Performance Option (Optional Subset 3)
The high performance option is applicable to network nodes only. It provides the ability for management services applications to use persistent conversations over dedicated sessions, thus improving the performance for management services applications with higher transaction rates. The base set uses short conversations over shared sessions to transport the management services units. In addition, it uses LU 6.2 confirmations for reliable delivery of the data. The overhead introduced this way is containable if the transaction rate remains low.

Transport Confirmation Option (Optional Subset 4)
The transport confirmation option is applicable to network nodes only. It provides the ability for management services application programs to omit the LU 6.2 confirmations for each management services unit, thus increasing the session throughput.

MS_CAPS (MS capabilities)
It provides the support for getting information from a focal point and to route this information to local application programs on a node. An APPN end node can either communicate directly with its focal point, using an LU-LU session, or indirectly through its network node server.

Have a Backup or Implicit FP (Optional Subset 1)
Support for backup or implicit focal point is applicable to end nodes and network nodes. It provides the support for a node to have a backup focal point or an implicit focal point.

Be a Sphere_of_Control End Node (Optional Subset 2)
Support for being a sphere of control node is applicable to end nodes. It provides the support for an entry point to directly communicate with its focal point. Normally, an entry point communicates indirectly with its focal point through its network node server.

Base Network Node Support (Optional Subset 3)
Support for base network node support is required for network nodes. It provides the support necessary for a network node to be an SOC node and enables the node to send and receive MS capabilities from the entry point side of the relationship.

Have a Subarea Focal Point (Optional Subset 4)
Support for subarea focal point is applicable to network nodes only. It provides the ability for the network node to act as a pseudo focal point for its domain on behalf of a subarea focal point. It will forward the data it receives on an SSCP-PU session to a subarea focal point.

FILE_SERVICES_SUPPORT
It provides the support to route management services requests and bulk data between nodes using SNA distribution services.

Network Operator Support (Optional Subset 1)
Network operator support is applicable to both end nodes and network nodes. It provides the support to interact with the node operator at the node, to receive request verbs, and return reply verbs.

SEND_DATA_SSCP_PU
It provides the support for sending network management vector transport RUs across an SSCP-PU session to a subarea CPMS.

RECEIVE_REQUEST_SSCP_PU
It provides the support to receive network management vector transport RUs and pass the vector to the appropriate function group set.

EP_ALERT
It is responsible for:

Detecting an alert condition for any resource controlled by its node

Building the alert major vector

Passing the vector to the Multiple Domain Support for further processing by a focal point

The following optional subsets are available for EP_ALERT:

Problem Diagnosis Data (Optional Subset 1)
Support for problem diagnosis data means that the alert vector contains a problem diagnosis section. The problem diagnosis section may contain, for example, a malfunction code.

Delayed Alert (Optional Subset 2)
This function is not supported for T2.1 nodes. Support for delayed alert means that an entry point can delay the alerts when the session with its focal point is lost. As soon as the session with the focal point is reestablished, the alerts held will be forwarded to the focal point.

Held Alert for PUMS (Optional Subset 3)
Support for held alert for PUMS means that the entry point is capable of holding alerts until the session with the PUMS is reestablished.

Operator-Initiated Alert (Optional Subset 4)
Operator-initiated alerts provide a mechanism for the network operator to initiate the reporting of an alert condition. Normally, these are conditions that cannot be detected by the control point.

Qualified Message Data (Optional Subset 5)
Support for the qualified message data provides the ability to generate alerts using indexed text messages and qualifier data. The receiver of the alert creates the alert message by using the index and qualifier data to

reconstruct the message from its local message table. For example, if the national language differs between focal point and entry point, this subset allows the focal point and entry point to generate the alert message in their own national language.

Text Message (Optional Subset 6)
Support for text message provides the capability to include, in the alert, a character string of 236 characters.

LAN Alert (Optional Subset 7)
Support for LAN alert provides the capability to send alerts for errors detected at the MAC layer of a token-ring, Ethernet, or bridged LAN.

SDLC/LAN LLC Alert (Optional Subset 8)
Support for SDLC/LAN LLC alerts provides the capability to send alerts for problems detected on SDLC and LAN logical link level control.

X.21 Alert (Optional Subset 9)
Support for X.21 alerts provides the capability to send alerts for problems detected on X.21 link connections. This will also include the alerts for X.21 short-hold mode.

Hybrid Alert (Optional Subset 10)
Support for hybrid alert is not available for T2.1 nodes. It provides support for nodes to send alerts in a form that can be both processed by the current version of CPMS as well as a back-level version.

X.25 Alert (Optional Subset 11)
Support for X.25 alerts provides the capability to send alerts for problems detected on X.25 connections.

Held Alert for CPMS (Optional Subset 12)
Support for held alerts for CPMS provides the capability to hold alerts when the focal point is not available and to send the alerts, with an indication that the alert was held, when the focal point is available again.

Resolution Notification Support (Optional Subset 13)
Support for the unsolicited notification of the correction of an error condition.

Operations Management Support (Optional Subset 14)
Support for operations management commands to be initiated as a direct result of an Alert or Resolution condition, thereby providing problem bypass and recovery capability in the network.

EP_RTM
It provides the capability to measure and monitor end user response times for type 2 LUs.

Local Display (Optional Subset 1)
Support for local display provides the capability to display the measurements at the node implementing this function set. The focal point can send commands to enable or disable the local display.

EP_QPI

It provides the capability to physically identify the SNA node and attached devices upon request.

EP_CHANGE_MGMT

It provides the capability to respond to change control and activation requests from a change management focal point or local operator interface.

Production-Only Activation (Optional Subset 1)

Support for production-only activation provides the capability to respond to requests from the focal point for activation of only those versions of components marked in-production.

Execution Window Timing (Optional Subset 2)

Support for execution window timing (including automatic acceptance delay and activate force or rejection delay).

Activation Reporting Support (Optional Subset 3)

Support for unsolicited reporting of activation results.

Alter Active Support (Optional Subset 4)

Support for responding to requests for installation that specify whether alteration of active components is allowed.

Alter Object Disposition Support (Optional Subset 5)

Support for responding to requests for installation that specify a change object disposition.

Initiate Command Support (Optional Subset 6)

Support for the capability to respond to initiation requests from a change management focal point or local operator interface.

Cancel Command Support (Optional Subset 7)

Support for the capability to respond to cancelation requests from a change management focal point or local operator interface.

Last-Used Activation Support (Optional Subset 8)

Support for responding to requests from the focal point for activation to either trial or production based on the setting used in the previous activation.

EP_COMMON_OPERATIONS_SERVICES

It provides the capability to support communication between network operators and served network management applications.

EP_OPERATIONS_MGMT

It provides the capability to receive operations management commands from network operators and replies or reports from second-level application programs. Unsolicited messages may also be received from application programs served by EP_OPERATIONS_MGMT and sent to the operations management focal point.

13.6 NetView Management of APPN Networks

IBM NetView V2R4 includes a feature for managing APPN networks called the NetView APPN Topology and Accounting Management (APPNTAM). This feature works with corresponding Communications Manager/2 (CM/2) functions to gather and record data about APPN networks.

NetView V3R1 was enhanced to include functions for managing the topology and status of both subarea and APPN networks. For more information on SNA and APPN management, please see *Dynamic Subarea and APPN Management Using NetView V3R1,* SG24-4520. For APPN, these enhancements include:

- Integration of the APPN Topology and Accounting Management (APPNTAM) feature into the Enterprise Option of NetView V3R1. It is now called the SNA Topology and Accounting Manager (SNATAM), and i provides support for both APPN and subarea topology.
- The CMIP services function is no longer part of NetView in V3R1. Instead, NetView utilizes the CMIP services function present in VTAM V4R3 in order to communicate with agents.
- Support for the VTAM SNATAM agent shipped as a part of VTAM V4R3.
- The CM/2 agent is now shipped as part of NetView and has been renamed the APPN Topology and Accounting Agent (APPNTAA). This agent is also available for the IBM 2217.
- Support for the dynamic topology and status of LUs. With the SNA topology manager in NetView Version 3, LU information is not automatically collected from the VTAM agent for all LUs. This choice was made in order to reduce the network traffic and the number of objects created and maintained in NetView's *Resource Object Data Manager* (RODM). Application LUs and APPN control points will automatically be reported by the VTAM agent to the SNA topology manager when local and network topology is being collected from the VTAM agent.

  Note: The NetView RODM is an object-oriented data cache, objects in RODM represent resources in the network. The data cache is located entirely in the memory of the host processor resulting in fast access to data and high transaction rates.
- Session monitor support for DLUR/S sessions, border nodes, and VR-TGs. The session monitor will be able to indicate whether the SSCP-PU and SSCP-LU sessions are using the Dependent LU Requester/Server (DLUR/S) pipe. The session monitor has also been enhanced to be able to indicate in the APPN route displays whether the APPN route for a session traverses VR-TGs or crosses APPN networks.

The *Topology Management* function provides the ability to obtain, monitor, control and graphically display the topology of your APPN networks:

- Collection and storage of APPN topology data, including real-time updates, in the RODM data cache
- Dynamic, graphical display of APPN topology, using the NGMF
- Control of SNA ports and links using commands on the NGMF pull-down menus, the operator console, and Command Tree/2

The *Accounting Management* function provides the ability to centralize collection of LU 6.2 session and conversation accounting information. This information is logged to the system management facilities (SMF) or a user-defined external log.

You can automate these functions using the NetView automation facilities such as command lists and the automation table. In addition, you can automate using methods and objects stored in RODM.

13.6.1 SNATAM Structural Overview

SNATAM provides APPN management functions according to a manager-agent relationship. This feature uses the Open System Interconnect (OSI) system management model. Management service is provided by one or more managing systems, which gather and correlate data from multiple managed systems. The managing systems provide this service through one or more management applications, called managers, which communicate using OSI Common Management Information Protocol (CMIP) with management applications at the managed systems, called agents.

The topology manager and accounting manager applications are separate entities that can be installed and initialized independently. You can install the topology manager application on a NetView central system. You can install the accounting manager application on a NetView central system and on a NetView distributed system.

The corresponding SNATAM agent applications reside on VTAM and on APPN network nodes and end nodes that use the OS/2 Communications Manager/2 platform. The SNATAM agent includes both the topology agent and the accounting agent applications that can be initialized independently.

In all cases, the CMIP services must be active to support the manager-agent communications. Communication between the manager and agent applications is over LU 6.2 sessions using OSI CMIP and the SNA multiple domain support (MDS).

Figure 128 on page 319 illustrates the structure of the SNATAM feature. The topology agent on the OS/2 system is gathering and forwarding topology information to the topology manager. The accounting agent is gathering and forwarding accounting data to the accounting manager. Note that each manager application can gather information from multiple agent applications; each agent application can forward data to multiple manager applications.

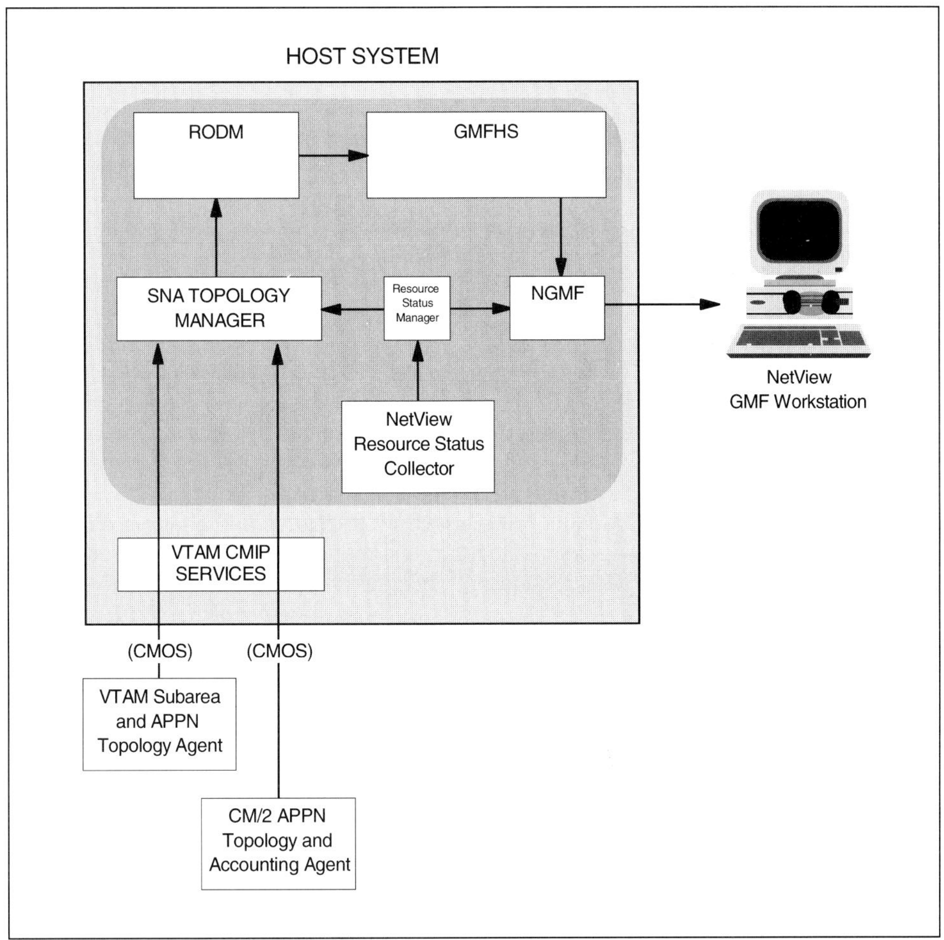

Figure 128. Structural Overview of SNATAM

13.6.2 VTAM CMIP Services

The VTAM CMIP services component allows communication between the SNATAM manager and agent applications using VTAM MS transport. MS transport uses LU 6.2 sessions for the actual communications between systems in the network. The CMIP data exchanged between the manager and agent applications is encapsulated in MDS-MUs and transported over these LU 6.2 sessions using the management services MDS-SEND and MDS-RECEIVE transaction programs. The CMIP services task or program comprises the OSI layers 5 to 7 and other services, such as internal MIB API.

13.6.3 SNATAM Topology Manager Overview

The topology manager works with one or more topology agents to gather the APPN topology information of your APPN networks, as well as to monitor the networks for any topology or resource status changes. Agent applications can be on APPN network nodes (NNs) and end nodes (ENs). NNs provide network and local topology support; ENs provide local topology support.

The topology agent forwards APPN topology and status information upon request to the topology manager. The topology manager correlates and stores this data in RODM according to the SNATAM topology data model. It dynamically creates objects in RODM and updates the status of these objects as information is received from the topology agents in the network.

The topology manager allows you to manage APPN resources, namely logical links and ports, at the agent nodes. When you issue a command to start monitoring network or local topology, the topology manager sends a request to the agent. The agent sends the requested topology data to the manager, then continues to send status and configuration updates to the manager. The agent also activates and deactivates ports and links when it receives those commands from the manager. An agent can interact with one or more managers, each requesting the same or different data.

13.6.3.1 SNATAM Topology Data

The SNATAM topology manager gathers topology data from the topology agent nodes in the network. The two types of topology being collected and monitored are:

Network topology
: That is, your APPN *backbone* topology. It contains information about network nodes (NNs), virtual routing nodes (VRNs), and transmission groups (TGs) between nodes that are part of an APPN intermediate routing network. Topology manager should request network topology from at least one agent network node in each subnetwork.

Local topology
: That is, *local* information about network nodes (NNs), end nodes (ENs), and low entry networking (LEN) nodes, the connections between nodes, and the ports and links that make up the connections. A node must have a topology agent installed to support local topology monitoring.

13.6.3.2 NGMF Graphic Views of APPN

The APPNTAM topology manager uses the NGMF to provide the graphical interface for displaying and monitoring APPN resources stored in RODM. APPN views are updated dynamically as changes occur in the network. This ensures that the most current status and configuration are available to the operator. Operators can use the views to monitor the status of the APPN network, navigate through the network, locate failed resources, activate and deactivate links and ports, and control topology monitoring.

13.6.3.3 Topology Manager Functions

The functions available with the topology manager enable you to do the following:

- Monitor APPN network topology to view the connectivity between APPN network nodes. The views are updated dynamically with configuration and status changes of the network nodes and the TGs between them.
- Monitor APPN local topology to view APPNTAM agent nodes and their TGs, ports, and logical links. Local topology also displays adjacent network nodes, end nodes, and low entry networking (LEN) nodes. These views are updated dynamically with configuration and status changes to nodes, TGs, links, and ports.
- Control the status of ports and links (activate, deactivate, and recycle).
- Navigate from high-level aggregate views to real resources, using functions such as the More detail, Fast path to failing resource, and Locate resource pull-down menu selections.
- Display views of an APPN network, including views of:
  - All APPN subnetworks being monitored (with each subnetwork as an aggregate object)
  - An individual APPN subnetwork (an aggregate view representing NN domains and the TG circuits between NNs)
  - A particular domain of an NN
  - Local connections of a node (TG, links, ports, and adjacent nodes)
  - A particular connection (a TG or link and the adjacent node)
- Display information about resources such as CP and link names, TG numbers, and the NETID of a subnetwork.
- Identify which NNs, ENs, and TGs have additional capabilities and display what they are. For example, NN capabilities can include border node and directory server. TG capabilities can include support for CP-CP sessions.
- Use existing NGMF functions to navigate and edit views.
- Automate operations using RODM objects.
- Create user-defined objects and views in RODM for customized operation.

13.6.4 APPN Accounting Manager Overview

The APPN accounting manager application offers the following functions:

- Provides operator commands to start and stop the collection of LU 6.2 session and conversation accounting data at agent nodes
- Retrieves LU 6.2 session and conversation accounting information from agent applications in the network
- Formats the data for output to an external record log (either SMF or a user-defined log)

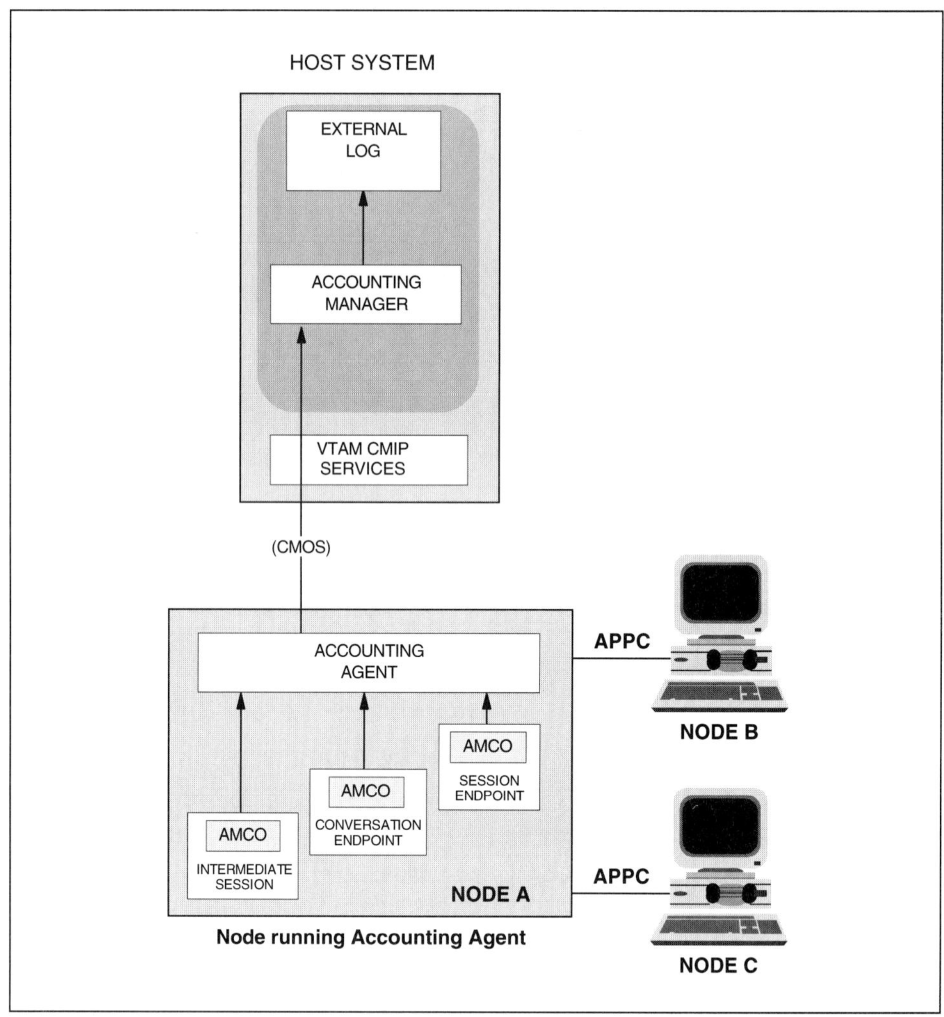

Figure 129. How the Accounting Function Works

You can use the accounting data for usage reporting and billing. A typical situation in which you might want to use the accounting manager application is where you are charging users for the use of an APPN network's resources. The APPN accounting agent collects session and conversation data such as when the session or conversation began, when and why it ended, and the number of bytes sent and received. Session data can be collected at an end point or at an intermediate node in the session path. Conversation data can be collected only at an end point of the conversation.

The node from which the manager retrieves the data must have the accounting agent installed. The agent function is installed, started, and maintained separately from the manager function. The agent application collects LU 6.2 accounting information in

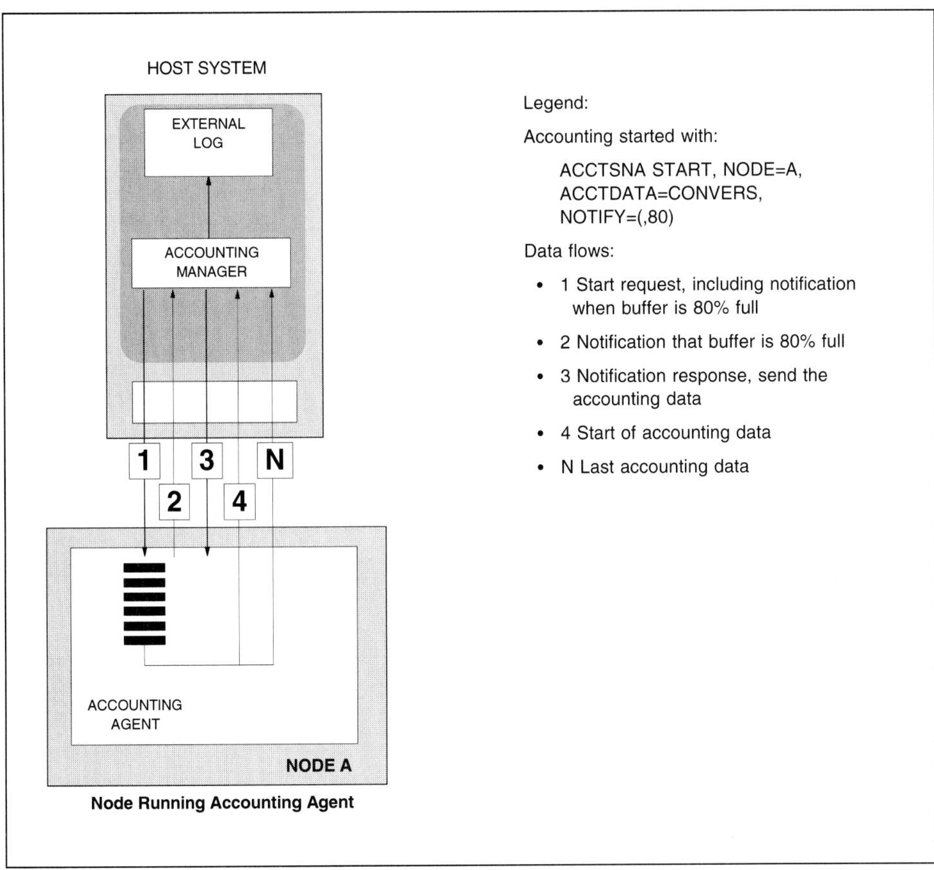

Figure 130. Accounting Data Flows

response to requests from the manager application. The agent application is installed on OS/2 with Communications Manager/2 V1.1 or above. Communication between the NetView system and the node containing the agent is through an SNA LU 6.2 session.

The accounting manager function uses the new NetView ACCTSNA command. With this command, operators specify the type of data (session, intermediate session, or conversation) to be collected at an agent and under what conditions the manager should retrieve the data.

You can set scheduled clock times when the accounting manager should automatically retrieve accounting data from a specified agent node. You can also specify the conditions for a specified agent node to notify the accounting manager based on the absolute and relative fullness of the buffer at the accounting agent. That means the manager can automatically retrieve data at a certain time of day or when a certain percentage of records have been collected.

You can collect more than one type of data at an agent. A manager can retrieve data from multiple agents, and multiple managers can retrieve data from the same agent. Operators can enter the commands from the NetView command line; however, the ideal way to operate accounting is to automate the function using command lists or other automated routines.

13.6.4.1 Accounting Manager Functions

An operator (or an automated routine) issues NetView ACCTSNA commands to perform the following functions:

- Start collecting accounting data at an agent node for a particular type of data (session, intermediate session, or conversation)
- Retrieve data from an agent:
  - According to scheduled times (for example, every morning at 5:00 a.m.) or periodic intervals
  - When a specified threshold is reached (for example, when the data collected reaches a specified number of records)
  - Immediately upon a manager request
- Stop collecting a particular type of accounting data at a given agent node
- Modify defaults, display information about data collection, and other maintenance tasks

In addition, the accounting manager has the ability to resynchronize data transactions as an error recovery mechanism. If communication between agent and manager is interrupted (for example, the connection goes down), once the communication is recovered, the manager resynchronizes its processing with the agent. The agent resends all data that the manager has not received and has not written to the external log at the time of failure.

13.6.4.2 How the Accounting Function Works

Figure 129 on page 322 shows how data is collected at the accounting agent and then sent to the accounting manager at NetView.

Assume the NetView operator has issued ACCTSNA START commands to start collecting session and conversation data at the agent. As a result, the agent creates separate accounting management control objects (AMCOs) to manage the collection of session endpoint data, intermediate session data, and conversation data. The AMCOs contain all the instructions for managing the data collection, such as under what conditions to notify the manager that data is ready to be retrieved.

In this example, the agent node collects data for:

- Sessions where the primary LU or secondary LU is Node A, for example, sessions between Node A and Node B, Node A and Node C, and Node A and the host.

- Sessions for which node A is an intermediate node, for example, sessions between Node B and Node C, the host and Node B, and the host and Node C.
- Conversations where Node A is one endpoint, that is, where the source or target APPC program is located at Node A.

13.6.4.3 How Accounting Data Flows between Manager and Agent

The manager and agent communicate data and data requests across an LU 6.2 session using OSI CMIP and SNA MDS. To support the CMIP services, APPN accounting manager uses the MS transport.

Accounting data is transferred between agent and manager based on a series of notifications and requests. In each case, the data transfer applies to a specified type of data, that is, conversation data, session data, or intermediate session data.

For example, a user specifies that the manager should be notified when the conversation data buffer at the agent becomes 80% full. As shown in Figure 130 on page 323, when the agent has collected enough data to fill its buffer to the specified threshold, the agent sends a notification to the manager. The manager then retrieves the accounting data from the agent.

13.7 SNMP Management Support of APPN Networks

IBM Nways Campus Manager - LAN for AIX now includes the functionality of *IBM Router and Bridge Manager/6000 V1.2 (RABM).* RABM is used to monitor the health and performance of bridges and routers in the campus network. Amongst support for other IBM and OEM devices through standard and enterprise specific MIBs, it also supports APPN and DLSw MIBs. In addition, it includes *Alert Manager*, which enables SNA alerts that are enveloped in SNMP traps to be displayed correctly on the NetView for AIX Event Desk. Although this function was provided specifically for IBM 3746 and AS/400 devices, it can be used by any SNMP agent.

With the APPN Topology feature, it is possible to view APPN networks end-to-end. APPN resources are discovered automatically and can be viewed with their status as color-coded icons. APPN protocol performance and error events (data and graphs) are also provided.

A single NN RABM client provides details of the complete APPN backbone. For local topology of network and end nodes, the RABM client must be installed in each network node.

13.8 APPN Topology Integrator

The APPN Topology Integrator (referred to as the *Integrator*) is an application that runs on any Operating System/2 (OS/2) Warp or Warp Connect workstation with Communications Manager/2 (CM/2) V1R1 or later and TCP/IP V3R0. The Integrator enables the management of SNMP devices via CMIP. Together with the NetView SNA

Topology and Accounting Manager (SNATAM) and the APPN Topology and Accounting Agent (APPNTAA), the Integrator is part of a complete solution providing for the management of APPN topology.

SNATAM provides APPN management functions according to a manager-agent relationship. This relationship is defined by the International Organization for Standardization (ISO) in terms of a managing system and a managed system, respectively. The manager applications for APPN topology are NetView applications. Agent applications, including APPNTAA and the Integrator, which collect information for transmission to NetView, reside on APPN network nodes and end nodes that use the CM/2 platform. Communication between the manager and agent applications is over APPC sessions using Open Systems Interconnection (OSI) Common Management Information Protocol (CMIP) and the Systems Network Architecture (SNA) Multiple-Domain Support (MDS). To support the CMIP Services, the Integrator uses the Management Services (MS) transport.

The Integrator is installed, started, and maintained entirely separately from the manager function (see 13.6, "NetView Management of APPN Networks" on page 317).

13.8.1 How the Topology Manager and Integrator Work Together

The Topology Manager application works with one or more Integrators to gather topology from the SNA network. The Integrator is needed to provide APPN topology information from SNMP devices. An Integrator can be located on an APPN network node (NN) or end node (EN).

When an operator issues a command to start monitoring topology at a node with an SNMP agent, the topology manager sends a request to the Integrator. The Integrator obtains the requested network or local topology data from the respective SNMP agent and sends the data to the manager. It continues to send status and configuration updates to the manager by polling the SNMP agent for topology changes. An Integrator can support approximately 200 concurrent monitor requests.

Note: Each monitor request is handled in a separate OS/2 thread. Although OS/2 can handle a theoretical maximum of 4095 processes or threads, the system default value is 256.

The Integrator can also activate and deactivate ports and links at an SNMP device upon receiving requests from the manager if these actions are supported by the SNMP agent at the device.

13.8.2 The Topology Integrator Packaging Information

The Integrator consists of the following:

- Graphical user interface implemented in OS/2 2.0 Presentation Manager (PM), NLS-enabled in English and Japanese.
- Application-executable files produced from C++ source code, including:

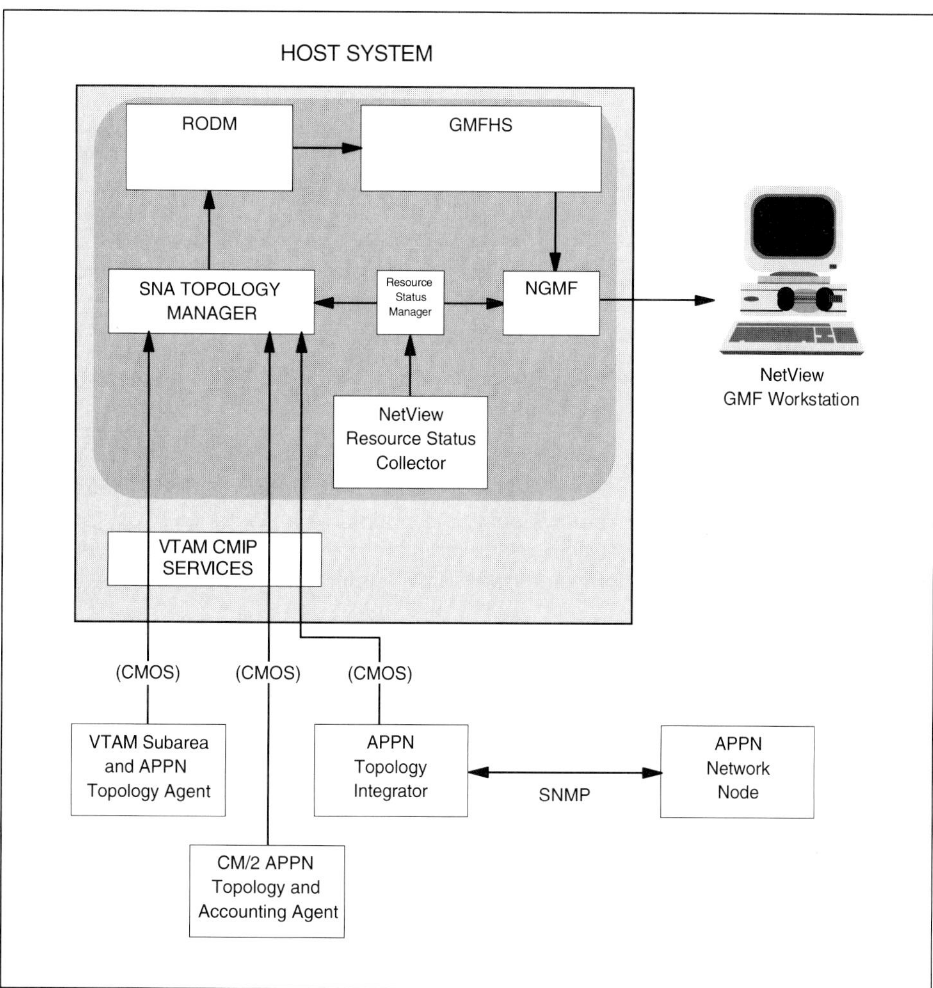

Figure 131. APPN Topology Integrator

- Attributes' callback code generated with MIBcomposer V4R3.
- Dispatcher, subtree manager, and snapshot action processing compiled and linked using IBM VisualAge C++ Version 3.0 for OS/2.
- CmipWorks, specifically the CMIP protocol stack from the IBM NetView TMN Portable Agent Facility (PAF), compiled with options to support sockets, multithread, and MDS; also included are ASN.1 files necessary for APPN network management.
- SNMP Libraries, specifically the SNMPv1 protocol stack providing transport over UDP, NetBIOS, and NetWare/IPX, developed by NetView for OS/2 based upon the TCP/IP Common Agent.

13.8.3 Proxy Agents

This section provides an historical perspective and design issues of proxy agents.

13.8.3.1 The History

While SNMP has become the telecommunications industry's de facto standard for management in the United States, CMIP is popular in Europe. Both SNMP and CMIP have been widely deployed; consequently some APPN nodes have SNMP agents while others have CMIP agents. These two different types of agents pose a problem: it is not possible for a CMIP-based manager (such as SNATAM) or an SNMP-based manager (such as NV/6000) to view the entire topology of an APPN network. A CMIP-based manager cannot find out about APPN end nodes that are "behind" an APPN network node containing an SNMP agent. Similarly, an SNMP-based manager cannot find out about APPN end nodes "behind" an APPN node containing a CMIP agent.

13.8.3.2 Proxying Techniques

The industry uses the term *proxy* to refer to a method of integrating CMIP agents and SNMP agents. A proxy agent is a system that provides the appearance of one type of agent for an agent of a different type. For example, the Integrator is a proxy agent that provides an CMIP agent appearance for an SNMP agent.

A proxy agent can do one of the following:

- Provide CMIP agent appearances for SNMP agents, or
- Provide SNMP agent appearances for CMIP agents.

In theory, both solutions are plausible; in reality, however, most of the industry has focused on the first approach, since the information that can be represented with SNMP is essentially a subset of the information that can be represented with CMIP.

The ISO/CCITT and Internet Management Coexistence (IIMC) groups have published two techniques for proxying SNMP agents:

Direct Translation

With the direct translation approach, an Integrator would only have to be written once. It can take any SNMP MIB and algorithmically convert it to a set of OSI managed objects. Direct translation has a number of disadvantages. First, in order for the algorithmic translation to work, a new set of managed object classes must be algorithmically generated from an SNMP MIB. If there are already existing managed object classes for a given type of resource, as in APPN topology, a CMIP-based manager would need to be bilingual, that is, it would have to support the new managed objects in addition to the existing ones. Second, if more than one application uses a set of managed object classes, you can see that direct translation has just pushed the problem of integrating the two types of agents into each application. And third, since direct translation generates a new set of managed object classes for each SNMP MIB, writing generic applications is not possible; the algorithm used in direct translation does not attempt to take advantage of common attributes (such as operational state) or inheritance.

Abstract Translation

The abstract translation approach, on the other hand, involves mapping between a set of managed object classes and an SNMP MIB. With careful analysis, the mapping process can take advantage of common attributes and inheritance. In the majority of cases, the abstract translation for an attribute in a managed object requires retrieving the appropriate MIB variable and performing some simple transformation on its value. For some attributes, it may be necessary to retrieve more than one MIB variable. Unless some attributes have no corresponding information in the SNMP MIB, default values can be specified in the mapping.

For APPN management, there were both existing SNMP managers and agents as well as existing CMIP managers and agents; the direct translation approach was not practical. The Integrator employs the abstract translation approach, thereby permitting existing managers and agents (both CMIP and SNMP) to continue working without any changes.

13.8.4 MDS Routing

The following section describes MDS routing at the host system and at the agent using Multiple-Domain Support (MDS).

13.8.4.1 At SNATAM (NetView V3R1 and VTAM V4R3)

The manager and Integrator communicate data and data requests across APPC sessions. A component called *CMIP Services* supports these transactions. For more information about CMIP Services, see 13.8.4.5, "cmipWorks" on page 333.

The Integrator, much like the APPN Topology Agent (APPNTAA) application, supplies topology information in response to requests from the manager application. The manager stores the information in the Resource Object Data Manager (RODM) data cache at the NetView host, enabling the NetView Graphic Monitor Facility Host Subsystem (GMFHS) to graphically display the information on the NetView Graphic Monitor Facility (NGMF) workstation. The topology information consists of the SNA nodes in an APPN network, the APPN transmission groups (TG s) between them, and the underlying logical links and ports supporting the TGs.

When an operator issues a command to start monitoring topology, the Topology Manager generates a snapshot action for ongoing local or network topology. The CMIP Services component of VTAM subsequently consults its Directory Definition File (DDF), in which all nodes that require proxying are mapped to the Integrator (see Figure 132 on page 330). As a result, the CMIP protocol data unit, called an *ROIVapdu*, is created including the managed APPN node address, that is, the fully qualified CP name. It is enveloped in an MDS-MU, which contains the address of the Integrator.

```
class managed object
       name '1.3.18.0.2.4.6=NET1;1.3.18.0.0.2032=ENDNODE'
      aetitle '1.3.18.0.2.4.6=NET1;2.9.3.2.7.4=(name INTEGR8R);1.3.18.0.2.4.12=OSISMASE'
```

Figure 132. Example of Entry in VTAM V4R3 DDF

For more information on NetView and VTAM, consult the following IBM publications: *Managing Your APPN Environments Using NetView*, GG24-2559 and *VTAM V4R3 Resource Definition Reference*, SC31-6552.

13.8.4.2 At the Integrator

Every MS application program that sends or receives MDS-MUs must register itself with MDS when it first becomes active. This enables MDS to route MDS requests, replies, and error messages to the application program when they are received. An application program registers itself with MDS via an internal MS protocol boundary. The application program registering itself passes its name and the ACTION indicator of ADD to MDS via this protocol boundary. Whenever it receives a registration request via the protocol boundary, MDS processes it, entering the application program name specified on the request into its application routing table.

The MDS Router provides send and receive services for MS application programs. It routes messages between MS application programs in the same node and uses the MDS service transaction programs to route messages between MS application programs in different nodes within a network. For outgoing messages, the router directs an instance of the MDS_SEND service transaction program to send the message over an LU 6.2 session. The router also delivers messages to application programs within a single node. The message may be incoming traffic from other nodes or intra-node traffic between local application programs.

The MDS-MU GDS variable (X'1310') contains the MDS Routing Information GDS variable (X'1311'), which contains a Destination Location Name MS subvector (X'82'). This in turn contains the NETID subfield (X'01'), NAU Name subfield (X'02'), and the MS application program name subfield (X'03'). Application program names in MS follow the LU 6.2 transaction program (TP) naming convention, which provides for 4-byte architecturally defined values or 1-to-8-character installation-defined names (LU 6.2 base support). In order for communication to take place between two MS application programs, the names by which the application programs are known to MDS must be understood. That is, the application program that initiates a unit of work must know the correct name of the target application program so that the message can be properly routed. The understanding of application program names is achieved implicitly, that is the application names are predefined or hardcoded when the functions are implemented. For architecturally defined functions that rely upon predefined application program names, the names are registered values. The application program name for the Integrator is the architecturally defined MS TP name X'23F0F1F8', also called the Session Layer Mapper for CMOS. It is hardcoded by both VTAM and the Integrator.

The MDS-MU is routed from the manager to the Integrator on an LU-LU session with the mode name SNASVCMG established on a link between MVS and the Integrator. It is received by the MDS_RECEIVE service transaction program at the Integrator. MDS_RECEIVE passes the MDS-MU to the MDS Router. The MDS Router verifies that the destination is the local node. Then it examines the destination application program name for the Integrator (X'23F0F1F8'), comparing it to the list of all MS application programs that are known in the local node. The MDS-MU is then passed to the MS application program known as the Integrator.

13.8.4.3 Sockets and SNMP

The Integrator makes extensive use of sockets for communicating with other processes and SNMP agents. Designed to be a generic communication programming interface, sockets were first introduced by the UNIX system. A socket is used to pass messages between two processes or two TCP/IP hosts. Sockets are similar to files: they can be opened, closed, read from and written to. The operating system references a socket by a file descriptor.

The datagram socket interface defines a connectionless service, such as UDP (User Datagram Protocol). Datagrams are sent as independent packets and the service provides no guarantees of delivery. The size of a datagram is limited to the size that can be sent in a single transaction (the default is 8 KB and the maximum is 32 KB). In contrast, the stream socket interface defines a reliable connection-oriented service, such as TCP (Transmission Control Protocol). SNMP is a standard application using UDP.

The OS/2 socket API supports both stream and datagram sockets (as well as raw sockets). The API includes the select() call, which has several parameters, of which the two most significant are: a pointer to a bit mask of file descriptors, and the maximum interval, in milliseconds, to wait for the selection to complete.

The select() function monitors the sockets flagged in the bit mask. If any data can be read from one or more of the sockets before the specified time elapses, control is returned to the function that called select() with a non-zero return code and the bit mask is modified to indicate which sockets have data pending. If the specified time elapses without any data becoming available on the flagged sockets, control is returned to the caller with a return code of zero and the bit mask set to all zeroes.

The dispatcher component of the Integrator maintains a list of sockets that are opened and the bit mask needed by select(). Every time a socket is opened, it is added to the socket queue. The dispatcher gets the file descriptor for the socket and turns on the respective bit in the bit mask. When a socket is closed, the socket is deleted and the corresponding bit is reset in the bit mask.

When the dispatcher selects a socket, data on the socket is read and processed. The type of processing depends upon the type of data: SNMP data, CMIP data, etc. The dispatcher implements a C++ pure virtual function, giving it a single way to invoke the necessary processing while allowing unique processing of different socket types.

The Integrator uses the Carnegie-Mellon SNMP API that is available with NV for OS/2. The SNMP operation GETNEXT is used extensively in the Integrator for walking through SNMP tables. By changing the operation type from GET_RSP_MSG to GETNEXT_REQ_MSG in the last SNMP response PDU, the next SNMP table row is retrieved. While the prefix of the first MIB variable in the response is the same as the prefix of the first MIB variable in the request, the same table is accessed. When the prefix varies, the end of the table has been reached.

13.8.4.4 Discovery

Before the Integrator can act as a proxy agent on behalf of an SNMP device, it must know the name and type of the APPN node. Once an SNMP agent is configured at the Integrator, the discovery of the agent proceeds. After an SNMP request and response for discovery is exchanged, the Integrator creates a managed object that represents the APPN node and registers it with cmipWorks, which will route requests pertaining to those registered objects to the Integrator.

If the discovery response contains the MIB variables for node name and type, the Integrator creates a pair of C++ objects that represent a managed object for the APPN node. There are three different types of classes and objects referenced by the Integrator:

1. Managed object classes
2. C++ classes generated by the MIBcomposer to represent managed object classes

   Instances of these classes are referred to as MIBcomposer objects.
3. C++ classes written by hand to represent real resources (such as an APPN node)

   This object performs the "real" work and sends out SNMP operations to get the information it needs. Instances of these classes are referred to as resource objects.

The combination of a MIBcomposer object and a resource object represents a managed object. A MIBcomposer object performs much of the processing needed for each incoming CMIP request, such as determining which attributes to retrieve or which action to invoke. A resource object is always created before its corresponding MIBcomposer object. Then, when a MIBcomposer object is created, it is passed a pointer to the resource object. In this way, the MIBcomposer object can call methods in the resource object to do the "real work" of simulating attributes and actions, for example, sending an SNMP request to get the MIB variable that corresponds to a particular attribute.

After the resource object and MIBcomposer objects are created, the Integrator registers a managed object with cmipWorks with the following information:

- The class of the managed object, inferred from the type of node returned in the SNMP response
- The distinguished name of the managed object, constructed from the NETID and CPNAME returned in the SNMP response
- The address of the MIBcomposer object, used as a subroute identifier

When a CMIP request is received for a managed object registered by the Integrator, cmipWorks passes the right MIBcomposer object pointer to the Integrator. In this way, the Integrator avoids searching for the MIBcomposer object that corresponds to the managed object that is the target of the CMIP request. Also, the managed object that represents the APPN node is flagged as a subtree manager, both with cmipWorks and in the MIBcomposer object.

Since every APPN node has a local topology, the Integrator also creates a local topology MIBcomposer object and resource object and registers the managed object representing them with cmipWorks. If the APPN node is a network node, the Integrator also creates a network topology MIBcomposer object and resource object and likewise registers their managed object with cmipWorks.

13.8.4.5 cmipWorks

The Integrator communicates with cmipWorks over sockets; sockets inter-process communication is supported in the cmipWorks MIB API.

After a manager sends a CMIP request encapsulated inside an MDS-MU, it is received by cmipWorks on the Integrator's system. The CMOS component of cmipWorks receives the MDS-MU, then hands the CMIP request to the cmipWorks dispatcher, which passes it to the Integrator over a socket. Along with the CMIP request, cmipWorks passes the subroute identifier for the managed object specified in the CMIP request; the subroute identifier is a pointer to a MIBcomposer object. If the discovery process has not yet registered the managed object, cmipWorks will respond with a "no such object" error and the Integrator will not receive the request from cmipWorks.

The managed objects that represent APPN nodes proxied by the Integrator are flagged as subtree managers.

Managed objects are arranged in a conceptual tree called the naming tree. The distinguished name (DN) of a managed object is the distinguished name of its parent in the naming tree, concatenated with a relative distinguished name (RDN) that uniquely identifies it with respect to all of the other managed objects contained under that parent. If a managed object indicates to cmipWorks that it is a subtree manager, the managed objects named under it do not have to be registered with cmipWorks. If the Integrator did not register the APPN node managed object as a subtree manager, it would be required to spend time and resources maintaining cmipWorks' awareness of contained managed objects (ports, logical links, and TGs). However, a managed object that registers as a subtree manager must perform routing and scoping for managed objects that are contained under it.

Managed objects contained under a subtree manager are not precluded from being registered with cmipWorks. The Integrator registers managed objects for local topology and network topology with cmipWorks. Consequently, these managed objects live for the duration of the node managed object. By registering these managed objects, cmipWorks assumes the responsibility of routing requests directly to them.

For more information regarding cmipWorks, the IBM NetView TMN Portable Agent Facility User's Guide is published on the Internet at:

`http://www.networking.ibm.com/paf/pafprod.html.`

Appendix A. APPN Base and Option Sets

This chapter identifies APPN functions and divides them into:

- A *base set* of functions, which every APPN node must implement according to its node type (end node or network node)
- Multiple *option sets*, which nodes may implement

The different functions are numbered for easy reference. Throughout the previous chapters references were made to the different functions using these numbers.

This chapter is organized as follows:

- Table 10 on page 336 lists base functions and briefly describes each one. (Some of these are base functions for network nodes, but only options for end nodes.)
- Table 11 on page 346 lists and describes option sets for APPN nodes.
- Table 12 on page 353 lists base and option function sets for the various APPN link types.
- Figure 133 on page 357, and Figure 134 on page 358, show dependencies among function sets for APPN end nodes. Figure 136 on page 359, and Figure 135 on page 358 show dependencies among function sets for APPN network nodes.

A.1 APPN Base Sets

All APPN nodes implement a base set of functions according to their node type. Table 10 on page 336 lists functions that are base for a network node or an end node and not applicable or optional for the respective other node type. For example, several base network node functions are optional for end nodes.

The contents of the APPN base has changed over time and products have normally implemented those functions to comply with the architecture, especially where the change significantly improved function. However, products that complied with the level of architecture at the time of implementation may not implement functions that have later been added to the base set, especially when those products are functionally frozen.

All new APPN implementations are expected to comply with the current level of APPN architecture, which is called Version 2. Information about APPN Version 1 is included as a reference to assist in understanding older implementations.

Table 10 (Page 1 of 10). Base Functions for APPN Architecture Versions 1 and 2					
No.	**Name**	**Description**	**Page**	**APPN EN**	**APPN NN**
Configuration Services					
001	**LEN-level XID3**	XID3 exchange with a LEN-level node.	63	base	base
002	**All XID3 States**	XID3 exchange with all exchange states.	63	base	base
003	**Link Station Role Negotiation**	Local link station role can be primary, secondary, or negotiable.	61	base	base
006	**CP Name on XID3**	Inclusion of a control point Name on XID3.	63	base	base
007	**TG Number Negotiation**	XID3 negotiation between adjacent link stations to assign a transmission group number for a link.	58	base	base
008	**Multiple TGs**	Connectivity to more than one node.	58	option	base
010	**Single-Link TG**	A transmission group consisting of a single physical link.	58	base	base
1001	**Secondary-Initiated Nonactivation XID**	Send or receive a nonactivation XID3 initiated by a secondary link station, that is, send or receive a nonactivation XID3 regardless of link station role.	64	Vers. 2: base Vers. 1: option	Vers. 2: base Vers. 1: option
1004	**Adjacent Node Name-Change**	Permits the adjacent node to change its name (but not its net ID) while remaining operational. A network node learning of its neighbor's name change via nonactivation XID3 sends a topology update. This might occur, for example, if the adjacent node is a composite network node and a Dynamic Name Change (option set 1006) occurs. One product feature implementing option set 1006 is called *SSCP-takeover.*	64	Vers. 2: base Vers. 1: option	Vers. 2: base Vers. 1: option
Intermediate Session Services					
011	**LFSID Addressing**	Using the local-form session identifier (LFSID) key to address the local node's DLC and path control layers.	34	base	base
013	**Priority Queuing for Transmission**	Queuing outbound packets for transmission based on transmission priority.	39	base	base
Address Space Manager					
020	**Extended BIND and UNBIND**	BIND and UNBIND RUs contain a Fully Qualified Procedure Correlation Identifier (FQPCID) control vector used to uniquely identify the session throughout its lifetime at every node it traverses.	140	base	base
021	**Adaptive Pacing for Independent LU BINDs**	Window-based flow control for independent LU BINDs prevents flooding the adjacent node with numerous BIND requests, assists the BIND receiver's buffer management, and prevents deadlocks.	52	base	base
023	**BIND Segmenting and Reassembly**	Segmenting and reassembly for BIND requests, which may exceed a link's configured maximum BTU size.	52	option	base

Table 10 (Page 2 of 10). Base Functions for APPN Architecture Versions 1 and 2					
No.	**Name**	**Description**	**Page**	**APPN EN**	**APPN NN**
024	**Adaptive Pacing for Dependent LU BINDs**	Window-based flow control for dependent LU BINDs, prevents flooding the adjacent node with numerous BIND requests, assists the BIND receiver's buffer management, and prevents deadlocks; required in APPN networks that carry dependent LU sessions.	52	Vers. 2: base Vers. 1: option	Vers. 2: base Vers. 1: option
Session Services					
030	**CP-CP Sessions**	Parallel sessions between adjacent CPs.	28	base	base
031	**CP Capabilities Exchange**	Exchange of CP capabilities GDS variable following the activation of CP-CP sessions.	63	base	base
033	**FQPCID Generation**	Generation of a FQPCID to identify all the flows associated with a session, including session initiation flows.	140	base	base
034	**CD-Initiate**	Support for the CD Initiate GDS variable.	146	base	base
035	**Reconstruct CD-Initiate Reply**	CD-Initiate reply based on the CP(DLU) node's level of APPN support.	146	base	base
036	**COS/TPF**	Support for class of service and transmission priority.	89	base	base
037	**BIND (ILU=PLU)**	Sending and receiving a BIND in which the initiating LU is also the primary LU.	267	base	base
038	**Limited Resource**	A link defined as a limited resource (typically, a switched link) will be brought down when it is no longer being used by active sessions in order to minimize connect charges. CP-CP sessions using the CPSVCMG mode name are exempt from deactivation by this function.	58	base	base
039	**BIND without RSCV from Any LEN or APPN Node**	Accepting a BIND without an RSCV from an adjacent LEN or APPN end node, or an APPN network node.	100	base	base
040	**Propagate Unrecognized CVs**	Nodes playing an intermediate role in a distributed procedure propagate any unrecognized control vectors.		n/a	base
041	**Session RU Segmenting and Reassembly**	Segmenting of RUs (other than BIND) as necessary for BIUs that exceed a link's configured maximum BTU size.	39	option	base
042	**Interleaved Segments**	Reassembly of segments on a session basis rather than on a link station basis.	41	base	base
1015	**CP-CP Session Activation Enhancements**	An improved mechanism for selection of a network node server by an end node that reduces the need for operator intervention when an NNS fails or becomes unreachable.	142	Vers. 2: base Vers. 1: option	Vers. 2: base Vers. 1: option
Directory Services					
050	**Register EN Resources**	End nodes may register their resources to a serving network node via the Register GDS variable.	111	base	base

Table 10 (Page 3 of 10). Base Functions for APPN Architecture Versions 1 and 2					
No.	**Name**	**Description**	**Page**	**APPN EN**	**APPN NN**
051	**Locate/Find/Found**	The Locate, Find, and Found GDS variables used to locate resources.	125	base	base
052	**Reconstruct GDS Variables for Locate Reply and CD-Initiate Reply**	Locate reply and CD-Initiate reply based on the CP(DLU) node's level of APPN support.		base	base
053	**Participate in Network Searches**	Distributed Locate searches to find resources.	118	base	base
054	**Send Wildcard Reply**	A Locate reply that indicates that *all* destination resources are located in the sender's domain. Send capability should be active for only one network node in a network.	125	n/a	base
055	**Broadcast and Directed Searches**	Distributed Locate search procedures to find a resource, the former used when the resource is unknown by the NNS(OLU), the latter when it is known.	118	base	base
056	**ENCP Search Control**	A control vector appended to the CP Capabilities GDS variable that indicates whether an EN wishes to allow its NNS to search the EN for resources unknown to the NN.	126	base	base
057	**Partial Directory Entries**	Defining and using directory entries in which the resource name is incompletely specified.	110	base	base
059	**Accept Unqualified LU Name**	Accepting an LU name that lacks a net ID from a LEN or APPN end node.		n/a	base
060	**Locate Chains — Locate(keep)**	Maintaining the chain of Locate control blocks established by an initial directed search in order to support subsequent session initiation flows for a given session setup. This is a prerequisite in *all intermediate routing nodes* along the path of directed searches between nodes implementing option set 1060, Prerequisites for Session Services Extensions CP Support.		n/a	base
061	**Sending Locate to a Gateway**	Sending Locate at an appropriate time in the NNS(OLU) network search logic to a node that has indicated, via the topology database, that it is a Gateway (option set 1017) to another network.		n/a	base
062	**Cache Resource Locations**	Retaining the results of successful Locate searches in the network node's directory database as cache entries.	114	n/a	base
063	**Favor Explicit Replies**	The NNS(OLU) function of favoring explicit replies to a broadcast search over wildcard replies.	125	n/a	base
064	**Network-Qualified LU Names**	Using, recognizing, sending, and receiving network-qualified LU names.	9	base	base

Table 10 (Page 4 of 10). Base Functions for APPN Architecture Versions 1 and 2					
No.	**Name**	**Description**	**Page**	**APPN EN**	**APPN NN**
065	**Central Directory Client**	The NNS(OLU) function of seeking to resolve directory queries by referring them to a central directory server, if one has identified itself via the topology database, before attempting a broadcast.	112	n/a	base
066	**Abbreviated Resource Hierarchy**	An abbreviated way to specify an origin or destination resource on Locate searches when CP = LU (see option set 1012).	110	n/a	base
068	**Inauthentic Net ID Indicator**	Setting the Inauthentic net ID Indicator field appropriately when adding an assumed network identifier to an unqualified LU name. Implementation of function set 068 by *every* network node in the network is a prerequisite before installing the Uservar product feature on *any* node in the network.		n/a	base
069	**DS Support for Domain LEN Resources**	Providing directory services for resources residing on adjacent LEN nodes. The LEN resources must be predefined at the serving network node and the owning LEN CP appears in the resource hierarchy.	108	n/a	base
1103	**Retry Referred Search**	If a referred search to a Central Directory Server fails due to session outage, the network node retries the referred search before dropping into the broadcast logic.	129	n/a	Vers. 2: base Vers. 1: option
1104	**Topology-Based Directory Nonverify**	Permits the establishment of a session with a DLU=NNCP without a prior Locate search, using only information from the network topology database.	111	n/a	base
1105	**PCID Modifier**	A control vector on Locate that increases the network's capacity to handle a larger number of possible distributed Locate subprocedures than the Search Number field permits.	269	option	Vers. 2: base Vers. 1: option
1109	**Surrogate Owner**	Suppressing network management Alerts for duplicate resources discovered during a given broadcast search if no more than one of the conflicting replies indicates that the owning CP is *not* a surrogate owner.		n/a	Vers. 2: base Vers. 1: option
1117	**Bypass of Directed Locate Not Allowed**	Allows an end-node to indicate that the Locate search must occur. If the base function 1104, Topology-Based Directory Nonverify function, locates the LU, a directed Locate search must still be sent to the NN.		option	Vers. 2: base Vers. 1: option
1119	**Report Branch Topology to Manager**	Network nodes with an SNMP or CMIP agent make the following two TDU fields available to their manager: • Branch Awareness Support, in the Node Characteristics X'4580' control vector • Additional Configuration Information indicator on TG Characteristics X'4680' control vector		n/a	added to base in May 1996

Table 10 (Page 5 of 10). Base Functions for APPN Architecture Versions 1 and 2					
No.	**Name**	**Description**	**Page**	**APPN EN**	**APPN NN**
1120	**Branch Awareness**	This function set is required in NNs that are or may be adjacent to nodes supporting option set 1121.		n/a	added to base in May 1996
1121	**Branch Extender Function**	Branch Extender permits larger APPN networks to be built by providing topology isolation between a branch network and a wide-area network, while permitting resource registration, searches, route selection, and RTP connections across the boundary. The branch network node defines TGs as branch downlinks or uplinks. Configurations are restricted. A node that supports option set 1121 and also has an SNMP agent supports the ibmBnaLocalTgConfGroup and the ibmBnaDirConfGroup in the ibmBna MIB module.	252	N/A	option

Table 10 (Page 6 of 10). Base Functions for APPN Architecture Versions 1 and 2					
No.	**Name**	**Description**	**Page**	**APPN EN**	**APPN NN**
Topology and Routing Services					
070	**Process Local Resource Change**	Processing information about routing-related resources local to the node, such as transmission groups (TGs) or significant changes in nodal congestion.	81	base	base
073	**Initial Topology Exchange**	A protocol for the exchange of topology database contents by adjacent network nodes after CP-CP session activation.	80	n/a	base
074	**Flow Reduction Sequence Numbers**	Checkpoint information that minimizes the amount of topology data flowing during an initial topology exchange occurring after reactivation of CP-CP sessions.	86	n/a	base
075	**Resource Sequence Numbers**	Information used to ensure the integrity and correctness of topology data in race conditions that can occur during the topology flood broadcast.	85	n/a	base
076	**Topology Broadcast**	A flood protocol by which network nodes distribute network topology information using Topology Database Update GDS variables.	81	n/a	base
077	**Garbage Collection**	A mechanism to remove stale or outdated information from the topology database.	87	n/a	base
078	**Topology Isolation at Net ID Boundaries**	Preventing the exchange of topology information by adjacent network nodes with different net IDs in their CP names.	233	n/a	base
079	**Build RSCV**	Building a Route Selection control vector describing a one-hop route (ENs and NNs) or a multi-hop route (NNs only).	104	base	base
080	**Calculate Route Using Connection Networks**	Using connection network information provided by other nodes via the topology database in computing routes.	89	n/a	base
081	**Class-of-Service Manager**	Managing COS definitions: includes defining classes of service and updating them in the local COS database, mode-to-COS resolution, and calculating resource weights.	89	option	base
082	**Route Randomization**	Random selection from equivalent routes.	99	base	base
083	**Member of Connection Network**	The ability to define the local node as a participant in a shared-access transport facility (such as a LAN) and (in NNs only) to distribute this information via Topology Database Updates.	66	base	base
084	**Select One-Hop Routes**	Select appropriate one-hop routes (including routes traversing a connection network) from the local node to an adjacent node based on the local topology database, the network topology database (NNs only), the destination node, and (if function set 081 is supported) the desired COS.	105	base	base

Table 10 (Page 7 of 10). Base Functions for APPN Architecture Versions 1 and 2					
No.	**Name**	**Description**	**Page**	**APPN EN**	**APPN NN**
085	**Select Network Routes**	The network node function of selecting an appropriate route between the local node, or a served end node, and a destination node, based on EN connectivity information (when applicable), the network topology database, the destination node, and (if function set 081 is supported) the desired COS.	95	n/a	base
086	**Topology awareness of CP-CP Sessions**	This function enables TRS to keep the current status of TGs carrying CP-CP sessions.		Vers. 2: base Vers. 1: option	Vers. 2: base Vers. 1: option
087	**Garbage Collection Enhancements**	A more efficient method of removing outdated information from the topology database.		n/a	Vers. 2: base Vers. 1: option
088	**TDU Flow Improvements During Topology Exchanges**	This reduces the amount of topology information that is transferred in some kinds of topology exchanges.		n/a	Vers. 2: base Vers. 1: option
1202	**Safe-Store of Topology Database**	A network node's topology database and related information is written to a permanent storage medium (option set 1201).	79	n/a	base (conditional on 1201)

Table 10 (Page 8 of 10). Base Functions for APPN Architecture Versions 1 and 2					
No.	**Name**	**Description**	**Page**	**APPN EN**	**APPN NN**
Node Operator Command Set					
090	**Common Node Operator Command Set**	The following Node Operator Facility (NOF) commands: • Define or delete an adjacent node • Define, delete, or query COS • Define, delete, or query a connection network • Define or delete a directory entry • Define, delete, query, start, or stop a data link control • Define, delete, query, start, or stop a link station • Define or delete a local LU • Start the local node • Define or delete a mode • Define or delete a partner LU • Change, initialize, or reset session limits • Query node statistics • Define, delete, query, or start or stop a port • Define, delete, or start a transaction program	26	product specific	product specific
091	**Network Node Operator Command Set**	The following NOF commands for network nodes: • Define or delete intermediate session routing tuning parameters • Define or delete node characteristics	27	n/a	product specific
Intermediate Session Routing					
100	**Extend/Unextend BIND and UNBIND**	Mapping between unextended and extended forms of BIND, UNBIND, and their responses when forwarding these RUs between nodes with varying levels of function.		n/a	base
101	**Fixed Session-Level Pacing**	IRS Support for fixed session-level pacing that may be selected by session endpoints via BIND.	33	n/a	base
102	**Adaptive Session-Level Pacing**	IRS Support for a window-based flow control protocol allowing the receiver to manage the necessary number of receive buffers for each session stage.	33	n/a	base
103	**Intermediate Session Segmenting/Reassembly**	IRS Support for segmentation and reassembly on each session stage for BIUs exceeding a link's configured maximum BTU size.	39	n/a	base
104	**Routing BIND and UNBIND**	Forwarding BIND and UNBIND RUs to the adjacent node in order to build or take down a chain of session stages for LU-LU data flow.	104	n/a	base
105	**Intermediate Session Routing for Dependent LU Sessions**	Functions necessary to perform APPN routing for LU-LU sessions between an SSCP-dependent SLU and a PLU when neither LU is in the local node.	31	n/a	base

No.	Name	Description	Page	APPN EN	APPN NN
Table 10 (Page 9 of 10). Base Functions for APPN Architecture Versions 1 and 2					
106	**Intermediate Session Routing for Type 6.2 LU-LU Sessions**	Functions necessary to perform APPN routing for LU-LU sessions between type 6.2 LUs when neither LU is in the local node.	31	n/a	base
Management Services - Multiple-Domain Support					
150	**SNA/MS MDS Common Base**	MULTIPLE_DOMAIN_SUPPORT function set common to both end node and network node implementations.	312	base	base
151	**SNA/MS MDS End Node Support**	That portion of MDS beyond the common base that is unique to end node implementations.	312	base	n/a
152	**SNA/MS MDS Network Node Support**	That portion of MDS beyond the common base that is unique to network node implementations.	313	n/a	base
153	**SNA/MS MDS High Performance Option**	This is an MDS optimization especially suited to management services application programs with very high transaction rates.	313	option	option
154	**SNA/MS MDS Transport Confirmation Option**	This is MDS optional subset 3. It allows application programs to override the default use of APPC confirmation on all data transported by MDS.	313	option	option
Management Services - MS Capabilities Function Set					
160	**SNA/MS MS_CAPS Base End Node Support**	Describes the level of MS_CAPS function required in end node implementations.	313	base	n/a
161	**SNA/MS MS_CAPS Have a Backup or Implicit Focal Point**	Describes MS_CAPS support needed for a node in the entry point role to acquire the services of either a backup focal point or an implicit focal point.	313	option	base
162	**SNA/MS MS_CAPS be a Sphere of Control (SOC) End Node**	This describes the MS_CAPS support needed in an end node in order to participate directly in the sphere of control of an explicit focal point.	313	option	n/a
163	**SNA/MS MS_CAPS Base Network Node Support**	Describes the MS_CAPS function required in every network node implementation.	313	n/a	base
164	**SNA/MS MS_CAPS Have a Subarea FP**	This describes a function which may be implemented by a network node product which also provides a T2.0 node appearance for attachment to the boundary function of a subarea network. It describes how the network node may act as a *pseudo focal point* to its served end nodes for the purpose of gathering SNA/MS alerts. The network node then forwards all these alerts to its SSCP over the SSCP-PU session.	313	n/a	option
Management Services - Entry Point Alert Function Set					
170	**SNA/MS EP Alert Base Subset**	Describes the base support required in every APPN node for sending generic Alerts for problems.	314	base	base

Table 10 (Page 10 of 10). Base Functions for APPN Architecture Versions 1 and 2					
No.	**Name**	**Description**	**Page**	**APPN EN**	**APPN NN**
171	**SNA/MS Problem Diagnosis Data in Alert**	Describes how implementations may also include *problem diagnosis* data in alerts.	314	option	option
174	**SNA/MS Operator-Initiated Alert**	Allows a product to provide an interface for human operators to enter text messages which are reported to a focal point within an alert.	314	option	option
175	**SNA/MS Qualified Message Data in Alert**	Allows an entry point to identify a product-unique message string that should be displayed.	314	option	option
176	**SNA/MS Self-Defining Message Text Subvector in Alert**	Provides a mechanism for an entry point to include a language-dependent text string in an alert. The coded character set in which the string is encoded and the national language are identified.	315	option	option
177	**SNA/MS LAN Alert**	Provides methods for reporting errors detected at the MAC layer of a LAN.	315	option	option
178	**SNA/MS SDLC/LAN LLC Alert**	Provides the capability to send alerts for problems detected on SDLC and LAN LLC logical connections.	315	option	option
179	**SNA/MS X.21 Alert**	Provides the capability to send alerts for problems detected on X.21 link connections.	315	option	option
180	**SNA/MS Hybrid Alert**	Provides method by which alert senders can specify elements of both basic and generic alerts in a manner that allowed for migration to focal point products which supported generic alerts. This optional subset was applicable only to a limited number of alert sending products for a particular period of time and may now be ignored completely by products which support generic alerts only.	315	option	option
181	**SNA/MS X.25 Alert**	Provides the capability to send alerts for problems detected on X.25 link connections.	315	option	option
182	**SNA/MS Held Alert for CPMS**	Provides the capability for an alert sender to hold alerts which occur when a focal point is not available, and then to send the alerts later when a focal point does become available.	315	option	option
183	**SNA/MS Resolution Notification Support**	Provides for sending an unsolicited notification of the correction of an error condition.	315	option	option
184	**SNA/MS Operations Management Support in Alert**	Provides a method for including operations management information in alerts.	315	option	option
Miscellaneous					
1013	**Interoperability with Peripheral Border Node**	This function set is needed if the network may be interconnected to other APPN networks by one or more peripheral border nodes (option set 1014).	233	n/a	Vers. 2: base Vers. 1: option

A.2 APPN Option Sets

APPN offers a number of functions that a product may implement; these functions are grouped into option sets. If an option set is chosen, it should be implemented in its entirety.

There are dependencies between some of the option sets. Some of these dependencies are complex, since they involve functions that are distributed among several nodes, but most dependencies are among functions implemented in one node. The dependencies among optional functions in a node are described in A.5, "Dependencies between Option Sets" on page 356.

Table 11 (Page 1 of 7). APPN Options

No.	Name	Description	Page	APPN EN	APPN NN
Configuration Services					
1002	**Adjacent Link Station Name**	Exchange of adjacent link station name control vector on XID3	61	option	option
1003	**Short-Hold Mode**	X.21 short-hold mode		option	option
1006	**Dynamic Name Change**	A function wherein a node may dynamically change its CP name (but not its net ID) without bringing down operational links.	64	option	option
1007	**Parallel TGs**	Connectivity to an adjacent node via more than one concurrently-active transmission group	58	option	option
CP Capabilities					
1011	**Multiple Local LUs, Session Manager for a Local Independent LU 6.2, and Intranode Routing**	One or more independent (type 6.2) LUs may reside in the local node.	31	option	option
1012	**LU Name = CP Name**	The node may be configured with a single LU that can support user sessions while simultaneously acting as the node's CP.	28	option	option
1014	**Peripheral Border Node**	This option set enables a network node to interconnect APPN network nodes with different net IDs. Implementation of function set 1013 (Interoperability with Peripheral Border Node) by other nodes in the network is a prerequisite	233	n/a	option
1016	**Extended Border Node**	Interconnecting multiple subnetworks with the same or different net IDs, while isolating network topology and enabling directory services and session establishment across multiple subnet boundaries.	244	n/a	option
1017	**Gateway**	Not yet architecturally defined. Provides enhanced network interconnection.		n/a	option

Table 11 (Page 2 of 7). APPN Options					
No.	**Name**	**Description**	**Page**	**APPN EN**	**APPN NN**
1018	**Delete EN Resources Before Registering**	End nodes implementing function set 1018 send a Delete GDS variable before sending a Register to reregister a resource that has been registered previously.	112	option	option
Dependent LU Support					
1060	**Prerequisites for Session Services Extensions CP Support**	Includes chasing Locate with discard, checking for backlevel adjacent node, intranode routing of negative Locate reply, sending/receiving resubmit on directed search and CD-Term/Cleanup, and appending the CP(PLU) name to BIND. Implementation of base function 060 by all network nodes along the path of the session initiation flows (Locate/CD-Initiate) is a prerequisite in order for endpoint implementations of option set 1060 to be effective.	263	option	option
1061	**Prerequisites for Session Services Extensions NNS Support**	Includes chasing Locate with discard, checking for backlevel adjacent node, intranode routing of negative Locate reply and routing requests that contain unrecognized GDS variables. Implementation of base function 060 by all network nodes along the path of the session initiation flows (Locate/CD-Initiate) is a prerequisite for implementations of option set 1061 to be effective.	263	n/a	option
1062	**Session Services Extensions CP Support**	The minimum set of CP(PLU) or CP(SLU) functions needed to support session services extensions for LU-LU sessions between *SSCP-independent LUs*.	263	option	option
1063	**Session Services Extensions NNS Support**	Enables a network node to act as NNS for the CPs of local or domain LUs supporting option set 1062 (Session Services Extensions CP Support). A CP supporting option set 1062 requires a network node server that supports option set 1063 in order to exercise option set 1062's functions.	263	n/a	option
1064	**Session Services Extensions PLU Node Support**	CP(PLU) support for sessions with non-6.2 LUs.	263	option	option
1065	**Session Services Extensions CP(SLU) (SSCP) Support**	Session services control point (SSCP) support for non-6.2 LUs. Includes SSCP support for SSCP-PU and SSCP-LU sessions, node type 2.0 formats and protocols, unformatted system services logon, and network management flows on the SSCP-PU session.	263	option	option

Table 11 (Page 3 of 7). APPN Options					
No.	**Name**	**Description**	**Page**	**APPN EN**	**APPN NN**
1066	**Dependent LU Server**	Server support for Dependent LU Requester clients (option set 1067), in which SSCP-PU and SSCP-LU flows to a T2.0 or T2.1 node externally attached to the Requester, or a T2.0 or T2.1 node image within the Requester, are encapsulated within LU 6.2 sessions.	270	n/a	option
1067	**Dependent LU Requester**	The client side of the Dependent LU Server (option set 1066) function, in which SSCP-PU and SSCP-LU flows to a T2.0 node attached to the Requester are encapsulated within LU 6.2 sessions.	270	option	option
1071	**Generalized ODAI Usage**	Ability to send and receive an ODAI value of 1 in flows associated with dependent LU-LU sessions, SSCP-PU sessions, SSCP-LU sessions, and in THs for adaptive BIND pacing IPMs and HPR ROUTE SETUP RUs. If the local and adjacent nodes both support this option, link station role for boundary TGs may be negotiable; otherwise the boundary node must assume the role of primary link station, and the node containing dependent SLUs must assume the role of secondary link station.		option	option
Cryptography Support					
1070	**Session Cryptography**	Managing and distributing keys for session cryptography to enable encipherment of the data on LU-LU sessions.		option	option
Directory Services					
1100	**Safe-Store of Directory Cache**	Cache entries in a network node's directory database are written to a permanent storage medium, permitting faster recovery after a network node failure or initial power-on.	115	n/a	option
1101	**Preloaded Directory Cache**	Ability to predefine, in a network node's directory database, initial values for information that may be learned and updated dynamically via the network search function.		n/a	option
1102	**EN Authorization**	If an end node is *unauthorized*, directory information about the EN's resources must be configured at its serving NN.	13	n/a	option
1106	**Central Directory Server**	Enables one or more designated network nodes to act as focal points for Locate searches in the native subnet, improving network performance by decreasing the number of broadcast searches.	112	n/a	option

Table 11 (Page 4 of 7). APPN Options					
No.	**Name**	**Description**	**Page**	**APPN EN**	**APPN NN**
1107	**Central Resource Registration (of LUs)**	An end node can designate that certain resources are to be registered to a Central Directory Server (see option set 1106). The NNS registers these, and other NOF-designated resources in its domain, to a Central Directory Server.	112	option	option
1108	**Nonverify**	In some cases this option lets a CP(OLU) indicate that verification of a destination resource, via directed Locate (either at the NNS(OLU) or the NNS(DLU) is not necessary. Also includes indications of resource availability and stability for caching in directory entries.	131	option	option
1116	**DLUS-Served LU Registration NNS Support**	An EN DLUR should be able to register its LUs to allow its NNS to handle locates for these LUs without having to forward the locates to the DLUR. This requires that the NNS be able to identify the type of LU and know how to handle Locates for it. This function is know as DLUS-served LU registration.		n/a	option
1118	**EN TG Vector Registration**	The EN registers its TGVs with its NNS, the NNS caches them to be used in building RSCVs.		option	option
Topology And Routing Services					
1200	**Tree Caching and TG Caching**	In a network node, precalculating, caching, and incrementally updating one or more trees representing all or part of the topology database, based on each defined COS. In a network node or end node, precalculating or caching a selected TG (for a one-hop route).	94	option	option
1201	**Permanent Storage Medium**	An APPN node's hardware may include a writable permanent storage medium such as tape, disk, flash RAM, EE-ROM. Other function sets are able to take advantage of such hardware to improve overall node and network performance after node restart.	79	option	option
1203	**Detection and Elimination of TDU Wars**	In a network node, this enables the detection of a TG war occurring because two or more network nodes are contending over the information contained in a topology (TG or node) record. This option set also ends the war and corrects any erroneous topology information that may have been transmitted during the war.	82	n/a	option
Intermediate Session Routing					

Table 11 (Page 5 of 7). APPN Options					
No.	**Name**	**Description**	**Page**	**APPN EN**	**APPN NN**
1300	**Tuning Values for Intermediate Session Routing (ISR)**	The ability to define, modify, and display the parameters used by the ISR function to set up session-level pacing and to negotiate the maximum send RU sizes during session activation.		n/a	option
1301	**Nonpaced Intermediate Session Traffic**	The ability of session connectors in an APPN network node to receive nonpaced session traffic.	33	n/a	option
High Performance Routing					
1400	**HPR Base**	See A.4.1, "Base Functions" on page 354	354	option	option
1401	**Rapid Transport Protocol**	See A.4.2, "RTP Option" on page 355	355	option	option
1402	**Control Flows over RTP**	See A.4.3, "Control Flows over RTP" on page 355	355	option	option
1403	**Dedicated RTP Connections**	See A.4.4, "Dedicated RTP Connections" on page 356	356	option	option
1404	**Multilink TG (MLTG)**	See A.4.5, "Multilink TG (MLTG)" on page 356	356	option	option
Management Services - File Services					
1500	**SNA/MS File Services Support Base**	The base subset of the FILE_SERVICES_SUPPORT function set which describes the interactions with SNA/File Services and SNA/Distribution Services that are required to route commands, reports, and bulk data for the SNA/MS change management discipline.	314	option	option
1501	**SNA/MS Network Operator Support for File Services**	Optional subset of FILE_SERVICES_SUPPORT which describes the capability to interact with the operator at a node for the purposes of file retrieval.	314	option	option
Management Services - Change Management					
1510	**SNA/MS Change Management Base**	The base subset of the EP_CHANGE_MGMT function set, which describes support for the SNA/MS change management discipline.	316	option	option
1511	**SNA/MS Change Management Production Only Activate**	Optional subset 1 of the EP_CHANGE_MGMT function set.	316	option	option
1512	**SNA/MS Change Management Execution Window Timing Support**	Optional subset 2 of the EP_CHANGE_MGMT function set.	316	option	option
1513	**SNA/MS Change Management Activate Report Support**	Optional subset 3 of the EP_CHANGE_MGMT function set.	316	option	option
1514	**SNA/MS Change Management Alter Active Install Support**	Optional subset 4 of the EP_CHANGE_MGMT function set.	316	option	option

No.	Name	Description	Page	APPN EN	APPN NN
1515	**SNA/MS Change Management Object Disposition Install Support**	Optional subset 5 of the EP_CHANGE_MGMT function set.	316	option	option
1516	**SNA/MS Change Management Initiate Command Support**	Optional subset 6 of the EP_CHANGE_MGMT function set.	316	option	option
1517	**SNA/MS Change Management Cancel Command Support**	Optional subset 7 of the EP_CHANGE_MGMT function set.	316	option	option
1518	**SNA/MS Change Management Activate Last Support**	Optional subset 8 of the EP_CHANGE_MGMT function set.	316	option	option

Table 11 (Page 6 of 7). APPN Options

Table 11 (Page 7 of 7). APPN Options					
No.	**Name**	**Description**	**Page**	**APPN EN**	**APPN NN**
Management Services - Operations Management					
1520	**SNA/MS Common Operations Services**	EP_COMMON_OPERATIONS_SERVICES function set provides the capability to support communication between network operators and served network management applications.	316	option	option
1521	**SNA/MS Operations Management**	The EP_OPERATIONS_MGMT function set extends the functions of common operations services and change management, improving a network manager's ability to control distributed resources.	316	option	option

A.3 Function Sets for APPN Links

Table 12. Functions for APPN Links

No.	Name	Description	ATM	Ether-net	Frame Relay	Token Ring	X.25
2001	**Native ATM DLC for HPR**	Enables HPR nodes to establish TGs over native ATM virtual channels. For native ATM virtual channels, HPR may specify the throughput and quality of service parameters. Functions 1400, 1401, and 1402 are prerequisites.	Base	n/a	n/a	n/a	n/a
2002	**IEEE 802.2 LLC type 2 (LLC2) Support**	Allows nodes to use LLC2 over APPN links. Use of LLC2 in a node with native ATM links (that is, function 2001) enables frame-relay-to-ATM service interworking and LAN-to-ATM service interworking between that node and APPN, LEN, and subarea boundary nodes with native frame relay or LAN capability.	option	base	base	base	n/a
2003	**ATM Forum User-Network Interface Specification, Version 3.0 (ATM UNI 3.0) Support**	Allows nodes implementing function 2001 to use ATM UNI 3 for managing native ATM switched virtual channels.	option	n/a	n/a	n/a	n/a
2004	**Multiprotocol Sharing**	Allows nodes to support multiprotocol sharing of APPN links. RFC 1483 (as extended) defines the multiprotocol encapsulation technique used for sharing of ATM virtual channels. RFC 1490 (as extended) defines the multiprotocol encapsulation technique used for sharing of frame relay virtual circuits.	option	n/a	option	n/a	n/a
2005	**Native ATM Dedicated Switched Virtual Channels (SVCs)**	Allows nodes implementing function 2001 to establish RTP connections over dedicated ATM SVCs (that is, no other RTP connection's traffic will be multiplexed onto the SVC.) This function is useful in conjunction with option set 1403 for application programs that are able to specify their needed throughput and quality of service.	option	n/a	n/a	n/a	n/a
2006	**Logical Data Link Control (LDLC) Support**	Allows nodes to use LDLC over APPN links. Use of LDLC in a node with native frame relay, token-ring, Ethernet, or X.25 links enables service interworking between that node and HPR nodes with native ATM capability.	base	option	option	option	option

A.4 HPR Base and Options

In order to facilitate implementation across a wide range of products, certain portions of HPR have been designated as optional functions. These options are:

- HPR Base - Option set 1400
- RTP Option - Option set 1401
- Control Flows over RTP Option - Option set 1402
- Dedicated RTP Connections - Option set 1403
- Multilink TG (MLTG) - Option set 1404

All new implementations of APPN are required to support at least the HPR base. HPR base functions are required in Version 3 of the architecture base and option set description. Base and option APPN sets are currently described in Appendix A of *APPN Architecture Reference*, SC30-3422.

The current intention is to include HPR options in the appendix.

A.4.1 Base Functions

The primary function of the HPR base is to provide ANR routing. Products that only implement the base can participate as intermediate nodes for RTP connections. Nodes that do not support the RTP option cannot be the endpoints of RTP connections. The following table summarizes the base functions:

Table 13 (Page 1 of 2). Base Functions for HPR - Option Set 1400

Name	Description
Intermediate ANR Routing for NLPs	HPR network layer packets (NLPs) may be efficiently routed, using ANR routing, through the node. The traffic that is ANR-routed is that which flows over RTP connections.
FID2 PIUs are Used for CP-CP and LU-LU Sessions	All CP-CP session traffic flows as in APPN using FID2 PIUs. APPN LU-LU session traffic not flowing over RTP connections also uses FID2 PIUs.
FID2 PIUs and NLPs share link (TG)	Both FID2 PIUs and NLPs may flow over a single link. They are distinguished by the first three or four bits in the packet (FID2 packet B'0010', NLP B'110').
Link and Node TDUs Indicate Level of HPR Capability	Link and node TDUs are sent indicating the appropriate level of HPR support.
FID2 Route Setup	Prior to establishing an RTP connection, a route setup protocol is executed in order to obtain the necessary ANR information associated with each link along the desired path. Every node along the path, including base HPR nodes, participates by adding the appropriate ANR information. When the route setup messages are exchanged between two nodes where one or both are base HPR nodes, it flows within a FID2 PIU.
Minimum Link Size 768 bytes	The smallest *maximum link size* allowed on any link that supports HPR is 768. This information is exchanged in XID3 just as in today's APPN.

Table 13 (Page 2 of 2). Base Functions for HPR - Option Set 1400	
Name	**Description**
HPR Capability Exchanged via XID3	A new control vector on XID3 indicates the HPR support level.
HPR Only Routes	NNs understand how to calculate HPR-only routes.
Link-level Error Recovery Support	In order to insure that all HPR nodes can be configured to interoperate, the following link-level error recovery support is defined. Link-level error recovery is always required for the following link types. (Not using link-level error recovery on these link types is not allowed.) • IBM compatible parallel (OEMI) and ESCON channels • X.25 The ability to send packets over a link without using link-level error recovery is required support for all other (not listed above) link types supported by HPR and using link-level error recovery is optional.

A.4.2 RTP Option

Nodes that support the RTP option are able to transport LU-LU session traffic across HPR networks over RTP connections, thus enabling the use of HPR's high-speed ANR routing and nondisruptive path switch functions. An RTP connection can only be made between nodes that support the RTP option, so it is essential that there be such nodes in the network. If all the HPR nodes in the network support only the base, there will be no advantages over APPN. (In fact, pure APPN protocols will be used.) All data flowing over an RTP connection is carried in a network layer packet (NLP). The following functions are included in the RTP option.

Table 14. RTP Functions for HPR - Option Set 1401	
Name	**Description**
Rapid Transport Protocol (RTP)	This is the transport protocol used in HPR for transporting data across HPR subnets.
Nondisruptive Path Switch	If the current path being used by an RTP connection fails, the connection may be switched to a new path automatically. Sessions that are being transported by the RTP connection are not disrupted.
Directory Reply with LU's Network Connection Endpoint (NCE) Identifier	An NCE identifier is part of an ANR routing label that allows an NLP to be routed to a specific component within a node. The component is uniquely identified by the NCE identifier. A search reply for an LU contains the NCE identifier associated with the LU.
APPN/HPR Boundary Function Support	APPN (FID2 PIU) traffic is mapped to HPR (NLP) traffic and vice versa.

A.4.3 Control Flows over RTP

This option extends RTP connectivity to control sessions.

Table 15. Control Flows over RTP - Option Set 1402	
Name	**Description**
Control Flows over RTP	RTP connections, between adjacent nodes, are used to carry CP-CP session traffic and route setup requests and replies.

A.4.4 Dedicated RTP Connections

This function allows the setup of dedicated RTP sessions.

Table 16. Dedicated RTP Connections - Option Set 1403	
Name	**Description**
Dedicated RTP Connections	Allows nodes implementing option set 1401 to establish dedicated RTP connections (that is, RTP connections that can be used by only one session). This function is useful for application programs that are able to specify their needed throughput and quality of service. See also option set 2005. Option set 1401 is a prerequisite.

A.4.5 Multilink TG (MLTG)

This function allows multiple links to be included in a single TG.

Table 17. Multilink TG - Option Set 1404	
Name	**Description**
Multilink TG	This function (a recent product feature) allows you to include multiple links, of any kind, in a single TG. Since HPR is a 1404 Multilink TG (MLTG) prerequisite, reordering of data that gets out of order (as a result of flowing over the MLTG) is done by the RTP endpoints. Option set 1402 is a prerequisite.

A.5 Dependencies between Option Sets

Figure 133 on page 357 through Figure 135 on page 358 show the dependencies between the different APPN functions for any given end node or network node implementation. These figures do not show any dependencies between functions in different nodes and any functions that apply only to subarea nodes and APPN-subarea interchange nodes. Also, not shown are functions that have always been part of the base functions. The numbers in the figures represent the functions as described in Table 10 on page 336 and Table 11 on page 346.

The dependencies between the different functions are indicated by the placement of the boxes representing the functions in the figures. A function is dependent on other functions if the box representing this function is placed directly above the boxes of functions on which it depends, or the functions are connected by a line. For example, in Figure 136 on page 359 function 1102 depends on functions 065 and 1103. No other functions are dependent upon function 1202. Also, function 1016 is dependent upon functions 1014 and 1063.

APPN architecture has been enhanced over time. The current APPN level described in *SNA APPN Architecture Reference*, SC30-3422 is APPN Version 2, which is the base for all new APPN implementations. APPN Version 2 is depicted in the following figures.

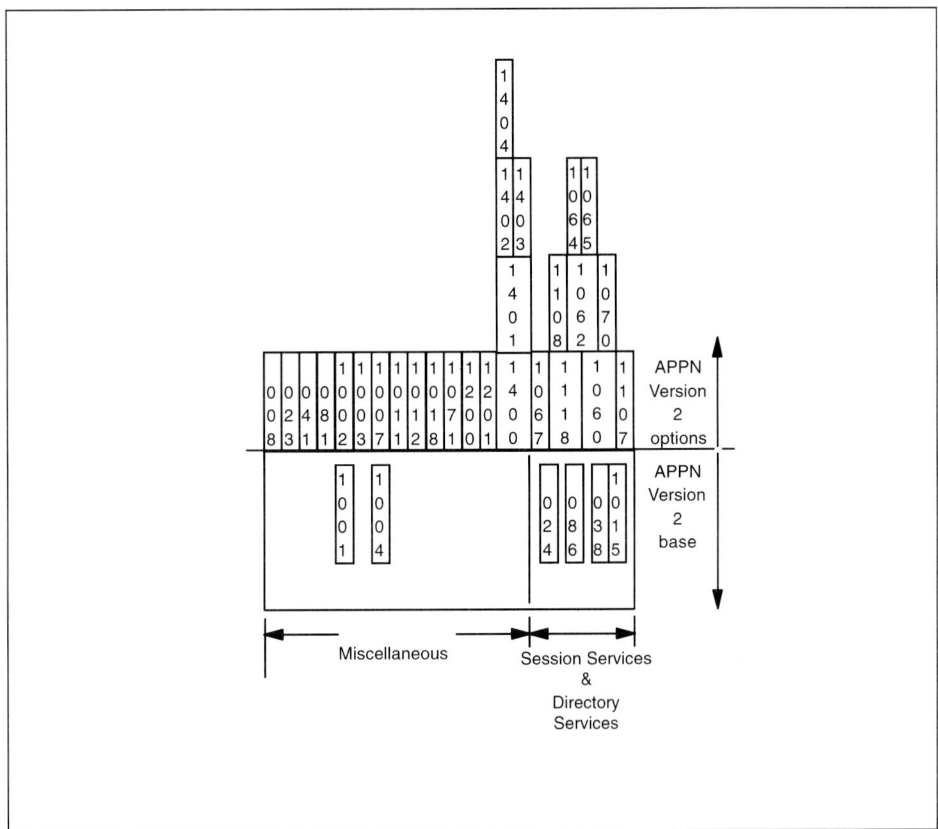

Figure 133. APPN End Node Base and Options

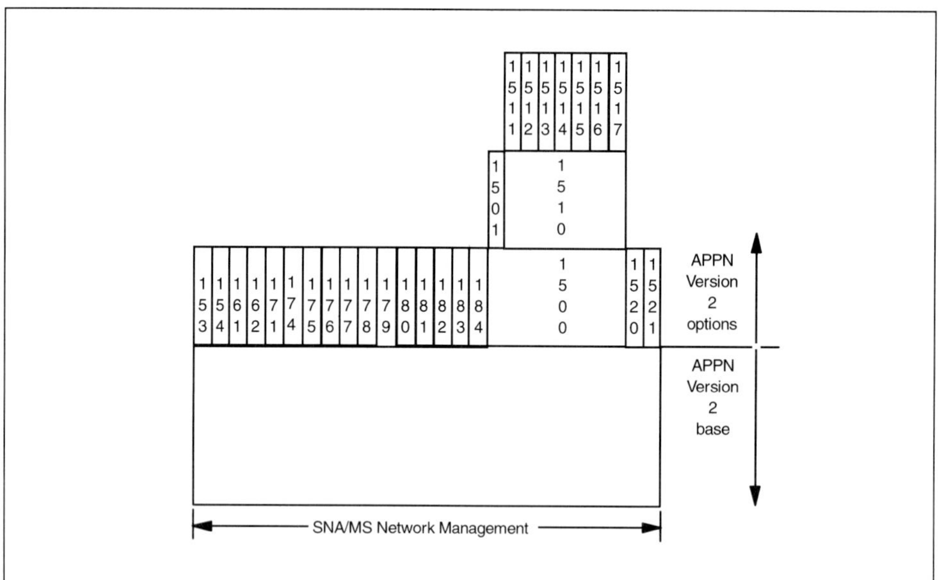

Figure 134. APPN End Node Base and Options (SNA/MS)

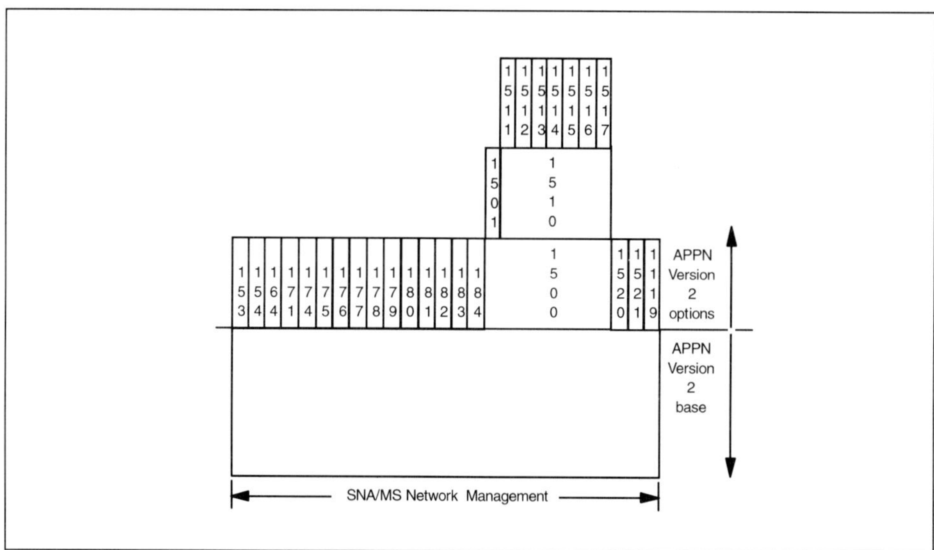

Figure 135. APPN Network Node Base and Options (SNA/MS)

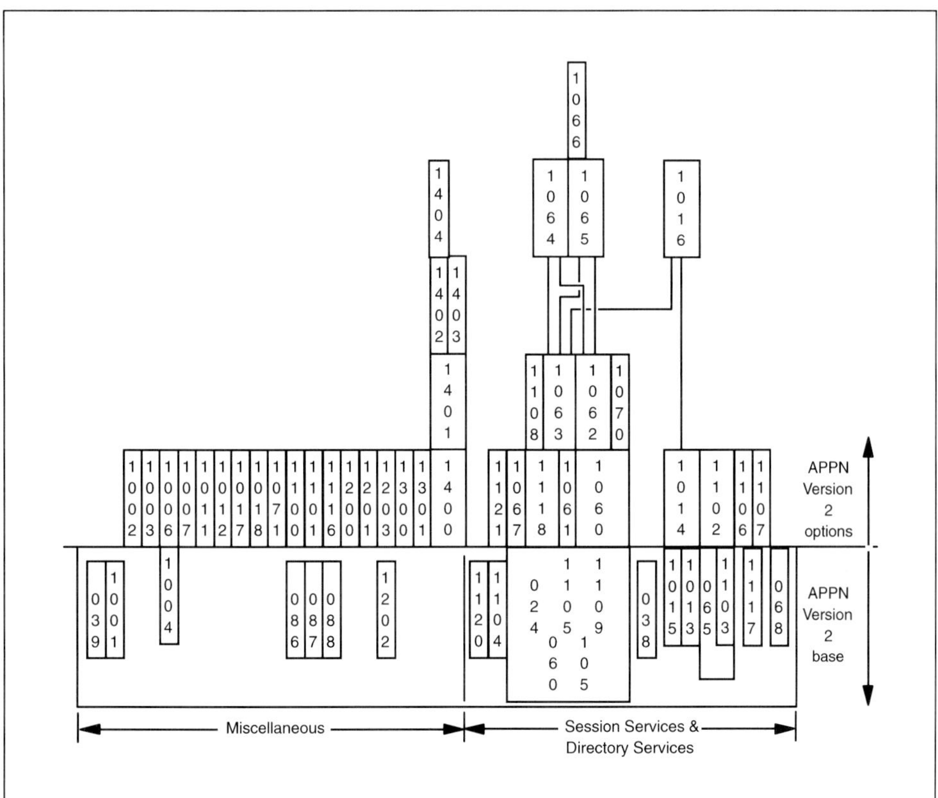

Figure 136. APPN Network Node Base and Options

Appendix B. APPN Implementations

Several products have implemented APPN and LEN functions, either as APPN nodes or as LEN end nodes. This chapter gives a brief overview of the implementation specifics of IBM products providing APPN functions. For an extensive description of APPN VTAM you should read Appendix C, "APPN VTAM" on page 409. APPN implementations in other manufacturer's equipment are not covered in this document.

The size of an APPN network may be limited by restrictions caused by implementations having limited storage and processor capacity. In the following section, we mention some limitations imposed by several APPN implementations. The values specified are maximum values, but for performance reasons use of lower values may be recommended.

APPN architecture groups functions into a base set and a number of optional function sets. The numbering of the different functions together with a brief description of each function can be found in Appendix A, "APPN Base and Option Sets" on page 335. In this chapter, each section describing the APPN implementation of a specific product contains a set of figures documenting which functions are implemented in the respective product. The functions are referenced by number only and the support for a specific function is indicated by a shaded box.

Table 20 on page 397 and Table 21 on page 404 at the end of this chapter give an overview of which functions have been implemented on IBM systems. For each of the functions, a reference has been made to the page where more information about the function can be found.

The evolution of SNA will continue and enhancements to APPN and APPN implementations will continue to be introduced. You should be aware that this chapter describes current hardware and software.

B.1 VTAM and NCP

VTAM and NCP announced LEN support in 1987. VTAM V4R1, announced in March, 1992, allowed VTAM and NCP V6R2 to portray itself as an APPN network node; a VTAM that does not own NCPs can also be an end node. VTAM V4R2 allows VTAM (and NCP) to portray itself as an extended border node.

VTAM V4R3 introduced the following major enhancements to APPN support:

- Non-Verify (Option Set #1108)
- HPR and RTP Support (Option Set #1400 and #1401)
- Topology Awareness of CP-CP Sessions (Option Set #086)

When referring to the APPN support introduced with VTAM V4R1 and enhanced with VTAM V4R2 and V4R3, we will use the term APPN VTAM. We will use the term APPN VTAM to refer to either VTAM V4R1, VTAM V4R2 or VTAM V4R3 unless a specific release is stated.

Information in this chapter is based on APPN VTAM. LEN functions were introduced with VTAM V3R2 and NCP V5R2.1.

Note: The following section gives a very condensed description of APPN VTAM; a more extensive discussion can be found in Appendix C, "APPN VTAM" on page 409.

B.1.1 Terminology and Implementation Specifics

APPN VTAM allows host systems to attach to APPN networks as APPN network nodes, end nodes, or LEN end nodes. The function within VTAM and NCP which allows nonsubarea (or peripheral) nodes to connect is called the VTAM or NCP boundary function.

APPN VTAM offers extended connectivity in a transparent manner for both APPN and subarea LUs, without loss of functionality. With a single exception, all LU-LU session capabilities present in a pure subarea or a pure APPN environment are also supported in a combined APPN/subarea networking environment. The only exception is Bisynchronous 3270 support, which is only supported when the session path is pure subarea.

To get full APPN connectivity requires CP-CP connectivity. APPN VTAM allows CP-CP sessions to be established between an APPN VTAM node and any adjacent APPN node.

For other APPN nodes in an APPN network, the VTAM/NCP complex is a composite network node (see Appendix C, "APPN VTAM" on page 409) or LEN end node; however, internally, subarea protocols are used. VTAM and NCP configured as an APPN network node or LEN end node allow intermediate session routing within the VTAM/NCP complex.

Dynamic Cross-Domain Resource

In VTAM all independent LUs owned by attached APPN nodes can be either explicitly or dynamically defined. Resources not explicitly defined will, during session establishment, be defined as dynamic cross-domain resources. The dynamic definition of independent LUs owned by adjacent APPN nodes has been introduced with VTAM V3R4 and NCP V5.4.

APPN versus Subarea Flows

Within a subarea network, LUs are located using CDINIT or DSRLST requests. The VTAM host (see, for example, NN1 or NN2 in Figure 137 on page 364) that transforms APPN requests into subarea requests and vice versa, is called an interchange node (ICN). CDINIT and DSRLST routing in a subarea network can be seen as a sequence of directed searches.

Surrogate Network Node Server

A subarea network may enable session establishment between two disjoint APPN networks by making all APPN resources in the distant APPN network (at the other side of the subarea network) appear to be ENs connected to the ICN; see, for example, Figure 137 on page 364. If the ICNs providing the boundary function, NN1 and NN2, are two separate VTAMs between which no CP-CP, only SSCP-SSCP, connectivity exists, then each of the APPN nodes in the *other* APPN network appears to its APPN endpoint partner as an end node that connects to a *surrogate network server.* For example, NNA *sees* NNB as an ENB connected to the surrogate network node server NN1, and NNB *sees* NNA as an ENA connected to surrogate network node server NN2.

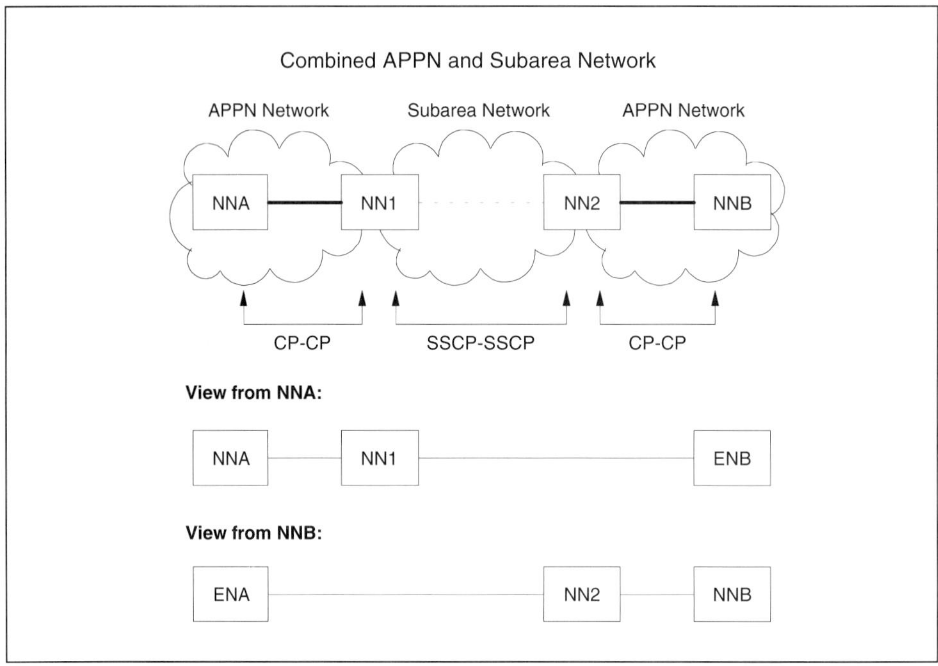

Figure 137. Surrogate Network Node Servers (NN1 and NN2)

Note that the LUs within the subarea that are owned by different VTAMs from the one providing the boundary function also appear to reside on an end node. For more details about the concept of a *surrogate network server* see page 419.

Transmission Priority and Class of Service

The COS name is obtained from a (VTAM) mode table (MODETAB). The class of service is used to select an operational route and a transmission priority from a list of predefined routes within a COS table (COSTAB). The transmission priority is used within the subarea part of the network (between VTAMs and NCPs) and optionally on the boundary links to attached APPN or LEN nodes. The latter part of a route within a subarea network is often called the *route extension*.

Rather than using a LOGMODE name to obtain the appropriate APPN and/or subarea COS name from a LOGMODE table, VTAM V4R3 introduced a new method of performing COS selection using subarea-to-APPN and APPN-to-subarea mapping tables (VBUILD TYPE SATOAPPN and APPNTOSA). A LOGMODE name is still used for the first lookup to obtain the subarea or APPN COS name. Once that is known, VTAM will use the mapping tables where it is possible to map APPN COS to subarea or vice versa. If mapping tables are not defined, then VTAM reverts back to using the LOGMODE name and LOGMODE tables.

Casual Connection

VTAM may portray itself as an APPN network node, an end node, or a LEN end node. VTAM/NCP may portray itself as a (composite) APPN network node or a LEN end node. A LEN connection between two (VTAM/NCP) composite nodes is called a *casual connection*; each side sees the adjacent side as one LEN end node.

Connection Networks

VTAM V4R1 does not allow the definition of its own attachment to a connection network; however, VTAM V4R1, as a network node server, is able to recognize a connection network and calculate a route through a virtual routing node. This restriction is removed with VTAM V4R2. A VTAM V4R2 APPN network node and end node can now define a TG towards a virtual routing node representing a connection network and activate a TG across the shared-access transport facility when a session is being established.

Adjacent Link Station (ALS) Selection Function

The ALS selection function in the VTAM session management exit can be programmed to select a route to a destination LU when multiple LEN connections exist to an adjacent APPN network. This is equivalent to selective wildcard routing.

VTAM High-Performance Routing

Within composite network nodes (CNNs), only ANR base (1400) is supported and only if the RTP path enters and exits the CNN through ANR-capable NCPs. In VTAM NNs (VTAMs with no subarea capability at all), both ANR base (1400) and RTP (1401) are supported. In VTAM ENs (with no subarea capability at all), only RTP (1401) is supported.

B.1.2 System Definitions

Generally, LUs are defined locally, that is, only once in a subarea network. For LEN connections, LUs have to be defined on both sides. Yet, there are some functions that provide dynamic network access and eliminate the need for multiple definitions.

Self-Defining Independent LUs

When a BIND from a LEN end node enters the subarea network, the OLU can automatically be defined (dynamic CDRSC). This function complements the wildcard search function in APPN networks. The DLU can be a predefined CDRSC, a dynamic CDRSC, or automatically defined by a VTAM exit.

Dynamic Switched Definition Support

Dynamic switched definition support simplifies adding switched devices to the network, including token-ring attached devices, which are treated as switched devices when connected through NCP's or VTAM's boundary function (not through a 3174 gateway). This support is for dependent or independent logical units. For dial-in support, reusable model definitions together with an installation exit routine are used.

B.1.3 Restrictions

Route selection between APPN networks and subarea networks is not seamless, as independent algorithms apply.

Multiple LEN connections from the APPN network to the subarea network require at least VTAM V3R4 and NCP V5R4.

B.2 AS/400

APPN functions were available when the first version of the AS/400 was announced in 1988. The core functions had already been implemented in the S/36, the AS/400's predecessor. The AS/400 can be configured as a network node, as an end node, or as a LEN node. Further information can be found in *AS/400 APPN Configuration Guide*, GG24-4024.

APPN support is part of OS/400, the operating system of the AS/400.

B.2.1 Terminology and Implementation Specifics

The term *location* is used for LU (logical unit).

A remote node is also called a *controller* or *control unit*.

A *device* is the representation of a remote location (LU) in the local node.

Wildcard routing is also called *ANY routing.

Session Cryptography
OS/400 releases V3R2 and V3R7 support session-level cryptography (option set 1070). Session cryptography requires the 2620 Cryptographic Processor (or 2628 Cryptographic Processor - Commercial) and PRPQ Common Cryptographic Architecture Services/400 (5799-XBY for V3R2 and 5799-FRF for V3R7).

Multinetwork Connectivity
The AS/400 is the first APPN system to implement border node functions with OS/400 V2.1. This capability is referred to as multinetwork connectivity. The AS/400 has implemented the peripheral border node function, also known as border node release 1.

Congestion
The maximum number of intermediate routing sessions supported by a network node can be defined by the network administrator. Network nodes are said to be congested if 90% of that number is reached. The node becomes uncongested, when the actual number of intermediate routing sessions becomes less than 80% of the defined maximum.

B.2.2 System Definitions

The AS/400 can be defined to have multiple local LU names. Local resources have to be defined. Remote LUs need to be defined only for:

- LUs in adjacent LEN end nodes
- LUs in adjacent end nodes without CP-CP sessions, if the LU name is different from the CP name
- LUs in adjacent end nodes that do not register and do not allow domain broadcast
- LUs in adjacent unauthorized end nodes

- LUs for which session security is defined
- Single-session LUs

Controller descriptions for LAN devices can be created automatically; however, their use is limited to independent LUs. Therefore, if an AS/400 connects to VTAM or NCP and dependent LU support is required, the controller and device descriptions need to be entered manually.

B.2.3 Restrictions

The maximum number of conversations between local and remote transaction programs is 512 per mode. (A mode name is used when an LU starts a session to indicate the required session characteristics.)

The maximum number of sessions that can be routed through an AS/400 network node is 9999.

The maximum number of modes simultaneously in use between local and remote LUs is 14.

The maximum number of *devices* that can be associated with a controller is 254.

The maximum RU length is 16,384 bytes.

B.3 IBM 3174 Establishment Controller

Note: Configuration Support-C Release 6.3 (referred to as C6.3) is applicable to the 3174 Establishment Controller and to the IBM 8250/8260 Multiprotocol Intelligent Hub Workstation Networking Module (WNM). All references to 3174 also apply to the WNM except where the specific function is not supported by the WNM (for example, Ethernet or S/390 channel attachment).

The Advanced Peer-to-Peer Networking Licensed Internal Code (LIC) adds APPN network node capabilities to the IBM 3174 establishment controller. The APPN LIC feature was a separately orderable, no-charge feature that requires Configuration Support-C LIC Release 5. Configuration Support-C LIC Release 6 integrated the APPN feature into the base support.

The APPN implementation allows the IBM 3174 to be customized as an APPN network node only. For detailed information, refer to *3174 Planning Guide Configuration Support C*, GA27-3918.

The IBM 3174 network node supports links to other APPN network nodes, end nodes, and LEN end nodes. Links supported are:

- SDLC
- S/370 channel
- Coax (using 3174 Peer Communications)
- Token-ring
- Ethernet
- Frame relay (requires CS C5)
- X.25 (requires CS C5)

The only restriction with SDLC and S/370 channel links is that the 3174 must be the secondary link station.

Configuration Support-C R5 LIC adds the Dependent LU Requester Function (option 1067) to the IBM 3174 APPN support, which provides a remote boundary function for dependent LUs that represent coax-attached devices. The IBM 3174 does not provide the DLUR function for LAN-attached down-stream PUs Type 2.0. The DLUR function requires the Dependent LU Server function (option set 1066) available with VTAM V4R2 for SSCP services. Together, these functions relieve the restriction that PU T2.0 nodes be directly attached (or bridged, or data link switched, or frame relayed) to the SSCP giving them SSCP services.

Notes:

1. To connect APPN or LEN nodes via coax attachment to the IBM 3174 network node requires the Peer Communication LIC feature.
2. Connections to APPN or LEN nodes via S/370 channel and SDLC links are supported only if the adjacent node is an AS/400, a VTAM, or a composite VTAM/NCP node. (LEN support for VTAM is introduced with VTAM V3R2, also called LEN VTAM; APPN is supported with VTAM in V4R1 and higher, here referred to as APPN VTAM.)

B.3.1 Terminology and Implementation Specifics

In the IBM 3174 context, the term gateway applies to the IBM 3174 LAN (token-ring or Ethernet) gateway feature.

Dependent and independent LU traffic is supported on the same link to an adjacent VTAM APPN or VTAM LEN node. If dependent LUs attach to the IBM 3174, an SSCP-PU session is requested when exchanging XIDs during link activation.

The IBM 3174 considers dynamic links as limited resources. When the number of sessions using a specific link goes to zero, the link is taken down.

The IBM 3174 assumes that all end nodes are authorized, meaning:

- Resource registration requests will be accepted from all end nodes within the domain of the IBM 3174 network node.
- An end node's requests to be included in a domain search for resources not known to the IBM 3174 network node will be granted.

Network Node Characteristic

The IBM 3174 network node uses two indicators within the node characteristics to regulate the number of sessions being routed through the network node. When the number of sessions concurrently being routed through the IBM 3174 network node reaches the maximum number configured, the IBM 3174 network node broadcasts TDUs indicating *intermediate routing resources depleted*; when the number of free buffers falls below a critical level, it broadcasts TDUs indicating *congestion*. Other APPN network nodes will use this information to avoid additional sessions from being routed through the IBM 3174 network node.

3174 HPR Support

ANR support (option set 1400) was added to 3174 as an RPQ in December of 1995. Configuration Support-C R6.3 LIC includes ANR as a base feature. HPR is supported on token-ring, Ethernet and frame-relay links; the 3174 only supports ISR on SDLC, S/390 channel and X.25 links.

B.3.2 System Definitions

The IBM 3174 does not allow users to enter system definitions through the node operator facility when the IBM 3174 is online; all definitions must be entered during offline customization.

B.3.3 Restrictions

The safe/store cache function is supported only if the IBM 3174 has a hard disk.

When connecting to a VTAM APPN or VTAM LEN node on SDLC and channel links, the IBM 3174 is always the secondary station (not negotiable).

The node's *route-addition resistance* is fixed at 128.

The maximum RU size is 8 KB.

The maximum number of sessions routed through the IBM 3174 network node is 1000.

The maximum number of links supported by the IBM 3174 is 255. If a 4-Mbps token-ring adapter is used, the limit is 140; when an 8-KB frame size is used, then the maximum number of links supported drops to 100.

The maximum number of adjacent network nodes is eight.

B.4 IBM 3746 Nways Controller

The Nways Controller APPN feature and APPN enhancements to the 3746 Model 900 provide the 3746-950 and the 3746-900 with the capability to participate in APPN/HPR networks. For more details about the APPN implementation in the IBM 3746, refer to *3746 Nways Controller Models 900 and 950: APPN Implementation Guide*, SG24-2536-01. The following set of APPN functions are supported:

- APPN network node
- APPN node interconnection using:
  - Token-rings, including connection networks
  - Leased and switched SDLC lines
  - ESCON channels
  - Frame relay lines
  - X.25 lines
- HPR base option capabilities (ANR) for ESCON, token-ring and frame relay, with SDLC support announced for a future release
- Dependent logical unit requester (DLUR)

The 3746 NN functions are provided on the 3746-900 in addition to the functions already provided to NCPs in the attached 3745, most notably the data link control (DLC) support. The adapters of the 3746 Model 900 can be shared by both APPN and subarea networking functions.

In 1997 the 3746 NN will be enhanced to support direct attachment to ATM networks at 155 Mbps, HSSI (T3/E3), FDDI, Fast Ethernet (100 Mbps) and worldwide primary ISDN. The ATM adapter will support the native ATM DLC for HPR traffic, as well as Classical IP and LAN Emulation (client).

With the introduction of the 3746 NN, the connectivity options for APPN networking have been greatly enhanced. Both the 3746 Model 900 and the 3746 Nways Controller can be used as high-performance APPN network nodes, offering ESCON, token-ring, frame relay, X.25 and SDLC attachments. These attachments provide access for any APPN devices, for example, AS/400, RS/6000, CS/2, 3174, 6611, etc., including the many non-IBM devices adhering to APPN. Access is also provided for non-APPN, SNA Type 2.0 and Type 2.1 nodes, similar to the boundary support available within NCP and VTAM.

In addition to the APPN network node function, 3746 NN dependent LU requester (DLUR) support enables dependent LUs residing on adjacent nodes to establish a control (SSCP-LU) session with a remote system services control point (VTAM).

The 3746 NN provides DLUR functions for *external* nodes. The 3746 DLUR support for dependent LUs on remote nodes simplifies migration to a peer-to-peer network. It obsoletes the requirement for remote nodes to support DLUR themselves, or to be adjacent to the VTAM or NCP boundary function. Figure 138 on page 373 shows both types of DLUR support.

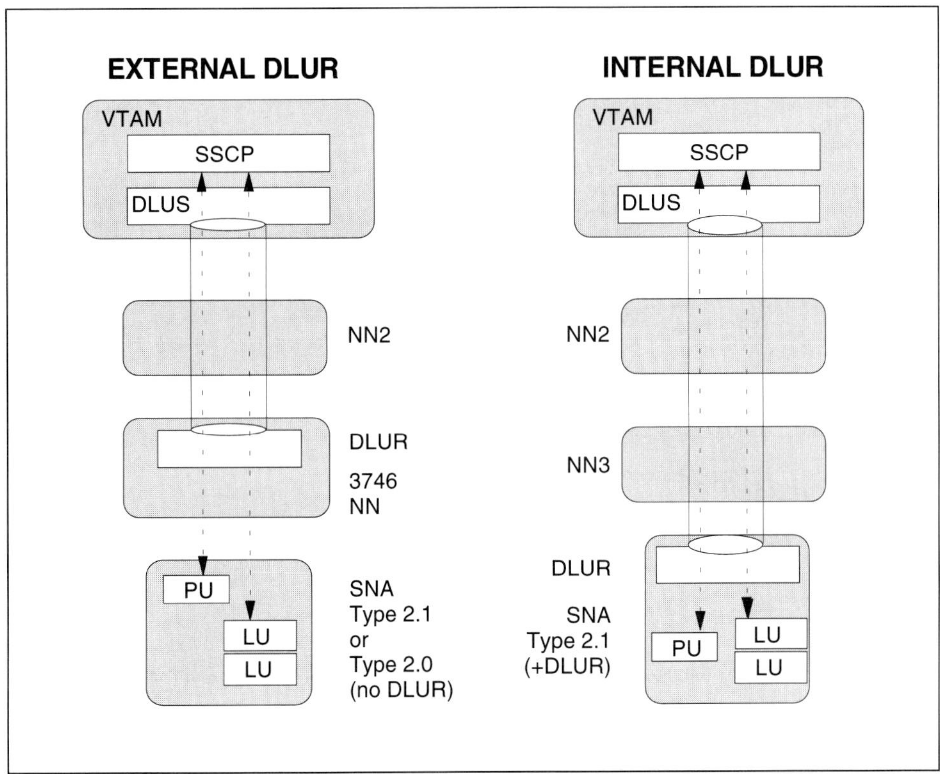

Figure 138. Internal and External DLUR Support

B.4.1 Terminology and Implementation Specifics

The 3746 NN is composed of a 3746 frame connected via a token-ring LAN to its service processor (SP) and network node processor (NNP). The token-ring LAN used for communication between the NNP and the service processor is referred to as the service LAN. The SP and NNP each contains a token-ring adapter attaching them to the same service LAN. MOSS-E traffic travels over the SP adapter and APPN traffic travels over the NNP adapter.

Figure 139 on page 374 depicts how the APPN functions are split up between the network node processor (NNP) and the adapters within the 3746 frame.

Note: By adapter we mean the CLP, TRP2, ESCP2, or CBSP2 processor and the associated line interface (LIC), token-ring interface (TIC3), or ESCON (ESCC) couplers.

Node Operator Facility (NOF) functions (for example, port and link activation), APPN topology and routing services, and session establishment tasks are executed in the NNP, while intermediate session routing is done within the 3746 frame.

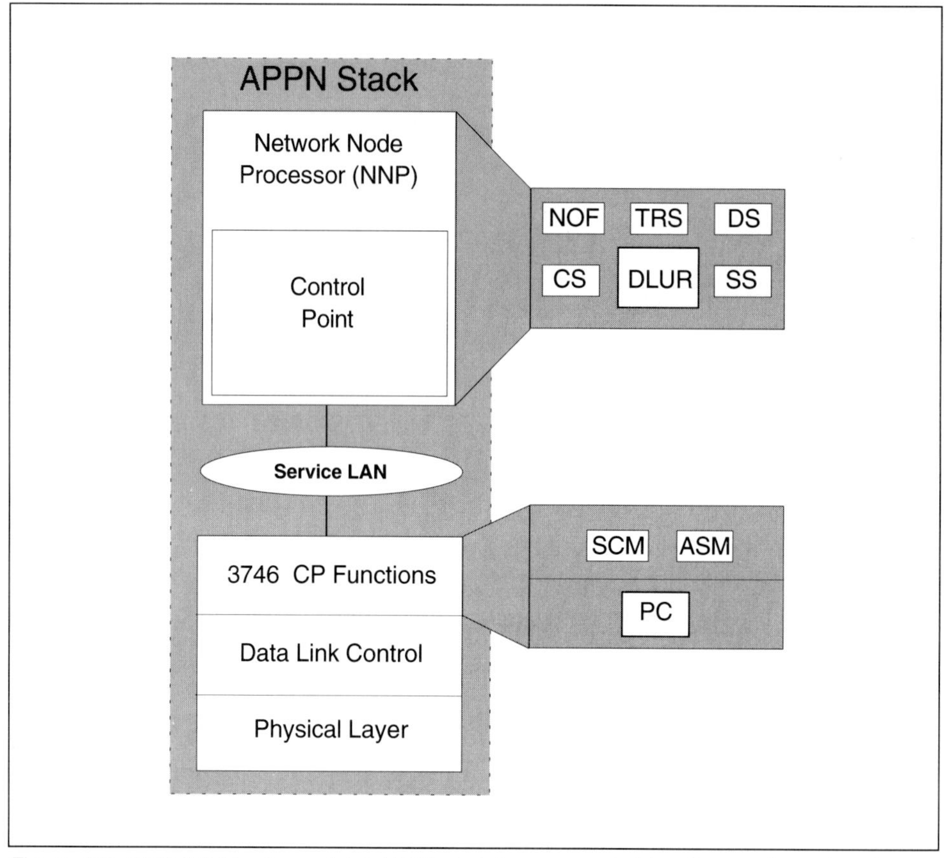

Figure 139. 3746 NN Structure. A full APPN stack is composed of functions performed on the network node processor (NNP) and within the 3746-9X0.

The APPN functions that run on the network node processor are:

- NOF - Node Operator Facility
- TRS - Topology and Routing Services
- DS - Directory Services
- CS - Configuration Services
- SS - Session Services
- DLUR - Dependent LU Requester

APPN functions performed within the 3746 frame are:

- DLC - Data Link Control

- PC - Path Control
- ASM - Address Space Manager
- SCM - Session Connector

The following section details how these components interoperate during session establishment and routing for APPN (independent LU 6.2) sessions.

B.4.1.1 Session Establishment and Routing

During APPN session establishment, CP functions on the NNP participate in locating session partners and are responsible for APPN route calculation. Figure 140 on page 376 depicts how CP-CP session data flows between the NNP and the control points of adjacent nodes. Irrespective of the coupler the node is connected to, CP-CP data will always traverse:

- The adapter (coupler and processor) the APPN node is attached to
- The communication switch
- CBSP2
- Token-ring port 2080
- Service LAN

Note: In only two cases CP-CP session data will not traverse the connectivity switch:

1. When APPN nodes connect via token-ring port 2080

   However, with the introduction of the APPN NN functions the attachment of user equipment via the service LAN is no longer supported.

2. When using an internal APPN link between the 3746-900 NN and any of the CCUs of the attached 3745 Model A

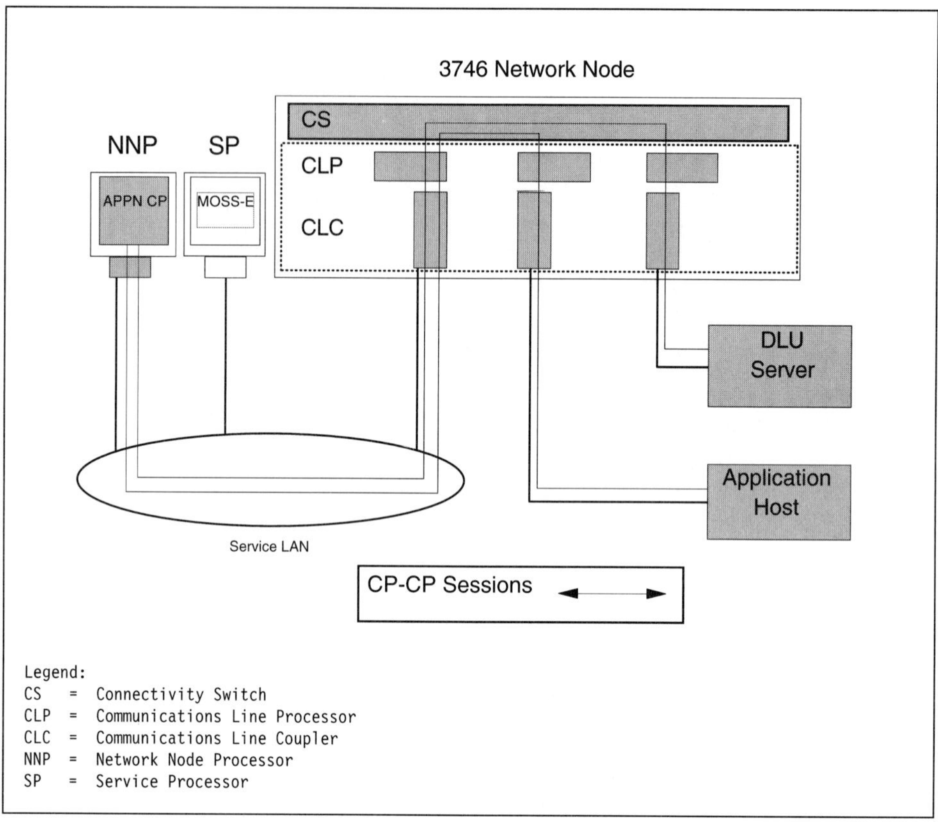

Figure 140. CP-CP Sessions

The BIND, which is the first SNA request unit flowing on the newly calculated route between two session partners, will trigger the address space manager (ASM) function running on the 3746 processors to assign LFSIDs. In addition, a session connector (SC) will be generated to enable intermediate session routing on the 3746 NN. The SC can be intra-processor (within the same 3746 processor), or inter-processor, (between two different processors connected via the 3746 connectivity switch (CS)). See Figure 141 on page 377.

Figure 142 on page 378 illustrates the data flows during and after session establishment. End node A (EN A) is token-ring-connected to 3746 NN, while end node C (EN C) is SDLC-connected. In both cases the 3746 NN (NN B) is providing the network node server function, having CP-CP sessions with both end nodes.

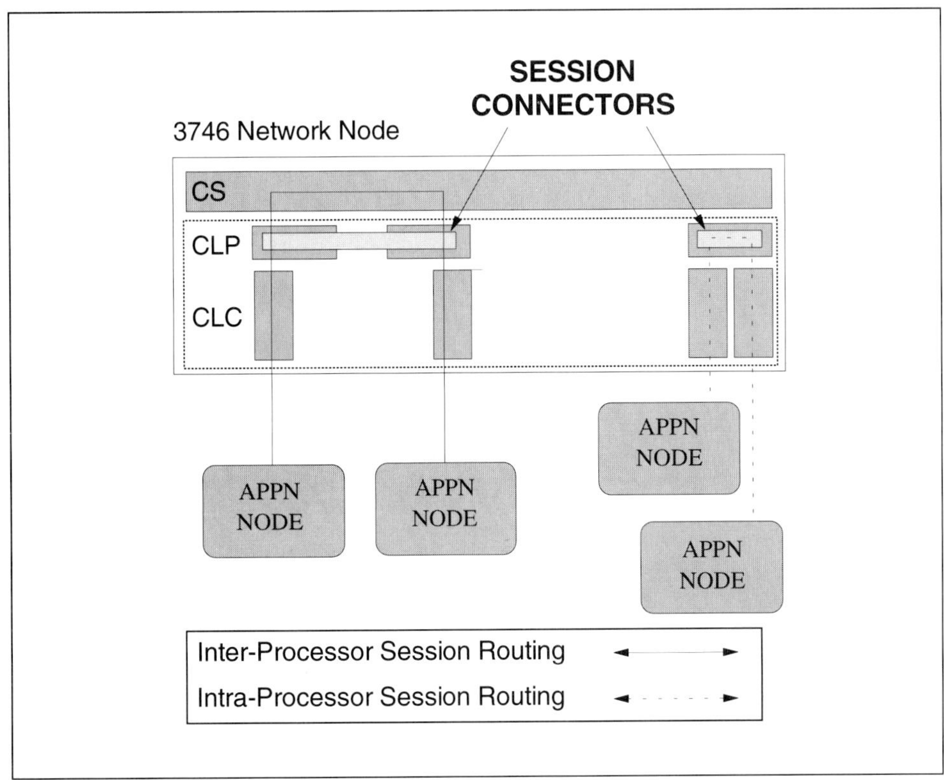

Figure 141. Intermediate Session Routing

To locate the session partner and calculate the best session path, APPN functions within the NNP are invoked. Initiated by the BIND, CP functions available on the 3746 processors will assign local-form session identifiers (LFSIDs) for this session and generate a session connector (SC). Note that for this session an inter-processor SC applies. If both EN A and EN C were connected to couplers controlled by the same processor, an intra-processor SC would result.

When the 3746 NN is performing intermediate session routing, the session connector manager (SCM) performs the LFSID swapping required to forward session data.

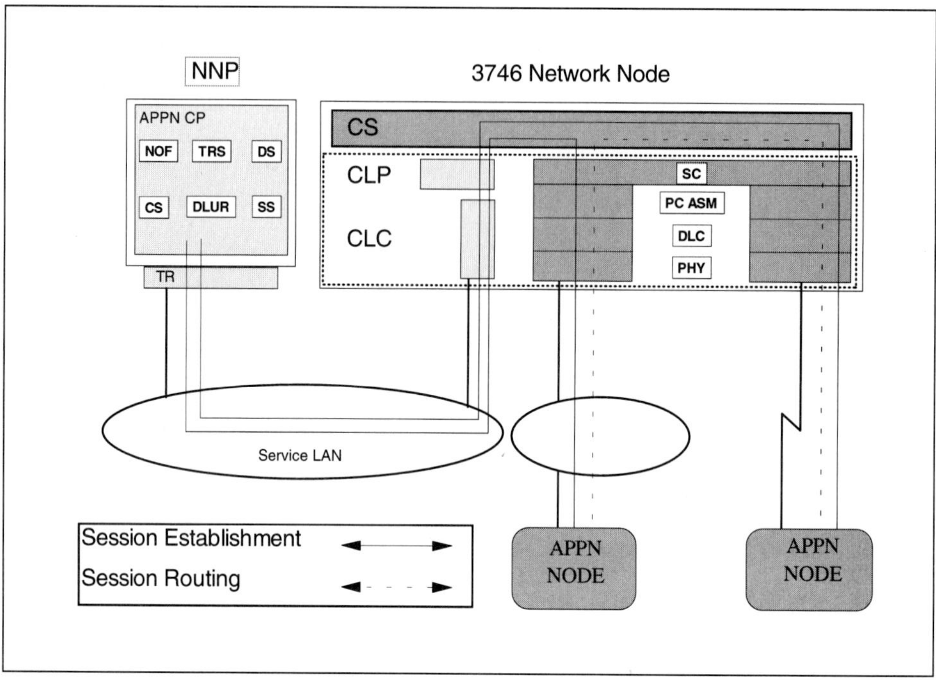

Figure 142. 3746 NN Intermediate Session Routing. All shaded components are involved in session setup. The dark-shaded components are also involved in intermediate session routing.

B.4.2 3746 Network Node Processor (NNP)

In order to provide the network node function in the 3746-9X0, the network node processor feature is used. This provides the network node processor (NNP) hardware resources and the licensed internal code required to support the APPN network node functions.

The NN processor feature includes the APPN CP and the APPN NN configuration control and management software (CCM) along with the hardware and token-ring interface. A keyboard and a display are not required on the network node processor; access is provided from facilities available on the service processor (SP).

Functions running on the control point can be accessed from the service processor. To allow configuration and management of the APPN NN functions the configuration control and management (CCM) tool which runs on the SP is used.

To provide additional resilience a second network node processor can be installed. The backup control point also attaches to the service LAN and can take over the functions from the primary control point. This process is controlled from the service processor; the CP backup can be done either manually or automatically. In case of a malfunctioning primary control point no new sessions can be established. To allow new session establishment, either the primary CP needs to be restarted, or the backup CP must take over. Once the original failing NNP again becomes available, it will be regarded as the backup network node processor.

B.4.3 Restrictions

The maximum number of ISR sessions that can be routed through the 3746 is 9000; during 1997 this will be increased to over 15000. There is no limit to the number of ANR sessions.

The maximum numbers of PUs supported is 3000; during 1997 this will increase to over 5000.

HPR multilink transmission groups will be supported in 1997.

HPR traffic over ESCON and SDLC and X.25 links are only supported with link-level error recovery (ERP). Frame-relay and token-ring links can be either ERP or non-ERP.

B.5 Personal Communications Family

The IBM Personal Communications (PComm) V4R1 family provides powerful client communications on all major PC operating systems. It offers 3270 and 5250 display and printer emulation and SNA-based client support for PCs running DOS (3270 only), Windows 3.1x, OS/2, and Windows 95. Personal Communications V4R1 for Windows 95 and Windows NT also provides 3270 and 5250 terminal emulation for Windows 95 and NT workstations.

One important enhancement to the PComm family is the inclusion of APPC3270 support. APPC3270 uses LU 6.2 sessions instead of LU 2 sessions as the underlying transport for 3270 sessions.

B.5.1 Personal Communications V4R1 for OS/2

The Personal Communications for OS/2 (PComm/2) product can be divided into two distinct parts, the 3270 and 5250 Emulation function and the communications function. There are two possible communications functions supported:

OS/2 Access feature

OS/2 Access Feature (AF) is shipped as a part of PComm/2. The AF includes SNA communications support and CM/2 APIs (including APPC and CPI-C support) and the AnyNet/2 Access Node, which allows SNA and TCP/IP workstation applications to communicate through the multiprotocol gateway to other computers.

AF support allows the workstation to be configured as an APPN LEN or end node. In addition, High Performance Routing (HPR) and Dependent LU Requester (DLUR) are supported.

Communications Server for OS/2

When running on communications server for OS/2 (CS/2), the APPN functions supported are those supported by the communications server software. For more information on the APPN features supported by CS/2, refer to B.6, “Communications Server for OS/2 Warp V4.1” on page 381.

To configure a PComm/2 workstation as an APPN network node, CS/2 must be used.

B.5.2 Personal Communications V4R1 for Windows 95 and NT

The Personal Communications for Windows 95 and NT (PComm95) product provides functions equivalent to the OS/2 Access Feature when run on Windows 95. The AF functions are integrated into PComm95.

PComm95 will also run on Windows NT using a TCP/IP connection or with Function Management Interface (FMI), LUA or APPC connections to a Microsoft SNA Server. For FMI, LUA or APPC support, the Microsoft SNA Server client software must also be installed on the workstation.

B.6 Communications Server for OS/2 Warp V4.1

The OS/2 support for LEN end nodes was announced in 1988 and the support for APPN network nodes and end nodes was announced in March, 1991. Originally (OS/2 V1.1, V1.2 and V1.3) LEN end node support was part of OS/2 Extended Edition (EE), which among other things offered Communications Manager support. APPN support for APPN network nodes and end nodes has been introduced with a separate product called Networking Services/2 (NS/2). NS/2 is an extension of the OS/2 V1.3 Communications Manager support. Since the introduction of OS/2 Extended Services (ES), LEN and APPN support both became part of Communications Manager/2 (CM/2) support.

Networking Services/DOS V1.0 announced in March, 1992, allows DOS workstations to participate, as LEN end nodes, in APPN as well as in SNA subarea environments.

In 1996, CM/2 functions were divided into two products. The *Desktop* function, including emulation and APPC support, was moved to the Personal Communications family of products (see B.5, "Personal Communications Family" on page 380). The *Server* function was moved to the Communications Server for OS/2 (CS/2) family of products. The following enhancements were made to CS/2:

- CS/2 V4.0 included multiprotocol support with AnyNet Sockets over SNA and SNA over IP gateway and Access Node support.
- CS/2 V4.1 added LAN Gateway (IPX and NetBIOS over IP and SNA), TN3270E Server support, frame relay support and SNA and APPN enhancements.

B.6.1 Terminology and Implementation Specifics

The following functions are specific to the CS/2 APPN implementation.

B.6.1.1 APPN Backup Link

A *backup link* is a link that CS/2 will attempt to activate if activation of the primary link fails, or if a primary link becomes inactive. Once the backup link is active, CS/2 will attempt to reactivate the primary link. If successful, sessions will be switched back to the primary link without disrupting traffic. If the primary link is deactivated by the user, by an inactivity timeout, or because it is a *limited resource* link, then the backup link will not be activated.

A primary link may only have one backup link. The backup link may never be defined as the preferred link to a NNS. A backup link is always defined as a limited resource link and it has a *connect cost* of 255 (maximum).

B.6.1.2 Non-Limited Resource Connection Network

Limited resource CNs disconnect after a conversation ends while non-limited resource CNs do not. This is designed for sessions which will be frequently used and therefore should be kept up. Keeping them up removes the performance overhead of constantly bringing them up and down. CS/2 V4R1 now supports the definition of Connection Networks as non-limited resources.

B.6.1.3 Substitute Network Node Server

During session initiation, an APPN or LEN end node tries to locate the partner LU within its local directory database and, if no information can be found, queries its network node server (APPN end node only). Session initiation will fail if the partner LU cannot be located. However, OS/2 end nodes can define, using a *local wildcard* definition, a *substitute network node server*. The substitute network node server is an adjacent APPN network node with which no CP-CP sessions have been established. If, during session initiation, the partner LU cannot be located locally, the OS/2 end node sends a BIND to the substitute network node server. The substitute network node server then becomes responsible for locating the partner LUs, route calculation, and forwarding the BIND to the destination node. The concept of substitute network node server can be used to define a backup network node server for OS/2 end nodes and provides a means of using wildcard definitions on a OS/2 LEN end node for its local use only.

B.6.1.4 Session Flow Control and Congestion

To manage the flow of data over a network, Communications Manager uses adaptive session-level pacing. The pacing occurs between each pair of adjacent nodes participating in the session route. When the APPC component of the Communications Manager is started, it determines the amount of memory that can be locked, that is, made nonswappable and nonmoveable. Communications Manager then computes 30% of this amount as *available memory*, that is, the memory that can be used to transmit and receive user data. The amount of available memory dictates how the adaptive pacing algorithm is used, as well as determining when the node becomes *congested*.

B.6.2 System Definitions

OS/2 can be defined as a primary, secondary, or negotiable link station.

B.6.3 Restrictions

Only one network node can be specified as server. But another server can be designated as a substitute server (by using the end node's local wildcard function).

Route-addition resistance is fixed at 128.

The cache directory can hold up to 255 LUs. When more are learned, the oldest ones are discarded. The cache directory is saved to disk after every 20 updates.

Transmission priority is not supported.

B.7 Communications Server/AIX

AIX SNA Services/6000 V1R2 allowed RS/6000s to function as LEN end nodes. AIX SNA Server/6000 V2R1 now provides full APPN support and enables the RS/6000 workstation to function as a network node or end node in an APPN network.

AIX SNA Server/6000 supports connection networks over token-ring and Ethernet.

B.7.1 Terminology and Implementation Specifics

The term *partner LU* is used for LUs in remote nodes.

The term *calling link station* is used for link stations that initiate activation of a link.

The term *dynamic calling link station* is used for link stations that initiate activation of a link over a connection network.

The term *listening link station* is used for link stations that accept link activation requests from remote link stations.

- A *selective listening link station* accepts a link activation request only from a specific remote link station.
- A *nonselective listening link station* accepts a link activation from any partner link station.
- A *dynamic listening link station* is not explicitly configured.

B.7.2 System Definitions

Configuration information is stored in *profiles* that are maintained in two databases: a working database that contains new or changed profiles and a committed database that contains verified profiles. Before new or changed profiles can be used to run SNA Server/6000, the entire profile database must be verified with the *update* option specified to place the profiles in the committed database.

To configure a RS/6000 workstation, you need to provide information about the node and the local control point, each link to an adjacent node, and the LUs that provide control for sessions with a remote node. In an APPN network, you also can use dynamic resource definition to access resources that have not been configured to SNA Server/6000 (for example, activating dynamic link stations or finding remote LUs that are not configured on the local node).

B.7.3 Restrictions

The maximum number of sessions supported by a node is 50,000. This number applies to sessions with local LUs and intermediate sessions (that is, sessions between remote LUs passing through a node).

The maximum number of node entries in the topology database is 65,535.

B.8 Communications Server for Windows NT V5

The APPN functions in Communications Server for Windows NT V5 (CS/NT) are comparable to those supported by Communications server for OS/2 V4R1 (see B.6, "Communications Server for OS/2 Warp V4.1" on page 381).

B.9 IBM 6611, 2210 and 2216

The IBM 6611 with IBM Multi-Protocol Networking Program V1R4 (MPNP), IBM 2210 with Multi-Protocol Routing Services V1R1 (MRS), and the IBM 2216 with Multi-Protocol Access Services V1R1 (MAS) are based on the same APPN software. The APPN support in MAS and MRS is a later version than that used by the MPNP. The routers have the capability of being APPN network nodes (NN) with intermediate routing functions and provides network services to both APPN and LEN end nodes.

We will use the term *router* in this section to refer to the above mentioned hardware and software.

B.9.1 Traffic Prioritization

The following two methods of traffic prioritization are used by the IBM 6611, 2210 and 2216. The 6611 supports priority queueing, the 2210 and 2216 support bandwidth reservation.

B.9.1.1 Priority Queueing

Priority queueing for FR and PPP on the 6611 has been enhanced for APPN. Three new APPN transmit queues were added in order to give the customer increased control over APPN and HPR data being sent over the serial line.

There are eight transmit queues on the 6611. Queue 7, the highest priority queue, is reserved for PPP and FR control frames. Queue 6 is reserved for high priority protocol control frames, including HPR network priority traffic. Queues 5, 4, and 3 are assigned to HPR's high, medium, and low data priorities, respectively. Direct DLC APPN ISR traffic is defaulted to queue 4. DLSw traffic is defaulted to queue 1. Queue 0 defaults to contain both non-SNA protocols and regular bridge data.

The customer can prioritize APPN ISR traffic over any of the six data queues (queue 5, 4, 3, 2, 1, 0). Queueing of APPN ISR traffic is done on a per link station basis. Likewise, IP traffic can be prioritized over any of the three generic data queues (queue 2, 1, 0).

B.9.1.2 Bandwidth Reservation System (BRS)

On serial connections, frame relay (FR) and PPP, the routers can implement a *Bandwidth Reservation (BRS)* mechanism. BRS enables the network administrator to reserve portions of the bandwidth of a circuit for specific types of data, differentiate between urgent, high, normal, and low-priority traffic within that bandwidth, and therefore favor the transmission of the highest-priority data.

BRS allows you to decide which packets to drop when demand (traffic) exceeds supply (throughput) on a network connection. Bandwidth reservation is not used until more than 100% of the available bandwidth is requested.

Bandwidth reservation *reserves* transmission bandwidth for a network connection. This reservation feature allocates minimum percentages of total connection bandwidth for specified classes of traffic.

BRS Components: BRS uses the following mechanisms to differentiate between traffic types and then to queue that traffic.

Circuit Classes
: Frame relay interfaces can be grouped into circuit classes and each circuit class is assigned a percentage of the frame relay interface's bandwidth. The sum of bandwidths reserved per link must be less than 100%. A *default* class is defined per frame relay interface and cannot be deleted. The bandwidth assigned to the DEFAULT class can be changed.

Traffic Classes
: Bandwidth reservation guarantees bandwidth for specific types of encapsulated traffic (classes) identified by either the protocol type or a filter. Traffic classes are defined for each PPP interface and each frame relay circuit.

  BRS supports the following protocols:

  - IP
  - ARP
  - IPX
  - Bridging
  - SNA/APPN-ISR (BAN and BNN)
  - APPN-HPR (BAN and BNN)
  - Appletalk
  - DECnet IV
  - Banyan Vines
  - OSI/DECnet V

  Note: By default, all protocols/applications are assigned to the DEFAULT class with priority normal. BRS also supports the following filters:

  - IP tunneling
  - SDLC tunneling over IP (SDLC Relay)
  - Rlogin
  - Telnet
  - SNA/APPN-ISR
  - APPN-HPR
  - SNMP

- IP Multicast
- DLSw
- MAC Address (through MAC filtering tags)
- MAC Filters
- NetBIOS
- Network-HPR
- High-HPR
- Medium-HPR
- Low-HPR
- X.25 Transport Protocol (XTP)

Using either the type of protocol, or a filter to differentiate between traffic types, traffic can be assigned to one of the *traffic classes*.

The reserved percentages for each class are a minimum slice of bandwidth for the network connection. When the network is operating to capacity, messages in any one class can be transmitted only until they use the configured bandwidth allocated for the class. In this case, additional transmissions are held until other bandwidth transmissions have been satisfied.

Priority Levels

Within each traffic class, the traffic can also be assigned a *priority level*. When BRS transmits packets for a traffic class, all packets with urgent priority are sent first, then all high priority, then all normal priority, and then all low priority. The following priority levels are defined:

- Urgent (U)
- High (H)
- Normal (N)
- Low (L)

Figure 143 on page 388 shows three traffic classes, each traffic class has its own set of data which has been given a priority (shown by the four queues, urgent(U), high (H), normal (N), and low (L).

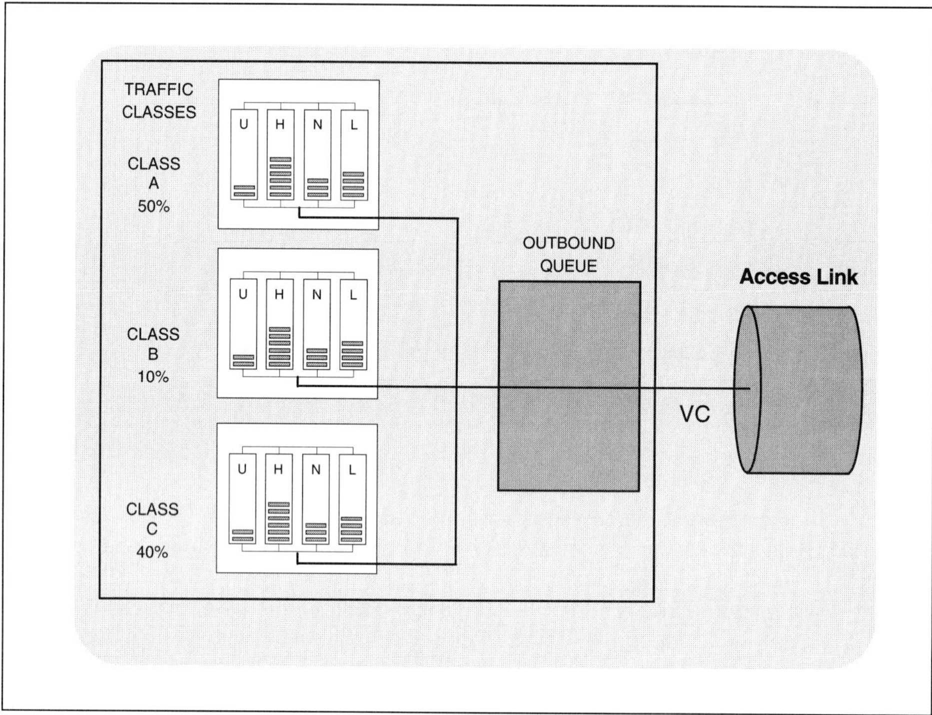

Figure 143. Traffic Class Queues

> Both *orphan circuits* (that is circuits that are not configured but are learned via LMI) and configured circuits with BRS explicitly disabled, use a default queueing mechanism where all frames are assigned to a default traffic class at the circuit level, and the circuits are assigned to the default circuit class.

Figure 143 shows three traffic classes, class A is assigned 50% of the bandwidth available to that DLCI, class B is assigned 10%, and class C is assigned 40%. Traffic bound for the DLCI shown is differentiated by the previously discussed protocol types or filters, and is assigned one of the four priorities. In the 2210 and 2216, each traffic class has a queue for each priority level.

BRS Support of APPN Traffic: When SNA/APPN-ISR is assigned to a traffic class, either APPN-ISR traffic that is being routed by the router's APPN code or SNA or APPN-ISR traffic that is being bridged will be assigned to this class. This is why SNA/APPN-ISR shows up as a protocol (the *routed* case) and as a filter (the *bridged* case). To identify SNA/APPN-ISR traffic that is being bridged, the BRS code looks for any bridging frames that use a DSAP or SSAP of 0x04, 0x08, 0x0C and a LLC (802.2) control field value that is NOT the un-numbered information (UI) type (i.e. NOT 0x03).

If SAPs other than 0x04, 0x08, or 0x0C are used for SNA/APPN-ISR bridge traffic, a sliding window MAC filter can be created to identify and tag SNA/APPN traffic. Using the BRS MAC filtering support, MAC filter tags can be assigned to a traffic class and priority.

When APPN-HPR is assigned to a traffic class, the BRS code looks for any bridging frames that use a DSAP or SSAP of 0x04, 0x08, 0x0C, and 0xC8 and a LLC (802.2) control field value that is equal to the un-numbered information (UI) type (i.e. 0x03).

If the user wants to differentiate between HPR HPR traffic depending on its transmission priority then the user can use the following HPR filters:

Network-HPR
: Used for HPR traffic that is using the network transmission priority.

High-HPR
: Used for high transmission priority.

Medium-HPR
: Used for medium transmission priority.

Low-HPR
: Used for low transmission priority.

This means that one of the above HPR transmission filters can be assigned to a different traffic class and/or priority than the other APPN HPR traffic.

B.9.2 APPN over DLSw

The routers support APPN over DLSw for connectivity to nodes through a remote DLSw partner. An example is shown in Figure 144 on page 390. The 6611 supports both remote and local DLSw, the 2210 and 2216 only support remote DLSw.

Note: It is recommended that you use APPN over direct DLCs when available instead of APPN over DLSw.

When APPN is configured on the router to use a Data Link Switching (DLSw) port, DLSw is used to provide a connection-oriented interface (802.2 LLC Type 2) between the APPN component in the router and APPN nodes and LEN end nodes attached to a remote DLSw partner.

When configuring a DLSw port for APPN on the router, the network node itself is assigned a unique MAC and SAP address pair that enables it to communicate with DLSw. The MAC address for the network node is locally administered and must not correspond to any physical MAC address in the DLSw network.

Figure 144 on page 390 shows how TCP/IP and DLSw are used to transport APPN traffic over an IP network.

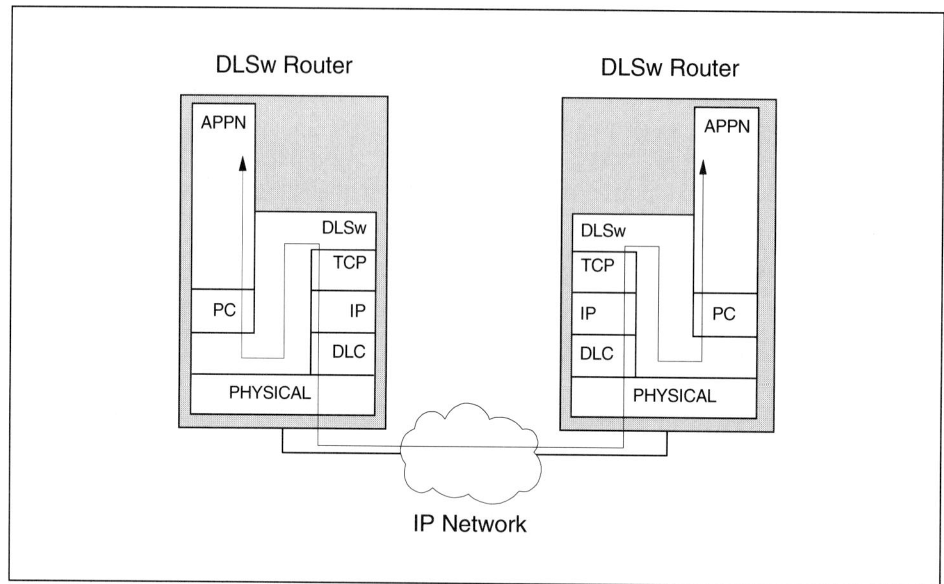

Figure 144. APPN over DLSw

B.9.3 Supported Traffic Types

APPN ISR uses the QLLC protocol for X.25 direct data link control, the IEEE 802.2 LLC Type 2 protocol for token-ring, Ethernet, PPP, and frame relay and SDLC protocol for the SDLC data link control. APPN HPR, which is supported on token-ring, Ethernet, PPP and frame relay, does not use LLC Type 2 protocol, but does use some functions of an APPN link station for XID and inactivity timeout. A single APPN link station is therefore used for ISR or HPR. Different mechanisms are used to distinguish between ISR and HPR traffic depending upon the DLC type:

For token-ring and Ethernet LAN ports

Each protocol that uses a port must have a unique SAP address, with the exception of DLSw (which may use the same SAP address as other protocols because DLSw frames will not be destined for the local MAC address, but rather a DLSw MAC address). A unique SAP address identifies the APPN link station for HPR traffic (Local HPR SAP address parameter). If ISR traffic is destined for a link station, then a different SAP address (Local APPN SAP address parameter) must be used. The ISR traffic uses LLC Type 2 LAN frames. The HPR traffic is handled in a similar fashion to LLC Type 1 LAN frames and must have a different SAP address. The default SAP address for HPR traffic is X'C8'. If X'C8' has already been used by another protocol on a port, the default must be overridden. Note that there is only one APPN link station even though APPN ISR and HPR traffic use different SAP addresses.

For frame relay ports

APPN ISR traffic and APPN HPR traffic transferred over a frame relay data link connection supports both the RFC 1490 bridged frame format and the RFC 1490 routed frame format. RFC 1490 routed frame format APPN ISR traffic will be transferred over a frame relay data link connection using the connection-oriented multiprotocol encapsulation method defined in RFC 1490 using:

- NLPID = X'08' (Q.933 encoding)
- L2PID = X'4C80' (Layer 2 protocol identifier indicating 802.2 LLC)
- L3PID = X'7083' (Layer 3 protocol identifier indicating SNA-APPN/FID2)

APPN HPR traffic transferred over a frame-relay data link connection does not use IEEE 802.2 LLC. It uses a different multiprotocol encapsulation as defined in RFC 1490 using:

- NLPID = X'08' (Q.933 encoding)
- L2PID = X'5081' (Layer 2 protocol identifier for no layer 2 protocol)
- L3PID = X'7085' (Layer 3 protocol identifier indicating SNA-APPN/HPR)

APPN HPR does not use a SAP for traffic transferred using the RFC 1490 routed frame format because there is no layer 2 protocol. APPN HPR uses a SAP for traffic transferred using the RFC 1490 bridged frame format.

The 2210 and 2216 support both the routed and bridged frame formats, the 6611 supports only the routed frame format.

For PPP ports

APPN ISR traffic uses 802.2 LLC over the PPP connection. Since there is no layer 2 protocol used in HPR's RFC 1490 encapsulation (non-ERP), no SAP is used for HPR traffic.

B.9.4 Functional Differences

This section details the functional differences between the router APPN implementations.

Network Control Layer

The Network Control Layer (NCL) is the HPR code component that implements the ANR function.

The portion of the NCL function that forwards packets is implemented on adapter cards in the 6611 and in the tasker in the 2210 and 2216.

In MPNP, MAS, and MRS, the NCL forwarder code takes advantage of the router's traffic prioritization mechanism. The mechanism to prioritize APPN/HPR traffic in the 6611 is different than that used in the 2210 and 2216. The 6611 uses a mechanism known as *priority queuing*, while the 2210 and 2216 use a mechanism know as *bandwidth reservation* (BRS).

The NCL is distributed between the 6611's system unit and adapter cards. The NCL manager that resides on the system unit is responsible for assigning and maintaining ANR labels. A copy of HPR's routing information table is propagated from the NCL manager to each adapter.

Topology Safestore

Topology Routing Services (TRS) can now store the APPN topology database on the 6611's and 2216's hard disks. In order to reduce the number of topology database updates (TDUs) transmitted over the network, the backup copy of the topology database is restored when the APPN topology database maintained in the router's memory is lost due to either a power loss or reboot. After the topology database is retrieved from the hard disk during startup, TRS advertises the last TDU sequence number received by the router. Only APPN network changes made after that sequence number will be broadcast. Without this feature, a complete set of TDU broadcasts are sent which significantly increases network traffic.

Since there is no DASD file system on the IBM 2210, the following functions cannot be supported:

- Topology safe store
- Explicit focal point recovery
- Session accounting using the DASD option (the memory option can be used)

The 2216 only saves the topology to its hard disk once a day during garbage collection, how often the topology is saved to disk on the 6611 is user configurable.

Table 18. Supported DASD Functions

Function	6611	2210	2216
Topology Safe Store	X	-	X
Session accounting - DASD Option	X	-	-
Session accounting - Memory Option	X	X	X

Direct DLC Support

In software releases of 6611 MPNP prior to V1R4, APPN traffic was routed over IP or Data Link Switching. Native SNA routing on the 6611, which means that APPN directly uses the DLC, is now supported for token-ring, Ethernet, frame relay (FR), and point-to-point protocol (PPP). Since direct DLC eliminates the need for DLSw, there is less processing overhead on LAN ports. Refer to Table 19 on page 396 for an overview of the DLCs supported.

SDLC Interfaces

IBM 6611 SDLC Support

Local DLSw is also used to support PU T2.0/2.1 nodes attached to the SDLC adapter which are serviced by the DLUR function. The remote SDLC station has an APPN connection established with the 6611 network node over the DLSw pseudo port. A local SNA link station terminates the SDLC link in the 6611, and DLSw performs SDLC-to-LLC conversion. The LLC frame is then switched to its destination, which in this case is the DLSw pseudo port of the 6611 network node containing the SDLC adapter.

IBM 2210 and 2216 SDLC Support

The IBM 2210 and 2216 both support native SDLC interfaces.

Route Test

Currently, HPR's route test can only be invoked through SNMP. Two variations of route test exist. The first tests the wrap around time of an established HPR connection. This route test is invoked specifying the NCL and RTP connection identifiers of an HPR connection. The NCL and RTP connection identifiers are unique identifiers used to identify HPR connections. These identifiers can be retrieved from the HPR RTP connection table MIB information.

The second tests the wrap around time of an APPN selected route to a specified destination node. This route test is invoked specifying the APPN network and LU name of the destination node and the mode used for the session. APPN's route selection algorithm is used to calculate the best route to the destination. If the selected route is an HPR connection originating at the 6611, the route is then tested.

When a route test is initiated, a separate time-stamped message is sent to each node within the HPR connection. At the destination node, the message is returned to the originating node. The route test message is only processed by the NCL forwarders in the intermediate and destination nodes. Upon receipt of the returned route test message, the wrap around time is recorded along with the corresponding node. The individual link rates can be calculated by comparing the round trip time for each route test message.

Operator Path Switch

Network operators can force an HPR connection originating at a 6611 node to be rerouted via SNMP's operator path switch. The NCL and RTP connection identifiers must be specified in order to invoke a path switch. A path switch attempt and result are reported in the HPR MIB's path switch status table.

B.9.5 Restrictions

The following restrictions apply to the router APPN support:

User API

The router implementation of APPN does not provide an application program interface to support user-written LU 6.2 programs.

Limited Resource Link Stations

On the IBM 2210 and 2216, limited resource link stations are supported on the following links:

- Connection network links
- X.25 SVC links (Previewed for APPN)
- PPP links running over ISDN or V.25bis
- Frame relay links running over ISDN

The IBM 6611 only supports limited resource link stations on connection network links.

Session-Level Security

A session-level security feature can be enabled for connections between the router network node and an adjacent node. Both partners require a matching hexadecimal key that enables each node to verify its partner before a connection is established.

Parallel TGs

Parallel TGs are not supported between two router network nodes using the same port on each router. However, parallel TGs are supported between two router network nodes using different ports on one or both routers. Also, parallel TGs are supported between a router network node and another non-router remote node over the same port using different remote SAP addresses, provided that the remote node has a mechanism to define or accept different local SAP addresses for APPN on the same port.

DLUR Restrictions

The DLUR option, as implemented on the router network node, has the following functional restrictions:

- Only secondary LUs (SLUs) can be supported by the DLUR function. An LU supported by DLUR cannot function as a primary LU (PLU). Therefore, the downstream physical unit (DSPU) should be configured as secondary.
- Because only SLUs are supported, Network Routing Facility (NRF) and Network Terminal Option (NTO) are not supported. Extended recovery facility (XRF) and XRF/CRYPTO are not supported.
- You must be able to establish an APPN-only or APPN/HPR-only session between DLUS and DLUR. The CPSVRMGR session cannot pass through a subarea network.

Connection Network Restrictions

The router APPN support has the following connection network restrictions:

- Connection networks defined on the router network node are only supported on token-ring and Ethernet LAN ports.
- The same connection network (VRN) can be defined on only one LAN. However, the same VRN can be defined on multiple ports having the same characteristics to the same LAN.
- The same connection network can be defined on a maximum of five ports to the same LAN on the router network node.
- There is only one connection network TG from a given port to a given connection network's VRN.
- The same connection network TG characteristics apply for each port on which a given connection network is defined on this router network node. The TG characteristics could be different on a different node.
- Because the VRN is not a real node, CP-CP sessions cannot be established with or through a VRN.
- When a connection network is defined on the router network node, a fully qualified name is specified for the connection network name parameter. Only connection networks with the same network ID as the router network node may be defined. The network ID of the VRN is then the same as the network ID of the router network node.

APPN over DLSw Restrictions

The following restrictions apply to APPN over DLSw:

- Connectivity through remote DLSw partners only
- Only 1 DLSw port per router
- Use of a locally administered MAC address
- HPR is not supported on DLSw ports
- DLSw ports cannot be members of connection networks
- Parallel TGs are not supported over more than one DLSw port

  A parallel TG may contain a single DLSw port, and any combination of other supported DLCs, but a parallel TG may never contain more than one DLSw port.

B.10 Summary of Supported DLCs and APPN Functions

The following table gives an overview of the DLC types supported by APPN capable hardware. The APPN function supported over these DLCs are listed.

Table 19. Summary of Supported DLCs and APPN Functions

DLC TYPE	6611	2210	2216	3746	CS/2.	CS/NT	3174
					6		
Token Ring	IHD	IHD	IHD	IHD	IHD	IHD	IH
Ethernet	IHD	IHD	IHD	IHD	IHD	IHD	IH
Twinax	n/a	n/a	n/a	n/a	ID	IHD	-
Frame Relay BNN	IHD	IHD	IHD	IHD	IHD	IHD 3	IH
Frame Relay BAN	-	IHD	IHD	IHD	IHD	IHD 3	IH
Point-to-Point Protocol	IH	IH	IH	IH 8	-	-	-
APPN over DLSw	ID	ID	ID	ID 8	IHD 2	IHD 2	-
SDLC Leased Line	-	ID	ID	IHD	ID	IHD	I
X.25 (PVC and SVC)	-	ID 7	ID 7	IHD	ID	IHD	I
APPN over PPP over ISDN	-	IH	IH	IH 8	-	-	-
APPN over Frame Relay over ISDN	-	IHD	IHD	IHD 8	ID	IHD 3	-
APPN over LAN Emulation 1	-	IHD	IHD	IHD 8	IHD	IHD	-
APPN over PPP over V.25BIS	-	IH	IH	IH 8	-	-	-
SNA over Asynch	n/a	n/a	n/a	n/a	ID	IHD	-
ESCON	n/a	n/a	n/a	IH	IHD 5	IHD 4	I

Notes:

I = Intermediate Session Routing

H = High Performance Routing

D = Dependent LU Requester, this refers to the port providing the connection to the downstream PU (DSPU)

1 Refers to ATM Forum Compliant LAN Emulation

2 Supported over Synaptel Adapters

3 Supported over Eicon Technology Adapters

4 Supported over BusTech Adapters

5 Escon adapters are supported by 3172 which can run CS/2

6 DLUR is supported by the GW feature of CS/2

7 This support has been previewed.

8 Supported by the Multiaccess Enclosure (MAE).

B.11 Summary of Implemented APPN Functions

Note: See the notes at the end of the tables (page 403) for abbreviations and explanation of terms used.

Table 20 (Page 1 of 7). Summary of Implemented Base Functions (APPN Version 2)

Function		VTAM	AS/400	3174	6611 MPNP	3746	PComm		CS			MRS MAS
							NT	AF	AIX	NT	/2	
No.	**Description**	**V4R3**	**V3R2**	**C6.3**	**V1R4**	**V4R2**	**11**	**12**	**13**	**14**	**15**	**16**
Configuration Services												
001	LEN-level XID3	B	B	N	N	N	E	B	B	B	B	N
002	All XID3 States	B	B	-	N	N	E	B	B	B	B	N
003	Link Station Role Negotiation	B	B	N	N	N	E	B	B	B	B	N
006	CP Name on XID3	B	B	N	N	N	E	B	B	B	B	N
007	TG Number Negotiation	B	B	N	N	N	E	B	B	B	B	N
008	Multiple TGs	B	B	N	N	N	E	B	B	B	B	N
010	Single-Link TG	B	B	N	N	N	E	B	B	B	B	N
1001	Secondary-Initiated Non-Activation XID	B	-	N	N	N	E	B	-	B	B	N
1004	Adjacent Node Name Change	B	B	N	N	N	E	B	-	B	B	N
Intermediate Session Routing												
011	LFSID Addressing	B	B	N	N	N	E	B	B	B	B	N
013	Priority Queuing for Transmission	2	B	N	N	N	E	B	-	B	B	N
Address Space Manager												
020	Extended BIND and UNBIND	B	B	N	N	N	E	B	B	B	B	N
021	Adaptive Pacing for Independent LU BINDs	3	B	N	N	N	E	B	-	B	B	N
023	Bind Segmenting and Reassembly	-	B	N	N	N	E	B	B	B	B	N
024	Adaptive Pacing for Dependent LU BINDs	-	B	N	N	N	E	B	-	B	B	N

Table 20 (Page 2 of 7). Summary of Implemented Base Functions (APPN Version 2)												
Function		**VTAM**	**AS/ 400**	**3174**	**6611 MPNP**	**3746**	**PComm**		**CS**			**MRS MAS**
							NT	**AF**	**AIX**	**NT**	**/2**	
No.	**Description**	**V4R3**	**V3R2**	**C6.3**	**V1R4**	**V4R2**	**11**	**12**	**13**	**14**	**15**	**16**
Session Services												
030	CP-CP Sessions	B	B	N	N	N	E	B	B	B	B	N
031	CP-CP Capabilities Exchange	B	B	N	N	N	E	B	B	B	B	N
033	FQPCID Generation	B	B	N	N	N	E	B	B	B	B	N
034	CD-Initiate	B	B	N	N	N	E	B	B	B	B	N
035	Reconstruct CD-Initiate Reply	B	B	N	N	N	E	B	B	B	B	N
036	COS/TPF	B	B	N	N	N	E	B	B	B	B	N
037	BIND (ILU=PLU)	B	B	N	N	N	E	B	B	B	B	N
038	Limited Resource	B	B	N	-	N	E	B	B	B	B	N
039	BIND without RSCV from Any LEN or APPN Node	B	B	N	N	N	E	B	B	B	B	N
040	Propagate Unrecognized CVs	N	N	N	N	N	-	N	N	N	N	N
041	Session RU Segmenting and Reassembly	B	B	N	N	N	E	B	B	B	B	N
042	Interleaved Segments	B	B	N	N	N	E	B	B	B	B	N
1015	CP-CP Session Activation Enhancements	B	B	N	N	N	E	-	B	B	-	N

Table 20 (Page 3 of 7). *Summary of Implemented Base Functions (APPN Version 2)*

Function		VTAM	AS/400	3174	6611 MPNP	3746	PComm		CS			MRS MAS
							NT	AF	AIX	NT	/2	
No.	**Description**	**V4R3**	**V3R2**	**C6.3**	**V1R4**	**V4R2**	**11**	**12**	**13**	**14**	**15**	**16**
Directory Services												
050	Register EN Resources	B	B	N	N	N	E	B	B	B	B	N
051	Locate/Find/Found	B	B	N	N	N	E	B	B	B	B	N
052	Reconstruct GDS Variables for Locate Reply and CD-Initiate Reply	B	B	N	N	N	E	B	B	B	B	N
053	Participate in Network Searches	B	B	N	N	N	E	B	B	B	B	N
054	Send Wildcard Reply	-	N	N	N	N	-	N	N	N	N	N
055	Broadcast and Directed Searches	B	B	N	N	N	E	B	B	B	B	N
056	ENCP Search Control	B	B	N	N	N	E	B	B	B	B	N
057	Partial Directory Entries	-	B	N	N	N	E	B	B	B	B	N
059	Accept Unqualified LU Name	B	N	N	N	N	-	N	N	N	N	N
060	Locate Chains - Locate(keep)	B	N	N	N	N	-	N	N	N	N	N
061	Sending Locate to a Gateway	N	N	-	N	N	-	N	N	N	N	N
062	Cache Resource Locations	N	N	N	N	N	-	N	N	N	N	N
063	Favor Explicit Replies	N	N	N	N	N	-	N	N	N	N	N
064	Network-Qualified LU Names	B	B	N	N	N	E	B	B	B	B	N
065	Central Directory Client	N	N	N	N	N	-	N	**5**	N	N	N
066	Abbreviated Resource Hierarchy	N	N	N	N	N	-	N	-	N	N	N
068	Authentic Net ID Indicator	B	-	N	N	N	-	N	N	N	N	N
069	DS Support for Domain LEN Resources	**6**	N	N	N	N	-	N	N	N	N	N
1103	Retry Referred Search	N	-	-	N	N	-	N	-	N	N	N
1104	Topology-Based Directory Nonverify	**9**	N	N	N	N	-	N	N	N	N	N
1105	PCID Modifier	B	-	-	N	N	-	-	-	N	-	N
1109	Surrogate Owner	N	-	-	N	N	-	-	-	N	-	N
1117	Bypass of Directed Locate Not Allowed	**9**	-	-	-	-	-	-	-	-	-	-

Table 20 (Page 4 of 7). Summary of Implemented Base Functions (APPN Version 2)												
Function		**VTAM**	**AS/ 400**	**3174**	**6611 MPNP**	**3746**	**PComm**		**CS**			**MRS MAS**
							NT	**AF**	**AIX**	**NT**	**/2**	
No.	**Description**	**V4R3**	**V3R2**	**C6.3**	**V1R4**	**V4R2**	**11**	**12**	**13**	**14**	**15**	**16**
Topology and Routing Services												
070	Process Local Resource Change	B	B	N	N	N	E	B	B	B	B	N
073	Initial Topology Exchange	B	N	N	N	N	-	N	N	N	N	N
074	Flow Reduction Sequence Numbers	B	N	N	N	N	-	N	N	N	N	N
075	Resource Sequence Numbers	B	N	N	N	N	-	N	N	N	N	N
076	Topology Broadcast	N	N	N	N	N	-	N	N	N	N	N
077	Garbage Collection	N	N	N	N	N	-	N	N	N	N	N
078	Topology Isolation at Net ID Boundaries	N	N	N	N	N	-	N	5	N	N	N
079	Build RSCV	N	B	N	N	N	E	B	B	B	B	N
080	Calculate Route Using Connection Networks	N	N	N	N	N	-	N	N	N	N	N
081	Class-of-Service Manager	B	B	N	N	N	E	B	B	B	B	N
082	Route Randomization	N	N	N	N	N	E	B	B	B	B	N
083	Member of Connection Network	B	B	N	N	N	E	B	B	B	B	N
084	Select One-Hop Routes	N	B	N	N	N	E	B	B	B	B	N
085	Select Network Routes	N	N	N	N	N	-	N	N	N	N	N
086	Topology Awareness of CP-CP Sessions	N	-	N	N	N	-	-	-	-	-	N
087	Garbage Collection Enhancements	N	-	-	-	-	-	-	-	-	-	-
088	TDU Flow Improvements	N	-	-	-	-	-	-	-	-	-	-
1202	Safe-Store of Topology DB	N	N	N	N	-	-	-	-	-	N	7
Node Operator Command Set												
090	Common Node Operator Command Set	B	B	N	-	N	E	B	B	B	B	-
091	Network Node Node Operator Command Set	N	N	-	-	N	-	-	-	N	-	-

Function		VTAM	AS/ 400	3174	6611 MPNP	3746	PComm		CS			MRS MAS
							NT	AF	AIX	NT	/2	
No.	Description	V4R3	V3R2	C6.3	V1R4	V4R2	[11]	[12]	[13]	[14]	[15]	[16]
Intermediate Session Routing												
100	Extended/Unextended BIND and UNBIND	B	N	N	N	N	-	N	N	N	N	N
101	Fixed Session-Level Pacing	B	B	N	N	N	-	N	B	N	N	N
102	Adaptive Session-Level Pacing	B	B	N	N	N	-	N	B	N	N	N
103	Intermediate Session Segmenting/Reassembly	-	N	N	N	N	-	N	N	N	N	N
104	Routing BIND and UNBIND	[6]	N	N	N	N	-	N	N	N	N	N
105	Intermediate Session Routing for Dependent LU Sessions	[6]	N	N	N	N	-	N	[5]	N	N	N
106	Intermediate Session Routing for Type 6.2 LU-LU Sessions	[6]	N	N	N	N	-	N	N	N	N	N
Management Services - Multiple-Domain Support												
150	MDS Common Base	[4]	B	N	N	N	E	B	B	B	B	N
151	MDS End Node Support	[4]	E	-	-	N	E	E	E	E	E	-
152	MDS Network Node Support	[4]	N	N	N	N	-	N	N	N	N	N
153	MDS High Performance Option	[4]	-	-	-	-	-	-	-	-	-	-
154	MDS Transport Confirmation Option	-	-	-	-	-	-	-	-	-	-	-

Table 20 (Page 5 of 7). Summary of Implemented Base Functions (APPN Version 2)

Table 20 (Page 6 of 7). Summary of Implemented Base Functions (APPN Version 2)												
Function		**VTAM**	**AS/ 400**	**3174**	**6611 MPNP**	**3746**	**PComm**		**CS**			**MRS MAS**
							NT	**AF**	**AIX**	**NT**	**/2**	
No.	**Description**	**V4R3**	**V3R2**	**C6.3**	**V1R4**	**V4R2**	[11]	[12]	[13]	[14]	[15]	[16]
Management Services - MS Capabilities												
160	MS_CAPS Base End Node Support	[4]	E	-	-	N	E	E	E	E	E	-
161	MS_CAPS Have a Backup or Implicit FP	[4]	B	N	[1]	N	E	B	[1]	B	B	[1]
162	MS_CAPS Be a Sphere of Control End Node	[4]	E	-	-	-	E	E	E	E	E	-
163	MS_CAPS Base Network Node Support	[4]	N	N	N	N	-	N	N	N	N	N
164	MS_CAPS Have a Subarea FP	[8]	N	N	-	-	-	N	-	N	N	-
Management Services - Entry Point Alerts												
170	EP Alert Base Subset	[4]	B	-	N	N	E	B	B	B	B	N
171	Problem Diagnosis Data in Alert	-	B	-	N	N	E	N	B	B	N	N
174	Operator-Initiated Alert	[4]	B	N	-	-	E	-	-	B	-	-
175	Qualified Message Data in Alert	-	B	-	-	-	E	-	-	B	-	-
176	Self-Defining Message Text Subvector in Alert	-	B	-	-	-	E	-	-	B	-	-
177	LAN Alert	-	B	N	-	-	E	B	-	B	B	-
178	SDLC/LAN LLC Alert	-	B	-	-	-	E	B	-	B	B	-
179	X.21 Alert	-	B	-	-	-	E	B	-	B	B	-
180	Hybrid Alert	-	-	-	-	-	-	-	-	-	-	-
181	X.25 Alert	-	B	-	-	-	E	B	-	B	B	-
182	Held Alert for CPMS	-	B	N	N	-	E	B	-	B	B	N
183	Resolution Notification Support	-	-	-	-	-	-	B	-	-	B	-
184	Operations Management Support in Alert	-	-	-	-	-	-	-	-	-	-	-

Table 20 (Page 7 of 7). Summary of Implemented Base Functions (APPN Version 2)												
Function		VTAM	AS/400	3174	6611 MPNP	3746	PComm		CS			MRS MAS
							NT	AF	AIX	NT	/2	
No.	Description	V4R3	V3R2	C6.3	V1R4	V4R2	11	12	13	14	15	16
Miscellaneous												
1013	Interoperability with Peripheral Border Node	N	N	N	N	N	-	N	-	N	N	N

Notes:

E = End Node

B = End and Network Nodes

N = Network Node

\- = Not Supported

1 Backup Focal Point only

2 Supported by NCP's BF only

3 VTAM will respond to a BIND pacing request received, but will never set the pacing request indicator on a BIND.

4 Function supported through NetView

5 Not supported by AIX SNA Server V2R1; supported by V2R1.1

6 VTAM NN, and VTAM EN providing LEN attachment

7 MAS only

8 NetView serves as the subarea focal point, but cannot have a subarea focal point using the APPN architecture. Instead, NetView supports using another NetView as a subarea focal point using a proprietary interface.

9 VTAM does perform topology database lookup (to see if an unknown resource is a NN CP), but does not skip sending the APPN locate. This locate is then sent as a directed search to the NN. Because of this processing, VTAM has implemented option set 1117.

11 Refers to PComm for Windows 95 and Windows NT

12 Refers to PComm for OS/2

13 Refers to Communications Server for AIX V2R1

14 Refers to Communications Server for Windows NT V5

15 Refers to Communications Server for OS/2 V4R1

16 Refers to IBM 2216 Multi-protocol access services V1R1 and IBM 2210 Multi-protocol routing services V1R1

Table 21 (Page 1 of 4). Summary of Implemented Optional Functions (APPN Version 2)

Function		VTAM	AS/ 400	3174	6611 MPNP	3746	PComm		CS			MRS MAS
							NT	AF	AIX	NT	/2	
No.	**Description**	**V4R3**	**V3R2**	**C6.3**	**V1R4**	**V4R2**	**11**	**12**	**13**	**14**	**15**	**16**
Configuration Services												
1002	Adjacent Link Station Name	B	B	N	N	N	E	B	-	B	B	N
1003	Short-Hold Mode	B	B	-	-	-	-	-	-	-	-	-
1006	Dynamic Name Change	B	-	N	-	-	-	-	-	-	-	-
1007	Parallel TGs	B	B	N	N	N	E	B	B	B	B	N
CP Capabilities												
1011	Multiple Local LUs	B	B	-	-	N	E	B	B	B	B	-
1012	LU Name = CP Name	-	B	N	N	N	E	B	B	B	B	N
1014	Peripheral Border Node	-	N	-	-	-	-	-	-	-	-	-
1016	Extended Border Node	N	-	-	-	-	-	-	-	-	-	-
1017	Gateway	-	-	-	-	-	-	-	-	-	-	-
1018	Delete EN Resources Before Registering	B	-	-	-	-	E	-	-	B	-	-
Dependent LU Support												
1060	Prerequisite for Session Services Extensions CP Support	B	-	-	-	-	-	-	-	-	-	-
1061	Prereqs. for SSE NNS Support	N	-	-	-	-	-	-	-	-	-	-
1062	Session Services Ext. CP Support	B	-	-	-	-	-	-	-	-	-	-
1063	Session Services Ext. NNS Support	N	-	-	-	-	-	-	-	-	-	-
1064	Session Services Ext. PLU Node Support	B	-	-	-	-	-	-	-	-	-	-
1065	Session Services Ext. CP(SLU) (SSCP) Support	B	-	-	-	-	-	-	-	-	-	-
1066	Dependent LU Server	N	-	-	-	-	-	-	-	-	-	-
1067	Dependent LU Requester	-	B	N	N	N	E	B	B	B	3	N
1071	Generalized ODAI Usage	-	-	-	N	N	-	-	-	-	-	N
Cryptography Support												
1070	Session Cryptography	B	B	-	-	-	-	-	-	-	B	-

Table 21 (Page 2 of 4). Summary of Implemented Optional Functions (APPN Version 2)												
Function		**VTAM**	**AS/ 400**	**3174**	**6611 MPNP**	**3746**	**PComm**		**CS**			**MRS MAS**
							NT	**AF**	**AIX**	**NT**	**/2**	
No.	**Description**	**V4R3**	**V3R2**	**C6.3**	**V1R4**	**V4R2**	**[11]**	**[12]**	**[13]**	**[14]**	**[15]**	**[16]**
Directory Services												
1100	Safe-Store of Directory Cache	N	N	N	-	-	-	N	-	N	N	-
1101	Preloaded Directory Cache	N	-	N	N	N	-	N	-	N	N	N
1102	EN Authorization	-	-	-	-	-	-	-	N	-	-	-
1106	Central Directory Server	N	-	-	-	-	-	-	-	-	-	-
1107	Central Resource Registration (of LUs)	B	-	-	N	N	E	-	-	B	-	N
1108	Nonverify	N	-	-	-	-	-	-	-	-	-	-
1116	DLUS-Served LU Registration NNS Support	-	-	-	N	N	-	-	-	-	-	N
1118	EN TG Vector Registration	B	-	-	-	-	-	-	-	-	-	-
Topology and Routing Services												
1200	Tree Caching and TG Caching	N	B	-	N	N	E	B	N	B	B	N
1201	Permanent Storage Medium	B	B	-	N	N	-	-	-	-	-	[6]
1203	Detection and Elimination of TDU Wars	-	-	-	-	-	-	-	-	-	-	-
Intermediate Session Routing												
1300	Tuning Values for ISR	B	-	-	-	N	-	-	-	-	-	-
1301	Nonpaced Intermediate Session Traffic	B	N	-	-	-	-	-	[7]	N	-	-
High Performance Routing												
1400	HPR Base (ANR)	[4]	B	N	N	N	E	B	[5]	B	B	N
1401	Rapid Transport Protocol	[4]	-	-	N	N	E	B	-	B	B	N
1402	Control Flows over RTP	-	-	-	N	N	-	-	-	-	-	N
1403	Dedicated RTP Connections	-	-	-	-	-	-	-	-	-	-	-
1404	Multilink TG (MLTG)	-	-	-	-	[17]	-	-	-	-	-	-
Management Services - File Services												
1500	File Services Support Base	-	[8]	N	-	-	-	-	[10]	-	[9]	-
1501	Network Operator Support for File Services	-	-	-	-	-	-	-	-	-	-	-

Table 21 (Page 3 of 4). Summary of Implemented Optional Functions (APPN Version 2)												
Function		VTAM	AS/400	3174	6611 MPNP	3746	PComm		CS			MRS MAS
							NT	AF	AIX	NT	/2	
No.	Description	V4R3	V3R2	C6.3	V1R4	V4R2	11	12	13	14	15	16
Management Services - Change Management												
1510	CM Base	-	8	N	-	-	-	9	10	-	9	-
1511	CM Production Only Activate	-	8	-	-	-	-	-	-	-	-	-
1512	CM Execution Window Timing	-	8	-	-	-	-	9	10	-	9	-
1513	CM Activate Report	-	8	N	-	-	-	9	10	-	9	-
1514	CM Alter Active Install	-	8	-	-	-	-	9	10	-	9	-
1515	CM Object Disposition Install	-	-	-	-	-	-	-	-	-	-	-
1516	CM Initiate Command	-	8	-	-	-	-	9	10	-	9	-
1517	CM Cancel Command	-	8	-	-	-	-	9	10	-	9	-
1518	CM Activate Last	-	-	-	-	-	-	-	-	-	-	-

Table 21 (Page 4 of 4). Summary of Implemented Optional Functions (APPN Version 2)													
Function		VTAM	AS/400	3174	6611 MPNP	3746	PComm		CS			MRS MAS
							NT	AF	AIX	NT	/2	
No.	Description	V4R3	V3R2	C6.3	V1R4	V4R2	11	12	13	14	15	16
Management Services - Operations Management												
1520	Common Operations Services	-	-	-	-	-	-	B	-	-	B	-
1521	Operations Management	1	-	-	-	-	-	-	-	-	-	-

Notes:

E = End Node

B = End and Network Nodes

N = Network Node

\- = Not Supported

1 Function supported through NetView

2 NetView serves as the subarea focal point, but cannot have a subarea focal point using the APPN architecture. Instead, NetView supports using another NetView as a subarea focal point using a proprietary interface.

3 DLUR for downstream devices is supported by the gateway feature, for local LUs by the LUA feature.

4 Within composite network nodes (CNNs), only ANR base (1400) is supported and only if the RTP path enters and exits the CNN through ANR-capable NCPs. In VTAM NNs (VTAMs with no subarea capability at all), both ANR base (1400) and RTP (1401) are supported. In VTAM ENs (with no subarea capability at all), only RTP (1401) is supported.

5 ANR is supported on Token Ring, Ethernet (standard and 802.3), FDDI, X.25 and SDLC DLCs. It is not supported on channel DLC.

6 MAS only

7 Receive nonpaced intermediate session traffic only; not supported by AIX SNA Server/6000 V2R1; supported by V2R1.1.

8 Function supported by Managed System Services/400

9 Function supported by NetView DM/2

10 Function supported by NetView DM/6000

11 Refers to PComm for Windows 95 and Windows NT

12 Refers to PComm for OS/2

13 Refers to Communications Server for AIX V2R1

14 Refers to Communications Server for Windows NT V5

15 Refers to Communications Server for OS/2 V4R1

16 Refers to IBM 2216 Multi-protocol access services V1R1 and IBM 2210 Multi-protocol routing services V1R1

17 Supported in 3746 V5.

Appendix C. APPN VTAM

VTAM V4R1 was the first implementation of APPN on an IBM mainframe. As its name implies, APPN architecture reverses the hierarchical nature of SNA. By using a peer-to-peer approach, APPN offers advantages over subarea SNA such as:

- Better performance during session initiation - APPN uses (in most cases) fewer line flows per LU-LU session during initiation.
- Improved performance during network activation - APPN can eliminate control sessions, such as SSCP-PU and SSCP-LU, thereby eliminating many control flows during network activation.
- Reduced system definitions - APPN does not use PATH decks as it learns about network topology dynamically.
- Increased availability - as the topology is learned dynamically, there is no need to shut down parts of the network in order to add a single node.

Note: In the following sections we will use the term APPN VTAM when referring to VTAM V4R3, unless there are reasons to mention a specific release.

C.1 Overview

Starting from VTAM V3R2, a VTAM or composite node (VTAM and NCP) can portray itself as a LEN node to APPN nodes. With the introduction of VTAM V4R1, VTAM can now present an APPN image, either end node or network node. In addition to this, VTAM will be able to maintain subarea connections.

APPN VTAM is able:

- To support APPN nodes attached to the boundary function supplied by VTAM itself or supplied by NCP. A FID2 connection between a VTAM node and any node that operates as an APPN node is referred to as a boundary function transmission group (BF-TG).
- To support multiple connections to the same APPN node, known as parallel TGs.
- To allow the exchange of levels of CP support (including the CP-CP session over the connection) during establishment of an APPN connection.

By supporting an APPN appearance to the APPN network and a subarea appearance to the subarea network, APPN VTAM (see Figure 145 on page 410):

- Enables subarea LU-LU sessions *through* and *into* an APPN network.

  LUs within any of the VTAM domains shown in Figure 145 can have sessions with either LUs on NNA or NNB, or any other LU in any VTAM domain.
- Enables APPN LU-LU sessions *through* and *into* the subarea network.

LUs on APPN network nodes NNA and NNB can have sessions with any LU, on either NNA or NNB, or with LUs in any VTAM domain.

- Creates a migration path from subarea to APPN networking.

  Only the VTAMs providing the APPN boundary function need to be on the current software levels. LUs controlled by backlevel VTAMs, (for example, VTAM6) can also establish LU-LU sessions with LUs in APPN or non-adjacent subarea networks.

APPN VTAM offers extended connectivity in a transparent manner for both APPN and subarea LUs, without loss of function. All LU-LU session capabilities present in a pure subarea or a pure APPN environment are also supported in a combined APPN/subarea networking environment. For details and limitations see C.5, "LU-LU Sessions" on page 427.

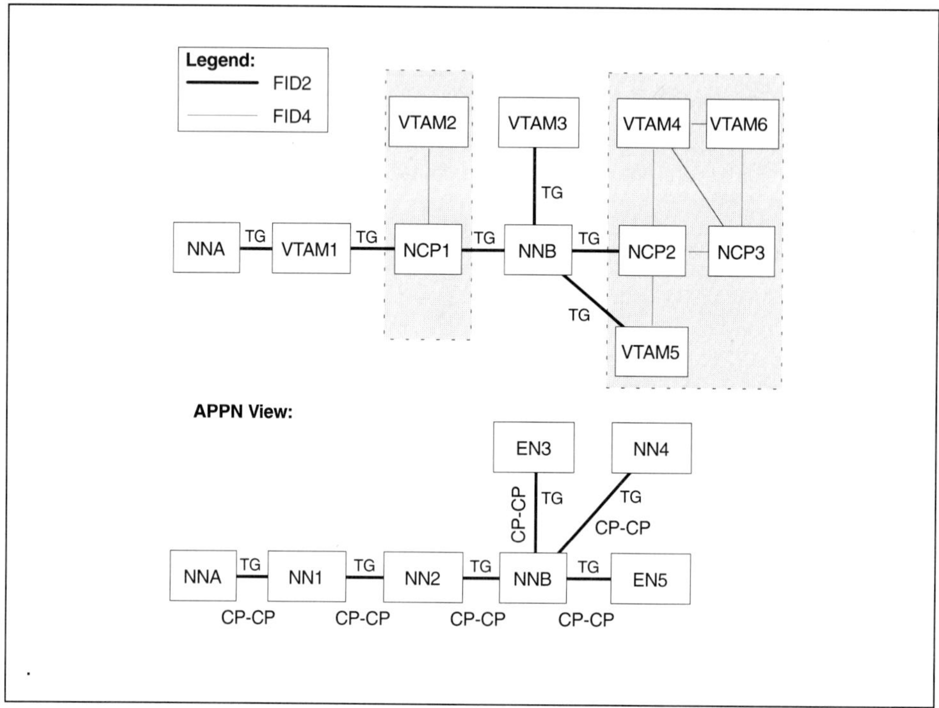

Figure 145. VTAM APPN Support

Note: In the APPN view, the VTAM and composite network nodes (CNNs) are represented by NNx (x=1, 2, 4) and ENy (y=3, 5).

In VTAM V4R2, a new type of connection can be defined between any two VTAM V4R2 interchange nodes or migration data hosts, namely a *VR-based transmission group* (VR-TG), which represents all predefined virtual routes between two VTAM V4R2 domains. The TG number associated with a VR-TG will always be 255. The VR-TG is reported being active in TDUs to all APPN network nodes as soon as the CDRM-CDRM session between the two VTAMs has been activated. Only one VR-TG will exist between any two VTAM V4R2 nodes, regardless of the number of active virtual routes, including VTAM-to-VTAM, VTAM-to-NCP, and NCP-to-NCP virtual routes.

A VR-TG can carry CP-CP sessions between the VTAMs' control points. Unlike subarea logic, which requires fully meshed CDRM-CDRM sessions (also in a VTAM V4R2 APPN network) between all VTAMs in a net ID subnetwork to achieve any-to-any session connectivity, APPN logic requires only CP-CP connectivity; that means that any two CPs can communicate across a sequence of CP-CP sessions without having established CP-CP sessions directly between themselves. Extreme care should be taken when designing which CDRM-CDRM sessions activate a VR-TG and which of those VR-TGs carry CP-CP sessions.

Figure 146 on page 412 shows an example of a VR-TG between two VTAM V4R2 interchange nodes. CP-CP sessions can be activated once the CDRM-CDRM session between the two SSCPs has been activated. TRS in other nodes will treat the VR-TG as a normal APPN transmission group when calculating the RSCV for an LU-LU session traversing this VR-TG.

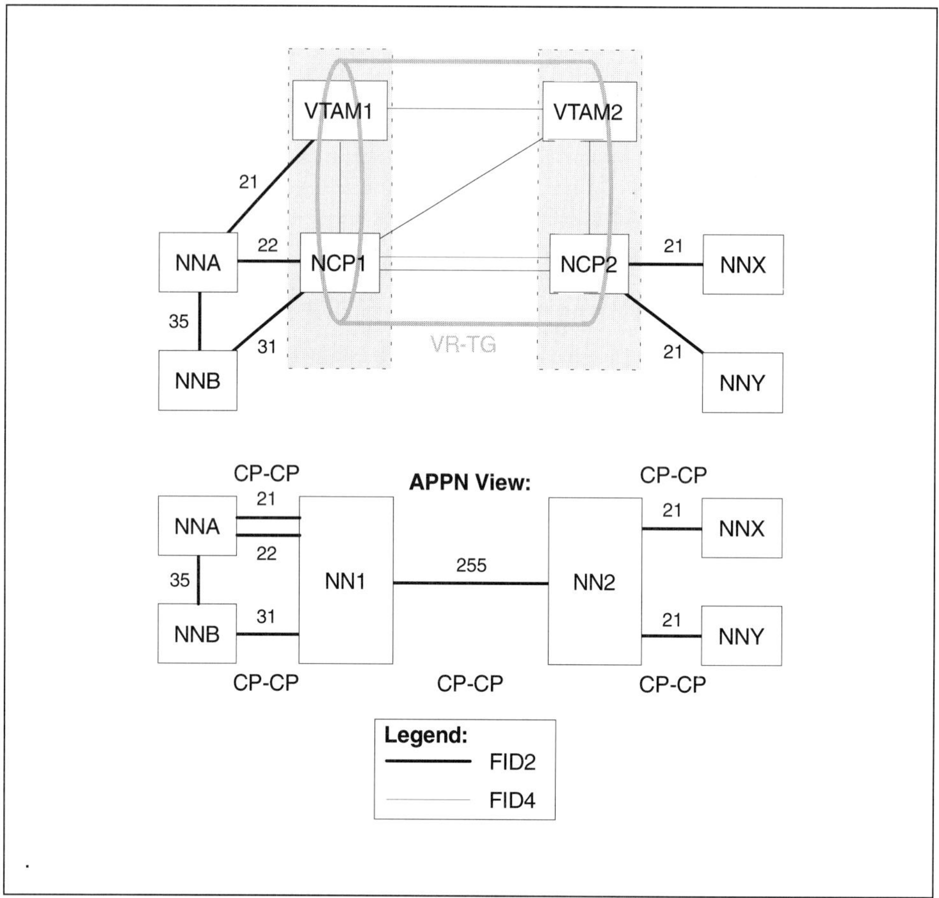

Figure 146. VTAM V4R2 VR-Based Transmission Group

To get full APPN connectivity requires full CP-CP connectivity. APPN VTAM allows CP-CP sessions to be established between an APPN VTAM node and any adjacent APPN node. The CP-CP sessions:

- Traverse an APPN VTAM or NCP boundary function to an adjacent node or a VR-TG between two VTAM V4R2 nodes
- Give APPN network connectivity into and across the subarea network
- Move APPN functions into the subarea network with full directory and session services functions

It is a user's choice to define existing subarea (FID4) links to T2.1 (FID2) links or use the existing FID4 links for VR-based transmission groups and establish CP-CP sessions. A mixture of SSCP-SSCP and CP-CP sessions may be used.

C.2 VTAM Node Types

Possible node configurations and their functional abilities are determined by the VTAM start options. An APPN VTAM host can be configured as:

Subarea VTAM

The default parameter setting is such that VTAM V4R1 continues to operate as a pure subarea node. APPN VTAM, when started as a subarea node, supports SSCP-SSCP sessions but cannot have CP-CP sessions. It supports LEN connections with the same support provided by VTAM V3R4.1.

As an example, see VTAM6 in Figure 145.

Interchange Node (ICN)

A VTAM host configured as an interchange node (ICN) can be:

- A stand-alone APPN VTAM node.
- A VTAM and one or more NCPs; an APPN VTAM node and one or more NCPs owned by this VTAM is called a *composite network node* (CNN).

An ICN is intended to replace the subarea CMC host. It may own NCPs and is the repository of all the functions provided by the CMC host. It provides ownership of dependent LUs, allowing these LUs to operate unchanged.

The ICN routes sessions from APPN nodes into and through the subarea network using subarea routing, without exposing the subarea implementation to the APPN part of the network. This is accomplished by making the APPN VTAM node, plus all its owned resources, appear to other nodes as a single APPN network node with multiple connections. At the same time the ICN and the NCPs it owns will maintain their subarea appearance to other subarea nodes.

The ICN supports SSCP-SSCP sessions with other VTAM nodes as well as CP-CP sessions with adjacent APPN network nodes and end nodes. This support allows the ICN to use both APPN and subarea data flows to locate LUs and to provide the best route between nodes. APPN session setup protocols, which flow on CP-CP sessions, are converted to the corresponding subarea protocols that flow on SSCP-SSCP sessions, and vice versa.

As an example, see VTAM2 and VTAM4 in Figure 145.

Migration Data Host (MDH)

A migration data host (MDH) is a VTAM host that acts as an APPN end node and maintains FID2 connections to adjacent APPN network nodes. An MDH is able to maintain FID4 connections to directly attached VTAMs and NCPs but is not able to own NCPs.

When maintaining FID2 connections to adjacent APPN network nodes, the MDH must have one of the following connections to these network nodes:

- A channel connection, when connecting to an NCP that is part of an adjacent composite network node
- A token-ring connection using a 3172

An MDH is able to maintain both SSCP-SSCP and CP-CP sessions.

MDHs do not provide intermediate session routing, and they do not transform the APPN session setup protocols to subarea session setup protocols or vice versa.

As an example, see VTAM5 in Figure 145.

APPN End Node Only

APPN VTAM configured as just an APPN end node has no subarea number assigned, is not able to maintain SSCP-SSCP sessions, does not support FID4 connections, and is not able to own NCPs. The VTAM end node is able to maintain CP-CP sessions and supports FID2 connections. It is added to the APPN network without requiring subarea network routing definitions.

As an example, see VTAM3 in Figure 145.

APPN Network Node Only

APPN VTAM configured as just an APPN network node has no subarea number assigned, is not able to maintain SSCP-SSCP sessions, does not support FID4 connections, and is not able to own NCPs. The VTAM network node is able to maintain CP-CP sessions and supports FID2 connections. It is added to the APPN network without requiring subarea network routing definitions.

As an example, see VTAM1 in Figure 145.

C.2.1 APPN VTAM Network Node

APPN VTAM configured as a network node, either as a network node only or as an interchange node:

- Is able to perform APPN intermediate session routing
- Maintains CP-CP sessions with adjacent network nodes and, optionally, with adjacent end nodes
- Providing it has active CP-CP sessions with adjacent end nodes, allows these ENs to register the EN's resources at the NN
- Is able to dynamically inform a directory server of its local resources and resources on served ENs
- Can be configured as a central directory server to receive dynamic resource information from NNs

- May own dependent LUs residing on the VTAM node itself or on nodes adjacent to the VTAM or NCP boundary function

C.2.2 APPN VTAM End Node

APPN VTAM configured as an end node, either as an end node only or as a migration data host:

- Is not able to perform APPN intermediate session routing.
- Can have only CP-CP sessions with the adjacent network node acting as its network node server.
- Registers its resources at its network node server. Resources explicitly excluded from being registered can be found by domain searches only if they are cached at their network node server because of an earlier session request originating in their EN.
- Requests not to be searched by its NN server when performing an APPN domain search.
- May own dependent LUs residing on the VTAM node itself or on nodes adjacent to the VTAM boundary function.

Possible node configurations and their functional abilities are summarized in the table below.

Table 22. Node Type Functional Summary

Node Type	APPN Nodetype	HOSTSA Number	CP-CP Sessions	SSCP-SSCP Sessions	NCP Ownership	Interchange Function[1]
Subarea Node Only	n/a	yes	no	yes	yes	no
Interchange Node	NN	yes	yes	yes	yes	yes
Migration Data Host	EN	yes	yes	yes	no	no
APPN EN Only	EN	no	yes	no	no	no
APPN NN Only	NN	no	yes	no	no	no

Note:

1. Interchange function allows APPN session setup protocols, which flow on CP-CP sessions, to be converted to the corresponding subarea protocols, which flow on SSCP-SSCP sessions, and vice versa.

C.3 CP-CP Sessions

APPN VTAM uses the same name for both the SSCP and the CP. The CP functions are similar to the subarea SSCP. APPN VTAM establishes CP sessions to increase connectivity into a network and to assist in LU-LU session initiation and termination.

CP-CP sessions, using APPC/VTAM support for the LU 6.2 sessions, help to create a contiguous APPN network. APPN directory services, topology services, and network management are dependent on CP-CP sessions.

CP-CP sessions are supported over FID2 links or over a VR-TG across FID4 links. The FID2 links (APPN TGs) are provided by either the boundary function of VTAM or the boundary function of NCP. Three different types of CP-CP sessions exist:

1. SNA Services Manager Session
2. CP Services Manager Session
3. DLUS-to-DLUR Session

SNA Services Manager sessions provide transport for network management data, such as ALERTS. The entry point CP and focal point CP can have an SNA Service Manager session even if they are not adjacent to one another. The sessions use mode name SNASVCMG.

CP Services Manager sessions provide a transport facility for directory (resource search and registry) and topology data. The sessions always exist in pairs, each CP being *contention winner* in one session and *contention loser* in the other. The two nodes must be adjacent, and the sessions may follow different BF-TGs, but both CP-CP sessions must use the same VR as the SSCP-PU session with the NCP that provides the boundary function. The sessions use mode name CPSVCMG.

DLUS-to-DLUR sessions provide a transport facility for SSCP-PU and SSCP-LU session flows between a dependent LU server (DLUS) and a dependent LU requester (DLUR). The sessions are always established in pairs between CPs that are not necessarily adjacent and can reside in different subnetworks connected via adjacent or extended border nodes. The sessions use mode name CPSVRMGR.

APPN architecture allows CP-CP sessions between network nodes having different net IDs, if at least one of the network nodes supports the border node function; VTAM V4R1 does not support the border node function, although it may, as an NN, attach to a border node. VTAM V4R2 implements the extended border node function.

An end node can establish CP-CP sessions with an adjacent NN that has a different net ID.

An end node can have CP-CP sessions with only one network node at a time, which then is called the end node's network node server. An APPN VTAM end node (either a pure APPN EN or a migration data host) can define a sequence of possible NN servers. VTAM starts to establish CP-CP sessions with the NN node listed first. If CP-CP sessions with its network node server fail, VTAM will try to establish sessions with either the first NN in the list or the next NN in sequence, depending on a user-defined service order.

The VTAM CP utilizes logic that is already implemented in subarea VTAM to provide the full CP function as defined by APPN architecture. A VTAM CP performs the following functions:

- Management Services Transport (MST)

- Directory Services (DS)
- Topology and Routing Services (TRS)
- Session Services for CP (SSC)
- Session Services for LU (SSL)

The APPN control point (CP) is treated in VTAM as an LU and internally represented as a VTAM application program. The VTAM CP functions are performed by different transaction programs.

C.3.1 Topology and Routing Services

The main purpose of topology and routing services is to maintain information about nodes, transmission groups (TGs), and classes of service (COS) so that appropriate routes through the network can be calculated. Topology and routing services is a function present in every network node and, with reduced functions, in every end node. There are two kinds of topology databases in an APPN network:

Local Topology Database

In APPN architecture, this data set exists on APPN LEN nodes as well as on APPN end nodes.

Note: In VTAM's current LEN implementation, local topology information about T2.1 nodes and TGs is kept with the rest of the subarea configuration. Because it is not a separate database, VTAM acting as a LEN node cannot strictly be said to have a local topology database.

In an APPN end node, TRS uses the local database to supply the endpoint transmission group vectors (TGVs) to the network node server during a search procedure.

APPN VTAM does not save the local topology database but rebuilds it when VTAM reinitializes.

Network Topology Database

The database contains information about NNs and TGs, and is identical on every NN in an APPN network. As the network topology changes, topology database updates are exchanged between adjacent NNs over the CP-CP sessions. To ensure that unnecessary topology updates are not propagated through the network, APPN VTAM has implemented APPN flow reduction mechanisms such as the flow reduction sequence number (*FRSN*) and resource sequence number (*RSN*).

After directory services has located a resource, topology and routing services in a network node will use the network topology database when calculating a route to that resource. APPN VTAM keeps routes it has calculated between nodes and reuses the routes if applicable. The user is able to limit the amount of storage used to save route trees. When the storage is exhausted, the least used tree is discarded to make room for new trees.

In the network topology database, information is also kept about endpoint TGVs. They are received from local ENs that register their endpoint TGVs. This information is not sent to other NNs in topology database updates (TDUs).

In APPN VTAM, the network topology database can be saved to disk via an operator command. VTAM will use the information on disk to rebuild its topology database at initialization time.

Note: The content of the network topology database is similar to other APPN implementations. One difference is the fact that VTAM has chosen to implement an architectural option that allows it to store the weight of TGs in the topology database, which reduces computing time when calculating routes.

C.3.1.1 Class-of-Service Functions

The COS database is an optional database as defined in the APPN end node architecture. If an EN does not support the COS/TPF (class of service / transmission priority field), then it relies on its NN server to provide a COS mapping. This mapping is done when the EN sends a request to set up a session with a resource using a certain mode name.

APPN VTAM provides a similar COS database on both its EN and NN implementations. VTAM allows COS definitions to be added or modified dynamically.

Mapping between the mode names and (APPN) COS names is done using the APPNCOS keyword from the MODEENT macro of a user-defined logmode table or the default logmode table (ISTINCLM). The existing COS keyword will be used to select routes through the subarea network.

Mode to Class of Service Mapping: There are two methods of mode to COS mapping:

APPN COS selection

When an interchange node is calculating the route to be used for a session that passes from a subarea network to an APPN network, an APPN class of service (APPNCOS) will be selected.

The mode name to APPN COS mapping is done on the APPN side of the interchange node.

Subarea COS selection

When an interchange node is calculating the route to be used for a session that passes from an APPN network to a subarea network, a subarea class of service (COS) will be selected.

The mode name to subarea COS mapping is done on the subarea side of the interchange node.

C.3.1.2 Route Selection Services

Route selection services is responsible for calculating the optimum route through the APPN network. The mode name specified in a session initiation request is mapped to a COS name. The COS selected indicates the *required* characteristics of the session. The information contained within the topology database contains the *actual* characteristics of the resources (NNs and TGs) in the APPN network. Together with TGVs obtained from the end nodes, an optimal route will be computed.

The route description is contained within a route selection control vector (RSCV). The RSCV contains a series of TG vectors from the node on which the PLU resides to the node which contains the SLU.

If there are multiple APPN networks separated by subarea networks, then in each APPN network a separate RSCV is calculated to describe the route through the network. For the connection to an LU that resides *in* or is accessible *through* the subarea network, TG number 254 will be used (see Figure 147 on page 420); for connections across a VR-TG, TG number 255 will be used (see Figure 146 on page 412).

Note: TG numbers 254 and 255 are reserved TG numbers, which cannot be defined by customers. To provide transparency to the APPN nodes in the APPN network, all LUs in or accessible through the subarea network, except the LUs owned by the ICN itself, are presented as if they reside on an end node that connects to the ICN using TG number 254. This ICN is also known as a *surrogate* network node server.

In Figure 147 on page 420, for example, assume an LU on NNA establishes a session with an LU on NNB. No end-to-end CP connectivity exists as VTAM1 and VTAM2 are connected via subarea (SSCP-SSCP) protocols.

Note: APPN topology database updates (TDUs) flow on CP-CP sessions and because there is no end-to-end CP connectivity between the two APPN nodes, NNA and NNB are topologically isolated. Also, APPN session setup messages flow on CP-CP sessions, but because the VTAM interchange nodes VTAM1 and VTAM2 convert the APPN message flows into subarea flows, and vice versa, LU-LU session establishment is possible between LUs owned by NNA and NNB.

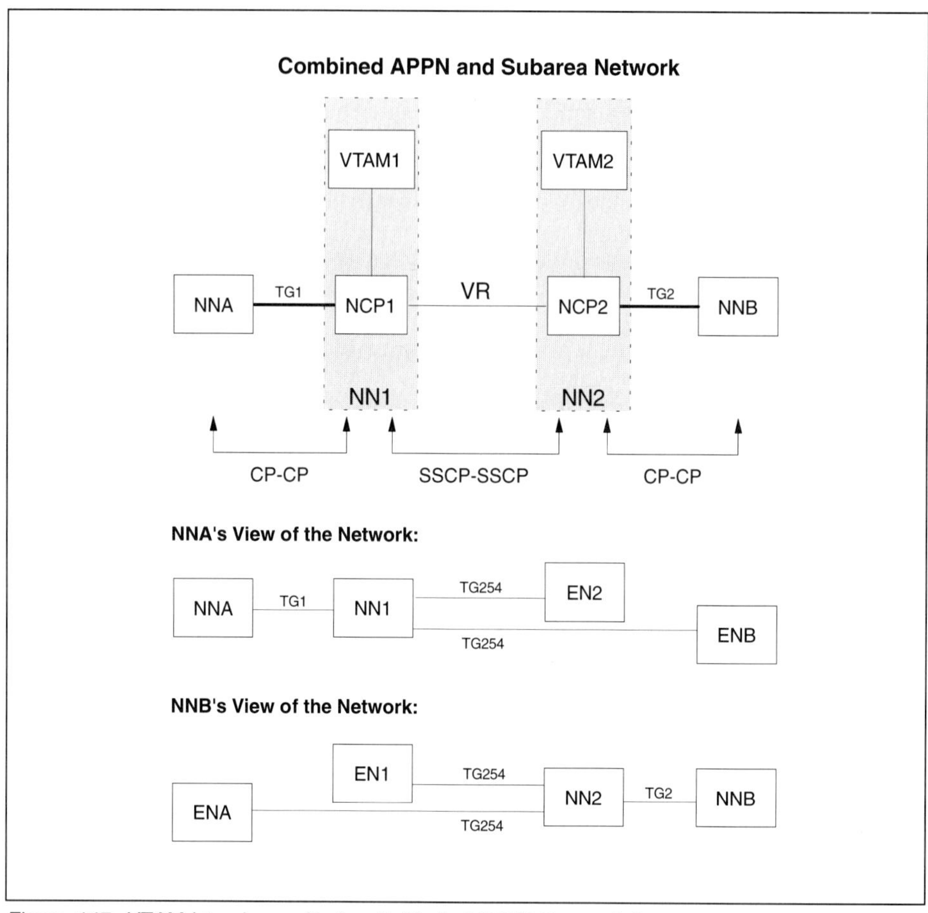

Figure 147. VTAM Interchange Node with Limited APPN Connectivity

Note: In the APPN view, the composite network nodes (CNNs) are represented by NN1 and NN2. Because the CNNs are connected using subarea (VR) protocols and have not established CP-CP sessions across a VR-TG, two (topologically) disjoint APPN networks result. LU-LU session establishment is possible between any LUs.

Composite network node NN1, which is the APPN representation of VTAM1 and NCP1, will function as a surrogate network node server for node NNB. From the perspective of NNA, the DLU resides on an APPN end node connected via TG254 to the composite network node NN1. The BIND received by interchange node VTAM1 contains in its RSCV two TG descriptions:

(TG1 to NN1) and (TG254 to CP(SLU))

From the perspective of NNB, the OLU resides on a APPN end node connected via TG254 to the composite (surrogate) network node server NN2. The BIND sent by interchange node VTAM2 contains in its RSCV the following two TG descriptions:

(TG254 to NN2) and (TG2 to NNB)

Route calculation in a base APPN network is the responsibility of the network node server of the PLU. In a combined APPN/subarea environment, route selection may become the responsibility of the network node server of the OLU (which is not necessarily the PLU). For details, see 5.7, "Route Computation: Overview" on page 95.

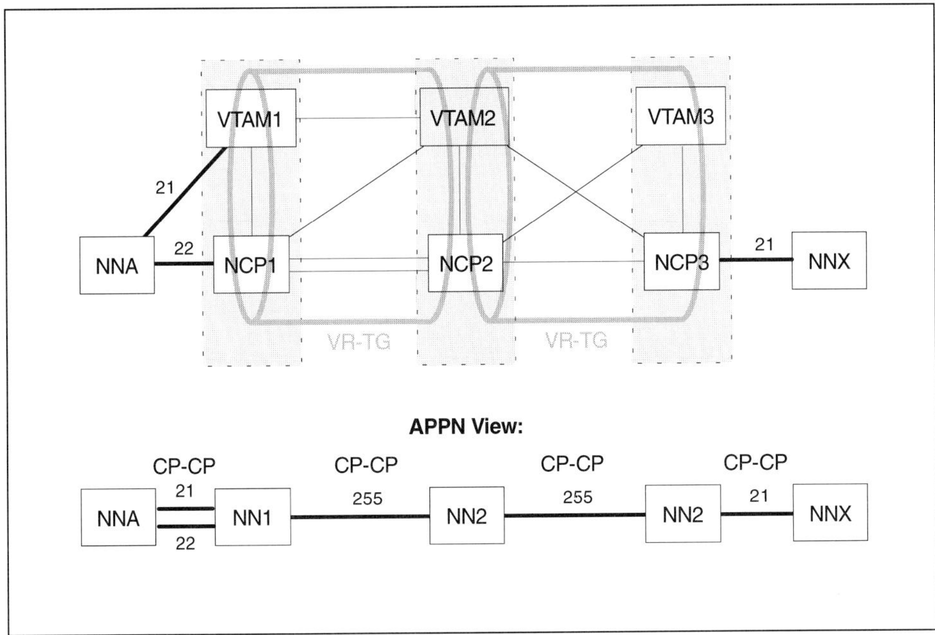

Figure 148. Multiple VTAMs Connected over VR-TGs

Figure 148 shows a network with three VTAM V4R2 interchange nodes connected over VR-based transmission groups. These VR-TGs are reported in TDUs to all APPN network nodes with the TG number 255. Unlike the previous example, there is one APPN network with full CP-CP connectivity and every network node is able to calculate a session path through the whole network. If NNA (as NNS(OLU)) had to calculate a path for an LU-LU session between itself and NNX as the CP(DLU), the resulting RSCV could contain the following TG descriptions:

(TG21 to NN1), (TG255 to NN2), (TG255 to NN3), and (TG21 to NNX)

When the BIND carrying this RSCV arrives at NCP1, the BIND must be forwarded over a virtual route through the subarea network. Subarea routing requires that the BIND be forwarded on one virtual route from NCP1 to NCP3 (between the subarea entry and exit boundary nodes on the session path). For that reason, VTAM1 has to combine the multiple VR-TGs into one VR-TG representing the virtual route through the subarea network. This process of combining two or more contiguous VR-TGs into one VR-TG is called RSCV pruning. The resulting RSCV will then be:

(TG21 to NN1), (TG255 to NN3), and (TG21 to NNX)

The BIND will be forwarded from NCP1 to NCP3 carrying this modified RSCV.

Note that the RSCV now describes a VR-TG from NN1 to NN3 (also with the TG number 255), although no TG between NN1 and NN3 is reported in the network topology database. To support the command flows that are necessary to establish subarea addressability, an SSCP-SSCP session between VTAM1 and VTAM3 must be active, or the session setup will fail.

RSCV pruning is also necessary when in the RSCV one or more VR-TGs are directly followed by a TG with the number 254 (indicating that the session path leaves the APPN network). The sequence of VR-TGs and the TG with number 254 will be combined into one TG with number 254.

C.4 Directory Services

The VTAM directory services component is responsible for managing the local directory database and controlling the search for network resources. One or multiple VTAM NNs may act as central directory servers. All central directory servers are considered to have equal capabilities. If multiple central directory servers exist, then a VTAM network node will query one of them. If this central directory server has no information about the resource or the verification of the resource's location fails, then it will search the other central directory servers in *sequence* before it starts a broadcast search.

The cache entries within VTAM's directory services show whether the resource is *available*, *unavailable*, or *unknown*. Knowledge of unknown resources will be maintained for a user-defined period. During this time the node will send a negative reply to Locate searches. This function is also known as *negative caching*.

C.4.1 Directory Services Database

APPN VTAM, if configured as a network node, maintains information about resources in its directory database. If configured as an end node, the resource information is kept in the VTAM resource definition table (RDT).

The database contains location and availability information about network resources. Each APPN network node (NN) contains a directory services database. The database learns about resources through predefinition, resource registration, and network searches. As a node learns new information about resources in the network, it will update its database to reflect the new information. The database serves as a dynamic means of keeping track of network resources. The database kept in storage will be written to disk via an operator command or during an orderly VTAM shutdown. When VTAM reinitializes, VTAM will use this information to rebuild its working database.

The resources kept in storage have an entry type associated with them as follows:

Register

These entries are written into the database as a result of end node registration. Resources are deleted on request of the EN or after the CP-CP session to the EN becomes inactive. Entries will be updated on request of the end node that did the registration, after an operator command, or after a directed Locate to the owning node returned a resource unknown.

These entries are *not* written to disk.

Defined

These entries are written into the database after activation of CDRSC major nodes. The resources are deleted after deactivation of the CDRSC major node. Entries will be updated after a directed Locate to the owning node returns a resource unknown, after a broadcast search discovers that the resource has been moved, or after an operator command.

These entries are written to disk. When VTAM is restarted, priority is given to the information stored, over predefinition, when both have an entry for a resource.

Dynamic

These entries are written into the database as a result of network searches or as result of central resource registration. Entries are deleted:

- After a search fails and this node is the network node server of both OLU and DLU
- After a search fails and this node is a directory server doing a search for the DLU
- If a DLU entry has not been used for eight days

Entries are updated after a search discovers that resources have been moved.

Dynamic entries are written to disk, with the exception of information obtained from OLU resource caching.

C.4.2 Resource Registry

APPN VTAM implements the following APPN resource registration functions, both as a requester and as a server:

- Registration of end node's resources at its network node server
- Registration of end node's and network node's resources at a directory server (also known as *central resource registration*)

  Note: An end node can only request its network node server to register resources at the directory server; it cannot register the resources itself.

Registering resources, most notably VTAM application programs (as LUs), as they are the most likely targets of LU-LU session setup traffic, will cut down the network traffic for session setup. VTAM allows resource registration to be user controlled. A resource can be:

- Not registered
- Registered at the network node server
- Registered at both the network node server and the central directory server

Registering CDRSC resources can be done to preload the DS database to avoid broadcast search processing for known LUs.

Dependent LUs owned by ENs need to be registered because a VTAM end node does not allow itself to be searched for resources. There is no need, except in order to reduce the number of setup flows, to register dependent LUs owned by an NN.

C.4.3 Network Searches

APPN VTAM gives the user extensive control over the order in which the network is searched for resources and has implemented a number of mechanisms to optimize search procedures and to avoid duplicate searches.

The APPN and subarea search forwarding algorithms are modified to allow the propagation of the search request into the APPN or subarea network. The VTAM interchange node (ICN) transforms resource search procedures and session setup protocols from APPN Locate formats to the corresponding CDINIT and DSRLST formats, and vice versa.

Although a VTAM interchange node (ICN) gives the external appearance of a single node, internally there are two logical nodes, an APPN side and a subarea side. As a result, when searching for a resource, special consideration is given to the way each side determines whether the other side owns a resource or knows about it. The APPN and subarea search algorithms are modified to interrogate the local database of the other side before forwarding a search request to other nodes.

Equivalent to the APPN local database at the APPN side is the resource definition table (RDT) at the subarea side. The VTAM RDT contains resources, same or cross-domain,that are either defined explicitly or learned dynamically. A cache search of the subarea side includes checking the RDT and resolving possible USERVARs. VTAM distinguishes two types of local subarea cache searches:

The Limited Subarea Cache Search:
: Only DLUs present in the ICN's domain are considered. These include application programs, dependent LUs, and independent LUs that have an active LEN connection from that ICN toward the DLU.

The Extended Subarea Cache Search:
: Both, same-domain,and cross-domain definitions cached in the ICN will be considered. VTAM will perform ALIAS translation, call its adjacent link

station (ALS) exit, and so on. No search will go into the subarea if the resource is not found. If an entry is found, VTAM will do a CDINIT/DSRLST type search to verify that the resource is available.

Besides a cache search, the ICN may perform a full search of the subarea network as well.

When an ICN receives a search request for a resource, then VTAM will always check its local directory services database and perform a local subarea search. A VTAM network node server will query topology and routing services for the resource in case an LU has the same name as its CP. If the resource has been found locally, then the request is immediately forwarded to the resource.

If VTAM has no knowledge of the resource, then VTAM will start querying the authorized end nodes that have not registered their resources before starting an APPN or subarea network search.

C.4.3.1 APPN and Subarea Search Order

For search requests originating from its subarea side, the ICN will use existing logic to scan through its adjacent SSCP tables. To direct VTAM to start an APPN network search, a special entry is used. When requested to start a network search from either its APPN or subarea side, VTAM will, at a user-controlled point, start to perform the APPN network search.

C.4.3.2 Subarea Search

When an ICN receives a search request from its APPN side during APPN searches, then it is a user's choice:

- To include the subarea side of the ICN in the network search
- To exclude the subarea side of the ICN from the network search
- To limit the subarea search to the cached entries the ICN has on its subarea side

C.4.3.3 Disjoint Subarea Networks

Two subarea networks are said to be *disjoint*, if they have the same net ID and are connected only by an APPN network; that means, no SSCP-SSCP sessions exist between VTAMs residing in different parts of the network. When an ICN receives a search request from the APPN network, it normally will not forward it into the subarea network if the request was sent into the APPN network by an ICN with the same net ID as the receiving ICN. This is done to prevent search requests looping between a subarea and APPN network connected by multiple interchange nodes. But the user has the option to explicitly specify a remote ICN as being disjoint. Search requests from the APPN network originating from this ICN will then be forwarded into the subarea network.

C.4.3.4 Serial Interchange Node Search

An ICN will never forward a search request into the subarea network when it has received a locate request with the *suppress subarea search* bit ON. The ICN will perform a local subarea search only.

This bit will be set by ICNs when starting an APPN broadcast search. If the APPN broadcast search is unsuccessful, direct searches are sent to ICNs to which APPN connectivity exists. This process is called *serial interchange node search*. The method described effectively splits the broadcast search into two parts:

1. An APPN broadcast, done in parallel
2. A subarea search, done sequentially

C.4.4 Avoiding Duplicate Searches

A VTAM interchange node may receive a search request at its subarea side from either a directory server or from another interchange node. If the request is received from another interchange node and APPN routes can be calculated to the origin interchange node, then the receiving interchange node will never forward the request into the APPN network through which connectivity exists. Topology and routing services provides a list of the interchange nodes in the APPN network from its topology database.

VTAM interchange nodes will use an *SSCP visit count* field in APPN Locate requests and subarea CDINIT/DSRLST to limit the number of SSCPs that are tried on a specific search path. Although APPN nodes do not use the SSCP visit count, they will pass its value unchanged. Each gateway SSCP performing SNI rerouting, or ICN performing an APPN/subarea (or vice versa) transformation of the search request, will decrease the count by one. If the count falls to zero, then VTAM will not propagate the request but return a negative reply or response.

To avoid duplicate searches in the subarea parts of the network, an ICN performs caching of searches whenever it transforms APPN to subarea searches, or vice versa. The node performs caching on the basis of:

Fully Qualified Procedure-Correlation Identifier (FQPCID)
The FQPCID is used to correlate a Locate search with its replies.

Procedure Resubmit Number (PRN)
PRN is used by subarea and interchange nodes to distinguish related search procedures. The use of PRN is part of base APPN architecture and only the NNS(OLU) and NNS(DLU) will modify the PRN.

PCID Modifier
The PCID modifier in the Locate request is used to distinguish subprocedures for a Locate procedure. Besides the origin and destination node, intermediate nodes may also start subprocedures.

SSCP visit count

It is a user's option to specify the period that the search request is cached (default 8 seconds). The ICN node will delay successive search requests for the same DLU in order to prevent multiple broadcast searches across the APPN and subarea part of the network.

C.5 LU-LU Sessions

Base APPN architecture limits sessions to PLU-initiated, LU 6.2 sessions. APPN VTAM extends existing subarea functions (such as SLU-initiated and third-party initiated sessions, autologon, session release request, etc.) for all LU types, currently supported by a subarea VTAM, to APPN networks. This has been accomplished by mapping APPN and existing subarea session setup protocols.

APPN VTAM will be able:

1. To work with other APPN nodes to establish LU-LU sessions through an APPN network
2. To work with prior releases of VTAM to establish LU-LU sessions through subarea networks
3. To work jointly with other APPN products and prior releases of VTAM to establish LU-LU sessions through combined APPN and subarea networks

APPN VTAM has implemented the functions described in 11.1, "Session Services Extensions" on page 263 to make sure that all LU-LU session capabilities present in either pure subarea or pure APPN networks are also supported in a combined APPN and subarea networking environment, independent of the APPN and subarea components connecting both session partners.

Only the VTAM interchange node providing the connection between the subarea and APPN network needs to be on the current software level; SSCPs having subarea connectivity to these boundary VTAMs may be backlevel VTAMs.

If one or both session partners are independent LUs, then LU-LU sessions are limited to PLU-initiated, LU 6.2 sessions. If both LUs are controlled by a VTAM SSCP, then any session type known to subarea SNA is supported.

C.6 Dependent LU Support

As mentioned in 2.3.1, "Dependent and Independent LUs" on page 30, all LUs depend on the services of a control point. The essence of a dependent LU is the fact that it is always dependent on the services of a control point outside of the node on which the LU resides. In this section we will focus on the case of an LU dependent on services offered by a VTAM SSCP and residing on either a VTAM node or on nodes adjacent to the VTAM or NCP boundary function.

Among other things, SSCP support includes SLU, PLU, and third-party initiation, autologon support, and session queuing/notification. It also includes interpret functions and unformatted and formatted session services support, for example, to allow a human operator to request an SLU-initiated, LU 2 session.

Currently, for dependent LUs residing on a node adjacent to the VTAM or NCP boundary functions, the LU sessions will always traverse the VTAM or NCP boundary function.

Note: APPN VTAM nodes configured as end nodes are not able to perform APPN intermediate session routing, but do allow nodes to attach using the VTAM boundary function. Dependent LU sessions may traverse the VTAM node via its boundary function.

C.6.1 Dependent LU Server

As mentioned in the previous chapter, current support for dependent LUs requires that the LUs reside on either a VTAM node, or on a node adjacent to the VTAM or NCP boundary function.

To allow the session capabilities currently provided by VTAM SSCPs to all LUs in an APPN network would require either that the SSCP functions be distributed to remote APPN nodes, or that the SSCP functions be enhanced allowing VTAM to serve nonadjacent nodes.

VTAM V4R2 provides extended APPN support for dependent LUs based on enhanced SSCP support by VTAM. The enhanced support allows traditional SSCP-PU and SSCP-LU data flows to be multiplexed in LU 6.2 CP-CP sessions to nonadjacent nodes. See 11.2, "Dependent LU Requester/Server" on page 269 for a detailed description.

Appendix D. APPN Information Resources

The single most comprehensive source of information for any person interested in APPN is the *APPN Implementers' Workshop* (AIW).

Members participate in the AIW to facilitate the availability of fully interoperable, high-quality APPN products from a wide variety of vendors. The AIW serves as a forum to share information about APPN, its implementations and customer experiences; to help one another with implementation problems; to develop any necessary enhancements; and to promote the use of APPN.

For information regarding APPN, the AIW Home Page is the place to look first. You can even ask the APPN architects questions (which they will answer vie e-mail) from this page. The AIW Home Page can be found at:

```
http://www.networking.ibm.com/app/aiwhome.htm
```

The *AIW Information Exchange* is a document that describes all forms (Web, e-mail, and FTP) of electronic access to AIW members, discussions, and documents. It describes each of the mailing lists and is the only place with an inventory of the FTP site. The AIW information exchange can be reached from the AIW Home Page or directly at:

```
http://www.networking.ibm.com/app/aiwinfo/aiwinfo.htm
```

For information about IBM software and hardware products, the two URLs listed below provide indexes to information sources:

```
http://www.networking.ibm.com/netprod.html
http://www.networking.ibm.com/netsoft.html
```

Appendix E. Special Notices

This publication is intended for system engineers, system planners, system programmers, and network administrators who need to know the APPN functions, the APPN node types, and their interworking. The information in this publication is not intended as the specification of any programming interfaces that are provided by the APPN architecture and product family. See the PUBLICATIONS section of the pertinent IBM Programming Announcement for more information about what publications are considered to be product documentation.

References in this publication to IBM products, programs or services do not imply that IBM intends to make these available in all countries in which IBM operates. Any reference to an IBM product, program, or service is not intended to state or imply that only IBM's product, program, or service may be used. Any functionally equivalent program that does not infringe any of IBM's intellectual property rights may be used instead of the IBM product, program or service.

Information in this book was developed in conjunction with use of the equipment specified, and is limited in application to those specific hardware and software products and levels.

IBM may have patents or pending patent applications covering subject matter in this document. The furnishing of this document does not give you any license to these patents. You can send license inquiries, in writing, to the IBM Director of Licensing, IBM Corporation, 500 Columbus Avenue, Thornwood, NY 10594 USA.

The information contained in this document has not been submitted to any formal IBM test and is distributed AS IS. The use of this information or the implementation of any of these techniques is a customer responsibility and depends on the customer's ability to evaluate and integrate them into the customer's operational environment. While each item may have been reviewed by IBM for accuracy in a specific situation, there is no guarantee that the same or similar results will be obtained elsewhere. Customers attempting to adapt these techniques to their own environments do so at their own risk.

The following terms are trademarks of the International Business Machines Corporation in the United States and/or other countries:

ACF/VTAM	Advanced Peer-to-Peer Networking
AIX	AnyNet
APPN	AS/400
ES/3090	ESCON
Extended Services for OS/2	Extended Services
IBM	IMS
NetView	Nways
OS/2	OS/400
PS/2	RS/6000
RT	S/370

S/390	SP
System/36	System/390
VTAM	400

The following terms are trademarks of other companies:

C-bus is a trademark of Corollary, Inc.

PC Direct is a trademark of Ziff Communications Company and is used by IBM Corporation under license.

UNIX is a registered trademark in the United States and other countries licensed exclusively through X/Open Company Limited.

Microsoft, Windows, and the Windows 95 logo
are trademarks or registered trademarks of Microsoft Corporation.

Java and HotJava are trademarks of Sun Microsystems, Inc.

IPX	Novell, Incorporated
MOSS	MOSS Systems, Limited

Other trademarks are trademarks of their respective companies.

Appendix F. Related Publications

The publications listed in this section are considered particularly suitable for a more detailed discussion of the topics covered in this redbook.

F.1 International Technical Support Organization Publications

- *3174 APPN Update*, SG24-4171
- *AS/400 APPN Configuration Guide*, GG24-4023
- *VTAM V4R3: HPR Early User Experiences*, SG24-4507
- *IBM VTAM APPN Handbook*, SG24-4823
- *Nways Controller Models 900 and 950: APPN Implementation Guide*, SG24-2536

F.2 General Publications

- *SDLC Concepts*, GA27-3093
- *Systems Network Architecture Formats*, GA27-3136
- *SNA/MS Formats*, GC31-8302
- *3174 Planning Guide Configuration Support C*, GA27-3918
- *IBM 6611 Installation and Service Guide*, GA27-3941
- *S/36 Advanced Peer-to-Peer Networking (APPN) Guide*, SC21-9471
- *SNA Technical Overview*, GC30-3073
- *SNA Transaction Programmer's Reference for LU Type 6.2*, GC30-3084
- *SNA Distribution Services Reference*, SC30-3098
- *SNA Management Services Reference*, SC30-3346
- *SNA APPN Architecture Reference*, SC30-3422
- *VTAM Resource Definition Reference*, SC31-6427
- *SNA File Services Reference*, SC31-6807
- *AIX SNA Server/6000: User's Guide*, SC31-7002
- *AIX SNA Server/6000: Configuration Reference*, SC31-7014
- *AS/400 Communications: APPN Guide*, SC41-8188
- *Communications Server for OS/2 V4.1 - Up and Running!*, GC31-8189
- *Communications Server for OS/2 V4.1 - Network Adminstration and Subsystem Management Guide*, SC31-8181
- *IBM 2210 Planning and Setup Guide*, GA27-4068

- *IBM 6611 Introduction and Planning Guide*, GK2T-0334

F.3 Non-IBM Publications

- *Computer Networks*, ISBN 0-13-166836-6
  by Andrew S. Tanenbaum
  Prentice Hall International Editions

Abbreviations

AAL ATM adaptation layer

ALS adjacent link station

AMCO accounting management control object

ANR automatic network routing

APPC advanced program-to-program communication

APPN advanced peer-to-peer networking

ARB adaptive rate-based

ASM address space manager

ATM asynchronous transfer mode

BECN backward explicit congestion notification

BF boundary function

BF-TG boundary function transmission group

B-ISDN broadband ISDN

BIU basic information unit

BN border node

bps bits per second

BrNN Branch Network Node

BSN byte sequence number

BTU basic transmission unit

CDRM cross-domain resource manager

CDRSC cross-domain resource

CIE connection identifier exchange

CIR committed information rate

CMIP common management information protocol

CN connection network

CNN connection network node

COB client out of band

COS class of service

COSM class-of-service manager

CP control point

CPCS common part convergence sublayer

CPMS control point management services

CQF connection qualifier field

CRC cyclic redundancy-check character

CRR central resource registration

CRSS composite route selection subvector

CS configuration services

CV control header

DAF	destination address field
DDB	directory database
DLC	data link control
DLCI	data link connection identifier
DLU	destination logical unit
DLUR	dependent LU requester
DLUR	dependent LU server
DS	directory services
DSE	data switching exchange
EBN	extended border node
EFCI	explicit forward congestion indicator
EFI	expedited flow indicator
ELLC	enhanced logical link control
EN	end node
ENCP	end node control point
EP	entry point
FECN	forward explicit congestion notification
FID	format identifier
FID2	format identifier type 2
FID4	format identifier type 4
FID5	format identifier type 5
FIFO	first in/first out
FP	focal point
FQPCID	fully qualified procedure correlation identifier
FRSN	flow-reduction sequence number
GDS	general data stream
HPR	high-performance routing
ICN	interchange node
ILU	initiating logical unit
INN	intermediate network node
IPM	isolated pacing message
ISDN	integrated services digital network
ISO	international standards organization
ISR	intermediate session routing
ISTG	intersubnetwork transmission group
LAN	local area network
LAPB	link access protocol - balanced
LAPD	link access protocol on the D-channel
LDLC	logical data link control
LEN	low-entry networking
LFSID	local-form session identifier
LLATMI	low-level ATM interface

LLER link-level Error Recovery

LU logical unit

LMS local management services

LN low-entry networking node

MAC medium-access control

MCPS maintain CP status

MDH migration data host

MDS multiple domain support

MIB management information base

MLTG multilink transmission group

MPOA multiprotocol over ATM

MS management services

MSU management services unit

MU message unit

NAU network accessible unit

NCE network connection endpoint

NCL network control layer

NCP network control program

NHDR network layer header

NLP Network Layer Packet

NMVT network management vector transport

NN network node

NNS network node server

NNCP network node control point

NNTDM network node topology database manager

NOF node operator facility

NRM normal-response mode

NS network search

OAF origin address field

ODAI OAF'/DAF' assignor indicator

OSI open systems interconnection

OLU origin logical unit

PBN peripheral border node

PC path control

PCM port connection manager

PCID procedure correlation identifier

PDU protocol data unit

PIU path information unit

PLU primary logical unit

PRN procedure resubmit number

PSDN packet switched data network

PT payload type

PU physical unit

PUMS physical unit management services

QLLC qualified logical link control

QoS quality of service

RDT resource definition table

RH request header

RI routing information

RR resource registration

RSCV Route Selection control vector

RSN resource sequence number

RSS route selection services

RTM response time monitor

RTP rapid-transport protocol

RU request unit

SABM set asynchronous balanced mode

SAP service access point

SAR segmentation and reassembly

SATF shared-access transport facility

SC session connector

SCM session connector manager

SDLC synchronous data link control

SDU service data unit

SI switching information

SIDH session identifier high

SIDL session identifier low

SLU secondary logical unit

SM session manager

SNA systems network architecture

SNA/DS SNA distribution services

SNA/FS SNA file services

SNMP simple network management protocol

SNRM set normal response mode

SOC sphere of control

SR status requested

SS session services

SSCF service specific coordination function

SSCOP service specific connection oriented protocol

SSCP system service control point

STP service transaction program

TCID transport connection identifier

TDB topology database

TDM topology database manager

TDU topology database update

TG transmission group

TGV transmission group vector

TH transmission header

THDR transport header

TP	transaction program
TPF	transmission priority field
TRS	topology and routing services
UBR	unspecified bit rate
UI	unnumbered information
UNI	user network interface
VBR	variable bit rate
VCC	virtual channel connection
VR	virtual route
VR-TG	VR-based transmission group
VRN	virtual routing node
VTAM	virtual telecommunications access method
XID	exchange identification
XID3	XID format 3

Index

Numerics

A

B

C

D

E

F

G

H

I

K

L

M

N

O

P

Q

R

S

T

U

V

W

X